★ THE ★
CONFEDERACY

A Guide to the Archives of the Government
of the Confederate States of America

Henry Putney Beers

National Archives and Records Administration
Washington, DC

PUBLISHED FOR THE
NATIONAL ARCHIVES AND RECORDS ADMINISTRATION
BY THE
NATIONAL ARCHIVES TRUST FUND BOARD
1986

First published in 1968 as *Guide to the Archives of the Government of the Confederate States of America* by the National Archives and Records Service, General Services Administration, through the U.S. Government Printing Office, publication number 0—320-005.

The paper used in this publication meets the minimum requirements of the American National Standard for Permanence of Paper for Printed Library Materials Z39.48–1984. ∞™

Cover photo detail from the Cook Collection, Courtesy of the Valentine Museum of the Life and History of Richmond, Richmond, Virginia.

Cover design by Stanley Copeland.

FOREWORD

Nineteen eighty six is the 125th anniversary year of the firing on Fort Sumter and the beginning of the U.S. Civil War. It has now been 20 years since the end of the Civil War centennial. The centennial generated a considerable variety of events. The National Archives had a major exhibition on the war for the centennial years, 1961-65, and there was extended publication activity. But, perhaps because of the frenetic nature of the celebration itself, public interest waned soon after 1965 and one does not find much attention paid to the war by the general public today. A recent television docu-drama about the war did not receive universal critical acclaim.

During the Civil War centennial, the National Archives completed and published the first volume of its comprehensive two-volume guide to records in the National Archives relating to the Civil War. The second volume was published in 1968. These guides pinpoint source material in the National Archives on almost any topic for the Civil War period.

Since 1965, many volumes pertaining to the Civil War have been prepared by editorial projects under the auspices of the National Historical Publications and Records Commission, which is associated with the National Archives by law and by the fact that the Archivist of the United States is Chairman of the Commission. To name but three editorial projects, they are *The Papers of Ulysses S. Grant,* edited by John Y. Simon, which has now completed documenting Grant's activities through 1865; *The Papers of Jefferson Davis,* edited by Linda Crist, which has five volumes published and considerable material gathered and ready to publish for the war years; and *The Papers of Andrew Johnson,* edited by Leroy Graf, which now has six volumes in print, taking Johnson through 1864.

In addition, the first two volumes of *Freedom, A Documentary History of Emancipation, 1861-1867,* are revealing considerable new material on the condition of slaves during and after the war. The Commission-funded *Mary Chesnut's Civil War,* edited by C. Vann Woodward, and publications such as *The Cormany Diaries: A Northern Family in the Civil War,* edited by James C. Mohr, provide considerable insight into the impact of the war on the civilian population, both North and South. There is an abundance of truly exciting source material in archival repositories across the nation, including photographic collections (6,000 Brady prints at the National Archives alone), maps, surviving newspapers, and early film treatments, such as "Birth of a Nation," all of which can support renewed research.

Perhaps every generation must review history in terms of its own experience, not so much rewriting history as reinterpreting it through emphasis on topics not previously thought important. At the time of the Civil War centennial, the civil rights movement had not yet fully blossomed and the women's movement was barely beginning. We can look forward to new treatments of the Civil War with those two experiences in our consciousness. And the "Roots" phenomenon, which was felt by all archives and many libraries across the country, has shown how traditional disciplines, such as genealogical research, can take on new life and meaning when an innovative approach is pioneered.

This reissue of the two-volume guide to the Civil War, therefore, appears at a propitious time, and we hope it will make available some information and sources for those who wish to restudy, or study for the first time, the Civil War. As with all coverage of topics that can be researched in the National Archives, this is but a hint of the vast resources available to the researcher. We hope that these resources will add to your knowledge and understanding of America's past.

FRANK G. BURKE

Acting Archivist
of the United States

PREFACE

This *Guide* is a companion volume to *The Union: Guide to Federal Archives Relating to the Civil War,* published by the National Archives in 1962 and reissued in 1986. Its organization is similar to that of the other volume. The general records of the Confederacy are described first; there follow descriptions of the records of the Confederate Congress, Judiciary, and executive branches. Each chapter begins with a statement of the functions and responsibilities of the branch or executive department concerned. Records of a more general character are then described, followed by records of a more particular description, such as those of component bureaus. These descriptions are followed by bibliographical references, notations of finding aids, documentary publications, and other pertinent information.

The reader will appreciate that many of the Confederate archives have been lost or destroyed. Every effort, however, has been made to present the most complete and comprehensive guide possible. In instances where no records respecting particular Confederate agencies and establishments have been found, those agencies or establishments have nevertheless been listed. Insofar as possible, the *Guide* describes all the records of the Confederacy in the National Archives, the Library of Congress, and in other custody. Records described under a record group number, such as Record Group 109, are in the National Archives unless stated to be in a Federal Records Center.

Confederate records maintained in the following repositories have been examined and are described in this volume. These respositories include the Alabama Department of Archives and History, the Columbia University Library, the Confederate Museum, the Duke University Library, the Emory University Library, the Federal Records Center at East Point, Ga., the Georgia Department of Archives and History, the Georgia Historical Society, the Louisiana Adjutant General's Office, the Louisiana State Museum, the Department of Archives of the Louisiana State University, the New York Historical Society, the New York Public Library, the North Carolina Department of Archives and History, the South Carolina Archives Department, the Archives Division of the Texas State Library, the Howard-Tilton Memorial Library of Tulane University, the Tulane University Medical School Library, the U.S. District Court at Austin, Tex., the P.K. Yonge Library of the University of Florida, the University of Georgia Library, the Southern Historical Collection of the University of North Carolina Library, the South Caroliniana Library of the University of South Carolina, the Texas Archives of the University of

Texas Library, the Valentine Museum at Richmond, the University of Virginia Library, the Virginia Historical Society, the Archives Division of the Virginia State Library, and the William and Mary College Library.

Information obtained from repository guides and registers, the *National Union Catalog of Manuscript Collections,* and from bibliographies regarding the holdings of other repositories has also been incorporated in this *Guide.* Addresses of all repositories referred to may be obtained from the following directories:

American Association for State and Local History, *Directory of Historical Societies and Agencies in the United States and Canada, 1985-86* (Nashville, 1986).

American Association of Museums, *Museums Directory of the United States and Canada* (Washington, 1986).

National Historical Publications and Records Commission, *Directory of Archives and Manuscript Repositories* (Washington, 1978).

R.R. Bowker and Company, *American Library Directory* (New York, 1985).

I wish to express appreciation for additional information concerning Confederate archives and the history of Confederate agencies to the following: Frank L. Byrne, Ralph W. Donnelly, H.B. Fant, Louis H. Manarin, Haskell Monroe, Horace Montgomery, Warren F. Spencer, William N. Still, Willard E. Wight, and Bell I. Wiley.

I am grateful indeed for the editorial assistance of Margaret Beyer Buerschinger without whose dedication and perseverance this work could not have been completed.

The suggestions of members of the staff of the National Archives have been invaluable. The outstanding typing ability of Rita Goldring Carr was a significant contribution to the publication of this *Guide* and is especially acknowledged.

H.P.B.

CONTENTS

CONTENTS   ix

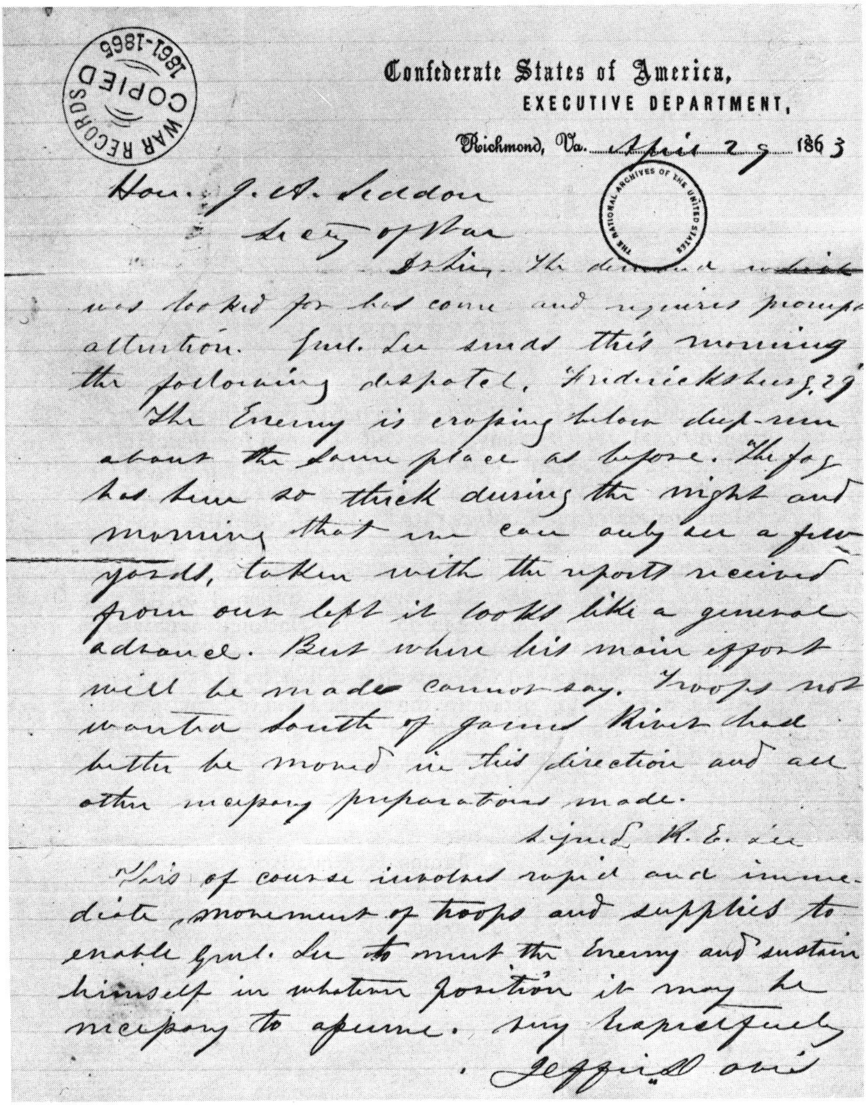

Confederate States of America,
EXECUTIVE DEPARTMENT,

Richmond, Va. April 2 5 1863

Hon. J. A. Seddon
Secy of War

[handwritten letter, partially legible]

A message to Secretary of War Seddon from President Davis in which he has copied an important dispatch from General Lee, preliminary to the Battle of Chancellorsville. It has been published in series I, volume XXV, of the Official Records of the Union and Confederate Armies, and it is now in Record Group 109, War Department Collection of Confederate Records, at the National Archives.

I

GENERAL RECORDS

OF THE

CONFEDERATE STATES GOVERNMENT

Even had the Government of the Confederate States of America been in a position to protect, evaluate, and organize its own archives at the end of the Civil War there probably would not have survived as intact and complete a collection of the general records of government as exists for the Government of the United States for the war period. Indeed, differing concepts within the Confederacy of the political character of national government, the greater autonomy of State government and a wartime situation all militated against the creation of complete documentation of a general character. Nevertheless, certain records that relate to the activities of the Confederate States Government as a whole constitute its general records. These include the records of the constitutional convention, conventions between the States and the Confederate Government, secession and ratification ordinances, Congressional laws and resolutions, Presidential proclamations, and other records as described in detail below. The records of the constitutional convention, the original Provisional and Permanent Constitutions, and the electoral returns were maintained at the time by the Congress. The other general records of the Government were maintained by the Department of State.

CONSTITUTIONAL CONVENTION

After the election of Abraham Lincoln as President of the United States, South Carolina seceded from the Union on Dec. 20, 1860. On the same day her secession convention adopted resolutions inviting other States holding secession conventions to meet in a general convention to form a provisional government for a Southern confederacy. By Jan. 26, 1861, five other Southern States--Georgia, Florida, Alabama, Mississippi, and Louisiana--had seceded from the Union and early in February 37 delegates from these six States assembled in convention at Montgomery, Ala. Additional delegates from these States were later admitted and by Mar. 2 six delegates had been admitted from Texas. Thus, before the adoption of the Permanent Constitution there were 50 delegates at the Montgomery convention.

At its first meeting on Feb. 4 the convention was called to order by William P. Chilton of Alabama; on his motion Robert W. Barnwell of South Carolina became temporary president. Another Alabama member,

1

John G. Shorter, moved the appointment of Albert R. Lamar of Georgia as temporary secretary. Robert Barnwell Rhett, Sr., delegate from South Carolina, nominated Howell Cobb of Georgia for permanent president, and he was elected by acclamation.

On Feb. 5 the convention adopted with modifications a resolution of Christopher G. Memminger of South Carolina providing for a Committee of Twelve to draft a constitution for a provisional government. The committee was composed of the following members (two delegates from each State): Richard W. Walker and William R. Smith of Alabama; James P. Anderson and James B. Owens of Florida; Alexander H. Stephens and Eugenius A. Nisbet of Georgia; John Perkins, Jr., and Duncan F. Kenner of Louisiana; William S. Barry and Wiley P. Harris of Mississippi; and Christopher G. Memminger and Robert W. Barnwell of South Carolina. On Feb. 7 Memminger, committee chairman, reported a draft of a constitution for a provisional government, and a motion to print it was passed. (It was printed also in Journal of the Provisional Congress, p. 25-30.) After debates in secret session on Feb. 8, changes in the wording of the draft were approved, and it was engrossed, read a third time, and adopted unanimously. The parchment copy was signed by the delegates of the several States in the order in which they appear in the preamble, geographically from east to west: South Carolina, Georgia, Florida, Alabama, Mississippi, and Louisiana. On Mar. 2 the Texas delegation signed. An interim government was organized under the Provisional Constitution while Congress drafted a permanent one.

The Committee on the Permanent Constitution was composed of the following members: Richard W. Walker and William R. Smith of Alabama; Jackson Morton and James B. Owens of Florida; Robert A. Toombs and Thomas R. R. Cobb of Georgia; Alexander De Clouet and Edward Sparrow of Louisiana; Alexander M. Clayton and Wiley P. Harris of Mississippi; and Robert B. Rhett, Sr., and James Chesnut, Jr., of South Carolina. Rhett, chairman of the committee, reported on Feb. 26 a draft of a Constitution (printed in the Journal of the Provisional Congress, p. 851-858). From Feb. 28 until the adoption of the Constitution, the Congress resolved itself at noon each day into a Constitutional Convention to debate and amend the draft. A resolution of Mar. 8 instructed the Committee on the Permanent Constitution to appoint a subcommittee of three to perfect the style and arrangement of the Constitution, have it printed, and report it for revision. On Mar. 9 the report of the subcommittee was ordered spread upon the record, but it has not been found among the extant records and it is not printed in the Journal. Two days later the Permanent Constitution was engrossed, read a third time, and unanimously adopted. Copies were sent to the States for approval and ratification and the Permanent Constitution was ratified by secession conventions or legislatures rather than by popular vote.

C.S.A. Congress, Journal of the Congress of the Confederate States of America, 1861-1865 (S. Doc. 234, 58 Cong., 2 sess., Serials 4610-4616; Washington, 1904-5). Serial 4610 (the first of seven volumes) contains the Journal of the Provisional Congress. E. Merton Coulter, The

Confederate States of America, 1861-1865 (Baton Rouge, 1950); Augustus L. Hull, ed., "The Correspondence of Thomas Reade Rootes Cobb, 1860-1862," Southern History Association, Publications, 11:147-185, 233-260, 312-328 (May, July, Sept. -Nov. 1907); Charles R. Lee, Jr., The Confeder-

ate Constitutions (Chapel Hill, 1963);
William M. Robinson, Jr., "A New
Deal in Constitutions, " Journal of
Southern History, 4:449-461 (Nov.

1938); Wilfred B. Yearns, The
Confederate Congress (Athens, Ga.,
1960).

Record Group 109. --A record of the proceedings of the Provisional
Congress relating to the drafting of the constitutions is available in its
journals preserved in the War Department Collection of Confederate
Records (see appendix I for an explanation of the classification of those
records in chapters). Congress appears to have kept a separate journal
of these proceedings, but only parts of it have been found. The proceedings of
Feb. 5-8, 1861, that pertain to the drafting of the Provisional Constitution and
those of Feb. 28-Mar. 7 that pertain to the drafting of the Permanent
Constitution are in this record group. A rough journal dated Mar. 1-9,
1861 (1 in.), may be only part of the original manuscript, for on the sheet
for Mar. 1 is the notation "23d Day Convention. " The complete proceedings
are recorded in the journal of the open and secret sessions of the Provisional Congress, however. This journal contains a draft of the Provisional
Constitution as reported by the Committee of Twelve and a record of the
actions amending the draft.

A Congressional resolution of Feb. 28, 1861, provided for keeping a
separate journal of the Constitutional Convention that framed the Permanent Constitution. Accordingly, after the dissolution of the Provisional
Congress on Feb. 17, 1862, the Convention proceedings were copied in a
bound volume. The smooth "Journal of the Constitutional Convention of
the Provisional Congress," Feb. 28-Mar. 11, 1861 (ch. VII, vol. 23),
contains the draft Constitution as reported by the Committee on the Permanent
Constitution on Feb. 26 and a record of actions taken to amend it.

Other records relating to the drafting of the Constitutions are among
the Provisional Congress legislative papers described below in the chapter on
the Congress. These include the report of the Committee of Twelve,
amendments to the report, and a few rough minutes of the Constitutional
Convention.

The proceedings of the Constitutional Convention, Feb. 28-Mar. 11,
1861, are in Journal of the Provisional Congress, p. 851-896. The debates
were not recorded; motions of Robert B. Rhett for the keeping of steno-
graphic records were defeated.

Records in Other Custody. --In Apr. 1865 the original Confederate
Constitutions, with other records, were abandoned by the Confederates in
charge of them as Federal troops approached the railroad depot at
Chester, S. C. Felix G. De Fontaine, a local newspaper publisher, rescued
some of the records, including the Constitutions, and kept them until he
was later forced by debt to offer them for sale. In 1884 he sold the original
parchment Provisional Constitution of Feb. 8, 1861, to William W. Corcoran
of Washington, D. C., for $800. Corcoran presented it to the Southern
Historical Society, founded in 1869 by ex-Confederates to preserve manuscripts relating to the Confederacy. In 1908 the Society, whose headquarters had been established in Richmond in 1873, transferred the Provisional
Constitution and other manuscripts to the Confederate Museum in Richmond.

In 1883, Mrs. George W. J. De Renne bought the original vellum
manuscript of the Permanent Constitution of Mar. 11, 1861, from George T.
Hanning, acting for Felix De Fontaine, for $1,500. It remained in the
possession of the De Renne family until 1939 when it was sold to the

University of Georgia Library for $25,000.

Copies of the Permanent Constitution are in other repositories. In 1908 a handwritten draft by Thomas R. R. Cobb, member of the Committee on the Permanent Constitution, was deposited in the University of Georgia Library by one of his descendants. In 1905 the Manuscript Division of the Library of Congress paid $100 for one of the 100 copies ordered printed on Mar. 9, 1861, containing longhand corrections; in 1935 it paid $500 for another of the printed copies containing interlinear additions that was once among the papers of Alexander B. Clitherall.

W. W. Corcoran Papers, Library of Congress; Wymberley J. De Renne, A Short History of the Confederate Constitutions of the Confederate States of America, 1861-1899 (Savannah, 1909); Jeremy F. Gilmer Memorial Volume, Confederate Museum, Richmond, Va., which contains a letter from Mrs. Mary De Renne to Mrs. Jeremy F. Gilmer, Sept. 4, 1883; Leonard L. Mackall, "The Wymberley Jones De Renne Georgia Library," Georgia Historical Quarterly, 2:73 (June 1918).

Both Constitutions have been published frequently. During the war they were printed in pamphlet form (bibliography in Marjorie L. Crandall, comp., Confederate Imprints; a Check List Based Principally on the Collection of the Boston Athenaeum, 1:3-5, 2 vols.; Boston, 1955; and Richard B. Harwell, comp., More Confederate Imprints, 1:3, 2 vols.; Richmond, 1957), in the compilation of the laws of the Provisional Congress edited by James M. Matthews, and in the proceedings of the ratifying conventions of the Southern States. They can be found in the Journal of the Provisional Congress, cited above, and in U.S. War Department, The

War of the Rebellion; a Compilation of the Official Records of the Union and Confederate Armies, ser. 4, vol. 1, p. 92-99, 136-147 (130 "serials" comprising 70 vols.; Washington, 1880-1901) cited hereinafter as Official Records... Armies, and the Permanent Constitution is in James D. Richardson, ed., A Compilation of the Messages and Papers of the Confederacy, Including the Diplomatic Correspondence, 1861-1865, 1:37-54 (2 vols.; Nashville, 1905). Both Constitutions are also in Jefferson Davis, The Rise and Fall of the Confederate Government, 1: 640-673 (2 vols.; New York, 1881), and in Alexander H. Stephens, A Constitutional View of the Late War Between the States, 2:714-735 (Philadelphia, 1868). The Permanent Constitution appears in parallel columns with the U.S. Constitution in Jabez L. M. Curry, Civil History of the Government of the Confederate States, p. 274-303 (Richmond, 1901), and in Russell H. Quynn, The Constitutions of Abraham Lincoln and Jefferson Davis; a Historical and Biographical Study in Contrasts, p. 242-275 (New York, 1959). Before selling the Provisional Constitution, De Fontaine permitted its publication by photolithographic process.

DOCUMENTS OF STATES

A resolution of the Provisional Congress dated May 20, 1861, provided that the State ordinances ratifying and adopting the Permanent Constitution were to be recorded and filed in the Department of State. The Confederate State Department also became the custodian of the secession ordinances and the conventions between the States and the Confederacy providing for the transfer to the Central Government of military forces and of former U.S. public property.

Records in Other Custody. --A file of secession ordinances, conventions between States and Confederacy, ratifications of the Permanent Constitution, correspondence, and Presidential proclamations on the admission of States, Jan. 1861-Jan. 1862 (1 1/2 in.) is in the Manuscript Division of the Library of Congress. Arranged alphabetically by State, this file includes Alabama, Arkansas, Florida, Kentucky, Mississippi, Missouri, North Carolina, South Carolina, Tennessee, Texas, and Virginia.

The texts of many of these documents are in the Journal of the Provisional Congress and in the proceedings of the secession conventions most of which were published during the war period by the States. Ordinances ratifying the Constitution are in Official Records ... Armies, ser. 4, vol. 1. The proceedings and ordinances are available on microfilm in the Library of Congress; see the section on "Constitutional Records" in U.S. Library of Congress, A Guide to the Microfilm Collection of Early State Records (Washington, 1950).

LAWS AND RESOLUTIONS OF CONGRESS

Publication of the laws and resolutions adopted by Congress was the responsibility of the Attorney General. Although the Secretary of State had initially been given the duty of preserving the original laws and resolutions and arranging for their publication in newspapers, an act of May 21, 1861 (Prov. Cong. C.S.A. Stat. 149), required the Attorney General to select from the laws and resolutions passed at each session those of a public nature and have them printed in newspapers in the State capitals and Confederate capital. Another act of the same date (Prov. Cong. C.S.A. Stat. 155), provided for the publication in pamphlet form of 500 copies of the acts of the session then ending, and their distribution to State and Confederate officials, with the remainder retained by the Department of Justice. An act of Aug. 5, 1861 (Prov. Cong. C.S.A. Stat. 172), continued the authority of the Attorney General to publish the laws in newspapers, vested the custody of the original laws and resolutions in the Department of Justice, and provided for the publication of the session laws by the Superintendent of Public Printing. The Attorney General continued to arrange for the publication of the laws in newspapers under terms stipulated by Congress and such publication continued into Apr. 1865.

Official compilations of most of the laws were published during the war. The acts and resolutions of the four sessions of the Provisional Congress were printed in pamphlet form in 1861 and 1862. An act of Feb. 17, 1862 (Prov. Cong. C.S.A. Stat. 277), authorized the publication in one volume of all acts, resolutions, and treaties of the provisional Government that were not secret. James M. Matthews edited a compilation of the statutes, Constitutions, and Indian treaties that was published in Richmond by Richard M. Smith in 1864.

Matthews also compiled the laws of the four sessions of the First Congress and the first session of the Second Congress from the originals in the custody of the Department of Justice, and they were published in Richmond by Smith in 1862-64. The laws of the First Congress and the Second Congress (first session) printed in pamphlet form were indexed and they were paged continuously so that they could be bound together.

The session laws were published in editions of 3,000 copies and were distributed in accordance with an act of Aug. 5, 1861 (Prov. Cong. C. S. A. Stat. 172). Some 1,100 copies were distributed among Members of Congress, Committees of Congress, officers and employees of Congress, the President and Vice President, the executive departments, the judiciary, and the Governors of States. Acting on a resolution of the House of Representatives, the Attorney General distributed copies to members of military courts in 1864. An act of Jan. 16, 1865 (Charles W. Ramsdell, ed. , Laws and Joint Resolutions of the Last Session of the Confederate Congress (November 7, 1864-March 18, 1865); Together with the Secret Acts of Previous Congresses, p. 15, Durham, 1941; cited hereinafter as Ramsdell, Laws and Joint Resolutions), authorized the distribution of the laws to judges and judge advocates of military courts, the commissioners of district courts, and the judges of supreme, superior, and circuit courts of the States.

Record Group 109. --In the War Department Collection of Confederate Records is a file of engrossed bills and resolutions of the Provisional Congress, Feb. 9, 1861-Feb. 17, 1862 (6 in.). These are on separate foolscap sheets bearing the dates on which they were read and passed and the signature of the Secretary, and they are arranged chronologically.

Records in Other Custody. --The original enrolled acts and resolutions of Congress, Mar. 16, 1861-June 14, 1864 (7 vols.), are in the Manuscript Division of the Library of Congress. The original enrolled acts and resolutions of the Second Session of the Second Congress, Nov. 7, 1864-Mar. 18, 1865, were purchased in 1930 by the library of Duke University after being for many years in private hands. That library also acquired an official register of the acts of the Confederate Congress, Feb. 1861-Mar. 1865, containing a chronological record of the titles of acts and the dates of passage and approval. The collection of statutes contains less than half of those adopted by the Second Session of the Second Congress.

The Confederate Government expired before the statutes enacted by the Second Session of the Second Congress could be published. Using the register of acts in Duke University Library as a guide and drawing on the collection of enrolled acts and resolutions in that library, on original bills, resolutions, and amendments in the records of Congress in the National Archives, on the texts published in the Journal of the Congress of the Confederate States of America, on Richmond newspapers, and on other printed and manuscript sources, Charles W. Ramsdell of the University of Texas published the compilation cited above in this section. It contains 198 enactments of the Second Session of the Second Congress and some earlier secret laws and resolutions.

Public and private laws, bills, resolutions, and amendments were printed in broadside or pamphlet form during the enactment process for the use of Members of Congress and for distribution. Bibliographies of these separately printed acts and resolutions are in Crandall, Confederate Imprints, 1:10-43, 47-105; Harwell, More Confederate Imprints, 1:3-27; and U. S. Library of Congress, A Catalog of Books Represented by Library of Congress Printed Cards, 32:86-99 (Ann Arbor, Mich. , 1943). See also William M. Robinson, Jr. , "The Second Congress of the Confederate States: Enactments at Its Second and Last Session, " American Historical Review, 41:306-317 (Jan. 1936).

PRESIDENTIAL PROCLAMATIONS

Presidential proclamations were issued to effectuate presidential policies or congressional enactments and to announce matters of public interest.
Records in Other Custody. --With the Confederate State Department
records in the Manuscript Division of the Library of Congress are Presidential proclamations for the period Apr. 17, 1861-Mar. 10, 1865 (1 in.).
Included is a bound volume of fair copies of Presidential proclamations for
the period Apr. 12, 1861-Jan. 25, 1865.

Presidential proclamations have been published in Richardson, ed., Messages and Papers of the Confederacy, vol. 1, passim; in U.S. Navy Department, Official Records of the Union and Confederate Navies in the War of the Rebellion, ser. 2, vol. 3, p. 96-134 (30 vols.; Washington, 1894-1922) cited hereinafter as Official Records ... Navies; and in Official Records ... Armies, ser. 3 and 4, passim.

ELECTORAL PAPERS

In accordance with Article II of the Permanent Constitution, Congress
by an act of May 21, 1861 (Prov. Cong. C.S.A. Stat. 122), provided for the
appointment of electors for President and Vice President on Nov. 6, 1861.
The electors then met in their respective States on Dec. 4 to vote. It was
also stipulated that the electoral returns were to be sent to the Vice President of the provisional Government, who was to deliver them on Feb. 18,
1862, to the President pro tempore of the Senate.
Record Group 109. --Returns of electors for President and Vice President, 1861 (1 in.), include proclamations of State Governors certifying the
results of the election on Nov. 6 and calling the electors to vote at the
State capitals on Dec. 4. Certified lists of the names of the electors show
the result of the votes by the State electoral colleges.

INDIAN TREATIES

The Confederacy negotiated nine treaties with Indian tribes in the
Trans-Mississippi West (see Bureau of Indian Affairs in the chapter on the
War Department, below). The original treaties have not been found.
Record Group 109. --Copies of some of the Indian treaties are in this
record group.

The treaties were published in 1864 in the compilation edited by James M. Matthews cited above. The treaties were reprinted in Official Records . . . Armies, ser. 4, vol. 1.

GREAT SEAL OF THE CONFEDERACY

Although the matter was referred to a committee in Feb. 1861, it was
more than 2 years before Congress (1 Cong. C.S.A. Stat. 167) authorized a
design for a Great Seal of the Confederate States. The design featured an
equestrian portrait of George Washington surrounded by a wreath composed
of the principal agricultural products of the Confederacy with the motto
"Deo Vindice" (God our Defender). On May 20, 1863, Secretary of State
Benjamin instructed James M. Mason to arrange for its manufacture in

London and this was duly accomplished. In the summer of 1864 Lt. Robert T. Chapman, C.S.N., safely conveyed the silver seal to Richmond, but the iron press and other materials shipped from Liverpool were captured. Without the press and mounting, the seal was difficult to use and for this reason the Department of State continued to affix the seal of the provisional Government to commissions of civilian appointees. This seal showed a scroll with the word "Constitution" above and "Liberty" below.

On the collapse of the Government in Apr. 1865, the Great Seal of the Confederacy was taken from Richmond by a State Department clerk. John T. Pickett later obtained possession of it and gave it to Thomas O. Selfridge in 1872. Years later, in 1912, a group of southerners bought it from Selfridge for $3,000 and presented it to the Confederate Museum in Richmond. A reproduction of this seal that was received by the War Department in July 1889 is now in the National Archives. The seal of the provisional Government was dropped in the Savannah River by Secretary of State Benjamin on his flight South in 1865.

John T. Pickett, Sigillologia; Being Some Account of the Great or Broad Seal of the Confederate States of America; a Monograph (Washington, 1873); Paul P. Walsh, "The Seal of the South," South Atlantic Quarterly, 38:392-402 (Oct. 1939).

II

CONGRESS

The convention of State delegates that assembled in Montgomery, Ala., in Feb. 1861 constituted itself a Provisional Congress. As such it adopted a Permanent Constitution under which an election was held for members of a Senate and a House of Representatives. Some of the records of the Confederate Congress relate only to the Provisional Congress, others relate both to it and the Congress of 1862-65, and others relate only to the Senate or the House of Representatives. The records are described here in those categories, and a separate section is included to show the availability of the papers of the individual Members.

PROVISIONAL CONGRESS

The Provisional Constitution vested the legislative power of the provisional Government in the convention assembled in Montgomery. On Feb. 4, 1861, Howell Cobb, as President of Congress, took the oath to support the Constitution and administered the same oath to the Members. Congress then unanimously elected Jefferson Davis President and Alexander H. Stephens Vice President of the Confederacy, and on Feb. 18 the President was inaugurated. Acts were approved 3 days later organizing the Confederate Government and establishing State, Treasury, War, Navy, Post Office, and Justice Departments.

The speedy launching of the provisional Government following upon the seizure of forts and arsenals in the South combined with other events to induce other Southern States to join the Confederacy. The successful Confederate attack on Fort Sumter, Apr. 12-13, 1861, was quickly followed by President Lincoln's call for 75,000 State militiamen. Commissioners went out from Montgomery to negotiate with several of the States: Alexander H. Stephens to Virginia, R. M. T. Hunter to Missouri, and Henry W. Hilliard to Tennessee. President Davis submitted to Congress conventions with those States providing for their alliance with the Confederacy and ratification of the Confederate Constitution. Other States adopted secession ordinances and elected delegates to the Confederate Congress, and by the end of 1861 the Confederacy reached its full strength. By acts of the Provisional Congress new States were admitted during 1861 as follows: Texas on Mar. 2, Virginia on May 6, North Carolina and Tennessee on May 17, Arkansas on May 21, Missouri on Nov. 28, and Kentucky on Dec. 10. In January 1862 Granville H. Oury took his seat as delegate from the newly created Territory of Arizona. The total number of men who served in the Provisional Congress was 117.

The Provisional Constitution vested in Congress the power to lay and collect taxes, duties, imposts, and excises; to borrow money; to regulate foreign and domestic commerce and the Indian trade; to enact naturalization and bankruptcy laws; to coin money and regulate its value and that of foreign coin and to fix the standard of weights and measures; to punish counterfeiting; to establish post offices and post roads; to adopt copyright and patent laws; to establish inferior judicial tribunals; "to define and punish piracies and felonies committed on the high seas, and offenses against the law of nations"; "to declare war, grant letters of marque and reprisal, and make rules concerning captures on land and water"; to raise and maintain an Army and a Navy and make rules for their regulation; to provide for calling forth the militia and for its organization, arming, and discipline; to admit other States; and to make laws necessary to carry out these powers and other powers expressly delegated by the Constitution to the provisional Government.

On Feb. 5, 1861, Congress adopted rules for the conduct of its business. The vote on questions in the Congress was to be taken by State, each State being allowed one vote. Each day the journal of the preceding day was to be read and corrected. After disposing of unfinished business, the regular order of business was to be first, the "call of the States alphabetically, for memorials or any matter, measure, resolution, or proposition"; second, the call of committees for reports, those not otherwise disposed of to be placed on the calendar; and third, the calendar or regular orders of the day. The titles of resolutions or other matters submitted were to be inserted in the journal. Stenographers and newspaper reporters wishing to record the proceedings of Congress were to be admitted by the President. On the motion of a Member, seconded by another Member, to close the doors for secret discussion, the President could close the doors and clear the gallery and floors of all except Members and officers of Congress. This rule led to the adoption of a resolution of Feb. 5, 1861, providing for keeping two journals: one for open sessions and one for secret sessions. A resolution introduced on the same day authorized the President to appoint two stenographers to record the proceedings and debates in both secret and open sessions, but it was not adopted and the debates were not recorded.

The Provisional Constitution contained no provision regarding the service of Cabinet members in Congress. Several Congressmen who were appointed to the Cabinet, including Hunter, Memminger, Reagan, and Toombs, continued to serve in Congress. The Permanent Constitution empowered Congress to give the heads of executive departments seats on the floor of either House with the privilege of discussing measures pertaining to their departments, but no legislation was passed on the subject.

A resolution of Feb. 9, 1861, authorized the President of Congress to appoint standing committees, and on Feb. 12 he announced the following standing committees:

Committee on Accounts; James B. Owens (Fla.), chairman.
Committee on Commercial Affairs; Christopher G. Memminger (S. C.), chairman.
Committee on Engrossment; John G. Shorter (Ala.), chairman.
Committee To Organize the Executive Departments; Alexander H. Stephens, chairman.
Committee on Finance; Robert Toombs (Ga.), chairman.
Committee on Foreign Affairs; Robert Barnwell Rhett, Sr. (S. C.), chairman.
Committee on Indian Affairs; Jackson Morton (Fla.), chairman.

Committee on the Judiciary; Alexander M. Clayton (Miss.), chairman.
Committee on Military Affairs; Francis S. Bartow (Ga.), chairman.
Committee on Naval Affairs; Charles M. Conrad (La.), chairman.
Committee on Patents; Walker Brooke (Miss.), chairman.
Committee on Postal Affairs; William P. Chilton (Ala.), chairman.
Committee on Printing; Thomas R. R. Cobb (Ga.), chairman.
Committee on Public Lands; Henry Marshall (La.), chairman.
Committee on Territories; James Chesnut, Jr. (S.C.), chairman.
On May 8, 1861, the Committee on Claims was appointed with John Gregg (Tex.) as chairman.

The standing committees inquired into the advisability of proposing legislation on matters referred to them and submitted bills, resolutions, and reports to Congress. They also considered the qualifications of persons nominated for public office and made recommendations to Congress. A resolution of Feb. 13, 1861 (Journal, 1:50), instructed the standing committees to consider and report on all matters relating to the purposes for which they were appointed. A resolution of Feb. 15, 1861 (Prov. Cong. C.S.A. Stat. 92), authorized the standing committees to print matters they wished to lay before Congress, but few committee reports were printed. At first the committees each had five members; this number was increased to six on Mar. 6 for some committees, and on July 23 nine members were authorized for all committees.

The Provisional Congress formed by resolution other committees for objects not coming within the purview of the standing committees. A Committee on Rules, created on Feb. 4, 1861, under the chairmanship of Alexander H. Stephens, submitted on the next day rules for procedure in Congress (Journal, 1:17-19). The Committee on Government Buildings, appointed on Feb. 9, 1861, with John G. Shorter (Ala.) as chairman, investigated the availability of office space for the executive departments in Montgomery. It submitted a report on Feb. 13 (Journal, 1:50), and on May 7 another report was referred to the Committee on Finance. Its resolution of May 3 providing for the acceptance of the offer of the hall of the Alabama House of Representatives was adopted. Shorter also became chairman on Feb. 9 of a committee whose task was to design a flag for the Confederacy. The committee was instructed on the next day to report also a device for a seal, arms, and motto; it did not complete its assignment, which was passed on to the Congress under the Permanent Constitution. A Committee on Inauguration, on Feb. 15, 1861, appointed under the chairmanship of William P. Chilton (Ala.), reported on the next day a program for the inauguration of the President-elect (Journal, 1:62). The Committee To Digest the Laws, to which William P. Chilton (Ala.) and John Hemphill (Tex.) were appointed on Mar. 12, 1861, was to digest laws of the United States applicable to the Confederacy, with changes and modifications. It did not complete its assignment, which was turned over to the Department of Justice. On May 6, 1861, a Committee on Pay and Mileage, with J. A. P. Campbell (Miss.) as chairman, was appointed to certify the pay and mileage due Members. It also reported bills to amend the act of Mar. 11, 1861, concerning the compensation of Congressmen. A committee headed by William H. Macfarland (Va.) helped to arrange for the transportation and care of men wounded at Manassas. A report was submitted by this committee on July 24, 1861 (Journal, 1:279). A committee appointed on Aug. 1 to investigate the condition of Army hospitals in Richmond submitted a report on Aug. 31

(Journal, 1:461-462). A Special Committee To Inquire into the Organiza-
tion and Administration of the Medical, Commissary, and Quartermaster's
Departments, appointed on Jan. 11, 1862, submitted a report on Jan. 29
(Journal, 1:720-727). A Special Committee on the Removal of the Seat of
Government presented a report on Aug. 16, 1861. The Journal contains references to other committees that were not very active, including a Committee on Ways and Means, a Committee To Inquire into the Amount of
Small Arms and Ammunition in Possession of and Distributed by the Government, and a Committee on Commercial and Financial Independence.
        A resolution of May 21, 1861 (Prov. Cong. C.S.A. Stat. 157), directed
that the books that had been purchased by the Committee To Digest the Laws
be turned over to the Secretary of Congress for the use of Members. A
few publications were sent to the Confederate Library of Congress that was
established by the stipulation of the copyright act of May 21, 1861, that one
copy of each copyrighted work delivered to the Department of State be
placed in the Library of Congress.

          Richard E. Beringer, "A   1952); Horace Montgomery, Howell
Profile of Members of the Confed-   Cobb's Confederate Career (Tusca-
erate Congress, " Journal of South- loosa, Ala., 1959); Wilfred B. Yearns,
ern History, 33:518-541 (Nov. 1967); The Confederate Congress (Athens,
William S. Hoole, Alias Simon   Ga., 1960). The printed Journal of
Suggs; the Life and Times of John-   the Provisional Congress is cited in
son Jones Hooper (University, Ala., chapter I of this Guide.

        An act of Congress of Feb. 27, 1861 (Prov. Cong. C.S.A. Stat. 39),
directed the Secretary of Congress to prepare copies of the journals of the
public sessions for publication. This preparation seems not to have been
done during the life of the Provisional Congress, and an act adopted at its
close, Feb. 17, 1862 (Prov. Cong. C.S.A. Stat. 277), authorized the President of Congress to have prepared two copies of its journals and those of
the Constitutional Convention, one copy to be deposited in the Department
of Justice and the other to be retained by the President. The original
journals were to be deposited with the Secretary of State, and all of the
journals were to be preserved until publication was ordered by Congress.
Howell Cobb assigned to Johnson J. Hooper, the former Secretary of Congress, the task of copying the journals. Hooper died in June 1862, however,
and Cobb engaged Maj. John C. Whitner of West Point, Ga., to copy the
journals. In July Major Whitner received some of the records of the Provisional Congress, and in August Robert E. Dixon delivered the journal of
the open and secret sessions to him. In 1864 Whitner obtained the original
proceedings of the Constitutional Convention. He procured other records
through the assistance of Dixon and Albert R. Lamar, another Assistant
Secretary of the Provisional Congress, but was unable to find many of the
papers referred to in the journals. Whitner's transcription was therefore
delayed by lack of records and, even more, by the need to protect them
from capture by the U.S. Army. From Augusta on Nov. 18, 1864, he reported to Cobb that part of the convention journal and two-thirds of the
journals of the open and secret sessions of Congress had been copied and
that he hoped to complete the work shortly (Official Records . . . Armies,
ser. 4, vol. 3, p. 1016-1018).
        In June 1865 at Athens, Ga., on instructions from Howell Cobb,
Whitner turned over the Provisional Congress records, the journal

transcripts, and the original proceedings of the Constitutional Convention to Maj. Charles L. Greeno, provost marshal of U. S. Army headquarters at Macon. Maj. Gen. James H. Wilson, the commander at Macon, shipped these records to Washington where they became part of the records entrusted to the Archive Office of the War Department.

General Wilson's letter of June 24, 1865, to the Assistant Adjutant General notifying him of the shipment of the records (Archive Office, Letters Received, W-45) was accompanied by a list of the records received from Major Whitner that is still on file with the letter cited.

Record Group 109. --Records of the Provisional Congress are in the War Department Collection of Confederate Records. In classifying those records the War Department placed the legislative records in chapter VII (see appendix I of this Guide for an explanation of chapter designations). The rules of the Provisional Congress provided for open and secret sessions, and since Congress passed on nominations for appointments it also held executive sessions. A finished copy of the journal of the open and secret sessions, Feb. 4, 1861-Feb. 18, 1862 (ch. VII, vols. 1, 3, 5, and part of vol. 6), contains more than 900 pages. A subject index to volumes 5 and 6 of the journal is in ch. VII, vol. 34 1/2, and a name index is in part of an unnumbered volume. The journal contains a chronological record of the proceedings of Congress for the admission of Members and the administering of oaths; the admission of additional States; the election of officers; appointment of employees; adoption of rules; appointment of committees; the drafting of the Provisional Constitution; votes; and the introduction and referral of memorials, petitions, and communications. The journal also contains the texts of bills, resolutions, motions, committee reports, and Presidential messages and a record of the action taken on them. The journal of the executive sessions, Feb. 21, 1861-Feb. 17, 1862 (ch. VII, vol. 21), contains Presidential nominations for appointments to civil and military positions, recommendations of Cabinet officers, reports of the standing committees to which the nominations were referred, and the record of confirmation or rejection. Some rough notes for the journal are in a separate file (3 ft. 4 in.); others are filed with notes for the House journal. A calendar of secret sessions, Feb. 9-Aug. 28, 1861 (1 vol.), contains data regarding bills and resolutions introduced, the name of the person introducing each one, and, occasionally, a notation of the action taken. A register of acts and resolutions, Feb. 6, 1861-Feb. 17, 1862 (ch. VII, vols. 2 and part of 4), gives in numerical order the number of the act or resolution and its title, date of passage, and date of approval. An index arranged by subject gives the number of the act or resolution.

Papers of the Provisional Congress are in a number of small files (sometimes part of larger series containing records of the House and/or the Senate). A file of legislative papers, Feb. 4, 1861-Feb. 17, 1862 (1 ft. 4 in.), arranged chronologically, contains bills and resolutions; reports of committees with communications from the executive departments; minutes of open and secret sessions; letters and telegrams to Members of Congress from Cabinet officers, other Government officials, and persons concerned with proposed legislation; and petitions, specifications, drawings, and correspondence for patent caveats. Some memorials and petitions are in this file, but most are in a separate file described below. (Papers on the Constitutional Convention in this file are described above.) A chronological file (5 in.) of messages from the President for this period contains approvals of acts and resolutions, nominations for appointments with letters of recommendation from heads of executive departments, transmittal letters covering communications and estimates from the executive departments, letters requesting the return of lists of nominations not acted on, speeches, veto messages, and letters from the executive departments. There are cross-reference cards for some original messages that were withdrawn for use in the Official Records . . . Armies. A file of Members' credentials, Jan. 1861-Feb. 1862 (1 in.), consists of Governors' commissions and certificates of elections, election returns, lists of State delegations, and printed lists of Members. Nominations for appointments and estimates for funds are in other files described in the section on joint committees. The Journal, cited below, serves as an index to the Provisional Congress files.

The journal of the open, secret, and executive sessions of the Provisional Congress is printed in C.S.A. Congress, Journal of the Congress of the Confederate States of America, 1861-1865, Volume 1, Journal of the Provisional Congress of the Confederate States of America (S. Doc. 234, 58 Cong., 2 sess., Serial 4610; Washington, 1904). See chapter IV of this Guide for information on Presidential messages.

Lists of Members of the Provisional Congress are in the following sources: Charles C. Jones, Jr., "Confederate Roster," Southern Historical Society Papers, 3:125-130 (May and June 1877); Official Records . . . Armies, ser. 4, vol. 3, p. 1185-1191; U.S. Record and Pension Office, Executive and Congressional Directory of the Confederate States, 1861-1865 (Tallahassee, 1899). An alphabetical list of the names of Members of Congress is in Bell I. Wiley and Hirst D. Milhollen, Embattled Confederates; an Illustrated History of Southerners, p. 258-273 (New York, 1964). Since some Members had served in the U.S. Congress, see also U.S. Congress, Biographical Directory of the American Congress, 1774-1961 (H. Doc. 442, 85 Cong., 2 sess., Serial 12108; Washington, 1961).

CONGRESS OF 1862-65

In contrast to the unicameral Congress of the provisional Government, the Permanent Constitution, adopted on Mar. 11, 1861, provided for a Senate and a House of Representatives. The Members of the House of Representatives were to be elected biennially by electors from each State. Until a census was taken within 3 years after the first meeting of the Congress, the States were to have the following number of Representatives: South Carolina, 6; Georgia, 10; Alabama, 9; Florida, 2; Mississippi, 7; Louisiana, 6; and Texas, 6. When vacancies occurred in House seats, special elections were to be held to fill them. Two Senators were to be chosen by each State legislature for terms of 6 years. So that one-third could be chosen every second year, the Senators chosen initially were to be divided into three classes as follows: those to serve 2 years, those to serve 4 years, and those to serve 6 years. If a vacancy occurred in the Senate, a State Governor could make temporary appointments until the next meeting of the legislature, which was then to fill the vacancy.

An election for Members of the House of Representatives and electors for the President and Vice President was held on Nov. 6, 1861, under the provisions of an act of May 21, 1861 (Prov. Cong. C.S.A. Stat. 122). The States admitted to the Confederacy since the adoption of the Permanent

Constitution were given the following representation: Virginia, 16; North Carolina, 10; Tennessee, 11; and Arkansas, 4. In States where no regular sessions of the legislatures were to be held before Feb. 18, 1862, Senators could be elected at any special or extra session.

Missouri and Kentucky, not as yet having been admitted to the Confederacy, did not participate in the general election. By acts of Nov. 29 and Dec. 21, 1861 (Prov. Cong. C. S. A. Stat. 221 and 226), Missouri was permitted 13 Representatives and Kentucky, 12. These States were then largely under U. S. control and their secession governments operated in exile. Their Governors appointed Senators and ordered Representatives elected by soldier and refugee votes.

No census was taken by the Confederate Government, and the representation continued to be based on the U. S. census of 1860: one Member for every 90,000 inhabitants and one additional Member for a fraction more than one-half of that number.

Each House was to judge the elections, returns, and qualifications of its own Members, determine the rules of its proceedings, punish Members for disorderly behavior, and expel a Member when necessary. Separate journals, to be kept by each House, were to be published from time to time--except for matter regarded as secret. The salaries of Senators and Representatives were to be determined by law. A two-thirds vote of each House was required to override Presidential vetoes of bills and of parts of appropriation bills.

Congress was given the same general powers to legislate as had been vested in the Provisional Congress, but some limitations were imposed. Congress could lay and collect taxes but could not grant bounties from the Treasury or levy customs duties for the purpose of fostering industry. Congress could regulate commerce but could not appropriate money for internal improvements intended to facilitate commerce--except for lighthouse services and river and harbor improvement. The expenses of the Post Office Department were to be paid from its own revenues after Mar. 1, 1863.

JOINT COMMITTEES OF CONGRESS

Joint Committee on Rules

The Committees on Rules of the two Houses, formed at the beginning of the First Congress, also served as the Joint Committee on Rules. As such, it prepared joint rules and orders that were adopted by the two Houses on Feb. 27, 1862 (printed in the Senate Journal, 2:26-27).

Joint Committee on Inauguration

Authorized by a House resolution of Feb. 19, 1862 (concurred in by the Senate on Feb. 21). The report of the committee in the form of a program for the ceremony is in the Journal, 5:17-18.

Joint Committee on Printing

Authorized by a House resolution of Feb. 24, 1862 (concurred in by the Senate on Feb. 25).

Joint Committee on Buildings

Authorized by a House resolution of Feb. 24, 1862 (concurred in by the Senate on Feb. 25).

Joint Committee on Flag and Seal

Authorized by a House resolution of Feb. 24, 1862 (concurred in by the Senate on Feb. 25). A report on a design for a Confederate flag is in the Journal, 5:272.

Joint Committee on Enrollment and Engrossment

Authorized by a Senate resolution of Mar. 13, 1862 (concurred in by the House on Apr. 14). Under the joint rules of Congress this committee had the regular task of examining enrolled and engrossed bills.

Joint Select Committee To Investigate the Management of the Navy Department

Authorized by a House resolution of Aug. 27, 1862 (concurred in by the Senate on Aug. 28), this committee conducted an extensive inquiry into the administration of the Department and prepared a lengthy report (cited in chapter VIII of this Guide).

Joint Select Committee To Prepare an Address to the People of the Confederate States

Authorized by a House resolution of Jan. 9, 1864 (concurred in by the Senate on Jan. 11). An address was adopted on Feb. 17, 1864, and the House ordered it printed. Another select committee for the same purpose was authorized in Jan. 1865. A report was submitted to the Senate on Mar. 17 and ordered printed.

Joint Special Committee on Impressments

Authorized by a joint resolution that originated in the House on May 10, 1864.

Joint Committee To Collect Intelligence Concerning Any Movement of the Enemy Threatening the Forcible Interruption of the Deliberation of Congress

Authorized by a House resolution of May 11, 1864 (concurred in by the Senate on May 13).

Joint Special Committee on the Means of Public Defense

Authorized by a House resolution of Dec. 28, 1864 (concurred in by the Senate with amendments on Dec. 30). Written reports were submitted to the House and Senate on Jan. 25, 1865.

Joint Select Committee To Investigate the Condition and Treatment of
 Prisoners of War

Authorized by a Senate resolution of Jan. 10, 1865 (concurred in by
the House on Jan. 12). Reports submitted to the Senate on Mar. 3 and 18
are cited under the Office of the Commissary General of Prisoners in
chapter VII of this Guide.

The committees prepared reports, bills, statutes, or resolutions.
Some reports were printed in small editions, some are cited elsewhere in
this Guide, and others are listed in the bibliographies by Crandall and
Harwell. Reports that were not printed are in the records of either the
House or the Senate; the Journal and the Statutes can be used as aids in
locating the reports, bills, and resolutions. The committees sometimes
were carried over from one session to another, a fact to be kept in mind
when using the Journal.

The bulk of the records of Congress of 1862-65 were moved south
from Richmond before or during its evacuation on Apr. 2, 1865. Some
records not thus removed were stolen; and some, found by U.S. Army units
that occupied the city, were forwarded to the Archive Office of the War
Department. Material awaiting printing in the hands of the public printer
in Richmond, including the evidence taken by the Joint Select Committee
To Investigate the Condition and Treatment of Prisoners of War (see above),
was burned while Richmond was being evacuated. Of the material moved
south, the records of both Houses, including their journals, most of the
enrolled acts and resolutions, and other papers, were recovered at Chester, S. C., and sent to the War Department at Washington.

Record Group 109. --Some records of Congress are for the years
1862-65, but other series cover the Provisional Congress also. A chronological file of messages from the President, Feb. 25, 1862-Mar. 20, 1865
(1 ft. 9 in.), is similar in content to messages of 1861-62 described under
the Provisional Congress. Papers concerning nominations are described
under the Senate. A file of memorials and petitions, 1861-65 (10 in.), is
arranged numerically. A register of memorials and petitions, Mar. 1861-
Feb. 1865 (ch. VII, vol. 10), is arranged alphabetically by the first letter
of the petitioner's name and shows the date presented, the committee to
which referred, the date reported, and the action of the committee. A
file of Congressional messages, Feb. 1862-Mar. 1865 (5 in.), consists of
messages from the Senate to the House and from the House to the Senate.
Arranged by session of Congress, they concern action on bills, resolutions,
and committee reports. A file of estimates of funds, 1861-65 (3 in.), contains communications from the executive departments and the officers of
Congress showing estimates of appropriations necessary and letters regarding additional needed employees. A file of miscellaneous letters and
reports, 1861-65 (1 in.), contains letters from departmental and bureau
heads and Army officers to Congressmen and applications for appointments
as Senate employees. Other letters from the Secretary of War, heads of
War Department bureaus, and Army officers, 1861-65 (1/3 in.), are accompanied by a chronological list.

Several volumes and files relate to legislation. A register of acts
and resolutions, Feb. 6, 1861-Mar. 18, 1865 (ch. VII, vols. 2 and 4), is
arranged numerically and shows the number of the act or resolution, its
title, the date passed, and the date approved. An index (ch. VII, another

vol. 2) is arranged alphabetically by subject and gives the number of the act or resolution. A calendar of bills and resolutions, Mar. 1862-May 1864 (ch. VII, vol. 32), contains separate chronological records for the Senate and the House, showing subject, name of introducer, date introduced, and action taken. Some rough notes on the action of Congress on bills and resolutions, 1861-65 (1 ft.), relate largely to bills and resolutions on which no final action was taken. Other files include Senate amendments to House bills and House amendments to Senate bills, 1862-63 (1 in.), enrolled and engrossed bills and resolutions, Feb. 1862-Mar. 1865 (4 1/2 in.), and reports of the Joint Committee on Enrollment and Engrossment, Mar. 1862-Mar. 1865 (3/4 in.).

Alphabetical indexes to subjects and names were prepared for some of the files described above and for the journals. These include an index to bills, resolutions, and committee reports, Feb. 1861-Mar. 1865 (1 vol.); an index to open sessions, Feb. 1861-Mar. 1865 (1 vol.); and an index to numbered memorials and petitions (1 vol.). It is more convenient, however, to use the indexes in the volumes of the published Journal. They are not so reliable as they might be, however, and paging through the Journal, particularly if the date of a document is known, might be of benefit.

Besides the printed materials in the Congressional files other material of this character is in separate files in this record group. A file of reports of executive departments, 1861-65 (1 ft.), includes printed and manuscript reports of the War, Treasury, and Post Office Departments, the Attorney General, the Commissioner of Patents, the Superintendent of Public Printing, the Secretary of State (Apr. 27, 1861), and the Second Auditor of the Treasury (Jan. 8, 1862). A larger file of printed documents, 1861-65 (3 ft.), includes House and Senate bills and resolutions, Presidential messages, committee reports, and speeches.

The journal of the Confederate Congress was eventually printed as a document of the U.S. Senate. In 1903 the Record and Pension Office of the U.S. War Department prepared copies of the journals for the printer. A Senate resolution of Jan. 28, 1904, introduced by Joseph B. Foraker, directed the Secretary of War to transmit to the Senate a copy of the journal of the Provisional Congress and the First and Second Congresses. On Jan. 30 the copy was transmitted to the Senate, and on Feb. 1 it was ordered printed. During 1904-5 the War Department Military Secretary's Office indexed the journal volumes, which were printed in the same years as S. Doc. 234, 58 Cong., 2 sess. Serials 4610-4616 (cited in chapter I of this Guide). Microreproductions of the printed journal may be purchased from the Louisville (Ky.) Public Library.

The Journal of the Confederate Congress can be supplemented by its "Proceedings," Feb. 18, 1862-Mar. 18, 1865, published in the Southern Historical Society Papers, vols. 44-52 (1923-59). As president of the Southern Historical Society, Douglas S. Freeman initiated the preparation of these proceedings from wartime reports in the Richmond Examiner, the Richmond Enquirer, and other newspapers. The newspaper accounts had been prepared by reporters admitted to the open sessions of Congress, and they include abstracts of debates, texts of bills, resolutions, memorials, military correspondence and telegrams, a record of the action of Congress on measures under consideration, and eulogies for deceased Members. The proceedings are most valuable for the summaries of Members' remarks on proposed legislation, which supplement the

minutes recorded in the Journal.
Other Congressional docu-
ments are published in Richardson,
ed., Messages and Papers; in
Rowland, ed., Jefferson Davis,
Constitutionalist, vols. 5-6; in
Official Records . . . Armies,
particularly ser. 2, vols. 2-8, and
ser. 4, vols. 1-3; and in the Journal of the Congress of the Confederate States of America, 1861-1865,
cited above. An extensive unpublished compilation by Raphael P.

Thian entitled "Documentary History
of the Flag and Seal of the Confederate States of America, 1861-1865"
(Washington, 1880) is in the Rare
Book Room of the Library of Congress.
Documents from the files of
Congress are in the compiled military service records and papers relating to Confederate citizens and
businesses described in the final
chapter of this Guide.

Records in Other Custody. --In the Archives Division of the Virginia
State Library is a typewritten manuscript (98 p.) entitled "Substance of
the Testimony of Col. Frank G. Ruffin, Late Lieut. Col. in the Confederate Bureau of Subsistence, Given Before the Joint Select Committee of the
Two Houses of the Confederate Congress, on the Means of Public Defense,
on the 23rd of January 1865."

SENATE

On Feb. 18, 1862, the Senate met in the Senate Chamber of tie Virginia State Capitol in Richmond and was called to order by Vice President
Stephens. Robert M. T. Hunter of Virginia was elected President pro
tempore, and he was reelected on May 2, 1864, at the beginning of the first
session of the Second Congress. Stephens was absent in Georgia during
much of 1862-64. The usual meetingplace of the Senate was on the third
floor of the State Capitol, but when the State senate was not in session its
chamber was used. Of the 26 Senators, 14 had served in the U.S. Congress.
A total of 36 men served in the Senate during the two Confederate Congresses.
Rules for conducting business in the Senate were adopted on Feb. 24,
1862. Rule I required the reading each day of the journal of the preceding day and the correction of errors. Rule XXXVI required secret sessions for confidential or executive business. Separate and distinct record
books were prescribed for the legislative proceedings, the executive proceedings, and the confidential legislative proceedings. The executive
sessions were devoted to passing on Presidential nominations for appointments. Stenographers and newspaper reporters could be admitted by the
President. The order of business was the same as that followed by the
Provisional Congress. Rules XLIX and L, adopted on Apr. 1, 1862, retained for the President pro tempore his right as a Member to vote on all
questions and provided that the Senator elected to that position should hold
it until the beginning of a new Congress and the election of his successor.
The division of Senators into classes to serve for 2, 4, or 6 years in accordance with the Permanent Constitution was done by balloting on Feb. 21,
1862.

Senate Standing Committees

On Feb. 25, 1862, the Senate adopted an order designating the following standing committees:

Committee on Accounts; Charles B. Mitchel (Ark.), chairman, 1st Cong., Allen T. Caperton (Va.), 2d Cong.

Committee on Claims; George Davis (N.C.), chairman, 1st Cong., Henry C. Burnett (Ky.), 2d Cong.

Committee on Commerce; Clement C. Clay (Ala.), chairman, 1st Cong., Williamson S. Oldham (Tex.), 2d Cong.

Committee on Enrollment and Engrossment; Landon C. Haynes (Tenn.), chairman, 1st Cong., William T. Dortsch (N.C.), 2d Cong.

Committee on Finance; Robert W. Barnwell (S.C.), chairman, 1st and 2d Congs.

Committee on Foreign Relations; James L. Orr (S.C.), chairman, 1st and 2d Congs.

Committee on Indian Affairs; Robert W. Johnson (Ark.), chairman, 1st and 2d Congs.

Committee on the Judiciary; Benjamin H. Hill (Ga.), chairman, 1st and 2d Congs.

Committee on Military Affairs (called Military Affairs and Militia in 2d Cong.); Edward Sparrow (La.), chairman, 1st and 2d Congs.

Committee on Naval Affairs; Albert G. Brown (Miss.), chairman, 1st and 2d Congs.

Committee on Patents (called Patents and Patent Office in 2d Cong.); Augustus E. Maxwell (Fla.), chairman, 1st and 2d Congs.

Committee on Post Offices and Post Roads; Williamson S. Oldham (Tex.), chairman, 1st Cong., Charles B. Mitchel (Ark.), 2d Cong.

Committee on Printing; James Phelan (Miss.), chairman, 1st Cong., John W. C. Watson (Miss.), 2d Cong.

Committee on Public Buildings (authorized May 20, 1864); James M. Baker (Fla.), chairman, 2d Cong.

Committee on Public Lands; John B. Clark (Mo.), chairman, 1st Cong., James M. Baker (Fla.), 2d Cong.

Committee on Territories; Louis T. Wigfall (Tex.), chairman, 1st and 2d Congs.

The standing committees considered bills, recommendations made by the President in his messages, and Presidential nominations for appointments. Rule XXXI of the Senate concerning the standing committees was amended on Jan. 20, 1863, to provide for the appointment of their members at the beginning of each Congress; therefore the membership was changed on May 3, 1864, by balloting in the Senate. The amended rule omitted the Committee on Public Buildings, but on May 20, 1864, the rule was again amended to include that committee, and its members were appointed on the same day.

Senate Special and Select Committees

Matters not assignable to the standing committees were placed in the hands of special and select committees for investigation and report. For the purposes of this Guide, the titles of the committees in the following list were devised from entries in the Journal describing their duties. The committees did not always submit written reports; they sometimes submitted oral reports, bills, or resolutions.

Special Committee on Pay and Mileage
Appointed on Apr. 3, 1862, to consist of Henry C. Burnett (Ky.), James L. Orr (S.C.), and Gustavus A. Henry (Tenn.).

Special Committee To Investigate the Complaints Made by the Sick and Wounded in the Army
Authorized and appointed on Aug. 26, 1862, to consist of William E. Simms (Ky.), Charles B. Mitchel (Ark.), and Benjamin H. Hill (Ga.). On Sept. 22, 1862, Simms submitted a report that on Sept. 27 was referred to the Committee on Printing.

Select Committee To Investigate Outrages Committed by the Enemy Upon the Persons and Property of Our Citizens
Authorized and appointed on Oct. 3, 1862, with 13 members under the chairmanship of Clement C. Clay (Ala.). On May 1, 1863, Clay submitted a report that was ordered printed.

Select Committee on the Cotton Bill
Appointed on Jan. 28, 1863, to consist of James Phelan (Miss.), Edward Sparrow (La.), Charles B. Mitchel (Ark.), Gustavus A. Henry (Tenn.), and James L. Orr (S.C.). The bill (S. 21) was "for the condemnation to public use of all cotton within the Confederate States, providing for the payment thereof, and for other purposes." On Feb. 11, 1863, Phelan submitted the bill with amendments.

Special Committee To Investigate the Recent Violation of the Dignity of the Senate
Authorized and appointed on Feb. 4, 1863, to consist of Robert W. Barnwell (S.C.), Edward Sparrow (La.), Gustavus A. Henry (Tenn.), Louis T. Wigfall (Tex.), and Albert G. Brown (Miss.). On the same day the committee reported resolutions expressing disapprobation and censure of the conduct of Benjamin H. Hill (Ga.) and William L. Yancey (Ala.).

Special Committee To Inquire into the Rights and Duties of Reporters Admitted to the Senate and Also To Inquire Whether There Has Been
Any Breach of Those Rights
Authorized and appointed on Feb. 25, 1863, to consist of Louis T.
Wigfall (Tex.), William L. Yancey (Ala.), and Robert W. Johnson (Ark.).
The committee's report of Mar. 12 (Journal, 3:157) expressed the opinion
that the reporter for the Richmond Enquirer had used improper language
in reporting the proceedings of the Senate and favored his exclusion from
the floor.

Special Committee To Investigate the Expediency of Providing for Reports
of the Senate Debates
Authorized and appointed on Apr. 13, 1863, to consist of Robert W.
Johnson (Ark.), James L. Orr (La.), and Albert H. Brown (Miss.).
During the summer the committee interviewed shorthand reporters, and
on Jan. 7, 1864, the committee submitted resolutions and a report that
were ordered printed. The proposed publication of reports of debates was
regarded as too expensive and was not undertaken.

Select Committee on Bill (H. R. 92) To Tax, Fund, and Limit the Currency
Appointed on Feb. 2, 1864, to consist of Robert M. T. Hunter (Va.),
Williamson S. Oldham (Tex.), William E. Simms (Ky.), James L. Orr
(S. C.), and Thomas J. Semmes (La.). On Feb. 4, 1864, Semmes reported
the bill with amendments.

Special Committee To Inquire into the Practicability of Employing Stenogra-
phers, by Contract, To Report the Debates and Proceedings of the
Senate
Authorized and appointed on June 4, 1864, to consist of James L. Orr
(S. C.), Albert G. Brown (Miss.), and Robert W. Johnson (Ark.).

Special Committee To Investigate the Price Paid for Army Clothing
Authorized and appointed on Nov. 25, 1864, to consist of William E.
Simms (Ky.), James M. Baker (Fla.), and William A. Graham (N. C.).
This committee was also to determine whether the compensation granted
women employed in the Ordnance Department was sufficient for their subsistence. On Jan. 5, 1865, Simms reported a bill (S. 155) to regulate the
pay and allowances of female employees of the Government.

Select Committee To Consider the Bill (S. 167) To Organize an Executive
Corps of the Provisional Army
Appointed on Jan. 24, 1865, to consist of Williamson S. Oldham
(Tex.), Waldo P. Johnson (Mo.), and Benjamin H. Hill (Ga.).

Special Committee To Confer with the President in Reference to the Pres-
ent Condition of the Country
Authorized and appointed on Mar. 2, 1865, to consist of William A.
Graham (N. C.), Robert M. T. Hunter (Va.), and James L. Orr (S. C.).
On Mar. 4, Graham submitted an oral report.

Select Committee on the Portion of the President's Message as Relates to
the Action of Congress
Appointed on Mar. 13, 1865, to consist of James L. Orr (S. C.),

Thomas J. Semmes (La.), William A. Graham (N.C.), Allen T. Caperton (Va.), and John W. C. Watson (Miss.). Orr submitted a report on Mar. 16 (Journal, 4:726-731).

Record Group 109. --Journals, other record books, and files of folded papers comprise the Senate records. The finished journal of the open sessions, Feb. 18, 1862-Mar. 18, 1865 (ch. VII, part of vol. 7, vols. 8, 9, and part of vol. 18) contains a chronological record of the proceedings. These minutes concern the admission of Members; appointment of committees and employees; election of officers; introduction of bills, resolutions, memorials, petitions, and amendments; and the record of votes. Also in the journal are the texts of a variety of documents including bills, resolutions, amendments, acts, motions, orders. Presidential messages and letters, communications from department heads, messages from the House, committee reports, and battle reports. The finished journal of the secret sessions, Feb. 27, 1862-Mar. 18, 1865 (ch. VII, parts of vols. 6 and 7), has similar contents but is much briefer. The finished journal of executive sessions, Feb. 25, 1862-June 14, 1864 (ch. VII, vols. 21 and 22), contains Presidential nominations for appointments with recommendations from department heads and the record of the Senate action. Rough journals of the open, secret, and executive sessions, 1862-65 (ch. VII, vols. 31, 33, 34, 34 1/2), are mostly in pencil. A file of rough journal notes, Feb. 18, 1862-Mar. 18, 1865 (4 ft. 6 in.), chronologically arranged, contains material on the open, secret, and executive sessions. An alphabetical name index to open and secret sessions, Feb. 1862-Mar. 1865 (1 vol.), contains chronologically arranged journal entries for the Senators. A calendar of bills and resolutions, Feb. 19, 1862-Feb. 17, 1864 (ch. VII, vol. 11), contains a record of the numbers, dates, and titles of bills and resolutions, the names of the committees to which referred, dates of reports, action of the committee and of the Senate, and the dates presented to and signed by the President. The legislative papers, Feb. 18, 1862-Mar. 16, 1865 (9 in.), referred to in the journal consist of original bills, resolutions, amendments, acts, and committee reports; letters and reports from Government officials and others; and resolutions of State legislatures proposing legislation. A file of nominations to Congress and related papers, 1861-64 (9 in., mostly for 1864), contains recommendations for appointments from Department heads--sometimes including the Presidential nominations, lists of assignments of military officers on nomination lists, and lists of officers not confirmed.

C.S.A. Congress, Journal of the Congress of the Confederate States of America, 1861-1865, vols. 2-4, Journal of the Senate . . . (S. Doc. 234, 58 Cong., 2 sess., Serials 4611-4613; Washington, 1904). This published journal contains the proceedings of the open, secret, and executive sessions. For bibliographical data concerning Senate documents that were printed during the war, see the preceding section of this chapter. Data regarding Senators appointed by the Governors of Missouri and Tennessee may be found in the Governors' papers.

HOUSE OF REPRESENTATIVES

The Congressmen elected in the State elections of Nov. 1861 assembled in the Virginia State Capitol in Richmond on Feb. 18, 1862. Howell

Cobb called the session to order and administered the oath of office to the 85 Members who were present from 13 States. The House elected Thomas S. Bocock of Virginia as Speaker, and he served in that position throughout the war. Other Representatives took their seats on later days; the total authorized membership was 102. Malcolm H. MacWillie took his seat as the delegate of Arizona Territory on Mar. 11, 1862, replacing Granville H. Oury. After the Union reconquest of Arizona in 1862, MacWillie continued to serve in Congress as the delegate of the nonexistent Confederate Territory of Arizona. The treaties of 1861 with Indian tribes west of the Mississippi allowed them nonvoting delegates. Accordingly, Elias C. Boudinot was admitted as Cherokee delegate on Oct. 9, 1862, Robert M. Jones as Choctaw-Chickasaw delegate on Jan. 17, 1863, and Samuel B. Callahan as the Creek and Seminole delegate on May 30, 1864. The total membership of the House from the 13 Confederate States, Arizona Territory, and the Indian nations was 106.

The total number of men who served in the House of Representatives during the First and Second Congresses was much larger than the authorized membership. Some Representatives did not run for reelection in 1863, and others were defeated in that election. The total number of men who served in the House during the two Congresses was 163; only 27 Representatives served continuously throughout the war.

House Standing Committees

A report of the Committee on Rules of Feb. 20, 1862, relating to standing committees, was accepted, and on the 25th the Speaker announced the following committees:

Committee on Accounts; John McQueen (S.C.), chairman, 1st Cong., Israel Welsh (Miss.), 2d Cong.

Committee on Claims; William Smith (Va.), chairman, 1st Cong., William N. H. Smith (N.C.), 2d Cong.

Committee on Commerce; Jabez L. M. Curry (Ala.), chairman, 1st Cong., Julian Hartridge (Ga.), 2d Cong.

Committee on Elections; William N. H. Smith (N.C.), chairman, 1st Cong., John A. Gilmer (N.C.), 2d Cong.

Committee on Flag and Seal; Alexander R. Boteler (Va.), chairman, 1st Cong., William P. Chilton (Ala.), 2d Cong.

Committee on Enrolled Bills; John M. Elliott (Ky.), chairman, 1st Cong., Marcus M. Cruikshank (Ala.), 2d Cong.

Committee on Foreign Affairs; Henry S. Foote (Tenn.), chairman, 1st Cong., William C. Rives (Va.), 2d Cong.

Committee on Indian Affairs; Otho R. Singleton (Miss.), chairman, 1st and 2d Congs.

Committee on the Judiciary; Lucius J. Gartrell (Ga.), chairman, 1st
     Cong., Charles W. Russell (Va.), 2d Cong.

Committee on Military Affairs; William P. Miles (S.C.), chairman, 1st
     and 2d Congs.

Committee on Medical Department (created Sept. 8, 1862); Augustus R.
     Wright (Ga.), chairman, 1st Cong., David Clopton (Ala.), 2d Cong.

Committee on Naval Affairs; Charles M. Conrad (La.), chairman, 1st
     Cong., William W. Boyce (S.C.), 2d Cong.

Committee on Ordnance and Ordnance Stores (appointed Sept. 8, 1862);
     Alexander R. Boteler (Va.), chairman, 1st Cong., John D. C.
     Atkins (Tenn.), 2d Cong.

Committee on Patents; Caspar W. Bell (Mo.), chairman, 1st Cong.,
     Joseph B. Heiskell (Tenn.), 2d Cong.

Committee on Pay and Mileage; Theodore L. Burnett (Ky.), chairman,
     1st and 2d Congs.

Committee on Post Offices and Post Roads; William P. Chilton (Ala.),
     chairman, 1st Cong., Franklin B. Sexton (Tex.), 2d Cong.

Committee on Printing; Ethelbert Barksdale (Miss.), chairman, 1st Cong.,
     Lucius J. Dupré (La.), 2d Cong.

Committee on Public Buildings; James Lyons (Va.), chairman, 1st Cong.,
     Fayette McMullin (Va.), 2d Cong.

Committee on Quartermaster's and Commissary Departments (appointed
     Sept. 8, 1862); William P. Chilton (Ala.), chairman, 1st Cong.,
     Willis B. Machen (Ky.), 2d Cong.

Committee on Rules and Officers of the House; George W. Jones (Tenn.),
     chairman, 1st Cong., John Perkins, Jr. (La.), 2d Cong.

Committee on Territories and Public Lands; John A. Wilcox (Tex.),
     chairman, 1st Cong., Augustus H. Garland (Ark.), 2d Cong.

Committee on Ways and Means; Duncan F. Kenner (La.), chairman, 1st
     Cong., Francis S. Lyon (Ala.), 2d Cong.

The complete membership of the committees is listed in the Journal under
the dates they were appointed (Feb. 25, 1862, and May 7, 1864). The
House amended its rules on Dec. 1, 1864, adding to Rule XXXVI the standing
committees that had been appointed on Sept. 8, 1862. Other committees
on the executive departments and prisons, prisoners, and the exchange
of prisoners were also added to Rule XXXVI, but these committees were
apparently not actually constituted. The committees of the First Congress
had 3 to 9 members and those of the Second Congress 3 to 12 members.
Members were frequently excused from or added to the committees.

House Special and Select Committees

House special and select committees were formed by resolution to consider matters outside the cognizance of the standing committees or to conduct investigations. The Journal does not always indicate the membership or the outcome of a committee's work. Some of the committees are not in the indexes except under subjects, and the indexing is not complete. A careful reading of the Journal would reveal more information concerning the committees.

Special Committee To Inquire into the Causes of the Capitulation of Roanoke Island

Authorized Feb. 26, 1862; report submitted by Burgess S. Gaither (N. C.), printed in House Journal, 5:238-243, and separately.

Special Committee on Recent Military Disasters

Authorized and appointed on Feb. 26, 1862, to consist of Henry S. Foote (Tenn.), Ethelbert Barksdale (Miss.), Thomas B. Hanly (Ark.), Thomas J. Foster (Ala.), and Horatio W. Bruce (Ky.). It was to "inquire into the late military disasters at Forts Henry and Donelson, and also into the circumstances connected with the supposed surrender of the city of Nashville." The committee's recommendation of Apr. 15 to print the testimony it had collected was accepted. On Feb. 23, 1863, the committee presented a supplementary report on charges against Maj. Vernon K. Stevenson, a quartermaster officer.

Special Committee on Waste and Destruction of Public Property

Appointed on Mar. 17, 1862, to consist of Lucius J. Dupré (La.), John D. C. Atkins (Tenn.), Julian Hartridge (Ga.), and Owen R. Kenan (N. C.). The committee was to investigate alleged wasteful practices of military officers.

Special Committee To Inspect Ordnance Establishments in Richmond and Vicinity

Appointed on Mar. 27, 1862, to consist of Joseph B. Heiskell (Tenn.), J. W. Clapp (Miss.), and Muscoe R. H. Garnett (Va.).

Special Committee To Visit Hospitals in Richmond

Authorized and appointed on Apr. 1, 1862, to consist of John P. Ralls (Ala.), Franklin B. Sexton (Tex.), Robert Johnston (Va.), Thomas Menees (Tenn.), and J. R. McLean (N. C.). The committee reported on Apr. 21 (printed in House Journal, 5:288-289, and separately).

Special Committee on War Tax

Authorized Aug. 20, 1862; appointed on Aug. 21 to consist of Lewis M. Ayer (S. C.), Francis S. Lyon (Ala.), Joseph B. Heiskell (Tenn.), Charles F. Collier (Va.), James S. Chrisman (Ky.), William Lander (N. C.), Franklin B. Sexton (Tex.), Israel Welsh (Miss.), William W. Clark (Ga.), Aaron H. Conrow (Mo.), Robert B. Hilton (Fla.), and Thomas B. Hanly (Ark.). Instructed to consider an allowance of just and equitable compensation to district collectors of the war tax, the committee reported a bill on Oct. 9.

Special Committee on Hospitals
      Appointed on Aug. 21, 1862, with Augustus R. Wright (Ga.), as chairman, this committee was instructed "to inquire into any abuses in the medical and surgical department." On Sept. 16 that duty was transferred to the standing Committee on the Medical Department.

Special Committee on Homesteads for Disabled Officers and Soldiers
      Appointed on Feb. 9, 1863, to consist of Charles M. Conrad (La.), William P. Chilton (Ala.), John D. C. Atkins (Tenn.), Augustus H. Garland (Ark.), Robert Johnston (Va.), Julian Hartridge (Ga.), Robert B. Hilton (Fla.), Peter W. Gray (Tex.), J. W. Clapp (Miss.), Thomas S. Ashe (N.C.), John McQueen (S.C.), Willis B. Machen (Ky.), and Caspar W. Bell (Mo.). On Apr. 22 Conrad reported a joint resolution.

Special Committee To Examine into Frauds in Transportation on Railroads
      Appointed on Feb. 11, 1863, to consist of John D. C. Atkins (Tenn.), Robert R. Bridgers (N.C.), Charles J. Munnerlyn (Ga.), William D. Simpson (S.C.), and Charles F. Collier (Va.).

Special Committee To Investigate the Chief War Tax Collector in Virginia
      Authorized on Mar. 28, 1863; appointed on Mar. 30 to consist of John Perkins, Jr. (La.), Waller R. Staples (Va.), Jabez L. M. Curry (Ala.), W. N. H. Smith (N.C.), and Otho R. Singleton (Miss.). On Apr. 14 Perkins submitted a report that was ordered printed.

Special Committee To Inquire into the Treatment of Prisoners at Castle
Thunder
      Authorized on Apr. 4, 1863; appointed on Apr. 6 to consist of Caleb C. Herbert (Tex.), William R. Smith (Ala.), Daniel C. De Jarnette (Va.), William W. Clark (Ga.), and William D. Simpson (S.C.). On May 1 the committee made majority and minority reports that were printed. The reports have been reprinted in Official Records . . . Armies, ser. 2, vol. 5, p. 871-924.

Special Committee on the Senate Bill Amending the Sequestration Act
      Appointed on Apr. 14, 1863, to consist of James Lyons (Va.), Augustus H. Garland (Ark.), Peter W. Gray (Tex.), J. W. Clapp (Miss.), and George B. Hodge (Ky.).

Special Committee To Inquire into Illegal Arrests
      Authorized Dec. 10, 1863; appointed on Dec. 12 to consist of Henry S. Foote (Tenn.), David Clopton (Ala.), Julian Hartridge (Ga.), Thomas S. Ashe (N.C.), and David Funsten (Va.). Reappointed as the Special Committee on Illegal Seizures on May 7, 1864, with Foote, Clopton, Hartridge, Funsten, and James M. Leach (N.C.) as members.

Special Committee on the Currency
      Appointed on Dec. 12, 1863, to consist of William W. Boyce (S.C.), Charles M. Conrad (La.), George W. Jones (Tenn.), John B. Baldwin (Va.), Francis S. Lyon (Ala.), Robert R. Bridgers (N.C.), and Peter W. Gray (Tex.). On Dec. 31 the committee reported a bill with a minority report and a substitute bill; the report was printed.

Special Committee on Deceased Soldiers' Claims
    Appointed on Dec. 15, 1863, to consist of William W. Clark (Ga.),
Otho R. Singleton (Miss.), Samuel A. Miller (Va.), William D. Simpson
(S. C.), and Thomas J. Foster (Ala.). On Feb. 10, 1864, Clark submitted
a report that was ordered printed.

Special Committee on the Manufacture of Salt
    Authorized Dec. 18, 1863; appointed on Dec. 19 to consist of Joseph B.
Heiskell (Tenn.), Waller R. Staples (Va.), and Horatio W. Bruce (Ky.).
The committee was to inquire into the feasibility of obtaining salt in Smyth
and Washington Counties, Va. On Feb. 15, 1864, Bruce submitted a report
that was ordered printed.

Select Committee on Veteran Soldiers' Home
    Authorized on Dec. 30, 1863; appointed on Dec. 31 to consist of J. W.
Clapp (Miss.), Jabez L. M. Curry (Ala.), George V. Vest (Mo.), John R.
Chambliss (Va.), and William G. Swann (Tenn.). On Jan. 15, 1864, Clapp
reported a bill (H. R. 94) that was enacted but vetoed in February.

Special Committee on the Manufacture of Arms in Richmond
    Appointed in 1863 to consist of Joseph B. Heiskell (Tenn.), Willis B.
Machen (Ky.), and Samuel A. Miller (Va.).

Select Committee on the Joint Resolution Relating to the War
    Appointed on Jan. 5, 1864, to consist of J. W. Clapp (Miss.), John
Goode, Jr. (Va.), Jabez L. M. Curry (Ala.), Julian Hartridge (Ga.), and
W. N. H. Smith (N. C.). The committee introduced a joint resolution on
Jan. 9.

Select Committee on the Charge of Corruption Made in the Richmond
        Examiner, Jan. 7, 1864
    Authorized Jan. 7, 1864; appointed on Jan. 8 to consist of James
Lyons (Va.), John McQueen (S. C.), and John D. C. Atkins (Tenn.). The
committee reported on Jan. 25 (printed in House Journal, 6:681, and separately.

Special Committee To Inquire into Certain Outrages of the Enemy
    Appointed on Jan. 8, 1864, to consist of W. N. H. Smith (N. C.),
James P. Holcombe (Va.), William R. Smith (Ala.), Horatio W. Bruce
(Ky.), and George G. Vest (Mo.). On Feb. 17 the committee submitted a
report and evidence that were ordered printed.

Special Committee on Increase of Clerks' Pay
    Appointed on Jan. 25, 1864, to consist of James Lyons (Va.), Joseph
B. Heiskell (Tenn.), John J. McRae (Miss.), William D. Simpson (S. C.),
and George W. Ewing (Ky.). On Jan. 27 Lyons reported a bill (S. 172)
with amendments.

Special Committee on Exemption of Printers
    Appointed on May 6, 1864, to consist of Henry S. Foote (Tenn.),
John B. Baldwin (Va.), and Henry C. Chambers (Miss.). The committee
was "to confer with the executive of the State of Virginia, for the purpose
of securing exemptions from service in the State militia [for] a sufficient

number of printers to do the necessary printing of Congress. "

Special Committee on Reporting the Proceedings of Congress

Appointed on May 7, 1864, to consist of John Perkins, Jr. (La.), Ethelbert Barksdale (Miss.), Thomas S. Gholson (Va.), Warren Akin (Ga.), and Burgess S. Gaither (N.C.). A report submitted by Perkins on Nov. 19 was laid on the table.

Special Committee Relative to Compensation for a Patent

Appointed on May 7, 1864, to consist of David Funsten (Va.), Thomas C. Fuller (N.C.), Joseph B. Heiskell (Tenn.), Henry E. Read (Ky.), and Israel Welsh (Miss.). On May 26 Funsten reported a bill "to compensate Charles E. Stuart, Israel C. Owings, and J. H. Taylor for the use of an improvement in instruments for sighting cannon. "

Special Committee To Inquire into Charges of Disloyalty against Mr. Williamson R. W. Cobb

Appointed on May 7, 1864, to consist of William P. Chilton (Ala.), Augustus H. Garland (Ark.), Robert L. Montague (Va.), James T. Leach (N.C.), and John P. Murray (Tenn.). A report submitted on May 31 was recommitted to the committee; Cobb failed to appear to claim his seat, and a resolution of Nov. 15 declared it vacant.

Special Committee on Impressments

Appointed on May 10, 1864, to consist of John B. Baldwin (Va.), Charles M. Conrad (La.), William P. Chilton (Ala.), Julian Hartridge (Ga.), John P. Murray (Tenn.), William D. Simpson (S.C.), and Burgess S. Gaither (N.C.). The committee was instructed on May 16 to "consider and report the true principle upon which 'just compensation' shall be made for private property taken or impressed for public use, " and was further instructed on Jan. 25, 1865, to "inquire into the expediency of so altering the impressment acts as to allow a fair market price for all articles taken for public use. " The committee reported a bill on Mar. 8.

Special Committee on Pay and Mileage

Appointed on May 30, 1864, to consist of Henry S. Foote (Tenn.) and 11 other members. The next day Foote reported back a Senate bill with amendments.

Special Committee on Violations of the Impressment Law in East Tennessee and Southwestern Virginia

Appointed on May 31, 1864, to consist of Joseph B. Heiskell (Tenn.), Samuel A. Miller (Va.), and John M. Elliott (Ky.). On Mar. 9, 1865, the committee reported a resolution.

Special Committee on the Payment of Claims

Authorized on May 11, 1864. and appointed on May 13 to consist of W. N. H. Smith (N.C.), Robert Johnston (Va.), and Otho R. Singleton (Miss.). The committee was to inquire into the payment of demands against the Government prior to Apr. 1, 1864. On May 26 Singleton submitted a report which was laid on the table and ordered printed.

Special Committee on the Exemption of State Officers
        Appointed on Nov. 11, 1864, to consist of Waller R. Staples (Va.),
Francis S. Lyon (Ala.), and James M. Smith (Ga.). On Nov. 19 Staples
submitted a report and a resolution.

Select Committee To Investigate the Condition of Stewart Hospital
        Authorized on Nov. 25, 1864, and appointed on Nov. 30 to consist of
Israel Welsh (Miss.), James Farrow (S.C.), Mark H. Blandford (Ga.),
Josiah Turner, Jr. (N.C.), and Caleb C. Herbert (Tex.).

Select Committee on Lessening the Number of Exempts
        Appointed on Nov. 30, 1864, to consist of 13 members with William
C. Rives (Va.) as chairman.

Select Committee on State Claims Against the Confederate Government
        Appointed on Nov. 30, 1864, to consist of 13 members with W. N. H.
Smith (N.C.) as chairman. The committee reported a bill on Jan. 23, 1865.

Select Committee on Impressments
        Appointed on Dec. 14, 1864, to consist of 13 members with John B.
Baldwin (Va.) as chairman.

Special Committee on Army Pay and Clothing
        Appointed on Dec. 5, 1864, to consist of Samuel A. Miller (Va.),
William D. Holder (Miss.), James H. Witherspoon (S.C.), Thomas Menees
(Tenn.), and John R. Baylor (Tex.). On Feb. 11, 1865, the committee sub-
mitted a report which was ordered printed.

Special Committee on Conscription
        Authorized and appointed on Dec. 12, 1864, to consist of John Goode,
Jr. (Va.), Lewis M. Ayer (S.C.), Lucius J. Dupré (La.), David Clopton
(Ala.), and Samuel St. George Rogers (Fla.). On Jan. 10, 1865, Goode
reported a bill.

Special Committee on the Relief of Taxpayers
        Authorized on Jan. 7, 1865, and appointed on Jan. 9 to consist of
Daniel C. De Jarnette (Va.), Clifford Anderson (Ga.), Aaron H. Conrow
(Mo.), Thomas J. Foster (Ala.), and John A. Orr (Miss.). The committee was to report legislation necessary "to relieve from the payment of
taxes the people residing in such districts, towns, or counties as have
been subject to depredations by the public enemy." On Feb. 14, 1865, the
committee reported a bill.

Special Committee on the Arrest of Henry S. Foote
        Appointed on Jan. 13, 1865. On Jan. 16 the committee submitted a
report (printed in House Journal, 7:458).

Special Committee on Passports Issued to Youths To Leave the Confederate
        States
        Appointed on Jan. 17, 1865.

Special Committee on the Exchange of Prisoners of War
        Appointed on Jan. 19, 1865, to consist of Humphrey Marshall (Ky.),

John Perkins, Jr. (La.), John A. Gilmer (N.C.), John B. Clark (Mo.), and David Funsten (Va.). The members of this committee also served as the House members of the Joint Select Committee To Investigate the Condition and Treatment of Prisoners of War. Perkins made a report on Mar. 3 that was ordered printed, and Marshall made a report on Mar. 15 that also was ordered printed.

Special Committee To Investigate the Fuel Supply at Chimborazo Hospital
        Authorized on Feb. 2, 1865, and appointed on Feb. 4 to consist of
William C. Wickham (Va.), David Clopton (Ala.), and Horatio W. Bruce
(Ky.).

Select Committee on the Increase of the Military Force
        Appointed on Feb. 11, 1865, to consist of a member from each State
with Ethelbert Barksdale (Miss.) as chairman. The inquiry made by this
committee was on the employment of Negroes as soldiers. The committee
reported a bill on Feb. 14.

Select Committee on Additional Taxes
        Appointed on Feb. 13, 1865, to consist of 13 members with Charles
W. Russell (Va.) as chairman.

        Besides attending meetings of the House and committees, Congress-
men performed many other duties. For example, the diary of Franklin B.
Sexton, Congressman from Texas, shows that he went to meetings of the
Texas delegation in Congress, accompanied other Congressmen from the
Trans-Mississippi West to confer with the President, called on the President about appointments and commissions, transacted business with the
executive departments, and procured discharges and performed many other
services for soldiers.
        Record Group 109. --The journal of the open sessions, Feb. 18, 1862-
Mar. 18, 1865 (ch. VII, part of vol. 13, and vols. 14, 16, 17, and part of
vol. 18), contains a record of the proceedings of the House. It concerns
the admission of Members; the election of officers; the appointment of employees and of committees; the introduction of bills, resolutions, memorials, petitions, and communications and their referral to committees; and
a record of the action of the House on legislation. Documents printed in
the journal include rules, Presidential messages and letters, bills, resolutions, committee reports, and letters from Government officials. Confidential transactions were recorded in a journal of the secret sessions,
Feb. 24, 1862-Mar. 17, 1865 (ch. VII, part of vol. 13 and vol. 15). In
addition to these finished journals there are rough minutes of open sessions,
Aug. 18, 1862-Dec. 31, 1863 (ch. VII, vols. 26 and 27), and secret sessions, Sept. 3, 1862-Mar. 17, 1865 (ch. VII, vols. 28 and 29). Journal
notes, Feb. 18, 1862-Mar. 18, 1865 (6 ft. 6 in.), are arranged chronologically. An index to personal names in the journals of the open and secret
sessions is available. A register of bills sent to the Senate by the House,
May 3, 1864-Mar. 18, 1865 (ch. VII, vol. 19), shows the title and number
of a bill and the dates when sent to the Senate, returned to the House, enrolled, returned to the Senate, and approved. A register of bills referred
to the Committee on Military Affairs, Feb. 25, 1862-Mar. 14, 1865 (ch.
VII, vol. 20), contains a record of action on such bills. A roll book of
Members (ch. VII, vol. 52) contains signatures of Representatives arranged

alphabetically by first letters of surnames, but the roll is very incomplete.
A file of legislative papers, Feb. 1862-Mar. 1865 (2 ft. 5 in.) contains original bills and resolutions, amendments, petitions, memorials,
committee reports with letters of Departmental officials, resolutions of
State legislatures, letters to Representatives, Senate messages, lists of
Members, clerks' correspondence, stationery accounts, and rough minutes.
Some of the memorials and petitions were withdrawn and placed in a special file, represented in this file only by cross-reference cards. Papers
showing the credentials of Members, 1861-64, are filed with similar papers
for Members of the Provisional Congress (for a description, see the section above on the Provisional Congress). A collection of letters from
William Porcher Miles, Representative from South Carolina, to Gen. P.
G. T. Beauregard, Sept. 9, 1862-Mar. 18, 1864 (1/2 in.), concerns military
affairs. A small quantity of election returns from several congressional
districts in Virginia, 1862-63 (1/2 in.), shows the names of candidates and
the number of votes received in elections held to fill vacancies. Papers
relating to the contested election for Representative from the Third District of Arkansas, involving Jilson P. Johnson and Augustus H. Garland,
1862-63 (1 in.), include testimony, reports of the House Committee on
Elections, the candidates' responses, affidavits, and exhibits.

C.S.A. Congress, Journal of the Congress of the Confederate States of America, 1861-1865, vols. 5-7, Journal of the House of Representatives . . . (S. Doc. 234, 58 Cong., 2 sess., Serials 4614-4616; Washington, 1905), contains the proceedings of the open and secret sessions. Separately printed House bills, resolutions, amendments, and committee reports are listed by title in Crandall, Confederate Imprints, 1:47-113, and in Harwell, More Confederate Imprints, 1:21-27. Acts, joint resolutions, and other documents of Congress are in the Official Records . . . Armies, passim.

Records in Other Custody. --In Emory University Library are some
copies of correspondence between the Secretary of State and Confederate
commissioners in Europe (Slidell and Mason), and Alfred Paul, the French
consul in Richmond, 1863-64. These were transmitted to the House by
President Davis on Dec. 15, 1864 (House Journal, 7:361).

Records of the House of Representatives that were taken from the
State Capitol in Richmond early in Apr. 1865 by Rev. William H. Ryder
and sent north for preservation are now in Tufts College Library. These
papers include House journal notes, bills, resolutions, memoranda, and
estimates submitted by Secretary of the Navy Mallory, 1861-64. Letters from
Capt. Sidney S. Lee, commanding at Drewry's Bluff, Va., to Secretary
Mallory, Sept. 23, 1863, and to Charles M. Conrad, Chairman of the
House Naval Affairs Committee, Feb. 20, 1863, also appear to be House
records.

Historical Records Survey, Massachusetts, A Calendar of the Ryder Collection of Confederate Archives at Tufts College Library (Boston, 1940).

PAPERS OF MEMBERS OF CONGRESS

Records in Other Custody. --The official archives can be supplemented by the papers of Members of Congress. Since some Members of the
Provisional Congress later served as Representatives or Senators and
some Representatives became Senators, a single alphabetical list is given
here, showing where their papers have been published or in what repository they may be found.

Akin, Warren. Bell I. Wiley, ed., Letters of Warren Akin, Confederate
 Congressman (Athens, Ga., 1959).
Anderson, James P. Papers in Southern Historical Collection, University
 of North Carolina Library.
Arrington, Archibald H. Papers in Southern Historical Collection, Uni-
 versity of North Carolina Library.
Baker, James M. Papers in Archives Division, Virginia State Library
 (Hammond collection).
Barnwell, Robert W. Papers in South Caroliniana Library, University of
 South Carolina.
Bonham, Milledge L. Papers in South Caroliniana Library, University of
 South Carolina.
Boteler, Alexander R. Papers in Manuscript Department, Duke Universi-
 ty Library.
Boudinot, Elias C. Papers in Division of Manuscripts, University of
 Oklahoma Library. See also the Bureau of Indian Affairs in chapter
 VII of this Guide.
Boyce, William W. Rosser H. Taylor, ed., "Boyce-Hammond Corre-
 spondence," Journal of Southern History, 3:348-354 (Aug. 1937).
Branch, Anthony M. Papers in Henry E. Huntington Library.
Campbell, Josiah A. P. Papers in Southern Historical Collection, Univer-
 sity of North Carolina Library.
Chesnut, James, Jr. Papers in Manuscript Department, Duke University
 Library.
Chisolm, William G. Papers in Virginia Historical Society collections.
Clay, Clement C. Papers in Alabama Department of Archives and History
 and Manuscript Department, Duke University Library.
Cobb, Howell. Papers in University of Georgia Library (Will Erwin depos-
 it). Ulrich B. Phillips, ed., "The Correspondence of Robert Toombs,
 Alexander H. Stephens and Howell Cobb," American Historical Asso-
 ciation, Annual Report, 1911, vol. 2 (Washington, 1913) and Robert P.
 Brooks, ed., "Howell Cobb Papers," Georgia Historical Quarterly,
 6:355-394 (Dec. 1922).
Cobb, Thomas R. R. Papers in Manuscript Department, Duke University
 Library; Southern Historical Collection, University of North Carolina Library; and University of Georgia Library. Augustus L. Hull,
 ed., "The Correspondence of Thomas Reade Rootes Cobb, 1860-
 1862," in Southern History Association, Publications, 11:147-185,
 233-260, 312-328 (May, July, Sept.-Nov. 1907) and "Thomas R. R.
 Cobb . . . Extracts from Letters to His Wife, February 3, 1861-
 December 10, 1862," Southern Historical Society Papers, 28:280-
 301 (1900).
Curry, Jabez L. M. Papers in Manuscript Division, Library of Congress;
 Southern Historical Collection, University of North Carolina; and

Virginia Baptist Historical Society Library.
De Clouet, Alexander. Papers in Southern Historical Collection, University of North Carolina Library.
Graham, William A. Papers in Southern Historical Collection, University of North Carolina Library.
Hanly, Thomas B. Willard E. Wight, ed., "Letters of Thomas B. Hanly, 1863-1864, " Arkansas Historical Quarterly, 15:161-171 (Summer 1956).
Harris, Thomas A. Papers in Henry E. Huntington Library.
Harrison, James T. Papers in Southern Historical Collection, University of North Carolina Library.
Hemphill, John. Papers in Southern Historical Collection, University of North Carolina Library.
Hill, Benjamin H. Benjamin H. Hill, Jr., Senator Benjamin H. Hill of Georgia; His Life; Speeches and Writings of B. H. Hill (Atlanta, 1891).
Hunter, Robert M. T. Papers in Manuscript Department, University of Virginia Library (available on microfilm).
Johnson, Herschel V. Papers in Manuscript Department, Duke University Library. Some letters are published in Percy S. Flippin, Herschel V. Johnson of Georgia, State Rights Unionist (Richmond, 1931).
Johnson, Waldo P. Papers in Manuscript Division, Library of Congress.
Jones, George W. Papers in Southern Historical Collection, University of North Carolina Library.
Keitt, Lawrence M. Elmer D. Herd, Jr., ed., "Lawrence M. Keitt's Letters from the Provisional Congress of the Confederacy, 1861, " South Carolina Historical Magazine, 61:19-25 (Jan. 1960).
Lyons, James. Papers in Henry E. Huntington Library.
McDowell, Thomas D. Papers in Southern Historical Collection, University of North Carolina Library.
McKee, Robert. Papers in Alabama Department of Archives and History.
McRae, Colin J. Papers in Alabama Department of Archives and History.
Memminger, Christopher G. Papers in Southern Historical Collection, University of North Carolina Library (available on microfilm). See also chapter VI of this Guide.
Miles, William P. Papers in New York Public Library and Southern Historical Collection, University of North Carolina Library. See also the section on the House of Representatives in this chapter.
Nisbet, Eugenius A. Papers in Manuscript Department, Duke University Library.
Oldham, Williamson S. Unpublished "Memoirs" in Texas Archives, University of Texas Library.
Orr, James L. Papers in Southern Historical Collection, University of North Carolina Library.
Oury, Granville H. Cornelius C. Smith, ed., "Some Unpublished History of the Southwest, " Arizona Historical Review, 4:18-38 (July 1931).
Perkins, John, Jr. Papers in Southern Historical Collection, University of North Carolina Library.
Ramsey, James G. Papers in Southern Historical Collection, University of North Carolina Library.
Reagan, John H. See chapter IX of this Guide.
Rhett, Robert B., Sr. Papers in Southern Historical Collection, University of North Carolina Library.
Rives, William C. Papers in Manuscript Division, Library of Congress,

and University of Virginia Library.

Semmes, Thomas J. Papers in Manuscript Department, Duke University Library.

Sexton, Franklin B. Mary S. Estill, ed., "Diary of a Confederate Congressman, 1862-1863," Southwestern Historical Quarterly, 38:270-301 (Apr. 1935), 39:33-65 (July 1935).

Shorter, John G. Papers in University of Alabama Library.

Simpson, William D. Papers in Duke University Library and South Caroliniana Library, University of South Carolina. Willard E. Wight, ed., "Some Letters of William Dunlap Simpson, 1860-1863," South Carolina Historical Magazine, 57:204-222 (Oct. 1956).

Smith, Robert H. Papers in Southern Historical Collection, University of North Carolina Library.

Smith, William E. Papers in Manuscript Department, Duke University Library.

Smith, William R. Mildred Easby-Smith, William Russell Smith of Alabama, His Life and Works (Philadelphia, 1931).

Stephens, Alexander H. See chapter IV of this Guide.

Turner, Josiah, Jr. Papers in Manuscript Department, Duke University Library, and Southern Historical Collection, University of North Carolina Library.

Tyler, John. Papers in Manuscript Division, Library of Congress.

Wigfall, Louis T. Papers in Manuscript Division, Library of Congress, and Texas Archives, University of Texas Library.

Wright, Augustus R. Papers in University of Georgia Library.

Yancey, William L. Papers in Alabama Department of Archives and History.

III

THE JUDICIARY

The judicial power of the Confederate States of America was vested by Article III of the Provisional Constitution in a supreme court, a system of district courts, and such inferior courts as Congress might establish. The district courts were to have the jurisdiction vested in both district and circuit courts by U. S. law, and appeals were to be taken from the district courts to the supreme court under procedures similar to those existing in the United States. The Judiciary Act of Mar. 16, 1861 (Prov. Cong. C. S. A. Stat. 75), set forth these procedures. The few changes made in the judicial system by the Permanent Constitution are discussed below in the section on district courts.

SUPREME COURT

The Provisional and Permanent Constitutions of the Confederate States of America provided for a supreme court to be composed of all the district judges, with powers similar to those of the U. S. Supreme Court. Bills for its establishment were considered by every session of Congress, but for many reasons, perhaps most notably the fear of centralization and the desire to protect States rights, no bill ever passed both houses and a supreme court was not established.

DISTRICT COURTS

The Judiciary Act of Mar. 16, 1861, established the system of district courts provided for by the Provisional Constitution. Although the Constitution stated that each State should constitute a district, the Judiciary Act required the district court judges to hold at least two terms annually in each of the U. S. judicial districts that had existed on Nov. 1, 1860. Some of the States were divided into two or more divisions, corresponding to the former districts, but in other States Congress established two or more districts in accordance with an amendment to the Constitution of May 21, 1861.

The judges designated the times and places at which the courts were to meet. Upon the U. S. occupation of parts of the South, Congress authorized the judges to change the times and places of holding court and to move records and files whenever public exigencies required.

Concerning the jurisdiction of Confederate courts the Permanent Constitution (Art. III, Sec. 2) provided that:

> The judicial power shall extend to all cases arising under this Constitution, the laws of the Confederate States, and treaties made, or which shall be made, under their authority; to all cases affecting

ambassadors, other public ministers and consuls; to all cases of admiralty and maritime jurisdiction; to controversies to which the Confederate States shall be a party; to controversies between two or more States; between a State and citizens of another State, where the State is plaintiff; between citizens claiming lands under grants of different States; and between a State or the citizens thereof, and foreign states, citizens or subjects; but no State shall be sued by a citizen or subject of any foreign state.

Certain changes in the jurisdiction of the district courts were concessions to States rights. Omitted from the Permanent Constitution was a provision giving the courts jurisdiction over controversies between citizens of different States; thus this jurisdiction ceased when the Provisional Constitution expired on Feb. 18, 1862. District courts continued to have jurisdiction over cases involving foreigners. Under the Judiciary Act no inhabitant of the Confederate States could be sued elsewhere than in his own district. Further, by requiring the amount involved in civil suits at common law or in equity to exceed $5,000, exclusive of costs, Congress greatly reduced the business of the district courts and increased that of the State courts.

The Judiciary Act gave the district courts exclusive jurisdiction in all crimes and offenses cognizable under Confederate law (Sec. 35) and adopted U. S. criminal law and mode of procedure (Sec. 37). The jurisdiction of the courts in offenses committed on waters over which the courts had admiralty and maritime jurisdiction was limited to those waters navigable by vessels of 100 tons burden or more (Sec. 39). Extensions and revisions of the criminal law provided penalties and punishments for offenses committed by privateersmen against the prize and revenue laws, counterfeiting, violations of the act imposing censorship over telegrams, fraudulent exportation of cotton, false swearing on tax returns, frauds by Government contractors, improper use of public transportation, aiding deserters, purchasing public property from a soldier, trading with the enemy, dealing in the enemy's paper currency, and violations of the revenue laws.

The district courts shared with State courts jurisdiction over the naturalization of aliens. The naturalization laws of the United States continued in effect in the Confederate States throughout the war: 5 years' residence was required of foreigners and a declaration of intention had to be made at least 2 years before admission to citizenship. An act of Aug. 22, 1861 (Prov. Cong. C. S. A. Stat. 189), waived the preliminary declaration for persons in military service and permitted them to take the oath before officers. These oaths were transmitted to the clerks of the district courts for recording and indexing.

An act of May 21, 1861 (Prov. Cong. C. S. A. Stat. 157), to secure copyrights to authors and composers gave to district courts original cognizance of all actions, suits, controversies, and cases arising under the law. Persons seeking a copyright were required to deposit the title of the work in the clerk's office of the district court of the district in which that proprietor resided and within 3 months to deposit a copy of the work itself.

In 1870 the U. S. Congress assigned the administration of copyright laws to the Library of Congress and directed that copyright records in the Department of the Interior and the registers of clerks of district courts be transferred to the Library. Some of the registers transferred contain entries relating to Confederate copyrights, and these are referred to in the sections on the courts below. Not all Confederate district courts kept separate registers of copyrights, however, and information regarding copyrights can sometimes be found in other court records. The registers of copyrights that were transferred to the Library of Congress are now in its Rare Book Room.

U.S. Library of Congress, Records in the Copyright Office Deposited by the United States | District Courts Covering the Period 1790-1870, comp. by Martin A. Roberts (Washington, 1939).

Another act of May 21, 1861 (Prov Cong. C.S.A. Stat. 136), to establish a Patent Office and provide for "the granting and issue of patents for new and useful discoveries, inventions, improvements, and designs, " vested in the district courts original cognizance over all actions, suits, controversies, and cases arising under that act.

The judges, who were appointed under the Provisional Constitution for terms that lasted only as long as the Provisional Government, held office under the Permanent Constitution "during good behavior." A marshal and a district attorney were appointed by the President for terms of 4 years. They were recommended by the Attorney General and confirmed by the Provisional Congress or the Senate. The judge appointed one or more clerks, a crier, a commissioner, and, when necessary, a substitute attorney. Any district attorney who desired to enter military service could appoint an attorney to serve during his absence. The marshal appointed a deputy marshal and a bailiff to attend the grand and petit juries. The marshal, the clerk, and the receiver appointed under the sequestration acts were required to give bond.

The officials of the courts performed varied duties. As administrative officer of the court, the marshal proclaimed the opening of sessions of the court, provided for its needs, served writs, executed its precepts, handled the sale of property, and took charge of civil prisoners and convicts. When no State or local prison was available he rented a suitable place for the confinement of prisoners. The marshal also attended to the deportation of alien enemies, prevented the illegal exportation of cotton, and had custody of and handled the sale of prizes. The district attorney prosecuted cases for the Government, represented the Confederate States in State courts, drafted indictments, collected moneys, prepared opinions on land titles and reports on local matters for executive officers, and attended the hearing of matters referred to masters or commissioners. The commissioners administered oaths, took acknowledgments and depositions, issued warrants of arrest against offenders for crimes against the Confederate States, and committed offenders to prison or admitted them to bail. The clerks kept the court's records, issued writs and subpenas, and swore in bailiffs, criers, and jurors.

The costs and fees established for marshals and clerks were the same as those allowed by State law for the officers on the highest court of original jurisdiction. The Attorney General recommended in his report of Feb. 26, 1862, that legislation be adopted to make fees uniform in order to encourage adequate compensation. An act of Apr. 19, 1862 (1 Cong. C.S.A. Stat. 41), required district attorneys, clerks, and marshals to make to the Attorney General semiannual returns of fees and emoluments received, distinguishing those received under the sequestration acts from those received for other services. District attorneys and marshals were not to retain more than $5,000 above expenses, and clerks, not more than $4,000; surplus fees were to be paid into the Treasury.

Acts of Aug. 30, 1861, and Feb. 15, 1862 (Prov. Cong. C.S.A. Stat. 201, 260), provided for the sequestration of alien-enemy property and credits within the Confederate States; it was declared to be the duty of every Confederate citizen to supply information regarding such property. Attorneys, agents, former partners, or trustees holding or controlling lands, goods, or credits, or any interest in them, were required to render accounts to the receivers and to place the property in their hands. Grand juries were to inquire into and report upon alien-enemy property within their districts.

The administration of the act fell chiefly upon receivers appointed by district judges. In most States, because of the volume of business involved, the judges had to divide the districts or divisions into a number of receivers' districts and appoint receivers in each. The receivers had to give bond and take an oath to perform "diligently, well and truly" the duties of their offices. Receivers took possession of alien-enemy property, transported it when necessary, had it guarded, advertised it for sale, and conducted auction sales. When a receiver was unable to obtain possession of property by other means, he petitioned the district court to sequester it. A notice was then issued with a copy of the petition to the person holding the property, and the case was docketed for trial. Receivers were allowed fees and expenses up to $5,000; any surplus was to be paid into the Treasury.

A clerk of the court, at the request of a receiver, issued writs of garnishment ordering persons to appear in court to explain under oath what property or funds of alien enemies they had in their control or what sums they owed alien enemies. The court could condemn the property, funds, or debts and have other persons involved brought into court to testify. If a receiver filed a statement claiming that the garnishee had not answered truthfully, the court could cause an issue to be made between the receiver and the garnishee and render judgment. In litigated cases the receiver could propound interrogatories to the adverse party.

The receivers rendered semiannual accounts showing collections and disbursements for each case, thus providing a record of the transactions regarding each alien enemy's property. The court could also require an account while litigation was pending. Clerks of courts recorded statements of accounts of receivers and forwarded copies to the Treasurer of the Confederate States. The district attorney also had to handle the settlement of sequestration matters. The act of Feb. 15, 1862, authorized judges to appoint attorneys in sections where no Confederate attorney resided to attend to duties imposed by the sequestration act.

The principal business of Confederate district courts after the latter part of 1861 was the sequestration of alien-enemy property. Thousands of cases were handled. The South had long made extensive purchases in the North and was heavily indebted to northern merchants; similarly, much property in the South was owned by northerners. The funds derived from sequestration cases amounted to millions of dollars. Under the Aug. 30, 1861, act, these funds were used for the general purposes of the Government. The Feb. 15, 1862, act set the money aside for use in indemnifying Confederates for losses resulting from U.S. confiscation acts. Its use was later extended to cover losses from hostile operations in the South.

Under the provisions of a U.S. act of July 17, 1862 (12 Stat. 590), which rendered all conveyances of real estate by the Confederate

Government null and void, original owners of land and buildings recovered their property after the war.

The Confederate courts continued to create the same types of records as those created by the U.S. courts, which had inherited their records systems from the English colonies. They often used the same record books that had been used by the U.S. courts, either beginning a new page with the heading "Confederate States of America" or substituting "Confederate" for "United."

The courts accumulated minute books, dockets, case files, and account books. Most useful for research purposes are the minute books containing data on court sessions and on such matters as the appointment and installation of officers, commissions, bonds, oaths, names of attorneys admitted, names of jurors drawn and impaneled, rules adopted, interrogatories served, declarations of intention to become citizens, and naturalization orders. The minute books also contain information about the cases tried and their disposition (including texts of orders, motions, decrees, and jury verdicts) and sequestration receivers' accounts. Sometimes separate order books were kept. When required by the volume of business, special minute books for admiralty, sequestration, and garnishment cases were maintained. Admiralty minutes contain rules for taking testimony, items of interrogatories, appointments and oaths of prize commissioners, motions, orders, decrees, and information concerning the activities of Confederate privateers and the U.S. vessels captured by them and by Confederate and State naval vessels.

Dockets contain brief chronological records of papers filed and actions taken. They usually cover all categories of cases, but some districts used special sequestration and garnishment dockets. Dockets show the number of the case, names of attorneys, style or title of the case, type of case, actions, and final disposition. Judgment dockets contain a record of judgments entered. Execution dockets record all executions (or orders to carry out judgments) sued out or pending in the marshal's or receiver's office and show case number and style, names of attorneys, date issued, amount of judgment, court costs, attorneys' fees, and marshal's returns. Less frequently used were motion, bar, and trial dockets.

The most voluminous case files among the Confederate archives are those of sequestration cases covering the seizure of alien-enemy property and debts. These files consist of receivers' petitions to sequester property or debts, summonses to appear in court, respondents' answers to receivers' petitions, writs of garnishment with the receivers' interrogatories, garnishees' answers to interrogatories with schedules of debts, receivers' petitions for and reports on the sale of property, court orders for receivers to take possession of property, respondents' affidavits regarding their interest in property, subpenas, bail bonds, exhibits, correspondence, schedules of writs of garnishment and petitions for sequestration served by deputy marshals, orders for the settlement of receivers' accounts, receivers' returns of moneys received and expended, decrees, papers regarding the settlement of estates, administrators' accounts, deeds to land, clerks' bills for preparing documents, and marshals' bonds for personal appearances.

Admiralty cases tried by district courts concerned prize vessels captured by Confederate privateers and by Confederate and State naval vessels. The Confederate courts followed U.S. procedures in libeling captured ships and their cargoes. The case files include libels setting forth the circumstances of the captures; orders to marshals to take possession of vessels and their tackle; testimony taken by prize commissioners; court orders; answers of interveners; affidavits; prize commissioners' reports and orders; orders of sale, release, and dismissal of libel; libelants' objections to the appointment of appraisers; stipulations for payment of cost and for the delivery of libeled vessels; and statements of the claims of other persons having an interest in libeled vessels.

Criminal case files of Confederate district courts contain grand-jury indictments, affidavits setting forth circumstances of cases, affidavits of sureties, orders to marshals to take custody of witnesses, depositions, writs of arrest, bonds, court orders, decrees, warrants of arrest, demurrers, notices to marshals to serve jurors, subpenas, orders of release on bail bond issued to marshals, bail bonds, jury venires, and pleas in abatement in treason cases.

Habeas corpus cases in Confederate district courts resulted from efforts of men to be released from military service particularly under the conscription acts, and from imprisonment for espionage and desertion. The case files contain petitions for writs of habeas corpus from persons claiming to be illegally held by enrolling or other military officers, copies of writs of habeas corpus directing enrolling officers to bring men before the court, orders to marshals directing the delivery of writs of habeas corpus, subpenas issued to military officers, answers of enrolling and other military officers, answers of respondents, and motions for judgment of costs against the defendants.

The transition from U.S. district court to Confederate district court was effected smoothly. Personnel of the old courts were usually retained by the new. The Confederate courts took over the criminal dockets of the U.S. courts, tried persons who had been indicted, and imprisoned those convicted. Judgments of the predecessor district courts were executed except those rendered in favor of the United States. The courts and the Department of Justice, adhering to the doctrine of stare decisis, continued to accept applicable decisions and opinions of ante bellum days. Because of the interruptions of war, a considerable part of the inherited dockets were carried over and continued after the war.

State courts also passed upon the constitutionality of acts of the Confederate Congress and assumed jurisdiction of suits arising under Confederate laws. The State courts claimed concurrent jurisdiction over all questions cognizable in Confederate courts when not prohibited by law. The State supreme courts upheld the constitutionality of the conscription act of Apr. 16, 1862 (1 Cong. C.S.A. Stat. 29), on the grounds that it was within the war powers of Congress. These courts also heard questions on whether men in the militia and reserve organizations of the States could be conscripted, and they challenged the power of the Secretary of War to interpret the conscription law. In a case before the North Carolina Supreme Court, in which the Confederate Government was represented by counsel, the court decided that it was within its jurisdiction to interpret the conscription law and to release persons who appeared to be unlawfully held. The Confederate Government acceded, and the North Carolina courts shared concurrent jurisdiction in issuing writs of habeas corpus inquiring into the detention of conscripts by Confederate officers. Other State courts took the same position and also issued writs. After the adoption of the second conscription act of Sept. 27, 1862 (1 Cong. C.S.A. Stat. 61), providing for the conscription of white males between the ages of 35 and 45, the

principals who had obtained substitutes went to court alleging violation of
contract by the Confederate Government. The courts generally held that
the Secretary of War had power, under the discretionary authority conferred upon him by Congress, to conscript the principals. The principals
again went to court, but without success, after Congress abolished substitution by an act of Dec. 28, 1863 (1 Cong. C. S. A. Stat. 172). Other suits
in State courts concerned persons interfering with conscription, aiding
and abetting desertion, trading with the enemy, making unlawful impressments, and violating emergency laws prohibiting the sale of liquor.

Information from William M.
Robinson, Jr. , Justice in Grey; a
History of the Judicial System of
the Confederate States of America
(Cambridge, Mass. , 1941) has been
used throughout this chapter. Information about the Confederate
district court records in the custody of the U. S. district courts is in
the Survey of Federal Archives,
Inventory of Federal Archives in
the States, Series II, the Federal
Courts. Among the Records of the
Work Projects Administration (Record Group 69) in the National Archives is a "Special Report on the
Location of Confederate Court Records Found by the Survey of Federal Archives. " The Federal Records Centers now having custody
of most of the Confederate district
court records supplied lists of them
for use in this Guide.

The decisions of Confederate
district courts were not published
except occasionally in pamphlet form
and in newspapers. A list of published reports on State supreme
court cases for the war period is in
Robinson, Justice in Grey, p. 635-
639. Information about other State
court records is in Old Law Naturalization Record Project, Mississippi,
Index to Naturalization Records, Mississippi Courts, 1798-1906 (Jackson,
1942), and U. S. Work Projects Administration, Arkansas, Index to
Naturalization Records in Arkansas,
1809-1906 (Little Rock, 1942).

Alabama

The Southern, Middle, and Northern Districts that had existed in
Alabama under U. S. law became divisions in the Confederate judiciary
system. William G. Jones, who had resigned as U. S. judge earlier in the
year, was commissioned as Confederate Judge of the district of Alabama.
His order of Apr. 4, 1861, directed that regular terms of the court for the
Southern Division were to be held in June and December in Mobile; for the
Middle Division, in May and November in Montgomery; and for the Northern Division, in May and November in Huntsville. At a special term of the
court for the Southern Division in Mobile in April 1861, the court was organized and an admiralty case was considered. Benjamin Pattison, who
had become marshal in 1861, died and was succeeded in Jan. 1864 by Robert
W. Coltart. John A. Cuthbert was reappointed as clerk and served probably throughout the war. A. J. Requier was the district attorney. During
the war the court for the Southern Division held lengthy sessions not only
at the regular times but at special terms when sequestration and garnishment, and some admiralty and criminal, cases were handled. At a special
term in the fall of 1861, the division was divided into three districts that
were placed in charge of Sequestration Receivers J. Little Smith, Decatur
C. Anderson, and J. T. Lomax. Lomax was later replaced by George G.
Lyon. Other special terms for admiralty cases were held in Apr. 1863 and

Sept. 1864.

Less is known about court terms in the Middle and Northern Divisions, for few records remain. The main business of the court at Huntsville, where the first session was held in Nov. 1861, consisted of garnishment and sequestration cases. After a lapse in 1862 when U.S. troops occupied the town, sessions were resumed in Jan. 1863. Sequestration receivers in the Northern Division were John Malone and Zebulon P. Davis. Existing records show that the court for the Middle Division at Montgomery was also chiefly concerned with sequestration cases. Sequestration receivers in that division were Jefferson Buford, Joseph R. John, William W. Knox, William H. Martin, P. Tucker Sayre, and Daniel M. Seals.

Record Group 21. --The records of the Confederate District Court for the Southern Division of Alabama at Mobile were transferred from the U.S. District Court at Mobile to the Federal Records Center at East Point, Ga., in 1953. A minute book, Apr. 18, 1861-Jan. 13, 1865 (1 vol.), is continued for Jan. 1-16, Mar. 6-9, Mar. 12, and Mar. 20, 1865, in the minute book of the U.S. Circuit Court, 1859-61, 1865-66 (p. 69-77). Separate docket books cover admiralty cases, 1861-63, chancery cases, 1861-65, garnishment cases, 1861-65, and sequestration cases, Dec. 1862-July 1863 (the last docket is part of a U.S. Circuit Court chancery docket, 1839-60 and 1865-66). A trial docket for Apr. 1861-June 1863 contains a record of admiralty, criminal, equity, law, garnishment, and sequestration cases. A writ docket for May 1861-June 1864 is mostly a record of writs of garnishment issued and sequestration petitions filed. An execution docket of sequestration cases, Apr. 1861-Mar. 1865, contains a record of judgments to be executed and an alphabetical index.

Documents relating to cases are in both case files and in volumes. The case files for 1861-65 (1 ft.) consist largely of sequestration and garnishment proceedings, but include some law, equity, criminal, habeas corpus, and admiralty cases. A record of garnishment and sequestration cases for May 1861-Jan. 1865 (1 vol.) contains copies of documents, such as writs of garnishment, garnishees' answers, petitions for sequestration, pleas, notices of trials, litigants' bonds, orders, decrees, and marshals' returns. In another volume, Apr. 22, 1861-Apr. 17, 1865, are copies of documents in admiralty, equity, criminal, sequestration, and garnishment cases; also included are the titles of works deposited for copyright.

Naturalization proceedings, 1861-62, are on p. 54-209 of a volume of declaration of intention, 1855-1929. Other naturalization proceedings are recorded in the minute book.

In the center at East Point there is only one record book of the Confederate District Court for the Middle Division of Alabama at Montgomery. This is a garnishment docket, Nov. 1862-May 1863, containing a record of cases involving the seizure of alien-enemy property and showing the names of garnishees, alien enemies, amounts owed them, attorneys and receiver concerned, and the kinds of property seized. The docket also contains a record of alien-enemy property received for the period Sept. 27, 1861-Jan. 25, 1862.

Records in Other Custody. --In 1913 the Manuscript Division of the Library of Congress received from the U.S. District Court of the Northern District of Alabama two record books of the Confederate District Court for the Northern Division of Alabama. A judgment docket shows court costs for Confederate Government cases in which judgments were rendered and contains notations regarding the dismissal of other cases for the Jan. 1863 term. A trial docket, May 1861-May 1863, contains entries for a few cases carried over from the U.S. court, but most were garnishment cases: 287 for the Nov. 1861 term, 561 for the Jan. 1863 term, and 593 for the May 1863 term.

Some entries for copyrights registered by the Confederate District Court for the Southern Division of Alabama are in Raymond V. Robinson, "Confederate Copyright Entries," William and Mary College Quarterly, 16:248-266 (Apr. 1936).

Arkansas

An act of May 21, 1861 (Prov. Cong. C.S.A. Stat. 152), divided Arkansas into Eastern and Western Districts with the limits and boundaries previously established by U.S. law. The seats of these districts were Little Rock and Van Buren. Daniel Ringo resigned his commission as Federal district judge and on May 21. 1861, was confirmed as the Confederate judge. Charles E. Jordan became district attorney for the Eastern District in May 1861 and was succeeded in Dec. 1861 by William M. Randolph. Randolph was removed for disloyalty and was succeeded by James H. Patterson in June 1864. John G. Halliburton was the marshal for that district from May 1861, and A. H. Rutherford was the sequestration receiver. The Senate confirmed Granville Wilcox as district attorney and James M. Brown as marshal of the Western District on May 21, 1861, and reconfirmed them on Apr. 11, 1862. Federal forces occupied Van Buren on Dec. 28. 1862, and Little Rock on Sept. 10. 1863, forcing the retirement of the State government to Washington in the southwestern part of the State. The district court probably met there or elsewhere south of the Arkansas River, but little is known of its activities.

No records of the Confederate courts for the Arkansas districts have been found.

Florida

Confederate judges replaced the U.S. judges who had served in the Northern and Southern Districts of Florida. Jesse J. Finley was confirmed as judge on Mar. 16, 1861, and presided over sessions of the court that were held in the old Northern District. James D. Westcott. Jr.. became clerk at Tallahassee on May 14, 1861. Although Robert H. M. Davidson was confirmed as district attorney on May 21, 1861, there is no evidence that he served, and Chandler C. Yonge was commissioned as district attorney on Aug. 13. 1861. Elias E. Blackburn was nominated as marshal in Apr. 1861 but was not confirmed and commissioned until Apr. 1862. Judge Finley entered the Army and was succeeded in Apr. 1862 by George S. Hawkins, who remained district judge until the end of the war. After Yonge's resignation, James F. McClellan was confirmed as district attorney on Mar. 6, 1865.

Northern Florida or the "Northern District, " as the minute books continued to refer to it, was divided into several divisions for the administration of justice. Sessions of the Middle Division were held at Marianna in Sept. 1861, at Tallahassee in Nov. 1861, at Madison in Sept. 1862, and again at Tallahassee in Oct. 1862, June and Nov. 1863, July and Oct. 1864, and Jan. and Mar. 1865. The business of this court was largely sequestration cases. Judge Finley and later Judge Hawkins presided over the sessions in the different divisions; an order of the court of Jan. 24, 1862, prescribed regular terms for the Western Division at Pensacola in April, for the Apalachicola Division at Apalachicola in May, for the Middle Division at Tallahassee in June, and for the Eastern Division at St. Augustine in July. Special terms were sometimes ordered by the court. Hugh A. Corley was appointed deputy clerk for the Middle Division in July 1861, but Charles H. Fisher became the clerk at Tallahassee in Nov. 1861. On Sept. 25, 1861, Judge Finley appointed John Beard and Barton C. Pope sequestration receivers for the Middle Division. In Nov. 1861 Hugh Corley became deputy district attorney and John H. Rhodes became deputy marshal for the Middle Division.

Most active of the divisions was the Apalachicola Division. The court met at Apalachicola in Sept. 1861 and Jan. 1862, but after the arrival there of U.S. naval forces sessions were held at Marianna. The bulk of the business was sequestration and garnishment cases, although the initial session was concerned with prize cases and, during the July 1864 term, cases involving aid to deserters. Samuel W. Spencer and, later, Joseph May served as clerks. Deputy district attorneys were J. F. McClellan and William E. Anderson, and in 1864 the deputy marshal was J. L. Wilson. Before his appointment as judge, George S. Hawkins served as sequestration receiver in this division; he was succeeded as receiver by G. F. Baltzell. Some prize cases were tried during a term of court in the Eastern Division at St. Augustine in Oct. 1861, but repeated Federal incursions in northeastern Florida after 1862 terminated Confederate judicial activities there. The court for the Western Division was organized at Pensacola in May 1861, when Maxcimo P. de Rioboo was appointed the deputy clerk and the commissioner; and C. C. Yonge, the deputy district attorney. Sessions held at Pensacola until late 1864 were concerned primarily with sequestration and garnishment cases. The sequestration receivers in the Eastern Division were R. R. B. Hodgson and George R. Foster, and, in the Western Division, George G. McWhorter.

An act of Mar. 11, 1861 (Prov. Cong. C.S.A. Stat. 60), authorized a court of admiralty at Key West, and on Mar. 16, 1861, McQueen McIntosh, who had been U.S. judge of the Northern District of Florida, was confirmed as judge of the admiralty court. When he arrived in Key West in May, he found the U.S. Army in control, and after a courtesy call on Judge William Marvin, who had remained loyal to the United States, he departed. The United States continued in control of Key West and no Confederate court was established there.

Record Group 21.--Records of the Confederate District Court in Florida were transferred in 1953 by the U.S. District Court at Tallahassee to the Federal Records Center at East Point, Ga. The records of the Middle Division include a minute book, May 14, 1861-Mar. 20, 1865 (part of a volume covering 1858-61 and 1867-68); a judgment docket, Dec. 15, 1862-Mar. 21, 1864 (part of a volume for the period 1849-68); an execution docket, Nov. 1861-Oct. 1864; a garnishment docket, 1861-62 (part of the last page of a volume for the years 1847-60); an order book, 1862-65, containing orders for the appointment of sequestration receivers and their oaths of office, bonds, and accounts. The minute book includes accounts of John Beard, the receiver, 1862-64. Also in this record group are correspondence, accounts, and other records of Beard, the clerk's account for the July 1864 term, admissions of attorneys, and appointments, 1861-64.

The records of the Apalachicola Division include a minute book, May 1861-Oct. 1864 (part of a book also used by the U.S. District Court, 1847-60 and 1867), and a sequestration judgment docket, Dec. 1862-Mar. 1864. A minute book of the court for the Western Division, Dec. 23, 1861-Oct. 25, 1864 (part of a book also used by the U.S. Circuit Court, 1846-1936), was found by the Survey of Federal Archives among the U.S. District Court records at Pensacola, but it was not among the records received by the center in 1953.

Records in Other Custody. --The papers of Chandler C. Yonge in the P. K. Yonge Library of the University of Florida contain answers to libels against the owners of the prize schooners Basilde, Three Brothers, Olive Branch, and Fanny.

Georgia

The two U.S. judicial districts in Georgia with seats at Savannah and Marietta became the Southern and Northern Divisions under a single Confederate judge. Henry R. Jackson, a former State circuit judge, was commissioned Confederate States judge in Mar. 1861. Judge Jackson resigned and became a brigadier general of the Provisional Army during the summer, and Edward J. Harden was commissioned to succeed him on Aug. 13, 1861. The court for the Southern Division met at Savannah from 1861 until Dec. 1864, when it moved to Augusta. Charles S. Henry was the clerk. John C. Nicoll served as district attorney from 1861 to 1863, William Dougherty from Dec. 1863, and Henry Williams from Nov. 1864. Thomas L. Ross, the marshal, was succeeded in Mar. 1863 by Philip A. Clayton. In Sept. 1861 William C. Daniell became the sequestration receiver.

The court for the Northern Division met at Marietta from Nov. 1861 to Dec. 1862 and at Atlanta from Mar. 1863 to Mar. 1864. David Irvin served as substitute district attorney of this court. The marshal designated William H. Dorsey as deputy for the Northern Division in Oct. 1861, and in November appointed John G. Jacoway as another deputy. William H. Hunt was the clerk. In Sept. 1861 James T. Nisbet was appointed sequestration receiver.

The bulk of the business of the Georgia courts was sequestration cases. The Savannah court also handled admiralty, equity, criminal, common law, and habeas corpus cases.

Warren Grice, "The Confed-   Georgia Historical Quarterly, 9:131-
erate States Court for Georgia, "   156 (June 1925).

Record Group 21. --Records of the Confederate District Court in Georgia were transferred to the Federal Records Center at East Point, Ga., by the U.S. District Court at Savannah in 1954 and from the court at Atlanta in 1952 and 1958. The records of the Confederate District Court for the Southern Division at Savannah include a minute book, May 2, 1861-May 22, 1862. Additional minutes for Aug.-Dec. 1861 are in a book containing minutes of the U.S. district court, 1849-60, which also contains some entries relating to the Northern Division. A record of the proceedings of the court in admiralty cases is in an admiralty minute book, Aug. 22, 1861-Jan. 15, 1863. One issue and information docket of equity, criminal, habeas corpus, and admiralty cases, Jan. 1862-Nov. 1864, also contains records of scire facias writs and claims (part of a judge's docket of the U.S. Circuit Court for the Southern District of Georgia, 1859-61). A briefer docket, June and Nov. 1861 (1 vol.), concerns cases transferred from the U.S. Circuit Court for the Southern District of Georgia and garnishment cases filed at the Nov. 1861 term. A fuller record of 2,037 garnishment cases is in a garnishment docket, Sept. 23, 1861-May 24, 1865 (2 vols.), for which there are alphabetical name indexes. The sequestration docket, Nov. 1861-Nov. 1862 and Aug. 1863-Nov. 1864 (2 vols.), is incomplete; the second volume, for 1862-63, is missing. The execution docket, Feb. 1862-Nov. 1864 (2 vols.), contains a record of judgments in sequestration cases.

Other records of the Southern Division consist chiefly of case files. These include sequestration and garnishment proceedings, 1861-64 (5 ft.), and admiralty, criminal, and habeas corpus case files. In addition, there are packets of orders, drafts of minutes, unfiled case papers, correspondence, financial papers, emolument returns, marshal's returns and accounts, receiver's accounts, and receipts for 1861-65 (9 in.).

Available at the Federal Records Center are preliminary inventories of the Georgia district court records in its custody.

Less extensive are the records of the Northern Division that were transferred by the U.S. District Court at Atlanta to the Federal Records Center at East Point in 1952. There are minute books for Dec. 11, 1861, to Mar. 9, 1864 (2 vols.), sequestration and garnishment dockets, Dec. 1861-Dec. 1863 (2 vols.), and sequestration and garnishment case files, Dec. 1861-Dec. 1864 (1 ft.). There are also orders, accounts of sequestration sales, receiver's accounts, oaths of commissioners, and powers of attorney, 1862-64 (1 in.).

Record Group 365. --After the war the records in the custody of W. C. Daniell, sequestration receiver for the Southern Division, were seized by the U.S. provost marshal at Augusta and sent to the War Department in Washington. The Georgia court records received by the Archive Office in Dec. 1866 numbered 13 volumes and included journals, ledgers, dockets, minute books, registers, and indexes. They were transferred in 1867 to the Treasury Department, and a schedule listing them by their titles was signed by the Secretary of the Treasury (Adjutant General's Office, Letters Received, 707 S 1866).

Six of these volumes are now in the National Archives in Record Group 365, Treasury Department Collection of Confederate Records. A sequestration receiver's minute and account book, Sept. 1861-Jan. 1864 (1 vol.), contains returns of property of alien enemies and debts owed them, W. C. Daniell's accounts, a report on sales of bank and railroad stock at auction, a list of bank and railroad stock sequestered, reports of moneys received on sequestration judgments, a list of returns delivered to the clerk, and monthly statements of receipts and payments of cash. The receiver's docket of sequestration cases, Nov. 1861-June 1862 (1 vol.), contains for each case the number, name of alien enemy or garnishee, nature of action, county, and disposition. An alphabetical index to the docket is in a separate volume. Returns of alien-enemy property submitted to the receiver, Oct. 1861-June 1863 (2 vols.), give the names of the alien enemies and the amounts of debts due or the value of other property owned. An alphabetical name index is in a separate volume. Another volume (without dates) contains returns of amounts of indebtedness to alien enemies, with

an index in the front of the volume. Ledgers, Oct. 1861-Nov. 1864 (2 vols.),
contain accounts showing amounts due the Confederate States by alien enemies, their trustees and agents, and persons indebted to northerners; a
chronological record of amounts of interest received, Mar. 1862-Jan. 1864;
and a chronological record of costs, Dec. 1862-Dec. 1863. Alphabetical
name indexes are in the fronts of the latter two volumes.

       National Archives, Prelim-   of Confederate Records, comp. by
inary Inventory [No. 169] of the   Carmelita S. Ryan (Washington,
Treasury Department Collection   1967).

       Records in Other Custody. --Emory University Library has W. C.
Daniell's account book, Sept. 1861-Nov. 1863, showing moneys received on
judgments in sequestration cases and expenditures made in connection
with the cases. The entries in the book show the names of the alien enemies whose property was sequestered, names of garnishees, and dates
and amounts of judgments. The expenditures were for district attorneys'
and marshals' fees, insurance, freight, store rent, a guard on board ship,
advertising sequestration notices, jury fees, county taxes on land, clerks'
services, and stationery. A letter book of Judge Harden, containing correspondence, 1861-65, with judges of Confederate courts in Alabama, South
Carolina, and Florida, with attorneys, and with Assistant Attorney General
Wade Keyes, was deposited by the judge's granddaughter in 1962 in the
Southern Historical Collection in the University of North Carolina Library.
       The Rare Book Room of the Library of Congress has a register of
copyrights for the Southern Division of Georgia, Aug. 1, 1861-Mar. 30,
1865 (parts of two volumes also used by the U.S. district court, 1825-65
and 1845-63), and a register for the Northern Division, Oct. 9, 1861-May
16, 1864 (part of a volume also used by the U.S. district court, 1849-70).

       Raymond V. Robinson, "Con-   liam and Mary College Quarterly,
federate Copyright Entries, " Wil-   16:248-266 (Apr. 1936).

Louisiana

       The former U.S. Eastern and Western Districts in Louisiana became
divisions under the Confederate judiciary system. When Louisiana seceded,
two Federal judges resigned. Passing over the former incumbents, President Davis appointed Edwin Warren Moise, a former attorney general of
Louisiana, as Confederate district judge. Moise presided over the court
in the Eastern Division, at New Orleans, handling civil, criminal, sequestration, and admiralty cases from May 1861 until Mar. 1862. Shortly after
that New Orleans fell to the enemy and it is unlikely that the court met
elsewhere in the Eastern Division.
       In the Western Division the court had met at Alexandria, Opelousas,
and Monroe, but those towns were frequently in enemy hands during 1863
and 1864, and no records have survived to show whether Judge Moise held
court there or in Shreveport. In May 1861 Henry C. Miller was appointed
district attorney and Constantine B. Beverly was appointed marshal.
Frank P. Stubbs replaced Beverly in Nov. 1864. The fact that Henry A. G.
Battle of Shreveport was confirmed as marshal in Apr. 1863 and James O.
Fuqua in Jan. 1864 suggests that court terms may have been held in western Louisiana. Sequestration receivers at New Orleans were John M.

Huger and George W. Ward; at St. Joseph, James W. Collier; at Bastrop, J. B. Matthews; at Clinton, John McVea; at Franklin, Robert N. McMillan; at Shreveport, John J. Kline; and at Alexandria, Thomas C. Manning.

Records in Other Custody. --Records of the Confederate District Court for the Eastern Division of Louisiana are in the custody of the U. S. District Court at New Orleans. These records include a docket, Oct. 1861-Apr. 1862; a court-costs book; case files, 1861-66; and venires of grand and petit juries, Nov.-Dec. 1861. In the Louisiana Historical Association Collection on deposit in the Howard-Tilton Memorial Library of Tulane University is a judgment docket, June 15, 1861-Feb. 12, 1862, containing the texts of judgments rendered by Judge Moise in prize cases involving the condemnation of vessels and their cargoes. A few documents relating to sequestration cases, chiefly writs of garnishment, Oct. 1861-Jan. 1862, are in the Manuscript Division of the Library of Congress.

Mississippi

In Mississippi the former U.S. Southern and Northern Districts with seats at Jackson and Pontotoc, respectively, became divisions under the Confederate judiciary system. In May 1861 Alexander M. Clayton, a Member of the Confederate Congress from Mississippi and a former judge in that State, was confirmed as district judge. Carnot Posey served as district attorney by deputy from 1861 to 1864. Killed while serving in the army in Virginia, he was succeeded by Robert Bowman. William H. H. Tison was the marshal. The first open sessions of the court at Jackson and Pontotoc were held in Aug. 1861. The court for the Northern Division moved from Pontotoc to Holly Springs in Feb. 1862 and held terms there until 1864 despite the town's intermittent occupation by the enemy. By an act of Feb. 13, 1862 (Prov. Cong. C.S.A. Stat. 260), the jurisdiction of Attala County was transferred from the Northern to the Southern Division. After the withdrawal of the Confederate forces from Jackson and the fall of Vicksburg in July 1863, the court for the Southern Division could no longer meet in that area. The State Government moved to Macon in Noxubee County, and to permit a session of the court to be held at Macon Congress transferred the jurisdiction of Noxubee County to the Southern Division in Feb. 1864. Judge Clayton set a term of the court for July, but not enough jurors reached Macon; he then set the term for Oct. 1864. Sequestration receivers were B. C. Buckley, Robert A. Clark, Charles R. Crusoe, H. T. Ellett, and John W. C. Watson.

Nannie M. Tillie, ed., "Letter of Judge Alexander M. Clayton Relative to Confederate Courts in Mississippi [Sept. 5, 1864]," Journal of Southern History, 6:396-401 (Aug. 1940).

Record Group 21. --Some records of the Confederate District Court of the Northern Division of Mississippi were received by the Federal Records Center at East Point, Ga., in 1954 from the U.S. District Court at Oxford, Miss. These include an issue and appearance docket, Aug. 1861-Apr. 1862 and 1864 (in a volume for 1857-68); an execution docket, Feb. 1862 term (in a volume for 1858-98); and a bar docket, Aug. 1861 term (in a volume for 1858-82).

Records in Other Custody. --In 1913 the Manuscript Division of the Library of Congress received from the U.S. District Court at Jackson

a minute book of the Confederate District Court of the Northern Division of
Mississippi. It is a general minute book for the period Aug. 12, 1861-Apr.
5, 1865, and does not include sequestration cases. The copyright register for
the Southern Division is in the Rare Book Room of the Library of Congress.

North Carolina

        The U.S. judicial districts of Pamlico, Cape Fear, and Albemarle,
with seats at New Bern, Wilmington, and Edenton, respectively, were retained as divisions in the Confederate judiciary system. Asa Biggs resigned as Federal judge in Apr. 1861 and in June was appointed Confederate
judge for all the North Carolina divisions. In July he organized the Pamlico Division in a session at New Bern and began hearing admiralty cases
involving ships captured by Confederate privateers and North Carolina
State gunboats. George V. Strong was district attorney, Wesley Jones was
marshal, and William M. Watson was clerk. H. C. Jones was the prize
commissioner. Wesley Jones was succeeded as marshal in Nov. 1864 by
Pride Jones. Sequestration receivers appointed on Sept. 20, 1861, were
B. B. Banon, J. H. Carson, Edward Connigland, John W. Cunningham, J.
L. Holmes, H. C. Jones, A. A. McCoy, John Manning, W. W. Peebles,
David Schenck, Benjamin M. Selby, Henry B. Short, and C. N. White.
After the Union capture of Hatteras Inlet in Aug. 1861 and of Roanoke Island
and New Bern early in 1862 the Pamlico Division Court met at Goldsboro.
Sequestration cases were its chief business.

        William M. Robinson, Jr.,   North Carolina, " North Carolina
"Admiralty in 1861; the Confederate   Historical Review, 17:132-138 (Apr.
States District Court for the Divi-   1940).
sion of Pamlico of the District of

        The first session in the Cape Fear Division was held at Wilmington
in Nov. 1861, but beginning in Feb. 1862 the sessions were held at Salisbury. John L. Cantwell was the first clerk; he was succeeded in June 1862
by Daniel M. Coleman, with William M. Coleman as deputy clerk. Man-
ger London, the district attorney, was succeeded in 1862 by A. A. McKay.
The deputy marshal was W. H. High, and Thomas W. Brown was prize
commissioner. The sequestration receivers were J. H. Carson, James
Calloway, DuBrutz Cutlar, Samuel L. Love, Darius F. Ramsour, David
Schenck, John J. Shover, and C. N. White. Admiralty, sequestration,
and garnishment cases were the business of the court.
        Little information is available concerning the Albemarle Division, for
no records have been found. The seat of the court was probably moved
from Edenton to Halifax in 1862. An order in the minute book of the Cape
Fear Division dated Mar. 10, 1862, set a term of the court for Halifax for
the following May. Sequestration receivers who were probably attached to
this division included W. H. Bailey, L. M. Scott, L. D. Starke, and G. H.
Wilder.
        Record Group 21. --In 1937 the National Archives received from the
North Carolina Department of Archives and History some records which it
had taken over from the U. S. District Court at Raleigh. These records are
now in the Washington National Records Center. Among them are the
minutes of the Confederate District Court, Pamlico Division, July 16-Sept.
20, 1861 (available on microfilm as M 436), concerning the organization of

the court at New Bern and its admiralty business, and minutes for the period Nov. 24, 1862-Nov. 3, 1864, concerning sessions held at Goldsboro. For the Nov. 1861 term at Goldsboro there is a brief trial docket covering civil, admiralty, criminal, and equity cases. Other Pamlico Division records were transferred in 1954 from the U.S. District Court at New Bern to the Federal Records Center at East Point, Ga., and these include minute books for 1861-65 (2 vols.), an admiralty record book, July 18-Sept. 18, 1861, an appearance docket, 1861-65, and an execution docket, 1861-65. A trial docket, 1861-65, contains a record of admiralty, jury, criminal, and sequestration cases set for hearing. The Survey of Federal Archives special report noted a record of copyrights, 1858-65, containing titles of some Confederate publications. Although this record is now missing, photocopies of certain titles are available in the North Carolina Department of Archives and History.

Some records of the Cape Fear Division were among the records received by the National Archives in 1950 from the U.S. District Court at Wilmington that are now in the Washington National Records Center. They include sequestration case files for 1861-64 (2 in.), writs of fieri facias for 1863-64 (3/4 in.) directing the marshal to enforce the payment of judgments in sequestration cases, and a group of papers for 1861-64 (1 in.) including case files of persons accused of harboring deserters, a mail robbery case, a treason case, jury lists, subpenas, grand jury presentments, receivers' bonds, depositions, and bills for fees connected with court cases. These records are available on microfilm as M 436.

Other records of the Cape Fear Division were transferred to the Federal Records Center at East Point in 1954 by the U.S. District Court at Wilmington. These include books also used by the U.S. District Court, such as minutes for 1862-63 and admiralty minutes, record of cases, and a trial docket for 1862-64. There are also sequestration, admiralty, and criminal case files.

Record Group 109.--A letter from Judge Biggs to George V. Strong, district attorney for the Pamlico Division, July 21, 1862, concerning Strong's compensation, is in the War Department Collection of Confederate Records (Confederate Department of Justice records).

Records in Other Custody.--Pamlico Division sequestration case files, 1861-65 (3,390 items), are in Duke University Library. A record of copyright entries for the Pamlico Division is in the Rare Book Room of the Library of Congress.

South Carolina

The former U.S. Eastern and Western Districts of South Carolina became divisions under the Confederate judiciary system. Andrew G. Magrath, who had been the U.S. judge, was appointed as Confederate district judge. In Apr. 1861 he organized the district court at Charleston, where privateers soon brought cases involving prize vessels and cargoes for adjudication. The court met at Columbia in Dec. 1861 and at Greenville in Feb. 1862 and during 1862-64 held sessions also at Charleston. Magrath became governor of South Carolina in Dec. 1864 and was succeeded as judge early in 1865 by Benjamin F. Perry. Serving as district attorney at different times were Perry, James Conner, and C. Richardson Miles. Daniel H. Hamilton was appointed marshal in May 1861. Sequestration receivers functioning throughout the State included James R. Aiken, John

Bauskett, John W. Caldwell, W. J. DeTreville, R. E. Fraser, E. P. Lake, J. J. Ryan, John B. Sitton, John Y. Stock, and S. J. Townsend.

Record Group 109. --The War Department Collection of Confederate Records contains material relating to the sequestration of alien-enemy property in South Carolina. A minute book of sequestration proceedings, Sept. 9, 1861-Dec. 16, 1864 (ch. X, vol. 210), contains verdicts of juries on the citizenship of persons whose property was involved; statements of cases; orders to marshals to seize alien-enemy property and deliver it to receivers and to receivers to sell the property and submit accounts; orders to continue cases; appointments of receivers; reports of receivers on sales; circulars; and decisions. An index in the front of the book is arranged alphabetically by name. A list of sequestration papers, 1861-63 (ch. X, vol. 216), covers petitions and writs of garnishment, reports of debts and property, and receivers' reports. A clerk's account book, 1861-64 (ch. X, vol. 215), contains sequestration receivers' accounts and accounts for the sale of prize vessels and their cargoes. An account book of sequestered debts, 1861-64 (ch. X, vol. 212), gives the names of southern debtors and northern creditors, the amounts owed, payments made to the receiver in cash, and the proceeds of sales. Other books include a record of writs of garnishment and sequestration petitions issued with amounts of money received, 1861-62 (ch. X, vol. 218 1/2); docket of sequestration cases, 1862-65 (ch. X, vols. 211, 213); alphabetical name index to writs of garnishment (ch. X, vol. 218); alphabetical name index to sequestration decrees (ch. X, vols. 213 1/2, 214); list of writs of garnishment and sequestration petitions issued by the second receiver's office, 1861-62 (ch. X, vol. 217); and accounts of sequestration receivers, 1862-64 (ch. X, vol. 208). On loose sheets in ch. X, vol. 214, is a trial balance of the cash ledger of Sequestration Receiver John Y. Stock, 1864. The sequestration case files, 1861-62 (more than 9 ft.), include many cross-reference cards as well as original papers.

No other records of the Confederate court in South Carolina have been found. On May 7, 1862, after the declaration of martial law in Charleston, the court moved to Columbia. Sessions were later held at Charleston, but the records may have been left at Columbia and destroyed when Columbia was burned in Feb. 1865.

Tennessee

After Tennessee joined the Confederacy in July 1861, the former U. S. judicial districts (Eastern, Middle, and Western) became divisions of the District of Tennessee under the Confederate judiciary system. West H. Humphreys, who had been U. S. district judge, was appointed Confederate judge. He opened court in the Eastern Division at Knoxville in Sept. 1861 and held the prescribed terms in October for the Middle and Western Divisions at Nashville and Jackson, respectively. John C. Ramsey served as district attorney and Jesse B. Clements as marshal during 1861-62. In Sept. 1861 William G. McAdoo was appointed clerk and William H. Crouch was appointed deputy marshal of the Eastern Division.

An act of Dec. 12, 1861 (Prov. Cong. C. S. A. Stat. 224), reestablished the three divisions as independent judicial districts under a single judge. Early in 1862 B. M. Estes became district attorney and W. W. Gates, William H. Crouch, and Jesse B. Clements became marshals of the Western, Eastern, and Middle Districts, respectively. On Mar. 29,

1862, Jesse G. Wallace was confirmed as district attorney of the Eastern District. John L. Sehon became district attorney of the Middle District in 1863. Sequestration receivers appointed on Sept. 23, 1861, were William A. Branner, Landon C. Haynes, Charles M. McGhee, Joseph A. Mabry, and Thomas L. Powell. Others who served later included T. J. Campbell, Sterling Cockrill, Matthew T. Haynes, and Howell E. Jackson.

In the Eastern District, Judge Humphreys held terms of court at Knoxville until July 27, 1863, and considered treason, sequestration, garnishment, espionage, habeas corpus, and criminal cases. By September of that year Confederate court sessions had ceased in Tennessee.

Record Group 21. --Records of the Confederate District Court for the Eastern District of Tennessee (Knoxville) in the Federal Records Center at East Point, Ga., include a minute book, Sept. 6, 1861-July 27, 1863 (part of a book also used by the U.S. district court, 1852-60); an index of minutes; and a docket of sequestration cases. In the Washington National Records Center is a trial docket of the court for the Middle District, Oct. 1861-May 1862, showing the names of parties, nature of cases, and their disposition. This docket had been left in Nashville when the Confederates withdrew in Feb. 1862 and was subpenaed by the U.S. Senate's High Court of Impeachment in June 1862 for use in the trial of Judge Humphreys (in absentia). It remained with the records of the Senate until it was reallocated to Record Group 21 after the transfer of the Senate records to the National Archives. No other records of the Confederate court in Tennessee have been found.

Texas

Texas was initially considered to be a single judicial district, but an act of May 21, 1861 (Prov. Cong. C.S.A. Stat. 127), divided the State into two judicial districts: a Western District composed of Matagorda, Wharton, Colorado, Fayette, Washington, Burelson, Milam, Falls, McLellan, Hill, Johnson, Tarrant, Wise, and Montague Counties and all territory west of them; and an Eastern District consisting of the rest of Texas. Officials to be appointed for the Western District were to hold terms twice a year at Austin and Brownsville. Thomas J. Devine was judge, John C. West was the district attorney, and John R. Jefferson was marshal of the Western District. William P. Hill and George Mason were judge and district attorney, respectively, for the Eastern District, and William T. Austin became marshal.

Judge Hill organized the court for the Eastern District at Galveston in July 1861. He and Mason were reconfirmed in their positions in Apr. 1862, and James W. Mosely became marshal of the Eastern District. Marcus F. Mott served as clerk. Sequestration receivers in the Eastern District were William P. Ballinger, Harris T. Garnett, Medicus A. Long, John McCreary, James M. Maxcy, and Trenton A. Patillo. An act of Sept. 30, 1862 (1 Cong. C.S.A. Stat. 65), transferred the counties of Matagorda, Wharton, Colorado, Washington, and Burleson to the Eastern District and provided for the appointment of a marshal for the Eastern District for the court at Galveston who was also to serve the court held at Tyler. In Oct. 1862 William T. Austin was confirmed as marshal for the court held at Galveston. James Masterson and W. B. Botts were appointed deputy clerks in the Eastern District. From its exposed seat at Galveston the court moved in Jan. 1862 to Houston, where sessions were held that year and later. After the recapture of Galveston on Jan. 1, 1863, the court again met there, and it also met at Tyler. The court for the Eastern District adjudicated admiralty, sequestration, garnishment, criminal, and habeas corpus cases.

The court for the Western District met at Brownsville in the fall of 1861 and at Austin in Jan. 1862. Judge Devine organized the court at Austin and appointed George Braine as clerk. An act of May 1, 1863 (1 Cong. C. S. A. Stat. 160), authorized the removal of the court from Brownsville to Corpus Christi. In Nov. 1863 U.S. forces captured both towns, and the judge moved the court inland to Gonzales. Sequestration receivers in the Western District were J. D. Giddings, W. S. Glass, John A. Green, M. O. Green, John Ireland, J. L. L. McCall, John S. McCampbell, Nestor Maxañ, William Milburn, Thomas Moore, William R. Reagan, J. C. Rushing, Junius W. Smith, and James A. Ware.

John N. Cravens, James Harper Starr: Financier of the Republic of Texas, p. 130-135 (Austin, 1950): T. R. Havins, "Administration of the Sequestration Act in the Confederate District Court for the Western District of Texas, 1862- 1865, " Southwestern Historical Quarterly, 43: 295-322 (Jan. 1940); Nowlin Randolph, "Judge William Pinckney Hill Aids the Confederate War Effort, " Southwestern Historical Quarterly, 68:14-28 (July 1964).

Record Group 365. --Records of the Confederate District Court for the Eastern District of Texas are among the Treasury Department Collection of Confederate Records. Admiralty case files, July 1861-May 1865 (3 in.), contain numerically arranged papers relating to prize vessels and to the payment of wages to seamen and payments for supplies. There are records of criminal and habeas corpus cases for Mar. 1862-May 1865 (4 in.).

Papers relating to sequestration cases are in several files. Sequestration case files, Nov. 1862-May 1865 (1 ft. 3 in.), are arranged numerically. A file of petitions for writs of garnishment against alien-enemy property, Nov. 1861-May 1865 (3 ft. 6 in.), arranged numerically, consists largely of the petitions submitted by the receiver but contains related papers for some cases, such as garnishees' answers and reports, schedules of notes and accounts, inventories of merchandise, interventions by creditors, writs of seizure, and receivers' reports. Some answers to writs of garnishment, 1861-65 (2 in.), are in a separate numerically arranged file (nos. 1-99, with many missing).

Other records of the Confederate District Court for the Eastern District of Texas in this record group concern the activities of the court and of the receivers regarding sequestration business. Minutes of the court in sequestration proceedings, Oct. 23, 1861-Jan. 31, 1862 (1 vol.), consist chiefly of judgments, and these give information about the parties and property involved and orders to receivers. The minutes also contain orders on keeping records, appointments of receivers, and the establishment of their districts, rules of proceedings under the sequestration act, affidavits of sureties, and appointments of commissioners. An alphabetical name index to the minutes is in a separate volume. A volume of receivers' accounts and reports, Nov. 30, 1861-June 7, 1864, shows receipts from the sales of sequestered property and receivers' expenses. The receivers were W. P. Ballinger, Harris T. Garnett, John McCreary, James M.

Maxcy, and William Milburn. In another small volume is an inventory of sequestered goods, wares, and merchandise of Chester N. Case of Austin, Feb. 1862. It had been an exhibit to one of H. T. Garnett's accounts. The accounts of Receivers Ballinger, Garnett, McCreary, Maxcy, and J. D. Giddings, Jan. 1862-Feb. 1865 (2 1/2 in.), show receipts from the sale of sequestered property and related expenses. Receipts for money paid out of the sequestration fund, June 1862-Mar. 1865 (3/4 in.), cover the district court clerk's fees and services, payments to the marshal for travel, serving writs, and attending grand juries, and abstracts of compensation paid to jurors and witnesses.

Several other small files are with the foregoing records. Some writs of fieri facias returned, Feb., May, and July 1864 (1/3 in.), show the results of the marshal's efforts to recover the amounts of judgments and costs from property. Oaths of office, July 1861-Feb. 1865 (1/2 in.), signed by court officials and others in the presence of either the judge or the clerk, are arranged by office. The marshal's accounts and related papers, July 1861-Dec. 1864 (2 in.), show compensation to jurors, witnesses, and contingent expenses; processes served by the marshal; receipts; returns of fees and emoluments; receipts and inventories relating to prize vessels Cavallo, Morning Light, and Elias Pike; the commissioner's report on the marshal's account in sequestration cases; and correspondence. There are writs for summoning juries (venire facias) and grand jury subpenas and reports, 1861-65 (1/2 in.). A file of receipts, 1862-64 (1/4 in.), includes those of the depositary, clerk, marshal, and proctors. Proceedings against defaulting jurors, June 1863-Mar. 1865 (1/2 in.), include citations, answers, excuses, affidavits, and related papers.

All of the above records are those of the court held at Galveston; no records of the court at Tyler have been found.

Record Group 21. --Records received from the U.S. District Court at Austin by the Federal Records Center at Fort Worth in 1963 included some record books and case files of the Confederate District Court for the Western District of Texas. The minute book, Jan. 6, 1862-June 13, 1863 (2 vols.), contains data on the administration of the court, but most of the case entries are sequestration cases. An index to the second minute book is in the "general index to court dockets." A docket, Jan. 1865 (2 vols.), contains records of cases numbered 93-2420 on p. 202 and 225-522, but entries for cases numbered 142-625 are missing. They are mostly sequestration and garnishment cases, with some trespass, debt, and injunction cases. Another docket, June 1862-May 1863 (1 vol.), shows the disposition of cases carried over from the U.S. district court and cases numbered 712-2882 for the sequestration of alien-enemy property. Other dockets include an undated bar docket for sequestration, garnishment, and criminal cases (1 vol.), a motion docket, Jan. 1862-June 1864, and an execution docket, June 1862-May 1863.

Other records include sequestration case files, 1861-65 (8 ft.), arranged numerically; an alphabetical name index to those files (1 vol.); a record of court costs, Oct. 1862-Dec. 1863 (1 vol.); a record of writs served by the marshal, Nov. 1861-June 1864 (1 vol.); and a record of the marshal's returns on the service of court orders, June 1862-May 1863 (1 vol.). The marshal's emolument accounts, Apr. 1862-July 1864 (1 vol.), contain a record of fees and emoluments received in connection with sequestration and other cases and receipts and expenditures. A receiver's account book,

Jan. 1862-Jan. 1863 (p. 7-43 of a book labeled "Journal, " also used by the
U.S. marshal, 1868-73), contains a record of receipts and expenditures,
funds received from the Department of Justice and other sources, and expenses of court terms at Brownsville and Austin, Nov. 1861-July 1864.
An alphabetical but undated list of alien enemies (persons or firms) whose
property was sequestered (1 vol.) contains references to case numbers and
the places of recording.

  Records in Other Custody.--Several collections of papers in the manuscript department of the University of Texas Library contain pertinent
material on the Eastern District. The papers of Philip C. Tucker, II,
prize commissioner of that district, include the minutes of a special grand
jury (Nov. 18, 1861-Jan. 11, 1862) impaneled to investigate and sequester
alien-enemy property, two reports, 40 indictments signed by W. P. Ballinger, and papers relating to the prize vessel Harriet Lane. The correspondence of W. P. Ballinger, sequestration receiver for Galveston and
Harris Counties, includes letters, 1861-63, about alien-enemy property,
and letters from Marshal William T. Austin giving lists of persons against
whom garnishments should be issued and lists of claims, property, and
debts. Press copybooks of letters sent by James H. Starr, receiver at
Nacogdoches, Aug. 15, 1861-May 17, 1863, and Feb. 22, 1862-Nov. 14, 1863
(2 vols.), contain letters to garnishees, other Confederate officials, and
postmasters; reports on sales of property; schedules of medicines ordered
to be sold; statements of debts due, receipts for payments received, and
alphabetical name indexes. Letters received by J. H. Starr, 1862-63, arranged alphabetically, also concern sequestration matters. A diary of
William P. Ballinger, Oct. 1861-Mar. 1865, is in the Rosenberg Library
at Galveston.

  Other records of the Confederate District Court for the Eastern District of Texas are in the custody of the U.S. District Court at Galveston.
They include a law and criminal docket, Nov. 1861-May 1865; a criminal
docket, Feb. 1862-May 1864; an admiralty docket, Feb. 1862-May 1864; the
clerk's cost docket, Feb. 1853-Dec. 1862; an execution docket, Nov. 1863-
May 1864; and a memorandum court ledger, June 1863-May 1867, containing expense accounts, cost records, reports of sales of property, and
grand jury reports and subpenas.

  Material in the custody of the U.S. District Court at Brownsville relating
to the Confederate District Court for the Western District of Texas includes
a minute book, 1852-67; a law docket, 1852-81, covering sessions in the fall
of 1861 and the spring of 1863; two chancery dockets, 1860-65 and 1862-81;
and a motion docket, 1853-63, containing motions filed in the spring of 1863.

Virginia

  An act of May 21, 1861 (Prov. Cong. C.S.A. Stat. 149), divided Virginia into Eastern and Western Districts, and on that date James D. Halyburton, the former U.S. judge, was confirmed as judge of the Eastern District, with Patrick H. Aylett as district attorney and John F. Wiley as
marshal. Loftin N. Ellett was appointed as clerk. The court opened at
Richmond on June 12, 1861; it continued to meet there until the end of Mar.
1865. It was concerned with sequestration, criminal, prize, and habeas
corpus cases. An act of Aug. 22, 1861 (Prov. Cong. C.S.A. Stat. 189),
providing for the naturalization of foreigners engaged in the military service of the Confederate States, required that oaths taken by them be filed

in the district court at Richmond. Sequestration receivers in the Eastern District of Virginia were Henry L. Brooke, Thomas H. Campbell, Thomas T. Giles, William A. Maury, Francis L. Smith, and John M. Speed.

John W. Brockenbrough of Lexington, former judge of the U.S. District Court of the Western District of Virginia, was commissioned as Confederate judge of the same district on May 23, 1861. In the same month Fleming B. Miller became district attorney and Jefferson T. Martin became marshal. The court met at Staunton in May 1861, and when it reconvened there in September the judge appointed Joseph W. Caldwell as court clerk. Sessions of the court were also held at Wytheville and Lexington, but the more western portion of the district espoused the Union side in the war and sessions normally scheduled at Wheeling, Clarksburg, Charleston, and Lewisburg were not held. On Sept. 26, 1861, the Western District was subdivided for the administration of the sequestration act, and the following men were appointed as receivers: Thomas T. Fauntleroy, William Gibboney, John W. Johnston, Jacob Keizer, John Kenney, Thomas J. Michie, James W. Shields, and Joseph G. Steele.

Record Group 21.--Records of the Confederate District Court for the Western District of Virginia transferred by the U.S. District Court at Abingdon, Va., to the National Archives in 1956 and 1961 are now in the Washington National Records Center. Sequestration case files, Dec. 1861-Oct. 1864 (3 ft.), are arranged alphabetically by initial letter of surname of party concerned. A common law and chancery docket, 1861-63 (3 p. of an "Issue Docket" also used by the U.S. District Court, 1839-78), shows for the spring 1861 term felony, debt, and ejectment cases and, for the spring 1862 and spring 1863 terms, law and chancery cases.

Also in the Washington National Records Center are records of the Confederate District Court sessions held at Staunton. An order book covering sessions for Sept. 24-30, 1861, and Jan. 6-14 and Mar. 6-11, 1862, contains the commissions of the judge and other court officers, orders for adjournment, minutes of proceedings in habeas corpus cases involving disloyal persons, admissions of attorneys, appointments of commissioners and receivers, abstracts of compensation paid to witnesses and grand jurors, and orders in civil suits. A witness book, also used by the U.S. District Court, contains brief entries for the May 1861, January 1862, and May 1864 terms showing the witnesses' names, number of days they served, number of miles they traveled, and amounts paid them. Letters, recognizances taken by the commissioner, grand jury indictments, petitions for writs of habeas corpus, bonds, summonses, rough notes of the court proceedings, commissions of justices of the peace of Rockingham County, injunctions, military orders prohibiting the impressment of corn, and court-martial proceedings are also included for 1861-64 (3/4 in.).

Records in Other Custody.--The U.S. District Court at Abingdon, Va., has some order books for sessions of the Confederate District Court held at Wytheville. An order book, May 29, 1862-May 30, 1863 (in a volume also used by the U.S. District Court, 1839-60), gives data regarding civil and criminal cases, indictments, appointments of judges and other court officials, admissions of attorneys, and names of witnesses and jurors. An order book, May 25, 1863-Nov. 9, 1864, concerns proceedings in criminal and sequestration cases. A chancery order book, July 30, 1862-Oct. 26, 1863 (part of a volume also used by the U.S. District Court, 1853-60), gives information regarding proceedings and orders of continuance.

Most of the records of the Confederate District Court for the Eastern

District of Virginia at Richmond were destroyed during the war. Many
were lost in a fire that destroyed the clerk's office in the summer of 1863.
Others were probably burned in the fires that swept the business district of
Richmond on Apr. 2-3, 1865. The deputy marshal saved an "order book"
that was later turned over to the U.S. District Court, which transferred it
in 1960 to the Archives Division of the Virginia State Library. It is for the
period June 12, 1861-Mar. 30, 1865 (820 p.), and the data are in chronological order, with an alphabetical name index. It contains appointments of
court officers, titles of cases, rules of the court in prize cases, jury lists,
indictments, decrees, pardons, orders for the division of the district into
receivers' districts and for the sale of alien-enemy property, and other
orders relating to the summoning of jurors, hearing of cases, imprisonment of offenders, and discharge of prisoners. A record of copyright entries, 1864-65, is in the Virginia Historical Society collections.

The titles of the copyrighted works are in "Confederate Copyrights," Virginia Magazine of History, 20:425-429 (Oct. 1912). See also Decisions of Hon. James D. Halyburton, Judge of the Confederate States District Court for the Eastern District of Virginia, in the Cases of John B. Lane and John H. Leftwich, in Relation to Their Exemption, As Mail Contractors, from the Performance of Military Service (Richmond, 1864).

TERRITORIAL COURTS

Arizona Territory

The Territory of Arizona as established by the Confederate Government consisted of the parts of the present States of Arizona and New Mexico that lie south of the 34th parallel. Since 1856 the people of this area
had urged the U.S. Congress to establish a Territory of Arizona separate
from the Territory of New Mexico. Their representatives met in convention at Mesilla on Mar. 16, 1861, and adopted resolutions of secession.
These resolutions and a constitution for the proposed Territory were sent
to the Confederate Congress, which referred them to the Committee on
Territories. Congress did not formally establish the Territory, however,
until the following January.
    In the meantime, Col. John R. Baylor, with a force of Texans, in-
vaded the area in July 1861 and, after driving out the Federal garrisons,
issued a proclamation on Aug. 1 declaring himself military governor of the
Territory of Arizona. The proclamation established a judicial system consisting of a supreme court, district and probate courts, and justices of the
peace. The district judges made up the supreme court. The Territory
was divided into a first district, east of Apache Pass with its seat at
Mesilla, and a second district, west of the pass with its seat at Tucson.
Probate courts established for the counties of Doña Ana and Arizona were
to meet at the same places, and the clerks of the district courts were to
serve also as clerks of the probate courts.
    The territorial court of the First Judicial District was organized at
Mesilla in 1861 by Judge H. C. Cook, an appointee of Governor Baylor.
He was succeeded by S. Hare before the court met at the end of the year.
In Dec. 1861 the grand jury returned seven indictments for murder and two
for assault, but only one assault case was tried before a petit jury. Orders

were issued by the court as late as Mar. 31, 1862, but it did not meet a-
gain in open session after the Dec. 1861 term.

No records of the court for the Second Judicial District that was to
meet at Tucson have been found, and its activities, if any, are unknown.

The first regular session of the probate court of Doña Ana County
met on Sept. 2, 1861, Judge Frank Higgins presiding. After holding other
sessions in Dec. 1861 and Jan. 1862, Higgins resigned and was succeeded
by John P. Deus. The court met in March, but the term scheduled for
May 1862 was adjourned to June because of disturbed conditions in the Territory. The judge resigned and the court did not meet again. Cases handled
by the court included attachment proceedings, actions for debt, fore-
closures, a suit in replevin, a damage suit, and appeals from the decisions
of justices of the peace. The court also performed such administrative
duties as auditing the accounts of officials, issuing ordinances for the public welfare, appointing officials, levying taxes, ordering road work, acting
as an election board, and supervising the work of public employees.

No records of the probate court of Arizona County that was to meet
at Tucson have been found, and its activities are unknown.

An act of Congress, approved Jan. 18, 1862 (Prov. Cong. C.S.A.
Stat. 245), to organize the Territory of Arizona, provided for a system of
courts similar to that created by Governor Baylor, but divided the Territory into three districts instead of two. The redistricting was not accomplished, however, for President Davis nominated only a chief justice,
Alexander M. Jackson, and one associate justice, Columbus Upson, leaving the third district unestablished. The justices were commissioned on
Mar. 21 along with Russel Howard as attorney and Samuel J. Jones as
marshal. Jurisdiction of the district courts was the same as that vested in
the district courts of the Confederate States. The supreme court and the
district courts were given chancery as well as common law jurisdiction.
The judges of the probate courts were appointed by the Governor; the
jurisdiction of these courts was very general. Justices of the peace were
to be appointed by the justices of the supreme court; their jurisdiction was
imited to disputes involving amounts not over $100, and they had no juris-
diction in suits over title to or boundaries of lands. Confederate jurisdiction ended in Arizona in the summer of 1862, when U.S. forces from Cali-
fornia occupied the Territory. The system of courts authorized by the act
establishing the Territory therefore did not become a reality.

William M. Robinson, Jr.,
Justice in Grey, p. 309-325; Benjamin Sacks, Be It Enacted; the
Creation of the Territory of Arizona, p. 62-69 (Phoenix, 1964). Edward D. Tittmann, "Confederate Courts
in New Mexico, " New Mexico Historical Review, 3:347-356 (Oct. 1928).

Records in Other Custody. --In the Doña Ana County Courthouse at
Las Cruces, N. Mex., are records of the courts that met at Mesilla during the Confederate period. "Doña Ana County Record A, " 1861-67, contains a record of the first judicial district court for Oct. 7-Dec. 21, 1861,
and Mar. 31, 1862, giving information on the impaneling of juries, appointment of court officials, admissions of attorneys, and civil and criminal
cases. The minutes of the Doña Ana County probate court, Aug. 8, 1861-
June 2, 1862, are in a volume containing also the record of the U.S. court
beginning in 1863.

Historical Records Survey, New Mexico, Inventory of the County Archives of New Mexico, No. 7, Doña Ana (Las Cruces) (Albuquerque, 1940). Charles S. Walker, ed., "Confederate Government in Doña Ana County, As Shown in the Records of the Probate Court, 1861-62, " New Mexico Historical Review, 6:253-302 (Apr. 1931), contains the text of the probate court minutes.

Indian Country

Treaties negotiated by Confederate Agent Albert Pike provided for the establishment of Confederate district courts in the Indian country, which had previously been attached to the Western District of Arkansas. The Cherokee treaty of Oct. 7, 1861 (Prov. Cong. C.S.A. Stat. 400), provided for the judicial district of Cha-lah-ki in the Cherokee Nation. The Creek, Seminole, Osage, Quapaw, Seneca, and Shawnee tribes agreed to accept the jurisdiction of that court. The treaty with the Choctaw and Chickasaw Nations of July 12, 1861 (Prov. Cong. C.S.A. Stat. 320), provided that their territory should constitute the judicial district of Tush-ca-hom-ma.

The Indian judiciary act of Feb. 15, 1862 (Prov. Cong. C.S.A. Stat. 272), empowered the President to appoint one judge for both districts for a term of 4 years and one marshal and one attorney for each district also for 4 years. The judge was authorized to appoint for each court clerks and interpreters who were to hold office at the pleasure of the court. Semiannual terms of the court for the Tush-ca-hom-ma District were to be held at Boggy Depot in the Choctaw Nation, and terms for the Cha-lah-ki District were to be held at Tahlequah or wherever the seat of government of the Cherokee Nation might be. The criminal jurisdiction of the courts was to extend to offenses against the Confederate States laws in force in the districts. Admiralty jurisdiction was to be the same as that of other district courts. Jurisdiction in civil cases was to extend to suits at law or equity, when more than $500 was involved, between a citizen of the Confederate States, or an alien, and a citizen or resident of the district. The jurisdiction of the courts was enlarged by the act for the organization of the Arkansas and Red River Superintendency of Indian Affairs of Apr. 8, 1862 (1 Cong. C.S.A. Stat. 20-21).

After the Indian nations ratified the treaties and their amendments, the President, on Sept. 26, 1862, nominated a judge and other officials, but these nominations were tabled by the Senate on Oct. 2. The President resubmitted nominations on Feb. 21, 1865. George A. Gallagher was confirmed as judge the next day and was commissioned 2 days later. The district attorney for the Tush-ca-hom-ma District was Campbell Laflore, and the marshal was H. M. U. C. Brown; William P. Adair was the attorney and Percy Brewer was the marshal for the Cha-lah-ki District. Gallagher was then serving on Gen. E. K. Smith's staff at Shreveport, La. His confirmation was probably too late for him to reach Tahlequah for the spring term, but he may have reached Boggy Depot in time to open the term there on Apr. 17. In the Tush-ca-hom-ma District the district court for the Western District of Arkansas had been exercising extraterritorial jurisdiction with the consent of the Choctaw and Chickasaw Indians; the other tribes had not agreed to this arrangement. Cases involving Indian nations or their citizens may have been tried in other district courts, for an act of Apr. 27, 1863 (1 Cong. C.S.A. Stat. 126), authorized Indians to sue at law or in equity, in the same manner as provided for with the Cherokee Nation, a citizen or resident of any State or Territory in any district court where litigation could be taken under the Constitution, laws, or treaties of the Confederate States.

No records of Confederate courts in the Indian country have been found.

BOARD OF CLAIMS COMMISSIONERS

The sequestration act of Aug. 30, 1861 (Prov. Cong. C.S.A. Stat. 205), authorized the President to appoint three commissioners to adjudicate claims presented by adherents of the Confederacy for losses sustained under the U.S. confiscation laws. The findings of the commissioners were to be prima facie evidence of the validity of the claims which, when approved by Congress, were to be paid by the Treasurer from money derived from the sequestration of alien-enemy property in accordance with the same act. The Attorney General or his assistant was to represent the interests of the Government before the Board of Commissioners. The Board was to function only until Congress provided for the court of claims authorized by the Permanent Constitution. Congress failed to enact such legislation, however, and the Board of Claims Commissioners continued to operate throughout the war. On Dec. 13, 1861, Congress confirmed as members of the Board George P. Scarburgh, the former presiding judge of the U.S. Court of Claims; Walker Brooke, a Delegate in Congress from Mississippi; and Thomas C. Reynolds, the lieutenant governor of Missouri. They were continued in office by appropriation acts of Feb. 10 and May 1, 1863, Feb. 17, 1864, and Mar. 13, 1865 (1 Cong. C.S.A. Stat. 97, 139, 201, Ramsdell, Laws and Joint Resolutions, p. 123). The act of Feb. 15, 1862 (Prov. Cong. C.S.A. Stat. 266), amending the sequestration act authorized the commissioners to appoint a clerk and examiners to hear witnesses. Edgar M. Garnett, who had been assistant clerk of the U.S. Court of Claims, was appointed clerk. Judge Scarburgh became the presiding commissioner.

The proceedings and other records of this board have not been found.

IV

THE PRESIDENCY

On Feb. 9, 1861, the Provisional Congress at Montgomery elected Jefferson Davis President and Alexander H. Stephens Vice President. Stephens, who was a delegate to Congress from Georgia, was inaugurated on Feb. 11. Davis was inaugurated on Feb. 18 upon his arrival from Mississippi, where he had gone upon his resignation from the U.S. Senate. Davis and Stephens were elected on Nov. 6, 1861, for 6-year terms, as provided by the Permanent Constitution. The Capital had been moved in June 1861 from Montgomery to Richmond, and the inauguration took place in Richmond on Feb. 22, 1862. The President's Office was located on the second floor of the U.S. customhouse on Main Street, a structure which also housed the Cabinet Room and the State and Treasury Departments. The City of Richmond purchased the Brockenbrough house for presentation to the Government for use as an executive mansion. Davis declined to accept the gift, but the house was leased for his use. Referred to as the "White House of the Confederacy" or the "Grey House," the mansion was used by President Davis throughout the existence of the Confederacy. Later it became a repository for documents, relics, and pictures relating to the history of the Confederacy, and in 1896 it was designated the Confederate Museum.

President Davis had a small personal staff to assist him in handling the business of the Executive Office. Alexander B. Clitherall served temporarily as his private secretary early in 1861. In approving an act of Feb. 20, 1861 (Prov. Cong. C.S.A. Stat. 29), authorizing the appointment of a private secretary, the President announced the appointment of Robert Josselyn of Mississippi. Josselyn was later appointed Secretary of the Territory of Arizona, however, and in Mar. 1862, on the recommendation of Col. Lucius Q. C. Lamar, Davis appointed Burton N. Harrison as his new secretary. Harrison, a native of New Orleans and a graduate of Yale University, was then teaching mathematics at the University of Mississippi. Harrison's duties included conveying messages to Congress, handling important documents, drafting communications, receiving visitors, acting as disbursing officer, and accompanying the President on horseback rides around Richmond. He served in this capacity throughout the war and was a resident of the executive mansion. Micajah H. Clark served as a clerk in the Executive Office.

The President also had a number of military aides, beginning with Col. Louis T. Wigfall of Texas early in 1861. An act of Aug. 21, 1861 (Prov. Cong. C.S.A. Stat. 188), authorized the appointment of two additional aides with the rank of colonel. On Aug. 31, George Washington Custis Lee, eldest son of Robert E. Lee, and Joseph R. Davis, a nephew of the President, were appointed to these positions. By the authority of an act of Apr. 9, 1862 (1 Cong. C.S.A. Stat. 7), additional aides were appointed on Apr. 19, including William Preston Johnston, son of Albert Sidney Johnston; Joseph C. Ives, a former engineer officer in the U.S. Army; James Chesnut, Jr., of South Carolina; and William M. Browne, who had had a short tenure as Assistant Secretary of State. In June 1864, Davis appointed Francis R. Lubbock, former governor of Texas, as an aide in order to have on his staff an officer acquainted with the people and affairs of the West. Lubbock reached Richmond in Sept. 1864 and remained on the President's staff until the end of the war. Lt. John T. Wood, C.S.N., became a Presidential aide in Jan. 1863, replacing Colonel Davis.

The military aides performed much the same duties as the private secretary, except that they also went on special missions connected with military operations. Colonel Lee advised the President on military engineering matters and from June 1863 commanded the Richmond Defense Brigade composed of employees of Government departments and of local industries. One or more of these officers presumably affixed the signature of the President to commissions in the armed forces in accordance with an act of Dec. 7, 1861 (Prov. Cong. C.S.A. Stat. 222). Robert B. Craddock served as the President's messenger in 1862.

The constitutional powers of the President were quite similar to those of the President of the United States. The Permanent Constitution made him the commander in chief of the Army and Navy and of the State militia when called into the service of the Confederate States. He was also empowered to grant reprieves and pardons for offenses against the Confederate States. He was authorized to make treaties; to nominate and appoint diplomatic representatives, judges, and other officers of the Confederate States (including the heads of the executive departments) by and with the advice and consent of the Senate; and to remove such representatives and officers. He could fill vacancies during a recess of the Senate, but he could not reappoint, during a recess, persons previously rejected by the Senate. He was to supply Congress with information, recommend legislation, receive Ambassadors and other public ministers, see that the laws were faithfully executed, and commission all officers of the military and naval forces of the Confederate States. Under his power to veto bills passed by Congress he vetoed 39 bills that he considered unconstitutional or unwise. Some bills received near the close of sessions went unsigned because there was not time to give them adequate consideration. As other duties continued to place increasing demands on his time, he arranged for Secretary of State Judah P. Benjamin to assist him in writing messages to Congress.

As military activities and other operations expanded, Congress authorized the President to appoint officers of the Provisional Army, of volunteers, of the Provisional Navy, and of the Volunteer Navy, and to grant letters of marque and reprisal to private armed vessels. Numerous acts of Congress, some of which are cited herein, authorized him to appoint various civilian officials, including heads of bureaus and offices, aides-de-camp, claims commissioners, collectors of customs, district attorneys, marshals, and officials of the Territory of Arizona. An act of Jan. 16, 1862 (Prov. Cong. C.S.A. Stat. 241), empowered the President to appoint the Assistant Secretaries of State, Treasury, and War by and with the advice and consent of Congress. An act of Feb. 15, 1864 (Ramsdell, Laws and Joint Resolutions, p. 170), appropriated $5 million for a secret service fund to be expended under the direction of the President.

Late on the evening of Apr. 2, 1865, President Davis, his aides, and members of the Cabinet, except Secretary of War Breckinridge, departed from Richmond on the Richmond and Danville Railroad. The party stayed at Danville, 140 miles southwest of Richmond, until Apr. 10 when, hearing of Lee's surrender, it continued farther south. At Greensboro, N. C., on Apr. 12 the Cabinet met with Generals Johnston and Beauregard and discussed the surrender of Johnston's army to General Sherman. As the railroad south of Greensboro had been ruined by U.S. forces, the flight from that place was on horseback and in ambulances, wagons, and carriages. The last Cabinet meetings took place at Charlotte, N. C., on Apr. 24 and 26, and on May 4, when Davis left Washington, Ga., the party consisted only of his aides and Postmaster General Reagan. A U.S. Army detachment captured Davis and his companions at an encampment near Irwinville, Ga., on May 10.

Davis was imprisoned at Fort Monroe, Va., until his release on bail on May 13, 1867. During his confinement the U.S. Government prepared to bring him to trial for treason and for complicity in the assassination of President Lincoln. He could not be tried in Virginia until the Federal courts were reestablished there, but by the time the circuit judges were prepared in May 1867 the Government decided that the outcome of a trial before a Virginia jury was too uncertain and dropped the proceedings. In Nov. 1868 Davis was brought to trial under a new indictment, but the judges disagreed and the case was referred to the Supreme Court. President Johnson issued a general amnesty in Dec. 1868, and the Supreme Court entered a nolle prosequi, thus freeing Davis.

Chester D. Bradley, "Dr. Craven and the Prison Life of Jefferson Davis, " Virginia Magazine of History and Biography, 62:50-94 (Jan. 1954); Jefferson Davis, The Rise and Fall of the Confederate Government (2 vols.; New York, 1881, reprinted, New York, 1958); Jonathan T. Dorris, Pardon and Amnesty under Lincoln and Johnson; the Restoration of the Confederates to Their Rights and Privileges, 1861-1898 (Chapel Hill, 1953); Seymour J. Frank, "The Conspiracy To Implicate the Confederate Leaders in Lincoln's Assassination, " Mississippi Valley Historical Review, 40:629-656 (Mar. 1954); Francis B. Harrison, Aris Sonis Focisque; Being a Memoir of an American Family, the Harrisons of Skimino, ed. by Fairfax Harrison ([New York], 1910); James L. Howe, "George Washington Custis Lee, " Virginia Magazine of History and Biography, 48:315-327 (Oct. 1940); Francis R. Lubbock, Six Decades in Texas, or Memoirs of Francis Richard Lubbock, Governor of Texas in War-Time, 1861-63; a Personal Experience in Business, War, and Politics, ed. by C. W. Raines (Austin, 1900); Roy F. Nichols, "United States vs. Jefferson Davis, 1865-1869, " American Historical Review, 31:266-284 (Jan. 1926); Rembert W. Patrick, Jefferson Davis and His Cabinet (Baton Rouge, 1944); Arthur M. Shaw, William P. Johnston; a Traditional Figure of the Confederacy (Baton Rouge, 1943); Hudson Strode, Jefferson Davis: Confederate President (New York, 1959).

The papers of Jefferson Davis were moved from Richmond on Apr. 2, 1865. At Abbeville, S.C., on the flight southward, Micajah H. Clark and Colonels Johnston and Wood of the President's staff destroyed many of the less valuable papers, leaving the remainder with a local resident.

Later, on his return to the north from Florida, Clark destroyed additional papers in this collection. After having been moved and held for a while near New Orleans, the remaining papers were shipped to Burton N. Harrison at New York. He also received a trunk containing some of his own and Davis' papers that had been left at Washington, Ga. In 1870 Harrison lent these papers to Charles C. Jones, Jr., a Georgian and an ex-Confederate artillery officer, who had opened a law office in New York. The official letter and message books of President Davis were taken from Georgia to Montreal, Quebec, by Margaret Howell, a sister of Mrs. Davis. In 1877 William T. Walthall, Davis' assistant in his work on a history of the Confederacy, recovered with Harrison's cooperation part of the papers deposited with Colonel Jones and delivered them to Davis. Davis also recovered his letter and message books from Canada. In 1874 Davis obtained from the U.S. War Department through Philip Phillips, a Washington attorney, some correspondence with Mrs. Davis, relatives, and others on personal and business matters. In 1880, after Davis had given the War Department copies of his papers, the Department returned an additional package of his private papers to him. Davis used these and other papers that he collected in writing The Rise and Fall of the Confederate Government.

Other papers of Jefferson Davis, seized by the U.S. Army in 1865, were delivered to the War Department in Washington. Papers taken from the baggage of Davis and his associates and from them personally at Irwinville were delivered by Col. Benjamin D. Pritchard to the Secretary of War on May 24, 1865 (see below under Record Group 109). Baggage of Davis that was located at Waldo, Fla., and found to contain Davis papers was shipped to Washington by steamer from Jacksonville in June. As stated above, the part of these papers that were of a private nature was returned to Davis; the remainder was added to the War Department Collection of Confederate Records.

Douglas S. Freeman, The South to Posterity; an Introduction to the Writing of Confederate History, p. 96-101 (New York, 1939); Alfred J. Hanna, Flight into Oblivion (Richmond, 1938); Dallas D. Irvine, "The Fate of Confederate Archives," American Historical Review, 44:823-826 (July 1939); Hudson Strode, ed., Jefferson Davis; Private Letters, 1823-1889 (New York, 1966).

Record Group 109.--The Jefferson Davis papers, Feb. 22, 1861-May 29, 1866 (1 ft.), in the War Department Collection of Confederate Records include letters and telegrams sent and received, nominations for appointments to Cabinet positions, notes on Cabinet meetings, lists of officers, and cross-reference cards for documents printed in the Official Records . . .Armies and placed by the War Department in a file of published documents. The correspondence is with military and civilian officials, Members of Congress, State Governors, and others, and it relates to military operations and troop movements, the procurement of war supplies in Europe, and Davis' imprisonment at Fort Monroe. These papers are arranged alphabetically by name, and with them is a name and subject index.

Records in Other Custody.--The Jefferson Davis papers, 1845-91 (4,270 items), in the Louisiana Historical Association collection on deposit in the Howard-Tilton Memorial Library of Tulane University, is the most important collection and includes several series of records. The official letters-sent books, Feb. 21, 1861-Apr. 24, 1865 (2 vols.), contain fair copies of letters and telegrams to heads of the executive departments, Army and Navy officers, Governors of States, Senators, Representatives, aides, judges, diplomatic agents, and other southerners. These books also contain appointments and orders. A few additional letters sent, Sept. 13, 1863-Nov. 21, 1864, are in another volume. The record of outgoing letters is not complete, for it was not begun until the end of 1861 when the Executive Office requested copies of letters sent by Davis to general officers; some of the papers of Gen. Joseph E. Johnston had already been destroyed. Confidential letters, such as those to Gen. R. E. Lee, were not recorded in the letter book but were kept with Davis' private papers. The message book, Feb. 25, 1862-Mar. 17, 1865, contains annual and other messages to Congress, nominations for appointments, and addresses to the people of the Confederacy. A correspondence file, Feb. 1861-Dec. 1865 (4 ft.), contains letters received by Davis from Confederate and State officials, Members of Congress, and general officers; drafts of outgoing letters; and copies of War Department correspondence. A chronological file of telegrams, Feb. 7, 1861-Nov. 8, 1865 (more than 1,200 items), includes both incoming and outgoing telegrams--many from prominent Confederate and State officials and Army officers. Some special and general orders, manuscript and printed, issued by the Adjutant and Inspector General's Office and by armies, departments, and brigades, July 21, 1861-Apr. 27, 1865 (2 in.), are with the Davis papers.

The Jefferson Davis papers, 1844-89 (562 items), in the Mississippi Department of Archives and History include 180 original letters and telegrams and copies of other outgoing and incoming letters and of other papers collected for publication by Dunbar Rowland, the director of the Department, from various repositories.

Most of the documents in this collection have been published in Dunbar Rowland, ed., Jefferson Davis, Constitutionalist; His Letters, Papers and Speeches (10 vols.; Jackson, Miss., 1923). Volumes 5 and 6 cover the war period and contain all of the letters in Davis' official letters-sent books. Most of the letters on other than military subjects were published for the first time in Rowland's compilation. Outgoing and incoming letters and telegrams on official subjects, public speeches, and some newspaper articles, instructions, and commissions are included. The correspondents include civil and military officials, Senators, Members of Congress, the Vice President, State Governors, and Mrs. Davis. The dispatches in the Official Records . . .Armies are not reprinted, but Rowland supplies a "List of Letters and Endorsements of Jefferson Davis Printed in the Records of the Union and Confederate Armies," (vol. 10, p. 169-281). Some letters to private individuals are printed, but most are omitted. The derivations of the papers are given.

Papers of Jefferson Davis, 1851-89 (700 items), in Duke University Library (on microfilm in the University of Texas Library) consist of official and personal correspondence. Mostly for the war period, the letters are from heads of executive departments, Army officers, State Governors, and other officials and private individuals. They relate to the organization of the Confederate Government, military and naval operations, public and personal affairs, appointments, conscription, foreign affairs, and economic conditions in the South. Telegrams received by Davis from Gen. R. E. Lee and copies of others received from Lee by the War Department and Gen. Braxton Bragg, June 26, 1862-Apr. 1, 1865 (295 items), in the same repository, were purchased from the Wymberley Jones De Renne Georgia Library, which had acquired them from Charles C. Jones, Jr.

Dispatches received by Davis from General Lee, telegrams, and special orders, June 3, 1862-Mar. 29, 1865 (152 items), are in the Archives Division of the Virginia State Library. These papers had also been in the De Renne Library until purchased by Bernard M. Baruch in 1949 and presented by him to the Virginia State Library.

The Jefferson Davis papers, 1847-89 (several thousand items), in the Confederate Museum collection in Richmond include original letters of the war years, family papers presented by Margaret Davis Hayes (Davis' eldest daughter), and typewritten copies of the official letter books, 1861-65, and the message book, 1862-65, in the Louisiana Historical Association collection. Papers collected by George Shea, associate counsel with Charles O'Conner, in preparing for the trial of Jefferson Davis, 1865-67, are also in the Confederate Museum collection.

Materials on Jefferson Davis were assembled for many years by Walter L. Fleming, a professor at Vanderbilt University, for use in writing a biography. He died before completing the biography, and his widow gave his collection to Robert M. McElroy, who used them in Jefferson Davis; the Unreal and the Real (2 vols.; New York and London, 1937). The Fleming collection and other items gathered by McElroy were deposited in the New York Public Library.

The Jefferson Davis papers in the Library of Congress consist only of a few letters and other documents of the war period, some printed broadsides, and a partly filled letter book, Jan.-Dec. 1861, in which are also recorded copies of letters sent by the War and other departments. The Edwin M. Stanton papers in the Library contain some letters written by Davis to his wife after the fall of Richmond.

Samuel Richey, a lumber dealer of Cincinnati, collected manuscripts of Jefferson Davis and military leaders of the Confederacy; his collection is now at Miami University. The Davis correspondence, 1847-89, includes, for the war period, letters to Southern Governors, Senators, Members of Congress, Cabinet officers, and aides. There are also many letters received, especially from Generals Beauregard, Bragg, J. E. Johnston, Pemberton, E. K. Smith, J. E. B. Stuart, Richard Taylor, William H. Thomas, and W. H. C. Whiting.

Fred B. Joyner, "A Brief Calendar of Jefferson Davis Letters in the Samuel Richey Confederate Collection of the Miami University," Journal of Mississippi History, 25: 15-32 (Jan. 1963).

Other Davis correspondence is in many other repositories. More than 800 telegrams and dispatches received by Davis are in the R. W. Norton Art Gallery in Shreveport, La. Nearly 50 letters received by Davis from generals, civilian officials, Governors, Vice President Stephens, and diplomatic commissioners in Europe, 1861-65, are in Emory University Library. A small quantity of original letters from similar correspondents is in the University of Georgia Library. Other repositories containing Davis material include the Alabama Department of Archives and History, Chicago Historical Society, Dallas Historical Society, University of

Kentucky Library, New Jersey Historical Society, New-York Historical Society, New York Public Library, North Carolina Department of Archives and History, University of North Carolina Library, Princeton University Library, Transylvania College Library, Tufts College Library, Howard-Tilton Memorial Library of Tulane University, Virginia Historical Society, University of Virginia Library, Western Reserve Historical Society (Palmer collection), and Yale University Library. The Jefferson Davis papers formerly in the possession of Jefferson Hayes-Davis of Colorado Springs have been given to the University of Alabama Library and Transylvania College Library. The Jefferson Davis shrine at Beauvoir, Miss., and the first executive mansion, at Montgomery, have some Davis manuscripts. Papers taken from Davis' office after the fall of Richmond are in the Lucy Chase collection in the American Antiquarian Society at Worcester, Mass. Papers relating to the proposed trial of Jefferson Davis other than those referred to above are in the University of Chicago Library.

Richard B. Harwell, "Brief Calendar of the Jefferson Davis Papers in the Keith M. Read Confederate Collection of the Emory University Library," Journal of Mississippi History, 4:20-30 (Jan. 1942).

Many wartime letters of Davis have been published. In Official Records . . . Armies are hundreds of letters not only from the captured Confederate records but also from the official letter books that Davis kept. This correspondence relates chiefly to military operations and does not contain all the confidential letters received by Davis from generals. Davis' messages, addresses, and other communications to Congress and nominations for appointments are in the Journal of the Congress of the Confederate States of America, 1861-1865 (S. Doc. 234, 58 Cong., 2 sess., Serials 4610-4616; Washington, 1904-5. 7 vols.). A selection of papers, including messages, addresses, instructions, proclamations, nominations, appointments, commissions, orders, and letters, is in James D. Richardson, ed., A Compilation of the Messages and Papers of the Confederacy, vol. 1 (2 vols.; Nashville, 1905; reprinted, New York, 1966). Douglas S. Freeman, ed., Lee's Dispatches; Unpublished Letters of General Robert E. Lee, C.

S. A., to Jefferson Davis and the War Department of the Confederate States of America, 1862-65 (New York and London, 1915), contains dispatches and telegrams received by Davis from Lee that are now in the Virginia State Library and Duke University Library.

Presidential proclamations; appointments of diplomatic representatives, special commissioners, and commercial agents; letters to the heads of foreign nations; some messages to Congress; and addresses to the people of the Confederacy and to soldiers are calendared in Official Records . . . Navies, ser. 2, vol. 3, p. 26-89 (cited in chapter I under the section on Presidential Proclamations). Concerning legal opinions addressed to the President, see chapter X.

Some addresses, messages, correspondence, and proclamations issued by Davis were published contemporaneously. A list of these publications with library locations is in Crandall, Confederate Imprints, 1: 113-119.

Correspondence between Davis and members of his Cabinet is in the records of the executive departments and in collections of personal papers described or mentioned elsewhere in this Guide. Correspondence between Davis and State Governors may be found in State archives and among the personal papers of the Governors in other repositories. Some letters received by Davis, such as applications and recommendations for appointments, were endorsed by him and referred to the appropriate departments. Many of these letters are now with the compiled military service records described in chapter XI. No minutes were kept of the meetings of the Confederate Cabinet. Some information on discussions is in the diaries or memoirs of Thomas Bragg, Josiah Gorgas, Stephen R. Mallory, John H. Reagan, and John B. Jones cited elsewhere in this Guide.

A more comprehensive publication of the Jefferson Davis papers is underway at Rice University under the editorship of Haskell Monroe.

PAPERS OF PRESIDENTIAL AIDES

Papers of some members of Davis' staff that are available contain correspondence with Davis and other letters that give information on the President, the executive office, and conditions in Richmond.

Records in Other Custody. --Papers of Burton N. Harrison and his wife are in the Library of Congress. The large collection of William Preston Johnston papers in the Howard-Tilton Memorial Library of Tulane University includes many letters to his wife that contain information about Davis and his family, trips with Davis, and events in Richmond. In the same collection of Johnston papers are letters from Army officers about commissions and letters to the President from Members of Congress. Other Johnston papers are in the Library of Congress and in the Southern Historical Collection in the University of North Carolina Library. A few letters of Joseph C. Ives are in the Library of Congress. The Texas State Archives and the San Jacinto Museum of History Association have papers of Francis R. Lubbock. Letter books of James Chesnut, Jr., are in the Library of Congress, the University of North Carolina Library, and Emory University Library. Letters sent by George Washington Custis Lee are in the Virginia Historical Society collections. Papers of John Taylor Wood are in the University of North Carolina Library; these papers include Wood's diary, Apr. 2-July 16, 1865. concerning the flight of Davis and the Cabinet to the south and Wood's escape through Florida to Cuba. Capt. Given Campbell, escort commander, kept a journal from Apr. 15 to May 10, 1865, of the flight of Davis and his party; a photostat of a typewritten copy of this journal is in the Manuscript Division of the Library of Congress. A sizable group of William T. Walthall papers is in the Mississippi Department of Archives and History.

ALEXANDER H. STEPHENS PAPERS

Alexander H. Stephens, a Georgia delegate to the Montgomery convention and a former Representative from that State in the U.S. Congress, was elected Vice President of the Confederacy on Feb. 9, 1861. As chairman of the Committee To Organize the Executive Departments of the Provisional Congress, he frequently conferred with President Davis on appointments to the Cabinet. In 1861 he traveled as a commissioner to the Georgia State convention meeting to ratify the Confederate Constitution, and to Virginia to arrange a military alliance to be operative until Virginia joined the Confederacy. After his election as Vice President on Nov. 6, 1861, he served for two periods (Nov.-Dec. 1861 and Jan.-Feb. 1862) as president pro tempore of the Provisional Congress. As Vice President of the

permanent Government after Feb. 1862, he was the presiding officer of the
Senate. But he grew antagonistic toward Davis' policies and returned to
Georgia in Oct. 1862, remaining there for more than 2 years except for
two brief visits to Richmond. In his absence, Robert M. T. Hunter, a
Senator from Virginia, presided over the Senate. While in Georgia
Stephens made speeches critical of Davis' administration and influenced
Gov. Joseph E. Brown against it. Hoping to aid in establishing peace,
Stephens returned to Richmond in Dec. 1864 and presided over the Senate
in Jan. 1865.

On visits to Richmond in 1863 and 1865 Stephens performed missions
for the Government. On July 3, 1863, he went down the James River with
Robert Ould (the Confederate "Agent of Exchange") to City Point to negotiate with Union representatives on the exchange of prisoners, but after the
battle of Gettysburg and the fall of Vicksburg the U.S. Government declined
to participate in such negotiations. Stephens had hoped to formulate
measures for establishing peace. Following visits by Francis P. Blair,
Sr., an unofficial U.S. representative, to Richmond, President Davis in
Jan. 1865 appointed Stephens, Assistant Secretary of War John A. Campbell, and Senator R. M. T. Hunter as peace commissioners. They met
President Lincoln and Secretary Seward on a steamship off Fort Monroe
on Feb. 3 for an informal conference of several hours' duration. No
agreement resulted from the meeting for Lincoln insisted on the restoration of national authority, emancipation of Negro slaves, and no armistice,
while Davis would accept nothing less than independence. After the defeat
of the Confederacy Stephens was arrested at Crawfordsville, Ga., and
confined at Fort Warren until Oct. 1865.

William H. Hidell began serving as secretary to the Vice President
in 1861, and after an act of Oct. 13, 1862 (1 Cong. C.S.A. Stat. 85), authorized the appointment of a secretary, he continued in the position until the
end of the war.

James Z. Rabun, "Alexander   290-321 (Jan. 1953); Rudolph R. Von
H. Stephens and Jefferson Davis, " Abele, Alexander H. Stephens, a
American Historical Review, 58:   Biography (New York, 1946).

Collections of papers of Alexander H. Stephens held for many years
by relatives are now divided among a number of repositories. Mrs. Mary
Holden, Stephens' niece, sold a large collection of his papers to Bernard
M. Baruch, who presented it to the Library of Congress. The papers of
Linton W. Stephens, Stephens' half brother, were presented by the former's
daughter, Mother Claude Stephens, to the library of Manhattanville College
of the Sacred Heart.

Records in Other Custody. --Alexander H. Stephens papers, 1834-83
(7,000 items), in the Manuscript Division of the Library of Congress consist almost entirely of letters received, both official and personal. Many
letters from Georgians and others requested assistance in obtaining appointments under the Confederate Government in the executive departments
and in the military service. There are letters of congratulation, inquiries,
comments on his speeches, requests for help in obtaining furloughs and relief for soldiers, and appeals from the parents of hospitalized U.S. soldiers. Letters from soldiers describe conditions in camps in various parts
of the Confederacy. A small number of letters from the heads of executive
departments and other officials are dated in the early part of the war. A

microfilm of this collection is in Emory University Library. Smaller collections of Stephens papers are in other repositories. The Linton W. Stephens papers in the library of Manhattanville College of the Sacred Heart contain correspondence of A. H. Stephens, 1834-72 (3,053 items), which reveals his attitude toward problems and policies of the Confederacy. Microfilm of this correspondence is in the Library of Congress and in the Libraries of the University of Arkansas, Duke University, the University of Georgia, Harvard University, Johns Hopkins University, the University of North Carolina, Princeton University, the University of Rochester, the University of Virginia, and the University of Washington. Alexander H. Stephens papers, 1837-82 (1,900 items), in Emory University Library include correspondence with Georgia and Confederate officials and with President Davis concerning Stephens' attempt in 1863 to confer with Abraham Lincoln on prisoner exchanges. The correspondence also includes applications and recommendations for appointments in the Army, the Navy, and the Confederate Government; appeals for aid in obtaining discharges from the military service; and letters of introduction. Stephens' prison diary of 1865 is also in Emory University Library. Alexander H. Stephens papers, 1822-1911 (3,029 items and 3 vols.), in Duke University Library include personal, legal, and political correspondence. The wartime correspondence concerns his activities as Vice President and as an opponent of the administration, his opinions on the conduct of the war, and his participation in the Hampton Roads conference in 1865. This repository also has letters of Stephens in other collections of personal papers. The papers of W. H. Hidell, Stephens' wartime secretary, in the Historical Society of Pennsylvania collections, include letters from Stephens, 1858-82 (300 items).

Myrta L. Avary, ed., Recollections of Alexander H. Stephens; His Diary Kept When a Prisoner at Fort Warren, Boston Harbor, 1865; Giving Incidents and Reflections of His Prison Life and Some Letters and Reminiscences (New York, 1910); Henry Cleveland, Alexander H. Stephens in Public and Private; With Letters and Speeches, Before, During, and Since the War (Philadelphia, 1866); Ulrich B. Phillips, ed., The Correspondence of Robert Toombs, Alexander H. Stephens, and Howell Cobb (American Historical Association, Annual Report, 1911, vol. 2, Washington, 1913); James Z. Rabun, ed., "A Letter for Posterity: Alex Stephens to His Brother Linton, June 3, 1864," Emory University Publications, Sources & Reprints, ser. 8, no. 3 (Atlanta, 1954); Alexander H. Stehens, A Constitutional View of the Late War Between the States; Its Causes, Character, Conduct, and Results Presented in a Series of Colloquies at Liberty Hall (2 vols.; Philadelphia, 1868-70); Rudolph R. Von Abele, Alexander H. Stephens, a Biography (New York, 1946); James H. Young, "Alexander H. Stephens Papers in the Emory University Library," Emory University Quarterly, 2:30-37 (Mar. 1946). Phillips, in the compilation cited here, gives a calendar of previously printed Stephens letters including those in the Official Records . . . Armies, ser. 2 and 4. Campbell's memorandum on the Hampton Roads conference of Feb. 1865 is in John A. Campbell, Reminiscences and Documents Relating to the Civil War during the Year 1865, p. 11-17 (Baltimore, 1887), and in "Papers of Hon. John A. Campbell--1861-1865," Southern Historical Society Papers, 42:45-52 (1917).

V

DEPARTMENT OF STATE

The Department of State was established by an act of Feb. 21, 1861 (Prov. Cong. C.S.A. Stat. 29), which provided for a Secretary of State who was to correspond with and direct Confederate representatives abroad and negotiate with ministers from foreign nations. An act of Feb. 27, 1861 (Prov. Cong. C.S.A. Stat. 42), authorized the appointment of an Assistant Secretary of State, and William M. Browne was appointed to the position in March. He resigned on Apr. 22, 1862, and the duties of the Assistant Secretary were performed thereafter by the chief clerk, a position filled successively by William F. Alexander, Philip P. Dandridge, and Lucius Q. Washington. William J. Bromwell became disbursing clerk after the departure of Alexander in 1861 and continued in that capacity throughout the war.

The Confederate Government sent representatives abroad to negotiate for recognition by the governments of Europe, promote commercial relations, and obtain loans of money. In Mar. 1861 William L. Yancey, Pierre A. Rost, and Ambrose Dudley Mann traveled to England and then to France. Mann went on to Belgium and Rost went to Spain. Yancey returned to the Confederacy early in 1862, and Rost resigned in May 1862. In Aug. 1861 James M. Mason was appointed commissioner to Great Britain and Ireland and John Slidell was sent to France. They stayed on in Europe but were no more successful than their predecessors in promoting the interests of the Confederacy. Lucius Q. C. Lamar was designated a commissioner to Russia in Nov. 1862. He spent some time early in 1863 in England and France, but since his appointment was not confirmed by the Senate he did not serve in Russia. From Belgium, A. Dudley Mann was sent to Rome in the fall of 1863 with a letter to Pius IX from President Davis. Another Confederate emissary to the Vatican, Bishop Patrick N. Lynch, was given a papal audience in 1864 but concluded no treaty. Robert Dowling was a commercial agent in Cork and Queenstown, Ireland. Other Confederate representatives abroad included Colin M. McRae, financial agent, and James Williams, both unsuccessful in an attempt to recruit Polish exiles in western Europe for Confederate service late in 1864. Duncan F. Kenner went to Europe on an abortive secret mission in 1865 to present to the governments of England and France an offer to abolish slavery in the South in exchange for recognition.

The Confederacy also employed propaganda agents in Europe to supplement the efforts of the commissioners. Henry Hotze promoted the publication in English newspapers of material favorable to the South and issued a weekly journal, The Index, containing news and comment on Confederate affairs. He sent James L. Capston, Father John Bannon, and others to

Ireland to frustrate Union recruiting efforts there. Other Confederates who contributed to the propaganda campaign in England included Comdr. Matthew F. Maury, Confederate Navy agent, Alfred T. Bledsoe, former Assistant Secretary of War, Robert B. Campbell, former U.S. consul in London, John L. O'Sullivan, former U.S. minister in Portugal, John R. Thompson, who became the editor of The Index, and Rose O'Neal Greenhow, who became associated with Commander Maury in aiding the Society for Promoting the Cessation of Hostilities in America. Mrs. Greenhow also went to France where she obtained an interview with Napoleon III, contacted French bankers and diplomats, and worked with Commander Maury in his efforts to obtain warships.

Edwin De Leon, journalist and former U.S. consul general in Egypt, served in France as a propagandist for the Confederacy from 1862 to 1864. He was assisted in this work by Charles F. Girard, Paul Pecquet du Bellet, Edward Gaulhac, and George McHenry.

The Confederate Government hoped to establish friendly relations with Mexico for supply purposes. John T. Pickett, a former U.S. consul at Vera Cruz, was sent to Mexico in 1861 to contact the Juarez Government. He reached Vera Cruz and Mexico City but through indiscretions became persona non grata and left the country at the end of 1861. He employed John S. Cripps as his agent at Mexico City. On his departure, Pickett appointed Charles Rieken acting Confederate agent in Vera Cruz to report on events in Mexico.

More important to the Confederacy was the northeastern area of Mexico bordering on Texas. Juan A. Quintero went to Monterrey as a Confederate agent in 1861 and was received by Gov. Santiago Vidaurri of Nuevo León and Coahuila, who upon obtaining control of the neighboring state of Tamaulipas in the spring of 1862 opened the port of Matamoras to Confederate trade. The Mexican border states thereafter furnished munitions and other supplies, and ordnance and small arms came in from abroad by way of Matamoras. Richard Fitzpatrick served as commercial agent of the Confederacy at that port. Bernard Avegno was appointed to a similar post at Vera Cruz in Dec. 1862 and was succeeded there in 1864 by Emile La Sère. Maj. Gen. William Preston was appointed minister to Maximilian's Government in Jan. 1864, but efforts to negotiate a treaty of friendship and commerce were unsuccessful.

A number of Confederate agents operated in Canada in 1864. James P. Holcombe, in Halifax, investigated the case of the Union steamer Chesapeake, believed to have been captured by escaped Confederates, and arranged for the repatriation of other Confederates who had escaped to Canada from U.S. prisons. He also visited border towns in Quebec and Ontario to find Confederates and arrange their return to the Confederacy. Jacob Thompson and Clement C. Clay, Jr., attempted to promote anti-Northern feeling in Canada and to direct raids on U.S. territory. Holcombe was associated with them as a third commissioner, and George N. Sanders worked with the commissioners. Thompson made an unsuccessful effort to subvert the Sons of Liberty through Clement L. Vallandigham and financed efforts by Benjamin P. Churchill, Lt. John W. Headley, Col. Robert M. Martin, and others to burn several hotels and Barnum's Museum in New York. A plot of Capts. Thomas H. Hines and John B. Castleman and other Confederates to free the Confederate prisoners at Camp Douglas, Ill., with the aid of Copperheads was foiled. Bennett Y. Young led a raid on the town of St. Albans, Vt., and escaped with more than

$200,000 from three banks. A group led by John Y. Beall and Bennett G. Burley, acting masters in the C.S. Navy, captured the steamers Philo Parsons and Island Queen on Lake Erie, but they were unsuccessful in using them to board the U.S.S. Michigan in a plan to free Confederate prisoners on Johnson's Island, off Sandusky, Ohio. George Dawson visited Quebec, Montreal, and Toronto in 1864 in an unsuccessful effort to promote the organization of an association favorable to recognition of the Confederacy.

Confederate agents in the Bermudas and the West Indies who were primarily engaged in the transshipment of munitions for the War and Navy Departments also functioned for the State Department. These agents included Charles J. Helm at Havana, Cuba; Louis Heyliger at Nassau, New Providence; and Maj. Norman S. Walker at Saint George, Bermuda. John T. Bourne, a local commission merchant of Saint George, acted as Confederate commercial agent there and was joined by Major Walker early in 1863.

Besides conducting the diplomatic and consular business of the Confederacy, the Department of State performed several domestic functions. The Secretary countersigned commissions and pardons and preserved record copies of those documents and the original texts of Presidential proclamations. An act of May 6, 1861 (Prov. Cong. C.S.A. Stat. 101), required captains of private armed vessels applying for letters of marque and reprisal to file applications with the Secretary of State. The Department became the depository of secession ordinances, ratifications of the Permanent Constitution, and conventions between the States and the Government of the Confederacy. It was the central depository of copyright records and of copyrighted works. The Great Seal of the Confederacy was also in the Department's custody. For a few months in 1861 the Department had custody of the original laws and resolutions adopted by Congress and arranged for their publication in newspapers. An act of Aug. 30, 1861 (Prov. Cong. C.S.A. Stat. 207), required judicial officers to prepare affidavits on the loss of slaves and other property seized by the enemy and forward them to the Department for preservation. Under an act of Mar. 17, 1862 (1 Cong. C.S.A. Stat. 2), owners of property destroyed to prevent its use by the enemy were authorized to file evidence of losses with the Department of State. It was also the duty of the Department to furnish Members and officers of Congress with passports permitting them to travel in the Confederacy and to arrange with the War Department for the issue of passes to foreigners for travel purposes.

Successive Secretaries of State:
Robert Toombs, Feb. 27, 1861.
Robert M. T. Hunter, July 25, 1861.
William M. Browne (acting), Feb. 19, 1862.
Judah P. Benjamin, Mar. 25, 1862.

Ephraim D. Adams, Great Britain and the American Civil War (2 vols.; London and New York, 1925); Charles P. Cullop, "Edwin De Leon, Jefferson Davis' Propagandist," Civil War History, 8:386-400 (Dec. 1962); Charles L. Dufour, "Rebel Propagandist: Henry Hotze," in Nine Men in Gray, p. 267-297 (New York, 1963); Charles F. Girard, A Visit to the Confederate States of America in 1863; Memoir Addressed to His Majesty Napoleon III, trans. and ed. by William S. Hoole (Tuscaloosa, 1962); Martin H. Hall, "Colonel James Reily's Diplomatic

Missions to Chihuahua and Sonora, " New Mexico Historical Review, 31: 232-242 (July 1956); Sheldon H. Harris, "John L. O'Sullivan Serves the Confederacy, " Civil War History, 10:275-290 (Sept. 1964); William W. Henry, "Kenner's Mission to Europe, " William and Mary Quarterly, 25:9-12 (July 1916); James D. Horan, Confederate Agent; a Discovery in History (New York, 1954); Charles L. Lewis, Matthew Fontaine Maury, the Pathfinder of the Seas (Annapolis, 1927); Ruth A. Nuermberger, The Clays of Alabama; a Planter-Lawyer-Politician Family (Lexington, Ky. , 1958); Frank L. Owsley, King Cotton Diplomacy; Foreign Relations of the Confederate States of America (Chicago, 1931); Paul Pecquet du Bellet, The Diplomacy of the Confederate Cabinet of Richmond and Its Agents Abroad, Being Memorandum Notes Taken in Paris During the Rebellion of the Southern States from 1861 to 1865, ed. by William S. Hoole (Tuscaloosa, 1963); Ishbel Ross, Rebel Rose; Life of Rose O'-Neal Greenhow, Confederate Spy (New York, 1954); Louis M. Sears, John Slidell (Durham, N.C. , 1925); William W. White and Joseph O. Baylen, "Pierre A. Rost's Mission to Europe, 1861-1863, " Louisiana History, 2:322-331 (Summer 1961); Robin W. Winks, Canada and the United States; the Civil War Years (Baltimore, 1960).

Nearly all the records of the Confederate Department of State were saved at the time of the evacuation of Richmond. Preparations for moving the records were made in Mar. 1865; William J. Bromwell removed records from Richmond for concealment at the end of March. He reported to Secretary Benjamin on Apr. 5, 1865, that he had deposited the records, including some placed earlier at the Danville Female Academy, at Charlotte, N.C. , and had arranged with A. C. Williamson for their removal if necessary. Papers on the secret activities of the Department were destroyed by Secretary Benjamin.

Evidence available indicates that Bromwell and John T. Pickett, former Confederate envoy to Mexico, planned to sell the Department's records. Bromwell returned to Richmond after the war and began the practice of law, but he moved to Washington toward the end of 1866 to become an associate in Pickett's law office (Isaac N. Morris & Co.). It is possible that he recovered the Department's records at this time and took them to Washington, where Pickett became the agent for their sale.

Pickett's initial efforts to sell the records to the U.S. Government were unsuccessful. Secretary of State Seward was not interested in 1868, and when Secretary of War Rawlins recommended the purchase in 1869 the price was considered too high. The President's offer of a small partial payment with an appropriation to be recommended later was not accepted. Pickett also failed to interest private persons, such as William W. Corcoran, the Washington banker to whom the records were offered for $25,000, and Jacob Thompson, ex-Confederate Army officer and agent.

After 1871, however, when Congress provided for the adjudication of the claims of Southern loyalists, the Government became interested in the possibilities of using the records in that connection. Comdr. Thomas O. Selfridge, U.S.N. Ret. , examined in Pickett's presence the records then deposited at Hamilton, Ontario, and reported on Apr. 15, 1872, that he believed them to be the entire archives of the Confederate Department of State. By an act of Congress of June 10, 1872 (17 Stat. 350), funds were appropriated to enable the Secretary of the Treasury to buy records relating to claims against the United States. At a meeting on June 26, 1872, in the office of James M. Edmunds, Washington postmaster, attended by Pickett, Secretary of the Interior Columbus Delano, Senator Zachariah Chandler, and Attorney Nathaniel Paige, it was agreed that $75,000 would be paid for the archives of the Confederate Department of State upon their receipt by Henry D. Cooke, a Washington banker. Selfridge examined the records that were received in Washington and on July 2 reported to the Secretary of the Interior that they were the same records he had previously inspected in Canada. Asa O. Aldis and Orange Ferriss, Commissioners of Claims, assured the Secretary of the Treasury on July 3 of the genuineness of the records and of the value they would have in proving the disloyalty of claimants by showing they had served the Confederacy. On that date $75,000 was paid to Pickett, who, according to W. J. Bromwell's affidavit of Sept. 3, 1872 (John T. Pickett Papers, Library of Congress), retained less than half of it. It is believed that Bromwell received the remainder. The records were placed in the Treasury Department and were used in later years by the Commissioners of Claims, the U.S. Court of Claims, and attorneys of the Justice Department in adjudicating war claims.

In 1904 the Librarian of Congress obtained an order from President Roosevelt for the transfer of the Confederate State Department records to the Library. Since some were still being used by the Treasury Department in the settlement of claims, it was agreed that only diplomatic records would be transferred. A schedule listing the records that were delivered to the Library was signed on Nov. 23, 1906. The Treasury Department transferred the remainder of the records on Oct. 26, 1910. Both groups of records are in the Manuscript Division of the Library of Congress and are described below.

At the time he sold the State Department records to the U.S. Government, Pickett retained some duplicates and copies of Department correspondence. He offered them to the Southern Historical Society in Aug. 1873, but the offer was declined. On Apr. 1, 1886, Pickett sold this collection to the War Department "for the sum of $5 & other valuable considerations." At an unknown date the collection was lent to John Hay, possibly for use in writing his biography of Lincoln. After Hay's death the records (14 vols.) remained in his Washington house that was used by his daughter, Mrs. James D. Wadsworth. In Apr. 1925 Senator Wadsworth informed the Library of Congress of their existence, and in May the Library acquired them.

John T. Pickett Papers and Causten-Pickett Papers, Library of Congress; James M. Callahan, "The Confederate Diplomatic Archives--The 'Pickett Papers, ' " South Atlantic Quarterly, 2:1-9 (Jan. 1903); Irvine, "Fate of Confederate Archives, " p. 826-828; Claude H. Van Tyne and Waldo G. Leland, Guide to the Archives of the Government of the United States in Washington, p. 73-74 (Washington, 1907). The schedule and the list accompanying the transfers of 1906 and 1910 are in the General Records of the Treasury Department (Record Group 56), Division of Bookkeeping and Warrants, Cotton and Captured Property Records.

Record Group 59. --A few letters of Confederate diplomats are among some intercepted papers of Confederates in the General Records of the (U.S.) Department of State in the National Archives. A letter to James M. Mason from Edgar P. Stringer, managing director of the Mercantile

Trading Co., Ltd., London, Sept. 16, 1863, and Mason's reply, Sept. 19, concern the agreement between that company and Caleb Huse, the War Department procurement agent in England. P. A. Rost's despatch no. 1 from Madrid, Mar. 21, 1862, reports on his arrival there and his interview with the Spanish Minister of Foreign Affairs. A letter from Rost to W. L. Yancey, Mar. 22, 1862, gives an account of his trip from Paris to Madrid and his reception by the Spanish Government. Edwin De Leon's despatch to Secretary Benjamin, Sept. 30, 1863 (no. 10), comments on affairs in England and France, the arrival of the Florida in France, and the movements of Napoleon III. John T. Pickett's despatch of Aug. 25, 1861 (no. 7), from Mexico is included.

Records in Other Custody. --Correspondence and other papers of Robert Toombs are in the University of Georgia Library. The Robert M. T. Hunter papers in the University of Virginia Library (available on microfilm) contain some correspondence relating to his activities as Secretary of State. A much smaller collection of Hunter papers in the Archives Division of the Virginia State Library contains little on diplomacy. Judah P. Benjamin had papers with him in England after the war and furnished some copies to Jefferson Davis and James M. Mason, but before his death he destroyed his manuscripts. An incomplete series of duplicate instructions from Benjamin to A. Dudley Mann, Apr. 1862-Oct. 1864, is in the Library of Congress. Copies of a few Benjamin letters of the war period have been collected from a number of repositories by the American Jewish Archives in Cincinnati. Other letters addressed to Benjamin during Jan. - Mar. 1865 on official matters are in the Ryder Collection of Confederate Archives in Tufts College Library.

DEPARTMENTAL RECORDS

The Confederate Department of State initiated many different series of records modeled after those maintained by its U.S. counterpart. Related series of records in the Manuscript Division of the Library of Congress are described below. Some series were subdivided when more emissaries were appointed.

Diplomatic Correspondence

Records in Other Custody. --The diplomatic correspondence in the Library of Congress consists of a number of series of instructions to envoys and despatches received from them. Instructions to commissioners and agents, Mar. 16, 1861-Mar. 29, 1862 (1 vol.), consist of fair copies of letters to Yancey, Rost, Mann, Mason, Slidell, Pickett, Quintero, Helm, and Hotze, giving directions on their duties, supplying information on measures taken by the Confederate Government, and transmitting useful papers and publications. Instructions to the commissioner to Great Britain (James M. Mason), Apr. 5, 1862-Dec. 30, 1864 (1 vol.), also contain instructions to the special commissioner to the British North American provinces (James P. Holcombe), Feb. 15, Feb. 24, and Apr. 20, 1864. Other series are instructions to the commissioner to France (John Slidell), Apr. 5, 1862-Dec. 27, 1864 (1 vol.), and instructions to the commissioner to Belgium (A. D. Mann), Apr. 5, 1862-Oct. 10, 1864 (1 vol.). The latter volume also contains instructions regarding missions to Denmark and the Vatican and copies of President Davis' correspondence with Pius IX. The instructions to the commissioner to Spain (P. A. Rost), Apr. 5-Sept. 26, 1862 (1 vol.), also contain instructions to the envoy to Mexico (William Preston), Jan. 7-July 22, 1864 (p. 200-233). With the instructions to the commissioner to Russia (L. Q. C. Lamar), Nov. 19, 1862-June 11, 1863 (1 vol.), is a letter from Burton N. Harrison to the Secretary of State concerning the failure of the Senate to confirm the nomination of Lamar. Instructions to commercial and confidential agents, Apr. 14, 1862-Jan. 3, 1865 (1 vol., p. 55-179), are addressed to Avegno, De Leon, Dowling, Fitzpatrick, Helm, Hotze, La Sère, Quintero, and Walker.

The 14 volumes received by the Library of Congress from Senator Wadsworth only partly duplicate the correspondence in other extant series. Volumes 3-5 and 7-14 contain copies of the diplomatic instructions and despatches; they may contain despatches missing from the regular files. Volumes 1-4 contain selected copies of other correspondence in the letters-sent books on domestic matters.

The despatches from the commissioners and agents in the Library of Congress are filed in chronological order in numbered series in document boxes. Most files are fairly complete, but some despatches were never received and others are missing. Despatches from the commissioners to Europe (Yancey, Rost, and Mann), May 21, 1861-Mar. 22, 1862, include some addressed to President Davis and some written by the commissioners' secretary, John W. Fearn. Despatches from Great Britain (James M. Mason), Oct. 5, 1861-May 1, 1865, include some written in 1864 from Paris. There are a few gaps in the despatches from France (John Slidell), Feb. 11, 1862-Feb. 24, 1865. The despatches from Belgium (A. D. Mann), May 5, 1862-Dec. 16, 1864, include letters from President Davis to Pius IX, Sept. 23, 1863, and the Pope's letter to Davis, Dec. 3, 1863. The despatches from Spain (P. A. Rost), Dec. 24, 1861-June 16, 1863, include some unofficial letters from France after he resigned from the post in Spain. The despatches from the commissioner to the Vatican (P. N. Lynch), Mar. 3-June 20, 1864, concern his journey to Europe and his visit to Paris but not his audiences with the Pope. The despatches from the commissioner to Russia (L. Q. C. Lamar), Mar. 2 and July 22, 1863, and a letter of Mar. 11, 1863, all originated in London. The commissioners' despatches concern travel to their posts, negotiations with foreign governments, propaganda activities, transactions with Confederate business agents, finances, the sale of cotton, the activities of the Confederate Navy, information about European affairs and public opinion, and reports on inventions. Related enclosures include copies and extracts of official correspondence with foreign governments, newspaper clippings, letters to officials of the Confederate Government, and letters from private companies about inventions. Despatches from William G. Mann of Dec. 23, 1861, and Jan. 10 and 27, 1862, concern both affairs in Italy and the attitude of the Italian Government and people toward the Confederacy.

The despatches in the Library of Congress from the commercial and other agents are not numerous. The largest group is that of Henry Hotze from London, including his official numbered despatches, Jan. 6, 1862-Sept. 17, 1864, and an unnumbered series, Mar. 17, 1862-Oct. 28, 1864. With Hotze's despatches are copies of his letters of June and Aug. 1863 to correspondents in Europe and in New York. Despatches from agents in Ireland include those from James L. Capston (Dublin and Queenstown), Oct. 1, 1863-Aug. 24, 1864; from Father John Bannon, Nov. 17, 1863-May 28, 1864; from Robert Dowling (Queenstown), Nov. 25, 1863, and Jan. 28,

1864; and James F. Lalor, undated. There are also Edwin De Leon's despatches from France, July 30, 1862-Feb. 3, 1864, no. 15 and no. 10, referred to above. Colin J. McRae, the Confederate financial agent in Europe, wrote on Apr. 15, 1864, concerning his efforts to recover funds from Edwin De Leon, and his letters of Oct. 19, Nov. 4, and Nov. 18, 1864, concern his and James Williams' recruiting activities.

Also in the Library of Congress are despatches from Mexico including those from J. T. Pickett, from Mar. 13, 1861, to Jan. 28, 1862; Juan A. Quintero in Monterrey, Chihuahua, Matamoros, and Brownsville, from June 1, 1861, to Dec. 7, 1864; Charles Rieken in Vera Cruz, from Sept. 9, 1862, to July 16, 1863, reporting on the operations of French military forces; from William Preston in Havana, from Feb. 13, 1864, to Jan. 31, 1865, including letters to the President; Richard Fitzpatrick in Matamoras, from Jan. 23, 1863, to Mar. 8, 1864; Emile La Sère in Vera Cruz, July 22, 1864; and Bernard Avegno in Matamoras, from Dec. 30, 1862, to Mar. 30, 1863, including letters of Jan. 10, Jan. 14, and Mar. 30, 1863, to the Secretary of the Treasury and Mar. 30, 1863, to the President. John S. Cripps wrote on Apr. 22, 1862, from Mexico City concerning the intervention of European countries in Mexico. Col. John S. Ford wrote to Assistant Secretary Browne from Fort Brown, Tex., Mar. 17 and Apr. 3, 1862, on behalf of Quintero regarding affairs in Mexico, enclosing copies of his correspondence with Quintero, with the Mexican commander in Matamoras, and with Col. Phillip N. Luckett, 3d Texas Infantry, then at Fort Brown.

There are files of numbered despatches and letters in the Library of Congress from the following agents in the West Indies and Bermuda: C. J. Helm in Havana, Sept. 30, 1861-Dec. 17, 1864; Louis Heyliger in Nassau, June 28, 1862- Dec. 19, 1864; and Norman S. Walker in Saint George, Feb. 23, 1863-Aug. 2, 1864. These communications relate to negotiations with officials of the islands regarding Confederate trade and naval vessels, the attitude of these officials, public opinion in the islands, materials that might be purchased there, the promotion of Confederate trade, the forwarding of despatches to and from Europe, and the shipment of books, stationery, and provisions.

From each of several agents sent to Canada in 1864 there are, in the Library of Congress, a few letters and telegrams. James P. Holcombe's communications are dated Feb. 29-June 18, 1864; others are from Clement C. Clay, June 17, Aug. 11, and Sept. 12, 1864; Jacob Thompson, Apr. 29, May 2, May 12, and Dec. 3, 1864; Thompson and Clay, May 3, 1864; Capt. George Dawson, July 26-Oct. 27, 1864, and Edwin G. Lee, Dec. 15, 1864.

Very little documentary material was published by the Confederate Department of State during the war. Its principal publication was Correspondence of the Department of State, in Relation to the British Consuls Resident in the Confederate States (Richmond, 1863). Much of the diplomatic correspondence has been published in Official Records . . . Navies, ser. 2, vol. 3, which also contains a list of the records of the Department of State (p. 19-26) and a calendar of diplomatic correspondence (p. 34-89). More correspondence is in Official Records . . . Armies, ser. 4, vols. 2-3. Volume 2 of Richardson's Messages and Papers of the Confederacy is devoted entirely to diplomatic correspondence; the compilation is incomplete, however, for it lacks important despatches of Mason and Slidell, and parts of other despatches are deleted. A long letter from John T. Pickett to Manuel de Zamacona, the Mexican Minister of Foreign Affairs, Sept. 16, 1861, is in His-panic American Historical Review, 2:611-617 (Nov. 1919). Bishop Lynch's despatches to Secretary Benjamin, Mar. 3, Mar. 25, and June 20, 1864, are published in "Reports of Bishop Lynch of Charleston, South Carolina Commissioner of the Confederate States to the Holy See, " American Catholic Historical Researches, n.s., 1:248-259 (July 1905).

The destruction of American merchant ships by Confederate cruisers built in England caused the U.S. Government to present claims to the British Government during and after the war. These claims became known as the Ala-bama Claims, because most of the losses were inflicted by the C.S.S. Alabama. The records of the U.S. Department of State and documentary publications concerning these claims are described in the Guide to Federal Archives Relating to the Civil War, p. 163-167, and in National Archives, Preliminary Inventory [No. 135] of Records Relating to Civil War Claims--United States and Great Britain, comp. by George S. Ulibarri and Daniel T. Goggin (Washington, 1962). The British Foreign Office also accumulated related records, which are described in Great Britain, Public Record Office, List of Foreign Office Records to 1878 Preserved in the Public Record Office, p. 19-20 (London, 1929).

Miscellaneous Correspondence

Records in Other Custody. -- Other correspondence of the Confederate Department of State in the Library of Congress concerns mainly domestic affairs of the Confederacy although some concerns foreign emissaries. Fair copies of letters sent and telegrams, Mar. 11, 1861-Feb. 23, 1865 (2 vols.), indexed by names of persons and offices, are arranged chronologically. The letters are to heads of departments and bureaus on official matters, to Members of Congress on subjects under consideration by Congress and on passports and letters of marque; to newspaper editors about subscriptions and the publication of laws and proclamations; to the public printers (Reid & Shorter) on the publication of laws and contracts for the Department's printing; to State Governors concerning the ratification of conventions with the Confederacy and political prisoners; to applicants for letters of marque; to collectors of customs regarding passports and letters of marque; to commissioners in Europe enclosing drafts for salaries; to secretaries of missions abroad regarding their accounts; to business firms making payments and ordering books; to the Comptroller of the Treasury concerning the Departmental accounts; to individuals concerning claims; and to Rose O'Neal Greenhow, Louis Heyliger, and Catherine V. Baxley on payments for their service. Resignations of the Secretaries and other officials, appointments, and letters on personnel matters are also in these books. Communications to the President and Congress, July 30, 1861-Jan. 5, 1865 (1 vol.), transmit information or documents requested by Congress, nominations of diplomatic representatives for confirmation by Congress, estimates of appropriations, and lists of diplomatic correspondence.

A file of miscellaneous letters received, Mar. 4, 1861-Feb. 23, 1865 (6 in.), in the Library of Congress, arranged chronologically, contains those received by the Secretary of State and his subordinates. Letters from Government officials, Members of Congress, and State Governors concern requests for information, foreign consuls in the Confederacy, passports, commissions of appointees to Government positions, conditions in the South, the activities of State agents and commissioners, the release of prisoners, and other matters. From Departmental employees there are applications for furloughs and resignations. Letters from political prisoners request explanations of their arrest and include petitions for release. Letters from collectors of customs concern applications for letters of marque. Letters on disbursing matters were addressed to W. J. Bromwell. Communications from Malcolm H. MacWillie, the delegate from Arizona Territory, concern Arizona and New Mexico. There are letters addressed to the President and referred by him or his aides to the Department of State. Other letters concern the confirmation of appointments of diplomatic representatives, foreign trade, Mexican affairs, the remuneration of agents, and foreign consuls in the Confederacy. A letter from Father John Bannon, Sept. 2, 1863, recommends enlisting the sympathies of the Holy See. Nathaniel B. Tucker's letter from Halifax of Mar. 7, 1864, concerns Confederates in Canada who had escaped from Federal prisons. An alphabetical index to these miscellaneous letters by name of person, office, or State is available.

There are smaller files of correspondence among the Confederate State Department records in the Library of Congress. Letters from William H. Trescott, Aug. 3-21, 1861, concern conversations with the British and French consuls at Charleston, S. C., on the admission of Confederate prizes to British and French ports and a proposal of Charleston merchants to use the steamer Nashville to break the blockade. There are letters from the Executive Office and from Congress communicating resolutions of Congress with texts of some resolutions, Feb. 1861-Nov. 1864. A few transmittal letters, Jan. 11, 1862-Feb. 14, 1864, relate to documents (not identified) regarding the loss of slaves and the destruction of property by Federal troops. Correspondence relating to Indian affairs includes a letter from Gov. Edward Clark to the President enclosing a report of the Texas Indian commissioners of Apr. 23, 1861, letters from Albert Pike of May 29 and Nov. 25, 1861, and a certificate of the election of Robert M. Jones as the delegate from the Choctaw and Chickasaw nations to Congress. Correspondence between Robert Ould and Lt. Col. William H. Ludlow, Sept. 25-Dec. 11, 1863, concerns the exchange of military prisoners. Correspondence between General Beauregard and Maj. Robert Anderson and the Confederate Secretary of War, Apr. 8-12, 1861, relates to the surrender of Fort Sumter. Correspondence of William M. Browne, as a member of the Board of Managers of the Georgia Relief and Hospital Association in Richmond, Dec. 6, 1861-Jan. 30, 1862, concerns the authority of the Board over hospitals in Richmond.

Personnel Records

Records in Other Custody. --In the Library of Congress are incomplete personnel records for all branches of the Confederate Government. Applications and recommendations for appointments, Feb. 11, 1861-Jan. 9, 1865 (3 in.), are arranged chronologically. Addressed to the Secretary of State, the President, heads of departments, and Congressmen, they relate to appointments in the executive departments, judiciary, Army, Navy, diplomatic corps, and territorial administration. The file includes Presidential nominations, Senate confirmations, and recommendations and memorials on behalf of applicants. Correspondence relating to appointments, nominations, and commissions of civil officials, Sept. 3, 1861-Mar. 11, 1865 (1 1/2 in.), with lists of persons recommended, concerns appointments to positions in Richmond and elsewhere. Commissions and appointments, Aug. 13, 1861-Mar. 28, 1865 (3 vols.), show name, position, and date and are signed by the President and the Secretary of State. These volumes are indexed by name. Commissions issued to special commissioners to the U. S. Government and to commissioners and agents to foreign nations, Feb. 27, 1861-Jan. 28, 1865 (1 vol.), are accompanied by letters of credence and special passports. A few acting appointments by the President, Mar. 19, 1861-Oct. 29, 1864 (1 vol., p. 29-35), are for positions in the executive departments. There are 33 oaths of office of Cabinet officers and Departmental clerks, Feb. 27, 1861-Feb. 7, 1865. Resignations of R. M. T. Hunter, Feb. 17, 1862, and William M. Browne, Apr. 22, 1862, are accompanied by acceptances by the President.

Financial Records

Records in Other Custody. --Accounts, receipts, and related correspondence of the Confederate Department of State, Mar. 18, 1861-Mar. 25, 1865 (1 1/2 in.), are in the Library of Congress. There are letters from the Secretary of the Treasury and from representatives abroad concerning financial matters; from the Comptroller of the Treasury regarding the adjustment of the disbursing officer's accounts; from John Fraser & Co. of Charleston and Fraser, Trenholm & Co. of Liverpool concerning the payment of accounts and drafts; from newspapers regarding subscriptions; and from postmasters about forwarding letters. There are memoranda by W. J. Bromwell, accounts of diplomatic and commercial agents and Department employees, receipts for salary payments, drafts of indemnity bonds, and bills for printing. There is an account of contingent expenses of the commission at London, Feb. 10, 1862-Nov. 16, 1863, submitted by J. E. McFarland on Feb. 9, 1864. An account book of William F. Alexander, Apr. 23-July 27, 1861, shows amounts deposited with the Confederate Treasurer and checks drawn, with a few warrants on the Confederate Treasurer by Alexander for June and July 1861. There are checkbook stubs, Mar. 19-May 19, 1861, showing checks drawn on the Bank of Montgomery for salaries and other Department expenses. Canceled checks, Apr. 30-June 27 and Aug. 10-Sept. 27, 1861, also show payments made by W. F. Alexander and W. J. Bromwell. Other items include duplicate drafts of the Treasurer in favor of commissioners and agents abroad, 1862-63, an estimate of Department expenses for 1865, foreign-currency exchange vouchers of John Slidell for Apr., June, and Sept. 1864, and payrolls of Department employees, Sept. and Dec. 1863. There are receipts for disbursements, Apr. 30, 1861-Mar. 31, 1865 (2 in.), for supplies, services, and salaries.

Additional financial records in the Library of Congress are in book form. A cashbook, Mar. 19, 1861-Apr. 1, 1865, contains a daily record of receipts and disbursements for salaries, telegraph expenses, publications, printing the laws, advertising, office furniture, and supplies. There is a ledger of disbursements, Mar. 19, 1861-Apr. 1, 1865 (1 vol.), under the foreign intercourse fund, for salaries, the expenses of foreign commissioners and agents, and other expenses. Foreign service personal accounts, Mar. 18, 1861-Apr. 1, 1865 (1 vol.), show payments made to individual commissioners, agents, secretaries, and Fraser, Trenholm & Co.

An appropriation expense record book, Feb. 1864-Mar. 1865, shows amounts of appropriations and amounts withdrawn for compensation and expenses of commissioners and secretaries, clerks, commercial agents, and the Secretary of State. Requisitions on the Treasury Department, July 31, 1862-Mar. 28, 1865 (1 vol.), show the appropriations to be charged.

A secret service account book, with the Chicago Historical Society collections, is a remnant; most of the pages have been removed.

Maritime and Naval Records

Records in Other Custody. --In the Library of Congress are applications for letters of marque and reprisal and related correspondence, Apr. 13, 1861-May 4, 1864 (2 in.). Among these are applications from owners of vessels, bonds of the principal and sureties, letters from collectors of customs with registers of commissions issued to privateers, requests for copies of commissions, and resignations. There are letters from collectors of customs at Beaufort, Brunswick, Charleston, Fernandina, St. Marks, Savannah, and Wilmington in reply to the Secretary of the Treasury, Oct. 16-30, 1861, regarding the effectiveness of the blockade. Statements of vessels entering and clearing southern ports, Jan. 1861-Mar. 1863, are accompanied by covering letters from the Secretary of the Treasury. They are available for Charleston, Darien, Fernandina, Galveston, Georgetown, Mobile, New Orleans, Pensacola, Port Lavaca, St. Marks, Savannah, and Wilmington. Declarations concerning an attack by a U.S. warship on the Margaret and Jessie in June 1863 are accompanied by a letter from Fraser & Co. of Charleston, June 24, 1863. There are records concerning the murder of William A. Andrews, commanding officer of the C.S.S. Sumter, by Joseph G. Hester at Gibraltar on Oct. 15, 1862. An affidavit, Jan. 13, 1862, of J. W. Zacharie, a New Orleans merchant, concerns Zacharie's apprehension on Dec. 7, 1861, aboard the British schooner Eugenie Smith in Mexican waters, by the commander of the U.S.S. St. Jago de Cuba. A proposal of Ernest de Bellot of Paris, Sept. 5, 1861, for a maritime postal service for the Confederacy accompanies a letter from Thomas H. Ellis of Richmond, Va., Oct. 5, 1861. A letter from George McHenry and his associates to President Davis, Jan. 13, 1863, presents a plan for the establishment of a steamship service between Queenstown, Ireland, and Norfolk, Va., after the end of the war. With it is a letter from J. H. Reagan to the President, Mar. 14, 1863, commenting on the proposal, which would have involved a postal contract with the Confederacy. Statements of claims of British merchants and other papers, 1863-64, relate to cargoes of the U.S. ships Amanda and Express destroyed by the C. S.S. Alabama. Letters sent by Comdr. Raphael Semmes, July 6, 1861-Jan. 24, 1862 (20 items), are addressed to officials and business firms in ports in Cuba, South America, and the West Indies and to Cádiz and Gibraltar-- all ports where the C.S.S. Sumter called during its voyage from New Orleans to Gibraltar--and to members of the ship's crew. They are accompanied by a transmittal letter from the Secretary of the Navy to the President, Mar. 25, 1862. Finally, there is a record of the arrival and departure of vessels at Bermuda and Nassau, 1861-65 (1 vol.).

Other Records

Records in Other Custody. --The duties of the Department of State resulted in the accumulation of certain other records that are in the Library of Congress. Copies of pardons, Dec. 9, 1862-Dec. 6, 1864 (1 vol.), are for such crimes as theft, forgery, mail robbery, counterfeiting, and bribery. Messages of the President to Congress, 1862-65, are in printed form. Letters received relating to copyright records, Oct. 21, 1863-May 20, 1864 (1/2 in.), are from clerks of district courts with lists of copyrighted works giving titles, dates of deposit, and names of depositors with information regarding titles published from 1861. Some title pages and sheet music are included. Applications for passports, Mar. 18, 1862-Mar. 23, 1865 (3 in.), are from individuals and from officials on behalf of others. They include affidavits of nativity or residence, surgeons' certificates of exemption from military service, physical descriptions, and military orders for leaves of absence. Stubs of passports granted, July 28, 1863-Mar. 28, 1864 (2 vols.), give age, physical description, date, and signature of bearer. These are for passports numbered 252-558; the earlier stubs are missing.

The papers relating to claims for property destroyed by the enemy, the property owners, and Confederate forces are missing, but two index volumes in the Library of Congress provide some information. An index to testimony concerning property taken or destroyed by the enemy, arranged alphabetically by name of claimant or agent, gives information on more than 1,400 claims. The property is noted only infrequently. A similarly prepared index to 338 claims for property destroyed by Confederates lists cotton, houses and other buildings, schooners, and timber and naval stores. Information concerning claims against Mexico is included in the latter index.

A diary of Judah P. Benjamin, Feb. 22, 1862-Dec. 12, 1864 (1 vol.), in the Confederate Department of State records in the Library of Congress, is mainly a record of events drawn from newspapers and official documents but includes notes on the policy to be adopted toward foreign consuls, the exemption of foreign residents, the departure of agents to foreign countries, and an interview with Count Henri Mercier, the French minister in Washington, who visited Richmond in Apr. 1862.

Letters from Foreign Consuls

The Confederate Government permitted foreign consuls residing in the South in 1861 to remain there. Most numerous were the British consuls at Richmond, Charleston, Savannah, Mobile, New Orleans, Galveston, Wilmington, and Key West. French consuls were at Richmond, Charleston, New Orleans, Galveston, Baton Rouge, Mobile, Key West, Savannah, Wilmington, and Norfolk. At Richmond consuls were able to serve as intermediaries between their own governments and the Confederacy. Among other activities, they issued passports and clearances for vessels. In Oct. 1863, however, the British consuls were forced to leave when they attempted to interfere with the recently adopted Confederate policy of conscripting foreigners who had overstayed their time limits.

An incomplete list of consuls and agents of foreign countries is in Official Records . . .Navies, ser. 2, vol. 3, p. 12. See also Milledge L. Bonham, Jr., The British Consuls in the Confederacy (New York, 1911) and "The French Consuls in the Confederate States," in Studies in Southern History and Politics; Inscribed to William

Archibald Dunning, p. 83-104 (New York, 1914); Great Britain, Parliament, Correspondence Respecting Removal of British Consuls From So-Styled Confederate States of America (House of Commons, Sessional Papers, 1864. vol. 23, London, 1864); Gordon Wright, "Economic Conditions in the Confederacy As Seen by the French Consuls," Journal of Southern History, 7:195-214 (May 1941).

Records in Other Custody. --Letters received by the Confederacy from foreign consuls, May 20, 1861-May 24, 1864 (4 in.), in the Library of Congress concern the seizure, imprisonment, and conscription of citizens of foreign countries; lawsuits involving British-owned vessels; claims for the destruction of ships and cargoes by the C. S. S. Alabama; the purchase and shipment of tobacco; the expulsion of British consuls; and the detention of British ships in Confederate ports. Besides such documentary enclosures as correspondence with State authorities and Army officers, court records, memorials, instructions to consuls, affidavits, and newspaper clippings, this file includes letters from State Governors and the War Department. The papers are arranged alphabetically by name of country and chronologically thereunder.

The records of the Department of State can be supplemented by other documentary materials. The records of the British Consulate at Savannah, Ga., dating from 1859, acquired by Emory University Library from Keith M. Read in 1938 consist largely of letters received. The correspondents include the Secretary of State, the Secretary of War, Richard B. P. Lyons (British minister in Washington), and Gov. Joseph E. Brown of Georgia. The letters relate mostly to the conscription of British subjects by the Confederate Army, the blockade of Confederate ports, and proofs of British citizenship. Other files of the same Consulate, dating from 1816, in Duke University Library include letters received from British citizens regarding conscription, redress for being unjustly punished or imprisoned on charges of being abolitionists or Union spies, and correspondence relating to British-owned cotton and timber seized during the war. The records of Alfred Paul, French consul in Richmond, in the New-York Historical Society collections contain chiefly copies of letters sent, 1860-63 (7 vols.), to officials in France but include some to the Secretary of State. Correspondence and other papers of Eugène Méjan. Feb. -May 1862 (85 items), are in the Library of Congress. He served as French consul at New Orleans. Reports of Laurent M. J. de Give are contained in Paul Evans and Thomas P. Goven, trans. and ed., "A Belgian Consul on Conditions in the South in 1860 and 1862," Journal of Southern History, 3:478-491 (Nov. 1937).

The reports sent by the consuls of European countries to their ministries of foreign affairs are with the records of those ministries. See Daniel H. Thomas and Lynn M. Case, eds., A Guide to Manuscripts Relating to American History in British Depositories Reproduced for the Division of Manuscripts of the Library of Congress, p. 52-53 (Washington, 1946). The reports from the British consuls and other records of the Foreign Office relating to the war in America were published in the British Sessional Papers; see P. and G. Ford, A Guide to Parliamentary Papers (Oxford, 1956), and Robert H. Jones, "The American Civil War in the British Sessional Papers; Catalogue

and Commentary," American Phi-
losophical Society Proceedings,
107:415-426 (Oct. 15, 1963). A

microprint edition of the British
Sessional Papers is available from
the Readex Corporation, Chester, Vt.

RECORDS OF COMMISSIONERS AND AGENTS

Commissioners to the United States

On Feb. 25, 1861, in an effórt to obtain a peaceful separation from
the Union, President Davis appointed André B. Roman of Louisiana, Martin J. Crawford of Georgia, and John Forsyth of Georgia commissioners
to the United States to obtain recognition of the Confederacy; to effect the
transfer of Federal forts, arsenals, and other public property; and to
arrange for the settlement of indebtedness and other matters that might
arise. President Lincoln refused to receive the commissioners, but Secretary of State Seward negotiated with them through Supreme Court Justices
John A. Campbell and Samuel Nelson. Lincoln's decision to relieve Fort
Sumter and the attack on the fort on Apr. 12-13 terminated the negotiations.

Records in Other Custody.--The records of the Commissioners to
the United States were deposited by their secretary, John T. Pickett, in the
Office of the Secretary of State on May 6, 1861, and are now in the Confederate Department of State's records in the Library of Congress. These
records, Feb. 27-Apr. 29, 1861, include instructions and letters from the
Secretary of State, letters and telegrams of the commissioners and their
secretary to the Secretary of State, letters to Secretary of State Seward
and to Jefferson Davis, notes of Justice Campbell, Pickett's memoranda,
and telegrams. Transcripts of part of the records for Mar. 3-Apr. 27,
1861 (labeled "R. Toombs Letter Book") are in the South Caroliniana
Library of the University of South Carolina and in the John G. Nicolay
papers in the Manuscript Division of the Library of Congress. Roman's
instructions, his appointment, and a few letters are among his papers in
the Louisiana State University, Department of Archives (La Villebeuvre
papers). Copies of the report of the Confederate commissioners on the
Hampton Roads conference and related documents are in the Burton N.
Harrison papers in the Library of Congress.

The commissioners' appointment order is in Official Records
. . . Armies, ser. 1, vol. 51, pt.
2, p. 8. Correspondence between
the commissioners and Seward is
in Davis, Rise and Fall of the Confederate Government, 1:675-685,
in Stephens, Constitutional View,
2:735-746, and in Rowland, ed.,
Jefferson Davis, Constitutionalist,
5:86-99. Justice Campbell's correspondence with Seward and Davis is
in the works of Stephens and Rowland and in "Papers of Hon. John A.
Campbell--1861-1865," Southern
Historical Society Papers, 42:30-41
(1917), which also contains a memorandum by Campbell on the part he
played in the negotiations.

Commissioners and Agents Abroad

Record Group 45.--In the Naval Records Collection of the Office of
Naval Records and Library are copies of some of John Slidell's official
records.

Record Group 109.--Correspondence of Clement C. Clay, Jr.,

Apr. 27, 1864-Mar. 26, 1865 (1/2 in.), is in the War Department Collection of Confederate Records. Included are letters from Jacob Thompson and James P. Holcombe, from agents assigned projects in the United States and from Confederates in Canada with information about U.S. prisons they escaped from.

Records in Other Custody. --The papers, 1838-70, of James M. Mason were purchased by the Library of Congress in 1912. They include a despatch book, letters received, and other records relating to his activities as Confederate commissioner at London. The despatch book, Feb. 2, 1862-May 1, 1865, contains fair copies of letters to the Secretary of State concerning Mason's negotiations with the British Government, his contacts with other Confederate commissioners and naval officers in Europe, his visits to Paris, the operations of Confederate cruisers, the activities of British sympathizers, the arrivals of Confederate ships in British ports, and inventions of possible interest to the Confederacy. Mason's papers for the period July 27, 1861-June 29, 1865, amount to 8 volumes (1 ft. 5 in.) of correspondence and other documents. Letters received are from the Secretary of State; heads of other executive departments; Lord John Russell; Clement C. Clay, Jr.; and James P. Holcombe in Canada; and from John Slidell in Paris; James Spence of Liverpool; Fraser, Trenholm & Co. of Liverpool; and Émile Erlanger of Paris. There are also letters from the Society for Promoting the Cessation of Hostilities in America to Members of Parliament, from the Reverend Francis W. Tremlett, the Society's secretary, from the Southern Independence Association of Manchester, and from William S. Lindsay, William Gregory, and other Englishmen who supported the Confederate cause. Other Confederates in Europe with whom Mason corresponded were James D. Bulloch, William G. Crenshaw, Henry Hotze, Caleb Huse, Lucius Q. C. Lamar, James E. McFarland, A. Dudley Mann, Matthew F. Maury, James H. North, Raphael Semmes, and George T. Sinclair. There are cotton certificates and warrants, statements and depositions concerning naval and marine matters, and lists of supplies to be furnished by contractors to the Confederate Government.

In Duke University Library are a few letters of Mason concerning his contacts with A. J. B. Beresford-Hope, a member of the London committee of the Society for Promoting the Cessation of Hostilities in America.

Virginia Mason, ed., The Public Life and Diplomatic Correspondence of James M. Mason, with Some Personal History, (Roanoke, 1903); Great Britain, Parliament, Correspondence with Mr. Mason Respecting Blockade and Recognition of Confederate States (House of Commons, Sessional Papers, 1863, vol. 72, London, 1863), Correspondence with Mr. Mason, Commissioner of the So-Styled Confederate States of America (House of Commons, Sessional Papers, 1864, vol. 62, London, 1864). Printed leaflets and letters of James Spence and Alexander Collie & Co. of London, 1863-65, are in the papers of Edward Stuart-Wortley-Mackenzie (1st Earl of Wharncliffe), the president of the Southern Independence Association, in the Sheffield City Libraries, Sheffield, England.

The William L. Yancey papers, 1846-63, in the Alabama Department of Archives and History include drafts of despatches to the Secretary of State and communications to P. A. Rost and Lord John Russell for 1861, letters of Rost, Apr. 7 and 24, 1862, and a letter of Caleb Huse, July 3, 1862, concerning his purchasing activities for the Confederate Government in Europe. A diary of Yancey, May 15-June 18, 1861, describes his journey to Europe and his travels there.

Papers of other Confederate representatives and employees in Europe also include official correspondence. P. A. Rost's papers, Aug. 24, 1861-May 29, 1862 (22 items), in the Royal Academy of History, Madrid, consist of instructions, letters, and a report on an interview with a Spanish official. A. Dudley Mann's correspondence, 1862-64, is in microfilm form in the Louisiana State University Department of Archives. Secretary Benjamin's commission to Bishop Patrick N. Lynch and letters concerning his mission to the Vatican are in the archives of the Roman Catholic Diocese of Charleston, S. C. Colin J. McRae's papers, 1837-66 (200 items), in the Alabama Department of Archives and History include correspondence and a letters-sent book, Oct. 9, 1864-Mar. 31, 1865, containing copies of letters and reports to Secretary Benjamin, letters received from James Williams, and McRae's account with Williams. The papers of Henri Vignaud, Slidell's secretary in Paris, in the Louisiana State University Department of Archives include letters of 1862 from Eugene Dumez concerning Confederate diplomatic missions in France and England and efforts to obtain recognition of the Confederacy. The Lucius Q. C. Lamar papers in the Alabama Department of Archives and History include his instructions and appointment and copies of his letters to Secretary Benjamin. The Lamar-Mayes papers in the Mississippi Department of Archives and History include some of Lamar's wartime correspondence. The Duncan F. Kenner papers in the Department of Archives of Louisiana State University and in the Louisiana State Museum Library include documents relating to his mission to Europe in 1865.

Ignacio Bauer, "Lista Cronológica de Documentos Encontrados en la Cartera C. S. A., Iniciales que Significan 'Confederate States of America, ' y Abandonados por el Delegado del Presidente Jefferson Davis en España, Mr. P. A. Rost, " Real Academia de la Historia Boletín, 76:161-162 (Feb. 1920); Joseph O. Baylen and William W. White, eds., "A. Dudley Mann's Mission in Europe, 1863-64; an Unpublished Letter to Jefferson Davis, " Virginia Magazine of History and Biography, 69:324-328 (July 1961), contains a letter of Feb. 12, 1864. A few documents from the Lamar papers are in Edward Mayes, Lucius Q. C. Lamar; His Life, Times and Speeches, 1825-1893 (Nashville, 1896).

George N. Sanders' papers, 1854-64 (mostly 1860-61, 1 1/2 in.), in Record Group 109 contain abstracts of outgoing letters from Paris during May-Aug. 1864 to the Secretary of State and others concerning the release from detention of the C. S. S. Rappahannock, the repair of the C. S. S. Alabama, the attitude of French officials toward the destruction of the Alabama, the construction of naval vessels, and Confederate finances and propaganda. Sanders appears to have had no official connection with the Confederate Government at the time he was in Paris.

Incomplete records of Henry Hotze as Confederate agent in London are in the Library of Congress. A despatch book contains copies of communications to the Secretary of State, James M. Mason, and Isaac Campbell; letters from Campbell and Edwin De Leon; and a record of expenditures for secret purposes, Nov. 1861-Dec. 1864. A letters-sent book, May 28, 1864-June 16, 1865, contains copies of letters to English, French, German, and Italian correspondents regarding the publication of material in The Index; letters to journalists in Brooklyn, Hartford, New York, and Philadelphia who also served as correspondents; and letters to James M. Mason, J. D. Bulloch, J. F. Lalor, Father John Bannon, Judah P. Benjamin, George McHenry, John George Witt, and T. B. Kershaw, the last-named of the Southern Independence Association, Manchester, England. Hotze's incoming letters, 1862-65 (65 items), are from John Slidell, M. F. Maury, J. D. Bulloch, George Eustis (apparently working for Slidell), George McHenry, Edwin De Leon, Colin J. McRae, and A. D. Mann.

Published papers of Henry Hotze include his secret service account and a letter to Judah P. Benjamin, Dec. 31, 1864, in J. Franklin Jameson, ed., "The London Expenditures of the Confederate Secret Service," American Historical Review, 35:811-824 (July 1930), and a letter of Aug. 11, 1864, to John G. Witt who did editorial work on The Index, in Richard B. Harwell, ed., "The Creed of a Propagandist; Letter from a Confederate Editor," Journalism Quarterly, 28:213-218 (Spring 1951).

Papers of other propaganda agents in Europe are also available. In the University of Virginia Library is the diary, Feb. 29-Dec. 29, 1864, of John R. Thompson, Hotze's assistant on The Index. James L. Capston's papers, Sept. 1863-Jan. 1865, in the Confederate Museum collections include his despatches to Secretary Benjamin from Dublin, Cork, and Queenstown; a list of men enlisted on the U.S.S. Kearsarge; a salary receipt; and a notice from the admiral of the port of Queenstown about the Queen's proclamation prohibiting the enlistment of men for Confederate cruisers. Matthew F. Maury's papers, 1825-74, in the Library of Congress include correspondence relating to his services as a Confederate agent in London. Especially numerous are his letters of Nov. 1863-Dec. 1864 to the Reverend Francis W. Tremlett, a Confederate sympathizer. Maury's diary, 1863-68, notes his official activities and contacts with other Confederate agents. Printed circulars issued by the Society for Promoting the Cessation of Hostilities are also among the Maury papers. Albert T. Bledsoe's papers in the University of Virginia Library include letters from James Spence and Edwin De Leon, and other Bledsoe papers (photostats) in the Library of Congress include a few wartime letters. The papers, 1862-64, of Edwin De Leon, Confederate agent in France, in the South Caroliniana Library of the University of South Carolina include letters from Secretary Benjamin, James M. Mason, Henry Hotze, and George McHenry; invoices for printing and other purposes; and account and diary books, Jan. 1861-Jan. 1865, showing disbursements, letters sent, money loaned, travel, and miscellaneous activities. In addition, there are photostat copies of a series of articles entitled "Secret History of Confederate Diplomacy Abroad" written by De Leon for the New York Citizen. Microfilms of these papers are in the American Jewish Archives at Cincinnati. There are De Leon papers, 1861-85 (20 items), in the Library of Congress.

In promoting the cause of the Confederacy in England the Reverend Francis W. Tremlett became acquainted with Confederate naval officers stationed there or passing through. Some of his manuscripts, acquired by the Virginia Historical Society in 1925, consist of letters received, 1862-65, from naval officers including J. H. North, R. B. Pegram, John J. McIntosh, William H. Murdaugh, George T. Sinclair, and Raphael Semmes. There are also letters from James M. Mason, Alfred T. Bledsoe, and John Slidell.

On his return from Mexico in 1862 John T. Pickett deposited two record books in the Confederate Department of State; these are with the Department's records in the Manuscript Division of the Library of Congress. A letters-sent book, June 15, 1861-Feb. 22, 1862, contains fair copies of letters he wrote to the Secretary of State from Vera Cruz and Mexico City. A long letter to the President, Jan. 11, 1864, in this book gives Pickett's observations on Mexican affairs, an account of his return from Mexico in 1862, and information regarding the loss of duplicates of his despatches mailed from a New Orleans post office. Enclosures to the despatches, such as correspondence with the Mexican Minister of Foreign Affairs and newspaper clippings, are also copied in this book. A letter and account book, June 15, 1861-May 5, 1862, contains fair copies of letters to the postmasters at Brownsville and New Orleans, to Asst. Secretary William M. Browne, to Mexican newspapers, to the ministers in Mexico from Prussia and France regarding Pickett's arrest by the Mexicans, to Thomas Corwin, (the U. S. minister) concerning the representation of the Confederacy in Mexico, and letters to the Secretary of the Treasury enclosing quarterly accounts of disbursements.

Among John T. Pickett's personal papers in the Manuscript Division of the Library of Congress is a press copy book of letters sent, June 12, 1861-May 14, 1862 (part of a vol. for 1861-67), containing badly faded copies of letters to the Secretaries of State and the Treasury, the President, W. M. Browne, John S. Cripps, Charles Rieken, and others concerning his activities as a Confederate agent. Pickett's despatch no. 17 of 1861, with eight enclosures, to the Secretary of State is in the Hackley Public Library, Muskegon, Mich.

Some of the papers of Confederate agents in Canada have been preserved. The Clement C. Clay, Jr., manuscripts acquired by Duke University Library from the Clay family in 1930 include correspondence on his activities in Canada. What appears to be the original copy of Jacob Thompson's report of Dec. 3, 1864, to Secretary Benjamin is in the Columbus Delano papers in the Library of Congress (printed in Official Records . . . Armies, ser. 1, vol. 43, pt. 2, p. 930-936). The Thomas H. Hines papers in the University of Kentucky Library include letters, expense accounts, a diary, notebooks, and unpublished memoirs. The memoirs of Bennett H. Young are in the Filson Club, Louisville, Ky. A microfilm copy of the diary of Edwin G. Lee from Dec. 5, 1864, to Dec. 31, 1865, is in the Southern Historical Collection in the University of North Carolina Library.

L. N. Benjamin, comp., The St. Albans Raid; or, Investigation into the Charges Against Lieut. Bennett H. Young and Command, for Their Acts at St. Albans, Vt., on the 19th October, 1864, Being a Complete and Authentic Report of All the Proceedings on the Demand of the United States for Their Extradition, Under the Ashburton Treaty (Montreal, 1865); John B. Castleman, Active Service (Louisville, 1917); John W. Headley, Confederate Operations in Canada and New York (New York, 1906); Thomas H. Hines, "The Northwestern

Conspiracy, " Southern Bivouac, 5:437-445, 566-574, 699-704 (Dec. 1886-Apr. 1887); Daniel B. Lucas, Memoir of John Yates Beall; His Life, Trial, Correspondence; Diary; and Private Manuscript Found Among His Papers, Including His Own Account of the Raid on Lake Erie (Montreal, 1865); Jacob Thompson, A Leaf from History; Report of J. Thompson, Secret Agent of the Late Confederate Government Stationed in Canada for the Purpose of Organizing Insurrection in the Northern States (Washington,

1868?). The proceedings of the military commission that tried George St. Leger Grenfel and others who conspired to release the Confederate prisoners at Camp Douglas, Ill., are in "George St. Leger Grenfel, " H. Ex. Doc. 50, 39 Cong., 2 sess., Serial 1290 (Washington, 1867). The proceedings of the military commissions that tried John Y. Beall and Robert C. Kennedy are in the Records of the [U. S.] Judge Advocate General (Record Group 153), files NN 3513 and 3729.

VI

DEPARTMENT OF THE TREASURY

The Department of the Treasury was established by an act of Feb. 21, 1861 (Prov. Cong. C.S.A. Stat. 30), which provided for the appointment of a Secretary of the Treasury, an Assistant Secretary, a Treasurer, a Comptroller, an Auditor, and a Register. As the Department expanded and acquired new functions by acts of Congress, other offices and bureaus were added. A Lighthouse Bureau, a Produce Loan Office, and a War Tax Office were organized in 1861, and a Second Auditor was appointed to audit War Department accounts. A Third Auditor was designated in 1864 to audit Post Office accounts. A Treasury Agent for the Trans-Mississippi West took over the management of Departmental functions in that region in 1864 after communication with it became difficult, and in the same year a Treasury Note Bureau was established. An act of Feb. 23, 1865 (Ramsdell, Laws and Joint Resolutions, p. 54), established an Office of Deposit to receive Treasury notes and drafts and funds of private persons, to make payments on depositors' checks, and to make loans to the Government, but actually little was accomplished by the Office.

Besides the many depositaries in the States of the Confederacy, depositaries were appointed in foreign countries where purchasing and other financial activities took place. The commercial agents of the State Department at Nassau, Havana, and Bermuda were designated as depositaries. Early in the war the firm of Fraser, Trenholm & Co. of Liverpool was appointed a depositary to serve Confederate agents abroad. In 1862 Colin J. McRae went to Paris to complete arrangements for the Erlanger loan, and in July of that year he was designated as the depositary to receive the funds obtained. Later McRae became the Government's financial agent in Europe, and Fraser, Trenholm & Co. became the sole depositary.

When Richmond was evacuated early in Apr. 1865 some Treasury Department records were shipped south by rail; other records were left in Richmond. Part of the Second Auditor's records and most of the Produce Loan Office records were destroyed by fire there, and records of the Treasury Note Bureau were destroyed at Anderson, S.C., by U.S. forces. In May 1865 Col. Richard D. Cutts, U.S.A., shipped to Washington from Richmond requisitions for funds, warrants, correspondence, printed Treasury Department documents, many boxes of records of the Second Auditor's Office relating to the settlement of quartermasters' and commissaries' accounts, books of the Register's Office relating to issues of Treasury notes, records of the tax collector of the 10th Virginia District, and some records of the Third Auditor relating to Post Office accounts. Other Treasury Department records that had been abandoned at Washington, Ga., were also sent to Washington, D. C. There they were placed in the custody of the War Department's Archive Office, which acquired also the records of the Produce Loan Office, the depository at Macon, the Commissioner of Taxes, and the First Auditor and certain canceled and uncanceled Confederate notes.

A record of Second Auditor's accounts and miscellaneous papers received by the Archive Office of the War Department in 1865 (Record Group 109, War Department Collection of Confederate Records, ch. VIII, vol. 34) contains lists of the accounts by names of quartermasters, commissaries, medical officers, ordnance officers, paymasters, and recruiting officers. This record shows that other boxes contained Confederate money, railroad vouchers, papers relating to claims filed on behalf of deceased soldiers, transportation accounts, company returns, and miscellaneous papers.

Most of the records that were received by the War Department remained in its custody until 1937, when they were transferred with other Confederate records to the National Archives and became part of Record Group 109.

The U.S. Treasury Department acquired other records of the Confederate Treasury Department soon after the war ended. Most of these were obtained through U.S. Treasury special agents who had been appointed to supervise trade and commerce in occupied areas of the Confederacy and to handle captured, abandoned, and confiscable property. When these agents closed their offices, they sent the Confederate records that they had acquired to the U.S. Treasury Department.

In the course of time the U.S. Treasury Department acquired still other Confederate records. In 1872 it purchased records of the Department of State, which it later transferred, in 1906 and 1910, to the Library of Congress. Records of the Cotton Bureau of the Trans-Mississippi Department, a geographical military command, were purchased by the Commissioners of Claims in 1873 and were later transferred to the Treasury Department. The Department also acquired records of the Confederate District Courts for the Southern District of Georgia and the Eastern District of Texas by transfer from the War Department. Other U.S. Treasury Department acquisitions included a few records of the States of Louisiana and Mississippi, paper currency of Confederate States, and other currency of Southern States and some counties, municipalities, and private corporations. Many indexes, lists, and other compilations were prepared by the U.S. Treasury Department to facilitate reference work on the Confederate records. In 1920 the Confederate Treasury Department records described below were transferred to the Library of Congress. Having received the Confederate currency in 1937, in 1939 the National Archives received from the Treasury Department the Confederate records that the Department had retained; these records constitute the Treasury Department Collection of Confederate Records (Record Group 365).

National Archives, Preliminary Inventory [No. 169] of the Treasury Department Collection of Confederate Records, comp. by Carmelita S. Ryan (Washington, 1967).

OFFICE OF THE SECRETARY OF THE TREASURY

The act establishing the Treasury Department stipulated that the Secretary of the Treasury was to have general superintendence of the collection of the revenue, the management of the Government's finances, and other duties vested in him by law. He was to appoint an Assistant Secretary who was to examine all letters, contracts, and warrants prepared for the signature of the Secretary and perform other duties that might devolve upon him. Philip Clayton was confirmed as Assistant Secretary on Apr. 2, 1861. He was succeeded by William W. Crump on May 20, 1864. The position of chief clerk was filled successively by Henry D. Capers, Charles A. Rose, John M. Strother, and John W. Hall. S. W. Hampton was disbursing clerk from May 1861 to Aug. 1862. He was succeeded, presumably, by Strother, who resigned from the positions of chief clerk and disbursing clerk in July 1864.

Successive Secretaries of the Treasury:

Christopher G. Memminger, Feb. 21, 1861.
George A. Trenholm, July 18, 1864.
John H. Reagan (acting), Apr. 27, 1865.

Reports by the Secretary of the Treasury were issued irregularly as were other special reports; these are listed in Crandall, Confederate Imprints, 1:192-194. The reports are in C.S.A. Treasury Department, "Reports of the Secretary of the Treasury of the Confederate States of America, 1861-65, compiled under the direction of Brev. Maj. Gen. E. D. Townsend, Adjutant General U.S. Army, by Raphael P. Thian, Chief Clerk, Adjutant General's Office," app. III (Washington, 1878), which is available at the National Archives and also on microfilm. Henry D. Capers, The Life and Times of C. G. Memminger (Richmond, 1893); John C. Schwab, The Confederate States of America, 1861-1865; a Financial and Industrial History of the South During the Civil War (New York, 1901); Samuel B. Thompson, Confederate Purchasing Operations Abroad (Chapel Hill, 1935); Richard C. Todd, Confederate Finance (Athens, 1954); U.S. War Department, Official Records . . . Armies, ser. 4, vols. 1-3.

Record Group 109.--The press copies of letters sent, Apr. 3, 1861-Aug. 2, 1864 (ch. X, vols. 159-162, 165, 167-170, 173, and parts of vols. 163 and 172, 1 ft. 8 in.), comprise a chronological record of outgoing letters, circulars, and regulations; name indexes appear in the front of the volumes. The letters concern advertising, appointments and other personnel actions, acquisition of buildings for Government offices, claims, collection of customs duties and war taxes, credits for European agents, designs for coins, detection of counterfeiting, establishment of assay offices, donations for the support of the Government, estimates of appropriations, fidelity bonds, purchase of war supplies, lighthouse districts, marine hospitals, the disposition of revenue cutters, suspension of the mints, settlement of accounts, subscriptions to loans, Treasury notes and bonds, purchase of vessels for the Navy, special reports to Congress, and other matters. Press copies of letters to customs collectors and depositaries, Mar. 21, 1861-Mar. 31, 1865 (ch. X, vols. 164, 166, 171, and 174), concern appointments, resignations, bonds of Produce Loan agents, examination of imported goods, export duties, counterfeit notes, transmission of funds, canceling notes, reduction of office forces, and other matters. A record of letters sent, Apr. 11, 1863-Oct. 8, 1864 (ch. X, vols. 171 1/2 and 175), shows name, position, and sometimes address of the person to whom letters were sent and the subjects of the letters. Press copies of telegrams sent, Feb. 23-May 24, 1861 (ch. X, vol. 163, p. 1-324), are addressed to Cabinet officers, collectors of customs, State Governors, the President, Members of Congress, loan commissioners, mint superintendents, Assistant Treasurers, and others. They concern appointments, payments, instructions, enforcement of the tariff act, import duties, official bonds of employees, subscriptions to loans, financing the Government, disposing of revenue cutters, and other matters.

A record of letters sent by the Chief Clerk's Office, June 6, 1861-Jan. 30, 1862 (ch. X, vol. 176), shows name, position, sometimes address of the person written to, and subject. A register of letters sent containing Treasury drafts, June 15, 1861-Feb. 5, 1864 (vol. 62A), shows date of the letter and name and address of the person to whom it was sent.

A selection of outgoing letters of the Secretary of the Treasury is in appendix IV of the compilation by Raphael P. Thian cited above. Correspondence of the Secretary of the Treasury is also in U.S. War Department, Official Records . . . Armies, ser. 4, vols. 1-3.

A file of orders, circulars, and regulations, 1863-65 (ch. X, vol. 264), consists chiefly of those of the Treasury Department but includes some issued by the Adjutant and Inspector General to officers assigned to carry out its regulations.

Other records include letters and reports received and related papers, Feb. 1861-Mar. 1864 (7 in.), from collectors of customs, depositaries, Assistant Treasurers, other Government officials, business firms, banks, Army officers, and receivers for sequestered alien-enemy property. The documents concern appointments and other personnel actions, operations, claims for services, construction of the New Orleans custom house, payment of salaries, deposits of funds, requisitions for funds, counterfeit currency, warrants, Treasury notes, estimates for funds, payrolls for contingent services, returns, and vouchers.

A register of letters received, Jan. 2, 1861-Mar. 18, 1865 (ch. X, vol. 158), shows by year the file number, name and address of the writer, and date and subject matter of the communication. A register of applications for clerkships, Feb. 1861-Feb. 1865 (ch. X, vol. 156 1/2), shows applicant's name, residence, and date of application. A register of applications for appointments, presumably for 1862 (ch. X, vol. 156), shows applicant's name, residence, position for which he applied, and sometimes names of recommenders and references. A register of applications for appointments, Feb. -Aug. 1861 (ch. X, vol. 157), is similar in content. The applications to which these registers refer were placed by the U.S. War Department in the file of Confederate papers relating to citizens or business firms described in chapter XI of this Guide.

Letters received from James D. B. De Bow, the general agent of the Produce Loan Office for Mississippi and Louisiana, Feb. 5, 1862-Jan. 20, 1865 (1/2 in.), relate to subscriptions to loans, appointments of subagents, cotton purchases and transfers, illegal cotton trade with New Orleans, and transmission of accounts, circulars, and reports.

Requisitions on the Treasury Department for funds are in several series. Civil and miscellaneous requisitions, Mar. 1861-Mar. 1864 (ch X, vols. 251-261, 1 1/2 ft.), show the date, by whom requested, amount, in whose favor, and appropriation charged. Interfiled with the requisitions in these volumes are certifications of balances due for payments for

services, Mar. 1861-Mar. 1864, showing on printed forms the date, name
of person to whom payment was due, his position in the Confederate Government or other employment, amount, and appropriation charged, with
the signatures of the First Auditor, the Comptroller, and the Register.
War Department requisitions for funds, Mar. 1861-June 1864 (ch. X, vols.
225-244, 3 ft. 8 in.), contain on printed forms requests that warrants for
funds be issued, showing date, requisition number, in whose favor to be
issued, purpose for which issued, amount, and appropriation charged.
Navy Department requisitions for funds, Mar. 1861-Sept. 1863 (ch. X, vols.
245 and 246), and customs service requisitions for funds, Mar. 1861-June
1864 (ch. X, vols. 248-250), contain printed forms with the same information. The requisitions were countersigned by the Comptroller and registered by the Second Auditor. Copies of appropriation warrants issued by
the Secretary of the Treasury, Mar. 25, 1861-Feb. 17, 1862 (ch. X, vol.
220), give title and date of the appropriation act, purpose and amount, and
instructions to the Register and the Comptroller who also signed the warrants.

Some accounting records supply additional information on the Department's financial operations. The disbursing clerk's ledger of accounts,
Mar. 1861-Jan. 1865 (ch. X, vol. 122), contains a record of accounts with
Departmental employees, depositaries, Treasury and other Government
officials, banks, and other persons and firms, showing account names and
debits for bonds and stocks issued under acts of Mar. 23 and Apr. 30,
1863, and Feb. 17, 1864. Disbursing clerk's receipts for contingent expenses, 1862-63 (ch. X, vol. 263), show date, to whom paid, amount paid,
purpose of payment, and payee's signature. Accounts of disbursing clerks
of the Secretary's Office, the War Department, the Executive Office, the
Treasurer, and Quartermaster James L. Calhoun, Mar.-Apr. 1861 (vol.
62A, p. 1-15), show for disbursements by checks the date, name of payee,
amount, and amounts of deposits. A list of claims, Oct. 1861-Dec. 1863
(ch. X, vol. 54), gives name of the claimant and date the claim was received.

Several files are miscellaneous in content. Returns and other records of Treasury depositaries, 1863-65 (4 ft.), relate to Treasury notes,
funds, the public debt, and claims. Besides returns addressed to the
Treasury Department in Richmond, this file includes letters to the Treasurer and the First Auditor. Miscellaneous returns and reports from collectors and surveyors of customs, 1861-64 (1 in.), relate to vessels
arriving and clearing, merchandise imported, customs duties received,
moneys received and paid, and the condition of the customhouses. A small
quantity of other records, 1862-65, includes lists of employees, estimates
of appropriations, financial statements, comparative statements of the
rates of import duties, and statements of unclaimed dividends of interest
on Government loans.

Record Group 365.--The Treasury Department collection contains
two volumes of letters sent, Mar. 1-Oct. 12, 1861, and Oct. 17, 1864-Mar.
31, 1865. They are available on microfilm at the National Archives as
M 500. These volumes, numbered 111 and 115, are part of what was evidently a long series of fair copies of outgoing letters, for vol. 115 refers to
vols. 110 and 112-114. The correspondents and subject matter are the same
as those in the press copies of letters sent described under Record Group
109. The two series duplicate each other. Fair copies of telegrams sent,
Feb. 23, 1861-July 30, 1864 (1 vol.), are addressed to collectors of

customs, Assistant Treasurers, depositaries, Governors of States, Army officers, banking and railroad officials, business firms, newspapers, and others. The telegrams relate to printing and distribution of Treasury notes and bonds, appointments, subscriptions to loans, advertising, administration of the customs service, suppression of counterfeiting, procurement of exchange, collection of the war tax, and financial arrangements for the procurement of supplies abroad.

The letters-sent book, 1864-65 (vol. 115), contains several other brief records. There are lists of temporary and permanent appointments and transfers, a record of leaves of absence, and a record of resignations, all concerning Treasury Department clerks for the period Oct. 1864-Mar. 1865. Some information regarding personnel is also in a record of office supplies delivered and on hand, 1863-64 (ch. X, vol. 260 1/2).

Letters and telegrams received and other papers, 1861-65 (12 ft.; available on microfilm as M 499), are from collectors of customs, Assistant Treasurers, depositaries, loan commissioners, mint officials, tax collectors, Produce Loan agents, the heads and other officials of the executive departments, Army and Navy officers, the President, Members of Congress, banks, business firms, Governors and other State officials, printers and engravers, foreign agents of the Treasury Department, foreign banking concerns, and private citizens. They concern printing and distribution of currency and bonds, subscriptions to loans, collection and remission or refunding of customs duties, negotiation of loans, problems of administration, collection of war taxes, shipment of cotton abroad, importation of supplies, investigations of the Department's activities, suppression of counterfeiting, blockade of Southern ports, personnel matters, manufacture of paper, transfer of former U.S. property to the Confederate Government, and management of Government finances. Documents in the letters-received file relating to personnel actions include applications and recommendations for appointments, applications for transfers, oaths of office, requests for leave, letters of resignation, and doctor's certificates. Other types of documents include reports of operations from bureaus, memoranda or reports prepared in the Department, drafts of regulations, lists of bids for cotton bonds, lists of employees, reports on destruction of spoiled Treasury notes, special orders of Army commands detailing men, reports on notes receipted for by the Treasury, reports on sales of bonds, and drafts of outgoing letters. An alphabetical name index to the letters received gives address of writer, number of letters in the file, and their subjects. A record of letters received, Oct. 1862-June 1864 (vol. 120D), shows the date of the letter, name and address of the writer, a brief of its contents, and endorsements for letters referred to other offices of the Department.

Several other small files consist of correspondence and other documents that were usually recorded in letter books. Some miscellaneous records, Feb. 1861-Mar. 1865 (1 1/3 in.), consist of correspondence, memoranda, circulars, regulations, instructions, blank forms, and other papers relating to the procedures of the Department and other subjects. Copies of resolutions, bills, acts of Congress and State legislatures, and related correspondence, Feb. 1861-Mar. 1865 (1 in.), concern finances and appropriations. Copies of regulations and circulars issued by the Department, Mar. 1861-July 1864 (1/4 in.), relate to the organization and administration of the Department, Government finances, foreign commerce, and other matters.

A selection of letters received by the Secretary of the Treasury is in appendix V of the compilation by Raphael P. Thian cited above, which is available at the National Archives and also on microfilm.

Registers of warrants issued by the Secretary of the Treasury are in several series. A register of civil warrants, Mar. 28, 1861-June 20, 1864 (vol. 104), concerns warrants for payment of salaries to the President, heads of the executive departments, Treasury Department and other Government officials, and other expenses of the departments, Congress, and the judiciary; payments to express, railroad, telegraph, and utility companies; newspaper advertising; rent of Government buildings; refunds on import duties; interest on loans and the public debt; and payment of Treasury notes. A register of war warrants, Apr. 14, 1862-Nov. 7, 1863 (vol. 63), concerns warrants for payment of salaries of Army officers, soldiers, and physicians; for subsistence, medical, and ordnance stores and supplies; for hospital expenses; for construction of river and coastal defenses; for bounties for soldiers; and for contingent expenses of the War Department. A register of Navy warrants, Mar. 26, 1861-Mar. 30, 1865 (1 vol.), concerns warrants for payment of salaries of navy and marine officers, seamen, and civilian employees of navy yards; for payment of prize money to crews that had captured enemy ships; for construction, alteration, purchase, and leasing of ships; and for purchase or manufacture of ordnance, provisions, fuel, and clothing. A register of miscellaneous warrants, Mar. 29, 1861-Apr. 6, 1864 (vol. 103), concerns warrants issued to cover donations made to the Government by churches and individual citizens and public funds received by collectors of customs, postmasters, depositaries, the Treasurer, Assistant Treasurers, superintendents of mints, disbursing clerks, district court officials, war taxes received by States, payments on the Erlanger loan received by European purchasing agents of the War Department, funds realized from the sale of sequestered alien-enemy property, subscriptions to Government loans, temporary gold loans from banks, and receipts from Treasury notes that were deposited with the Treasurer and Assistant Treasurers; and counterwarrants issued to Army and Navy officers permitting them to adjust their accounts. A compiled record of donations and loans made to the Confederate Government includes lists of donations by churches and by private individuals and a list of churches, theological seminaries, and other institutions that subscribed to the Confederate loans.

A few other small files relate to Confederate Government finances. Copies of estimates of appropriations submitted to Congress, Jan. 1863-Feb. 1865 (1/2 in.), concern the legislative and executive appropriations and some others. Some miscellaneous records of Treasury Department disbursing officers, Apr. 1861-Jan. 1865 (3 in.), include accounts, statements, correspondence, lists, and other papers. Accounts of the Department of Justice disbursing clerk with supporting vouchers and other papers, Sept. 1861-Oct. 1864 (1/2 in.), include accounts of Robert Josselyn, Secretary of Arizona Territory. Records relating to the expenses of district courts, May 1861-Dec. 1864 (2 in.), contain marshals' accounts and returns of sales of sequestered alien-enemy property for judicial districts in Alabama, Florida, Georgia, Mississippi, North Carolina, South Carolina, Tennessee, and Virginia. Statements of accounts of State Department commissioners and agents in foreign countries, Oct. 1861-Mar. 1865

(1 in.), contain information regarding salaries and other expenses. Miscellaneous records relating to War Department disbursements and the procurement of supplies, Apr. 1861-Mar. 1865 (2 in.), consist of accounts, payrolls, reports, correspondence, vouchers, contracts, First Auditor's reports, and statements and vouchers for supplies purchased by the armory at Tallassee, Ala., from Barnett, Micon and Co., among other papers.

Accounts and other records of the military telegraph lines, 1862-64 (1 in.), include accounts for salary payments to employees (Nov. 1863 and Mar. 1864), showing names of employees, their stations, and amounts paid to them; vouchers for payments made to the Southern Telegraph Co. for materials furnished to telegraph offices and lines, showing kinds of materials supplied and their cost; a few receipts; statements of accounts for the quarters ending Sept. 30 and Dec. 31, 1864, showing expenditures for salaries and other purposes; and a report by William S. Morris on the operations of the military telegraph lines, Apr. 1, 1863. Other records relating to the lines are described in chapter IX of this Guide.

Other records in this record group relate to Confederate activities in Europe and elsewhere. Records relating to Confederate agents in Europe and the West Indies, June 1863-Jan. 1865 (2 in.), include correspondence between the agents and the Secretaries of Treasury, War, and State and others concerning the Union blockade of the Confederate coast, shipment of cotton to Europe, negotiation of the Erlanger loan, sale of bonds, construction of ships, and payment of the agents; other documents include contracts, proposals for loans, loan agreements, agents' accounts, and loan accounts. Records relating to the construction of Confederate ships in Europe, 1862-65 (1 1/2 in.), include correspondence, accounts, agreements, warrants, vouchers, and reports. Records relating to the Erlanger loan, Jan. 1863-Oct. 1864 (1 in.), consist of correspondence received by the Secretary of the Treasury from Confederate agents in Europe and Émile Erlanger and Co., loan contracts and agreements, statements of payments on loans, accounts, reports on purchase of bonds, and memoranda of bonds on hand.

Related files of the U.S. Treasury Department concern its attempts to locate and obtain Confederate property in Europe and Nassau, funds paid to Paul Armanto build a warship for the Confederate Navy, and the sale of the C.S.S. Georgian.

Records in Other Custody. --A letters-sent book, Nov. 8, 1862-Feb. 15, 1864, is in the Auburn Public Library, Auburn, Maine. Press copies of letters sent, Sept. 17-Nov. 28, 1864, and Jan. 23-Apr. 2, 1865 (2 vols.), in the Confederate Museum include letters sent by the Assistant Secretary and the chief clerk. These evidently continue the series of letters sent described under Record Group 109 and are similar in content. Other correspondents found in these books include Fraser, Trenholm & Co. (depositary in Liverpool), the Treasury agent for the Trans-Mississippi West, and Colin J. McRae (depositary in Paris). Incoming and outgoing correspondence of the Secretary of the Treasury and other Treasury officials, Dec. 2, 1861-Feb. 21, 1865 (1/4 in.), is in the Confederate records collection in the Manuscript Division of the Library of Congress.

Most of Christopher G. Memminger's wartime papers were destroyed when his library in Columbia, S.C., burned in 1865. His papers in the Southern Historical Collection in the University of North Carolina Library include reports to Congress, some correspondence, his resignation of June 15, 1864, and the President's acceptance of his resignation on June 21. The entire collection is available on microfilm. Correspondence of C. G. Memminger, 1861-78 (17 items), in Duke University Library concerns official business, applications for office, and the salary of Thompson Allan, Commissioner of Taxes. Letters sent by Memminger are in the Louisiana State Museum collections. The papers of George A. Trenholm, Aug. 13, 1864-Apr. 27, 1865 (parts of 2 vols.), in the Manuscript Division of the Library of Congress include original incoming letters and press copies and drafts of outgoing letters, statements of drafts drawn on Fraser, Trenholm & Co., accounts and statements of cotton shipped from the Confederacy, and copies of communications from the Second Auditor to the Comptroller reporting the names of quartermaster officers and agents who had failed to render accounts. The George A. Trenholm papers, 1864-1923 (77 items), in the South Caroliniana Library of the University of South Carolina include correspondence of the war period.

OFFICE OF THE TREASURER

The duties of the Treasurer were to receive and keep the moneys of the Confederacy, to disburse them upon warrants drawn by the Secretary of the Treasury, to receipt for moneys paid out, and to render his accounts to the Comptroller. The Treasurer transmitted Treasury notes, bonds, and specie to Assistant Treasurers and depositaries and received funds from them. Before the establishment of the Treasury Note Bureau the Treasurer's Office was concerned with preparing, signing, and numbering Treasury notes. Another task connected with Treasury notes was the verification of schedules of canceled notes. William D. Nutt served as chief clerk until Jan. 1865 when he was succeeded by John Ott. A teller exchanged bonds for Treasury notes, received money, and paid checks on the Treasury.

Successive Treasurers:
　　　Edward C. Elmore, Mar. 6, 1861.
　　　John N. Hendren, Jan. 9, 1865.
　　　Micajah H. Clark (acting), May 4, 1865.

Record Group 109. --Letters received by the Treasurer, Feb. 1861-Dec. 1862 (2 in.), are from the Secretary of the Treasury, Treasury Department and other Government officials, Army officers, banks, Assistant Treasurers, collectors of the customs, and private citizens. The letters concern requests for funds, removal of deposits, counterfeiting, payment of interest, procurement of coin, sterling, and gold, issue of bonds and certificates of stock, personnel matters, transmittal of checks, notices of deposit, receipts for Treasury drafts, and certificates of deposit. A register of letters received, Jan. 9, 1861-Mar. 22, 1865 (ch. X, vol. 158, p. 259-348), shows name and address of the writer, date, and subject matter. The letters for 1863-65 for which there are entries have not been found. Other letters to the Treasurer of those years are in the letters received file of the Secretary of the Treasury. There are letters received by the Treasurer, Mar. 16-Nov. 14, 1861 (ch. X, vol. 178). A register of letters received by the Treasurer, Apr. 1861-Sept. 1864 (ch. X, vol. 179), shows date, name of writer, subject of letter, and date of reply.

Other records appear to be incomplete series. A record of warrants drawn on the Treasurer for Jan. 20-July 3, 1862, and Jan. 1-Mar. 31, 1864 (ch. X, vols. 221 and 222), shows warrant number. purpose, and amount. A record of balances in the hands of depositaries, Sept. 1861-Jan. 1863 (ch. X, vol. 180), shows date, name of the depositary or fund, place, and amount held. A disbursing journal, Oct. 1861-July 1862 (ch. X, vol. 177), contains a record of expenditures made in Richmond to Army officers and departmental disbursing clerks. There are stubs of War Department warrants for Jan.-Oct. 1862 (ch. X, vols. 223 and 224) and stubs of Navy warrants for Aug. 1861-Jan. 1865 (ch. X, vol. 247).

Record Group 365. --Miscellaneous records of the Treasurer's Office, June 5, 1861-Mar. 8, 1865 (1 in.), include correspondence, telegrams, reports, memoranda, vouchers, warrants, schedules of coin and bullion at mints and ports in 1861-62, statements of interest paid on the public debt, and copies of forms. A journal of receipts and expenditures, Oct. 1, 1862-June 30, 1863 (vol. 60), shows source of the receipts, date of receipt, name of the person who paid in the money, and amount, date, and number of warrant under which the money was paid out. A group of miscellaneous receipts for Jan. 1863-Dec. 1864 (1 in.), are for interest payments on interest-bearing Treasury notes and for office rent and supplies, canceled bonds, and money deposited by tax collectors.

Also in this record group are registers of certificates of stock issued under the loans of Feb. 28, May 16, and Aug. 19, 1861, Apr. 12, 1862, Feb. 20 and Mar. 23, 1863, and Feb. 17, 1864. They show date of issue, name of the purchaser, number and denominations of stock required, total value, and date interest began. Alphabetical name indexes are in separate volumes.

A register of call certificates and bonds issued, June 1863-Jan. 1865 (1 vol.), concerns 4- and 5-percent call certificates issued under acts of Mar. 23, 1863, and Feb. 17, 1864, 4- and 6-percent bonds under an act of Feb. 17, 1864, 6-percent bonds under an act of Nov. 28, 1864, and 6-percent nontaxable certificates, and shows date of issue, name of person or corporation to whom issued, and amount. A stub book for interest payments on Confederate loans, May 2-Sept. 24, 1864 (1 vol.), concerns payments on the loans of Aug. 19, 1861, and Feb. 20 and Mar. 23, 1863. It shows name of the payee, date and amount of payment, date of the loan, and date interest was due. Included also is a record of balances of new currency credited to Army and War Department disbursing officers.

Records in Other Custody. --A letters-sent book, Nov. 5, 1862-Feb. 15, 1864 (1 vol.), in the Confederate Museum contains fair copies of outgoing communications. They are to the Secretary of the Treasury, Treasury and other Government officials, collectors of customs, depositaries, Army officers acting as disbursing officers, bank officials, and others concerning appointments, administrative matters, warrants, and customs receipts. The same repository has check stubs for Feb. 17, 1862-Jan. 20, 1863, showing the name of the payee and the purpose for which paid. Other check stubs, Feb. 19, 1864-Jan. 18, 1865, are in Emory University Library. A few letters and receipts of officials who handled funds, 1863-64, are in the Ryder Collection of Confederate Archives in Tufts College Library. Receipts for the disbursement of the last specie funds of the Confederacy, May 3-4, 1865 (22 items), are with the Micajah H. Clark papers in the Manuscript Division of the Library of Congress.

OFFICE OF THE COMPTROLLER

The act of Feb. 21, 1861, establishing the Treasury Department provided: "That it shall be the duty of the Comptroller to superintend the adjustment and preservation of the public accounts; to examine all accounts
settled by the Auditor, and certify the balances arising thereon to the Register; to countersign all warrants drawn by the Secretary of the Treasury
which shall be authorized by law; to report to the Secretary the official
forms of all papers to be issued in the different offices for collecting the
public revenue, and the manner and form of keeping and stating the accounts of the several persons employed therein. He shall, moreover,
provide for the regular and punctual payment of all moneys which may be
collected, and shall direct prosecutions for all delinquencies of officers of
the revenue, and for debts that are or shall be due to the Confederate
States."

In the Confederate Government the Comptroller performed duties
that in the U.S. Treasury Department were divided among the First and
Second Comptroller, the Solicitor of the Treasury, and the Commissioner
of Customs. He revised and settled auditors' accounts; attended to the
correspondence, returns, and estimates of collectors of customs including
those relating to lighthouses; prepared requisitions for funds for collectors,
lighthouses, and war tax collectors; examined requisitions and warrants
of the departments to determine their legality and recorded them in requisition and warrant books; preserved the bonds of military and civilian disbursing officers; examined and decided questions of laws and supervised
suits against defaulters; and received and preserved contracts executed by
Government departments. The Comptroller's office also acquired the
functions of examining and recording claims on behalf of deceased soldiers,
registering accounts of deceased soldiers, counting canceled Treasury
notes and burning them, and calculating interest on bonds. The Comptroller also approved applications for reissue of certificates, warrants, and
registered bonds.

Lewis Cruger served as Comptroller throughout the war.

Record Group 109. --Correspondence and other papers of the Comptroller for 1861 and 1863-65 (3/4 in.) consist chiefly of letters from the
Secretary, other Treasury Department officials, and other Government
officials concerning the execution of contracts, official bonds, personnel
matters, the rent of Government buildings, and check forgeries; opinions
of the Attorney General; drafts of letters sent and of reports; and regulations. There is also a register of money received and counted for 1863-65
(ch. X, vol. 123).

Record Group 365. --In the Treasury Department Collection of Con-
ederate Records are incomplete correspondence files of the Comptroller.
Fair copies of letters and circulars sent, Mar. 23-Dec. 16, 1861 (vol. 121A),
are mainly to collectors of customs, other customs service officers, the
Secretary of the Treasury and other Treasury Department officials, the
heads and other officials of other executive departments, superintendents
of mints, Assistant Treasurers, railroad presidents, and bank officials.
The letters concern operations of the Comptroller's Office, the customs
service, lighthouses, marine hospitals, and mints; disposition of revenue
cutters; execution, receipt, and approval of fidelity bonds; appointments
and other personnel actions; provision of funds for the collectors of customs
and the examination of their accounts; and filing of contracts by Government

officials. Other records of collectors of customs are described below in this chapter as records of filed offices.

Files of incoming letters of the Comptroller are also incomplete. There are letters received from Cabinet officers, Jan. 10, 1862-June 11, 1863 (1 vol.), and from collectors of customs, May 19-Oct. 14, 1863 (1/4 in.).

A small file of miscellaneous records, Mar. 31, 1861-Mar. 31, 1865 (2 in.), includes letters received, copies and drafts of letters sent, reports, memoranda, copies of laws, lists and timetables of employees, warrants, claim papers, registers of warrants and requisitions, and other documents.

Other series of records also appear to be incomplete. There is a register of claims made on behalf of deceased soldiers by their next of kin or attorneys for pay, clothing, bounties, and horses, Mar. 1864-Mar. 1865 (vol. 124D). The register shows the soldier's name, rank, company, and regiment; claimant's name and address; date and nature of the claim, and amount awarded. A similar register is described as a part of the records of the Second Auditor's Office. The register in the Comptroller's records is labeled as a "continuation," indicating that there were other registers that are now missing. Applications for the reissue of certificates, warrants, drafts, and registered bonds that were lost, destroyed, or stolen, 1863-65 (1 1/2 in.), consist of affidavits regarding the circumstances of the loss, the official notice of the original issue, and a bond of indemnity to bind the person to return the lost document if recovered. Lists of depositaries (3 items) give the name of the depositary and his location.

There are penalty bonds and related records concerning officers. Penalty bonds of civil officers, Feb. 1861-Oct. 1864 (6 in.), show the names and signatures of the principal and his sureties and the date and amount of the bond. The bonds are sometimes accompanied by oaths of office of the principals and certifications by local judges. The bonds are for Assistant Treasurers, depositaries, collectors of the war tax, Produce Loan agents, collectors of customs and other officers of the customs service, employees of the Patent Office, and disbursing officers of the executive departments. Penalty bonds of Army and Navy officers, June 1861-Feb. 1865 (3 1/2 ft.), give similar information. These bonds are for quartermasters, commissaries, military storekeepers, contractors for military supplies, civilian agents of the War Department, and Army and Navy paymasters. A register of bonded officials of the executive departments, Feb. 1861-Nov. 1864 (vol. 66), shows the name of the principal, his location, name of his office, names of sureties and their places of residence, and date and amount of the bond. The register includes depositaries, collectors of customs and other customs service officers, keepers of marine hospitals, Produce Loan agents, collectors of taxes, and disbursing clerks of the executive departments. A record of bonded officers of the War and Navy Departments, June 1861-Feb. 1865 (vol. 65), gives similar information.

Civil, military, and naval contracts, Mar. 1861-Nov. 1864 (4 in.), show the name of the contractor and the officer who negotiated the contract, the date, a description of the goods or services to be furnished or manufactured, the amount of the compensation, and sometimes specifications. These contracts were negotiated by the Quartermaster General, the Commissary General of Subsistence, the Surgeon General, the Secretaries of the Navy and the Treasury, the Chief Medical Purveyor, quartermasters, commissaries, medical purveyors, and civilians employed by the War and

Navy Departments. Some bonds are filed with the contracts. A register
of civil, military, and naval contracts, Mar. 1861-Nov. 1864 (vol.
68), gives the name and residence of the contractor, a description of the material or service furnished, and the date of the contract and the bond, if one
was required.

Fiscal reports, correspondence, and other records relating to the
customs service, Mar. 1861-Mar. 1865 (8 ft.), include accounts of receipts
and disbursements, emolument returns, statements of moneys received
and deposited, abstracts of duties received on goods imported, abstracts
of moneys received for lighthouses, and accounts of warehouse bonds taken.
Other returns include estimates of funds required to defray expenses of
collecting the revenue, requisitions for funds to pay expenses of collecting
the revenue, lists of persons employed, payrolls, registers of bonds, ship
crew lists, inventories of customhouse property, transcripts of revenue
cutter logbooks, registers of merchandise imported, receipts for disbursements, receipts for military and naval expenses, warrants covering the
payment of moneys into the Treasury, and First Auditor's reports on collectors' accounts. The fiscal reports concern lighthouses and marine
hospitals in addition to customhouses. Besides correspondence between
collectors and Treasury Department officials, there is some personal
correspondence of collectors and other customs employees. Some earlier
records relating to the U.S. Customs Service are included.

Collectors of customs' weekly reports of export duty collected on
cotton, Dec. 1861-Feb. 1865 (6 in.), show the date, entry number, the name
of the exporter, name and destination of the vessel, quantity of cotton
exported, and amount of the duty. They are from the customs districts of
Apalachicola, Charleston, Eagle Pass, Galveston, Georgetown, Mobile,
New Orleans, Sabine, St. Marks, Saluria, and Savannah. The file includes
some collectors' transmittal letters and certificates covering deposits
made by them.

Records in Other Custody.--Letters received by the Comptroller
from collectors of customs and other customs service officers, Apr. 15,
1861-Jan. 10, 1862 (1 1/2 in.), are in the Manuscript Division of the Library of Congress. The letters concern bonds and oaths of allegiance,
accounts, estimates of funds required, and the transmission of accounts
and statements. Collectors of customs' estimates of funds required and
Comptroller's requests for funds, Mar. 8-Aug. 6, 1861 (1 vol.), in the
same repository, cover funds required for customhouses, lighthouses,
marine hospitals, inspection of steamboats, and operations of revenue cutters. This volume also includes other documents, such as letters from
collectors, lists of employees, payrolls, and receipts.

OFFICE OF THE REGISTER

The act of Feb. 21, 1861, establishing the Treasury Department provided for a Register who was to keep accounts of the receipts and expenditures of the public money and of debts of the Confederate States, to preserve accounts received from the Comptroller, to record all warrants for
the receipt or payment of moneys at the Treasury, and to transmit to the
Secretary of the Treasury copies of the certificates of balances of accounts
adjusted as herein directed. Employees of the Register's Office signed
Treasury notes and coupon bonds, prepared and signed certificates for the
interest on Government loans, and prepared stock, call, and cotton

certificates. The Office also received accounts from receivers of sequestered alien-enemy property and customs collectors' returns of the export
trade of the Confederate States. The administration of the produce loan
and the printing and distributing of Treasury notes, originally the responsibility of the Register, were assigned to separate bureaus in 1863 and 1864.

Acts of Congress authorized loans payable in specie and produce at
different rates of interest and directed the Secretary of the Treasury to
issue bonds or certificates of stock to subscribers. On Mar. 18, 1861, the
Secretary of the Treasury appointed boards of commissioners in the States
who opened subscription books at the cities where their offices were located
and named agents to open subscription books at interior points. The boards
of commissioners appointed on that date included:

> William Knox, John Whiting, and Joel Riggs at Montgomery, Ala.
> Henry Hyer, A. E. Maxwell, and Richard L. Campbell at
> Pensacola, Fla.
> Andrew Denham, William Bailey, and John Beard at Tallahas-
> see, Fla.
> Ebenezer Starnes and Joseph Milligan at Augusta, Ga.
> William B. Johnston at Macon, Ga.
> Samuel Smith, James D. Denegre, John J. Nobel, and Edmond
> J. Forstall at New Orleans, La.
> Richard Griffith, M. L. Haynes, E. R. Burt, and James D.
> Stewart at Jackson, Miss.
> Edward Frost, Charles M. Furman, and George A. Trenholm
> at Charleston, S. C.
> E. B. Nichols, James Sorley, and A. W. Spaight at Galveston,
> Tex.

Loan commissioners who were soon appointed for the other States
included the following:

> William H. MacFarland, James Lyons, Wyndham Robertson,
> John Rutherford, and Thomas W. McCance at Richmond,
> Va.
> John Porterfield, William W. Berry, and Hugh Douglas at
> Nashville, Tenn.
> P. K. Dickinson, William A. Wright, and A. G. Parsley at
> Wilmington, N. C.

The efforts of the commissioners were supported by banks, and by
Oct. 1861 the $15 million authorized on Feb. 28, 1861, was fully subscribed.

The Treasury Department also exchanged bonds and stock for Treasury notes (paper currency) in order to reduce the quantity of notes in circ-
ulation. Under an act of Feb. 20, 1863, more than $163 million in Treas-
ury notes were funded in 8-percent and 7-percent coupon bonds and 8-per-
cent and 7-percent stock. Under the loan provisions of an act of Mar. 23,
1863, more than $20 million in Treasury notes were funded in 6-percent
and 4-percent coupon bonds and 6-percent stock. Under an act of Feb. 17,
1864, noninterest-bearing Treasury notes were funded in 20-year 4-percent
bonds, 30-year 6-percent nontaxable bonds were sold in an effort to raise
$500 million, nontaxable certificates of indebtedness were issued to con-
tractors who supplied the Government, and 20-year 6-percent bonds and
4-percent coupon bonds and stock were issued. An act of June 13, 1864,
permitted holders of registered bonds issued under the produce loan act of
May 16, 1861, to exchange them for coupon bonds, and an act of Feb. 23,
1865, permitted a similar exchange to holders of registered bonds of the

loan of Feb. 28, 1861. The Treasury Department regularly made interest payments that came due on bonds.

Successive Registers of the Treasury:

Alexander B. Clitherall, Mar. 16, 1861.

Robert Tyler, Aug. 1861.

C. J. Affleck and B. M. Douglas, Confederate Bonds and Certificates; a Listing with a Description of the Confederate States of America Bonds and Certificates, Showing the Degree of Rarity and Price (Winchester, Va., and Washington, D.C., 1960); Grover C. and Clarence J. Criswell, Confederate and Southern State Bonds; a Descriptive Listing, Including Rarity (St. Petersburg Beach, Fla., 1961).

Record Group 109.--Letters-sent books of the Register of the Treasury, Mar. 18, 1861-Apr. 1, 1865 (ch. X, vols. 116 and 118-120), contain fair copies, except volume 120 which contains press copies. The letters are addressed to loan commissioners and agents, depositaries, Assistant Treasurers, bank officials, the Secretary of the Treasury, and the Assistant Secretary of the Treasury, the Treasury Agent at Marshall, Tex., the Chief of the Treasury Note Bureau at Columbia, S. C., collectors of customs, Members of Congress, printing establishments, the chief clerk of the Treasury Department, district court clerks, receivers of sequestered property, and others. The letters concern appointments, subscriptions to loans, deposits of funds, certificates of stock and coupon bonds, registered bonds, Treasury notes, payment of interest on loans, administrative matters, advances to depositaries, transmission of returns and accounts, redemption of notes, and other matters.

A number of journals relate to the Confederate Government loans. They show the ledger folio number, identify the loan by the act of Congress authorizing it, give names of subscribers to whom certificates were issued, date of the commencement of interest, voucher and certificate numbers, the number of certificates issued, amount of the certificates, and amount of each credit or loan. They include journals of transferable stock and coupon bonds, loan of Feb. 28, 1861, 1861-65 (ch. X, vols. 55 and 57); a journal of transferable stock, loan of May 16, 1861, 1861-65 (ch. X, vol. 63); a journal of coupon bonds, loan of Aug. 19, 1861, 1861-63 (ch. X, vols. 64 and 71); a journal of 8-percent registered stock, loan of Apr. 12, 1862, 1863-65 (ch. X, vol. 73); a journal of loans of Feb. 20, Mar. 23, and Apr. 30, 1863, 1863-64 (ch. X, vol. 83); a journal of 7-percent transferable stock, loan of Feb. 20, 1863, 1863-65 (ch. X, vol. 79); a journal of 8-percent transferable stock, loan of Feb. 20, 1863, 1863-65 (ch. X, vol. 75); a journal of 6-percent transferable stock, loan of Mar. 23, 1863, 1863-65 (ch. X, vol. 84); a journal of 4-percent transferable stock, loan of Feb. 17, 1864, 1864-65 (ch. X, vol. 88); a journal of the loan of Feb. 17, 1864, 1864-65 (ch. X, vol. 86); and an unidentified journal of 1864-65 (ch. X, vol. 86).

Loan ledgers show names of persons to whom stock or bonds were issued or transferred, date, and amount. They include a ledger of the loan of Aug. 19, 1861, 1862-65 (ch. X, vols. 65, 67-70, and 72); ledger of coupon bonds, loan of Feb. 28, 1861, 1861-62 (ch. X, vol. 58); ledger of transferable stock, 1861 (ch. X, vol. 56); ledger of 8-percent registered stock, loan of Apr. 12, 1862, 1863 (ch. X, vol. 74); ledger of 7-percent transferable stock, loan of Feb. 20, 1863, 1863-65 (ch. X, vols. 80-82);

ledger of 8-percent transferable stock, loan of Feb. 20, 1863, 1863-65 (ch. X, vols. 76-78); ledger of 6-percent transferable stock, loan of Mar. 23, 1863, 1863-65 (ch. X, vol. 85); and ledgers for the loan of Feb. 17, 1864, 1864-65 (ch. X, vols. 87 and 89-97).

Other records also relate to loans. Registers of subscriptions to the loan of Feb. 28, 1861, n.d. (ch. X, vols. 125-151 and 152-154), show place of subscription, subscribers' names, amounts subscribed for coupon bonds or transferable bonds, and notations on payment. A record of coupon bonds issued in exchange for registered stock, loan of May 16, 1861, Aug. 29, 1864-Feb. 28, 1865 (ch. X, vol. 62), shows the name of person and amount of bonds. A record of dividend-of-interest on loans, 1861-64 (ch. X, vols. 59-61), shows the name of the creditor (or subscriber), amount of principal, rate of interest, date interest began, and amount of interest. These books cover interest payments made at Charleston, Jackson, Montgomery, Mobile, New Orleans, Raleigh, Richmond, Savannah, and Wilmington. A register of unclaimed dividends under loans of 1861, 1861 (ch. X, vol. 117), shows the place, name of person, amount of certificates, date due, date of loan, total amount of interest, and acknowledgement of receipt of interest. Other records include a record of stock maturing Jan. 1, 1864, n.d. (ch. X, vol. 121 1/2); stubs of certificates relating to unclaimed interest, Sept. 27, 1862-Apr. 1, 1865 (ch. X, vol. 117 1/2); stubs of certifications of interest payments, Mar. 1, 1865 (ch. X, vol. 117 3/4); and lists of loan commissioners and agents, 1861 (ch. X, vol. 64, p. 21-31).

An alphabetical card index to subscribers to Confederate States loans, 1861-64 (16 ft.), compiled by the U.S. Adjutant General's Office, shows names of the subscribers, place of subscription, date and amount of subscription, and page reference to the volume in chapter X where the transaction was recorded. Subscribers included associations, business firms, churches, individuals, institutions, and life insurance companies. This index also identifies loan commissioners and depositaries. Other records of the Register's Office include accounts of receivers under the sequestration act, 1862-64 (ch. X, vol. 207), showing the receiver's name, his district, date, amount received and source of receipt, amount spent, and purpose of expenditure. A list of signers and numberers of 8-percent bonds issued under the act of Feb. 20, 1863, May 7-Oct. 23, 1863 (ch. X, vol. 267), shows the numbers of bonds signed.

Record Group 365. --Miscellaneous records, Sept. 1861-Oct. 1864 (1/2 in.), consist of depositaries' receipts for Confederate bonds, correspondence, vouchers for supplies and services bought, payrolls, and lists of employees. A list of warrants drawn on the Treasurer, July 1-Dec. 31, 1863 (1 vol.), shows appropriation title, warrant number, name of payee, and amount of warrant. Records of loan commissioners and reports of depositaries to the Register are described below in this chapter under records of States.

Records in Other Custody. --There are letters received by the Register, Mar. 20, 1861-June 18, 1862 (1 vol.), in the Confederate Museum collections. They are from the Secretary of the Treasury, Assistant Treasurers, collectors of customs, loan commissioners, Colin J. McRae, banks, insurance companies, depositaries, business firms, and individuals. They concern appointments of clerks, conversion of stock into bonds, execution of bonds, arrangements for raising the Government loan, redemption of notes, substitution of sureties, receipt of funds, and transmission of receipts, certificates of deposit, warrants, and blank registers.

A letters-sent press copy book, Nov. 26, 1863-June 1, 1864, in the Manuscript Division of the Library of Congress contains chiefly communications from the Register to depositaries, Assistant Treasurers, agents, and bank officers concerning transmission of stock, bonds, coupon bonds, call certificates, and schedules of interest payable on Government loans. Other letters to the heads of the executive departments acknowledge the receipt of certificates that an act of Jan. 30, 1864, had required to be submitted to obtain increases in the salaries of departmental employees. A record of warrants issued, Sept. 19, 1861-Jan. 18, 1862 (1 vol.), in the same repository shows warrant number, name of the individual to whom issued, purpose of expenditure, and amount. A record of warrants drawn, Mar. 29, 1861-Dec. 31, 1864 (1 vol.), in the collections of the Confederate Museum, is for miscellaneous, customs, War Department, and Navy expenditure. A record of interest payments on the loan of Aug. 19, 1861 (1 vol.), in the same repository shows subscribers' names, amounts of subscriptions, date of commencement of interest, payments of interest made in Jan.-Feb. 1865, and signatures of payees.

A list of bonds and stocks conveyed to Europe by James G. Gibbes of Columbia, S. C., Nov. 14, 1862, is in the South Caroliniana Library of the University of South Carolina.

OFFICE OF THE FIRST AUDITOR

The act of Feb. 21, 1861, establishing the Treasury Department provided for an Auditor to receive and examine public accounts, certify the balances, and transmit the accounts and accompanying vouchers and the certificates to the Comptroller for his decision. A Second Auditor was authorized in Mar. 1861 to audit accounts of the War Department, and the First Auditor audited accounts of the State, Treasury, Navy, Justice, and Post Office Departments. An act of May 16, 1861 (Prov. Cong. C.S.A. Stat. 113), prescribed the manner in which the Post Office Department accounts were to be audited. These accounts, unlike those of other departments, were finally adjusted by the First Auditor, who informed the Postmaster General about postmasters' delinquencies. The first Auditor retained the Post Office accounts and handled legal proceedings for collecting sums due the Department. The same act also directed him to "register, charge and countersign all warrants upon the treasury for receipts and payments by the Postmaster General," and to certify accounts of moneys paid pursuant to appropriations by postmasters. Under the provision of an act of Aug. 30, 1861 (Prov. Cong. C.S.A. Stat. 200), moneys collected by postmasters for U.S. postage were to be accounted for to the First Auditor. The moneys collected were to constitute a separate fund to pay for postal services rendered while the United States still controlled the postal system, and claims for such services were to be filed with the First Auditor. In Jan. 1864 the Office had a Customs Division, an Interest Division, a Navy Division, a Miscellaneous Division, a Canceling Division, and a registering clerk. In the same month a Third Auditor was appointed to settle Post Office Department accounts.

William W. Lester, appointed chief clerk on Apr. 19, 1861, was succeeded in Nov. 1862 by James W. Robertson, who continued until the end of the war. On May 21, 1861, Thomas Higham, Jr., was appointed chief clerk to aid the First Auditor in auditing accounts of the Post Office

Department.
  The appointment of Bolling Baker as First Auditor was confirmed on
Mar. 16, 1861, and he served throughout the war.

Reports of the First Auditor are in C. S. A. Post Office Depart-ment, Report of the Postmaster General, 1861-63 (Richmond, 1861-64).

  Record Group 28. --In the Records of the U. S. Post Office Department is a letters-sent book, Sept. 30, 1862-Apr. 7, 1863, containing fair
copies of outgoing letters signed by Bolling Baker and by James W.
Robertson as Acting Auditor. These letters are to postmasters, route
agents, contractors for carrying the mail, Members of Congress, State
legislators, railroad officials, Post Office Department employees, and
newspapers. They concern the settlement of accounts, drafts for funds,
payment for the services of postmasters before June 1, 1861, payments due
postmasters and mail messengers, transmission of certificates of service
and vouchers, salaries of Post Office employees, postage stamps on hand,
unpaid postage on dead letters, payments to newspapers, and other matters
connected with the settlement of Post Office Department accounts.
  Record Group 45. --Several records of the First Auditor are in the
Naval Records Collection of the Office of Naval Records and Library. A
register of letters received, Feb. 1862-July 1864 (1 vol.), shows the date
received, name of writer, vessel or station from which written, date of
the letter, and summary of contents. The entries in this register relate
to letters received from paymasters and assistant paymasters attached to
naval vessels and stations and from Navy and Marine Corps officers. A
register of allotments by Navy and Marine Corps officers, seamen, and
marines, June 1861-Nov. 1864 (1 vol.), shows the name and rank of officer
or man, name of paymaster registering the allotments, date of first payment, amount alloted each month, number of months, name of vessel,
where and to whom payable, and remarks on stopping, discharge, and
desertion. A register of allotments made by officers and seamen of the
Confederate States Navy, Aug. 1861-Oct. 1864 (1 vol. labeled "Auditor's
Book No. 2"), contains the same information as the register just described.
Copies of certifications of naval accounts sent to the Comptroller, May 15,
1861-Dec. 5, 1864 (1 vol. labeled "C. S. Auditor's Book 1861-2-3-4 Navy
Report Book"), certify accounts of Navy and Marine Corps officers and
paymasters and others and show the amount due them or by them to the
Confederate Government, the purposes of the expenditures, and the appropriation to be charged.
  Record Group 109. --A memorandum of moneys received from depositories, July 1, 1863-Mar. 27, 1865 (ch. X, part of vol. 181), shows the
name of person and place from which received, number of boxes received,
and the amount. A list of certificates issued by the First Auditor's
canceling commission, July 10, 1863-July 22, 1864 (ch. X, vol. 181, p. 336-
352), shows the date, name of official, location, and amount. Accounts of
Navy and Marine Corps officers, Mar. 1861-May 1862 (ch. X, vol. 46, p.
2-135), show the name of disbursing officer, amounts and kinds of credits,
and amounts of disbursements and the appropriations charged. A record
of the amounts of funded money received and turned over to the Canceling
Division, June-Nov. 1864 (ch. X, vol. 46, p. 139-147), also shows the
date and name of sender.
  Record Group 365. --Some miscellaneous records, July 1861-Mar.

1865 (3 in.), include incoming and outgoing correspondence, reports of
work done by divisions of the office, reports on the operations of the office
(Dec. 11, 1861, and Jan. 10 and Nov. 5, 1864), instructions to employees,
statements of accounts, reports on delinquent paymasters and disbursing
officers, employees' time reports, payrolls, lists of employees, and lists
of clerks in military organizations. Certifications of accounts, Mar. 30,
1861-Dec. 31, 1862 (vol. 64), contain copies of the First Auditor's certifications that were sent to the Comptroller. The accounts are those of
Government employees, newspapers, printing establishments, railroads,
and private persons. Records relating to the payments of expenses of
Congress, Mar. 1863-Jan. 1865 (3 in.), include warrants on the Treasurer;
an abstract of expenditures for pay and mileage of Members and Delegates,
May 1, 1863-June 14, 1864, with accompanying vouchers; and stubs for payments made to Members and employees of Congress and to others for
supplies and materials.

Miscellaneous records relating to Navy payments, Apr. 1862-May
1863 (1 1/2 in.), include an abstract of disbursements by Douglas F.
Forrest, assistant paymaster at Richmond, for payments under an appropriation for building 100 gunboats; vouchers for payments made by James
A. Semple, paymaster at Drewry's Bluff on the James River, to workmen,
seamen, petty officers, officers, and others for pay, hospital fund,
clothing, personal items, supplies, telegraphic messages, and equipment;
copies of letters of appointment of the Secretary of the Navy; copies of
orders issued by the Office of Orders and Detail; a few vouchers of D. C.
Seymour, paymaster at Savannah, for payments made, and a return by him
of men transferred from the Oconee; some paymasters' certificates of payments; and correspondence of Capt. Sidney Smith Lee, commandant at
Drewry's Bluff. Pay, receipt, transfer, and muster rolls of Confederate
naval personnel, Nov. 1862-Mar. 1865 (2 in.), are for the Firefly, Florida,
Georgia, Isondiga, Jackson, Oconee, Resolute, Sampson, Savannah, and
Spray and for Mobile Naval Station marines. The rolls are similar in
content to the rolls described under the Office of Orders and Detail in
chapter VIII of this Guide. With the rolls of the Florida are vouchers dated Aug. 1862 for expenditures for repairs, supplies, services, transportation, hospital and funeral fees, and equipment obtained in Nassau, N. P.,
and Cárdenas, Cuba. Payrolls of civilian employees at navy yards, Jan. -
June 1864 (1 in.), show the worker's name, his occupation, number of days
worked, amount of pay, signatures or marks of payees, and signatures of
witnesses, paymasters, and commanding officers. These were for workmen engaged in constructing naval vessels at McIntosh Bluff, Mobile, and
Selma and on the Tombigbee River.

Other muster rolls of naval personnel are in the Naval Records Collection of the Office of Naval Records and Library (Record Group 45), and payrolls of civilian personnel of navy yards are with the records of the Quartermaster General's Office in the War Department Collection of Confederate Records (Record Group 109).

Records in Other Custody. --Letters received by the First Auditor,
Mar. 21, 1861-Nov. 1, 1862 (3 in.), in the Manuscript Division of the Library of Congress include letters from collectors of customs and other
officials regarding the transmission and settlement of accounts and from
individuals recommending appointments.

OFFICE OF THE SECOND AUDITOR

An act of Mar. 15, 1861 (Prov. Cong. C.S.A. Stat. 66), authorized the appointment of a Second Auditor who was to audit accounts for the War Department. After examining these accounts and certifying the balances the Second Auditor was to transmit the accounts with vouchers and certificates to the Comptroller for his decision. The duty of auditing accounts and claims of States against the Confederate States for advances and expenditures made on behalf of the Confederacy in preparing for and waging war against the United States was assigned to the Second Auditor under the provisions of an act of Aug. 30, 1861 (Prov. Cong. C.S.A. Stat. 197). Claims for the arrears of pay filed on behalf of deceased soldiers were also examined by the Second Auditor. By the end of 1863 there had been received 42,433 claims for arrears of such pay, and 11,651 of these claims had been settled. Other claims audited were those of officers and soldiers for horses killed in battle and private claims for supplies, animals, and wagons furnished to or impressed by the Army.

In Mar. 1864 the 128 employees of the Second Auditor's Office were distributed among the following divisions: Bookkeepers; Claims; Quartermasters; Subsistence; Pay; Ordnance, Engineers, and Medical; and Claims of Deceased Soldiers. The chief clerk then was Robert Graeme.

Second Auditors:

> Walter H. S. Taylor, Mar. 27, 1861. (Resigned on Feb. 27, 1865.)
>
> George B. Hodge. (Confirmation denied by the Senate on Mar. 14, 1865.)

C.S.A. Treasury Department, Second Auditor's Office, Report of the Second Auditor of the Treasury of the Confederate States, to the Honorable Secretary of the Treasury, Exhibiting the Operations of His Office from Its Creation to the 31st of December, 1861, Inclusive, Its Present Condition, etc., etc., Made January 8th, 1862. (Richmond, 1862).

Record Group 109.--A register of letters received by the Pay Division, 1862-64 (ch. X, vol. 50), shows name, rank and organization of writer; date of letter and date of its receipt; subject of letter; and action taken. The letters concern pay of military personnel, bounty payments, and transmission of returns. Registers of requisitions for Army expenses, Feb. 1861-Mar. 1865 (ch. X, vols. 48 and 49), show date, number of requisition, date received, name of person submitting requisition, description of requisition, appropriation to which charged, and amount of money requisitioned. A register of payments to officers and soldiers, 1861-63 (ch. X, vol. 43), shows name, rank, organization, by whom paid, period of service, amount paid, date of settlement, number of settlement, voucher number, and remarks. A record of payments to discharged soldiers, 1862-63 (ch. X, vol. 45), shows soldier's name and regiment, by whom paid, date of settlement, number of settlement, and voucher number. An undated record of payments to soldiers (ch. X, vol. 38),shows voucher number, soldier's name and State, number of certificate, by whom paid, and number of settlement. Payrolls of officers, 1861-63 (ch. X, vols. 40-42). show officer's name, rank, organization, by whom paid, period of service, amount paid, and voucher number. Abstracts of drafts, transfers, and acknowledgments of moneys disbursed to and received from officers, Oct. 1862-Mar. 1864 (ch. X, vol. 36), show date of draft, by whom drawn, amount, account drawn on, when accounted for, on whom drawn or by whom received, date paid, and by whom paid. A record of payments to troop units, 1861-64 (ch. X, vols. 37 and 44), shows name of organization, month for which paid, and by whom paid. A register of company and bounty rolls received for payment, 1861-62 (ch. X, vol. 1), shows captain's name, organization, period covered, name of paymaster, and voucher number. A register of accounts of Army disbursing officers, 1861-65 (ch. X, vols. 35 and 39), shows name and rank of officer, his station, period for which disbursements were made, account, date received, dates of report to and return by the Comptroller, amount of balance, settlement number, and remarks. Miscellaneous records, 1861-65 (1/4 in.), consist of outgoing letters, a printed letter of instruction, drafts of statutes, statements, memoranda, and blank forms. A record of accounts reported to and returned by the Comptroller, 1861-64 (ch. X, vol. 47), shows date reported, name and rank of person whose account was reported, description and amount of account, and date account was returned. A record of bonded quartermasters and commissaries, 1861-65 (ch. X, vol. 12), shows officer's name, rank, State from which appointed, date of bond, names of sureties, and amounts of penalty bonds. Returns of deceased officers and soldiers received from hospitals, regimental and company officers, and others, 1861-65 (ch. X, vols. 2-11, 1 ft. 9 in.), show name of deceased officer or soldier; his company and regiment; sometimes his birthplace; date, place, and sometimes cause of death; amount of money and other effects and in whose charge they were left; date return was received; certificate number; and remarks. A record of deceased soldiers' money effects turned over to quartermasters, 1862-65 (ch. X, vol. 21), shows date money was received, receipt number, soldier's name, rank and organization, and amount of money received.

Other records relate to claims. There are letters sent relating to claims filed on behalf of deceased soldiers, Oct. 9, 1862-Mar. 28, 1865 (ch. X, vols. 13-20, 1 ft. 3 in.). Registers of claims filed on behalf of deceased officers and soldiers, 1861-65 (ch. X, vols. 22-34, 1 ft. 3 in.), show soldier's or officer's name, rank, by whom the claim was presented, date claim was filed, place of birth and death of deceased, company and regiment, date claim was reported to the Comptroller and date returned by him, amount found due, and remarks. Registers of claims, Apr. 1863-Jan. 1865 (ch. X, vols. 51-53), show name of claimant, date claim was received, nature and amount of claim, and sometimes the notation "confirmed." These are claims by military personnel for horses killed in action or captured by the enemy, by States for money advanced to troops, and by others for providing transportation for troops and for supplies, equipment lost, Negroes escaped to the enemy, horses impressed, steamers sunk as obstructions to navigation, property seized by soldiers, and medical, legal, and other services.

The U.S. War Department abstracted information from some of the records described above on index record cards that were filed in the compiled military service records of Confederate soldiers and general and staff officers described in chapter XI of this Guide. Original letters received by the Second Auditor are among the compiled military service records.

Record Group 365. --Miscellaneous records, Jan. 1862-Feb. 1865
(2 in.), include reports to the Comptroller and the Secretary of the Treasury on disbursing officers and agents who had failed to render accounts,
payrolls, a list of clerks of the Second Auditor's Office, claim papers,
correspondence, muster roll of the reserve company composed of the staff
of the Second Auditor's Office (Sept. 30, 1864), and vouchers for salary
payments made by Maj. Thompson Harrison, chief paymaster for the District of Texas, New Mexico, and Arizona (Apr. -Sept. 1864). A register of
claims filed on behalf of deceased soldiers and others, Jan. 3-Nov. 14,
1862 (1 vol.), shows date; claim number; name of the soldier or claimant;
name of the soldier's attorney or administrator; soldier's rank, company,
and regiment; and nature and amount of the claim. The register covers
claims for soldier's pay, allowance for clothing, use or loss of horses and
equipment, food, and lodging; of physicians for services rendered at hospitals or posts and to soldiers; and by others for the hire of slaves and for
supplies and provisions.

Records in Other Custody. --A diary of William W. Cleary, a Ken-
tuckian who served as an accountant in the Claims Division of the Second
Auditor's Office in 1863, is in the Virginia Historical Society collections.

OFFICE OF THE THIRD AUDITOR

An increase in the business of the First Auditor's Office resulted in
an act of Jan. 8, 1864 (1 Cong. C. S. A. Stat. 173), authorizing the appointment of a Third Auditor who was to audit the Post Office Department accounts, including those of postmasters, contractors for regular mail routes
and special mail routes, route and express agents, and mail messengers
and local agents.

By Nov. 1864 the Third Auditor's Office was composed of the following divisions: Collecting, Pay, Examining, Error, Register, Bookkeeper's,
and U. S. Pay and Collecting. The chief clerk was A. Julian Moise, Jr.
There were also a warrant and draft clerk, route agent and special mail
clerk, and a letter book clerk.

J. W. M. Harris became Third Auditor on Jan. 21, 1864.

Record Group 365. --Miscellaneous records, June 1861-Nov. 1864
(1/2 in.), include reports, lists of employees, payrolls, employees' exemption certificates, and correspondence. Treasurer's warrants covering
moneys deposited by postmasters with depositaries, Apr. -Dec. 1864 (1/4
in.), show name and address of depositary, warrant number, amount deposited, and date. A journal of Post Office Department accounts, June
22, 1861-Mar. 30, 1865 (vol. 61C), shows date, names of depositaries,
names and locations of postmasters making deposits, dates and amounts
drawn by the Post Office Department on depositaries, warrant numbers,
and names of payees.

LIGHTHOUSE BUREAU

An act of Mar. 6, 1861 (Prov. Cong. C. S. A. Stat. 47), authorized
the organization of a Lighthouse Bureau under a captain or commander of
the Navy to be detailed by the President. The Bureau was to have charge
of all lighthouses, light vessels, buoys, and other aids to navigation and
matters connected with their administration, construction, repair, illumi-
nation, and inspection The seacoasts of the Confederacy were to be

divided into five lighthouse districts under the command of Navy lieutenants to be appointed by the President. The district inspectors were designated in April, and on May 20, 1861, Thomas E. Martin reported for duty as chief clerk.

The Bureau administered a lighthouse system that had been established by the United States and operated by its Lighthouse Board. By Apr. 1861 action by the States had already resulted in the seizure of lighthouses and lightships along the seacoasts from Virginia to Texas and the removal or destruction of lighting apparatus and supplies. Lightships and tenders were transferred to the Navy and Army for use in their operations. To maintain the lighthouses would have aided the blockading vessels of the U. S. Navy, therefore by July 1861 most lights appear to have been extinguished, and the district inspectors returned to the Navy. Thereafter the Bureau was engaged primarily in a caretaking operation. Equipment and supplies were removed from the exposed positions occupied by the lighthouses to interior storage points where they were more secure from seizure by enemy raiders. Keepers became caretakers, and some of them were forced to leave when U. S. forces occupied the coast and seized the lighthouses. The work of the Bureau steadily declined, and on Feb. 5, 1864, its Chief was transferred to the First Auditor's Office.

Successive Chiefs of the Bureau:

> Comdr. Raphael Semmes, Apr. 1861.
> Comdr. Ebenezer Farrand, Apr. 1861.
> Thomas E. Martin, Sept. 21, 1861.

U. S. Lighthouse Board, List of Light-Houses, Lighted Beacons, and Floating Lights, of the Atlantic, Gulf, and Pacific Coasts of the United States (Washington, 1861); George Weiss, The Lighthouse Service; Its History, Activities and Organization (Baltimore, 1926).

Record Group 45. --Records relating to lighthouses, 1861-64 (subject file KL, 1/4 in.), in the Naval Records Collection include correspondence of the Chief of the Lighthouse Bureau, superintendent of lights' accounts, estimates of expenses, abstracts of expenditures, vouchers, and a list of lighthouses in the District of Norfolk and Portsmouth, Va.

Record Group 365. --Correspondence, Apr. 12, 1861-Feb. 5, 1864, consisting of incoming and outgoing correspondence with the Secretary of the Treasury, other Treasury Department officials, superintendents of lights, lighthouse keepers, naval and military officers, and others. These letters concern such matters as the operation and maintenance of lighthouses, removal of equipment and property, compensation of caretakers, personnel matters, inventorying of lighthouse property, and adjustment of lighthouse superintendents' accounts. Records (10 in.) relating to lighthouses, 1861-65, include correspondence between the Chief of the Bureau and superintendents of lights, lighthouse keepers, Treasury Department officials, Army and Navy officers, and other persons relating to the maintenance of lighthouses and lightships, removal and concealment of lighthouse property, repairs, transfer of oil to the Navy and the Army, compensation of keepers, and other matters. Fiscal reports in this file include superintendents' abstracts of disbursements with vouchers, statements of accounts, returns of light money collected from vessels, accounts current, and estimates of funds required. Other documents include returns of stores received, consumed and on hand, and inventories of lighthouse property. A list of the

lighthouses for which records are available in this series is in National
Archives, Preliminary Inventory [No. 169] of the Treasury Department
Collection of Confederate Records.

PRODUCE LOAN OFFICE

An act of Congress of May 16, 1861 (Prov. Cong. C.S.A. Stat. 117),
authorized the Secretary of the Treasury to issue $50 million in 8-percent
bonds payable in specie, military stores, or the proceeds of the sale of
raw produce or manufactured articles. The amount of the loan was increased by an act of Aug. 19, 1861 (Prov. Cong. C.S.A. Stat. 177), to
$100 million. Subscriptions to the loan were obtained by having Members
of Congress and prominent citizens circulate lists among planters. To
direct the work of making collections and obtaining new subscriptions the
Secretary of the Treasury in 1861-62 appointed general agents in the States.
Subagents were appointed by the general agents, but only the latter reported direct to the Produce Loan Office in Richmond. Under the provisions
of an act of Apr. 21, 1862 (1 Cong. C.S.A. Stat. 47), authorizing the
exchange of bonds or stock for articles in kind, the subagents or special
agents provided for by that act also purchased cotton and tobacco.

In Jan. 1863 the general agents were as follows: Alabama: John Scott,
general agent for the State at Mobile; James A. Farley, agent for Montgomery County at Montgomery; J. J. Donegan, agent for northern Alabama
at Huntsville. Arkansas: David Block at Washington. Florida: Thomas J.
Perkins at Tallahassee, agent to collect subscriptions; James B. Gladney,
agent to purchase cotton. Georgia: Phinizy & Clayton at Augusta. Mississippi and eastern Louisiana: James D. B. De Bow at Jackson, and after
May 1863 at Columbus. North Carolina: A. J. DeRosset at Wilmington,
agent to collect subscriptions; L. S. Williams at Charlotte, agent to purchase cotton. South Carolina: Isaac S. K. Bennett at Charleston. Texas:
Henry Sampson at Houston, agent to collect subscriptions. Virginia: J. A.
Lancaster & Son at Richmond. Western Louisiana and eastern Texas:
Andrew W. McKee at Alexandria.

In Aug. 1864 J. W. Clapp was appointed general agent at Columbus,
Miss., superseding De Bow. In Feb. 1863 cotton purchases in eastern
Texas were placed under the supervision of Henry Sampson. In Aug. 1864
James T. Belknap replaced McKee at Alexandria, La.

The large quantities of cotton that were obtained were stored in
buildings on plantations, in municipal warehouses, and at railheads. Some
was shipped abroad to pay the Confederacy's foreign debt and purchase
Army supplies. But much of it was captured by U.S. forces or burned by
Confederate authorities. Produce Loan agents also handled cotton acquired
under the tax in kind. Special agents were appointed to purchase and process tobacco of which a much smaller quantity was obtained. Allen S.
Gibbes served as Treasury agent for the export of cotton at Wilmington, N.
C. After the resignation of James D. B. De Bow as head of the Produce
Loan Office in Jan. 1862, the Office was placed under the supervision of
the Register of the Treasury. On Jan. 21, 1862, Archibald Roane was
designated the acting chief clerk and instructed to prepare lists of subscriptions for each general agency. An act of May 1, 1863 (1 Cong. C.S.A.
Stat. 135), placed the Office under the chief clerk, and the Register was
informed that he was relieved of responsibility for the Office.

Successive Chiefs of the Office:
James D. B. De Bow, Aug. 1861.
Robert Tyler, Jan. 3, 1862.
Archibald Roane, May 1, 1863.

C. S. A. Produce Loan Office, Report (Richmond, 1864). An alphabetical list of persons who sold cotton to the Confederate States in the States of Alabama, Arkansas, Florida, Georgia, Louisiana, Mississippi, and South Carolina is in S. Doc. 987, 62 Cong., 3 sess., Serial 6348, p. 6-260 (Washington, 1913). Documents relating to the sale of cotton to the Confederate Government are among the records of the Civil War Special Agencies of the Treasury Department (Record Group 366). Records of Gazaway B. Lamar, cotton trader, blockade-runner, president of the Bank Conventions of the Confederate States, and president of the Bank of Commerce of Savannah, are also in that record group (see Guide to Federal Archives Relating to the Civil War, p. 238). See also Edwin B. Coddington, "The Activities and Attitudes of a Confederate Business Man: Gazaway B. Lamar," Journal of Southern History, 9:3-36 (Feb. 1943).

Record Group 365. --Miscellaneous records, Jan. 1862-Jan. 1865 (1 in.), consist of incoming and outgoing correspondence with Treasury Department and other Government officials, Produce Loan agents, cotton agents, subscribers to loans, and private individuals regarding accounts, reports, personnel matters, bonds of Produce Loan agents, instructions, and other matters; a list of clerks in the Office and a report by the Chief of the Office, Oct. 30, 1864; statements of sales of bonds; accounts of the Treasury cotton agent at Wilmington; receipts for the payment of commissions; oaths of office; a statement of subscriptions to the produce loan, Mar. 15, 1862; estimates of expenses; lists of bids for cotton bonds; a list of subscribers to the produce loan; and other papers.

Records in Other Custody. --An extensive collection of James D. B. De Bow's papers in Duke University Library includes correspondence with the Secretary of the Treasury. (After serving as the head of the Produce Loan Office in Richmond, De Bow became its agent in Mississippi and Louisiana.)

OFFICE OF THE COMMISSIONER OF TAXES

An act of Congress of Aug. 19, 1861 (Prov. Cong. C. S. A. Stat. 1/7), authorized the levying of a war tax for the redemption of Treasury notes and the support of the Government. A tax of $0.50 was to be levied on each $100 of value of real estate, slaves, merchandise, stocks, securities, money, and other property. Each State was to constitute a tax division under a chief collector who was to divide the State into collection districts and appoint collectors to assess all taxable property by Nov. 1, 1861. The tax collectors could appoint assessors. In Sept. 1861 the President appointed the following chief collectors: Joseph C. Bradley in Alabama, William H. Halliburton in Arkansas, E. E. Blackburn in Florida, Ebenezer Starnes in Georgia, Robert A. Lusher in Louisiana, John H. Handy in Mississippi, William K. Lane in North Carolina, William E. Martin in South Carolina, Isaac B. Williams in Tennessee, George J. Durham in Texas, and Henry T. Garnett in Virginia. Joseph D. Pope became the chief

collector in South Carolina after Martin declined the appointment.
Subsequent legislation increased the taxes. In Apr. 1863 taxes were
levied on agricultural products, on many occupations, trades, and businesses, and on income. In Feb. 1864 additional taxes were imposed on
gold and silver plate and jewelry, corporation shares, solvent credits,
paper currency, gold and silver coin and bullion, gold dust, real estate,
and Confederate bonds.

The enlargement of the tax structure necessitated a reorganization
of the tax-collecting organization. An act of May 1, 1863 (1 Cong. C.S.A.
Stat. 140), authorized the appointment of a Commissioner of Taxes in the
Treasury Department to have charge of the preparation and distribution of
instructions, regulations, and directions and of other matters connected
with the assessment and collection of the taxes. A system of State tax
collectors, district collectors, and assessors similar to that established
in 1861 was organized; some former chief collectors were reappointed.
Chief collectors confirmed by the Senate on May 20, 1864, included the
following: Abram Martin in Alabama, A. R. Greenwood in Arkansas,
Robert H. Gamble in Florida, E. G. Cabaniss in Georgia, Robert M.
Lusher in Louisiana, G. F. Neill in Mississippi, W. K. Lane in North
Carolina, Joseph D. Pope in South Carolina, D. N. Kennedy in Tennessee,
George J. Durham in Texas, and T. C. Green in Virginia. Henry Sparnick
was the chief clerk under the Commissioner. The tax in kind was collec-
ted by quartermasters (see the section on the Quartermaster General's
Department in chapter VII of this Guide). By Apr. 1864 471 collection
districts had been established.

Thompson Allan became chief clerk of the War Tax Office on Oct. 1,
1861, and Commissioner of Taxes on July 2, 1863.

Record Group 109. --Letters-sent books, Sept. 24, 1861-Feb. 24,
1865 (ch. X, parts of vols. 165, 172, vols. 189, 191, and 193-201), contain letters mainly to chief collectors of States and district collectors but
also to Members of Congress, State Governors, receivers of sequestered
property, tax assessors, Government officials, and others concerning
appointments and commissions, bonds, payment of taxes, reports of collections, corrections to assessment lists, sequestered property, compensation, and other matters. Letters and telegrams received, 1861-65 (2
ft.), are from Confederate Government and State officials and concern
appointments, the establishment of collection districts, bonds, tax laws,
tax collections, and administrative matters. A register of letters received,
Sept. 25, 1861-Feb. 15, 1865 (ch. X, vol. 192), shows name of writer,
date and file number of letter, and its subject. Reports of the Commissioner of Taxes and other papers, 1863-65 (1 in.), include regulations
issued to the field staff and letters of the Commissioner to the Secretary
of the Treasury. A file of miscellaneous records, 1861-65 (3 in.), contains instructions and regulations issued by the Commissioner of Taxes,
reports of work done by his clerical staff, decisions of the Secretary of the
Treasury on tax matters, accounts of collection offices, certified lists of
counties from State Comptrollers, statements of taxes collected and to be
collected, assessment rolls of counties, lists of appointments of district
collectors and assessors, lists of counties not assessed because of occupation by the enemy, and correspondence. Also in this record group is a
record of the receipt and distribution of printed instructions and regulations, 1863-64 (ch. X, vol. 190, p. 316-399).

Reports and statements of taxes collected, 1861-65 (17 ft.), show the date, name of taxpayer, amount of tax collected, and sometimes amounts for different kinds of taxes. With these reports are State collectors' monthly statements of money received from district collectors, estimates of funds needed for office expenses, requisitions for funds, refund certificates for taxes wrongfully paid and refunded, depositions regarding the receipt of counterfeit money in payment of taxes, letters from State collectors submitting lists of district collectors and assessors, letters from district collectors regarding collections, and copies of correspondence between State collectors and district collectors. There are oversize tax returns in the form of rolls or folded papers for districts in Alabama, Georgia, North Carolina, South Carolina, and Virginia. Among those for Virginia are individual tax returns by taxpayers of Richmond, 1863-65, showing the kinds of taxes, rate, salary, amount of tax, occupation and address, name of assessor, and signature of the taxpayer. There are abstracts of estimates of articles due as tax in kind, 1863-64, for Alabama, Georgia, North Carolina, and Virginia.

A list of collectors, sureties, and assessors of the war tax, 1863-65 (ch. X, vol. 190), shows the State; number of the collection district; counties in the district; names of collectors, deputy collectors, and assessors; sureties; and amount of and date of bond. Sales tax registers for district no. 10, Richmond, Va. , Aug. 1863-Feb. 1865 (ch. X, vols. 202-206), show the names of businessmen, corporations, and firms liable to the sales tax, date of registry, residence, time, place, type of business, number and names of persons in the firm, amount of capital invested, amount of specific tax, amount of gross sales and receipts at time of registry, tax due on sales, and a certification of the genuineness of the information.

Record Group 365. --Miscellaneous records, Jan. 1862-Mar. 1865 (7 in.), consist of correspondence regarding accounts of State collectors and their estimates of funds needed for expenses, accounts of tax assessors, and other accounts; quarterly abstracts of disbursements by State collectors and assessors, and of the Office of the Commissioner of Taxes showing the purposes of expenditures and amounts, with supporting vouchers; and payrolls of the Office, showing names of employees, the amounts paid to them, and their signatures. Records of State collectors are described below as records of field offices.

Records in Other Custody. --Confederate tax declarations filed in Wythe County, Va. , 1864-65 (275 items), are in the Archives Division of the Virginia State Library.

TREASURY NOTE BUREAU

Under legislation adopted by the Confederate Congress during 1861-64 the Treasury Department issued Treasury notes or paper currency in different denominations and designs totaling more than $1 1/2 billion. Contracts for printing the notes were made with private companies including the National Bank Note Co. of New York, the Southern Bank Note Co. of New Orleans, J. Manouvrier of New Orleans, Hoyer & Ludwig of Richmond, J. T. Paterson of Columbia, S. C. , Keatinge & Ball of Richmond (later Columbia), Blanton Duncan of Richmond (later Columbia), Evans & Cogswell of Charleston, Archer & Daly of Richmond, and Dunn & Co. of Richmond. The Secretary of the Treasury superintended the printing with the assistance of Principal Clerks Thompson Allan (July-Sept. 1861) and

B. F. Slocumb (Sept. 1861-1862). For greater security some of the printing establishments were moved in Apr. 1862 to Columbia, and thus two Treasury Note Divisions came to exist. That at Columbia supervised the printers and engravers and prepared the Treasury notes and had them taken by courier to Richmond. The office at Richmond was concerned with dating and numbering the notes and keeping them secure until they had been signed by the Treasurer's and Register's clerks and turned over to the Treasurer for distribution.

An act of Feb. 3, 1864 (1 Cong. C. S. A. Stat. 178), created the Treasury Note Bureau, which was to have charge of printing and preparing Treasury notes and bonds. The Bureau was moved from the capital to Columbia at the end of Apr. 1864. W. Y. Leitch, the Assistant Treasurer at Charleston, was directed to move to Columbia to take charge there of the distribution of Treasury notes. All printing of Treasury notes ceased when General Sherman's army attacked Columbia on Feb. 20, 1865.

Heads of the Treasury Note Divisions:

Sanders G. Jamison (Richmond), Mar. 1, 1862.
Joseph D. Pope (Columbia), May 10, 1862.
Charles F. Hanckel (Columbia), May 23, 1862.

Sanders G. Jamison became the head of the Treasury Note Bureau on Feb. 10, 1864.

Philip H. Chase, Confederate Treasury Notes; the Paper Money of the Confederate States of America, 1861-1865 (Philadelphia, 1947); Grover C. Criswell, Jr., and Clarence L. Criswell, Criswell's Currency Series, Vol. I, Confederate and Southern States Currency; a Descriptive Listing, Including Rarity (Pass-A-Grille Beach, Fla., 1957); Arlie R. Slabaugh, Confederate States Money; a Type Catalog of the Paper Money Issued by the Confederate States During the Civil War, 1861-1865 (Racine, 1961); Raphael P. Thian, Confederate Note Album for a Complete Collection (With Descriptive Letter-Press) of the Various Designs for Face and Back Selected by the Confederate Treasury Authorities for the Currency of the Confederate States of America, 1861-1865 ([Washington, 1876]); U. S. Adjutant General's Office, Register of Issues of Confederate States Treasury Notes, Together With Tabular Exhibits of the Debt, Funded and Unfunded, of the Confederate States of America, comp. by Raphael P. Thian (Washington, 1880).

Record Group 39. --There are Treasury notes, bonds, and certificates, 1861-64 (1 vol.), in the records of the Bureau of Accounts of the Treasury Department.

Record Group 109. --Registers of Treasury notes issued under acts of Congress, 1861-63 (ch. X, vols. 98-114, 2 1/2 ft.), show the names of signers for the Treasurer and the Register; to whom issued (usually "To Bearer"), registered number of the notes; and the number, denomination, and value of the notes. A schedule of Treasury note plates, Sept. 2, 1861-Apr. 7, 1864 (ch. X, vol. 121), shows the denomination of the notes and the name of the platemaker. Other records include a record of Treasury note redemption, July 31, 1862-Feb. 18, 1865 (ch. X, vol. 115); a record of Treasury notes signed by John W. Jones, Mar.-Sept. 1862 (ch. X, vol. 186); a memorandum of Treasury notes signed by Thomas D. Walford and T. F. Grayson, June 1862-June 1863 (ch. X, vol. 265); certifications of Treasury notes returned for redemption, Jan. 3-Mar. 31, 1865 (ch. X, vol.

266); and a list of schedules of interest paid on 7/30 Treasury notes, 1864-65 (ch. X, vol. 60A).

Record Group 365.--Miscellaneous records, Aug. 1861-Mar. 1865 (6 in.), include correspondence relating to personnel matters and the printing and shipment of Treasury notes, payrolls of the offices of the Bureau at Columbia and Richmond, accounts of the disbursing clerk in Columbia, reports by Comptroller's Office clerks on canceled Treasury notes counted, regulations for organizing the Bureau, and other documents. Bonds, stocks, and certificates of indebtedness, 1861-65 (5 ft.), include printed coupon and registered bonds and stock, nontaxable certificates of indebtedness, and call certificates issued by the Confederate Government to subscribers to loans authorized by acts of Congress and to other persons who turned in Treasury notes. Most of the bonds were issued to "Bearer" and have unused interest coupons attached, but some show the names of bondholders and the persons to whom the bonds were assigned. Treasury notes issued by the Confederate States of America, 1861-64, consist of canceled notes in denominations of $0.50, $1, $2, $5, $10, $20, $50, and $100. Most of the notes are expected to be transferred to the Smithsonian Institution, but samples will be retained by the National Archives. Chronological lists of the notes prepared by the U.S. Treasury Department show the number of notes of different denominations in the collection. Other records relating to Treasury notes and to the Treasury Note Bureau at Columbia are described below as records of field offices.

TREASURY AGENT FOR THE TRANS-MISSISSIPPI WEST

An act of Congress of Jan. 27, 1864 (1 Cong. C.S.A. Stat. 176), authorized the President to appoint an agent of the Treasury Department to serve as the deputy of the Secretary of the Treasury in the region west of the Mississippi River. An act of Feb. 17, 1864 (1 Cong. C.S.A. Stat. 230), authorized the establishment in the War Department's Trans-Mississippi Department of a Bureau of the Auditor and a Bureau of the Comptroller under officers who were to be appointed by the President. The auditor was to receive and examine all public accounts, including those of the Post Office Department, arising in the Trans-Mississippi Department and "to keep all accounts of the receipts and disbursements of the public money and of all debts due to or from the Confederate States within the trans-Mississippi department; to receive from the comptroller the accounts which shall have been adjusted by him and to preserve such accounts with their vouchers and certificates subject to the orders of the Secretary of the Treasury; to record all warrants for the receipts of payment of moneys at the Treasury on account of expenditures made within the said trans-Mississippi department, certify the same thereon and transmit to the Secretary copies of the certificates of balances of accounts adjusted as herein directed." The auditor was also to preserve the evidence of claims against the Confederate Government for the loss of slaves and other property to the enemy and of property destroyed under military necessity. The comptroller was "to superintend the adjustment and preservation of public accounts; to examine all accounts settled by the auditor, except those relating to the Post-Office Department, and certify the balances arising thereon to the auditor; to countersign all warrants drawn by the agent of the Treasury for the trans-Mississippi department, which shall be authorized by law; to report to the agent of the Treasury the official forms of all papers to be issued in the

different offices for collecting the public revenue and the manner and form
of keeping and stating the accounts of the several persons employed therein. " By a regulation of May 1, 1864, the auditor and comptroller were
made responsible to the agent of the Treasury. The agent was also to
superintend the collection of taxes in the Trans-Mississippi district and
the State collectors were to make their reports through him to the commissioner of taxes. The agent also had general supervision of all depositaries, collectors, and Treasury agents in his department, exercising such
authority over them as was entrusted to the Secretary of the Treasury but
subject to his revision and control. An act of June 14, 1864 (2 Cong. C.S.
A. Stat. 272), directed that claims for supplies furnished to the Army
originating west of the Mississippi were to be settled by the accounting
officers of the Treasury agency for the Trans-Mississippi West.

Peter W. Gray took the oath of office as agent of the Treasury Department on Mar. 2, 1864, and established his office at Marshall, Tex., on
July 1. The region over which he had authority included Texas, Arkansas,
and western Louisiana. David F. Shall assumed the duties of auditor in
July, and Thomas H. Kennedy became the comptroller. Late in 1864 Capt.
W. C. Black reported to the Treasury agent at Marshall to head a
Foreign Supply Office, whose function was to export cotton and purchase
supplies for the Army in foreign markets. The Treasury agency destroyed
or abandoned its books and papers and moved westward from Marshall on
May 22, 1865.

Record Group 109. --In this record group is an account book of the
Bureau of the Auditor, July 1864-May 1865 (ch. II, vol. 201 1/2).

Records in Other Custody. --Letters to P. W. Gray from the Secretary of the Treasury, June 2, 1864, regarding the appointment of additional
depositaries, and from C. W. West, Jan. 12, 1865, concerning the rights
of States to export cotton, are in the Louisiana Historical Association collection on deposit in the Howard-Tilton Memorial Library of Tulane University. A diary of John Brown, the Confederate depositary at Camden,
Ark., in 1864-65, is in the Southern Historical Collection of the University
of North Carolina Library. Papers of Capt. W. C. Black, 1863-65 (6
items), are in the same repository. Press copies of letters sent by the
Foreign Supply Office, Jan. 7-May 22, 1865 (2 vols.), are in the Confederate Museum. These are letters from Captain Black to agents of the Office
at Houston, San Antonio, and Goliad, C. J. Helm in Havana, Colin J. Mc-
Rae in Europe, Maj. J. F. Minter in England, Lt. Col. W. A. Broadwell,
Chief of the Cotton Bureau, other Army officers, Fraser, Trenholm & Co.
in Liverpool, and others.

RECORDS OF FIELD OFFICES

Records of Treasury Department field offices and agents and records
of the Department relating to field operations were arranged by the U.S.
Treasury Department on a geographic basis. To facilitate the use of the
records in the investigation of claims against the U.S. Government special
index volumes were prepared. Though imperfect in some respects, these
indexes are still considered useful, and the geographic arrangement of the
records has been retained. Other records relating to Treasury Department field operations are described below by States.

Customhouses at Confederate ports were seized and operated by the
State governments before being transferred to the Confederate Government

in Feb-Mar. 1861 for administration by the Treasury Department. Besides collecting duties on merchandise imported, the collectors of customs sometimes served as depositaries, received crew lists from outgoing vessels and passenger lists and cargo manifests from incoming vessels, superintended lighthouses, issued documents to vessels, collected funds for marine hospitals, attempted to suppress smuggling, and submitted returns on commerce and navigation and the efficacy of the Union blockade.

Lists of customs collectors are in Thian, "Correspondence of the Treasury Department, " appendix IV, p. 32-34; Todd, Confederate Finance, p. 195-196; and National Archives, Preliminary Inventory of the Treasury Department Collection of Confederate Archives. Forrest R. Holdcamper, "Registers, Enrollments and Licenses in the National Archives, " American Neptune, 1:275-294 (July 1941); National Archives, Customhouse Marine Documentation; a List by Series Showing Ports for Which Documents Are Available in Record Group 41, comp. by Forrest R. Holdcamper (Washington, Nov. 1962).

The Confederate collectors of customs in such ports as Charleston, Mobile, and New Orleans continued to use record books and to add to files that had been initiated by U.S. collectors. After the war the records remained in the customhouses, and records for those ports and others have been accessioned by the National Archives and are now part of Record Group 36 (Bureau of Customs). Vessel documents received with the customhouse records have been transferred by the National Archives to Record Group 41 (Bureau of Marine Inspection and Navigation). Other customs collectors' records are in Record Groups 109 and 365.

Prize case files among the records of the U.S. District Courts for the Southern District of New York and the District of Maryland contain documents relating to Southern merchant ships that were seized by U.S. naval vessels (see Guide to Federal Archives Relating to the Civil War).

Assistant Treasurers and depositaries represented the Treasury Department locally to receive public revenue collected from taxes, customs, and the sale of stocks and bonds and to disburse funds on warrants received from the Treasury Department. In Mar. 1861 Anthony J. Guirot and Benjamin C. Pressley were appointed Assistant Treasurers at New Orleans and Charleston, respectively. Guirot later had to move his office to Jackson, then to Mobile, to Selma, and finally to Meridian, Miss. Pressley was succeeded in June 1862 by W. Y. Leitch, who moved his office the next year to Columbia and in 1865 to Chester.

A list of depositaries is in National Archives, Preliminary Inventory of the Treasury Department Collection of Confederate Records.

Some functions that had been carried on in the South by the U.S. Treasury Department were not continued by the Confederate Treasury Department. Confederate or State forces seized the mints at New Orleans, Dahlonega, and Charlotte, but an act of May 14, 1861 (Prov. Cong. C.S.A. Stat. 110), directed the suspension of the operations of those mints.

Assay offices that were opened at the mints did very little business during 1861-62. About the beginning of Oct. 1861 the employees of the Charlotte mint were dismissed, and later that month the bullion and coins on hand were deposited with the Assistant Treasurer at Charleston. In May 1862 the Charlotte mint was turned over to the Navy Department for use by the navy yard. In 1861 there were marine hospitals at Norfolk, Ocracoke, Wilmington, Charleston, Key West, St. Marks, Mobile, New Orleans, and Napoleon. A congressional resolution of May 16, 1861, limited their expenses to funds received from seamen for their support and authorized placing them under any corporate or State authority that might undertake to keep them open as hospitals (Prov. Cong. C.S.A. Stat. 163). The revenue cutters William J. Duane at Norfolk, William Aiken at Charleston, Minot at New Bern, Lewis Cass at Mobile, Robert McClelland, Morgan, and Washington at New Orleans, and Dodge at Galveston were seized by State authorities. The Minot (renamed the Manassas), the Lewis Cass, the cutters obtained at New Orleans and the Dodge were turned over to the Confederate Navy, and their officers were largely transferred to the Navy.

In Dec. 1860 the State of North Carolina seized the U.S. Coast Survey vessels Petrel and Firefly at Charleston. The Petrel became a privateer and was sunk by the U.S.S. St. Lawrence off the coast of South Carolina on July 28, 1861. The Firefly was turned over to the Confederate Navy and became attached to the Savannah River Squadron. The Confederate Government did not engage in coast surveying.

Records Relating to Alabama

Record Group 21.--A letters-sent book of Abram Martin, the chief tax collector for the State of Alabama at Montgomery, May 16, 1863-Jan. 24, 1865, is in the Federal Records Center at East Point, Ga., which received it in 1953 from the U.S. District Court at Montgomery. The book contains fair copies of outgoing letters, lists of tax collectors and assessors, lists of collectors' bonds and assessors' accounts, a list of drafts drawn by the Confederate Treasurer, a memorandum of drafts for collectors and supervisory assessors, a report of certificates of deposit, lists of certificates for 4-percent bonds deposited by the chief collector with the depository at Montgomery, and a statement showing the amount of certificates of deposit and of certificates for bonds returned to Martin.

Record Group 36.--An extensive collection of records of the collector of customs at Mobile includes some Confederate materials, such as an account book, Mar. 1, 1861-May 30, 1862 (part of a volume for 1860-62), and a daybook, Mar. 5, 1861-Aug. 1, 1864 (part of a volume for 1860-65). Records relating to merchandise imported include an abstract of duties, Oct. 1862-Oct. 1864 (1/4 in.); inward and outward cargo manifests, 1861-64 (1 1/2 ft.); entry papers, 1861-64 (1 ft.); inspector's returns, Mar. 1861-Aug. 1862 (part of a volume for 1857-62); invoices of cargo, 1861-64 (1/2 in.); a register of merchandise brought into the district of Mobile, Mar.-July 1861 (part of a volume for 1857-69); a warehouse book, Mar. 1-June 20, 1861 (part of a volume for 1856-68); and warehouse bonds, 1861-64 (3 in.; part of a volume for 1859-61). There are records relating to vessels cleared, Mar. 1861-June 1864 (parts of a volume for 1857-64) and entered, Mar. 1861-June 1864 (part of a volume for 1857-64). There are also crew lists for 1861-64 (1 in.). Other records include a record of exports of domestic produce in foreign vessels, Apr. 1861-June 1864 (part of a volume for 1861-75); a record of exports of domestic produce in foreign and American vessels, Mar. 2-29, 1861 (part of a volume for 1850-61); copies of bonds of consignors for the export of cotton, Jan. -May 1862 (1 vol.); copies of oaths of masters of vessels concerning the entering of cotton for exportation and the payment of the export duty, Jan. 24-May 5, 1862, and Apr. 10, 1863 (1 vol.); and a return of hospital money collected, Jan. 1861-Mar. 1862 (part of a volume for 1857-72).

Record Group 41. --Marine documentation accumulated by the collector of customs at Mobile and now among the records of the Bureau of Marine Inspection and Navigation includes duplicate certificates of enrollment of vessels, Mar. 11, 1861-Jan. 1, 1864 (part of a volume for 1857-65); bonds for enrolled vessels, Mar. 11, 1861-Nov. 24, 1863 (part of a volume for 1854-66); duplicate certificates of registry of vessels, Mar. 22, 1861-Nov. 9, 1864 (part of a volume for 1859-65); duplicate licenses of vessels, Feb. 28, 1861-July 26, 1864 (part of a volume for 1859-68); duplicate licenses of vessels, Mar. 8, 1861-July 26, 1864 (1/2 in., part of a file for 1860-65); bonds for licensed vessels, Feb. 26, 1861-July 26, 1864 (part of a volume for 1860-66); copies of enrollments and licenses of vessels, May 1861-Nov. 1863 (1/4 in., part of a file for 1858-68); a record of certificates of registry and enrollment and licenses issued and surrendered, 1861-64 (part of a volume for 1854-64); bills of sale of enrolled vessels, Mar. 4, 1861-Apr. 10, 1862 (p. 190-310 of a volume for 1859-62); bills of sale of enrolled vessels, Mar. 21-Apr. 20, 1861 (p. 53-66 of a volume for 1853-61); bills of sale of enrolled vessels, Mar. 8, 1862-Sept. 3, 1863 (1 vol.); bills of sale of registered vessels, Sept. 19, 1861-June 30, 1864 (part of a volume for 1856-65); and oaths of ownership of vessels, Feb. 26, 1861-Jan. 13, 1862, and Feb. 8, 1862-Mar. 1, 1865 (parts of volumes for 1856-62 and 1862-66).

Record Group 365. --Miscellaneous accounts and receipts of Anthony J. Guirot, Assistant Treasurer at Mobile, Jan. 1864-Jan. 1865 (1 in.); receipts for the payment of interest on Treasury notes by Guirot, Jan. 1862-Jan. 1865 (1 ft. 6 in.); miscellaneous lists and statements, Mar. 1, 1864-May 1, 1865 (vol. 9A), consisting of lists of Treasury notes funded by Guirot and Charles Walsh (the depositary at Mobile), accounts of interest payments on Treasury notes made by Guirot, statements of 4-percent stock certificates delivered to Guirot by Henry Barnewall (tax collector in the 49th district of Alabama), and a list of coupon bonds for loan subscribers at Mobile; miscellaneous reports, June 29, 1863-Mar. 6, 1865 (1/2 in.), consisting of reports and statements prepared by or received by Walsh and Guirot concerning Treasury notes funded, certificates of 4-percent registered bonds received in payment of taxes and forwarded to the Assistant Treasurer for deposit, and receipts for bonds issued under the loan provision of the act of Feb. 17, 1864; weekly reports of Treasury notes funded into 4-percent stock by Charles Walsh, Mar. 7-July 1, 1864 (vol. 1); and stub books for certificates issued by A. J. Guirot, Mar. 2, 1863-Mar. 6, 1865 (15 vols.).

Other records accumulated at Mobile by John Scott, general agent of the Produce Loan for the State of Alabama, include accounts and receipts, Mar. 1863-Apr. 1865 (1 in.); reports on cotton purchased in Alabama and Mississippi, Oct. 20, 1862-Mar. 31, 1864 (vols. 4A-4B); a cash book, Aug. 4, 1862-Apr. 3, 1865 (1 vol.); a journal of Produce Loan accounts, Aug. 23, 1862-Mar. 30, 1865 (1 vol.); a ledger of Produce Loan accounts, Nov. 1, 1862-Mar. 30, 1865 (1 vol.); and a record of cotton transactions, June 15, 1863-Apr. 8, 1865 (vol. 5C).

Records of James A. Farley, general agent of the Produce Loan for the State of Alabama at Montgomery, include miscellaneous accounts, Feb. 4, 1862-Dec. 30, 1864 (1/3 in.), relating to the purchase of cotton and other disbursements; invoices of cotton purchased by subagents, Oct. 13, 1862-June 27, 1863 (1/3 in.); a record of cotton transactions, Oct. 13, 1862- May 27, 1865 (vol. 5D); an alphabetical list of subscribers to the produce loan, Feb. 1862-July 1863 (vol. 8); certificates (receipts) issued to subscribers under the loan of Aug. 19, 1861, Jan. 24, 1862-Feb. 29, 1863 (4 in.); stub books of certificates issued to subscribers, Jan. 24, 1862-Nov. 26, 1863 (2 vols., numbered 4C); certificates issued to subscribers under the loan of Feb. 20, 1863, Mar. 26-July 30, 1863 (3/4 in.); stub books of certificates issued to subscribers under the loan of Feb. 20, 1863, Mar. 17-July 31, 1863 (4 vols., numbered 3D); receipts for the delivery of coupon bonds to subscribers to the loans of Aug. 19, 1861, and Feb. 20, 1863, Feb. 8, 1862-Feb. 23, 1865 (vols. 3A-3B); and quarterly reports of bonds received and issued in payment of cotton purchased, Jan. 15-Mar. 31, 1863 (vol. 3E).

In May 1862 Thaddeus Sanford moved the depository from Mobile to Montgomery. Reports, correspondence, and other papers of Sanford, Dec. 1861-Mar. 1865 (1 1/2 in.), concern the payment of interest on bonds and Treasury notes, delivery of bonds to subscribers, and redemption of call certificates. Reports, lists, and statements, Sept. 1864-Mar. 1865 (vol. 7), concern balances due disbursing officers, interest paid on bonds and Treasury notes, and canceled Treasury notes. Receipts for the payment of interest on Treasury notes, Jan. 1862-Jan. 1865 (1 1/2 ft.), are mostly those of Sanford but include some by Assistant Treasurer Guirot at Mobile. Other records include schedules of certificates deposited by Abram Martin, chief tax collector for Alabama, May 5, 1864-Jan. 28, 1865 (vol. 6); a record of interest payments to subscribers to loans of 1861 and 1863, Dec. 1863-Dec. 1864 (3 vols.); and stub books of certificates issued for stocks and bonds exchanged under various loans, Mar. 19, 1863-Mar. 28, 1865 (2 vols.).

Other Treasury Department records relating to various localities in Alabama include bills of sale and consolidated lists of sales of cotton to Produce Loan agents, Oct. 1862-Mar. 1865 (6 in.); a record of cotton purchased by Gray A. Chandler, a subagent of the Produce Loan, Nov. 17, 1862-Jan. 22, 1864 (vol. 4C); loan commissioners' and Produce Loan agents' receipts for the delivery of coupon bonds, May 14, 1861-Dec. 3, 1864 (1 in.); depositaries' weekly reports of certificates issued, Mar. 5, 1864-Jan. 7, 1865 (vol. 2); certificates issued by depositaries throughout the State of Alabama for bonds and registered stock, Dec. 1862-Dec. 1864 (2 ft. 6 in.); and vouchers for cotton purchased by military officers, June 30, 1862-Apr. 12, 1865 (1 in.).

Records Relating to Arkansas

Record Group 109.--Accounts, returns, and correspondence of Edward Cross, depositary at Little Rock, Jan. 1863-Jan. 1864 (ch. X, vol. 74).

Record Group 365.--Lists of cotton purchased by David Block, Produce Loan agent, Oct. 1862-Jan. 1864 (1/2 in.); and weekly reports and vouchers of Edward Cross, Sept. 21, 1861-Apr. 1, 1864 (1 1/2 in.), concerning bonds issued and interest paid on Treasury notes and call loan certificates.

Records Relating to Florida

Record Group 365. --Weekly reports of 4-percent bond certificates issued under the loan of Feb. 17, 1864, by William R. Pettes, depositary at Tallahassee, Mar.-Apr. and June 1864 (vol. 11), show the date, number and amount of certificate issued and the name of the subscriber. A report of certificates issued by Isaac R. Harris, depositary at Quincy, Mar.-Apr. 1864 (vol. 11), contains similar information. Certificates for stocks and bonds issued by depositaries in Florida, Apr. 1861-Feb. 1865 (10 in.), were issued under the provisions of various loan acts but mostly under the act of Feb. 17, 1864. The certificates give the name of the purchaser, the location of the depositary's office, the amount paid, and the name of the assignee (usually the tax collector).

Records in Other Custody. --Records of Alonzo B. Noyes, collector of customs at St. Marks, 1859-65 (250 items), in the P. K. Yonge Library of Florida History at the University of Florida include accounts, reports, returns, vouchers, payrolls, and some correspondence as collector and superintendent of lights, and accounts as disbursing agent of the Treasury Department. Other papers of Noyes, 1859-61 (78 items), in the Southern Historical Collection in the University of North Carolina Library include letters received and other documents relating to his activities as collector and superintendent of lights.

Records Relating to Georgia

Record Group 109. --Records of the depositary at Macon consist of a record of cash on hand, Mar. 21, 1863-Mar. 25, 1864 (ch. X, vol. 182), and an order book of the $500 million loan, July-Sept. 1864 (ch. X, vol. 155), showing payments made on 6-percent bonds issued under the act of Feb. 17, 1864. An account book of William B. Johnston, loan commissioner at Macon, Oct. 1862-Apr. 1863 (ch. X, vol. 184), shows the names of bond purchasers, bond numbers, and amounts of bonds sold. Letters received by John Boston, the depositary at Savannah, Dec. 30, 1862-Mar. 16, 1864 (ch. X, vol. 183), are chiefly from the Treasurer and the Register. Copies of certificates of ship registries for the port of Savannah, June 11, 1861-June 6, 1864 (ch. X, vol. 187), contain a variety of information regarding the ships. An account of bonds taken in the district of Savannah on merchandise warehoused, Nov. 1860-Nov. 1862 (ch. X, vol. 188), shows the names of the principal and the surety.

Record Group 365. --This record group contains lists of certificates for 4-percent bonds issued by Henry Hull, depositary at Athens, under the loan of Feb. 17, 1864, for Feb.-July 1864 (1 in.); an account of Jesse Thomas, depositary at Atlanta, June-July 1863; lists of 4-percent bonds issued by and interest paid on Treasury notes by Thomas S. Metcalf, depositary at Augusta, June 30, 1863-Dec. 31, 1864 (vol. 13), including a schedule by John Boston, depositary at Savannah, of interest payments on the loan of Feb. 29, 1861, for the half year ending June 30, 1863; receipts for payments by Metcalf of interest on 7/30 Treasury notes issued under the act of Apr. 17, 1862, Jan. 1-Mar. 31, 1864 (4 in.); weekly reports of stock certificates issued by William H. Young, depositary at Columbus, Feb. 19-July 5, 1864, and by David R. Adams, depositary at Eatonton, Mar. 18-Apr. 1, 1864 (vol. 18); a stub book for coupon bonds issued by the La Grange depositary under the loan of Aug. 19, 1861, Mar. 6, 1862-Jan.

22, 1863 (vol. 17); and lists of certificates issued by depositaries at La Grange, Milledgeville, Thomasville, and Savannah, Mar.-July 1864 (1 in.). Records of John Boston, depositary and collector of customs at Savannah, and of his successor, James R. Sneed, include miscellaneous records, Apr. 1861-Feb. 1865 (5 1/2 in.), concerning payments of interest on loans, bond sales, bond certificates and receipts redeemed, payments made, and receipts of funds, and comprise statements, lists, vouchers, receipts, accounts current, drafts, and correspondence; and a ledger of loan transactions, Feb. 1, 1862-Feb. 23, 1864 (vol. 15).

Other records relating to various places in Georgia include receipts of the Confederate Treasurer for the delivery by depositaries of coupon bonds under the loans of Feb. 28 and Aug. 19, 1861, 1861-62 (1 in.); receipts for the payment of interest on Treasury notes issued by the depositaries at Savannah and Augusta and the loan commissioners for the State of Georgia, July 1861-July 1864 (11 in.); lists of subscriptions to the produce loan, 1861-62 (1/4 in.); and certificates for stocks and bonds issued by depositaries, Sept. 1862-Aug. 1864 (4 ft.).

Records in Other Custody.--Emory University Library has a receipt book of the depositary at Savannah, Mar. 28, 1864-Mar. 13, 1865, containing stubs of receipts issued to persons making deposits; stubs for certificates of deposit issued by the same depositary for Treasury notes received under the act of Nov. 28, 1864, for Feb. 2-Apr. 14, 1865; and a receipt book of Charles S. Harden, the deputy collector of customs at Savannah, Apr. 13-Oct. 24, 1864. An extensive collection of records of the collector of customs at Savannah, 1754-1920, in Duke University Library includes some material of the war period. Cargo manifests of the same official are in the collections of the Georgia Historical Society. Letters and telegrams received by John Boston, the collector of customs at Savannah, Jan. 24, 1861-Mar. 17, 1864 (6 in.), are in the Manuscript Division of the Library of Congress.

Records Relating to Louisiana

Record Group 36.--On Feb. 1, 1861, the former U.S. collector of customs at New Orleans came under the control of the State of Louisiana, and at the beginning of March he began working for the Confederacy. A large collection of records of the collector of customs at New Orleans includes some materials relating to the Confederacy. Among them are press copies of letters sent, May 22-June 24, 1861 (p. 473-479 of a volume for 1859-61), to customs officers at New Orleans and to the Secretary of the Treasury. Records relating to cargoes and vessels include foreign and coastwise outward cargo manifests, Mar.-Sept. 1861 (2 ft.); foreign and coastwise inward cargo manifests, Mar.-July and Sept. and Nov. 1861 (1 ft.); an invoice register, Feb. 1-June 29, 1861 (1 vol.); a measurer's journal relating to cargoes imported, Mar. 1-Aug. 16, 1861 (parts of volumes for 1859-79 and 1854-80); an alphabetical register of arrivals of foreign and American vessels, Mar. 1861-Mar. 1862 (part of a volume for 1859-62); and a register of the tonnage of coastwise and foreign vessels cleared, Mar. 1, 1861-Apr. 23, 1862 (part of a volume for 1856-62). Passenger lists of vessels arriving at New Orleans, Feb. 23-May 31, 1861 (2 in., part of a file for 1820-1913; available on microfilm as M 259), cover only part of the Confederate period.

Record Group 41.--Marine documentation kept by the collector of customs at New Orleans and now in the records of the Bureau of Marine Inspection and Navigation includes duplicate certificates of enrollment of vessels, Apr. 3, 1861-Apr. 22, 1862 (1 vol.); bonds for enrolled vessels, Apr. 3, 1861-Apr. 22, 1862 (2 vols.); duplicate certificates of registry of vessels, Apr. 26, 1861-Apr. 15, 1862 (1 vol.); bonds for registered vessels, Apr. 26, 1861-Apr. 19, 1862 (1 vol.); bonds for licensed vessels, Apr. 4, 1861-Apr. 29, 1862 (1 vol.); bonds for licensed vessels, Apr. 1, 1861-Apr. 23, 1862 (1 vol.); bills of sale of enrolled vessels, Apr. 18-June 14, 1861 (two documents in a volume for 1858-61); bills of sale of enrolled vessels, Jan.-Apr. 1862 (1/2 in.); bills of sale of licensed vessels, Apr. 13, 1861-Apr. 17, 1862 (part of a volume for 1857-62); and bills of sale of all types of vessels, Feb. 25, 1861-Apr. 19, 1862 (part of a volume for 1860-62 and three documents, June-Sept. 1861, in a bundle for 1857-61).

Survey of Federal Archives, Louisiana, Ship Registers and Enrollments of New Orleans, Louisiana (Baton Rouge, 1941-42. 6 vols.).

Record Group 109. --Financial returns, May 1861-Nov. 1864 (4 in.), of Anthony J. Guirot, Assistant Treasurer at New Orleans, Jackson, Mobile, Selma, and Meridian, consist of returns of receipts and disbursements and returns of balances to the credit of disbursing officers. An account book, Sept. 1854-June 1861 (ch. X, vol. 187 1/2), of R. W. Adams, surveyor of the port of New Orleans, shows amounts of moneys received and disbursed, with copies of a few letters sent by Adams, July-Nov. 1861.

Record Group 365. --Records of Assistant Treasurer Anthony J. Guirot include copies of letters sent, Mar. 2, 1861-May 1, 1865 (with earlier correspondence of Guirot and his predecessor dating back to 1853); press copies of letters sent, Apr. 4, 1861-Sept. 12, 1862 (1 vol.), with his earlier outgoing letters as U. S. Assistant Treasurer and the depositary of the State of Louisiana, Jan. 31-Mar. 30, 1861; press copies of letters sent and statements relating to the mint at New Orleans, Apr. 4-Oct. 29, 1861 (1 vol.); letters received from disbursing officers and paymasters, Apr. 4, 1861-Apr. 18, 1862 (part of a volume for 1858-62); stub books of certificates of deposit, Apr. 9, 1864-May 8, 1865 (1 vol.); a journal of accounts of Confederate disbursing officers, Mar. 28, 1861-Nov. 22, 1862 (1 vol.); duplicate receipts for the payment of public revenue warrants, Apr. 1, 1861-May 2, 1865 (vol. 61B); a journal of Post Office Department accounts, July 27, 1861-May 10, 1865 (1 vol.); a record of payments of Post Office Department warrants, Aug. 29, 1861-Feb. 17, 1865, and in the same volume a record of the payment of public revenue drafts, Mar. 16, 1861-June 8, 1863 (1 vol.); duplicate receipts for the payment of Post Office Department warrants, Sept. 6, 1861-Apr. 22, 1865 (vol. 61A); a schedule of Treasury notes received and issued, Apr. 12, 1861-Dec. 29, 1862 (part of a volume also for the period Feb. 6-July 1, 1858); a journal of accounts for interest payments on Treasury notes and call certificates, Feb. 26, 1862-Mar. 31, 1865 (vol. 9); duplicate receipts for the payment of 6-percent call certificates, Feb. 15, 1862-June 30, 1863 (1 vol.); and a journal of interest payments on loans, June 30, 1861-Dec. 31, 1864 (vol. 83).

Records relating to cotton transactions include bills of sale, Dec. 1862-Sept. 1864 (8 in.); agents' reports of cotton purchased, Sept. 1862-Jan. 1864 (10 vols., numbered 23); other reports of cotton purchases, Nov. 11, 1862-Mar. 10, 1865 (2 in.); abstracts of cotton purchases and disposals, Jan. 12, 1862-Dec. 30, 1863 (3 vols., numbered 24); and letters received,

Dec. 1, 1862-May 19, 1865 (1/2 in.), by Ulger Lauve and James T. Belknap, cotton agents at Shreveport, and by James T. Belknap, general agent of the Produce Loan at Shreveport, chiefly from Andrew W. McKee, P. W. Gray, M. M. Rhorer (subagent at Alexandria, La.), W. A. Broadwell, and W. C. Black.

Small quantities of bond and stock certificates and receipts include certificates for 4-percent registered bonds issued, Mar. 24-Oct. 21, 1864, by Francis H. Hatch, depositary at Tangipahoa; receipts for coupon bonds issued to subscribers to the Confederate loan in New Orleans, Aug. 1861-Mar. 1862; and statements of interest paid on Treasury notes and bonds by H. J. G. Battle, depositary at Shreveport, 1864.

Records in Other Custody. --Records relating to Louisiana in the Confederate records collection in the Manuscript Division of the Library of Congress include letters and telegrams received by Assistant Treasurer A. J. Guirot, Apr. 21, 1861-Mar. 6, 1862 (4 in., mostly for 1862, with some earlier letters beginning Nov. 29, 1860); press copies of letters and telegrams, Feb. 2, 1861-Apr. 22, 1862 (3 vols.), sent by Francis H. Hatch, collector of customs at New Orleans; and letters and telegrams received by the collector of customs at New Orleans, Feb. 21-Dec. 31, 1861 (6 in.).

Records Relating to Mississippi

Record Group 109. --Schedule of certificates for 4-percent registered bonds received by the depositary at Columbus, Mar.-Nov. 1864 (ch. X, vol. 151 1/2).

Record Group 365. --List of bond certificates issued by T. W. Williams, depositary at Aberdeen, for Treasury notes under the act of Feb. 17, 1864, Mar. 17-31, 1864. Records of the general agent of the Produce Loan (James D. B. De Bow and J. W. Clapp) accumulated at Jackson and Columbus include correspondence and other papers, Aug. 1862-Feb. 1865 (7 in.); an undated list of cotton subscriptions (vols. 25-26); a list of subscriptions to the produce loan, n. d. (vol. 26); a record of cotton and cash transactions, July 1862-Feb. 1865 (vol. 26); cotton bills of sale, Sept. 1862-Dec. 1863 (8 in.); agents' expense receipts, Aug. 1862-June 1864 (1/4 in.); an account book, Oct. 1862-July 1864 (vol. 25), of Charles Baskerville, district agent, containing his accounts with subagents and with the Ordnance Department for cotton purchases; cotton inspection reports, Sept. 1862-Mar. 1865 (2 in.); and abstracts of cotton purchases and disposals, Oct. 1862-Mar. 1865 (vol. 25).

Other records include miscellaneous reports and receipts, Jan. 1861-Jan. 1865 (1 in.); certificates for stocks and bonds issued by depositaries under the loans of Feb. 20, 1863, and Feb. 17, 1864, Apr. 1863-Nov. 1864 (4 in.); and a stub book of stock certificates issued by Assistant Treasurer A. J. Guirot, Apr.-July 1863, while he was in Jackson; lists of interest payments on Confederate loans made by A. J. Guirot, June 1863-May 1865 (vol. 30A); receipts for the payment of the tax in kind, Mar. 1864-Mar. 1865 (2 in.); and Yazoo River claim papers, Feb. 1863-Apr. 1864 (1/2 in.), relating to cotton, boats, timber, and other materials taken by the military forces for use in the defense of the Yazoo River and for services rendered.

Records Relating to North Carolina

Record Group 36. --An account of marine hospital money collected at Edenton from the masters and owners of vessels, Jan. 7-June 10, 1861 (part of a volume for 1858-80).

Record Group 41. --Bonds for registered vessels, Jan. 21 and Apr. 22, 1861 (two documents in a volume for 1849-68).

Record Group 104. --Records of the Charlotte mint among the records of the Bureau of the Mint in the National Archives include several volumes containing information relating to the activities of the mint during 1861-62. G. W. Caldwell, the former superintendent of the U.S. branch mint, continued as superintendent until Oct. 1861 and thereafter as caretaker of the mint until the spring of 1862. The records include a ledger of ordinary accounts, Apr. 1, 1861-Mar. 31, 1862 (part of a volume for 1837-92); a register of gold bullion deposits, Apr.-May 1861 (part of a volume for 1857-61); a journal of transfers of bullion and coins, Apr.-Oct. 1861 (p. 235-241 in a volume for 1852-61); a daybook of disbursements, Apr., May, and Sept. 1861 (part of a volume for 1848-61); and a gold bullion weigh book, May 1-28, 1861 (part of a volume for 1846-61).

Record Group 365. --Other records relate to the activities of depositaries. Miscellaneous records, June 1861-Jan. 1865 (2 in.), consist of letters, reports, and accounts submitted by depositaries to Treasury Department officials in Richmond; Treasurer's warrants, surety bonds, vouchers, estimates of expenses, statements of Treasury notes funded and coupons paid, and certificates of the adjustment of accounts; and schedules of certificates canceled and forwarded to the Treasury Department on account of tax collectors. Miscellaneous lists, July 1861-Mar. 1865 (1 1/3 in.), include lists of interest paid on Treasury notes, schedules of hypothecated bonds, depositaries' accounts, receipts for the delivery of bonds, and salary lists for war tax assessors. Reports of stock and bond certificates issued by depositaries, Nov. 1863-Feb. 1865 (vols. 33 and 34), relate to various Confederate loans but mostly to the loan of Feb. 17, 1864. Volume 34 of these reports also contains a record of interest payments made at Wilmington on the loan of Feb. 20, 1863, and a list of wages due war tax assessors. Other records include bond certificates issued by depositaries under various Confederate loans, 1863-64 (2 ft.), mostly for the loan of Feb. 17, 1864, and receipts for the payment of interest on Treasury notes, 1863-64 (4 in.).

Records in Other Custody. --The papers of Joseph Ramsey in the Southern Historical Collection of the University of North Carolina Library include materials of 1861-62 relating to his activities as collector of customs and superintendent of lights at Plymouth, N.C.

Records Relating to South Carolina

Record Group 26. --With the records of the U.S. Coast Guard is a logbook of the revenue cutter William Aiken, Jan. 1, 1859-Apr. 21, 1861. This record shows that the cutter was seized by the State of South Carolina on Dec. 27, 1860, and continued in service as a State cutter. Beginning on Jan. 28, 1861, the logbook entries refer to the vessel as a "Coast Police Cutter," and from Mar. 4 the entries are headed "Journal of the C.S.A. Cutter Wm Aiken," Capt. Napoleon L. Coste commanding. The logbook gives information about shipping in the channel leading to the port of Charleston and the attack on Fort Sumter on Apr. 12-13, in addition to the activities of the vessel and its officers and crew.

Record Group 36.--Records of William F. Colcock, the collector of customs at Charleston, form part of the collection of records of the U.S. collector for that port. Colcock began functioning as the Confederate collector toward the end of Feb. 1861. Letters received, Feb. 15-May 6, 1861 (part of a volume for Dec. 1860-May 1861; 1 in.), are a remnant. Financial records include a journal, Feb. 1861-Dec. 1864 (1 vol.); a ledger, Feb. 1861-Dec. 1864 (1 vol.); a cashbook, Feb. 22-Nov. 28, 1861 (p. 198 of a volume for 1859-61); fee books relating to payments received from vessels, June 11, 1862-Dec. 31, 1864 (parts of volumes for 1862-71 and 1863-73); a record of receipts and expenditures, July 1, 1862-Mar. 2, 1863 (part of a volume for 1856-69); and a statement of Treasury notes received for the payment of duties, May 25-Oct. 12, 1861 (part of a volume for 1858-61). Records relating to cargoes include inward cargo manifests, July 1862-Feb. 1863 (1 vol.); monthly statements of the value of imports and exports, Mar. 1861-Sept. 1863 (1 vol.); a register of merchandise entering, Aug. 10-Nov. 5, 1861 (a page in a volume for 1855-67); a record of imports for foreign merchandise in foreign vessels, Mar. 1861-June 1863 (part of a volume for 1858-63); a record of goods ordered to customhouse stores for appraisement, Feb. 1861-Dec. 1864 (part of a volume for 1854-64); a record of appraisements of goods imported, Apr. 30, 1863-Aug. 5, 1863 (part of a volume for 1854-66); returns of railroad iron imported, Feb.-Apr. 1861 (part of a volume for 1855-71); a measurer's record of cargo weights (Feb. 22, 1861-Aug. 15, 1862 (part of a volume for 1848-67); summary statements of the value of imports and exports, Mar. 1861-Aug. 1863 (part of a volume for 1857-67); a surveyor's and guager's record of cargoes of liquids imported, Feb. 26, 1861-Nov. 21, 1862 (part of a volume for 1859-71); a warehouse book relating to quantities of merchandise entered for warehousing and withdrawn, Feb.-May 1861 (part of a volume for 1856-61); and a weigher's record of cargoes imported, Mar. 5, 1861-Aug. 29, 1862 (p. 259-274 of a volume for 1853-66). Records relating to import duties include an impost book, Feb. 1861-Mar. 1862 (part of a volume for 1860-62); a register of ascertained and unascertained duties, Feb. 22-June 29, 1861 (part of a volume for 1859-61); a record of imports entered and duties collected under the act of Mar. 31, 1863, Sept. 7, 1863-Dec. 19, 1863 (1 vol.); and abstracts of duties on goods imported in foreign vessels and Confederate vessels, Apr. 1861-Oct. 1864 (1 vol.). Records relating to vessels include an abstract of Confederate vessels cleared for foreign countries, Aug. 1861-June 1862 (parts of volumes for 1854-79 and 1854-81); an abstract of coastwise vessels cleared, Feb.-Oct. 1861 (parts of volumes for 1856-65 and 1854-70); an abstract of foreign vessels cleared for foreign countries, Feb. 22, 1861-June 6, 1863 (part of a volume for 1854-64), and Feb. 22, 1861-Mar. 31, 1862 (part of a volume for 1854-81); an abstract of foreign vessels entered from foreign countries, Feb. 22, 1861-Mar. 31, 1862 (part of a volume for 1854-82); an abstract of duties collected on the tonnage of vessels, Feb. 1861-July 1863 (part of a volume for Dec. 1860-July 1863); and an abstract of coastwise vessels entered, Feb. 22-Dec. 31, 1861 (part of a volume for 1854-70).

Record Group 41.--Marine documentation kept by the collector of customs at Charleston and now preserved among the records of the Bureau of Marine Inspection and Navigation include duplicate licenses of vessels, May 24-July 27, 1861 (part of a volume for 1853-61); bonds for licensed vessels, Feb. 26, 1861-July 26, 1864 (part of a volume for 1860-66); oaths and bonds of owners of registered vessels, May 15, 1861-Dec. 16, 1864 (part of a volume for 1860-64); bills of sale for enrolled vessels, May 28, 1861-Jan. 14, 1862 (p. 274-337 of a volume for 1858-62); bills of sale for registered vessels, May 21, 1861-Mar. 28, 1862 (p. 95-133 of a volume for 1859-62); bills of sale for vessels sold by the deputy marshal of the Confederate district court, Aug. 23-Dec. 20, 1861 (part of a volume for 1852-61); vessel mortgages, Apr. 25-Oct. 23, 1861 (p. 248-258 of a volume for 1850-68); shipbuilders' certificates for vessels, Oct. 2 and Nov. 6, 1861 (two documents in a volume for 1844-69); affidavits of masters relating to the loss of marine documents, May 17, June 29, July 17, and Aug. 24, 1861 (four documents in a volume for 1856-69).

Record Group 365. --Records relating to the activities of Assistant Treasurers Benjamin C. Pressley and W. Y. Leitch include a record of interest payments on Confederate loans, June 30, 1861-Feb. 28, 1865 (vols. 39 and 40); receipts for the payment of interest on Treasury notes, Jan. 1862-Jan. 1865 (2 ft.); receipts for the payment of the expenses of the Treasury Note Bureau in Columbia, S. C., Nov. 1863-July 1864 (1 in.), with a payroll of employees of the Bureau, Apr. 30, 1864; and a list of bond certificates issued by W. Y. Leitch to depositaries throughout the State, Jan. 5-31, 1865 (1/2 in.).

Records of the collector of customs at Charleston include copies of enrollment bonds for licensed vessels, June 11, 1861-May 13, 1863 (vol. 38); inward and outward cargo manifests with related correspondence, 1861-64 (part of a file for 1858-64); copies of cotton export bonds, Nov. 20, 1861-Nov. 25, 1864 (2 vols., numbered 42); and a register of export duty on cotton, Nov. 20, 1861-Feb. 7, 1865 (1 vol.).

Other records include stub books of certificates for 4-percent registered bonds issued by H. L. Charles, depositary at Darlington, under the loan of Feb. 17, 1864, Mar. 30, 1864-Jan. 19, 1865 (2 vols.); miscellaneous records relating to cotton purchased on behalf of the Navy Department, 1862-63 (1 in.); depositaries' reports of stock and bond certificates issued under Confederate loans, July 1862-Feb. 1865 (1 ft.); certificates for bonds issued by depositaries, Feb.-Dec. 1864 (2 ft.); and receipts for the delivery of coupon bonds under 1861 loans, July 1861-Mar. 1863 (3/4 in.).

Record Group 366. --Among the records of the Civil War Special Agencies of the Treasury Department (Eighth Special Agency) is a record of cotton shipped from Charleston, 1861-65 (1 vol.), which was copied from a record of the Confederate collector of customs at that port.

Records in Other Custody. --A receipt book of William R. Godfrey, depositary at Cheraw, July 8, 1864-Feb. 9, 1865, in the South Caroliniana Library of the University of South Carolina, shows the purposes for which funds were expended.

Records Relating to Tennessee

Record Group 45. --Letters received by James G. M. Ramsey, depositary at Knoxville, Apr. 1, 1863-Aug. 10, 1864 (1 vol.), in the Naval Records Collection include letters from Treasury Department officials and others.

Record Group 365. --Small quantities of records relating to the activities of depositaries include receipts for the payment of interest on Treasury notes and for the delivery of coupon bonds, 1861-64; certificates for registered bonds issued under the act of Feb. 17, 1864, Mar.-Apr. 1864;

and accounts current of Jesse Thomas, depositary at Nashville and Chattanooga, Jan.-Aug. 1863.

Records in Other Custody.--Papers of James G. M. Ramsey in the University of Tennessee Library include materials on services performed for the Treasury Department.

Records Relating to Texas

Record Group 36.--A register of imports at Laredo, Tex., 1861-65 (part of an "Impost Book" for 1851-69), contains a chronological record showing the names of importers, kinds of merchandise, quantities, invoice cost, invoice charges, duty rates, dutiable value, and amount of duty. The port of Laredo was under a deputy collector who was subordinate to Francis W. Latham, the collector in charge of the district of Brazos Santiago; Latham's office was in the customhouse at Point Isabel.

Record Group 41.--Duplicate certificates of registry of vessels, July 11, 1861-May 15, 1865 (1 vol.), kept by the collector of customs at Galveston are in the records of the Bureau of Marine Inspection and Navigation.

Record Group 109.--An account book of Benjamin F. McDonough, collector of customs at Sabine, Aug. 1861-Dec. 1864 (ch. X, vol. 268), shows the amounts and sources of receipts and the amounts and purposes of expenditures.

Record Group 365.--Abstracts of disbursements of George W. Palmer, depositary at San Antonio, relating to the payment of interest on Treasury notes and receipts for the payments, Apr. 1862-Sept. 1863 (1 in.); estimates of the tax in kind on the corn crop of Fort Bend County, Feb. 1864-Feb. 1865 (1/4 in.); and oaths of allegiance of officers and men of the 15th Texas Infantry, Jan.-Mar. 1862 (1/4 in.).

Records Relating to Virginia

Record Group 365.--Lists of 4-percent bond certificates issued by the Rockingham Bank, depositary at Harrisonburg, under the loan of Feb. 17, 1864, Mar. 7-Sept. 1, 1864 (vol. 56); a list of 4-percent bond certificates issued by William M. Blackford, depositary at Lynchburg, under the loan of Feb. 17, 1864, Feb. 24-Mar. 31, 1864 (vol. 55); abstracts of certificates issued by Daniel Dodson, depositary at Petersburg, under the acts of Feb. 20, Mar. 3, and Apr. 30, 1863, n.d. (vol. 55); a record of semiannual interest payments on loans of Aug. 19, 1861, and Feb. 20 and Mar. 23, 1863, made by E. C. Elmore, depositary at Richmond, June 1863-Apr. 1865 (vols. 76-78, 80-82, and 84-86); a record of interest payments on loans of Dec. 24, 1861, and Mar. 23, 1863, made by E. C. Elmore (1/4 in.); receipts of Alexander F. Kinney, depositary at Staunton, for the delivery of bonds and the transportation of currency and bonds, Feb. 1862-Dec. 1864 (1/4 in.); receipts of subscribers for the delivery of coupon bonds issued under various loans, June 1861-Oct. 1864 (1 ft.); lists of Treasury notes funded under the loan of Feb. 17, 1864, Feb.-Sept. 1864 (1 1/3 in.); depostaries' certificates for stocks and bonds issued under various Confederate loans (mainly the loan of Feb. 17, 1864), June 1862-Sept. 1864 (3 ft. 9 in.); stub books for stock and bond certificates issued under the loans of Feb. 20, 1863, and Feb. 17, 1864, Feb. 23, 1864-Feb. 25, 1865 (7 vols.); and miscellaneous records, Jan. 1864-Mar. 1865 (1 1/3 in.).

VII

WAR DEPARTMENT

An act of Feb. 21, 1861 (Prov. Cong. C. S. A. Stat. 32), established the War Department under a Secretary of War who was to have charge of all matters connected with the Army and with the Indian tribes in the Confederacy. An act of Feb. 26, 1861 (Prov. Cong. C. S. A. Stat. 38), for the establishment and organization of a general staff authorized an Adjutant and Inspector General's Department, a Quartermaster General's Department, a Commissary General's Department, and a Medical Department. Other subdivisions added to the War Department as the conflict widened included the Engineer Bureau (1861), the Bureau of Indian Affairs (1861), the Bureau of Ordnance and Ordnance Department (1861), the Signal Bureau (1862), the Army Intelligence Office (1862), the Bureau of Exchange (1862), the Bureau of Conscription (1862), the Niter and Mining Bureau (1863), the Bureau of Foreign Supplies (1863), and the Office of the Commissary General of Prisoners (1864).

A number of War Department agents were sent to Europe to procure war supplies. In Apr. 1861 Caleb Huse went abroad to procure ordnance and other supplies in Great Britain and on the Continent. He remained abroad throughout the war and concluded arrangements for large quantities of war supplies. Others became involved in the shipment of war supplies to Confederate ports. The practice developed of transporting the supplies in large steamers to Nassau, New Providence, St. George, Bermuda, and Havana, Cuba, where they were transferred to smaller steamers for the run through the Union blockade. Agents stationed at those places to attend to shipping matters usually served also as purchasing agents, acquiring goods that were brought in on private account for transshipment to the Confederacy. These agents were C. J. Helm at Havana, Louis Heyliger at Nassau, and Norman Walker at St. George. Walker was assisted by John T. Bourne, a local commission merchant who later became an official Confederate agent.

Successive Secretaries of War:
    Leroy P. Walker, Feb. 21, 1861.
    Judah P. Benjamin, Sept. 17, 1861.
    George W. Randolph, Mar. 18, 1862.
    Gustavus W. Smith, Nov. 18, 1862.
    James A. Seddon, Nov. 21, 1862.
    John C. Breckinridge, Feb. 6, 1865.
Assistant Secretaries of War:
    Robert Ould, Jan. 1862.
    Albert T. Bledsoe, Apr. 2, 1862.
    Lt. Col. George Deas, Oct. 22, 1862.

John A. Campbell, Oct. 1862.

Reports submitted irregularly by the Secretary of War were published as pamphlets (Crandall, Confederate Imprints, 1:230-231) but are more readily available in Official Records... Armies, ser. 4: Apr. 27, 1861, vol. 1:247-254. Dec. 14, 1861, vol. 1:790-797. Feb. 1862, vol. 1:955-964. Aug. 12, 1862, vol. 2:42-49. Jan. 3, 1863, vol. 2:279-294. Nov. 26, 1863, vol. 2:990-1018. Apr. 28, 1864, vol. 3:324-344. Nov. 3, 1864, vol. 3:756-771. See also Henry G. Connor, John Archibald Campbell, Associate Justice of the United States Supreme Court, 1853-1861 (Boston, 1920); Roy W. Curry, "James A. Seddon, a Southern Prototype," Virginia Magazine of History and Biography, 63:123-150 (Apr. 1955); William C. Harris, Leroy Pope Walker, Confederate Secretary of War (Tuscaloosa, Ala., 1962); Archer Jones, "Some Aspects of George W. Randolph's Service as Confederate Secretary of War," Journal of Southern History, 26:299-314 (Aug. 1960); John B. Jones, A Rebel War Clerk's Diary at the Confederate States Capital (2 vols.; New York, 1935); Robert D. Meade, Judah P. Benjamin; Confederate Statesman (New York, 1943); Harry E. Pratt, "Albert Taylor Bledsoe, Critic of Lincoln," Illinois State Historical Society Transactions, 1934: 153-183; Lucille Stillwell, John Cabell Breckinridge (Caldwell, Idaho, 1936); Edward Younger, ed., Inside the Confederate Government; the Diary of Robert Garlick Hill Kean (New York, 1957).

Early in Mar. 1865 War Department clerks began boxing some of the records in preparation for removing them from Richmond. On Apr. 2, the day of the evacuation of the city, Robert G. H. Kean attended to the packing of other records and placed them aboard the train on which President Davis and members of the Cabinet left for Danville at 11 p.m. Kean traveled by rail with the boxes of records as far as Greensboro, N.C., and from there by wagon to Charlotte. Kean wrote in his diary that on Apr. 26 he left the records at Charlotte in charge of C. T. Bruen, assistant secretary of the Senate, who stored them in a warehouse. Adjutant General Samuel Cooper wrote to Gen. Joseph E. Johnston from Charlotte on Apr. 27 stating that the President and the Secretary of War had impressed on him the necessity for preserving the records for the history of the war and asked his advice on their disposition (AIGO, Telegrams Sent). General Johnston notified Maj. Gen. John M. Schofield on May 8 that the Confederate War Department records were at Charlotte ready to be turned over to U.S. authorities. Lt. C. P. Washburn took charge of the removal of the records from Charlotte to Raleigh. On instructions from General Halleck, General Schofield sent 81 boxes of records to New Bern whence they were shipped on the steamer John Tracy to Washington, D.C. (letter, Schofield to Assistant Secretary C. A. Dana, May 17, 1865, Archive Office, Letters Received, N 4, with an inventory).

The records of the Secretary's Office and of the Adjutant and Inspector General's Department were found to be more completely preserved than those of other War Department offices. Dr. Francis Lieber reported in Jan. 1866 that several of the registers of letters of the Secretary's Office and its letters-sent books for the periods May 21-Sept. 12, 1862, and Jan. 21-Apr. 21, 1863, were missing. According to a note on its flyleaf, the letter book for 1863 was later presented to the War Department by a Union soldier. When he left Charlotte, N.C., for Virginia on Apr. 26, 1865,

Robert Kean carried with him a volume of reports submitted by the heads
of War Department bureaus to Secretary of War Breckinridge in Feb. 1865.
Soon afterward he copied the reports and delivered the originals to the
commanding officer at Charlottesville, Va. In 1873 he gave the copies to
the Southern Historical Society (letter, R. G. H. Kean to Jubal A. Early,
Nov. 15, 1873, Southern Historical Society Papers, 2:56-57, July 1876).

OFFICE OF THE SECRETARY OF WAR

The Secretary of War was concerned with the superintendence of the
War Department, the procurement of supplies, and the direction of Army
operations. His attention was given to nominating men for appointment as
Army officers, handling important correspondence of the Department, con-
sulting with the heads of bureaus, Members of Congress and the President,
and obtaining the cooperation of State Governors. On most of the affairs of
the Army he was guided by the President.

An act of Mar. 7, 1861 (Prov. Cong. C.S.A. Stat. 52), authorized for
the War Department a Chief of the Bureau of War and some additional clerks.
Albert T. Bledsoe and Robert G. H. Kean, successive Chiefs of the Bureau
of War, handled the Secretary's correspondence and Army officers' bonds
and supervised the clerical staff. One of the clerks was designated the
disbursing clerk, and the principal incumbents of that position were James
E. Peebles and Alfred Chapman. Beverly R. Wellford, Jr., examined
contracts and bonds and attended to other legal matters.

In Dec. 1861 (by Prov. Cong. C.S.A. Stat. 222) the Secretary of War
was authorized to appoint an Assistant Secretary of War to administer the
conscription law, act on cases involving political prisoners, and superintend the Secretary's correspondence, among other duties. The Secretary's
Office was involved throughout the war in issuing passports to persons
desiring to leave the Confederacy. Most of the passports were issued by
John B. Jones, a clerk, particularly during 1861-62.

Record Group 109.--The records of the Secretary's Office constitute
chapter IX in the War Department Collection of Confederate Records. They
are described below by type:

Correspondence. Letters-sent books, Feb. 21, 1861-May 3, 1865
(ch. IX, vols. 1-4, 6-19, 3 ft; available on microfilm as M 522), contain
fair copies of letters and some telegrams sent; some of the volumes have
indexes. Additional letters for Feb. 9-Apr. 22, 1865, were copied into
these volumes after the war by the U.S. War Department. From Feb. 18,
1862, to Jan. 23, 1865, two series of letter books were maintained--one
for correspondents with surnames beginning with the letter "A-K" or "A-L"
and one for those with names beginning with "L-Z" or "M-Z." The letters
concern the administration of the War Department and the Army, recruitment, conscription, procurement, prisoners of war, and other matters.
The letter books include letters signed by the Assistant Secretary, by the
Chief of the Bureau of War, and by clerks. Besides the names of address-
ees, the indexes contain the names of persons referred to in the letters.
There is a separate index to appointment letters. There are no letters of
this type for the period May 22-Sept. 12, 1862. Letters to the President,
Nov. 20, 1861-Apr. 14, 1865 (ch. IX, vols. 39 and 40; available on microfilm as M 523), include letters and reports on nominations, the operations
of the War Department, comments on proposed legislation, and estimates
of appropriations. Some of the letters on nominations are extracts of

communications the full texts of which are in the "letters-sent books"; others are accompanied by lists of the names of men nominated for appointment in the military services. Many are transmittal letters covering reports and statements that are in the files of Congress. The reports of the Secretary of War (cited above) are copied in these books. Letters to the President presenting nominations for appointment and promotion in the Army, Mar. 1, 1861-Mar. 17, 1865 (ch. I, vol. 147, ch. IX, vol. 99; available on microfilm as M 523), contain lists of names by rank. The confirmation dates are entered on the lists. An index is also on the microfilm. A letters-sent book of the Chief of the Bureau of War, Nov. 27, 1861-Mar. 10, 1862 (ch. IX, vol. 5; available on microfilm as M 522), contains fair copies of letters written by A. T. Bledsoe at the direction of the Secretary of War to Army officers, Government officials, Congressmen, heads of departmental bureaus, State Governors, railroad and business companies, and individuals concerning appointments, assignments, exemptions, claims, contracts, details of men, correction of bonds, and raising troops. These letters are indexed. There are telegrams sent, Feb. 21, 1861-Apr. 1, 1865 (ch. IX, vols. 33-35; available on microfilm as M 524), concerning subjects similar to those in the letters-sent books.

The Secretary's letters received, Feb. 1861-Apr. 1865 (42 ft.; available on microfilm as M 437), are from heads of War Department bureaus, Army officers, heads of executive departments, Government officials, Members of Congress, State Governors, State and local officials, commissioners to examine prisoners, businesses, and individuals. The file also includes letters to Assistant Secretary Campbell and to War Department offices referred to the Secretary for reply. Among the letters are communications addressed to the President, including applications and recommendations for military commissions, offers to organize military units, petitions for the discharge of persons in the Army, and appeals for protection against raids and reprisals by the U.S. Army. The communications from commissioners appointed to examine political and other prisoners include letters and reports on interrogated prisoners with supporting letters, affidavits, depositions, and petitions. For the period Feb. 1861-Feb. 1862 the letters are filed by registration number. The letters for Feb. 1862-Apr. 1865 are filed alphabetically by name of writer and thereunder by date of receipt. The file is not complete, for some letters were referred to other offices of the War Department, others were removed for publication in the Official Records . . . Armies and thereafter kept in a file of published documents, and others were put in the compiled military service records of Confederate soldiers and in other compiled files such as the vessel papers described in chapter XI of this Guide. Registers of letters received, Feb. 3, 1861-Apr. 1, 1865 (ch. IX, vols. 20, 20 1/2, and 21-32), show the date of receipt, name of writer, file number assigned, date and purport of letter, and sometimes information on action taken. In volumes 20-22 for Feb. 1861-Feb. 1862, the entries are arranged numerically by the numbers assigned the letters on the date of receipt, and volumes 23-31 for Feb. 1861-Apr. 1865 are arranged alphabetically by writer's name and thereunder numerically by the numbers assigned the letters on the date of receipt. The register entries are indexed in 13 volumes. Index cards, prepared by the Adjutant General's Office in 1892 (available on microfilm as M 409), contain the names of signers of letters, enclosures, and endorsements; the cards also show the names of some persons mentioned in the letters. Registers of letters referred, 1862-65 (ch. IX, vols. 91 1/2, 92-97, 246-248, and three index vols.), contain information regarding letters referred to other offices for action. Three volumes of this series are missing.

Much less voluminous is a file of telegrams received, Feb. 1861-Apr. 1865 (4 ft.; available on microfilm as M 618). Besides those received by the Secretary's Office, these include others that were forwarded to the Secretary of War. They are arranged in two numerical sequences: 1-4853 (Feb. 1861-June 1862) and 153-4210 (July 1862-Apr. 1865). After the war some of the telegrams were removed and placed in other files--many in the file of published documents used in the Official Records . . . Armies. Registers of telegrams received, Feb. 22, 1861-Apr. 2, 1865 (ch. IX, vols. 36-38), are indexed in separate books.

Personnel Records. The correspondence files described above contain much material relating to personnel of the War Department and the Army; few records pertaining specifically to personnel were kept by the Secretary's Office. There are a register of applications for appointment in the Army, Apr. 1-June 23, 1861 (ch. IX, vol. 89), with alphabetical entries and a separate index, and a register of applications for appointment and promotion, July 1, 1863-Mar. 30, 1865 (ch. IX, vol. 90), also with a separate index. Both of these volumes contain notes dated 1900 to the effect that the papers registered therein had been filed (when found) in a file of "personal papers" (incorporated later into the compiled military service records described in chapter XI of this Guide).

Prisoner Records. A register of political prisoners arrested in the Department of East Tennessee, 1861-62 (ch. IX, vol. 219 1/2), gives the prisoner's name, residence, date of arrest, by whom arrested, age, and date sent to prison or discharged. It includes lists of prisoners sent to Tuscaloosa and a list of those in the Knoxville prison on Mar. 15, 1862, and those committed later. A register of Federal citizens, sutlers, teamsters, and others taken prisoner, July 21, 1861-Sept 3, 1862 (ch. IX, vol. 219), shows the prisoner's name, occupation, place and date of capture, residence, disposition, and, when applicable, death. The register also includes laborers, telegraph operators, boatmen, and deserters.

Other records relating to political and other civilian prisoners are described in the sections of this chapter on the Office of the Commissary General of Prisoners and the Department of Richmond.

Disbursing Records. Certain records supply information regarding the disbursing activities of the War Department. War Department payrolls, July 1862-Mar. 1865 (ch. IX, vols. 87 and 88), show disbursements made by the disbursing clerk to employees of the Secretary's Office and other offices of the War Department. The payrolls give the name of employee, his or her position, yearly salary, period served, amount paid, and signature. Other records of the disbursing clerk, July 1863-Mar. 1865 (5 in.), contain receipts of individuals and firms for payment for services, office supplies, advertising, utilities, equipment, and postage. With the foregoing papers is a memorandum of agreement between the Confederate Government and the Virginia Mechanics' Institute, June 1, 1861, for leasing its building.

Requests for funds, 1861-65 (2 1/2 ft.), include those from the Ordnance, Commissary General's, and Quartermaster Departments. They show the amount requested, in whose favor the requisition was to be issued, and the purpose for which it was to be used. Requests for funds, Mar. 1861-

Mar. 1865 (ch. IX, vol. 98), are copies of letters from the Secretary of War to the Secretary of the Treasury requesting the issue of warrants to the disbursing clerk of the War Department for the payment of employees' salaries and incidental expenses. Lists that accompany the letters show name of person to be paid, period of service, and amount to be paid. Requisitions on the Treasury Department for funds, Feb. 23, 1861-Jan. 6, 1865 (ch. IX, vols. 45-86, 5 ft. 2 in.), are for quartermaster, subsistence, and other officers for pay, transportation, recruiting, stores, clothing, telegrams, construction, forage, services, armament, and secret service. Appropriation accounts, 1861-65 (ch. IX, vols. 40 1/2, 41-44, 9 in.), show the amounts and purposes of expenditures, and the persons to whom paid. Vol. 40 1/2 (Mar. 1, 1862-Mar. 23, 1865) gives daily balances. Volumes 41 and 43 (Mar. 5, 1861-Mar. 19, 1863, and June 1, 1863-Mar. 23, 1865) show general appropriations for the Army, volume 42 (Apr. 2, 1861-Sept. 15, 1864) covers appropriations for the volunteer forces, and volume 44 (Apr. 4, 1861-Jan. 1, 1865) covers appropriations for War Department bureaus. Volumes 41-43 are indexed.

Records in Other Custody. --Two volumes of records of the Confederate Secretary of War are in the Manuscript Division of the Library of Congress. A register of letters and telegrams received, Feb. 27, 1864-Jan. 31, 1865 (1 vol.), contains a chronological record of abstracts of the communications and a record of endorsements showing the action taken. A letters-sent book, Feb. 21-Sept. 15, 1861 (1 vol.), was purchased by the Library in 1929 and is probably the copy that Leroy P. Walker had made before he left office (Jones, A Rebel War Clerk's Diary, 1:79).

Small collections of papers of those who served as Secretary of War are in other repositories. A few pieces of correspondence of Leroy P. Walker are in the Alabama Department of Archives and History and Duke University Library. Correspondence of Judah P. Benjamin at the American Jewish Archives includes a few wartime items. Letters of George W. Randolph are in Duke University Library, in the Confederate Museum, and with the Edgehill-Randolph papers in the University of Virginia Library. James A. Seddon reported to John W. Jones on Mar. 27, 1876, that his papers had been almost completely destroyed during his imprisonment after the war (Southern Historical Society Papers, 1:203). Some of his papers, however, including correspondence with Jefferson Davis and Bradley T. Johnson, are in Duke University Library. A few other papers of Seddon, Jan. 1863-Dec. 1864, are in the Chicago Historical Society collections. A fire in John C. Breckinridge's house in Lexington, Ky., after the war destroyed certain papers and mementoes, but some Breckinridge papers in the Chicago Historical Society include items for the war period. Other Breckinridge papers in the Library of Congress are dated 1821-75, with a gap for 1857-62.

Papers of other War Department officials are also available. The John A. Campbell papers in the Southern Historical Collection in the University of North Carolina Library include a letter to John C. Breckinridge, Mar. 5, 1865, on the condition of the Confederacy and recommending its surrender, his recollections of the evacuation of Richmond and meetings with Lincoln and Seward, and letters to his family, May-Oct. 1865, written while he was imprisoned. Papers of Campbell, Jan.-Apr. 1865, concerning negotiations for peace are in the Illinois State Historical Library. Other Campbell papers are in the Alabama Department of Archives and History, the Confederate Museum collections, and Yale University Library.

The University of Virginia Library contains papers of Albert T. Bledsoe, and a few letters are in the Henry E. Huntington Library and Miami University, Oxford, Ohio. The diary and correspondence, 1861-65, of Robert G. H. Kean are in the University of Virginia Library; Dr. Robert H. Kean of Richmond, Va., has other correspondence. A diary of Maj. Edward C. Anderson, May 26-Nov. 14, 1861, in the Southern Historical Collection at the University of North Carolina Library concerns his activities as a purchasing agent in England associated with Caleb Huse. Beverly R. Wellford's diary, Apr. 2-May 19, 1865 (on microfilm), in the same repository, relates the escape of the Confederate Cabinet to Charlotte, N. C.

ADJUTANT AND INSPECTOR GENERAL'S OFFICE

The Adjutant and Inspector General's Office, established under an act of Feb. 26, 1861 (Prov. Cong. C.S.A. Stat. 38), became the custodian of records concerning officer and enlisted personnel of the Army. Such records included orders for the assignment and transfer of officers, reports of deaths with inventories of personal effects, applications for leave, certificates of disability signed by surgeons, resignations of officers, copies of orders issued by army commands, muster rolls and payrolls, returns of prisoners, and inspection reports.

AIGO Special Order 46 1/2 of Feb. 26, 1864, authorized a number of subordinate offices. The Reception Office, under Capt. John W. Riely, was charged with receiving, opening, endorsing, abstracting, and distributing correspondence and official papers, keeping the files and general records, and receiving visitors. The Office of Orders, under Lt. Col. John Withers, recorded general and special orders and actions on applications for leaves of absence, furloughs, transfers, details, discharges, and return of soldiers and the resignation and assignment of officers. The Appointment Office, under Lt. Col. Edward A. Palfrey, kept the register of commissioned officers. The Office of Organization, to which Maj. Samuel W. Melton was assigned initially, had charge of muster rolls, rosters, returns, and reports and matters related to the military organizations of the Army. The Judge Advocate's Office, under Maj. Charles H. Lee, handled papers and applications relating to courts-martial and courts of inquiry. Maj. William S. Barton succeeded Major Lee on Apr. 23, 1864. The Adjutant General's Office, under Lt. Col. Hugh L. Clay, acted upon matters that could not be handled by other offices and prepared general orders. The Office of Inspection, to which Col. Robert H. Chilton was assigned on Apr. 4, 1864, attended to inspection duties in the several armies and staff departments and had charge of inspection reports.

An act of Oct. 13, 1862 (1 Cong. C.S.A. Stat. 89), authorized the President to bestow medals upon officers for courage and good conduct on the field of battle. He was also to confer a badge of distinction upon a private or noncommissioned officer elected by each company participating in victories. AIGO General Order 131 of Oct. 3, 1863, announced that the names of those considered worthy of medals and badges were to be inscribed in a roll of honor to be preserved in the Adjutant and Inspector General's Office. Such a roll accompanied the order, and another was published with General Order 64 of Aug. 10, 1864; others are in the Official Records . . . Armies. No actual medals appear to have been issued, however.

The records of the Adjutant and Inspector General's Office were surrendered to Maj. Gen. John M. Schofield at Charlotte, N. C., on May 13, 1865.

Successive heads of the office:
Maj. George Deas (acting), Mar. 7, 1861.
Brig. Gen. Samuel Cooper, Mar. 16, 1861.

Bauman L. Belden, War Medals of the Confederacy (New York, 1915); C. S. A. War Department, Articles of War for the Government of the Army of the Confederate States (Montgomery, 1861); Thomas Parks, "The Confederate Roll of Honor, " Chronicles of Oklahoma, 34:234-238 (Summer 1956); William M. Robinson, Jr., Justice in Grey; a History of the Judicial System of the Confederate States of America, p. 359-382 (Cambridge, Mass., 1941).

Record Group 109. --The very extensive records of the Adjutant and Inspector General's Office became part of the War Department Collection of Confederate Records. They are described below by type:

Correspondence. Fair copies of letters and telegrams sent, Mar. 2, 1861-Apr. 1, 1865 (ch. I, vols. 35-41, 43-44, 2 ft.; available on microfilm as M 627), are addressed to Army officers, heads of War Department offices, the Secretary of War, Members of Congress, State Governors, Government officials, private individuals, and industrial firms. The volumes are indexed. There are other letters sent by the Recruiting Service, Feb. 18, 1862-Mar. 26, 1864 (ch. I, vol. 175), and letters sent by the Inspection Office, May 23, 1864-Mar. 28, 1865 (ch. I, vol. 24). An indexed volume of telegrams sent, Jan. 3-Apr. 28, 1865 (ch. I, vol. 23), mainly to general officers, continues the record of correspondence just described.

Letters received, 1861-65 (34 ft.; available on microfilm as M 474), include original letters received, some telegrams, and other documents from Army officers, War Department officials, Members of Congress, State Governors, Government officials, and individuals. Many letters in this file were addressed to the Secretary of War, the President, heads of War Department offices, and Gen. Braxton Bragg; they were referred to the Adjutant and Inspector General for action. Some letters from Navy officers relate to details of soldiers. Transmittal letters cover many different kinds of returns that were submitted to AIGO. The letters in this file concern personnel matters, orders, military movements, Army administration and organization, civilian personnel, and other matters. Other documents in the file include accounts current and reports of the Recruiting Service, oaths of office, officers' bonds, orders, medical certificates granting furloughs, soldiers' discharges, affidavits, requisitions for forage, applications for leave, reports on staff officers, and medical certificates. There are also many cross-reference cards for letters published in the Official Records . . .Armies and in the compiled military service records described in chapter XI of this Guide. Registers of letters received, Mar. 26, 1861-Apr. 28, 1865 (ch. I, vols. 45-74, 6 ft.), are arranged chronologically within 3-month periods, thereunder alphabetically by name of writer, and thereunder numerically. There is an index to letters of resignation, Oct. 1, 1861-June 14, 1862 (ch. I, vols. 162-164), for vols. 47 and 48 of the registers of letters received. Endorsement books, Mar. 1864-Apr. 1865 (ch. I, vols. 29-34, 1 ft.), contain abstracts of letters received and endorsements recorded thereon; name indexes accompany these volumes. A card index to the letters received, 1861-65 (95 ft.; available on microfilm as M 410; also for letters received by the Quartermaster General's Office), was compiled by the Confederate Archives Division of the Adjutant

General's Office in 1893. It contains cards for the signers of letters, enclosures, and endorsements for persons and organizations referred to in the letters. Since it is a consolidated index it is more useful than the registers and endorsement books, but the latter contain data about letters that are missing from the letters-received file.

Telegrams received and drafts of telegrams sent, 1861-65 (9 in.), are numerically arranged on message forms. There is an indexed record of telegrams received, Jan. 1, 1862-Apr. 28, 1865, in this record group (ch. I, vols. 21 and 22).

Other letters are recorded in a register of letters received by the Recruiting Service, Jan. 1862-Apr. 1864 (ch. I, vol. 174); these are usually reports from recruiting officers.

Inspection Reports. The Inspection Office, set up in 1864, became the custodian of records relating to inspections. Besides the letters-sent book, already described, it kept a register of letters received, May 1, 1864-Apr. 10, 1865 (ch. I, vol. 25). This book contains a record of inspection reports and abstracts of letters received. A file of inspection reports, 1863-65 (5 ft.), concerns all types of military organizations and field installations and offices of the Confederate Army. The reports sometimes include lists of officers, property returns, returns of small arms, morning reports, reports of employees, rolls of extra-duty men, and printed rules and regulations. A catalog of inspection reports (2 vols.) shows the name of the inspecting officer, the unit or installation inspected, the file symbol of the report, and its date. The reports are indexed (1 vol.). Other records relating to inspections include extracts from inspection reports, Oct. 5, 1864-Mar. 28, 1865 (ch. I, vol. 26). The names of inspecting officers of armies, corps, and divisions and those on general inspection duty, 1864, are listed (ch. I, vol. 26 1/2).

Courts-Martial, Military Courts, and Courts of Inquiry. The Articles of War adopted by the Confederate Congress on Mar. 6, 1861 (Prov. Cong. C. S. A. Stat. 51), provided for the use of courts-martial to try Army personnel charged with offenses against military law. Generals commanding armies and officers commanding departments could appoint the members of general courts-martial. Officers commanding a corps, regiment, fort, garrison, or barracks composed of troops from different services could appoint special courts-martial. The original proceedings of courts-martial with testimony and documentary exhibits were sent to the Adjutant and Inspector General's Office for any necessary review and preservation.

Because courts-martial procedure proved to be inefficient, an act of Oct. 9, 1862 (1 Cong. C. S. A. Stat. 71), authorized a military court for each army corps in the field, with three members and a judge advocate appointed by the President. Each court could appoint a provost marshal to execute its orders and a clerk to record its proceedings and adopt rules. The jurisdiction of these courts extended to offenses against the Articles of War, the customs of war, and Confederate and State law. Appointments of judges and judge advocates were announced by the War Department on Dec. 20, 1862 (AIGO General Order 109), and Feb. 13, 1863 (AIGO General Order 17). In 1864 military courts were authorized for A. P. Hill's corps in the Army of Northern Virginia, for northern Alabama, and for Nathan B. Forrest's and Stephen D. Lee's cavalry divisions. An authorization for the appointment of military courts in each of the geographical military departments and army corps (1 Cong. C. S. A. Stat. 157) was followed by a further authorization for military courts in each State within those departments

(1 Cong. C. S. A. Stat. 193). The appointments of personnel for a military court for the Trans-Mississippi Department were confirmed on Feb. 17, 1864 (Senate Journal, 3:806, 812). The military courts had unrestricted jurisdiction over military personnel except corps and department commanders, and they exercised civil jurisdiction in occupied hostile areas. Their power was similar to that of Confederate States district courts. After review by corps commanders the records of their proceedings were sent to the Adjutant and Inspector General's Office.

Courts of inquiry were established to investigate transactions or accusations against military personnel. These courts consisted of one or more officers, not more than three, and a judge advocate or other suitable person as a recorder. Although they could examine witnesses, these courts could not express an opinion unless so directed; ordinarily they were no more than factfinding bodies.

Charles H. Lee, The Judge Advocate's Vade Mecum; Embracing a General View of Military Law, and the Practice before Courts Martial, With an Epitome of the Law of Evidence, As Applicable to Military Trials (Richmond, 1863). While attached to the Adjutant and Inspector General's Office, Lee compiled this publication for the guidance of officers serving on courts. A revised and enlarged edition with a chapter on naval courts-martial and courts of inquiry was published in 1864.

The Judge Advocate's Office had charge of the records relating to courts-martial. Letters, telegrams, and endorsements sent, Mar. 24, 1864-Mar. 24, 1865 (ch. I, vol. 42), contain fair copies of communications relating to the convening of courts-martial, the suspension or execution of sentences, and the transmission of records. A volume of endorsements on court-martial correspondence, Mar.-Nov. 1864 (ch. I, vol. 201), contains abstracts of letters received and a record of endorsements on them. A record of courts-martial, Apr. 1861-May 1865 (ch. I, vols. 194-199, 1 ft.), gives the date and number, name, rank and organization of person tried, the finding, and sentence. Separate name indexes are available for vols. 195 and 196. A brief record of court-martial cases submitted to the Secretary of War, Jan. 9-Mar. 30, 1865 (ch. I, vol. 200), includes a name index.

Most court-martial proceedings are to be found in the compiled military service records of officers and soldiers described in chapter XI of this Guide. Proceedings involving more than one person are filed in the miscellaneous collection of manuscripts also described in chapter XI; these are cross-referenced in the pertinent compiled military service records. Orders presenting charges, specifications, and findings of courts-martial and courts of inquiry are in the AIGO general orders and the orders of Army headquarters.

Orders. During the war the AIGO preserved manuscript copies of the general and special orders that were distributed in printed form throughout the military establishment in numbered annual series.

General orders were used to disseminate instructions of general applicability and to publish acts of Congress; Presidential proclamations; findings of courts-martial, military courts, and courts of inquiry; rolls of honor; schedules of prices for impressed articles, labor, and services; lists of officers appointed, promoted, dropped, and resigned; changes in

regulations; administrative and procedural changes; and notices regarding
the exchange of prisoners. General orders, Mar. 25, 1861-Mar. 24, 1865
(ch. I, vols. 202 and 203), are numbered serially as follows:
Vol. 202: nos. 1-22, Mar. 23-Dec. 27, 1861; nos. 1-112, Jan. 1-Dec.
30, 1862; nos. 1-164, Jan. 3-Dec. 29, 1863.
Vol. 203: nos. 1-87, Jan. 4-Dec. 10, 1864; nos. 1-9, Jan. 6-Mar. 10,
and, unnumbered, Mar. 24, 1865. A similarly arranged printed set is
also available (ch. I, vols. 1-5) with a name and subject index (vol. 1A).
Vol. 5 contains an order of Mar. 30, 1865, that is not in vol. 203.

Special orders relate to individual officers and enlisted men and concern appointments, assignments, transfers, discharges, leaves of absence,
and the like. Some orders concern the establishment of and appointments
to general courts-martial, courts of inquiry, boards of survey, and medi-
cal examining boards, and the release of paroled prisoners of war. In
Record Group 109 are manuscript copies of special orders, Mar. 7, 1861-
Apr. 1, 1865 (ch. I, vols. 204-219, 4 1/2 ft.); other copies are also available (ch. I, vols. 6-20). The special orders are numbered serially as
follows:
Vol. 204: nos. 1-279, Mar. 7-Dec. 31, 1861.
Vols. 205 and 206: nos. 1-306, Jan. 2-Dec. 31, 1862.
Vols. 207 and 208: nos. 1-310, Jan. 2-Dec. 31, 1863.
Vols. 209-211: nos. 1-310, Jan. 2-Dec. 31, 1864.
Vol. 212: nos. 1-78, Jan. 3-Apr. 1, 1865.
These volumes have name indexes. Vols. 213-219 contain an incomplete
set for Jan. 2, 1862-June 14, 1864. Other manuscript special orders, 1861-
65 (2 1/2 ft.), with many duplicates are arranged by year and thereunder
by order number. A brief record of special orders issued, 1862-65 (ch.
I, vol. 220), gives some information about the individuals concerned.

The general orders were printed in Richmond from the files of the AIGO and in Charleston or Columbia, S.C., from the files of the Department of South Carolina, Georgia, and Florida. Library locations of copies of these compilations are given in Crandall, Confederate Imprints, 1:218-219, and in Harwell, More Confederate Imprints, 1:66-67. Special orders were also printed in Richmond and can be found among the records of Army commands, but they are not available in bound volumes in libraries. Five volumes of special orders, 1861-65, were printed by the U.S. War Department in the 1870's as "preliminary prints" for the use of the War Records Office in compiling the Official Records . . . Armies. Sets of these printed special orders are in Record Group 109, in the National Archives Library, and in the Rare Book Room of the Library of Congress. General orders and special orders are also printed in Official Records . . . Armies.

Muster Rolls and Payrolls. The Confederate States Army adopted
the practice of the U.S. Army in using muster rolls and payrolls to report
the strength of military organizations and units and payments made to noncommissioned officers and privates. Inspectors-general or other officers
conducted musters of troops usually at bimonthly intervals when after an
inspection and review the names of the men were called and checked off on
rolls. The combined muster rolls and payrolls were then prepared on
printed forms by the adjutant, signed by the mustering officer, certified by
the commanding officer, and forwarded to the Adjutant and Inspector

General's Office. Muster rolls deposited in that office by recruiting officers served as certificates of enlistment. When new organizations such as the local defense forces were authorized, they were required to forward muster rolls. Payments made by post commanders to soldiers who had been retired under the act of Feb. 17, 1864, were to be reported on muster rolls.

Muster rolls and payrolls, 1861-65 (folded papers, 805 ft.), show the designation of the unit, names of officers and noncommissioned officers, and enlisted men, rank, dates and places of enlistment, name of enlisting officer, period of enlistment, date of last payment, remarks as to those absent, amount paid, signatures, strength of the unit, its station, casualties, a record of events, and the inspecting officer's report. Company rolls make up the bulk of the file, but some rolls of battalions, legions, and other units are included. The rolls are arranged by State, thereunder by arm of service, and thereunder by unit. The file also includes some morning reports, regimental returns, correspondence, miscellaneous papers, and cross-reference cards for material placed in compiled files relating to individuals. There are also rolls, arranged by State, of militia and reserve organizations and State troops. There are other rolls of Confederate infantry, cavalry, and artillery organizations; engineer troops; sappers and miners; pioneers; the Signal Corps; bands; foreign battalions; the Invalid Corps; Scouts; prison, provost, and hospital guards; Indian organizations; the Infantry School of Practice; and hospital personnel and patients. Also available is a list of officers of the Niter and Mining Bureau. The file includes some copies of muster rolls that were made from originals lent to the Record and Pension Office after the compilation of military service records was begun in 1903. Some rolls of a number of State organizations have been repaired and filed separately. The information relating to individual servicemen on the muster and payrolls has been abstracted on cards that are filed in the compiled military service records described in chapter XI.

An incomplete card catalog of muster rolls, 1861-65 (6 ft. 5 in.), shows the organization, date of roll, station, name of commanding officer, and sometimes names of other officers. It is arranged by State (Alabama, Florida, Georgia, Maryland, North Carolina, and Virginia) and thereunder by organization.

Appointment Records. Officers were appointed or elected under Confederate or State laws. An act of Mar. 6, 1861 (Prov. Cong. C.S.A. Stat. 47), providing for the organization of the Regular Army, authorized the President to appoint Army officers with the advice and consent of the Congress. Under an act of Mar. 6, 1861 (Prov. Cong. C.S.A. Stat. 45), volunteers accepted into Confederate service could be organized by the President, who was authorized to appoint commanding officers of brigades and divisions with the advice and consent of the Congress. The same act authorized the President to appoint additional officers for quartermaster, commissary, and medical departments for volunteers or militia called into Confederate service. On May 8, 1861 (Prov. Cong. C.S.A. Stat. 104), the President was authorized to appoint field and staff officers of additional volunteer forces. Company officers were to be elected.

William F. Amann, ed., Personnel of the Civil War, Volume 1: The Confederate Armies, Volume 2: The Union Armies (New York, 1961). Volume I of this work contains reprints of the U.S. War Department compilations entitled Local Designations of Confederate Troops

(Washington, n.d.) and Memorandum of Armies, Corps, and Geographical Commands in the Confederate States from 1861 to 1865 (Washington, n.d.). C. E. Dornbusch, Military Bibliography of the Civil War, Volume 2: Regimental Publications and Personal Narratives: Southern, Border, and Western States and Territories; Federal Troops, Union and Confederate Biographies (New York, 1967). Ellsworth Eliot, Jr., West Point in the Confederacy (New York, 1941); Claud Estes, List of Field Officers, Regiments and Battalions in the Confederate States Army, 1861-1865 (Macon, Ga., 1912). Charles C. Jones, Jr., "A Roster of General Officers, Heads of Departments, Senators, Representatives, Military Organizations, etc., in Confederate Service . . .During the War Between the States," Southern Historical Society Papers, 1-3 (1876-77); U.S. War Department, List of Field Officers, Regiments and Battalions in the Confederate Army, 1861-1865 (Washington, ca. 1890), and List of Staff Officers of the Confederate States Army, 1861-1865 (Washington, 1891)--both of these compilations are very incomplete. U.S. War Department, "Memorandum Relative to the General Officers Appointed by the President in the Armies of the Confederate States--1861-1865," (S. Doc. 244, 60 Cong., 1 sess., Serial 5241; Washington, 1908). U.S. War Records Office, Memorandum of Field Officers in the Confederate States Service (Washington, 189?). Ezra J. Warner, Generals in Gray; Lives of the Confederate Commanders (Baton Rouge, 1959). See also the bibliography following the section of this chapter on Territorial Commands and Armies. Besides the series already indicated, other AIGO records bound into volumes (vols. 56-191) are on negative microfilm.

The appointment process involved several types of records. A record of appointments to be confirmed, 1861-62 (ch. I, vol. 148), shows organization, officer's name, to whom to report, and date of rank. A record of confirmations, 1861-64, (ch. I, vol. 149), shows name, assignment, date of appointment, date of rank, date of confirmation, and frequent notations about later personnel actions. A register of applications for appointment and promotion, 1863-65 (ch. I, vols. 156-158), shows name of person recommended, for what position, name of recommender, and disposition of the application. Vol. 156 includes a list of promotions for valor and skill. Endorsements on applications for appointment and promotion, 1863-64 (ch. I, vols. 160-162), are accompanied by name indexes. There are registers of applications for appointment as major or brigadier general and for regimental positions, 1863-65 (ch. I, vols. 155 and 159). A record book relating to officers (ch. I, vol. 150), contains the following sections: copies of letters of appointment and recommendation, chiefly from the Secretary of War, Mar. 1-Sept. 4, 1861; a list of promotions for valor and skill, 1863-64; and a list of officers granted authority to raise troops, 1863-64, with name indexes for the second and third sections. A record of the election of officers, 1862-65 (ch. I, vols. 152-154), gives the place and date of election, with rank and organization.

Registers of Appointments. Registers of appointments of officers give name, rank, date of appointment, confirmation and acceptance, arm of service, State, to whom to report, and sometimes information on declination, promotion, resignation, death, or other circumstances. The information on individuals in these registers has been abstracted on cards filed in the compiled military service records described in chapter XI of

this Guide. The contents of the volumes (all in ch. I) are as follows:
> Vol. 86. General officers and corps and department officers, 1861-
> 65.
> Vol. 88. Regular Army, 1861-65.
> Vol. 93. Field and regimental appointments of State and Confederate
> States organizations, Jan. 1864-Mar. 1865.
> Vol. 94. Field and staff officers, Jan. 1864-Mar. 1865.
> Vols. 116-120. Record of notifications of appointments sent to field
> and staff officers with notations on dates of acceptance, confir-
> mation, declination, or resignation.
> Vol. 123. Rough record of appointments and promotions for valor
> and skill, 1861-64. Most entries are crossed through.
> Vol. 124. Rough record of appointments, May 1862. Most pages are
> crossed through to indicate that the information was entered in
> another record.
> Vol. 128. Record of all types of appointments in all officer ranks,
> with name index.

Some of the above volumes are indexed by name in separate volumes, but most of them are included in a card index to appointments of officers, 1861-65 (17 ft.), that was compiled by the U.S. Adjutant General's Office.

Separate registers are available for staff officers of field commands, 1861-65 (ch. I, vol. 99); staff officers, 1861-65 (ch. I, vol. 133); division and brigade staff officers, 1862-64 (ch. I, vol. 122); officers appointed to temporary rank, 1861-65 (ch. I, vol. 115); aides-de-camp, 1862-65 (ch. I, vol. 114); quartermasters, 1861-65 (ch. I, vol. 135); commissaries of subsistence, 1861-65 (ch. I, vol. 134); drillmasters, 1862-65 (ch. I, vol. 131); chaplains, 1861-65 (ch. I, vol. 132); and officers of partisan rangers, n.d. (ch. I, vol. 113). A record of quartermasters, Apr. 27, 1861-Mar. 11, 1865 (ch. I, vol. 137), contains lists of brigade quartermasters, assistant quartermasters, and quartermasters by State and regiment. A chronological list of quartermasters, July 15, 1861-Jan. 10, 1863 (ch. I, vol. 138), shows the State, organization, or office to which assigned, with remarks such as declined, dropped, promoted, dead, resigned, and disbanded. A typewritten copy of an undated list of quartermasters (ch. I, vol. 136), gives the quartermasters of a few divisions. There is also a record of appointments made after the adjournment of the third session of the First Congress, May 1, 1863, 1863-64 (ch. I, vol. 127). A register of officers reporting at the Adjutant General's Office in Richmond, Jan. 1864-Feb. 1865 (ch. I, vol. 102), gives information on rank, corps, last station, post office, or residence. Most of these volumes are indexed in the card index to appointments of officers noted and have been microfilmed.

Regimental Rosters. Rosters of commissioned officers of regiments contain information about rank, date of appointment or election, resignation, and sometimes other matters. Volumes 75, 76, and 78 also contain similar information on successor officers. The coverage of the rosters (all in ch. I) is as follows:
> Vol. 75, 1861-65, Ala., Fla., Ga., Miss., and S.C.
> Vol. 76, 1861-65, Ark., La., and Tex.
> Vol. 78, 1861-65, N.C. and Va.
> Vol. 80, 1864-65, Ala., Ga., N.C., and Va.
> Vol. 81, 1861-65, Ark., Miss., Mo., and S.C.
> Vol. 82, 1861-65, Ala., Ark., Ga., Ky., La., Md., Miss., and Mo.
> Vol. 83, 1861-65, Ala., Ark., Fla., Ga., and Ky.

Vol. 84, 1861-65, Ala., Ga., La., Miss., and N.C.
Vol. 87 1/2, 1861-62, Ark., La., and Tenn.
Vol. 92, 1861-65, Ala., Ark., Fla., Ga., Miss., Mo., N.C., S.C.,
Tenn., Tex., and Va.
Vol. 95, 1863-65, Ga. and Va.
Vol. 96, 1863-65, Ala., Ark., Fla., Ga., La., Miss., Mo., S.C.,
Tenn., Tex., and Va.
Vol. 99, n.d., N.C. and Tex.
Vol. 101, n.d., Ala., Ark., Fla., Ga., La., Miss., Mo., N.C.,
S.C., Tenn., Tex., and Va.
Vol. 104, n.d., N.C., S.C., Tenn., Tex., and Va.
Vol. 105, n.d., Ala., Ark., Fla., Ga., Ky., La., Md., Miss.,
and Mo.
Vol. 107, n.d., Ala., Ark., Fla., Ga., La., Miss., Mo., N.C.,
S.C., Tenn., Tex., and Va.
Vol. 107 1/2, 1861-62, Ark., La., Miss., Mo., and Tex.
Vol. 113, n.d., Ala., Ark., Fla., and Ga.

Some of the rosters include battalions, batteries, reserves, local defense forces, and Indian troops. Most of them were used by the U.S. War Department in preparing the compiled military service records described in chapter XI of this Guide.

A record of the arrival and departure of troops at Richmond and roster of officers, 1861-62 (ch. I, vol. 103), contains a record of the arrival and departure of regiments (p. 98-113), and a roster of officers of regiments and battalions (p. 117-125, 300-343). Regiments and battalions are indexed in the back of the book, and an alphabetical name index is in a separate volume.

Battalion Rosters. A roster of battalion officers, 1861-65 (ch. I, vol. 79), shows name, date of entry or muster into State or Confederate service, whether elected or appointed, date and cause of vacancy, and similar information for the successor officer. Information is sometimes given on mergers with other organizations, including battalions of infantry, cavalry, artillery, partisan rangers, and sharpshooters. Another roster of battalion officers, 1861-65 (ch. I, vol. 87), supplies similar information regarding officers of the same types of organizations and also engineer troops, foreign battalions, and the Confederate States First Battalion. Name indexes are in separate volumes. Another roster of battalion officers, n.d. (ch. I, vol. 98), shows officers of the local defense forces (infantry, cavalry, mounted infantry, and reserves) of Alabama, Georgia, North Carolina, and Virginia; Confederate States battalions; artillery battalions of the Army of Northern Virginia and the Army of Tennessee; and the First Foreign Battalion.

Resignations, Discharges, and Deaths. Army Regulations required the transmission to the Adjutant and Inspector General of resignations of officers, reports of deaths and inventories of effects, certificates of disability warranting discharges, and returns of casualties. Registers of resignations of officers, 1862-65 (ch. I, vols. 166-168, 170, and a supplementary vol.), show rank and organization, date and place of resignation, and date of its acceptance. Lists of resignations accepted during 1862 (ch. I, vol. 165) and for 1862-65 (ch. I, vols. 169 and 171) and a register of resignations, 1865 (ch. I, vol. 172), show similar information. A record of discharges on surgeons' certificates of disability, 1861-65 (ch. I, vols. 176-185), shows date, name, rank, organization, date and place of discharge,

and name of surgeon. A register of deaths and effects reported, 1861-65
(ch. I, vols. 27 and 28), contains similar information regarding deaths.
Casualty lists, 1861-65 (folded papers, 1 1/3 ft.), consist of lists of men
killed, wounded, and missing. The lists give information on individuals
and are arranged by State and thereunder by name of battle or engagement.
Reports on operations accompany many of the lists. Citations to the place
of publication in the Official Records . . . Armies are on these documents.
The information on individuals in these records has been abstracted on
cards that are in the compiled military service records described below
in chapter XI of this Guide.

Invalid Corps. Several registers relating to the Invalid Corps are
available. A register of applications from officers and soldiers for transfer to the Corps, 1864-65 (ch. I, vols. 190 and 191), shows date, number,
name, rank, and organization, date and place of application, and notes on
the duty applied for. A register of officers of the Invalid Corps, Mar. 19,
1864-Apr. 1, 1865 (ch. I, vol. 192, rough copy in vol. 97), gives name, rank,
and organization, date of retirement, station, sometimes post office,
county and State, when and where assigned to duty, notes on disabilities
and requests for assignments, and date of renewal of form for retirement.
An alphabetical name index is in a separate volume. A register of enlisted
men of the Invalid Corps, Mar. 28, 1864-Mar. 23, 1865 (ch. I, vol. 193),
indexed, contains similar information. The information in the last two
registers is included in the compiled military service records described
in chapter XI of this Guide.

Boards to Examine Officers. The election of officers and promotion
by seniority resulted in the commissioning of many incompetent officers.
AIGO General Order 39 of May 26, 1862, authorized brigade and division
commanders to form boards of not less than three officers to examine the
qualifications of officers elected or promoted by reason of seniority in the
Provisional Army. "An Act to relieve the army of disqualified, disabled
and incompetent officers" of Oct. 13, 1862 (1 Cong. C.S.A. Stat. 85), directed commanders of departments to appoint boards to examine the qualifications of officers whose cases were brought to their attention. Their reports
were transmitted to the Department for examination and decision, resulting
in the removal of many officers; under threat of examination, others resigned. Lists of officers who resigned or were removed appear in the
special orders. General Order 49 of June 4, 1864, contains the names of
425 officers who were dropped, and General Order 51 of June 10, 1864, lists
the names of 1,300 officers who resigned. Officer examining boards were
also formed to examine candidates for appointments as artillery officers
for ordnance service and appointments as engineers.

Decisions of examining boards for promotion, 1862-65 (ch. I, vols.
186-188 and 189), show name, rank, and organization of the officers examined, whether the decision was favorable or unfavorable, sometimes the
date and place of the board's meeting, and the rank and organization to
which the person was to be promoted. There is an alphabetical name index
in a separate volume for vols. 186-188.

Cadets. An act of May 16, 1861, to increase the military establishment (Prov. Cong. C.S.A. Stat. 115) authorized the President to appoint
cadets from the States in numbers proportionate to their representation in
the House of Representatives plus 10 others. Until the opening of a military
academy the cadets were to be attached to companies in any branch of the
Army as supernumerary officers. No military academy was established,

but cadets served in both the Regular Army and the Provisional Army.

Registers of applications, appointments, and promotions of cadets are available. A register of applications for cadetships, 1861-65 (ch. I, vol. 129), gives the date, name and age of applicant, residence, number of the congressional district, name of recommender, and information about the cadet's service. A register of cadet appointments, 1861-65 (ch. I, vol. 130), shows the name of cadet, State, name of person to whom to report, and some notations on the duty; it contains an index.

Records Relating to Army Organization. A record of the organization of the Confederate Army, n. d. (ch. I, vols. 143-145), shows the composition of armies, corps, divisions, brigades, and territorial commands. Vols. 144 and 145 contain indexes to names of officers. An undated register of troop organizations (ch. I, vol. 14 1/2) shows for regiments and battalions the names of brigade and division commanders and the army to which they were attached.

Other Records. A record of the arrival of companies in Virginia, June 7-Nov. 4, 1861 (ch. I, vol. 113), gives information about the companies and their commanders and arms. A record of the receipt of returns, Oct. 1861-Jan. 1864 (ch. I, vol. 142), gives information on returns from regiments, battalions, companies, some brigade and departmental commands, and posts. An account book relating to telegrams, Sept. 1862-Mar. 1864 (ch. I, vol. 112), shows date of telegram, name of officer who sent or received it, and its cost. A register of requests received for authority to raise troops, Jan. 23-Apr. 22, 1865 (ch. I, vol. 151), contains names of persons making requests, names of troop units to be raised, and indications of acceptance or rejection, or referral. There is an undated roster of the President's Guard (ch. I, vol. 112). Also available is a record of the distribution of blank forms and general orders, Apr. 4, 1862-Mar. 3, 1865 (ch. I, vol. 221), endorsement forms for the Invalid Corps, 1864-65 (ch. I, vol. 193), a record of troops offered to the Confederate War Department. Copies of documents in a book labeled "Prison pens, Canada raids, secret operations" (ch. VII, vol. 24) include a consolidated return for Andersonville military prison, Aug. 1864, three letters of July and Aug. 1864 relating to that prison, and letters of K. J. Stewart to Jefferson Davis from Toronto, Nov. 30 and Dec. 12, 1864, with suggestions about operations against the United States. A book of memoranda on battle reports, 1863-64 (ch. VIII, vol. 354), gives name and rank of reporting officer, subject, date delivered, date returned, date original was sent to the Adjutant and Inspector General, and date copies were sent to Congress. Requests to the Secretary of War for requisitions for funds, Apr. 3, 1861-Oct. 13, 1862 (ch. I, vol. 173), show amount, purpose, and fund to be charged.

Among additional records are those relating to officers and cadets, 1861-64 (3 in.), which include a list of U. S. Army officers who resigned to join the Confederate Army; lists of applications for lieutenancies and captaincies; copies of notifications of appointments as cadets, lieutenants, and captains; lists of officers appointed to different grades; and lists of officers whose appointments were confirmed. Material relating to conscription and recruiting, 1861-65 (3 in.), includes correspondence, orders and circulars relating to conscription in various States, special orders and circulars issued by the Bureau of Conscription and the Richmond Conscript Office, orders and circulars relating to the Volunteer and Conscript Bureau of the Army of Tennessee, abstracts of payments, accounts current, and summary statements. Powers of attorney, 1861-65 (3/4 in.), authorize the

designated officers to receive and receipt for money due the signers for
their services. Records of boards of survey, 1861-65 (3 in.), contain orders appointing boards and reports concerning their investigations of the
losses of supplies and equipment, of deliveries of defective materials and
stores, and of the condition of supplies and equipment. A diary kept by
Lt. Col. John Withers, Jan. 1856-Dec. 1862 (3 notebooks), contains some
references to AIGO and to Government officials.

    Records in Other Custody. --In the Manuscript Division of the Library
of Congress is a miscellaneous collection of Confederate muster rolls,
1861-65, consisting of 61 rolls of organizations of various States. A list
of these rolls is in Ralph W. Donnelly, "Confederate Muster Rolls, " Military Affairs, 16:132-135 (Fall 1952).

    The Valentine Museum, Richmond, Va., has the proceedings of a
general court-martial convened in Petersburg, Va., in Mar. 1864 to adjudicate the case of Capt. William J. Malone. The Southern Historical Collection in the University of North Carolina Library has papers of Maj.
Garnett Andrews, containing correspondence and other documents relating
to the courts-martial of Maj. Gen. Lafayette McLaws and Brig. Gen.
Jerome B. Robertson. The Confederate Museum has papers relating to the
court-martial of Lt. Col. Richard B. Garnett on charges brought by Lt.
Gen. Thomas J. Jackson after the battle of Kernstown. In the same repository are correspondence and special orders, 1863-64, concerning the
court-martial of Daniel L. Russell.

    Chaplains. In his report of Apr. 27, 1861, Secretary of War Walker
recommended legislation empowering the Department to appoint chaplains
in order to promote "morality, good order, and general discipline of the
army in the camp or in the field. " An act of May 3, 1861 (Prov. Cong. C.
S. A. Stat. 99), authorized the President to appoint chaplains to serve with
the armies and to assign them as he thought necessary. Assignments of
chaplains were made in special orders issued by the Adjutant and Inspector
General's Office, but there was no office in the War Department for the
general supervision of chaplains. An act of May 31, 1864 (1 Cong. C.S.A.
Stat. 256), authorized the President to appoint chaplains to battalions and
general hospitals. State organizations entering Confederate service already had chaplains, who were then commissioned by the Adjutant and Inspector General. Men chosen as chaplains by military units from civilian
pastorates, from the unit or other military organization, or volunteers,
were certified to the Adjutant and Inspector General for appointment.

Herman A. Norton, Rebel
Religion; the Story of Confederate
Chaplains (St. Louis, 1961); Charles
F. Pitts, Chaplains in Gray; the
Confederate Chaplains' Story
(Nashville, 1957); Sidney J. Romero,
"Louisiana Clergy and the Confederate Army, " Louisiana History,
2:277-300 (Summer 1961). Rosters
of Confederate chaplains compiled
from published sources are in the
books by Pitts (p. 137-157) and Norton (p. 115-134). Manuscript papers
of chaplains and published diaries
and other materials are listed by
those authors.

Signal Bureau

An act of Congress of Apr. 19, 1862 (1 Cong. C. S. A. Stat. 38), authorized the organization of a Signal Corps. Signal personnel were assigned to corps and division staffs. Squads of mounted signalmen organized lines of communication for field armies and connected their headquarters with existing privately owned telegraph lines. Signalmen operated signal stations, tapped Union wires, and read Union signals. Signal operators also served on the coast and aboard blockade runners to facilitate the entry of vessels into port.

AIGO General Order 40 of May 29, 1862, announced that the Signal Corps would be attached to the Adjutant and Inspector General's Department. The assignment of Capt. William Norris to Richmond for duty with the Corps resulted in the development of a Signal Bureau. The Bureau procured communication equipment and supplies. It conducted a secret service operation to obtain information about enemy activities and plans from agents in the North and in other countries. It sent and received cipher messages and operated a courier service between the Confederacy and the United States. The couriers also brought back northern newspapers, which were examined in the departments for whatever intelligence they might yield. The newspapers were sometimes used as vehicles for the transmission of messages by Confederate agents in the United States. One propaganda agent in the Bureau wrote letters for publication in northern newspapers in an effort to influence public opinion concerning the war. The couriers also conveyed private letters, which after examination in Richmond were delivered through the regular postal system. Official communications and newspapers were distributed by the Signal Bureau to the President and the Government departments. Toward the end of 1864 Lt. Charles H. Cawood had charge of the "Secret Line" to the North (AIGO Special Order 285, Dec. 1, 1864), and commanded a Signal Corps camp on the Potomac River.

Successive heads of the Signal Bureau:
Capt. William Norris, July 31, 1862.
Capt. William N. Barker, Apr. 1864.
Maj. William Norris, Jan. 21, 1865.

The Signal Bureau office and files were destroyed by fire on Apr. 3, 1865. Correspondence of Signal Corps officers is in other correspondence files of the War Department, particularly those described under the Office of the Secretary of War and the Adjutant and Inspector General's Office. Additional records are in the compiled military service records described in chapter XI of this Guide.

J. Willard Brown, The Signal Corps, U. S. A., in the War of the Rebellion (Boston, 1896); H. V. Canan, "Confederate Military Intelligence," Maryland Historical Magazine, 59:34-51 (Mar. 1964); Edwin C. Fishel, "The Mythology of Civil War Intelligence, " Civil War History, 10:344-367 (Dec. 1964); Charles E. Taylor, The Signal and Secret Service of the Confederate States (North Carolina Booklet, vol. 2, no. 11, Hamlet, N. C., 1903).

Records in Other Custody. --A scrapbook of William Norris in the University of Virginia Library contains for the war period his commissions, orders, some correspondence, an invoice dated May 21, 1864, for signal equipment bought by S. B. Tennant from Negretti & Zambri of London, England, letters from Tennant to Norris dated Apr. 23 and May 27, 1864, and printed instructions to signal operators of the Army of the Peninsula, Jan. 31, 1862. The same repository has some letters written by Charles E. Taylor to his mother during 1863-64 while on duty at the signal station at Hamilton's Crossing, Orange County, Va., and at the Signal Bureau. In the Ryder Collection of Confederate Archives in Tufts College Library are letters of William Norris to Secretary of State Benjamin and correspondence with subordinates in the Signal Bureau, Mar. 7, 1865.

QUARTERMASTER GENERAL'S OFFICE AND THE QUARTERMASTER GENERAL'S DEPARTMENT

An act of Feb. 26, 1861 (Prov. Cong. C.S.A. Stat. 38), established the Quartermaster General's Department as part of the Army's General Staff. That act and other legislation provided for the appointment of quartermaster officers to serve in the office in Richmond and with the Army in the field. Assistant quartermasters general attached to the Richmond office included Capt. H. H. Sheldon, Lt. Col. Larkin Smith, and Lt. Col. Aurelius F. Cone.

The Quartermaster General's Department procured supplies and arranged for the transportation of supplies and personnel. It constructed buildings, including hospitals, on Army installations and furnished storage for military supplies. Quartermasters were also charged with the duties of paymasters, and the Department carried on extensive financial and accounting operations. A Quartermaster General's Circular of Nov. 13, 1861, directed quartermasters to pay for private property, except slaves, impressed into or expended in Confederate service. Contested claims for compensation for seized property were referred to the Quartermaster General's Office for settlement. In June 1864 Congress authorized a claims agent for each congressional district to investigate claims for supplies and animals furnished to or impressed by the Army.

The Quartermaster General's Department set up depots to store and distribute supplies and sometimes to manufacture them. By Jan. 1862 there were depots at Richmond, New Orleans, Memphis, Charleston, Savannah, Columbus, Montgomery, Staunton, San Antonio, and Ft. Smith (Prov. Cong., Journal, p. 720). AIGO General Order 13 of Jan. 31, 1863, placed the depots at Augusta, Atlanta, Columbus, Montgomery, and Huntsville, which had been established by the War Department to supply the wants of the Army at large, under the control of the Quartermaster General though they remained subject to the inspection of commanding generals of departments in which they were located.

To avoid competition in the purchase of Army supplies, a Quartermaster General's Circular of Mar. 24, 1863 (Official Records . . . Armies, ser. 4, vol. 2, p. 453-456), constituted the States as separate purchasing districts under principal purchasing officers as follows:

Virginia: Lt. Col. Larkin Smith, Richmond.
North Carolina: Maj. W. W. Pierce, Raleigh.
South Carolina: Maj. Hutson Lee, Charleston.
Georgia: Maj. Isaac T. Winnemore, Augusta.
Alabama: Maj. J. L. Calhoun, Montgomery.
Mississippi: Maj. Livingston Mims, Jackson.
Florida: Maj. H. R. Teasdale, Lake City.

Louisiana: Maj. G. W. Grice, Alexandria.
Texas: Maj. T. A. Washington, San Antonio.
Arkansas and Missouri: Maj. J. B. Burton, Little Rock, Ark.
Tennessee and Kentucky: Maj. James Glover, Knoxville, Tenn.
The purchasing officers were to regulate the prices to be paid for Army supplies, and monthly reports of supplies purchased or manufactured and quantities issued and on hand were to be prepared. Main depots of supplies were to be established at Richmond, Staunton, Raleigh, Columbus, Atlanta, Huntsville, Montgomery, Jackson, Alexandria (La.), Little Rock, Knoxville, and San Antonio, and smaller depots could be established at other points when necessary.

A Quartermaster General's Office memorandum book (Record Group 109, ch. V, vol. 227, p. 3), contains the following undated list of quartermaster officers in charge of depots:

Richmond, Va.: Lt. Col. Aurelius F. Cone
Staunton, Va.: Maj. H. M. Bell
Raleigh, N.C.: Maj. H. R. Hooper
Charleston, S.C.: Capt. G. J. Crafts
Columbus, Ga.: Maj. F. W. Dillard
Augusta, Ga.: Maj. Lemuel O. Bridewell
Savannah, Ga.: Maj. Hermann Hirsch
Montgomery, Ala.: Capt. W. M. Gillaspie
Enterprise, Miss.: Maj. Livingston Mims
Columbus, Miss.: Maj. W. J. Anderson
Camp Lawton, Ga.: Mr. Henry DeVeuve

The practice adopted early in the war of impressing supplies became so widespread and abusive that legislation had to be enacted to control it. An act of Mar. 26, 1863 (1 Cong. C.S.A. Stat. 102), empowered the Secretary of War to authorize the proper subordinate officers (quartermasters and commissaries) to take private property for public use and provided that in cases where the owner and the impressing officer failed to agree upon its value they were to select local appraisers to set the price. The impressing officer was to give to the owner certificates of payment showing the military organization for which the property was taken, the circumstances of the transaction, and the amount paid or owed. Officers could appeal decisions of local appraisers to State boards of commissioners, composed of one member appointed by the Confederate President and one appointed by the Governors. The Governors were also to establish schedules of prices to be used in compensating persons other than the producers from whom property was taken. This act also provided for the payment of compensation for property taken for temporary use and destroyed or damaged while in the hands of the Government.

As a result of complaints against the prices fixed by the State commissioners, AIGO General Order 161 of Dec. 10, 1863, allowed appraisements fixed by the local boards for property belonging to the producer or to a person who had bought it for his own use or consumption. An act of Congress of Feb. 16, 1864 (1 Cong. C.S.A. Stat. 192), amending the act of Mar. 26, 1863, allowed the commissioners on appeals from impressing officers to summon and examine witnesses to enable them to fix prices that would be just compensation at the time and place of impressment. The impressment system did not work well; opposition to it increased, and finally an act of Mar. 18, 1865 (Ramsdell, Laws and Joint Resolutions, p. 151), terminated impressment and directed that market prices be paid.

The large number of slaves and of free Negroes in the Confederacy provided a huge labor pool that was used increasingly by the Army. Slaves were impressed for work from the beginning of the war. The act of Mar. 26, 1863, regulating impressment provided that when slaves could not be hired by the consent of the owner or agent they could be impressed under the laws of the States. An act of Feb. 17, 1864 (1 Cong. C.S.A. Stat. 202), appropriated $3,108,000 to compensate owners for the loss of slaves who had been impressed for labor on public defenses and had escaped or died. Another act of Feb. 17, 1864 (1 Cong. C.S.A. Stat. 235), made free Negroes between 18 and 50 years of age liable for work under the Army on fortifications, in war plants, or in military hospitals at a compensation of $11 a month. The Secretary of War was authorized to employ up to 20,000 slaves, who were to be given rations and clothing and whose wages were to be paid to their owners. The owners were also to be compensated for the full value of the slaves in the event of their death or escape. Where slaves could not be hired, free Negroes were to be impressed; and when free Negroes were insufficient, slaves could be impressed under the same conditions of allowances and compensation. An act of Mar. 1, 1865 (Ramsdell, Laws and Joint Resolutions, p. 69), provided an additional $1 1/2 million to pay compensation for slaves lost while in Government service.

AIGO Special Order 77 of Apr. 1, 1864, appointed a Slave Claims Board to examine and report upon the validity and amount of claims for slaves who had escaped to the enemy or died from injuries received or disease contracted while in Confederate service. This board, which met in Richmond, was composed of Col. James D. Waddell, Maj. J. B. Brockenbrough, and Surg. W. A. Spence.

Successive Quartermasters General:

Lt. Col. Abraham C. Myers, Mar. 25, 1861.

Brig. Gen. Alexander R. Lawton, Aug. 10, 1863.

Rebecca Christian, "Georgia and the Confederate Policy of Impressing Supplies, " Georgia Historical Quarterly, 28:1-33 (Mar. 1944); C.S.A. War Department, Regulations for the Army of the Confederate States, for the Quartermaster's Department, Including the Pay Branch Thereof (Richmond, 1862); Florence F. Corley, Confederate City, Augusta, Georgia, 1860-1865 (Columbia, 1960); William Diamond, "Imports of the Confederate Government from Europe and Mexico, " Journal of Southern History, 6:489-491 (Nov. 1940); Bernard H. Nelson, "Confederate Slave Impressment Legislation, 1861-1865, " Journal of Negro History, 31:392-410 (Oct. 1946); Official Records . . . Armies, ser. 4, vols. 1-3, passim; Charles W. Ramsdell, "The Control of Manufacturing by the Confederate Government, " Mississippi Valley Historical Review, 8:231-249 (Dec. 1921); Diffee W. Standard, Columbus, Georgia, in the Confederacy; the Social and Industrial Life of the Chattahoochee River Port (New York, 1954).

Quartermaster General's Office

Record Group 109.--Records of the Quartermaster General's Office that were captured at Lynchburg, Va., in May 1865 and forwarded to Richmond and shipped thence by Col. Richard D. Cutts to Washington are now in the War Department Collection of Confederate Records (ch. V). They are described below by type:

Correspondence. Letters and telegrams sent, Mar. 25, 1861-Mar. 29, 1865, are in 20 vols.: ch. V, vols. 13-21, 22-31, and 42, measuring 2 ft. 8 in. (available on microfilm as T 131); vols. 13-21 contain fair copies and the others, press copies. Letters to quartermaster officers concern appointments, duties, returns, bonds, and instructions; other letters are to general and other officers, the Secretary of War, State Governors, manufacturers, railroad executives, business firms, and individuals. Fair copies of letters to the Secretary of War, Apr. 1, 1861-Jan. 6, 1864 (ch. V, vol. 157), concern estimates, requisitions for funds, appointments of quartermasters, and the issuance of instructions. Letters sent relating to remittances, Oct. 17, 1861-Mar. 13, 1862, and Nov. 13, 1862-Aug. 6, 1863 (ch. V, vol. 41), contain press copies of letters to quartermasters informing them of amounts of remittances requested for them on their estimates and acknowledgments of estimates with directions that applications for funds be made to field quartermasters. Letters sent relating to accounts current, June 20-Dec. 22, 1863 (ch. V, vol. 41), contain press copies of letters to quartermasters calling for accounts current that were required by regulations to be sent in with abstracts and vouchers and letters to the Second Auditor transmitting quartermasters' accounts for settlement. Letters sent relating to claims, Feb. 8, 1864-Mar. 31, 1865 (ch. V, vol. 126), contain fair copies of letters to claimants, quartermasters, and others relating to claims and accounts approved for payment or disapproved. There is a small quantity of unbound letters sent, July 1861-Mar. 1865, copies of which are in the letters-sent books. A record of letters answered, Mar. 1862-Mar. 1865 (ch. V, vols. 99-101), gives information regarding the writers of the letters and their contents. A small file of orders and circulars, 1861-65, contains both manuscript and printed copies and many duplicates.

There are also letters and telegrams received, Apr. 1861-Apr. 1865 (4 ft.; available on microfilm as M 469). Besides many letters from quartermasters transmitting returns and reports, there are letters from the Secretary of War, other War Department officials, the Second Auditor, Congressmen, State officials, textile mills, business firms, and individuals. Other documents in this file include certificates, invoices, and inventories of quartermaster stores, inspection reports, accounts current, lists of quartermasters failing to make returns, AIGO general orders, receipts for supplies, certificates of insurance, and insurance policies. Cross-reference cards are present for many letters, relating to individual officers, that were later removed from this file and placed in the compiled military service records described in chapter XI of this Guide. This file contains reports from quartermasters giving their stations and describing their duties and, from principal quartermasters and chief quartermasters of armies, lists of subordinate quartermasters submitted in response to AIGO General Order 118 of Sept. 1, 1863. Letters from transportation officers to A. H. Cole are also in this file.

The registers of letters received cover the period Mar. 1861-Feb. 1865 (ch. V, vols. 1-12, 2 ft. 4 in.). A register that was kept for Mar.-Apr. 1865 is missing. Some letters that were registered were forwarded to other War Department offices for action or returned to the writers with endorsements that took the place of letters of reply. An index to the Quartermaster General's letters received (also to letters received by the Adjutant and Inspector General), prepared by the Adjutant General's Office of the U.S. War Department (available on microfilm as M 410), indexes not only the names of writers but also the names of persons referred to in the letters. A small quantity of telegrams received, 1861-65 (1 1/2 in.), is arranged chronologically. A volume of endorsements on letters received, Mar. 1862-Mar. 1864 (ch. V, vol. 222), contains abstracts of communications that were referred to or returned to the Secretary of War or to quartermasters and endorsements that were made on muster rolls and accounts.

Records. Books and files provide information regarding quartermasters and others working with them. An appointment record of quartermasters, 1861-63 (ch. V, vol. 231), gives the name, rank, duty to which assigned, whether bonded, date appointed, and other information. An undated station book of quartermasters (ch. V, vol. 228) describes duties performed. An undated list of quartermasters in the field and at posts (ch. V, vol. 229) shows the names of the officers to whom they were assigned. An undated assignment record of quartermasters (ch. V, vol. 230), contains a State list of regimental quartermasters, a State list of post quartermasters, a list of quartermasters serving in the Army of Northern Virginia, and lists of quartermasters of various commands. A list of clerks in the Quartermaster General's Office, Aug. 1, 1861-May 28, 1864 (in front of letters-sent book, ch. V, vol. 13), shows name, date of appointment, salary, State of residence, and other data. Some lists of quartermasters, 1861-65 (folded papers, 1 1/2 in.), show quartermasters on duty in various commands, assistant quartermasters, and quartermasters on duty with field transportation, Nov. 4, 1864. A register of applications for details in the Quartermaster's Department, 1864 (ch. V, vol. 207), shows name and address of applicant, nature of application, date and notation of action taken. A volume showing "names and residences of quartermasters, register of officers and agents of tax in kind, and men detailed for duty in Q. M. Department," 1864 (ch. V, vol. 199), contains an alphabetical list of the names of quartermasters with stations and remarks, an alphabetical register of officers collecting the tax in kind, a list of persons reporting to quartermasters for duty giving date and place and indexed by quartermasters' names, an alphabetical list of persons recommended for detail in the Quartermaster's Department for whom there were no vacancies, and copies of circulars issued by the Quartermaster General's Office and other subdivisions of the War Department. An alphabetical record of resignations of officers, 1862-65 (ch. V, vol. 122), shows officer's name, rank, and organization, date of resignation, and AIGO special order number. A numerical file of official bonds and related papers, 1861-65 (folded papers, 8 in.), contains notarized bonds of quartermasters, commissaries, and agents, showing names of principal and sureties, date and place, and amount of bond, with some related correspondence. A memorandum book, 1861-63 (ch. V, vol. 233), contains the following miscellany: pay and allowance table for the Confederate Army, copies of Quartermaster General circulars with a record of the names and stations of officers to whom they were sent, a record of applications for service in the Quartermaster's Department, a record of the cost of telegraphic despatches, a record of officers to whom the Regulations of the Quartermaster General's Department were sent, a list of officers on duty in the department, a record of the names and stations of officers to whom the laws relating to the War Department were sent, and a record of the distribution of the publication on the Uniform and Dress of the Army (Richmond, 1861). An undated record of detailed men and bonded officers (ch. V, vol. 234) shows for detailed men the name, rank and organization, and destination; and for the officers, the name, rank, whether he was bonded, and further personal information.

Records Relating to Accounts. Financial transactions connected with operations of the Quartermaster General's Department are recorded in a number of series. Requisitions for funds, Sept. 23, 1861-Mar. 30, 1865 (ch. V, vols. 80-92, 2 ft.), contain on printed forms requisitions drawn on the Secretary of War. These volumes have name indexes, except vols. 81 and 88. A ledger of moneys advanced, 1861-64 (ch. V, vols. 93-95), shows the names of officers and others to whom money was advanced, date, amount, and purpose. There are abstracts of drafts, transfers, and acknowledgments of moneys to and from officers, 1861-65 (ch. V, vols. 102-104), and abstracts of disbursements, Apr. 26, 1862-Mar. 13, 1865 (ch. V, vol. 210). There is a detailed account book relating to leather goods, Apr. 1863-Dec. 1864 (ch. V, vol. 116). Abstracts of purchases, payments, and expenditures, 1862-65 (folded papers, 2 1/2 ft.), show the kinds of articles and services, amounts paid, and by whom paid. This file also contains some invoices of medical and hospital supplies issued and requisitions for commissary supplies for the use of officers. A record of line officers failing to account for bounty funds, 1862-63 (ch. V, vol. 206), shows date, name, rank, and organization of officer receiving such funds, from whom received, amount received, and explanatory remarks. Abstracts of remittances to quartermasters and agents, Apr. 3, 1861-Feb. 3, 1865 (ch. V, vol. 243), are finely detailed. An account book, Sept. 1862-Oct. 1863 (ch. V, vol. 136), covers debit accounts of paymaster funds, accounts of purchases, accounts of quartermaster funds, accounts of expenditures, credit accounts of paymaster funds, and a record of the receipt of Hoyer & Ludwig money. An indexed ledger, 1861-62 (ch. V, vol. 130), contains many miscellaneous accounts. Railroad accounts, 1861-65 (folded papers, 7 ft.), show usually on printed forms the name of the railroad, date, number of voucher, number of men or quantity of materials transported, points between which carried, and the charge. Some miscellaneous quartermaster and commissary papers, 1861-65 (folded papers, 5 1/2 ft.), contain abstracts of provisions issued or sold, quartermaster stores transferred, and articles issued on special requisition; returns of quartermaster stores; returns and vouchers relating to the tax in kind; requisitions for forage; provision returns; invoices of subsistence stores; and some transmittal letters addressed to the Quartermaster General. Special requisitions of the Louisiana Army, Sept. 1861 (1/2 in.), are for clothing, camp and garrison equipage, and other equipment, showing the organization for which requisitioned, the kind and quantity of articles, the place of issuance, and name of issuing officer. An account book of Col. Larkin Smith, Jan. 1862-July 1863 (ch. V, vol. 247), contains a record of amounts expended for bounty and transportation of enlisted men. There are also abstracts of articles purchased, received, issued, sold, lost, and expended by Capt. Richard P. Waller, assistant quartermaster at Richmond, 1861-62 (ch. V, vol. 244).

Accounts of quartermasters, 1861-64 (39 vols.: ch. V, vols. 159-196, vols. 162, 169, 189 missing; 2 ft. 10 in.), contain quarterly analyses of quartermasters' accounts, showing names and stations, date, amounts of funds expended, transferred, on hand, and how expended. These books give the expenditures for supplies, postage, rent, services, stationery, furniture, transportation, fuel, repairs, burials, and extra-duty men. They include name indexes, but an index to the entire series is in vol. 196 1/4 and partial indexes are in vols. 118 and 196 1/2. A record of accounts rendered by quartermasters, 1861-64 (ch. V, vol. 96), shows whether he was bonded, his station, the date of his commission, and the dates of the accounts received. A register of returns and accounts received from quartermasters, Apr. 1863-Apr. 1865 (ch. V, vols. 123-125), is also available. Acknowledgments of accounts, 1863-64 (ch. V, vol. 97), give the date of receipt, name and rank of quartermaster, period covered by account or type of account, and the station of the quartermaster. Remarks on quartermasters' accounts, 1861-63 (ch. V, vols. 114, 115, and 117-121 1/2, 1 ft. 4 in.), concern corrections, inadmissable items and discrepancies, and reports and explanations received. Most of the books have indexes. A register of quartermasters' and agents' money accounts and property returns, 1861-64 (ch. V, vol. 142), gives names, stations, and dates when quarterly accounts were received. A record of the status of quartermasters' accounts, 1863-64 (ch. V, vol. 202), gives name and rank of quartermaster, date of last account, amount disbursed or transferred, and balance. A chronological analysis of expenditures of quartermasters at military posts, fourth quarter, 1861-third quarter, 1862 (ch. V, vol. 118 1/2), shows name, station, balance from quarter, remittances from Treasury acknowledged, amount and source of receipts, amount deposited, and how expended.

Rolls and Payrolls. Rolls transmitted by quartermasters to the Quartermaster General's Office supply information regarding military personnel and civilians employed by the Army. There are payrolls for extra-duty men, 1861-65 (folded papers, 32 ft. 8 in.), detailed for work under quartermasters, commissaries, surgeons, medical purveyors, ordnance officers, provost marshals, and other officers. The rolls show name, rank, and organization; by whose order employed; term of employment; and rate and amount of pay. They are in two sections; the first section contains 3,938 rolls and the second, 5,316. There are also rolls of civilian employees. Clothing rolls, 1861-65 (folded papers, 20 ft.), contain a record of clothing issued to soldiers with date, names, quantity and kind of articles, signatures of soldier and witness, place of issuance, and name of issuing quartermaster. The payrolls of extra-duty men and the clothing rolls were carded for inclusion in the compiled military service records described in chapter XI of this Guide. Commutation rolls, 1861-65 (folded papers, 3 ft.), contain lists of soldiers who received commutation of rations while on furlough or hospitalized. Another file containing payrolls of extra-duty men, hospital employees, and clerks and clothing rolls of soldiers, 1861-65 (folded papers, ca. 140 ft.), is arranged in two groups: those that were carded by the U.S. War Department for the compiled military service records and those that were not. Bounty rolls, 1862-65 (folded papers, 1 ft.), show payment of bounty for enlisting and reenlisting and give organization, date and place, names, amount of bounty, and certification that payment had been made by the recruiting officer.

Payrolls of civilian employees, 1861-65 (folded papers, 16,239 rolls, 86 ft.), show name of employing officer, name and occupation of employee, period of service, rate and amount of pay, and signatures of payee and witnesses. Slave payrolls, 1861-65 (folded papers, 23 1/2 ft.), give similar information and name of owner, with his signature or that of his attorney for the receipt of wages. An alphabetical name index to payrolls of civilian employees and slaves, 1861-65 (85 ft.), prepared by the U.S. Adjutant General's Office, gives names of employees and slaves and slaveowners. An incomplete record of the payrolls of civilian employees (1 ft. 7 in.), shows name of disbursing officer, office (or place), and date and number of roll.

Lacking an index to the places to which they relate, the payrolls are difficult to use for research, however.

Records Relating to Supplies. Some record books relate to the procurement, issuance, and transportation of supplies. A register of contracts, Apr. 1, 1861-Dec. 12, 1864 (ch. V, vol. 113), gives date, names of contracting parties, and an abstract of terms. The contracts relate to the purchase or manufacture of supplies; transportation of men, horses, supplies, cattle, powder, and other freight; construction and repair of Government buildings; chartering of vessels; rent for buildings and lease of warehouses; telegraphic communications; laying railroad track and use of railroads; and ballast for sinking boats as obstructions to navigation. Abstracts and quarterly returns of materials purchased, received, or expended, 1863-64 (ch. V, vol. 245), give name of persons or firm and kind and quantity of materials and their value. A memorandum book relating to agents and supplies, 1864 (ch. V, vol. 227), contains information regarding quartermaster officers and agents at home and abroad, arrivals of supplies from Europe on blockade runners, contracts and requests for supplies, depot officers, details of soldiers to factories, and bonded agents. A record of stores issued by quartermasters at Camps Utley and Freemont, Sept. 1861-Oct. 1862 (ch. V, vol. 133), shows date, type, quantity, and place of issuance, the organization to which issued, on whose requisition, and voucher number. A record of issues for current service, Nov. 6, 1862-Mar. 31, 1865 (ch. V, vol. 134), shows kinds and quantities of articles issued and to whom issued. A shipping book, Oct. 2, 1863-Mar. 31, 1865 (ch. V, vol. 218), is a chronological record of issues of leather and woolen goods, clothing, and cotton yarn, and it shows the name of the person or firm to whom shipped. A record of clothing issued to slaves, Oct. 1863-Dec. 1864 (ch. V, vol. 129), gives the overseer's name and county, name of slave and owner, and quantity of clothing, shoes, and tobacco issued. Some incompletely identified records include a record of stores received, Oct. 1, 1863-Sept. 24, 1864 (ch. V, vol. 217), and a record of stores delivered, 1864-65 (ch. V, vols. 200 and 201). A small file of papers relates to the valuation of horses and related equipment, 1861-65 (2 in.).

A register of claims, Sept. 1861-Sept. 1864 (ch. V, vols. 43 and 44), shows the claim number (1-4521), claimant's name, nature of claim, amount, date of receipt, and action taken. The claims are for supplies and services purchased by the Quartermaster Department.

Records in Other Custody. --The papers of Alexander R. Lawton in the Southern Historical Collection in the University of North Carolina Library contain a few items dated 1864-65 regarding his official status and the work of the Quartermaster General's Office, with letters of 1862 to his wife. Small miscellaneous collections of documents relating to that office are in Duke University Library, the Library of Congress, and the Valentine Museum at Richmond, Va. Papers of Frank W. Battaile for 1863-64 (12 items) relating to his activities as a quartermaster purchasing agent in Yazoo County, Miss., are in the Mississippi Department of Archives and History.

Family papers sometimes contain accounts or reports relating to the tax in kind, and records of some industrial plants that supplied the Quartermaster General's Department are available (see the indexes in the National Union Catalog of Manuscript Collections and guides to individual repositories).

Pay Bureau

In his report of Apr. 27, 1861, the Secretary of War recommended that a separate Pay Department be established or that more quartermasters be authorized. Quartermasters continued throughout the war to disburse pay to military personnel and make bounty payments and other disbursements, however, and the office so responsible was designated the Pay Bureau.

Maj. Richard S. Cox had charge of the Pay Bureau.

Record Group 109.--Records of the Pay Bureau that were sent from Richmond to Washington in May 1865 became part of the War Department Collection of Confederate Records. Letters-sent press copy books, Nov. 22, 1862-Aug. 9, 1864 (ch. V, vols. 35 and 37-40), contain letters to quartermasters, Army officers, and others regarding the pay of soldiers, deceased officers and soldiers, sick and wounded soldiers in hospitals, and pay returns and accounts. A small file of letters received, 1862-65 (2 1/2 in.), relates to bounties and quartermasters' accounts and returns. Letters sent by Maj. John Ambler, Jan. 10-Oct. 23, 1863 (ch. V, vol. 219), contain fair copies of letters to officers, soldiers, discharged soldiers, the Quartermaster General, Congressmen, and others regarding pay, bounties, claims, and other business of the office.

More voluminous are the pay accounts. A record of payments to officers, noncommissioned officers, and enlisted men, 1861-65 (35 vols.: ch. V, vols. 45-79, 6 ft. 8 in.), shows payee's name, rank, and organization; period for which paid and date paid; and name, rank, and organization of person making payment, amount paid, and remarks. Payments to noncommissioned officers and enlisted men are recorded in vols. 46-48, 53, 54, and 79, and payments to officers are recorded in the other volumes. Some volumes include lists of the quartermasters making the payments. A record of payments to company officers, 1861 (ch. V, vol. 132), shows the name and organization of the officer, period for which paid, paymaster's name, voucher number, and date of settlement. A register of payments to discharged soldiers, 1861-64 (ch. V, vols. 110-112), shows the soldier's name, rank, organization, date of discharge, date of payment, and by whom paid. The entries in this register have been carded for inclusion in the compiled military service records described in chapter XI of this Guide.

Other pay records concern the paymasters' accounts or summarize the information in them. There are registers of paymasters' accounts, 1861-65 (ch. V, vols. 127, 128 and 239), and a register of the receipt of pay accounts, Jan. 28-Nov. 29, 1864 (ch. V, vol. 236). An undated record of military organizations paid (ch. V, vol. 232) shows by State the number of the regiment, arm of service, company or other unit, and the name of person by whom paid. A record of payments to troops, 1863-64 (ch. V, vol. 131), shows by State the military organization, year paid, and the names of the disbursing officers. A record of accounts current, 1861-65 (ch. V, vols. 105-109), shows by name of quartermaster the date; amount received, transferred, and expended for pay, subsistence, clothing, and forage; and the balance on hand.

Other records of payments were kept by officers stationed in Richmond who appear to have been subordinate to the chief paymaster. During 1863-64 Maj. J. B. Cary was on duty in that city as paymaster at the hospitals. There is an abstract of payments made by him from Apr. 6, 1863, to Dec. 31, 1864 (ch. V, vol. 98). His monthly accounts current for

Apr. 1863-Dec. 1864 are in the back of this volume. Major Cary's cashbook, Apr. -Dec. 1863 (ch. V, vol. 87), is a complete record of expenditures.
A record of payments to soldiers by Capt. Samuel R. Chisman, June 4-
Sept. 30, 1862 (ch. V, vol. 197), shows voucher number; date of payment;
name, rank, and organization of soldier paid; period for which paid; amounts
for pay, clothing, and bounty; and total amounts paid.

Records in Other Custody. --An account book of Capt. George A.
Barksdale, Oct. 8, 1861-Sept. 1, 1862 (1 vol.), in the Business Library of
Columbia University shows disbursements by check numbers made, appar-
ently, when he served with the Pay Bureau in Richmond.

Office of the Inspector General of Field Transportation

It became increasingly difficult as the war progressed to provide
field transportation for the Army. Quartermasters were designated as inspectors of field transportation in an effort to improve the situation, but
more effective measures were required. Accordingly, AIGO General Order
76 of Oct. 17, 1862, announced the appointment of Maj. A. H. Cole as Inspector General of Field Transportation at Richmond. The order directed
all officers of the Quartermaster's Department to report to him on the
quantity and condition of animals, wagons, and harness in their possession.
Major Cole sought to coordinate the activities of quartermasters and inspectors of field transportation. He set up a district system in Oct. 1863
(approved retroactively by AIGO General Order 142 of Oct. 30, 1863) under
which he was responsible for all inspections, purchases, impressments,
and issues of field transportation, except for officers specifically authorized to purchase and dispose of field transportation property. District
officers were to control field transportation within their respective districts, and inspection officers were authorized to order to be turned in to
the nearest post quartermaster all artillery horses and other transportation
property found unserviceable. Chief quartermasters of armies or quartermasters at posts other than those in the field were to provide chief inspectors with their estimates for field transportation requirements.

A QMGO Circular of Nov. 1, 1863, established the inspection districts
with the limits already outlined by Major Cole as follows:

First Inspection District, consisting of North Carolina and Virginia,
under Maj. George Johnston at Richmond.

Second Inspection District, consisting of Florida, Georgia, South
Carolina, that part of Alabama north of the Tennessee River, and that part
of Tennessee east and north of the Tennessee River, under Maj. Norman
W. Smith at Augusta, Ga.

Third Inspection District, consisting of that part of Alabama south of
the Tennessee River, Mississippi, that part of Louisiana east of the Mississippi River, and that part of Tennessee west of the Tennessee River,
under Maj. A. M. Paxton at Brandon, Miss., and later at Selma, Ala.
AIGO Special Order 255 of Oct. 26, 1864, directed Maj. E. H. Ewing to
relieve Paxton.

Fourth Inspection District, consisting of the Trans-Mississippi
West, under Maj. C. D. Hill at Shreveport, La.

The Inspector General of Field Transportation thus exercised greater control of the field transportation of the Army. Post and other quartermasters
were relieved of the purchase, impressment, recruiting, repairing, and
issuing of field transportation. Inspectors of field transportation assigned

to the chief inspectors of the districts made regular inspections of the field transportation at posts and camps. Major Cole continued as Inspector General until the end of the war. While he was absent on a long tour of inspection, ca. Apr. -Oct. 1864, Maj. William H. Gibbons served as Acting Inspector General of Field Transportation. AIGO Special Order 299 of Dec. 17, 1864, designated Major Gibbons as Assistant Inspector General of Field Transportation.

Record Group 109. --Records of the Office of the Inspector General of Field Transportation were among the records of the Quartermaster General's Department that were received in Washington in 1865. Now a part of the War Department Collection of Confederate Records, they include letters-sent press copy books, Nov. 14, 1862-Apr. 2, 1865 (ch. V, vols. 146-150 and part of 155), containing letters from A. H. Cole to chief inspectors and inspectors of field transportation, agents, quartermasters, and other officers, the Quartermaster General, the Secretary of War (in vol. 155), and others. Each volume except vol. 155 has a name index in front. Telegrams sent by Major Cole, Dec. 23, 1862-Mar. 31, 1865 (ch. V, vols. 151-153), are fair copies of outgoing telegrams to inspectors, quartermasters, general officers, and others. Telegrams and letters received, 1863-64 (1 1/2 in.), are incoming communications received by Major Cole from inspectors of field transportation, quartermasters, and other officers. Endorsement books relate to letters received, Aug. 1863-Apr. 1865 (ch. V, vols. 144-145, and part of 155). Telegrams received, 1862-65 (1 in.), concern the supply of horses and mules and the affairs of the office. A small file of correspondence, Dec. 1862-Apr. 1865 (1/2 in.), includes letters sent by Major Cole, Capt. Richard V. Gaines, inspector of field transportation at Richmond, Maj. James N. Edmondston, inspector of field transportation at Greensboro, N. C., and Maj. George Johnston, chief inspector of field transportation at Richmond. An order, letter, and endorsement book, Oct. 7, 1863-Mar. 27, 1865 (ch. V, vol. 225), contains copies of orders of Major Cole relating to the assignment of inspectors, other orders, letters of Cole to the Quartermaster General recommending appointments, Cole's endorsements on letters of inspectors of field transportation, and in the back of the volume the assignments of chief inspectors and inspectors of field transportation.

A few other book records furnish other kinds of information. A record of estimates of funds required for field transportation, Oct. 31, 1862-Feb. 28, 1865 (ch. V, vol. 238), pertains to the estimates submitted by officers attached to the field transportation service. There is a record of transportation property inspected and condemned in the Army of Northern Virginia, Oct. 28, 1862-Apr. 1, 1865 (ch. V, vol. 154 and part of 155). General orders relating to transportation allowances, Aug. 26, 1863-Nov. 3, 1864 (ch. V, vol. 154 1/2), contain copies of orders of various commands, chiefly of the Army of Tennessee and the Army of Northern Virginia, showing the number of vehicles and animals allowed. There is an undated record of artillery horses issued and condemned (ch. V, vol. 156). A brief record of transportation approved, Apr. 5, 1864-Mar. 28, 1865 (ch. V, vol. 224), shows amount of funds approved for transportation for a number of chief inspectors and inspectors of field transportation. An order and endorsement book of Capt. Richard V. Gaines, inspector of field transportation at Richmond, Sept. 20, 1864-Mar. 28, 1865 (ch. V, vol. 223), is a record of extracts of orders and communications he received, his endorsements on them, and orders issued by him. Captain Gaines kept a record of horses or mules captured or impressed, Aug. 1864-Apr. 1865, and a record of forage drawn, 1863-64 (ch. VIII, vol. 36).

Records in Other Custody. --In the Louisiana Historical Association deposit in the Howard-Tilton Memorial Library of Tulane University are official papers of Capt. John T. Purves, assistant inspector of field transportation at Mobile from about the end of July 1864. Letters-sent books, Jan. 22-Oct. 23, 1864, and Nov. 11, 1864-Apr. 1865 (2 vols.), contain fair copies of letters to quartermaster officers in Alabama, Georgia, and Mississippi, the headquarters of the District of the Gulf, and to Quartermaster General Lawton. Other papers of Captain Purves for Mar. 11-Dec. 16, 1864 (45 pieces), include additional letters to Lawton. Purves had served earlier as a quartermaster officer at Vicksburg, with Brig. Gen. Francis A. Shoup's command in the Army of Tennessee, and in the District of the Gulf. The same repository has papers of Maj. Edward A. Burk, a quartermaster officer who performed field transportation duties in Texas during 1863-65.

Railroad Bureau

Early in 1861 the Confederacy had nearly 9,000 miles of railroad, but the many lines did not constitute a system because of gaps between important cities, differences in guage, and breaks between lines that entered cities. No stockpile of supplies necessary for repairs and replacements existed, and there were no railroad shops in the South. The transportation of military stores, other materials, and personnel was arranged by quartermaster officers. In 1862 the Quartermaster General established a Government locomotive shop at Raleigh under Capt. Thomas R. Sharp to repair captured rolling stock.

AIGO General Order 98 of Dec. 3, 1862, designated Col. William M. Wadley as superintendent of railroad transportation for the Government, and the office he headed became known as the Railroad Bureau. He was to report through the Adjutant and Inspector General to the Secretary of War. Neither Wadley nor his successor had real authority over most of the officers in the field or over superintendents of railroads, who continued to manage their lines with an eye to profits. Wadley, who had been a prominent railroad official, did what he could to improve railroad transportation, however.

An act of May 1, 1863 (Ramsdell, Laws and Joint Resolutions, p. 167), authorized the Secretary of War to require railroads to provide "transportation of freight, supplies, material and men for the Government" and authorized the seizure of noncomplying railroads for operation by the Quartermaster General, who was also empowered to transfer rolling stock from one railroad to another when necessary for public use and to remove rails or railroad machinery to prevent their capture by the enemy. In July 1863 the superintendent of railroad transportation was transferred to the Quartermaster General's Office. He negotiated rates to be charged by railroads for carrying Government traffic and informed the accounting officer of the Quartermaster General's Office about them He distributed supplies for use in rebuilding railroads and arranged for the repair of engines and the manufacture of railroad cars. In 1864 the Bureau also became involved in transferring prisoners of war by rail. In Sept. 1864 Capt. W. G. Gray was assigned as an assistant in the Railroad Bureau and took charge when the superintendent was absent.

A number of officers who were stationed at different places in the South as railroad transportation officers were subordinate to the Railroad Bureau. In mid-1863 Maj. John D. Whitford was assigned to Goldsboro, N.C., and Maj. Thomas Peters to Atlanta; somewhat later Capt. John M. Hottel went to Montgomery. In May 1864 Peters was succeeded by Captain Hottel. In Dec. 1863 Capt. George A. Cuyler went to Savannah to take charge of railroad transportation from Macon to Wilmington via Savannah and Charleston. Beside facilitating the movement of Government freight, these officers had rolling stock removed from railroads in territory invaded by the enemy and supervised the rebuilding of railroad track. In May 1864 Capt. John M. Robinson was given supervision of railroad transportation between Wilmington and Richmond. The Bureau sent Capt. John Frizzell to Augusta in Jan. 1865 to audit and pay accounts of railroads in Florida, Georgia, and South Carolina. He had served in the transportation office at Atlanta in 1863.

Despite the efforts of the Railroad Bureau and its transportation officers, the condition of the railroads steadily worsened. An act for public control of the railroads was finally approved on Feb. 28, 1865 (Ramsdell, Laws and Joint Resolutions, p. 60), but by then it was too late.

Successive superintendents of the Railroad Bureau:

Col. William M. Wadley, Dec. 3, 1862.

Maj. (later Lt. Col.) Frederick W. Sims, June 4, 1863.

Robert C. Black, III, The Railroads of the Confederacy (Chapel Hill, 1952); Angus J. Johnston, II, Virginia Railroads in the Civil War (Chapel Hill, 1961).

Record Group 109.--Most of the records of the Railroad Bureau were lost in the burning of Belvin's Block, the office building in Richmond in which the Bureau had been housed. But Lieutenant Colonel Sims carried some records with him when he accompanied the Confederate officials on their flight southward on Apr. 2, 1865, and captured Confederate records shipped to Washington from Charlotte included Railroad Bureau records. A letters-sent press copy book, Dec. 30, 1864-Feb. 20, 1865 (1 vol., p. 193-304), contains a partial record of letters sent by Sims and Captain Gray to transportation officers, quartermasters, presidents and superintendents of railroads, the auditing quartermaster of the Quartermaster General's Office (C. M. Smith), general officers, the Bureau of Conscription, and individuals. Some other records of the Bureau were filed by the U.S. War Department in the officers' records described below.

Papers relating to the heads of the Bureau and most of the transportation officers who served under it are in the compiled military service records of Confederate general and staff officers described in chapter XI of this Guide. These officers' files contain correspondence, instructions, orders, receipts, mileage vouchers, and abstracts of articles received, purchased, or expended. Lieutenant Colonel Sims' file contains handwritten copies of telegrams sent, Feb. 1-13 and 23-27, 1864. Quartermaster officers' files also contain material on railroad transportation. Other letters-sent and letters-received files of the War Department, including those of the Secretary of War, the Adjutant and Inspector General, and the Quartermaster General, contain letters of officers concerned with railroad transportation.

Other material relating to railroads is in the Confederate papers relating to citizens or business firms, another large file compiled by the U. S. War Department described in chapter XI of this Guide.

The list of names of railroads on the map in the back of Black's The Railroads of the Confederacy is useful in searching this file. See also the railroad accounts described under Office of the Quartermaster General.

Records in Other Custody. --The Valentine Museum, Richmond, Va., has telegrams sent and received by the Railroad Bureau, Sept. 8, 1863-Jan. 31, 1864 (1 in.). The papers of Maj. John D. Whitford in the North Carolina State Department of Archives and History contain for the Civil War period much correspondence relating to transportation.

Tax in Kind Bureau

A comprehensive tax act of Apr. 24, 1863 (1 Cong. C. S. A. Stat. 122-125), levied a tax in kind on agricultural produce. After reserving specified quantities for their own use, farmers and planters were required to pay and deliver to the Confederate Government one-tenth of the wheat, corn, oats, rye, buckwheat, or rice, sweet and Irish potatoes, cured hay and fodder, sugar, molasses made of cane, cotton, wool, tobacco, peas, beans, and ground peas. In case of disagreement between the tax assessor (an officer of the Treasury Department) and the taxpayer in fixing the quantity, quality, and value of the crops, each was to select a freeholder of the neighborhood, who in the event of yet another difference of opinion could choose a third person. These appraisers were then to estimate the quantity, quality, and value of the crops.

The act required Army quartermasters to collect and distribute the produce received in payment of the tax in kind. Post quartermasters were to receive from the assessors the estimates of tax in kind and were to give receipts to the assessors for filing with the chief collectors. The collectors were to furnish copies of the receipt to the auditor settling the post quartermaster's account. The post quartermasters were to receive the produce paid as tax in kind and hold it in safe custody until delivered to other quartermasters responsible for distributing it to Army supply points and delivering cotton and tobacco to Treasury Department agents. Quartermasters could sell products that might spoil, and in places where it was not practicable to collect produce the Treasury Department could collect the tax in money. An amendatory act of Feb. 17, 1864 (1 Cong. C. S. A. Stat. 226), authorized the Secretary of War to appoint the assessors of taxes in kind; they were to be separate and distinct from the assessors of money taxes and were to be under the exclusive direction and control of the War Department.

In 1863 the Quartermaster General assigned a controlling quartermaster (a major) to each State and a post quartermaster (a captain) to each congressional district in the States where it was practicable to collect the tax. The controlling quartermaster was to establish himself in a central position, assign post quartermasters to districts, designate depots at which supplies were to be delivered, and prescribe measures necessary for safekeeping the produce and transporting it to the nearest shipping point. Post quartermasters were to divide their districts into sections and establish depots at which the taxpayer could deliver his produce.

Lt. Col. Larkin Smith had general charge of the duties of the Quartermaster General's Department relating to the tax in kind.

C. S. A. War Department, Communication from the Secretary of War [Transmitting a Report from the Assistant Quartermaster General Relative to the Collection and Distribution of the Tax in Kind, Richmond, 1864]; Instructions to Officers and Agents Receiving the Tax in Kind ([Richmond?], 1863).

Record Group 109. --Incomplete records relating to the tax in kind are in the War Department Collection of Confederate Records. Abstracts of estimates for tax in kind received from assessors at Tuscaloosa, 1864 (ch. V, vol. 199 1/5), show taxpayer's name and kind and quantity of produce received during the second quarter of 1864. Abstracts of estimates of tax in kind received from assessors by the quartermaster at Selma during the quarter ending Dec. 31, 1864 (unnumbered vol.), are also available, as are abstracts of estimates, assessments, and collections of articles due as tax in kind, received at Aberdeen, Miss., 1864-65 (ch. V, vol. 199 2/5). A similar volume relates to bacon received at Aberdeen, 1865 (ch. V, vol. 199 1/4). Another volume relates to Mississippi counties, 1864-65 (ch. V, vol. 158). A file of tax in kind papers, 1864-65 (folded papers, 3 1/2 ft.), consists of estimates of the quantity of produce to be taxed, quality, total amount, and value; reports of articles received as tax in kind at depots in congressional districts; and lists of collectors and assessors in the States.

Records in Other Custody. --A Rockbridge County (Va.) tax in kind book, 1864-65, is in the University of Texas Library, Texas Archives. Letter books of Maj. Chandler C. Yonge, who became controlling quartermaster at Tallahassee, Fla., in 1863, are in the P. K. Yonge Library of the University of Florida. Estimates of tax in kind and reports of tax in kind collected in Virginia, 1863-64, are in Duke University Library.

COMMISSARY GENERAL'S OFFICE AND SUBSISTENCE DEPARTMENT

The act of Feb. 26, 1861 (Prov. Cong. C. S. A. Stat. 39), organizing the general staff of the Confederate Army, provided for a Commissary General's Office under a Commissary General with the rank of colonel. Officers who served in the Commissary General's Office in Richmond included Lt. Col. Frank G. Ruffin, Maj. S. B. Brewer, Maj. Seth B. French, and Maj. Thomas G. Williams. A commutation office under Capt. John H. Wayt paid commutation of rations to army personnel. Additional appointments of commissaries for service throughout the military establishment were authorized by several acts of Congress.

The Subsistence Department obtained provisions for the Army chiefly from the domestic output of the Confederacy. In 1861 it began purchasing meat in areas where the Army was undertaking operations, and some salt meats that were acquired in enemy territory were still being used early in 1862. Meatpacking plants were established at Thoroughfare Gap and Richmond, and arrangements for obtaining meat were made with packing houses in Tennessee and Kentucky. During 1861-62 cattle were brought from Texas and Louisiana, and a slaughterhouse at Alexandria, La., packed meat for the Confederate Army, but this source was cut off when U. S. forces acquired control of the Mississippi River. Messrs. Haxall, Crenshaw & Co. of Richmond was a large supplier of flour; other contracts for grinding wheat were made in Lynchburg and Petersburg. Salt was obtained from the works operated by Messrs. Stuart, Buchanan & Co. near Saltville, Va., from newly developed salt mines on Avery Island near New Iberia, La., and from evaporating basins along the coasts into which sea water was run. Both the salt basins and fisheries that were developed along the coast were easily raided by Federal gunboats. Commissary officers impressed subsistence stores and collected other supplies under the legislation levying a tax in kind on agricultural produce. In importing food from abroad the Commissary General's Office had to depend upon War Department procurement officers.

An act of Feb. 17, 1864 (1 Cong. C.S.A. Stat. 194), transferred from the Quartermaster General to the Commissary General the responsibility for providing food for prisoners of war. An arrangement to this effect had been agreed upon in the preceding fall (Official Records . . . Armies, ser. 2, vol. 6, p. 456).

In the field the operations of the Subsistence Department were carried on by commissary officers and agents (civilians) whose assignments were specified in AIGO special orders. Some of them worked directly under the Commissary General's Office and others were attached to Army commands. They competed with each other and with the procurement officers of other War Department bureaus in purchasing supplies. To correct this situation a system of chief purchasing commissaries was introduced by a circular of Apr. 15, 1863. Chief purchasing commissaries were assigned to each State, which was divided into districts under chief purchasing commissaries or agents, and the districts were subdivided. The chief purchasing commissaries nominated commissaries or agents to have charge of the districts, and the latter nominated their subcommissaries or subagents. Chief commissaries of armies were to apply to the chief purchasing commissaries for supplies and designate points where they would be needed. The officers designated as chief commissaries were as follows:

Alabama: Maj. John J. Walker, Mobile.
Florida: Maj. P. W. White, Quincy.
Georgia: Maj. Joseph L. Locke, Savannah.
       Maj. R. S. Moses (Oct. 13, 1864), Columbus.
Mississippi and eastern
    Louisiana: Maj. W. H. Dameron, Meridian.
North Carolina: Maj. James Sloan, Greensboro.
South Carolina: Maj. H. C. Guerin, Charleston.
Tennessee: Maj. R. T. Wilson, Loudon (?).
Texas: Maj. Sackfield Maclin, Houston.
Virginia: Maj. W. H. Smith, Richmond.
       Maj. B. P. Noland (Oct. 7, 1863), Richmond.

Depots for the storage of commissary supplies were maintained at a number of places. In Virginia there were depots at Richmond, Danville, Lynchburg, Dublin, Boykins, Milford, Charlottesville, and Staunton; in North Carolina, at Charlotte, Greensboro, and Fayetteville; in Alabama, at Mobile and Selma; in Tennessee, at Nashville and Trenton; and in Texas, at San Antonio.

Successive Commissaries General:
    Col. Lucius B. Northrop, Mar. 27, 1861.
    Brig. Gen. Isaac M. St. John, Feb. 16, 1865.

C.S.A. War Department, Regulations for the Future Guidance of Officers of the Subsistence Department [Richmond, 1864], Regulations for the Subsistence Department of the Confederate States of America (Richmond, 1861); William Diamond, "Imports of the Confederate

Government from Europe and Mexico," Journal of Southern History, 6:470-503 (Nov. 1940); Charles L. Dufour, "The Peevish Commissary: Colonel Lucius B. Northrop," in Nine Men in Gray, p. 197-229 (Garden City, N. Y., 1963); Thomas R. Hay, "Lucius B. Northrop: Commissary General," Civil War History, 9:5-23 (Mar. 1963); Official Records . . . Armies, ser. 4, vols. 1-3, passim. For reports of the Subsistence Department, see ibid.: Jan. 18, 1862, vol. 1, p. 870-879; Nov. 18, 1862, vol. 2, p. 192-193; Nov. 20, 1863, vol. 2, p. 968-972; and May 4, 1864, vol. 3, p. 379-380.

According to reports that were made to Jefferson Davis by former Commissaries General after the war, the Subsistence Department's letter books, endorsement books, and other papers were destroyed in 1865 in Richmond and during the retreat southward (Rowland, Jefferson Davis, 7: 350, 8:181). As may be seen below, however, some letters received did survive.

Record Group 109. --In the War Department Collection of Confederate Records is a letter and order book of Capt. John H. Wayt, Nov. 6, 1861-June 22, 1863 (ch. II, vol. 230). Part of this volume relates to his services as assistant commissary with the Army of the Peninsula, Nov. 1861-Aug. 1862. The part of this volume dating from Oct. 27, 1862, relates to his work in the commutation office in Richmond. The volume includes letters to and from Colonel Northrop, S. B. Brewer, S. B. French, and W. H. S. Taylor (the Second Auditor), and transmittal letters covering returns, estimates, and accounts.

Other War Department files in Record Group 109 contain considerable documentation relating to the Subsistence Department. A collection of circulars, orders, and regulations, Oct. 1, 1861- Feb. 25, 1865 (1/2 in.), was collected from various sources. Communications to and from the Commissary General, his subordinates in the Richmond office, and other commissary officers are in the correspondence files of the Office of the Secretary of War, the Adjutant and Inspector General's Office, and the Quartermaster General's Office, described in other sections of this chapter. Files of commissary officers in the compiled military service records of Confederate general and staff officers contain correspondence and other documents. Included are letters addressed to the Commissary General and other officers of the Bureau of Subsistence. The file of Confederate papers relating to citizens and business firms compiled by the U. S. War Department from several sources relates to commissary agents and business firms that furnished subsistence stores or transportation to the Subsistence Department. Further description of these compiled files is in chapter XI of this Guide.

Records in Other Custody. --In 1915 the New York Public Library bought some papers, 1861-84 (64 items), of Lucius B. Northrop, which include his wartime correspondence with the Secretaries of War, commissaries, and other officers and persons relating to commissary matters. In the New-York Historical Society collections is a letters-sent book of Maj. Seth B. French, Sept. 12, 1862-May 9, 1863 (1 vol.), largely relating to the Department of Richmond, but containing fair copies of letters sent by French after he became attached on Apr. 20, 1863, to the Commissary

General's Office. A copybook of telegrams sent by Major French, July 4, 1864-Apr. 1, 1865, in the same repository contains fair copies of telegrams to commissary officers on the procurement, transportation, and distribution of subsistence stores. The collections of the Virginia Historical Society contain wartime papers of L. B. Northrop, F. G. Ruffin, and Capt. Herbert A. Claiborne, another officer who served as a commissary officer in Richmond during the war. Correspondence of F. G. Ruffin is also in the Henry E. Huntington Library, and other papers of Ruffin are in the Southern Historical Collection in the University of North Carolina Library. Papers of Maj. Henry C. Guerin, including correspondence, orders, invoices of subsistence stores delivered, receipts, and reports of boards of survey on provisions, are in the South Caroliniana Library of the University of South Carolina. Papers of Maj. Joseph L. Locke are in the Southern Historical Collection in the University of North Carolina. Papers of Capt. John Emmerson in Duke University Library concern the purchasing of commissary supplies in western Virginia where he was stationed at Tazewell Courthouse, Newbern, and Dublin. Papers of John M. Orr in Duke University Library concern in part his activities in procuring meat for the Confederate Army.

Willard E. Wight, ed.,   Magazine of History and Biography,
"Some Letters of Lucius Bellinger   68:456-477 (Oct. 1960).
Northrop, 1860-1865," Virginia

SURGEON GENERAL'S OFFICE AND THE MEDICAL DEPARTMENT

The act of Feb. 26, 1861, establishing a general staff for the Confederate Army (Prov. Cong. C. S. A. Stat. 39), authorized a Medical Department consisting of a Surgeon General, four surgeons, and assistant surgeons as required. In 1861 Congress authorized the appointment of more surgeons for the Regular Army and Provisional Army and appropriated funds for the employment of private physicians under contracts--a practice that continued throughout the war.

The Surgeon General administered the Medical Department, managed hospitals, regulated the duties of medical officers, appointed acting medical officers, supervised inspections, and procured and distributed supplies. Successive Surgeons General:
David C. De Leon (acting), May 6, 1861.
Charles H. Smith (temporary), July 12, 1861.
Samuel P. Moore, July 30, 1861.

C. S. A. War Department,   1863); Horace H. Cunningham, Doc-
Regulations for the Medical Depart-   tors in Gray; the Confederate Medi-
ment of the C. S. Army (Richmond,   cal Service (Baton Rouge, 1958).

Most of the records of the Surgeon General's Office were destroyed by fire after the evacuation of Richmond by the Confederates on Apr. 2-3, 1865, but some were saved and sent to Washington by Col. Richard D. Cutts in May 1865. These included books of the Medical Director's Office in Richmond, the Medical Purveyor's Office, records of hospitals in Richmond and throughout Virginia and some hospitals in Wilmington, N. C., reports of the examining board for the Invalid Corps, and a few packages labeled "Surgeon General's & Medical Director's Papers." On Nov. 22, 1865, the

Archive Office of the War Department transferred these records to the U. S. Surgeon General's Office for use in preparing a medical history of the war. An inventory of the records appears as appendix C of Francis Lieber's report of Jan. 18, 1866, in the records of the Archive Office. When these records were returned to the Adjutant General's Office in 1872, 184 other books containing Confederate medical records, which had been received from various sources by the Surgeon General's Office, were included among them. These and other Confederate records received later from the Surgeon General's Office became part of the War Department Collection of Confederate Records (Record Group 109).

Surgeon General's Office

Record Group 109. --A file of letters, telegrams, orders, and circulars sent, Aug. 3, 1861-Mar. 31, 1865 (ch. VI, vols. 739-741, 4 in.), relates to the Medical Department in general. It consists of communications from the Surgeon General to medical directors, medical purveyors, the Medical Bureau of the Trans-Mississippi Department, surgeons in charge of hospitals, and other surgeons relating to the establishment, construction, discontinuance, and inspection of hospitals, requisitions for funds, submission of reports, and other matters. This file was evidently compiled by the U. S. War Department from materials that came into its custody, since it contains original letters received by medical directors and copies and drafts of their outgoing communications.

Circulars and other printed issuances of the Surgeon General's Office are listed in Crandall, Confederate Imprints, 1:159-175; and in Harwell, More Confederate Imprints, 1:50-59. Other correspondence of the Surgeon General is described below.

Other records supply information regarding hospitals and their staffs and patients. There are hospital muster rolls, other rolls, and reports, 1861-65 (folded papers, 33 ft.). The muster rolls and payrolls are for stewards, wardmasters, cooks, nurses, matrons, detached soldiers serving at hospitals, and patients. This file also contains many reports of sick and wounded men showing the numbers of patients with certain diseases, the total during the month, their disposition, and discharges with names, rank, military organization, disease, and time of death if applicable. Other documents in this file include several types of rolls, lists of deceased soldiers, reports of furloughs granted by medical examining boards, and morning reports of patients. There are hospital clothing-receipt rolls, other rolls, and returns, 1861-65 (folded papers, 14 ft.). Information regarding military personnel in these documents has been abstracted on cards filed in the compiled military service records of Confederate soldiers described in chapter XI of this Guide. A file of miscellaneous medical records, 1861-65 (folded papers, 24 ft.), contains surgeons' requisitions and receipts and invoices of medical and hospital stores issued by medical purveyors. Included also are returns of medical and hospital property; morning reports; abstracts of vouchers of medicines issued and received by medical purveyors; railroad, drayage, and express receipts; medical purveyors' accounts; medical directors' consolidated reports of sick and wounded; consolidated provision returns of hospitals; printed circulars; and some correspondence.

Lists of medical officers recommended for appointment or promotion by the Surgeon General, Jan. 1863-Dec. 1864 (ch. VI, vol. 370 1/2), show the officer's name, rank, date of rank, place to report, and usually his native State.

A record of reports received from medical officers, 1863-64 (ch. VI, vol. 644), was evidently compiled in the office of Surg. Francis Sorrel, inspector of hospitals at Richmond. It contains a record of reports returned for correction, Apr.-July 1863; a list of the names of clerks in Surgeon Sorrel's office; a record of surgical reports and registers received during 1863-65, showing the name of hospital or regiment and the date of receipt; a record of quarterly reports of sick and wounded men, showing the names of medical officers, hospital or organization, and station, 1863-64; a list of the names of medical directors in the field, Oct. 19, 1863; and a record of reports received from medical directors, Jan. 1863-Aug. 1864.

Records in Other Custody. --In the Rudolph Matas Medical Library of Tulane University is a manuscript by Dr. Joseph Jones entitled "Investigation upon the Nature, Causes and Treatment of Hospital Gangrene as It Prevailed in the Confederate Armies 1861-1865 with Observations upon and Comparisons with Pyaemia, Small Pox and Malarial Fever. Augusta, Ga., 1865" (1 vol., 800 p.). Jones was a Confederate surgeon.

The papers, 1861-63, of Surg. Augustus C. Evans in the Southern Historical Collection in the University of North Carolina Library include some letters written from London in 1862 concerning the procurement of medicines for the Confederacy.

Letters and other papers relating to the administration of the Medical Department, 1861-64 (150 items), are in the Illinois State Historical Library.

Medical Directors

During the early part of the war medical directors of armies and military departments exercised general control over all medical officers and hospitals within the geographical limits of their commands. Regulations adopted on Mar. 26, 1862, provided for the assignment of medical directors to army corps and military departments and placed divisions of army corps under chief surgeons, who were to be recommended by the medical directors, and brigades under senior surgeons of brigades. The medical directors of army corps and departments, the chief surgeons of divisions, and the senior surgeons of brigades were to inspect and supervise the hospitals of their commands. They also assigned surgeons to duty, appointed members of medical examining boards, and executed contracts with private physicians. One surgeon and one assistant surgeon were assigned to regiments.

Eventually, medical directors were also placed in charge of general hospitals in cities. They were responsible only to the Surgeon General and were in direct control of the surgeons in charge. In the fall of 1864 medical directors of hospitals were stationed as follows:

Surg. William A. Carrington, Richmond, Va.
Surg. Frank A. Ramsey, Bristol, Tenn.
Surg. Peter E. Hines, Raleigh, N. C.
Surg. N. S. Crowell, Charleston, S. C.
Surg. Samuel H. Stout, Macon, Ga.
Surg. S. A. Smith, Alexandria, La.

Surg. James F. Heustis, Mobile, Ala.

Surg. P. B. Scott, Meridian, Miss.

Medical Director of General Hospitals in Virginia. AIGO Special Order 65 of Mar. 17, 1863, directed Surg. William A. Carrington to assume the duties of Medical Director of general hospitals in Richmond and on Apr. 2, 1863, he was ordered to take on the management of all general hospitals in Virginia. During Jan.-Mar. 1863 he had been Acting Medical Director of Maj. Gen. Gustavus W. Smith's command in the Army of Northern Virginia. Before being assigned to that position he had served in the same command as Inspector of Hospitals.

Record Group 109. --Records of the Medical Director at Richmond are in the War Department Collection of Confederate Records. Letters-sent books, Dec. 8, 1862-July 22, 1863, and Feb. 13, 1864-Apr. 1, 1865 (ch. VI, vols. 416 and 364), contain fair copies of inspection reports by Surgeons William A. Carrington and E. S. Gaillard and of letters from Carrington to the Surgeon General, the Secretary of War, Medical Directors E. S. Gaillard and Thomas H. Williams, surgeons in charge of hospitals and other surgeons, commandants of posts, Maj. Gens. G. W. Smith and Arnold Elzey, Brig. Gen. John H. Winder, commanders of Richmond prisons, Army officers, the Quartermaster General, the Commissary General, Medical Purveyor E. W. Johns, the Superintendent of Railroad Transportation, Maj. W. H. Wood (transportation officer at Richmond), Lt. Col. Frank Ruffin, and others. Volume 416 contains copies of some letters received by Carrington and some general and special orders of the Department of Henrico and of the Adjutant and Inspector General's Office. Volume 364 contains some statements of hospital funds. Letters received by the Medical Director, Apr. 9, 1864-Mar. 30, 1865 (ch. VI, vol. 364, p. 492-557, 563-640), are copies of letters, mostly from the same correspondents. A register of letters received, Aug. 1863-Apr. 1865 (ch. VI, vol. 145), arranged by subjects (Details, Furloughs, Leaves of Absence, etc.), identifies each communication and gives information about action taken. Endorsements on letters and orders received, 1863-65 (ch. VI, vol. 363), show the writer's name, date and subject of letter, and action taken. Volume 363 also contains on p. 550-551 and 559-560 a record of assignments of detailed soldiers, Feb. 6-Apr. 1, 1865. There is a copybook of orders, telegrams, and circulars issued, Mar. 19, 1863-Oct. 18, 1864, and received, Jan. 3, 1863-Mar. 15, 1865 (ch. VI, vol. 362). Among special orders and circulars issued and received, 1864-65 (ch. VI, vol. 365), are special orders issued by the Medical Director, Oct. 19, 1864-Apr. 1, 1865; special and general orders received from the Adjutant and Inspector General, the Surgeon General, and the headquarters of the Department of Henrico and the post of Richmond, July 1, 1864-Mar. 24, 1865; and circulars received from the Surgeon General, Sept. 29, 1864-Feb. 9, 1865.

The Medical Director's Office also kept records relating to hospital patients. In Record Group 109 are a list of patients admitted to hospitals, 1862-63 (ch. VI, vols. 146 and 153); a register of patients from Virginia organizations in hospitals, 1862-63 (ch. VI, vol. 152); a register of patients by regiments in Virginia hospitals, 1862-63 (ch. VI, vol. 357); a list of patients in Richmond hospitals, Sept. 1862-Mar. 1863 (ch. VI, vols. 150 and 155-157); a register of furloughs and discharges from Richmond hospitals, 1863 (ch. VI, vol. 465); a register of discharges, 1862-63 (ch. VI, vols. 144 and 645); a register of approved furloughs, 1862-63 (ch. VI, vols. 148 and 149); and a register of furloughs from Richmond hospitals, 1864 (ch. VI, vol. 177). In ch. VI, vol. 154, are a register of soldiers furloughed from Richmond hospitals, Jan. 1864-Mar. 1865, a register of men examined for admission to hospitals, Jan. -Mar. 1865, a register of officers recommended for leaves of absence, Nov. 1864-Mar. 1865, and a register of certificates of disability granted by a medical examining board, Oct. 1864-Mar. 1865. In ch. VI, vol. 140, are registers of assignments for treatment, officer patients, and transfers to private quarters, 1862-63.

Statistical reports of hospitals in Virginia, 1862-64 (ch. VI, vols. 151 and 548), show the number of patients remaining, admitted, transferred, returned to duty, furloughed, discharged, deserted, and deceased.

Other volumes concern medical officers and other Medical Department personnel. A register of medical officers' appointments, 1861-63 (ch. VI, vols. 141 and 143), shows officer's name, rank, date of appointment, assignment, and remarks. Lists of medical officers, 1861-64 (ch. VI, vol. 142), give name, rank, assignment, date of commission, and remarks. In this volume is a list of surgeons and assistant surgeons of the Volunteer Forces of Virginia appointed by the Governor and Council, May-June 1861, showing name, residence, date of appointment, and assignment. A medical examining board record, Feb. 25, 1863- May 26, 1864 (ch. VI, vol. 370), shows the date, name, rank, and organization of patient examined, disease or injury and its duration, and finding. Names of members of the board are sometimes shown. This volume also contains a record of officers who wished to resign, Apr. -Aug. 1863. Reports and other papers of the board for examining hospital stewards, Aug. 27, 1863- Feb. 20, 1864 (ch. VI, vol. 557), are mainly reports on persons examined showing name, age, whether a civilian or an enlisted man, date of appointment, and finding. The reports are preceded by a few circulars, orders, and letters relating to the board, Aug. 27-Sept. 11, 1863. A list of officers, Dec. 19, 1864, shows names, powers and duties, and residence; and a time record of clerks is dated Dec. 19, 1864-Apr. 2, 1865 (ch. VI, vol. 371). A page near the end of this volume contains a postage account of the Medical Director's Office, Jan. 1-Mar. 25, 1865. In ch. VI, vol. 179, are a register of officers recommended for leaves of absence, Aug. 1863-Oct. 1864; a register of examination of detailed soldiers, Sept. 1863-Nov. 1864; a register of examination of detailed men employed at the C. S. Shoe Factory, Nov. 1864; a register of soldiers recommended for detail or transfer from various hospitals, 1862-64; a register of discharges from various hospitals, 1863-64; and a list of permanently disabled soldiers examined by medical examining boards at different hospitals and recommended for transfer to Eufaula, Ala., Mar. 28, 1864.

Other volumes concern reports and requisitions for supplies. A record of the receipt of surgeons' reports, July 1863-Feb. 1865 (ch. VI, vol. 464), concerns surgical and medical cases. A record of requisitions for supplies issued to Virginia hospitals, Jan. 1864-Mar. 1865 (ch. VI, vol. 469), also shows persons to whom they were sent; and there is a record of requisitions for fuel for Richmond hospitals, Jan. 1864-Apr. 1865 (ch. VI, vol. 358).

Surgeon Carrington served as corresponding secretary of the Association for the Relief of Maimed Soldiers. The Association's record book (ch. VI, vol. 463) contains his correspondence, Jan. 1864-Mar. 1865, his reports, minutes of meetings, the constitution of the A. R. M. S., the treasurer's account of receipts and expenditures, Feb. 1864-Jan. 1865, and a register of beneficiaries, 1861-65.

Other correspondence is that of Surg. Thomas H. Williams, Inspector of Hospitals in Virginia. Letters-sent books, May 17, 1862-Jan. 22, 1863 (ch. VI, vols. 366 and 461), contain fair copies of letters sent by Williams from Lynchburg and Danville to surgeons in charge of hospitals, the Surgeon General, contract physicians, Army officers, and others relating chiefly to conditions in hospitals. Letters received by Surgeon Williams, June 7, 1861-Dec. 6, 1862 (ch. VI, vol. 369), are mainly copies of incoming communications from the Surgeon General and surgeons in charge of hospitals.

Records in Other Custody. --Some records of the Medical Director at Richmond are in other repositories. A correspondence and order book, 1861-64, in the Confederate Museum contains copies of outgoing and incoming communications, July 24-Sept. 10, 1863; Surgeon General's circulars, Jan. 23, 1863-Feb. 15, 1864; orders of the Army of the Potomac, Aug. 11-Nov. 1, 1861; and a list of sick and wounded men allowed to remain in private quarters, 1862. A roster of surgeons at the general hospitals in Virginia, Jan.-Apr. 1864, and consolidated statistical reports of sick and wounded men in hospitals in and around Richmond, Dec. 1862 and Feb. 1863, are in the same repository. A few William A. Carrington papers, 1863-64, are in Duke University Library. Other records of Surgeon Carrington relating to hospitals in Virginia, in the W. P. Palmer collection in the Western Reserve Historical Society, include reports of sick and wounded men and a return of medical officers, Department of Virginia, Jan. 1863-May 1864; morning reports of general hospitals in the Department of Henrico, Jan.-Nov. 1864; and requisitions and abstracts of hospitals in Danville, Lynchburg, and Charlottesville.

Medical Directors of the Army of Tennessee. As Medical Director of the Army of Tennessee, Surg. Andrew J. Foard had charge of the surgeons attached to the Army and its hospitals. He was relieved of the responsibility for hospitals in July 1862 on the appointment of Surg. Samuel H. Stout as Medical Director of Hospitals. Stout directed many hospitals in Tennessee and Georgia and was stationed successively at Chattanooga, Macon, Marietta, Atlanta, and Columbus. About the beginning of 1863 Surg. Edward A. Flewellen became Medical Director of the Army of Tennessee and served at its headquarters. In Nov. 1863 Surgeon Foard was assigned to relieve Flewellen.

Record Group 109. --In 1903 Surgeon Flewellen donated records that are now in the War Department Collection of Confederate Records. Letters, orders, and circulars sent and received, Jan. 9, 1862-Feb. 20, 1865 (ch. VI, vol. 748), include fair copies of outgoing communications (the letters are to the Surgeon General) and letters, orders, and circulars from the Surgeon General and the Adjutant and Inspector General. A letters-sent book, Jan. 20, 1863-Aug. 15, 1864 (ch. VI, vol. 749), consists mainly of fair copies of letters sent and some of orders and circulars. The letters and telegrams are to medical directors of corps, surgeons, Chief Medical Purveyor E. W. Johns, the medical purveyor at Chattanooga, and other Army officers. Service records, with an alphabetical index, of medical officers of the Army of Tennessee, 1861-65 (ch. VI, vol. 747), give information on individual officers including rank, date of appointment, command to which appointed, and date and place of examination by medical examining board. Index record cards prepared from this volume and volume 748 are in the compiled military service records of Confederate officers described in chapter XI of this Guide.

Records in Other Custody. --Papers of Surg. A. J. Foard, Apr. 1861-July 1862, in the Confederate Museum contain a few wartime letters. These and microfilm of other communications addressed to him, now in the Stout papers in the Southern Historical Collection in the University of North Carolina Library, relate partly to his activities as Medical Director of Department No. 2 in Tennessee.

In 1915 Surgeon Stout's collection of medical records of the Army of Tennessee was sold to several repositories and individuals. The extensive Stout collection in the Texas Archives in the University of Texas Library relates to hospitals in Tennessee, Alabama, Georgia, and Mississippi. The records relating to Stout's activities as Medical Director of Hospitals of the Army of Tennessee are described here; those relating to hospitals are described below. There are correspondence and order books, Dec. 16, 1862-July 14, 1863, July 24, 1863-Mar. 22, 1865, and Jan. 1, 1864-July 19, 1864 (3 vols.). Part of the first volume relates to his services as post surgeon at Chattanooga before he became medical director, and other records for 1862-63 that are described below also relate to that assignment. An order book, Apr. 12-May 1, 1865, contains copies of orders issued by Stout at Columbus and Atlanta. Correspondence and other papers, Jan. 9, 1862-Dec. 18, 1864 (2 in.), include letters received and sent, orders, vouchers, statements of provisions issued, and summaries of accounts current of hospital funds. Morning reports of the Medical Director, Apr. 1, 1863-July 19, 1864, contain statistical data on men in hospitals in Tennessee, Georgia, and Alabama. Another small file of S. H. Stout papers, 1861-65, includes letters, telegrams, orders, circulars, and contracts with private physicians. Some of the communications in this file are addressed to Surg. A. J. Foard.

Original manuscripts of Medical Director Stout are in several other repositories. Correspondence and other papers, Dec. 21, 1861-June 12, 1865 (2 in.), in the Confederate Museum include letters and circulars from the Surgeon General; special orders and circulars from the Adjutant and Inspector General's Office, the Army of Tennessee, the Department of East Tennessee, and Department No. 2; letters from hospital surgeons, post surgeons, medical purveyors, and other Army officers; and some hospital provision returns and property returns. Correspondence and orders, May 30, 1861-Apr. 27, 1865, in the Keith Read Confederate Collection in Emory University Library include letters from hospital, post, and regimental surgeons and the medical directors of the Department of East Tennessee and Department No. 2; copies of letters to the Surgeon General and to hospital and other surgeons; copies and drafts of circulars issued; receipts for payments; and AIGO and Army of Tennessee special orders. The S. H. Stout papers, 1863-65 (13 items), in the Georgia Historical Society collections consist mainly of letters and telegrams sent and received. Other S. H. Stout papers, 1861-65 (3 ft. 3 in.), in the W. P. Palmer Collection of the Western Reserve Historical Society consist of correspondence, special orders, circulars, lists of medical officers and other hospital employees, registers and lists of employees, and hospital reports of medical and hospital supplies, requests and invoices for provisions, diets and prescriptions, furlough papers, and registers of deaths, relating mostly to Georgia hospitals during 1863-64.

Microfilm of Stout papers that were privately owned is in other repositories. The University of North Carolina Library, Duke University Library, and Emory University Library have microfilm of correspondence

and other papers, 1861-65, that were owned by Col. Thomas Spencer of
Atlanta, Ga. The collection includes incoming and outgoing correspondence,
orders, reports, requisitions, and other papers relating to Stout's services
as surgeon at the Gordon Hospital in Nashville, post surgeon in Chattanooga,
and Medical Director of Hospitals of the Army of Tennessee. A register
of surgeons, 1862-65, containing service records, has an alphabetical name
index. Other S. H. Stout papers, 1861-65 (microfilm), in Emory University Library were obtained from W. E. Thomas of Medford, Oreg., who had
purchased the original papers from Mrs. Katherine Stout Moore.
Records of Other Medical Directors. Records of only a few other medical
directors have been found.

Record Group 109. --Two records concern hospitals in North Carolina where Surgeons Edward N. Covey and Peter E. Hines served successively during 1863-65 as medical directors of general hospitals at Raleigh.
Statistical reports concerning hospital patients and attendants, 1863-65
(ch. VI, vol. 280), include the following: (1) consolidated weekly reports,
Apr. 1863-Mar. 1865; (2) record of discharges on surgeons' certificate and
deaths, Apr. 1863-Mar. 1865; (3) consolidated monthly reports of sick and
wounded men, Apr. 1863-Feb. 1865; (4) return of hospital stewards, Nov.
1863-Feb. 1865; and (5) returns of medical officers of the Regular Army
and contract physicians, Apr. 1863-Feb. 1865. The first and third sections
of the foregoing record are statistics only; the second and fourth give additional information about individuals. Lists of sick and wounded patients
and attendants in Mobile hospitals, 1863-64 (1 vol.), give information about
individuals for the Nott, LeVert, Ross, Canty, Moore, and Miller Hospitals. Surg. Frank A. Ross was the medical director in Mobile in 1863.

Records in Other Custody. --In the Archives Division of the Virginia
State Library is a correspondence and order book of the Medical Director
of the Western Department, Jan. 10, 1862-Feb. 3, 1864. Surgeons David
W. Yandell and Andrew J. Foard served as Medical Directors of the West-
ern Department at different places in Kentucky, Tennessee, and Alabama.
A volume of copies of letters and orders sent and received by Surgeon
Foard, June 25-Dec. 24, 1862 (1 vol.), with a return of medical officers on
duty in the hospital at Tullahoma, Tenn., is in the Stout collection in the
University of Texas Library, Texas Archives.

Several officers served as medical director of the Army of the
Potomac and the Army of Northern Virginia. Surg. Thomas H. Williams
filled the position from June 1861; he was followed briefly by Surg. David C.
De Leon. Surg. Lafayette Guild was assigned in June 1862 and continued
until the end of the war. Letters-sent books, Sept. 22, 1861-May 18, 1862
(ch. VI, vols. 367 and 460), contain fair copies of letters sent by Surgeon Williams to the Surgeon General, surgeons in charge of hospitals, regimental surgeons, acting surgeons, Army officers, and others. Orders and circulars received and issued, 1861-62 (ch. VI, vol. 368), contain copies of special orders,
general orders, and circulars issued, Nov. 30, 1861-Dec. 15, 1862, and special
orders, general orders, and circulars received from the Adjutant and Inspector General, the Surgeon General, and Headquarters Army of the Potomac, Nov. 7, 1861-Dec. 20, 1862. A register of assignments of medical
officers, Aug. 1861-Apr. 1862 (ch. VI, vol. 147), shows the assignments of
surgeons and assistant surgeons to regiments. Lists of brigade and hospital surgeons are in the back of this volume. Lafayette Guild's letters-sent
books, June 28, 1862-Apr. 1, 1865 (ch. VI, vols. 641 and 642) contain fair
copies of letters to the Surgeon General and to medical and other officers,

and to John Enders, chairman of the Committee for Our Wounded (better
known as the Richmond Ambulance Committee), which transported wounded
soldiers from battlefields to interior hospitals. Index record cards embodying personal information derived from most of the foregoing records
are in the compiled military service records described in chapter XI of
this Guide.
    Records in Other Custody.--An order book, 1861, of Surg. Thomas
H. Williams in the Schenectady County Historical Society collections,
Schenectady, N.Y., contains orders issued from his office at Manassas
Junction and general and special orders received from Richmond. Surg.
Hunter H. McGuire served as Medical Director of the 2d Corps of the Val-
ley District during 1861-65. McGuire's papers, May 1861-Oct. 1862, in the
Confederate Museum include returns, reports, and registers; and other
papers are in the Virginia Historical Society collections.

Medical Purveyors

        Early in the war the Surgeon General appointed medical purveyors
to procure and distribute medical and hospital supplies. AIGO Special •
Order 79 of Apr. 7, 1862, directed medical purveyors to obey instructions
of Surg. Edward W. Johns, the medical purveyors in Richmond, regarding
the distribution of medical supplies. For nearly a year Surgeon Johns
functioned as Chief Medical Purveyor, but on Feb. 25, 1863, the Surgeon
General resumed direct authority (AIGO General Order 23). A circular
issued by the Chief Medical Purveyor on Apr. 12, 1862, was addressed to
medical purveyors in charge of depots at Richmond, Charlotte, Charleston,
Savannah, Atlanta, Montgomery, Jackson, New Orleans, and San Antonio
and to field purveyors in Virginia, North Carolina, Tennessee, Arkansas,
and Alabama. Field purveyors were responsible for furnishing supplies to
the Army commands to which they were attached, and they drew on the depots for that purpose. Medical purveyors also served at other points including Demopolis and Mobile, Ala.; Lake City, Quincy, and Tallahassee,
Fla.; Macon, Ga.; Wilmington, N.C.; Columbia, S.C.; Chattanooga and
Memphis, Tenn.; Fredericksburg, Petersburg, and Winchester, Va.; and
Houston, Tex.
        Medical purveyors were concerned also with the manufacture of
medicines and other supplies. They had charge of pharmaceutical laboratories at Atlanta, Macon, Columbia, Charleston, Charlotte, Lincolnton,
Montgomery, Mobile, Tyler, Arkadelphia, Little Rock, and Richmond and
of distilleries at Charlotte, Macon, and Salisbury. They supervised the
collection of indigenous herbs, roots, and barks for the manufacture of
medicines. The supply of medicines and surgical instruments derived from
home manufacture was augmented by importations from Europe and from
the United States in exchange for cotton.
        Record Group 109.--Records of a number of medical purveyors are
in the War Department Collection of Confederate Records. A record of
requisitions for hospital supplies made on the purveyor's depot at Macon,
1862-65 (ch. VI, vols. 567, 569, 571, 574, and 575), shows the name and
organization of the surgeon making the requisition and the kinds and quantities of articles requisitioned. A record of requisitions for medical and
hospital supplies, Sept. 2, 1864-Apr. 17, 1865 (ch. VI, vols. 630-632),
contains similar information. For the same place there are invoices of
hospital supplies issued, Apr. 4, 1863-Aug. 10, 1864 (ch. VI, vols. 570,

578, and 579); inventories of packages shipped and medicines on hand, June 21, 1862-Sept. 1, 1862 (ch. VI, vol. 565), and in the same volume a list of remedies on hand, July 31, 1863-May 31, 1864; an inventory of medical and hospital supplies on hand, June 25-Oct. 29, Dec. 25, 1862 (ch. VI, vol. 622); an inventory of medical and hospital supplies on hand and expended, 1862 (ch. VI, vol. 622); undated inventories of hospital supplies (ch. VI, vols. 568 and 598); a record of hospital and medical supplies, 1864 (ch. VI, vol. 581); and an inventory of medical and hospital supplies, Jan. 25, 1863-Apr. 1, 1865 (ch. VI, vol. 176). These records show kinds and quantities of supplies. A record of whiskey and alcohol received, Feb. 16-Apr. 1, 1865 (ch. VI, vol. 626), gives the names of firms, the quantities received, and the dates of receipt. Accounts books, 1862-65 (ch. VI, vols. 296, 623, and 632 1/2), contain a chronological record of expenditures for hospital and medical supplies and services, showing the date, person or firm paid, and the amount paid.

There are records of Surg. E. W. Johns, who continued as medical purveyor at Richmond until 1865. A record of medical and hospital supplies issued and received, 1864-65 (ch. VI, vol. 577), shows kinds and quantities of articles. In this volume are letters from Surgeon Johns to Surg. J. M. Holloway, Winder Hospital, May 10 and 12, 1862. A record of whiskey and other supplies received and issued, 1864-65 (ch. VI, vol. 656), and a record of clothing, bedding, and linens issued to hospitals, Jan.-Aug. 1863 (ch. VI, vol. 636 1/2), show kinds and quantities of articles.

The medical purveyor at Savannah was Surg. William H. Prioleau. For the office at that place there are a file of letters, telegrams, orders, and circulars received, Mar. 18-June 30, 1862 (ch. VI, vol. 6), abstracts of medical and hospital supplies received, June 30, 1862-Mar. 31, 1865 (ch. VI, vol. 580), and abstracts of medical and hospital supplies issued, 1862-65 (ch. VI, vol. 621). A cashbook of Medical Purveyor William H. Prioleau, Apr. 12, 1863-Feb. 23, 1865 (ch. VI, vol. 633), shows amounts received by Treasury drafts and expenditures with name of person or firm paid, voucher number, and amount paid. In this book there are also accounts for expenditures for alcoholic stimulants, July 23, 1863-Mar. 31, 1864, hospital clothing, July 29-30, 1863, and contract physicians, June 10, 1863-Mar. 7, 1864.

The medical purveyor's office of the Western Department, to which Surg. Richard Potts was appointed in Dec. 1861, was located at different places in Tennessee, Mississippi, Alabama, and Georgia. Its records include press copies of letters sent from Macon and Montgomery, Nov. 18, 1863-Mar. 31, 1865 (ch. VI, vol. 629); accounts of medical and hospital supplies purchased, Oct. 1861-July 1862 (ch. VI, vols. 611 and 613); abstracts of medical and hospital supplies issued, Aug. 1861-Mar. 1864 (ch. VI, vol. 576); a record of supplies furnished, Sept. 5, 1861-Mar. 26, 1862 (ch. VI, vol. 636); and mess accounts, June-Aug. 1863 (ch. VI, vol. 620). Accounts of medical and hospital supplies issued and purchased, 1861-6:' (ch. VI, vol. 624), contain the following: abstracts of supplies issued, June-Sept. 1861; accounts of supplies, equipment, and tools purchased, Sept.-Oct. 1861; drayage account, Aug.-Sept. 1861; articles purchased for cash, Aug.-Oct. 1861; a list of articles broken and lost; a postage account, June 1861-Mar. 1862; and a telegraph account, Aug. 1861-Mar. 1862.

Records are available for the offices of two other purveyors. A file of letters, telegrams, orders, and circulars received and sent by Surg. George S. Blackie at Atlanta, Nov. 20, 1862-Aug. 1863 (ch. VI, vol. 750), contains communications with the Surgeon General, Chief Purveyor E. W. Johns, Edward A. Flewellen (Medical Director of the Army of Tennessee), other medical purveyors, hospital surgeons, Army officers, and business firms. For the medical purveyor of the Army of Northern Virginia (Surg. W. H. Geddings) there is an undated receipt roll of cloth issued to medical officers (ch. VI, vol. 143).

Records in Other Custody. --The papers of Surg. J. E. A. Davidson, medical purveyor at Quincy, Fla., in the P. K. Yonge Library of Florida History of the University of Florida contain some wartime correspondence with the Surgeon General. Surg. James K. Hall's inspection report of Sept. 2, 1864, on the depot at Demopolis, Ala., is in the Southern Historical Collection in the University of North Carolina Library.

Hospitals

An act of Sept. 27, 1862 (1 Cong. C. S. A. Stat. 64), provided that hospitals were to be numbered as hospitals of particular States and that whenever possible sick and wounded soldiers were to be sent to hospitals representing their States. Many sick and wounded men from camps and battlefields were transported, however, to general hospitals in towns and cities where admission was not restricted to soldiers from particular military units. An act of May 1, 1863 (1 Cong. C. S. A. Stat. 162), authorized the establishment of way hospitals along railroad routes to care for sick and wounded soldiers who had been furloughed or discharged. Officers of both the Army and the Navy were eligible for treatment in any hospital. Personnel employed in hospitals under various acts of Congress included hospital stewards, nurses, cooks, laundresses, and matrons. Soldiers were detailed to hospitals for work as nurses, pharmacists, and other duty.

An act of May 1, 1863 (1 Cong. C. S. A. Stat. 153), provided for the formation of boards of examiners for hospitals to determine the eligibility of sick, wounded, and disabled soldiers for furlough or discharge. Such boards, as organized by the surgeons in charge of hospitals, were to visit the hospitals and examine applicants for furloughs and discharges; they could grant furloughs of not more than 60 days and could recommend discharges.

Hospitals kept the similar records on forms prescribed by the Regulations for the Medical Department of 1861 and 1863. Since these records were uniform in content, they are described here and will be referred to below in connection with individual hospitals only by title. Registers of patients show the patient's name, rank, organization, complaint, date admitted, and disposition made. The prescription book shows the date, patient's name, complaint, and daily medication; a diet book on the same form prescribed the daily diet. Case books contain information on the treatment given to individual patients with description of disease or wound, history of the case, and results of treatment. Hospitals sometimes kept registers of deaths and personal effects. Morning reports of sick and wounded men contain statistical information on the number of men present and the number returned to duty, transferred, furloughed, discharged, deserted, and deceased. Similar information is in weekly statistical reports of sick and wounded men, which also denote the patients living in private quarters.

The information concerning individuals in the hospital records described below was abstracted on index record cards filed in the compiled military service records of Confederate soldiers. These records and the compiled military service records of general and staff officers, which contain files for the surgeons who were attached to hospitals in addition to those who served with the Army commands, are described in chapter XI of this Guide. In some instances, significant documents relating to the establishment and operation of hospitals are filed in these compiled records. There were many hospitals for which no records have been found. Lists prepared by the U. S. War Department of hospitals (one by local names of hospitals and another by place names) are in Record Group 109.

Records of other military hospitals are described in this chapter under Office of the Commissary General of Prisoners and Territorial Commands and Armies.

W. J. Donald, "Alabama Confederate Hospitals," Alabama Review, 15:271-281 (Oct. 1962), 16:64-78 (Jan. 1963).

Alabama

Fort Morgan Hospital

Record Group 109. --The records include a register of patients, Feb. 3, 1863-Aug. 21, 1864 (ch. VI, vol. 3), and a miscellaneous record book, 1862-64 (ch. VI, vol. 5), containing rolls of hospital personnel, 1862-64, a wash list, 1862-63, statistical morning reports of patients, 1863-64, receipts and invoices of medical supplies, 1862, and copies of letters sent, 1862.

General Hospital (Marion)

George V. Irons, "Howard College as a Confederate Military Hospital," Alabama Review, 9:22-32 (Jan. 1956).

Records in Other Custody. --A prescription book, Aug. 1863-Dec. 1864, is in Howard College Library.

Engineer Hospital (Mobile)

Record Group 109. --Register of patients, Jan. 13, 1864-Apr. 25, 1865 (ch. III, vol. 20), including slaves and Federal Negro prisoners.

Ross General Hospital (Mobile)

Record Group 109. --The records include a register of patients, Sept. 1, 1863-Apr. 12, 1865 (ch. VI, vol. 2); an account of clothing and equipment of patients, Mar. 1-30, 1865 (ch. VI, vol. 1); requisitions for medical supplies, July 1861-Nov. 1864 (ch. VI, vol. 536); a daily record of the receipt and issue of hospital stores, Jan. 1-Apr. 8, 1865 (ch. VI, vol. 555); and diet books, Sept. 14, 1863-Apr. 25, 1864, Jan. -Mar. 1865 (ch. VI, vols. 592 and 139).

Wayside Hospital (Montgomery)

Records in Other Custody. --A register of patients, Jan. 1864-Apr. 1865 (3 vols.), is with the Texas Archives at the University of Texas Library (S. H. Stout collection).

General Hospital (Shelby Springs)

Record Group 109. --The records include letters, orders, and circulars received, Feb. 28, 1864-May 10, 1865 (ch. VI, vol. 462); and a prescription book, Apr. 4-Nov. 24, 1864 (ch. VI, vol. 643, p. 61-201).

Arkansas

Rock Hotel Hospital (Little Rock)

Record Group 109. --The records include letters and orders sent and received and receipts for deceased soldiers' effects, Dec. 1862-May 1863 (ch. VI, vol. 695), and a register of patients, Nov. 14, 1862-June 3, 1863 (ch. VI, vol. 721).

Florida

Camp Simkins Hospital

Records in Other Custody. --Reports, 1863-64, are in Duke University Library.

General Hospital (Lake City)

Records in Other Custody. --A case book, Mar. 1864-Jan. 1865, an account book, Mar. 1864-May 1865, and a medical furlough book, July 2-Oct. 22, 1864, are in the Confederate Museum at Richmond.

General Hospital (Pensacola)

Records in Other Custody. --Correspondence, orders, and reports, Apr. 1861-Jan. 1862 (photostats), are in the P. K. Yonge Library of the University of Florida.

Georgia

Military Prison Hospital (Andersonville)

Records in Other Custody. --Correspondence and orders, Oct. 29, 1864-Apr. 13, 1865 (microfilm from S. H. Stout papers), are in the Southern Historical Collection in the University of North Carolina Library. A manuscript volume incorporating the results of investigations in 1864 by Surg. Joseph Jones at the Andersonville Military Prison Hospital on gangrene, malarial fevers, diarrhea, and dysentery is in the Department of Archives of Louisiana State University. In the same repository are Surgeon Jones' diary, Sept. 17-22, 1864, containing descriptive matter regarding Andersonville and information on autopsies of Federal prisoners, a scrapbook of official documents, 1861-65, and other papers concerning his studies on Confederate medical history.

Other records of this hospital are described in this chapter under Commissary General of Prisoners.

Fairground Hospital No. 1 (Atlanta)

Records in Other Custody. --Letters and orders received, May 17, 1864-Mar. 17, 1865 (1 vol.), a register of patients, Aug. 22, 1862-Mar. 31, 1863, Apr. 1, 1863-June 24, 1864, and Sept. 22, 1863-Mar. 29, 1865 (3 vols.), and a baggage register, 1863-64 (1 vol.), are in the Texas Archives in the University of Texas Library (S. H. Stout collection).

Fairground Hospital No. 2 (Atlanta)

Records in Other Custody. --The Stout collection contains for this hospital a register of patients, Sept. 1, 1862-May 26, 1864 (2 vols.), a register of patients, Feb. 15-Sept. 22, 1863 (1 vol.), and a miscellaneous record book, Feb. 1863-Dec. 1864 (2 vols.). An order book, Aug. 1862-Aug. 1864, is in the Robert Battey papers in the William P. Palmer collection in the Western Reserve Historical Society.

General Hospital (Atlanta)

Records in Other Custody. --Letters and orders sent and received by Surg. John P. Logan, Aug. 14, 1862-Mar. 17, 1864, Jan. 2-Nov. 1, 1864 (2 vols.), are in the S. H. Stout collection with the Texas Archives at the University of Texas Library. Order books of Surgeon Logan, Aug. 1862-Feb. 1863, July-Oct. 1863 (2 vols.), are in the W. P. Palmer collection in the Western Reserve Historical Society.

Receiving and Distributing Hospital (Atlanta)

Records in Other Custody. --Records of this hospital are in the S. H. Stout collection with the Texas Archives at the University of Texas Library. They include letters and orders received, May 16-July 22, 1863, and May 14-Oct. 16, 1864 (3 vols.), a register of patients, Nov. 1863-June 1864 (3 vols.), a list of sick and wounded received, Dec. 15, 1863-Feb. 23, 1864 (1 vol.), and a miscellaneous record book, Aug. 1863-May 1864.

Walker General Hospital (Columbus)

Record Group 109. --Letters, orders, and circulars sent and received, Aug. 15, 1863-Apr. 22, 1865 (ch. VI, vol. 763).

Hood Hospital (Cuthbert)

Record Group 109. --Report on wounded men, Jan.-Mar. 1865 (ch. VI, part of vol. 663).

Post Hospital (Dalton)

Record Group 109. --Register of patients, July 29, 1862-Jan. 30, 1863 (ch. VI, vol. 292).

St. Mary's Hospital (Dalton)

In 1863 this hospital was moved to La Grange and in 1864 was located successively at Union Springs, Ala. (Aug. 17), Meridian, Miss. (Nov. 5), and West Point, Miss. (Dec. 4). Other records of this hospital are described under West Point.

Record Group 109. --A miscellaneous record book, 1862-63 (ch. VI, vol. 4). Other records include letters, orders, and circulars received, Nov. 5, 1863-Nov. 5, 1864, and Dec. 4-19, 1864 (ch. VI, vols. 746 and 551), and accounts of medical and hospital supplies, 1863-64 (ch. VI, vol. 542).

Hospitals (Dalton)

Record Group 109. --A medical examining board record relating to patients in Dalton hospitals, 1863-64 (ch. VI, vol. 543).

Fort Gaines Hospital (Ga.)

Records in Other Custody. --Papers of Surg. James M. Gaston, who helped to establish this hospital, are in the Southern Historical Collection in the University of North Carolina Library.

Empire Hospital (Macon)

Originally located at Atlanta, this hospital was moved from Macon in 1864 and located successively thereafter at Tuscumbia, Corinth, Meridian, and Opelika.

Records in Other Custody. --An order and letter book of the surgeon in charge (William P. Harden), Jan. 1863-Apr. 1865, was recently in the hands of a grandson (Cunningham, Doctors in Gray, p. 297).

Ocmulgee Hospital (Macon)

Record Group 109. --Records of this hospital were presented to the War Department in 1908 by Dr. Stanford E. Chaillé, who had been the surgeon in charge during the war. They include letters, orders, and circulars sent and received, July 24, 1863-Apr. 30, 1865 (ch. VI, vol. 757), orders and circulars received, Apr. 30, 1862-Oct. 31, 1863 (ch. VI, vol. 758), regulations and orders relating to records, Jan.-Mar. 1865 (ch. VI, vol. 760), regulations for the guidance of personnel, 1865 (ch. VI, vol. 759), register of patients, Sept. 23-Dec. 18, 1863, and Jan. 21, 1864-Apr. 30, 1865 (ch. VI, vols. 751 and 752), reports on surgical cases, Mar.-Dec. 1864 (ch. VI, vols. 754-756), account book of the hospital fund, Jan. 1864-Apr. 1865 (ch. VI, vol. 762), and a medical examining board record for Floyd House Hospital and Ocmulgee Hospital, Jan. 1, 1864-Apr. 4, 1865 (ch. VI, vols. 751 and 753).

Records in Other Custody. --In Emory University Library are reports on surgical cases, Feb. 1863-Mar. 1865, and a miscellaneous record book, Feb. 1864-Apr. 1865.

May Hospital (Madison)

Records in Other Custody. --A medical board record, July 1864-May 1865 (microfilm), is in the Georgia Department of Archives and History.

Foard Hospital (Marietta)

Records in Other Custody. --Registers of patients, including a general register, Oct.-Nov. 1863, are in the S. H. Stout collection with the Texas Archives at the University of Texas Library.

General Hospital No. 1 (Savannah)

Record Group 109. --The records include letters sent and letters, orders, and circulars received, Mar. 6, 1862-Aug. 27, 1864 (ch. VI, vol. 648); and a letter, report, and account book, Jan. 24, 1863-Mar. 7, 1864 (ch. VI, vol. 647), containing press copies of outgoing letters, statistical reports on patients, and accounts of the hospital fund.

Hospital (Tunnel Hill)

Record Group 109. --A register of patients, May-Aug. 1863 (ch. VI, vol. 663, p. 124-161), with a record of surgical cases.

Kentucky

Hospital (Bowling Green)

Record Group 109. --A register of patients, Oct. 22, 1861-Feb. 5, 1862 (ch. VI, vol. 295A).

Louisiana

General Hospital (Shreveport)

Record Group 109. --The records include orders, circulars, and letters received, Oct. 29, 1863-Apr. 29, 1865 (ch. VI, vol. 296 1/2), including requisitions for medical and hospital supplies, Aug. 8-Dec. 2, 1865, a list of detailed men, 1864-65, and a register of patients, Jan. 1, 1864-June 12, 1865 (ch. VI, vol. 297).

Mississippi

Hospital (Brooksville)

Records in Other Custody. --Letters and orders sent and received, July 8-Aug. 16, 1862 (1 vol.), are in the S. H. Stout collection with the Texas Archives at the University of Texas Library.

Hospital of the 1st Mississippi Regiment (Jackson)

Record Group 109. --Register of patients, Jan. 6, 1863-May 6, 1865 (ch. VI, vol. 298).

General Hospital (Lauderdale Springs)

Record Group 109. --A prescription book, 1862-63 (ch. VI, vol. 643, p. 1-60).
Records in Other Custody. --An order book, 1862-64, is in the Minnesota Historical Society.

Way Hospital (Meridian)

Record Group 109. --A register of patients, Jan. 7-Apr. 1, 1865 (ch. VI, vol. 665, p. 7-360).

Yandell Hospital (Meridian)

Record Group 109. --A register of patients, Apr. 1-12, 1865 (ch. VI, vol. 665, p. 361-406).

University Hospital (Oxford)

Record Group 109. --A register of patients, Mar. 17-Apr. 8, 1862 (ch. VI, vol. 298, p. 2-51).

St. Mary's Hospital (West Point)

Record Group 109. --A register of patients, June 14, 1864-Mar. 11, 1865 (ch. VI, vol. 274), and a steward's record of commissary supplies received and issued, Oct. 1864-Apr. 1865 (ch. VI, vol. 552).

Territory of New Mexico

General Hospital (Doña Ana)

Record Group 109. --A prescription book, Oct. 13, 1861-Feb. 7, 1862 (ch. VI, vol. 556, p. 22-53).

Hospital (Fort Fillmore)

Record Group 109. --A prescription book, Aug. 1-Oct. 12, 1861 (ch. VI, vol. 556, p. 1-20).

North Carolina

General Hospital No. 11 (Charlotte)

Record Group 109. --A register of patients, May 15, 1864-Apr. 28, 1865 (ch. VI, vol. 281).

Fort Fisher Hospital

Record Group 109. --Morning reports of patients, Dec. 1, 1863-Aug. 31, 1864 (ch. VI, vol. 400).

College Hospital (Goldsboro)

Record Group 109. --An undated list of men to be detailed as nurses (ch. VI, vol. 659).

General Hospital No. 3 (Goldsboro)

Record Group 109. --Letters received and sent, Mar. 8-Oct. 20, 1864 (ch. VI, vol. 137).
Records in Other Custody. --In the Southern Historical Collection in the University of North Carolina Library are correspondence and orders of William A. Holt, the surgeon in charge of this hospital after Mar. 12, 1864.

General Hospital No. 3 (Greensboro)

Record Group 109. --A register of patients, Jan. 1-Mar. 20, 1865 (ch. VI, vol. 291).

Wayside Hospital (High Point)

This hospital opened in the Barbee Hotel on Sept. 1, 1863.
Records in Other Custody. --The Southern Historical Collection in the University of North Carolina Library has a register of patients, Sept. 1863-Mar. 1865 (1 vol., microfilm), that includes a register of deaths, Mar.-May 1865.

General Hospital No. 7 (Raleigh)

Originally opened in 1861 by the State of North Carolina as a general hospital, this hospital was transferred in the next year to the Confederacy. It was known also as the Fairground Hospital and, apparently, as the Baptist Grove Hospital.
Record Group 109. --Reports on surgical cases (ch. VI, vol. 526) concern treatment given during 1863-65 at both General Hospital No. 7 and Pettigrew Hospital. A miscellaneous record book (ch. VI, vol. 523) contains weekly statistical reports of patients and attendants, Aug.-Dec. 1863, receipts for clothing issued to patients, Aug. 1863-June 1864, and quarterly returns of clothing, camp, and garrison equipage received and issued, Dec. 31, 1863, and Mar. 31, 1864. A record of the disposition of cases in General Hospitals Nos. 7 and 13, 1861-65 (ch. VI, vol. 395), contains a record of discharges and deaths, May 6, 1861-Apr. 26, 1864, and a record of patients returned to duty, furloughed, transferred, deserted, and deceased, May 21, 1864-Mar. 23, 1865.
Records in Other Custody. --Records that were kept by Edmund B. Haywood, the surgeon in charge of this hospital, are in the Southern Historical Collection in the University of North Carolina Library. They include letters sent and letters and orders received, June 25, 1863-May 20, 1864 (part of a vol.); a register of patients, Nov. 1, 1861-July 1862 (part of a vol.); a prescription and diet book, Dec. 1861-Oct. 1863 (2 vols.); and an account book, Dec. 1861-June 1864. Other papers, 1861-65, of Surgeon Haywood include correspondence, orders, circulars, accounts, requisitions, and other official documents.

General Hospital No. 13 (Raleigh)

Construction of this hospital was begun in 1863. Personnel were transferred from General Hospital No. 7 in June 1864. It was known also as Pettigrew Hospital.

Record Group 109.--The records include special orders sent and orders and circulars received, 1862-65 (ch. VI, vol. 394), consisting chiefly of orders issued by Surg. E. B. Haywood; a register of patients, June 1864-Apr. 1865 (ch. VI, vols. 224 and 290); a case book of wounded patients, 1864-65 (ch. VI, vols. 287 and 397); receipts for clothing issued to soldiers, June 26, 1864-Apr. 10, 1865 (ch. VI, vol. 523, p. 188-195); requisitions for and returns of medical and hospital supplies, 1864-65 (ch. VI, vol. 524); a record of hospital supplies issued to wards, 1864-65 (ch. VI, vol. 396 1/2); a baggage register, 1864-65 (ch. VI, vol. 396); and miscellaneous record books, 1864-65 (ch. VI, vols. 525, 288, and 289).

Records in Other Custody.--Records of this hospital are also in the Haywood collection in the Southern Historical Collection at the University of North Carolina Library. They include letters, orders, and circulars sent and received, June 8, 1864-Apr. 8, 1865 (part of a vol.); provision accounts, Jan. 2-Apr. 1865 (1 vol.); and a volume labeled "Provision Returns, Milk Acct. and Contingent Fund," June 1864-Apr. 1865, containing also requisitions for funds, records of employees, and a record of provisions and other materials contributed to the hospital.

Military Prison Hospital (Salisbury)

Record Group 109.--The records include letters, orders, and circulars sent and received, May 1, 1864-Mar. 22, 1865 (ch. VI, vol. 35); and accounts current of the hospital fund, Apr. 1864-Apr. 1865 (ch. VI, vol. 398).

General Hospital No. 4 (Wilmington)

Record Group 109.--The records of this hospital include a letters-sent book, Sept. 12, 1863-Feb. 19, 1865 (ch. VI, vol. 399), containing fair copies of letters signed by Thomas R. Micks, surgeon in charge; letters, telegrams, and orders received, Sept. 5, 1863-Feb. 19, 1865 (ch. VI, vol. 401); reports of the officer of the day, Oct. 16, 1863-May 10, 1864 (ch. VI, vol. 402), concerning conditions at the hospital; a register of patients, Feb. 3, 1862-Feb. 19, 1865 (ch. VI, vols. 282, 285, and 286); a register of patients, Jan. 1, 1863-Jan. 13, 1864 (ch. VI, vols. 278 and 244 1/2); a register of deaths and reports on deaths, June 1864-Feb. 1865 (ch. VI, vol. 284), containing also a list of money received from men, May 5-July 2, 1864, and a record of clothing drawn, Aug. 1864-Feb. 1865; record of transfers of patients to other hospitals, Jan.-Feb. 1865 (ch. VI, vol. 277), with a record of money received from patients, Sept.-Dec. 1863, and from deceased soldiers, Dec. 1864-Mar. 1865; reports of sick and wounded men and register of deaths, Jan. 1864-Jan. 1865 (ch. VI, vol. 279), with statistical statements of gunshot wounds and operations and reports of vaccinations; morning reports of sick and wounded, Apr. 1, 1864-Dec. 31, 1864 (ch. VI, vol. 404, p. 90-290); case books, 1863-64 (ch. VI, vols. 446 and 447); and copies of vouchers for supplies and services purchased, June 8-Aug. 21, 1863 (ch. VI, vol. 283). The following records are for General Hospitals

Nos. 4 and 5: account book, 1862-64 (ch. VI, vol. 404), charges, 1863-65 (ch. VI, vol. 527), medical examining board record, Sept. 1, 1864-Feb. 16, 1865 (ch. VI, vol. 528), and letters sent and received by the medical examining board, Feb. 26, 1864-Feb. 17, 1865 (ch. VI, vol. 403).

Military Prison Hospital (Wilmington)

Records in Other Custody. --A list of Confederate prisoners, Mar. 1865, is in the University of Virginia Library (William C. Rives papers).

General Hospital No. 2 (Wilson)

Record Group 109. --Letters, orders, and circulars received, Jan. 13, 1864-Mar. 1, 1865 (ch. VI, vol. 415).

South Carolina

First Louisiana Hospital (Charleston)

The Wayside Hospital at Charleston became on Jan. 13, 1864, the First Louisiana Hospital and was used as a receiving, distributing, and transfer hospital.

Records in Other Custody. --Records in the South Carolina Archives Department at Columbia include letters sent and letters and orders received, Dec. 14, 1863-Sept. 5, 1864 (1 vol.); registers of patients, July 1862-Feb. 1865 (2 vols.); prescription and diet book, Jan. 1864-Aug. 1864 (3 vols.); inventory and appraisement of effects of deceased soldiers, Nov. 1863-Feb. 1865 (1 vol.), with a list of deceased soldiers, Mar. 7-Dec. 30, 1863; account book of expenditures for provisions, materials, and medicine, June 1, 1863-Feb. 22, 1865 (1 vol.); and a miscellaneous record book, Jan. 1863-July 1864 (1 vol.).

Soldiers' Relief Hospital (Charleston)

Records in Other Custody. --Letters received, Sept. 26, 1864-May 10, 1865 (6 items), are in the South Caroliniana Library of the University of South Carolina.

Second North Carolina Hospital (Columbia)

Records in Other Custody. --A volume of letters sent and letters, orders, and circulars received, Aug. 15, 1863-Feb. 15, 1865, is in the South Carolina Archives Department.

Wayside Hospital (Columbia)

Records in Other Custody. --An account book, 1862-65, is in the South Caroliniana Library of the University of South Carolina.

Tennessee

Foard Hospital (Chattanooga)

Records in Other Custody. --A register of patients, Nov. 2, 1861-
Mar. 15, 1863 (1 vol.), is in the Texas Archives at the University of Texas
Library (S. H. Stout collection).

Newsom Hospital (Chattanooga)

Records in Other Custody. --In the University of Texas Library is a
register of patients, July 26, 1862-July 14, 1863 (4 vols.). The register
for Dec. 1, 1862-Jan. 8, 1863, includes a list of sick and wounded Federal
prisoners received.

Smallpox Hospital (Chattanooga)

Record Group 109. --Orders and circulars received, May 22-Aug. 15,
1863 (ch. VI, vol. 274, p. 3-18).

Overton General Hospital (Memphis)

Record Group 109. --Register of patients, Dec. 31, 1861-Mar. 31,
1862 (ch. VI, vol. 9 1/2), with a register of deaths, Mar. 3-31, 1862.

Southern Mothers Hospital (Memphis)

Record Group 109. --Undated inventory of furniture (ch. VI, vol. 274,
p. 27), with an undated memorandum regarding the hospital buildings and
a roll of the sick men at the State Hospital, Jan. 31, 1862 (p. 25).

Texas

General Hospital (El Paso)

Record Group 109. --A register of patients, Apr. 5-July 16, 1862 (ch.
VI, vol. 417 1/2, p. 20-23).

General Hospital (Franklin)

Record Group 109. --A register of patients, Apr. 5-June 30, 1862
(ch. VI, vol. 417 1/2, p. 8-18).

General Hospital (Galveston)

Record Group 109. --A register of patients, Sept. 13-Nov. 28, 1861
(ch. VI, vol. 275, p. 1-25); and a return of wounded men admitted, Jan. 1,
1863 (ch. VI, vol. 276).

General Hospital (Houston)

Record Group 109. --A register of patients, Dec. 1, 1861-Jan. 4, 1864
(ch. VI, vol. 275, p. 28-195, 200-205); and a miscellaneous record book,

1861-65 (ch. VI, vol. 276), containing requisitions for medical and hospital supplies, 1862-64, returns of medical and hospital property, 1861-65, and statistical reports of sick and wounded men, 1862-65.

13th Regiment, Texas Infantry, Hospital (Velasco)

This was the hospital of Lt. Col. Joseph Bates' regiment of Texas volunteers organized as the 4th Regiment, Texas Infantry, becoming later the 13th Regiment, Texas Infantry.

Record Group 109. --A register of patients, Dec. 1861-Oct. 1864 (ch. VI, vols. 480-482); and a record of rations drawn and required, May 1862-May 1865 (ch. VI, vol. 637), with memoranda regarding stores issued to hospital attendants, May 1862-Dec. 1864.

Virginia

Hospital of the 4th Regiment, Georgia Infantry (Camp Jackson, near Portsmouth)

Record Group 109. --A register of patients, July 1861-May 1862 (ch. VI, vol. 294), with a register of deaths, May 1861-Apr. 1862, and a record of discharges, Oct. 1861-Nov. 1861.

Delevan Hospital (Charlottesville)

Record Group 109. --A case book, 1864 (ch. VI, vol. 649, p. 46-51).

General Hospital (Charlottesville)

Established in July 1861 in buildings of the University of Virginia.

Record Group 109. --Records presented to the War Department in 1877 by Dr. James L. Cabell, who had been the surgeon in charge of the hospital, include a register of patients, July 22, 1861-Aug. 2, 1865 (ch. VI, vols. 214 and 215), with an alphabetical name index (ch. VI, vol. 216).

Records in Other Custody. --Duke University Library has a press copy book of letters sent by Surgeon Cabell, Sept. 15, 1861-Apr. 25, 1862; a register of patients, Jan. 1862-May 20, 1865; a descriptive list and account of pay and clothing of hospital personnel, 1862-64; accounts of supplies, equipment, tools, and services purchased, Aug. 28-Dec. 4, 1861; and invoices of medicines purchased and issued, Nov. 15, 1862-July 20, 1863. The Department of Archives of Louisiana State University (Joseph J. Jones papers) has a letters-sent book of Surgeon Cabell, Mar. 20, 1863-Apr. 8, 1865 (1 vol.). The Louisiana State Museum Library at New Orleans has letters sent and letters and orders received by Division 2 of the General Hospital, Jan. 16, 1863-Feb. 3, 1865 (1 vol.).

General Hospital (Culpeper Courthouse)

Established in June 1861; discontinued in Mar. 1862.

Record Group 109. --A miscellaneous record book, Sept. -Oct. 1862 (ch. VI, vol. 587), containing several brief records relating to supplies and a register of deaths and effects; and an undated list of employees (ch. VI, vol. 266, p. 69-70).

General Hospital (Danville)

Record Group 109.--Orders and circulars sent and received, Mar.
12, 1862-Apr. 7, 1865 (ch. VI, vol. 436); a register of patients, May 1862-
Apr. 1865 (ch. VI, vols. 207, 209, and 660); a register of patients, 1864-
65 (ch. VI, vol. 212), including both Confederate and Union soldiers; register of patients, 1861-62 (ch. VI, vol. 512); lists of Confederate and Union
patients and employees, 1862-65 (ch. VI, vol. 208); lists of patients, 1862-
65 (ch. VI, vol. 213); a register of deaths and effects, 1862-63 (ch. VI, vol.
208 1/2); weekly statistical reports of patients and attendants, 1863-65 (ch.
VI, vol. 550); monthly and quarterly statistical reports of sick and wounded
men, 1864-65 (ch. VI, vol. 511); and a register of deaths of Union soldiers,
General Hospital, Division 2, 1863-65 (ch. VI, vol. 210).
Records in Other Custody.--Duke University Library has papers of
Surg. Jefferson H. De Votie, 1856-65, that concern in part the Confederate
hospitals at Danville.

General Hospital (Emory)

This hospital occupied buildings at Emory and Henry College.
Records in Other Custody.--The Confederate Museum has a register
of patients, Dec. 1862-Apr. 1865 (1 vol.).

General Hospital (Farmville)

Established in May 1862.
Record Group 109.--The extensive records of this hospital include
letters sent and letters, orders, and circulars received, May 2, 1862-Mar.
22, 1865 (ch. VI, vols. 546 and 513); a register of patients, July 1861-May
1863 (ch. VI, vol. 269), covering also the General Hospital at Orange Courthouse; a register of patients, Jan. 1, 1863-May 1, 1864 (ch. VI, vol. 41, p.
7-382); a register of patients in ward no. 7, 1864-65 (ch. VI, vol. 48); a
register of deaths and discharges, 1862-65 (ch. VI, vol. 49); a record of
disposition of cases, 1864-65 (ch. VI, vol. 43), with a list of attendants; a
list of patients returned to duty, furloughed, discharged, and deceased,
Dec. 1862-June 1864 (ch. VI, vol. 544), with a list of medical and hospital
supplies received and issued, July 1862-Dec. 1863, and a return of medical
and hospital property, June 30, 1863, reports on surgical cases, 1862 and
1864 (ch. VI, vols. 520 1/2 and 520); a medical examining board record,
1862-65 (ch. VI, vols. 520 1/2, 578, and 579); a register of patients retired
from service by the medical examining board, 1864 (ch. VI, vol. 517); morning
reports of patients, 1862-65 (ch. VI, vol. 393); morning reports of patients
and attendants, 1865 (ch. VI, vol. 545); returns of hospital property, 1862-
65 (ch. VI, vols. 514-516); accounts of the hospital fund and record of clothing issued, 1862-65 (ch. VI, vol. 522); a prescription book, 1863-65 (ch.
VI, vol. 40), with a register of patients, Dec. 1862-Aug. 1863, p. 157-162;
a clothing book, 1863-64 (ch. VI, vol. 617); a miscellaneous record book,
1862-63 (ch. VI, vol. 42), containing a record of the disposition of cases,
a list of men in private quarters, a list of soldiers discharged on certificates of disability, and accounts for clothing furnished to soldiers; and
miscellaneous record books, 1863-65 (ch. VI, vol. 235 and parts of vols.
513 and 546), containing lists of sick and wounded men in private quarters,
a list of Reserve Corps men referred to conscript board, a list of detailed

men, a list of applications for the retired list, a list of invoices of medicines and supplies received, a list of free Negroes and slaves employed and of other employees, returns of medical officers and stewards, and regulations for the general hospital. The following records are of the 1st Division of the General Hospital: letters sent and orders and circulars received, Feb. 11-Sept. 26, 1864 (ch. VI, vol. 45); orders received, June-Dec. 1864 (ch. VI, vol. 521); a register of patients in ward no. 1, Apr. 1865 (ch. VI, vol. 47); and a register of patients, 1862-64 (ch. VI, vol. 46). Records of the 2d Division include registers of patients, 1862-65 (ch. VI, vols. 50 and 51), and a prescription and diet book, 1863 (ch. VI, vol. 44). A register of patients of the 3d Division, Sept. 1862-Apr. 1865 (ch. VI, vol. 39), also contains a list of hospital attendants.

Wayside Hospital (Farmville)

Record Group 109. --Register of patients, 1863-65 (ch. VI, vol. 32, p. 1-48).

General Hospital (Front Royal)

Established Sept. 1, 1861; discontinued Mar. 4, 1862.
Records in Other Custody. --A letters sent and letters and orders received book, Sept. 10, 1861-Jan. 6, 1865, was presented to the Confederate Museum by Surg. Benjamin Blackford, who had charge of the hospital.

General Hospital (Gordonsville)

Records in Other Custody. --The Confederate Museum has a register of patients, June 1, 1863-May 5, 1864 (1 vol.).

Hospital (Hanover Junction)

Records in Other Custody. --The University of Virginia Library has a miscellaneous record book, June 30, 1863-Oct. 18, 1864 (1 vol.), containing an invoice of medical and hospital supplies issued to Samuel H. Moffett, the surgeon in charge, inventories of clothing and money belonging to deceased soldiers, returns of medical and hospital property, and returns of quartermaster stores.

Fairview General Hospital (Lexington)

Record Group 109. --A diet book, 1863-64 (ch. VI, vol. 549); and a baggage register, 1863-64 (ch. VI, vol. 262).

General Hospital (Liberty)

Records in Other Custody. --A letters sent and letters and orders received book, Jan. 2, 1864-Mar. 2, 1865, is in the Confederate Museum. A diary of Henry C. Sommerville, who was a steward and later a surgeon at the Confederate hospitals at Liberty, Danville, and Lynchburg, is in the Archives Division of the Virginia State Library.

General Hospitals (Lynchburg)

General Hospital No. 1 was established at Lynchburg in May 1861; Nos. 2 and 3, in Apr. 1862. These hospitals occupied tobacco factories, warehouses, and fairground buildings.

Record Group 109.--Weekly reports of patients and attendants, General Hospitals Nos. 1-3, Camp Nicholls, Ladies Relief, Pratt, and Way Hospitals at Lynchburg, 1862-65 (ch. VI, vol. 724); and a miscellaneous record book, 1864-65 (ch. VI, vol. 529), containing statistical reports of patients, attendants, diseases, and wounds, lists of deaths and discharged men, and lists of medical officers and stewards.

Records in Other Custody.--A letters and orders sent and received book for General Hospital No. 2, July 27, 1862-Apr. 7, 1865, is in the Confederate Museum. Correspondence of Surg. George K. Turner, who was attached to General Hospital No. 1 in 1863-64 and later served in the field hospital at Kinston, N.C., is in the University of Virginia Library.

Hospital (Mount Jackson)

Record Group 109.--A register of patients, June 1-2, 1862 (ch. VI, vol. 266, p. 9-12).

General Hospital (Orange Courthouse)

Established on July 22, 1861; transferred to Farmville on Apr. 23, 1862.

Record Group 109.--Letters sent and letters, orders, and circulars received, Aug. 8, 1861-Apr. 23, 1862 (ch. VI, vol. 546, p. 1-37); a register of patients, July 1861-May 1863 (ch. VI, vol. 41, p. 1-6, vol. 269); a register of patients, Mar. 4-Apr. 23, 1862 (ch. VI, vol. 42, p. 109-114, 137-139); a record of disposition of cases, Oct. 10, 1861-Mar. 12, 1862 (ch. VI, vol. 42, p. 2-9); and a list of medical and hospital supplies received and issued, July 1861-Apr. 1862 (ch. VI, vol. 544, p. 1-13).

Confederate States Hospital (Petersburg)

Established on Mar. 27, 1861.

Record Group 109.--Reports on surgical cases, 1863-65 (ch. VI, vol. 272 1/2); and a baggage register, 1862-65 (ch. VI, vols. 271 and 272).

Records in Other Custody.--Correspondence, casebooks, a register of patients, an account book, reports, and orders of Surg. Warner L. Baylor, who was attached to this hospital, are in the Virginia Historical Society collections. Some correspondence of John H. Claiborne, who was surgeon in charge during 1862-63, is in the University of Virginia Library.

General Hospital (Petersburg)

Established on Oct. 1, 1861.

Record Group 109.--A register of patients, 1861-65 (ch. VI, vols. 265, 270, and 273); and morning reports of patients and attendants, 1863-65 (ch. VI, vol. 554).

First North Carolina Hospital (Petersburg)

Established in Oct. 1861.
Records In Other Custody. --William and Mary College Library has orders issued and orders and circulars received, Aug. 8, 1862-Sept. 4, 1863 (1 vol.).

Hoke's Division Hospital (Petersburg)

Records in Other Custody. --The Confederate Museum has a miscellaneous record book, June 1863-Apr. 1865 (1 vol.), containing ration returns, accounts current, a statement of the hospital fund, and copies of vouchers for provisions.

Second North Carolina Hospital (Petersburg)

Established on Mar. 21, 1862.
Records in Other Custody. --The Southern Historical Collection in the University of North Carolina Library has a prescription book, Aug.-Sept. 1864 (microfilm). Duke University Library has papers of John G. Brodnax, surgeon in charge.

South Carolina Hospital (Petersburg)

Established on May 10, 1862.
Record Group 109. --Statistical reports of sick and wounded men, 1863-64 (ch. VI, vol. 264), with lists of discharged patients and deceased patients; and a register of surgical cases, 1863-64 (ch. VI, vol. 487).

Alabama Hospital (Richmond)

Record Group 109. --A prescription book, 1864-65 (ch. VI, vol. 425); and an undated register of vaccinations of Union prisoners, Second Alabama Hospital (ch. VI, vol. 419).
Records in Other Custody. --Juliet Opie Hopkins and her husband, Arthur F. Hopkins, administered the Alabama hospital in Richmond during the war. The papers of Mrs. Hopkins in the Alabama Department of Archives and History include correspondence with Confederate and Alabama officials, accounts with the State of Alabama relating to the First, Second, and Third Alabama Hospitals, a record of deaths at those hospitals, and a record of receipts and expenditures.

Military Prison Hospital (Belle Isle, Richmond)

Record Group 109. --Morning reports of sick and wounded U.S. prisoners, Sept. 1, 1864-Feb. 1, 1865 (ch. VI, vol. 712, p. 162-280).

Camp Lee Hospital (Richmond)

Record Group 109. --Weekly reports of sick and wounded men, May 7, 1864-Jan. 31, 1865 (ch. VI, vol. 712, p. 281-311).

Chimborazo General Hospital (Richmond)

Opened in Oct. 1861 on Chimborazo Heights overlooking the city, this hospital became the largest in the Confederacy and contained five separate divisions or hospitals.

Edgar E. Hume, "Chimborazo Hospital, Confederate States Army-- America's Largest Military Hospital," Military Surgeon, 75:156-166 (Sept. 1934); Frank S. Johns and Anne P. Johns, "Chimborazo Hospital and J. B. McCaw, Surgeon- in-Chief," Virginia Magazine of History and Biography, 62:190-200 (Apr. 1954); Richmond Civil War Centennial Committee, Confederate Military Hospitals in Richmond, by Robert W. Waitt, Jr. (Richmond, 1964).

Record Group 109. --Records relating to the hospital generally include letters received and sent, Oct. 1861-July 1864 (ch. VI, vols. 707-709); orders and circulars received, 1861-65 (ch. VI, vols. 7 and 553); registers of patients, Feb. 1863-Aug. 1864 (ch. VI, vol. 33), and 1865 (ch. VI, vol. 54); index to registers of patients, 1861-65 (ch. VI, vols. 52, 76, 93, and 234); a record of employees, 1861-64 (ch. VI, vol. 33); a list of detailed men, 1861-64 (ch. VI, vol. 98), with lists of slaves and matrons employed; morning reports of patients and attendants, 1863-65 (ch. VI, vols. 305, 318, 322 1/4, 589, 705, and 706); receipts for payment, 1862-63 (ch. VI, vols. 313, 314, and 314 1/2); registers of the guard, 1862-64 (ch. VI, vol. 26); another register of the guard, 1864 (ch. VI, vol. 90); a record of the guard, 1865 (ch. VI, vol. 639); a record of clothing issued to patients, 1864-65 (ch. VI, vol. 618); accounts of clothing issued to patients, 1864-65 (ch. VI, vol. 322 3/4); a record of hospital property condemned, 1863-65 (ch. VI, vol. 304); accounts current, 1864 (ch. VI, vol. 245 1/2); bakery accounts, 1864-65 (ch. VI, vol. 638); an account book, 1861-63 (ch. VI, vol. 315); check stubs, 1863 (ch. VI, vol. 299); a prescription book, 1863-65 (ch. VI, vol. 32, p. 49-142, and vol. 322); and a record of monthly requisitions for hospital supplies, Jan.-June 1864 (ch. VI, vol. 26).

Records of Chimborazo Hospital No. 1 include orders and circulars received, July 30, 1863-July 16, 1864 (ch. VI, vol. 7); a register of patients, 1861-65 (ch. VI, vols. 20, 65, 71, and 78 and three index volumes: ch. VI, vols. 27, 29, and 77); reports on surgical cases, 1864 (ch. VI, vols. 449-453); a register of deaths, 1861-63 (ch. VI, vol. 83); a register of deaths and effects, 1863-64 (ch. VI, vol. 82); a list of paroled prisoners furloughed, 1865 (ch. VI, vol. 99); morning reports of patients and attendants, 1862-65 (ch. VI, vols. 30, 301, 303, and 306); a prescription book, 1862 and 1864 (ch. VI, vols. 323 and 619); lists of slaves employed, 1862-65 (ch. VI, vols. 79 and 307); a memorandum book of Steward William E. Toombs, 1862-63 (ch. VI, vol. 316), containing a list of slaves hired and accounts for food purchased; some miscellaneous record books, 1862-65 (ch. VI, vols. 310 and 448), containing information on medicine given to patients, a list of Negroes hired, lists of patients, a record of wood received and purchased, statistical reports of diseases and patients, lists of detailed attendants, lists of medical officers, reports on surgical cases, statements of patients vaccinated, tabular statements of operations, and reports on deceased patients.

Records of Chimborazo Hospital No. 2 include letters, orders, and circulars sent and received, Nov. 23, 1861-Feb. 25, 1865 (ch. VI, vol. 408); orders and circulars received, 1862-65 (ch. VI, vols. 9 and 18); reports of officers of the day, 1864-65 (ch. VI, vol. 324); registers of patients, 1861-65 (ch. VI, vols. 17, 24, 55, 75, and 87); a register of deaths and effects, 1863-65 (ch. VI, vol. 321); morning reports of patients, 1864-65 (ch. VI, vol. 86); a register of applications for furlough, 1863-65 (ch. VI, vol. 94); reports on surgical cases, 1862-65 (ch. VI, vol. 437 1/2 and 454); clothing accounts of patients, 1864-65 (ch. VI, vol. 410); a medical record book, 1864 (ch. VI, vol. 456), containing reports on surgical cases, a record of prescriptions and a statement of vaccinations; a miscellaneous record book, 1864-65 (ch. VI, vol. 80); and lists of employees, 1862-65 (ch. VI, vol. 85).

Records of Chimborazo Hospital No. 3 include registers of patients, 1861-65 (ch. VI, vols. 19, 21, 53, 60, 62, 64, 69, 95, 101, 103, 105, 132, 226, 661, and index vols. 88 and 89, 2 ft.); register of deaths, 1861-65 (ch. VI, vol. 31); morning reports of patients and attendants, 1862-65 (ch. VI, vols. 311 and 359); morning reports of patients, 1864-65 (ch. VI, vol. 100); a register of applications for furlough, 1862-64 (ch. VI, vol. 438); a record of provisions received, 1864 (ch. VI, vol. 409); an account book of funds, 1861-65 (ch. VI, vol. 96); a miscellaneous record book, 1862-64 (ch. VI, vol. 455 1/4); and a register of patients and prescription book, wards K and L, 1864 (ch. VI, vol. 84).

Records of Chimborazo Hospital No. 4 include letters sent and letters, orders, and circulars received, Feb. 1, 1862-Mar. 16, 1865 (ch. VI, vols. 72 and 302); registers of patients, 1861-65 (ch. VI, vols. 22, 28, 68, 74, 221, and index vols. 73, 92, and 242); a register of patients and prescription book, 1864 (ch. VI, vol. 63); lists of deaths, discharges, retirements, and patients in private quarters, 1864-65 (ch. VI, vol. 56); lists of patients returned to duty, transferred, furloughed, and deceased, 1862-64 (ch. VI, vol. 67); an undated record of patients transferred (ch. VI, vol. 66); reports on surgical cases, 1862-64 (ch. VI, vol. 434); case books, 1862-65 (ch. VI, vols. 439, 441, 444, 450, 451, 455, and 494); a register of surgical cases with lists of patients returned to duty and transferred, 1863-65 (ch. VI, vol. 437); morning reports of patients and attendants, 1862-65 (ch. VI, vols. 308, 309, 321, and 322 1/2); morning reports of nurses and patients, 1863-65 (ch. VI, vol. 300); a prescription book, 1864-65 (ch. VI, vol. 590); a miscellaneous record book, 1863-65 (ch. VI, vol. 317); and a memorandum book, 1863-65 (ch. VI, vol. 615).

Records relating to Chimborazo Hospital No. 5 include orders, letters, and circulars received, June 8, 1863-Oct. 29, 1864 (ch. VI, vol. 8); registers of patients, 1861-65 (ch. VI, vols. 23, 25, 34, 57, 70, 97, 228, and index vol. 232); a record of payments to patients, 1863-65 (ch. VI, vol. 104); morning reports of patients, 1864-65 (ch. VI, vol. 58); case books of wounded patients, 1862-64 (ch. VI, vols. 442, 443, and 445); a record of vaccinations, 1863-65 (ch. VI, vol. 319); a prescription book for U.S. colored troops, Apr. 1865 (ch. VI, vol. 325); and miscellaneous record books, 1861-64 (ch. VI, vols. 61, 91, 220, and 440).

Records in Other Custody. --An account current of the hospital fund, Aug. 1863-Feb. 1865 (1 vol.), is in Duke University Library. A few papers, 1863-64, concerning Dr. L. C. Crump, a contract physician at the hospital, are in the Archives Division of the Virginia State Library. Correspondence of George S. and Lucien Barnsley, who served as hospital stewards, are in the Southern Historical Collection in the University of North Carolina Library, which also has letters of Mrs. Phoebe Y. Pember, matron, 1861-65.

Clopton Hospital (Richmond)

Records in Other Custody. --A register of patients, May-Sept. 1862
(1 vol.), and an undated prescription and diet book are in the Confederate
Museum.

General Hospital No. 1 (Richmond)

Record Group 109. --Reports of resection cases, 1862-64 (ch. VI, vol.
764), and morning reports of patients and attendants, General Hospitals
Nos. 1-4, 7-8, 12-30, 22-23, and 25-27, 1862-65 (ch. VI, vol. 711).

General Hospital No. 4 (Richmond)

Record Group 109. --A register of patients, 1862 (ch. VI, vol. 180);
registers of officers treated, 1863-64 (ch. VI, vols. 178 and 240); morning
report of patients in Institute Hospital, 1862-63 (ch. VI, vol. 248); morning
reports of patients and attendants, 1865 (ch. VI, vol. 386); a record of
accounts with officer patients for board, 1864 (ch. VI, vol. 384); an account
book of officers' board and provisions purchased, 1863-64 (ch. VI, vol. 385);
prescription book, 1863 (ch. VI, vol. 119); and a miscellaneous record book,
1863-64 (ch. VI, vol. 181), containing a register of officer patients, a register of aides-de-camp and battery commanders who were patients, a list
of hospital attendants, a record of surgical cases, copies of correspondence,
reports of examining boards on attendants, statistical reports of sick and
wounded men, and lists of deaths.
    Records in Other Custody. --An account book, Sept. 1863-Dec. 1864,
in the Georgia Historical Society collections has sections on the hospital
fund, provisions issued to officers, commutation of rations for attendants,
returns of medical and hospital property, clothing issued to soldiers, returns of clothing, and provision prices.

General Hospital No. 7 (Richmond)

Record Group 109. --Register of patients and endorsements on communications relating to patients, 1863-65 (ch. VI, vol. 252), and morning
reports of patients and attendants, 1862-63 (ch. VI, vol. 389).

General Hospital No. 8 (Richmond)

Record Group 109. --Letters, orders, and circulars received, 1862-
63 (ch. VI, vol. 498); a register of patients, 1862-63 (ch. VI, vol. 251);
lists of patients returned to duty, sent to private quarters, transferred,
furloughed, and deceased, 1862-63 (ch. VI, vol. 510); morning reports of
patients and hospital personnel, 1862 (ch. VI, vol. 123); and an account of
the hospital fund, 1862-63 (ch. VI, vol. 120).

General Hospital No. 9 (Richmond)

Also known as Receiving and Wayside Hospital.
    Record Group 109. --The extensive records of this hospital include
letters sent books, Jan. 22, 1863-Nov. 24, 1864, and Dec. 1, 1864-Apr. 5,
1865 (ch. VI, vols. 387 and 424); letters received and sent, May 8, 1864-

Feb. 3, 1865 (ch. VI, vol. 337); letters, orders, and circulars received, Feb. 29, 1864-Apr. 2, 1865 (ch. VI, vols. 421 and 423); registers of patients, 1863-65 (ch. VI, vols. 106-109, 124, 126, and 128-131); lists of patients transferred, 1862-63 (ch. VI, vols. 113, 114, and 117); lists of patients, 1864 (ch. VI, vol. 112); registers of deaths and personal effects, 1862-65 (ch. VI, vols. 115 and 118); reports on surgical cases, 1863-64 (ch. VI, vol. 466); morning reports of patients and attendants, 1864 (ch. VI, vol. 718); a medical examining board record, June 1864-Apr. 1865 (ch. VI, vol. 335); a list of patients for examining board, Apr. 16-June 28, 1864 (ch. VI, vol. 111, p. 92-98); a report of transfers and admittances, 1864-65 (ch. VI, vol. 116); a record of detailed men examined and of hospital fund accounts, 1863-65 (ch. VI, vols. 339 and 341); an account book of expenditures for provisions, fuel, and other items, 1862-64 (ch. VI, vol. 651); a steward's account book, 1865 (ch. VI, vol. 655); cash and supply accounts, 1862-64 (ch. VI, vol. 388); copies of vouchers for hospital supplies, 1863-65 (ch. VI, vols. 390 and 490); copies of requisitions and property accounts, 1863-65 (ch. VI, vol. 489); accounts for rations received and issued, 1864-65 (ch. VI, vol. 386 1/2); records of supplies and accounts, 1862-65 (ch. VI, vols. 336 and 340); receipts for the personal effects of deceased soldiers, 1862-65 (ch. VI, vol. 420); a record of the receipt of hospital supplies, 1864 (ch. VI, vol. 391); diet books, 1864 (ch. VI, vols. 127, 338, and 488); miscellaneous record books, 1862-65 (ch. VI, vols. 81 and 110); check stubs, 1863 (ch. VI, vol. 334); and a register of patients, ward no. 3, 1865 (ch. VI, vol. 125).

General Hospital No. 11 (Richmond)

Also called Globe Hospital and Florida Hospital.
Record Group 109.--Letters, orders, and circulars received, Sept. 15, 1862-Oct. 1, 1863 (ch. VI, vol. 361), with copies of some letters sent.

General Hospital No. 12 (Richmond)

Also called Banner Hospital, Grant Hospital, and Wayside Hospital.
Record Group 109.--Reports on surgical cases, 1862-63 (ch. VI, vol. 468).

General Hospital No. 13 (Richmond)

Also known as Castle Thunder Hospital, Eastern District Military Prison Hospital, and Lunatic Hospital.
Record Group 109.--Registers of patients, 1862-65 (ch. VI, vols. 230 and 257); register of Union and Negro patients, 1863-65 (ch. VI, vol. 249); accounts current and a register of surgical cases, 1862-64 (ch. VI, vol. 467); accounts of provisions, hospital stores, and other supplies, 1863-64 (ch. VI, vol. 231); and miscellaneous record books, 1862-65 (ch. VI, vols. 256 and 455).

General Hospital No. 18 (Richmond)

Also known as Greaner's or Greanor's Hospital.
Record Group 109--Letters, orders, and circulars sent and received, Apr. 2, 1861-June 30, 1863, a register of deaths and effects, 1862, lists of patients treated in private quarters, 1862, and statistical reports of patients,

July 1863-Feb. 1864 (ch. VI, vol. 414 1/2); a register of patients, 1861-63
(ch. VI, vol. 217); and morning reports of patients and attendants, 1862-63
(ch. VI, vol. 250).

General Hospital No. 21 (Richmond)

   Established in Feb. 1862 as the Maryland Hospital; also known as the
Gwathmey Factory Hospital and Confederate States Military Prison Hospital.
   Record Group 109.--Letters sent and letters, orders, and circulars
received, Feb. 2-Oct. 7, 1863 (ch. VI, vol. 484); letters and orders sent
and received, May 12, 1862-May 13, 1863 (ch. VI, vol. 333); letters, orders,
and circulars received, Feb. 7, 1863-Oct. 6, 1863, and a register of patients, 1862 (ch. VI, vol. 483); a register of patients, 1862-63 (ch. VI, vols.
16 and 253); registers of Union patients, 1864-65 (ch. VI, vols. 161, 166, 236,
and 254); a register of Union patients, Division 3, 1864-65 (ch. VI, vol.
163); a register of Union patients, Division 4, 1864 (ch. VI, vol. 261); a
register of Union patients, ward A, 1864-65 (ch. VI, vol. 169); a register
of Union patients, ward D, 1863-65 (ch. VI, vols. 162 and 165); a register
of deaths and effects, 1862-63 (ch. VI, vol. 15); morning reports of patients
and attendants, 1861-63 (ch. VI, vols. 120, 327, and 331); morning reports
of Union patients and attendants, 1864-65 (ch. VI, vol. 720); a list of employees, 1862-64 (ch. VI, vol. 13); a list of colored employees, 1862-63 (ch.
VI, vol. 14); a record of clothing and equipment received from and issued
to patients, 1863 (ch. VI, vol. 332); a record of clothing and linen issued,
1864-65 (ch. VI, vol. 329); an account book of supplies purchased, 1862-63
(ch. VI, vol. 326); accounts for provisions, clothing, and supplies issued
to stewards, 1862-63 (ch. VI, vol. 413), with lists of articles received
from and sent to the laundry; accounts of hospital supplies on hand and
issued, 1862 (ch. VI, vol. 381); provision accounts, 1862-63 (ch. VI, vols.
380 and 383); prescription books, 1862-65 (ch. VI, vols. 159, 160, 229, 328,
330, 382, 382A, 382B, and 596); a record of disposition of cases, 1863
(ch. VI, vol. 12); a register of surgical cases of Union patients, ward E,
1864 (ch. VI, vol. 170); a register of surgical cases of Union patients, wards
1-3, 1864 (ch. VI, vol. 168); a case book of Union patients, ward 3, 1864
(ch. VI, vol. 167); a case book of Union patients, ward A, 1864-65 (ch. VI,
vol. 485); and lists of Union patients remaining in ward A, 1864 (ch. VI,
vols. 158 and 164).

General Hospital No. 23 (Richmond)

   Also known as Ligon's Factory Hospital.
   Record Group 109.--An undated prescription book (ch. VI, vol. 559).

General Hospital No. 24 (Richmond)

   Also known as Harwood Hospital, Moore's Hospital, and North Carolina Hospital.
   Record Group 109.--Letters, orders, and circulars sent and received, June 12, 1862-Mar. 16, 1865 (ch. VI, vols. 10, 422, and 491); registers of patients, 1862-64 (ch. VI, vols. 173 and 175); morning reports of
patients and attendants, 1862-65 (ch. VI, vol. 719); a case book, 1863-64
(ch. VI, vol. 493); a register of surgical cases, a list of officers and detailed men, and laundry accounts, 1863-64 (ch. VI, vol. 492); a register of

deaths and effects, 1862-64 (ch. VI, vol. 652); a record of the receipt of effects of deceased soldiers and of payment for services and hire of slaves, 1863-64 (ch. VI, vol. 640); a record of requisitions for rations and statements of the hospital fund, 1862-65 (ch. VI, vol. 495); a record of payment of hired hands and accounts, 1862-63 (ch. VI, vol. 653); an account book of supplies purchased, 1863-65 (ch. VI, vol. 650); provision and fuel accounts, 1862-64 (ch. VI, vol. 654); a prescription book, 1863-64 (ch. VI, vol. 496); requisitions for medical and hospital supplies, 1862-65 (ch. VI, vol. 122 1/2); an account of daily issues of hospital stores, Apr. 1863-Feb. 1865 (ch. VI, part of vol. 422); and miscellaneous record books, 1862-65 (ch. VI, vols. 171, 172, and 122), containing statistical reports of patients and attendants, lists of patients and employees, invoices of hospital property, a record of the receipt of clothing, and a record of donations by the Ladies Cumberland Hospital Association of North Carolina.

General Hospital No. 25 (Richmond)

Also called Randolph's Hospital and Texas Hospital.
Record Group 109.--A prescription and diet book, 1863 (ch. VI, vol. 417).

Howard's Grove Hospital (Richmond)

Record Group 109.--Letters sent, July 5-17, 1862 (ch. VI, vol. 414, p. 1-6); letters sent and orders issued, Sept. 16, 1863-June 23, 1864 (ch. VI, vol. 429); orders, letters, and circulars received, May 24, 1864-Mar. 25, 1865 (ch. VI, vol. 376 1/2); endorsements on communications received, 1863-65 (ch. VI, vol. 430); registers of patients, 1862-65 (ch. VI, vols. 192-194, 200, and 344); lists of patients admitted, 1863-65 (ch. VI, vols. 245, 201, and 219); reports on amputation cases, 1862 (ch. VI, vol. 478); a prescription book and register of patients, 1864-65 (ch. VI, vol. 205); rosters of employees, 1862-64 (ch. VI, vol. 342); requisitions for supplies and lists of employees, 1862-63 (ch. VI, vol. 355); clothing accounts, 1863-64 (ch. VI, vol. 585); accounts for supplies purchased, 1864-65 (ch. VI, vol. 133); a baggage register, 1863-65 (ch. VI, vols. 725 and 225); inventories of hospital supplies and equipment and morning reports of attendants, 1863-65 (ch. VI, part of vol. 429); prescription books, 1862-63 (ch. VI, vols. 351, 379, 564, and 593); and miscellaneous record books, 1862-65 (ch. VI, vols. 343, 344, 378 1/2, 414, and 423).

Records of Division No. 1 include a register of patients, 1863-64 (ch. VI, vols. 202 and 344); lists of patients, 1863-65 (ch. VI, vols. 199 and 239); a case book of wounded, 1863-64 (ch. VI, vol. 428); a record of delivery of equipment to departing patients, 1863-64 (ch. VI, vol. 238); prescription books, wards B, I, and O, 1863-65 (ch. VI, vols. 475, 477, 479, and 597); requisitions for and invoices of medical and hospital supplies, 1864-65 (ch. VI, vol. 471); a prescription book, ward H, 1864-65 (ch. VI, vol. 347); a prescription book, ward M, 1864 (ch. VI, vol. 356); and miscellaneous record books, 1864-65 (ch. VI, vols. 197, 203, and 345).

Records of Division No. 2 include letters sent and orders and circulars received, May 14, 1864-Apr. 3, 1865 (ch. VI, vol. 134); a register of patients, 1862-65 (ch. VI, vol. 204); a register of surgical cases, 1863-65 (ch. VI, vol. 431); morning reports of patients and attendants, 1863-65 (ch. VI, vols. 342 1/2 and 354); clothing accounts, 1864-65 (ch. VI, vol. 426);

a passport register, 1864-65 (ch. VI, vols. 190, 206, and 427); and prescription books, 1864 (ch. VI, vols. 346, 348-350, 352, 353, 472-474, and 476).

Records covering more than one division include letters, orders, and circulars sent and received, Division Nos. 1-2, Nov. 9, 1862-Jan. 2, 1864 (ch. VI, vol. 411); a register of patients, Division Nos. 1-3, 1862-64 (ch. VI, vols. 195, 196, and 198); a medical examining board record, Division Nos. 1-3, 1864-65 (ch. VI, vol. 432); morning reports of patients and attendants, Division Nos. 1-3, 1862-65 (ch. VI, vol. 713); lists of medical officers and detailed men and accounts current, Division Nos. 1-3, 1861-65 (ch. VI, vol. 191); and requisitions for hospital supplies, laborers, and funds, Division Nos. 1-3, 1862-65 (ch. VI, vol. 470).

Jackson General Hospital (Richmond)

Record Group 109. --The records of this hospital include letters, orders, and circulars sent and received, June 5, 1863-Apr. 2, 1865 (ch. VI, vols. 376, 406, and 407), including some correspondence of the U.S. officer in charge after the war; letters and orders sent and received, 1863-64 (ch. VI, vol. 414 1/2), containing also personnel lists; orders and letters received, 1864-65 (ch. VI, vol. 138); a register of communications received and transmitted, 1864-65 (ch. VI, vol. 377); correspondence of Maj. H. C. Scott, 1865 (ch. VI, vol. 378); reports of officers of the day, 1864-65 (ch. VI, vol. 373); a register of patients, 1864-65 (ch. VI, vols. 183 and 186); a register of Confederate sick and wounded, Apr. 4, 1865 (ch. VI, vol. 185); morning reports of patients and attendants, 1864-65 (ch. VI, vols. 701-704 and 726-728); morning reports of the guard, 1864-65 (ch. VI, vol. 375); invoices of medicines, instruments, furniture, and hospital stores, 1863-65 (ch. VI, vol. 374); a register of patients furloughed, detailed, retired, and recommended for discharge, Division Nos. 1-4, 1864-65 (ch. VI, vol. 184); lists of employees, Division Nos. 1-4, 1863-64 (ch. VI, vol. 187); orders and circulars received and issued and lists of employees, Division No. 4, 1863-65 (ch. VI, vol. 405); registers of patients, Division No. 4, 1864-65 (ch. VI, vols. 102, 182, and 189); and lists of patients, Division No. 4, 1864-65 (ch. VI, vol. 188).

Louisiana General Hospital (Richmond)

Also called Baptist College Hospital and Richmond College Hospital.
Record Group 109. --Morning reports of patients and attendants, Sept. 1, 1864-Mar. 31, 1865 (ch. VI, vol. 712, p. 7-161); and prescription books, 1861 (ch. VI, vols. 418 and 458).

Medical College Hospital (Richmond)

Records in Other Custody. --The Medical College of Virginia has records regarding the wartime operations of its hospital. Military personnel were treated there under contract with the Confederate Government.

Mississippi Soldiers' Hospital (Richmond)

Record Group 109. --A register of patients, 1863 (ch. VI, vol. 246).

Robertson Hospital (Richmond)

Record Group 109.--Morning reports of patients and attendants, 1863-65 (ch. VI, vol. 717).
Records in Other Custody.--In the Confederate Museum are a register of patients kept by Miss Sally L. Tompkins, Aug. 3, 1861-Apr. 2, 1865 (1 vol.), containing also a list of the names of "ladies," surgeons, and stewards; and account books, Jan. 1862-Aug. 1864 (3 notebooks).

St. Francis de Sales Hospital (Richmond)

Also known as St. Francis, Catholic, and Brook Hospital.
Record Group 109.--Morning reports of patients and attendants, 1864-65 (ch. VI, vol. 714).

Smallpox Hospital (Richmond)

Record Group 109.--A register of patients, 1862-64 (ch. VI, vol. 247), with lists of employees and a record of tobacco issued to patients.

Soldiers' Home Hospital (Richmond)

Record Group 109.--A register of patients, Apr. 1862-Feb. 1863 (ch. VI, vol. 463, p. 2-30).

Stuart General Hospital (Richmond)

Also called Old Fairground Hospital, Fort Stuart Hospital, and Barracks Hospital.
Record Group 109.--A register of patients, 1864-65 (ch. VI, vol. 662); morning reports of patients and attendants, 1864-65 (ch. VI, vol. 715).

Winder General Hospital (Richmond)

Record Group 109.--The records of this hospital include morning reports of patients and attendants, Division Nos. 1-6, 1863-65 (ch. VI, vol. 710); letters, orders, and circulars sent and received, Division No. 2, May 6, 1862-Oct. 10, 1864 (ch. VI, vols. 457 and 547); registers of patients, Division No. 2, 1861-65 (ch. VI, vols. 233, 258-260, and 435, and index vol. 243); lists of employees, Division No. 2, 1863-64 (ch. VI, vol. 218); and steward's accounts, Division No. 2, 1862-64 (ch. VI, vol. 412).

Hospital (Romney)

Records in Other Custody.--Papers, 1861-64 (100 items), of Surg. John H. Hunter in the University of Virginia Library relate to his services in the hospitals in Romney, Warm Springs, and White Sulphur Springs.

Baptist Church Hospital (Williamsburg)

Record Group 109.--Morning reports of patients in the Baptist Church, Episcopal Church, Methodist Church, and Seminary Hospitals, 1861-62 (ch. VI, vol. 562); morning reports of patients and attendants, Baptist Church,

Methodist Church, and New Courthouse Hospitals, 1861-62 (ch. VI, vol. 560); a prescription book, 1861-62 (ch. VI, vol. 561); and a record of medical and hospital supplies furnished to Williamsburg hospitals, 1861 (ch. VI, vol. 625).

Episcopal Church Hospital (Williamsburg)

Record Group 109. --Register of patients, 1861-64 (ch. VI, vols. 263 and 268); morning reports of patients and attendants, 1861-62 (ch. VI, vols. 557 1/2 and 563); laundry accounts of patients, 1862 (ch. VI, vol. 558); a prescription book, 1861-62 (ch. VI, vol. 558 1/2); and a miscellaneous record book, 1861-62 (ch. VI, vol. 559 1/2); containing inventories of hospital furnishings, a list of patients boarding outside the hospital, a record of quilts given to patients, and an inventory of the personal effects of deceased soldiers.

Seminary Hospital (Williamsburg)

Record Group 109. --A register of patients, 1861-62 (ch. VI, vol. 267); and a prescription book, 1861 (ch. VI, vol. 541).

Hospital (Winchester)

Record Group 109. --A register of patients, May 27-31, 1862 (ch. VI, vol. 266, p. 1-8).

General Hospital (Winchester)

Record Group 109. --A register of patients, July 20-Aug. 4, 1864 (ch. VI, vol. 265 1/2).

Lovingston Hospital (Winchester)

Record Group 109. --A register of patients, Aug. 8-Sept. 13, 1862 (ch. VI, vol. 266, p. 13-41).

ENGINEER BUREAU

The act of Mar. 6, 1861 (Prov. Cong. C.S.A. Stat. 47), establishing and organizing the Army provided for a Corps of Engineers with a colonel as Chief Engineer. In the next month the Engineer Bureau was set up to furnish the Corps with necessary supplies and services. Engineer officers and civilians were employed by both the Bureau and the Corps, and in 1861 the Bureau employed civil engineers for fieldwork. The number of engineer officers was increased by acts of Congress until by Feb. 1865 there were 246.

Under the direction of commanders of armies and departments, engineer officers were responsible for improving and strengthening existing fortifications; planning and constructing other military works, batteries, roads, and bridges; reconnoitering the terrain in the vicinity of armies and preparing topographic maps; erecting barriers in rivers and harbors; surveying routes for and constructing links between railroads; repairing damaged railroads; and preparing maps of battlefields for inclusion with battle reports. The large labor forces required by the Engineer Corps were supplied by fatigue parties of soldiers, engineer troops, details of soldiers for mechanical service, and slaves and free Negroes. Engineer officers transmitted reports and other records to the Engineer Bureau.

The Engineer Bureau undertook to supply maps to the Confederate Army, badly handicapped by the lack of them. The Bureau's draftsman prepared some maps, but more were obtained from the Department of Northern Virginia's Topographical Department, which was established in Richmond in 1862 under Capt. Albert H. Campbell. The officer in charge sent out surveying parties in Virginia and North Carolina, and copies of the maps that were based on these surveys were supplied not only to General Lee but also to the Engineer Bureau. On the request of the Chief Engineer, Campbell also had tracings made of maps for other general officers and for the Bureau. Maps of battlefields in Virginia were also supplied to the Bureau. On Feb. 5, 1864, R. S. Sanxay and Adolph Gomert patented a process for duplicating maps by photography. Immediately afterward the Bureau began using their services for obtaining many prints of the maps that had been prepared. These prints presumably were distributed to whatever Army commanders needed them. Engineer officers attached to Army commands made reconnaissances and sent maps and sketches to the Bureau.

The Engineer Bureau also engaged in procurement and manufacturing functions. It bought shovels, other tools, rope, and hardware. A. H. Rahm of Richmond made shovels and the Tredegar Iron Works furnished other hardware. The Bureau also supplied survey and drafting equipment and paper to engineers in the field. In the winter of 1862-63 the Bureau was involved in the procurement of ice for Richmond hospitals. In 1863 Capt. John M. Robinson, Corps of Engineers, went to England and arranged for the shipment of intrenching tools, technical books, and surveying and drafting equipment. The Bureau had workshops at Richmond, Charleston, Augusta, Mobile, and Demopolis for the manufacture of tools, implements, and the preparation of material for pontoon bridges. A torpedo plant at Charleston manufactured torpedoes that were distributed to engineer officers along the coast of the Confederacy. During 1862-63 arrangements were made with Prof. Richard Wells and Charles Cevor for experimental use of balloons for aerial observation, but Confederate officers did not cooperate and these efforts were abandoned.

Successive Chiefs of Engineers:
    Maj. Josiah Gorgas (acting), Apr. 8, 1861.
    Maj. Danville Leadbetter, Aug. 22, 1861.
    Capt. Alfred L. Rives, Nov. 13, 1861.
    Col. Jeremy F. Gilmer, Sept. 25, 1862.
    Lt. Col. Alfred L. Rives (acting), Aug. 18, 1863.
    Col. Jeremy F. Gilmer, July 18, 1864.

James L. Nichols, Confederate Engineers (Tuscaloosa, Ala., 1957); "Confederate Engineers and the Defense of Mobile," Alabama Review, 12:181-195 (July 1959); "Confederate Engineer Odd Jobs," Military Engineer, 53:12-15 (Jan.- Feb. 1961); Official Records . . . Armies, ser. 4, vols. 1-3, passim; William M. Robinson, Jr., "The Confederate Engineers," Military Engineer, 22:297-305, 410-419, 512-517 (July-Dec. 1930).

Some of the Engineer Bureau's records were recovered by the U. S. Army. On May 12, 1865, Col. Richard D. Cutts sent two boxes of correspondence and vouchers from Richmond to the War Department in Washington. These records became part of the War Department Collection of Confederate Records.

Record Group 56. --With the captured and abandoned property records (file no. 5997) of the records of the U. S. Department of the Treasury are a few payrolls of civilians employed at Drewry's Bluff, Richmond Bar, Warwick Bar, on pontoon bridges, and as crew members of the W. W. Townes and the Seaboard in 1863-64. The rolls show the occupations and the amount of the payments made by Lt. J. B. Stanard and Capt. Charles T. Mason.

Record Group 109. --The records of the Engineer Bureau in the War Department Collection of Confederate Records consist of correspondence and some other materials. Letters and telegrams sent, Aug. 22, 1861-Aug. 13, 1864 (ch. III, vols. 1-5; available on microfilm as M 628), are fair copies of outgoing communications. The letters are addressed to engineer and other Army officers, officers of the Virginia Engineer Corps, the Secretary of War, the agent in charge of the engineer warehouse in Richmond, chiefs of War Department bureaus, the Secretary of the Treasury, the First and Second Auditors, other Government officials, State Governors, industrial firms, the commission for removing railroad iron, and individuals. Much of the early correspondence is concerned with the arming of fortifications and ordnance. These outgoing communications include some letters written by officers attached to the Bureau and letters written to Colonel Gilmer during his absence from Richmond. These volumes also contain many endorsements for communications referred to other subdivisions of the War Department and to engineer officers. Registers of letters received, 1861-64 (ch. III, vols. 7, 7 1/2, and 7 1/4), show the file number, writer's name, place written, date of receipt, date of answer, and abstracts of the contents. These registers contain short summaries of the contents of the letters which were received from the same types of correspondents as those mentioned above. There is, however, no separate file of letters received. Many of the letters are filed in the compiled military service records described in chapter XI of this Guide. A large part of the incoming communications appear to have been lost, however.

Letters received and other documents relating to engineer officers, assistants, and troops are in the compiled military service records of Confederate organizations (see the description of these and other compiled files in chapter XI of this Guide). Part of that file for "Engineers, C. S. A. " (cards and folded papers, 10 ft.), consists of alphabetically arranged files for engineer officers, acting engineers, engineer assistants, clerks, and some privates. Envelope-jackets for officers include correspondence, requisitions for forage, certificates for the commutation of quarters and fuel, rolls of detailed men, accounts current, pay accounts, receipts for payments made to assistant engineers, forage returns, abstracts of provisions issued, abstracts of materials expended, pay vouchers, abstracts of purchases, special orders, invoices of engineer property, lists of engineer officers, Second Auditor's reports, cross-references to other officers' files, and index record cards embodying information in record books of the Confederate States War Department. The section of the same file for "Engineer Troops" (cards and folded papers, 23 ft.), containing envelope-jackets for individual troops and officers, consists largely of index record cards. A smaller file for "Sappers and Miners" (cards and folded papers, 3 1/2 ft.), contains envelope-jackets for privates, sappers, artificers, and officers. The papers of other engineer officers are in the compiled military service records of Confederate general and staff officers, and their contents are similar to the file described above. The papers of some engineer officers are described under the commands or departments to which they were attached.

A chronological record of provisions issued from the commissary store of the Engineer Bureau, Richmond, Sept. 1, 1862-Mar. 27, 1865 (ch. III, vol. 21), supplies information regarding the rations issued, on whose requisition, for what station, and under whose command or management. A small file of miscellaneous papers, 1862-65 (2 in.), consists of returns of officers and hired men, reports of operations on defenses, survey reports, accounts current, estimates of the cost of engineer projects, receipts for issues of engineer property, reports of proceedings of boards of survey, invoices of engineer stores, lists of applications for appointments as engineers, reports of money received and expended, and abstracts of disbursements, correspondence, telegrams, and circulars.

Records in Other Custody.--Papers of Jeremy F. Gilmer presented to the Confederate Museum in Richmond by his daughter include a small quantity of wartime correspondence, commissions, and orders. A larger collection of Gilmer papers is with the Southern Historical Collection in the University of North Carolina Library. For the war period it includes correspondence with engineer officers; correspondence on military operations in Tennessee, Kentucky, South Carolina, Alabama, and Georgia; and letters to his wife containing some information of official matters. Plans of engineer equipment, machinery, and defenses are also in this collection. The papers of Alfred L. Rives in Duke University Library include correspondence on his service as a Confederate engineer officer.

The States of Virginia, North Carolina, and South Carolina appointed their own engineer officers to work on fortifications and batteries in 1861. After the establishment of the Confederate Provisional Corps of Engineers, most of the State officers were commissioned in that body. The records of the State Engineer Departments are useful for study of the early activities of these officers. The Archives Division of the Virginia State Library has a letter book, May 14-Aug. 30, 1861; letters received, Mar. 9-Dec. 28, 1861; invoices, May-Dec. 1861; payrolls of slaves employed on defensive works, May-Sept. 1861; and payrolls of persons employed on fortifications, May-Aug. 1861.

Cartographic Records

Most of the Confederate maps in the National Archives are in collections consisting chiefly of maps prepared by agencies of the U.S. Government. These Confederate maps were prepared probably by the Engineer Bureau and Captain Campbell's Topographical Department in Richmond and in engineer offices and commands in the field.

Record Group 77.--The records of the U.S. Office of the Chief of Engineers include large map files. The "Headquarters (Civil Works) Map File" contains maps captured from Confederates during the war and other maps received from Confederate officers by the U.S. War Department after the war. The "Fortifications Map File" in this record group contains items relating to Confederate defenses. Since many of the Confederate fortifications had been U.S. forts before the war, the U.S. maps in these files are also useful for information on those places.

Record Group 92. --In the records of the Office of the Quartermaster General the "Post and Reservation Map File" contains a few items relating to the Southern States. A sketch map shows the railroad and steamboat terminals and Confederate defenses of Bridgeport, Ala., in 1863. A railroad map of the Southern States shows the different railroad gauges in 1862. See the catalog cited below for other maps in this file relating to places in the Confederacy occupied by Union forces.

Record Group 94. --In the records of the Adjutant General's Office is a collection of 800 Union and Confederate maps used in compiling the atlas for the Official Records . . . Armies. The Confederate maps include manuscript maps donated or lent for the purpose by Confederate officers or repositories and published maps with additions or corrections by Confederate officers. The collection includes battlefield maps, maps of local terrain and campaign routes, and plans and views of defenses. They are arranged by the plate numbers used in the Atlas, and the index of that work serves as an index to the collection.

For descriptions of some of the items in the record groups mentioned above, see National Archives, Civil War Maps in the National Archives (Washington, 1964). The U.S. War Department's Atlas to Accompany the Official Records of the Union and Confederate Armies, comp. by Capt. Calvin D. Cowles, (H. Misc. Doc. 261, 52 Cong., 1 sess., Serial 2998; 3 vols., Washington, 1891-95; reprinted New York, 1958), contains 202 Confederate maps of campaigns, battles, and skirmishes.

Record Group 109. --In the War Department Collection of Confederate Records is a small collection of other Confederate maps, 1861-65, of battlefields, fortifications, marches, reconnaissances, and cities. These are manuscript maps received with the papers of Confederate officers or copies of maps that were lent by officers, the Southern Historical Society, and others.

Records in Other Custody. --Original hand-drawn, colored maps prepared by topographers working under the direction of Maj. Albert H. Campbell, head of the Topographical Department of the Department of Northern Virginia, and maps prepared in the Engineer Bureau together with contemporary copies of maps originating in both of those offices are in a number of repositories. In 1912 a daughter of Maj. Gen. Jeremy F. Gilmer, Confederate Chief of Engineers, presented 75 topographic maps to the Virginia Historical Society. Most of these are of Virginia counties and besides geographic features show railroads, roads, fords, ferries, bridges, and some structures with names of householders. Other Gilmer-Campbell maps saved by Mrs. J. F. Gilmer are in the Confederate Museum in Richmond. These also are chiefly of Virginia and particularly of the defenses of Richmond and Petersburg. Other collections are in the U.S. Military Academy Library and William and Mary College Library. The Map Division of the Library of Congress has photostats of some of the same maps. Copies of maps of Virginia counties prepared under the direction of Major Campbell are in the Hotchkiss collection in the Library of Congress (see below under Army of Northern Virginia).

Lawrence Martin, "The Gil-mer-Campbell Maps--Virginia, Parts of West Virginia, North Carolina, South Carolina, and Georgia, " in U. S. Library of Congress, Noteworthy Maps No. 1; Accessions for the Fiscal Year Ending June 30, 1926, p. 7-17 (Washington, 1927). The maps in the Confederate Museum are listed in Douglas S. Freeman, A Calendar of Confederate Papers, p. 486-490 (Richmond, 1908). Confederate maps of Virginia and West Virginia are listed in Earl G. Swem, "Maps Relating to Virginia in the Virginia State Library and Other Departments of the Commonwealth, " Virginia State Library Bulletin, 7: 138-162 (Apr., July 1914).

Other published maps of the Confederacy and some manuscript official maps prepared by the Corps of Engineers are in other repositories. Small collections are in Duke University Library, the Valentine Museum in Richmond, the University of Virginia Library, the Louisiana Historical Association collection on deposit in the Howard-Tilton Memorial Library, Tulane University, and the Virginia State Library. Manuscript maps received with the papers of Confederates by the Southern Historical Collection in the University of North Carolina have been left with the papers but have been separately cataloged. The Jeremy F. Gilmer papers in that repository include topographic and battlefield maps of Virginia and North Carolina; maps of the Shiloh, Corinth, and Davis' Bridge battlefields; maps of Mobile defenses; and maps of Arkansas, western Louisiana, and Texas. The Map Division of the Library of Congress has a few manuscript or photocopy maps and published Confederate maps in addition to photostats of the Gilmer-Campbell maps.

U. S. Library of Congress, Map Division, Civil War Maps; an Annotated List of Maps and Atlases in Map Collections of the Library of Congress, comp. by Richard W. Stephenson (Washington, 1961). The papers of engineers and of general officers often contain maps; see the index to this Guide.

Commission for the Collection and Distribution of Railroad Iron

To coordinate the activities of the War and Navy Departments connected with the collection of railroad iron, a commission was established. AIGO Special Order 18 of Jan. 22, 1863, designated Col. William M. Wadley, supervisor of railroad transportation, and Maj. Isaac M. St. John, chief of the Niter and Mining Bureau, and an officer who was to be designated by the Navy Department as a commission to determine what railroads could best have their rails removed for use elsewhere. The rails collected were to be used on roads indispensable for military operations, and defective rails were to be rolled and used for ironcladding naval vessels. Colonel Wadley was soon replaced by Col. Jeremy F. Gilmer, chief of the Engineer Bureau (AIGO Special Order 36, Feb. 12, 1863). Major St. John was active for only a few months, and Gilmer was succeeded in 1863 by Col. Charles F. M. Garnett. During 1863-64 D. H. Kinney served as the commission's agent to purchase railroad iron. The Navy representative for a time was George G. Hull, superintendent of the Atlanta & West Point Railroad. Capt. George E. Walker served as commissioner in the deep South during mid-1863. After his death he was succeeded in Nov. 1863 by Maj. Minor Meriwether, an engineer officer who had had experience on

Southern railroads. Meriwether was instructed to purchase railroad iron and, when negotiations failed, to impress it and to obtain necessary legal assistance in doing so. He traveled around the South collecting and distributing rails and other materials and supervising the rebuilding of track and bridges. AIGO Special Order 37 of Feb. 13, 1864, assigned Lt. William N. Bolling to the Engineer Bureau for duty in collecting railroad iron. On Sept. 30, 1864, Capt. E. T. D. Myers, Corps of Engineers, was assigned to duty with the commission, and he was also to be employed under the Engineer Bureau in replacing bridges and repairing railroads damaged by the enemy (AIGO Special Order 232). Railroads that were threatened with the loss of rails resisted by suing out injunctions and employing other legal measures.

> Black, Railroads of the Confederacy, p. 205-208.

> No records of this commission have been found.

Correspondence and other documents relating to the commissioners are in Confederate War Department records. Many letters to the commissioners are in the Engineer Bureau's letters sent, and information regarding letters received from them by the Bureau is in its register of letters received.

Some correspondence and other documents are in the compiled military service records of Confederate engineers (files of Minor Meriwether and E. T. D. Myers). A few letters from Colonel Garnett are in the Secretary of War's letters-received file.

BUREAU OF INDIAN AFFAIRS

Under the act of Feb. 21, 1861, the War Department was to have charge of matters connected with Indian tribes (Prov. Cong. C. S. A. Stat. 32), and an act of Mar. 15, 1861 (Prov. Cong. C. S. A. Stat. 68), established a Bureau of Indian Affairs in the Department. Appointed and confirmed as Commissioner of Indian Affairs, David Hubbard began negotiations with the Indians in the spring of 1861.

Long before the Civil War the large Indian tribes of the southeastern States had been removed by the U. S. Government to the region west of Arkansas and north of the Red River. At the opening of the war this region was the home of the Cherokee, Creek, Choctaw, Chickasaw, and Seminole, who had immigrated from east of the Mississippi, and of the Quapaw, Seneca, mixed Seneca and Shawnee, Comanche, and Osage. The Indians in the southern part of the Indian Territory bordering on the Confederacy were estimated by the Confederate Commissioner of Indian Affairs in 1862 to number 71,520. Although the U. S. Office of Indian Affairs was still responsible for relations with these tribes in 1861, most of these Indians became Confederate allies. The United States was compelled to withdraw its troops from the southern part of the Indian Territory, and there were delays in the payment of annuities. The Confederacy with the aid of Indian officials who changed sides stepped into the void.

A resolution of Congress of Mar. 5, 1861 (Ramsdell, Laws and Joint Resolutions, p. 157), authorized the President to send a special agent to the Indian tribes west of Arkansas. Albert Pike of Arkansas was appointed commissioner to negotiate with the Indians and during the summer and fall of 1861 he concluded a series of treaties. They were ratified in Dec. 1861 and their terms became the responsibility of the Commissioner of Indian Affairs and of Indian agents and Army officers in the Indian Territory. Congress appropriated funds for annuity and other payments, but legislation adopted in 1865 provided for payments in cotton delivered at a Gulf port from which it could be exported. In Jan. 1862 Albert Pike conveyed the initial consignment of specie to the Indian Territory for distribution to the Indians. The Commissioner made annual visits in 1862-64 to the tribes in the Indian Territory where he disbursed funds to the treasurers of the Indian tribes and conferred with Indian chiefs and the Army officers commanding the District of Indian Territory and the Trans-Mississippi Department. In Oct. 1864 at his request Gen. E. Kirby Smith appointed Robert C. Miller, a quartermaster agent, as disbursing agent at the headquarters of the District of Indian Territory.

During the war most of the Indian country was a battleground, forcing the Indian inhabitants to flee. Creeks under Chief Opothleyohola loyal to the United States were attacked by Confederate Indian troops and Texas cavalry late in 1861 and fled during the winter to Kansas. Some Cherokees joined the Creeks in flight, and men of these and other tribes enlisted in the Union military forces. A Union expedition marched south from Kansas in 1862 and in July captured the Cherokee chief, John Ross. Stand Watie, the leader of the southern faction of the Cherokees and colonel of the First Cherokee Mounted Rifles, was elected chief of the Cherokees at Tahlequah in Aug. 1862 to succeed Ross. In the fall of 1862 other Cherokees of the Union faction fled to the neighborhood of Fort Scott, Kans. About half of the Seminole and smaller numbers of Quapaw, Seneca, Shawnee, Delaware, Wichita, and Kickapoo Indians also took refuge in Kansas where they received relief from the U.S. Government. The Union occupation of the Cherokee Nation in 1863 forced the Cherokee who had remained there to escape to the Choctaw and Chickasaw Nations in the valley of the Red River and south of that river into Texas. Most of the Choctaw and Chickasaw tribes remained loyal to the Confederacy, and in 1864 when much of the Indian country was under U.S. control part of those and the Seminole tribe moved southward. By the end of 1864 there were 15,000 to 16,000 Indian refugees in camps in the southern counties of the Choctaw and Chickasaw Nations, and the task of feeding them was a considerable burden to the Confederate Army.

Successive Commissioners of Indian Affairs:
David Hubbard, Mar. 16, 1861.
Sutton S. Scott, Nov. 3, 1861.

Annie H. Abel, The American Indian As Slaveholder and Secessionist (Cleveland, 1915); C.S.A. Bureau of Indian Affairs, Report of S. S. Scott, Act'g Com'r of Indian Affairs to Hon. J. P. Benjamin, Secretary of War, Richmond, Mar. 8, 1862 [Richmond, 1862] also contains reports of Indian agents and some correspondence. Other commissioner's reports in the Official Records . . . Armies include the following: Jan. 12, 1863, ser. 4, vol. 2, p. 352-357; Dec. 12, 1863, ser. 1, vol. 22, pt. 2, p. 1095-1096; Dec. 1, 1864, ser. 1, vol. 41, pt. 4, p. 1086-1090. See also Morton Ohland, "Confederate Government Relations with the Five Civilized Tribes, " Chronicles of Oklahoma, 31:299-322 (Autumn 1953); Sutton S. Scott, "Some Account of Confederate Indian Affairs, " Gulf States Historical Magazine, 2:137-154 (Nov. 1903); Grace S. Woodward, The Cherokees (Norman, Okla., 1963). Pike's report to the

President, Dec. 12, 1861, is in Message of the President, and Report of Albert Pike, Commissioner of the Confederate States to the Indian Nations West of Arkansas, of the Results of His Mission (Richmond, 1861). Concerning the Indian treaties of 1861 see the chapter of this Guide on the General Records of the Confederacy. See also in this chapter the correspondence of the Confederate Secretary of War which contains letters to and from Albert Pike and the Commissioners of Indian Affairs; some of this correspondence is published in Official Records . . . Armies, passim. A map drawn by J. T. Cox of the retreat of the Creeks and other Indians under Opothleyohola in the winter of 1861 is in Record Group 75, Records of the Bureau of Indian Affairs.

No records of the Bureau of Indian Affairs have been found. They were probably destroyed at the time of the evacuation of Richmond.

Arkansas and Red River Superintendency

An act of Apr. 8, 1862 (1 Cong. C.S.A. Stat. 11), designated the Indian lands west of Arkansas and north of Texas that had been annexed to the Confederacy as the Arkansas and Red River Superintendency of Indian Affairs. The superintendent was to reside at Fort Smith or Van Buren and supervise the activities and accounts of all officials of the Indian Bureau in that area. Elias Rector, who had been superintendent of the Southern Superintendency under the United States, continued as Confederate superintendent in 1861 and after assisting Albert Pike in negotiating the Indian treaties returned to Fort Smith. Pike assumed command of the Indian Territory in 1861 and acted as superintendent of Indian affairs until his resignation in the fall of 1862. After Jan. 1863 the commanders of the Indian Territory (Brig. Gen. William Steele, Maj. Gen. Samuel B. Maxey, and Brig. Gen. Douglas H. Cooper) acted as Superintendent of Indian Affairs. In his report of Dec. 1, 1864, the Commissioner of Indian Affairs stated that he had sought unsuccessfully for a suitable man for appointment as superintendent and that the lack of one had complicated the administration of Indian affairs.

During part of 1864 when General Maxey acted as superintendent, Col. Roswell W. Lee served as assistant superintendent of Indian affairs and bore most of the administrative burden. To assist the refugee Indians, General Maxey also appointed an issuing agent, a superintendent of issues, and an inspector of camps.

On his arrival in the Indian country in the spring of 1861 Commissioner Pike arranged with the men who were then serving as agents for the different Indian tribes to continue in their posts. After his return from Washington in 1861, Douglas H. Cooper was requested to continue as agent to the Choctaw and Chickasaw tribes and was appointed colonel of the 1st Choctaw and Chickasaw Mounted Rifles. John Crawford carried on as Cherokee agent. William H. Garrett, the incumbent agent to the Creeks, died Jan. 23, 1862; R. P. Pulliam then acted as agent until 1862 when Israel G. Vore replaced him. Samuel H. Rutherford continued as Seminole agent but was replaced in 1862 by Rev. J. S. Murrow, who had been a Baptist missionary in the area since 1859. Matthew Leeper served as agent to the Wichita, Comanche, and other Reserve Indians until he was killed in Oct. 1862 by a party of northern Indians. In 1864 some of the Reserve Indians were located between the Red and Canadian Rivers in the southwestern part of the Indian country under the supervision of Capt. L. G. Harmon; other bands had become wanderers. Andrew J. Dorn was given a Confederate appointment as agent to the Osage, Seneca, Shawnee, and Quapaw tribes.

The act organizing the Arkansas and Red River Superintendency of Indian Affairs confirmed the arrangements made by Albert Pike with the Indian agents. They were to reside on the reserves selected for agencies and to conduct relations with the Indians under instructions from the Secretary of War, the Commissioner of Indian Affairs, and the Superintendent of Indian Affairs. The act prescribed in detail the manner in which relations and trade with the Indians were to be conducted.

Annie H. Abel, The American Indian as Participant in the Civil War (Cleveland, 1919); C. S. A. War Department, Regulations Adopted by the War Department, on the 15th of April 1862, for Carrying into Effect the Acts of Congress of the Confederate States Relating to Indian Affairs, etc., etc. (Richmond, 1862); Angie Debo, The Rise and Fall of the Choctaw Republic (Norman, 1934) and The Road to Disappearance (Norman, 1941); Muriel H. Wright, "General Douglas H. Cooper, C. S. A.," Chronicles of Oklahoma, 32:142-184 (Summer 1954).

Record Group 75. --Captured records of the Arkansas and Red River Superintendency and of the Wichita Agency are now among the records of the Bureau of Indian Affairs. The records of the superintendency may have been captured when Fort Smith was occupied by U. S. forces on Sept. 1, 1863. The Delaware and Shawnee Indians who attacked the Wichita Agency in Oct. 1862 carried off papers, but they turned them over to the Delaware Indian agent, who transmitted them to the U. S. Commissioner of Indian Affairs. Correspondence and other records of the superintendency, July 5, 1861-Mar. 4, 1862 (1 in.), include letters from Indian agents and Albert Pike to Elias Rector, other correspondence of Pike, vouchers for Rector's expenses, Indian agents' receipts for funds, copies and drafts of Rector's letters to Indian agents, Indian chiefs, and S. S. Scott, and bills and invoices for supplies furnished to the Indians. A file of papers of the Wichita Agency, May 26, 1861-Sept. 28, 1862 (1/2 in.), consists of letters received by Matthew Leeper from Albert Pike, Elias Rector, commissary and quartermaster officers, and others; copies of letters to Pike, Rector, and the Commissioner of Indian Affairs; and vouchers for payments for services. Another file, Apr. 18, 1861-Jan. 25, 1862 (1 in.), consists mainly of papers relating to trade licenses issued by William H. Garrett, the agent to the Creek Indians, including applications, licenses, and inventories of stock held by traders. This file also contains invoices for supplies and services obtained by the superintendency.

Some of the documents in the superintendency and Wichita Agency files described above are printed in Annie H. Abel, The American Indian as Slaveholder and Seccessionist, p. 298-357 (Cleveland, 1915). The U. S. Bureau of Indian Affairs letters-received file (C757/1868) contains a statement of Confederate Creek leaders concerning the flight north of loyal Creeks in the winter of 1861-62. Letters sent by the commanders of the District of Indian Territory regarding Indian affairs are in their letter books, described in the section of this chapter on Territorial Commands and Armies.

The admission of the Indian and Oklahoma Territories as the State of Oklahoma in 1907 resulted in the dissolution of the tribal governments of the Five Civilized Tribes. Consequently the records of the Creek, Cherokee, Chickasaw, Choctaw, and Seminole tribes were placed in the custody of the Superintendent of the Five Civilized Tribes at Muskogee, Okla. In 1929 the Oklahoma Historical Society began classifying and calendaring these tribal records, and as a result of the efforts of the Society an act of Congress of Mar. 27, 1934 (48 Stat. 501), authorized the transfer of the records to the Society. In 1948 additional records of the Five Civilized Tribes were transferred to the Society. Indian tribal records and papers of Indian chiefs of the war period are in other repositories. Records of the Creek Nation, 1861-99, in the Creek Indian Museum, Okmulgee, Okla. include the treaty of 1861 with the Confederate Government.

Other records relating to Indians in Oklahoma that were formerly in the Wollaroc Museum in Bartlesville, Okla., have been transferred to the University of Oklahoma Library. Materials relating to the Cherokee in the University of Oklahoma Library include tribal records and papers of John Ross, Stand Watie, James M. Bell, and Randolph Bunch, leaders of the Nation. These records include correspondence with Albert Pike, David Hubbard, Elias C. Boudinot, and Army officers serving in the Indian Country. Some of this correspondence has been published in Edward E. Dale and Gaston Litton, eds., Cher-

okee Cavaliers; Forty Years of Cherokee History as Told in the Correspondence of the Ridge-Watie-Boudinot Family (Norman, Okla., 1939). Other papers, 1820-66, of John Ross are in the Tennessee State Library and Archives. The University of Oklahoma Library has papers of Peter P. Pitchlynn, chief of the Choctaw Nation during the war period. The same repository has in the Roscoe S. Cate collection papers relating to the Creek Indians that include correspondence of Albert Pike and other officials concerned with Indian affairs. Documents relating to Cherokee relations with the Confederacy in 1861 that were supplied by John Ross to Col. William Weer, commander of the Union expedition into the Cherokee Nation, are published in Official Records . . . Armies, ser. 1, vol. 13, p. 489-505, and documents on the same subject are in Joseph B. Thoburn, ed., "The Cherokee Question," Chronicles of Oklahoma, 2:141-242 (June 1924), which is a reprint of a document published by the U.S. Office of Indian Affairs in 1866. A report by Col. Roswell W. Lee, Aug. 20, 1864, is in Allan C. Ashcraft, "Confederate Indian Department Conditions in August, 1864," Chronicles of Oklahoma, 41:271-285 (Autumn 1963).

In 1932 the Oklahoma Historical Society undertook a survey of the records of Indian agencies in western Oklahoma. Under the act of 1934 referred to above the Society became custodian of records relating to the Cheyenne, Arapahoe, Comanche, Shawnee, Kiowa, Sauk and Fox, Pawnee, and Quapaw Indians.

Record Group 109. --In the War Department Collection of Confederate Records is a copy of the proceedings of the grand council of the Confederate Indian tribes at Cherokee Town, Washita River, on Aug. 8, 1864. This record was sent to General Maxey by Israel Folsome on Aug. 17, 1864.

Records in Other Custody. --Some correspondence on relations between the Cherokee and the Confederate and U.S. Governments, 1861-63, found at Fort Gibson by a captain of Wisconsin volunteer infantry, is in the State Historical Society of Wisconsin collections. Accounts and receipts, 1861-65, relating to provisions and other supplies issued to Osage and

Seminole Indians by Confederate officials at Sherman, Tex., are in Duke University Library. Manuscripts relating to Confederate Indian affairs are in the Louisiana Historical Association on deposit in the Howard-Tilton Memorial Library of Tulane University.

Albert Pike's papers in the Library of the Supreme Council, Scottish Rite of Freemasonry, Southern Jurisdiction, Washington, D.C., contain accounts relating to his expenditures as Indian commissioner, 1861-62, and his autobiography containing some data on the war period. In the same repository is a negative photostat of the treaty of Aug. 12, 1861, with the Comanche and other Indians obtained from the Newberry Library, Chicago, Ill. Other Pike letters are in the R. S. Cate collection in Oklahoma University Library, and microfilm of his correspondence including some relating to Indian and military affairs is in the Texas Archives in the University of Texas Library.

Letters of Pike, 1861-62, are published in Official Records . . . Armies, passim; Abel, American Indian as Slaveholder, passim;

Edward M. Coffman, ed., "Ben McCulloch Letters," Southwestern Historical Quarterly, 60:118-122 (July 1956).

BUREAU OF ORDNANCE AND ORDNANCE DEPARTMENT

The Bureau of Ordnance was established on Apr. 8, 1861, when Josiah Gorgas was assigned to duty as its Chief (AIGO Special Order 17). He served also as Acting Chief of the Engineer Bureau until the beginning of Aug. 1861. The Bureau of Ordnance was organized under the 44th article of the Army Regulations, which provided that the senior officer of artillery should be charged with the Bureau's administration. It never had specific legislative authorization although it was referred to in statutes.

In May 1861 Capt. Smith Stansbury became assistant to the Chief of the Bureau, and Lt. Robert Talley became the draftsman. Capt. Edward B. Smith, who succeeded Stansbury in 1862, and Capt. R. H. Glenn were in 1864 given the responsibility of revising estimates, applying appropriations, disbursing funds, and examining contracts and property and cash accounts and returns. Capt. Thomas L. Bayne joined the Bureau in 1861. In the next year Col. Thomas S. Rhett was assigned as inspector of ordnance and Maj. Gen. Benjamin Huger, as inspector of ordnance and artillery. Lt. Col. Julius A. DeLagnel, who became inspector of arsenals in Nov. 1863, was relieved by Lt. Col. James L. White in Sept. 1864. In Sept. 1863 Maj. F. F. Jones was assigned as inspector of small arms. Officers on ordnance duty throughout the Confederacy were concerned with the procurement, manufacture, storage, distribution, and use of ordnance stores.

An act of Feb. 20, 1861 (Prov. Cong. C.S.A. Stat. 28), authorized the President or the Secretary of War to contract for the purchase and manufacture of heavy ordnance, small arms, and machinery for the manufacture or alteration of small arms and munitions; to employ agents and artisans; and to contract for the establishment of powder mills and the manufacture of powder. An act of Apr. 17, 1862 (1 Cong. C.S.A. Stat. 33), to encourage the production of saltpeter and small arms, authorized the Confederate Government to advance 50 percent of the cost of constructing works and machinery. This act resulted in the opening of new mines and the reopening of old ones, the discovery and working of niter caves, and the establishment or enlargement of blast furnaces, rolling mills, foundries, forges, and shops throughout the Confederacy but particularly in Virginia, Georgia, and northern Alabama.

The Ordnance Bureau procured ordnance and ordnance stores from factories in the Confederacy and from Europe. Contracts were made for the manufacture at plants throughout the Confederacy of rifles, revolvers, heavy guns, gun carriages, caissons, projectiles, and machineguns. Edged weapons including swords, sabres, knives, and bayonets were fabricated at many different plants and blacksmith shops. Other manufacturers produced powder, percussion caps, knapsacks, horseshoes, paper, hardware, wagons, and saddles. Large quantities of arms, munitions, and other supplies were imported from England and the Continent through Maj. Caleb Huse, the War Department procurement agent in England, and in June 1862 Maj. Smith Stansbury went to Bermuda to take charge of the ordnance depot established there to handle these supplies.

The Chief of the Bureau throughout the war was Lt. Col. (later Brig. Gen.) Josiah Gorgas.

Reports of the Ordnance Bureau, Nov. 15, 1863, and Oct. 13, 1864, are in Official Records . . . Armies, ser. 4, vol. 2, p. 955-959, and vol. 3, p. 733-734. William A. Albaugh, III, and Edward N. Simmons, Confederate Arms (Harrisburg, Pa., 1957); John D. Capron, "Virginia Iron Furnaces of the Confederacy," Virginia Cavalcade, 17:10-18 (Autumn 1967); C. S. A. Ordnance Department, The Field Manual for the Use of the Officers on Ordnance Duty (Richmond, 1862); C. S. A. Ordnance Department, Regulations for the Government of the Ordnance Department of the Confederate States of America (Richmond, 1862); C. S. A. War Department, The Ordnance Manual for the Use of the Officers of the Confederate States Army (Richmond, 1863); Charles B. Dew, Ironmaker to the Confederacy; Joseph R. Anderson and the Tredegar Iron Works (New Haven and London, 1966); Josiah Gorgas, "Notes on the Ordnance Department of the Confederate Government," Southern Historical Society Papers, 12:67-94 (Jan.-Feb. 1884); Official Records . . . Armies, ser. 4, vols. 1-3, passim; Samuel B. Thompson, Confederate Purchasing Operations Abroad (Chapel Hill, 1935); Frank E. Vandiver, Ploughshares Into Swords; Josiah Gorgas and Confederate Ordnance (Austin, 1952).

Office of the Chief of Ordnance

Record Group 59. --A file of intercepted letters among the general records of the Department of State contains some documents regarding the importation of war supplies by the Confederacy. These include a letter from Caleb Huse to Josiah Gorgas, Apr. 1, 1862; an agreement between Huse and the Mercantile Trading Co. of London, July 23, 1863, with four letters from Huse to Edgar P. Stringer concerning that agreement, July-Sept. 1863; and an agreement between the Ordnance Bureau and C. E. Thorburn on behalf of himself and Messrs. Charles H. Reid & Co. and other parties of London to run steamers on joint account between St. George, Bermuda, and Nassau, N. P., and either Charleston or Wilmington, and two letters from Stringer to Thorburn, Oct. 3, 1863.

Record Group 109. --Some records of the Richmond office of the Bureau of Ordnance are in the War Department Collection of Confederate Records, but the Bureau's records were not preserved intact.

Miscellaneous ordnance records, 1861-65 (2 in.), consist of Ordnance Bureau circulars, general orders, and special orders embodying instructions to commanding officers of arsenals and other ordnance officers; a few pieces of correspondence; inventories of ordnance and ordnance stores; inventories of ammunition; property returns; and abstracts of ordnance and ordnance stores issued, articles fabricated, and articles purchased and not paid for. Some papers relate to ammunition supply, 1862-64 (3 1/2 in.), and include drawings for irons for gun carriages, irons for limber, a 24-pounder carriage wheel, a 24-pounder gun carriage, and a 12-pounder gun carriage. Other ordnance drawings in this record group depict a 6-pounder bronze field gun, a 12-pounder Napoleon with carriage, irons for field carriages, a 24-pounder howitzer carriage and irons, a carriage wheel, and a design of a submarine vessel bearing a torpedo. There is a book of invoices of ordnance supplies sent to various stations, Dec. 25, 1861-Aug. 30, 1862 (ch. IV, vol. 108). An abstract of ordnance and stores received at Enterprise, Miss., and Selma, Ala., during the first quarter of 1863 (ch. IV, vol. 149) is available as are other abstracts, 1862-64, for arsenals or depots at Charleston, Columbus (Miss.), Memphis, Richmond, Selma, and the Macon Central Laboratory.

Correspondence of the Chief of the Bureau of Ordnance and of ordnance officers is in a number of other files described elsewhere in this chapter. These include the letters-sent books and the letters-received files of the Secretary of War, the Adjutant and Inspector General, and the Quartermaster General. Because there are so many original letters addressed to Josiah Gorgas in the compiled military service records of Confederate general and staff officers (described in chapter XI of this Guide) it is probable that there survived at least a partial file of letters received of the Bureau of Ordnance. Other letters from that file were placed in other compiled files, such as the naval service records (Record Group 109), in which the file for Comdr. John M. Brooke contains letters to Gorgas dated Apr. 18, Apr. 19, May 9, Nov. 4, Nov. 20, and Nov. 27, 1863, and letters dated Dec. 17, 1862, and Jan. 6, 1864, to Maj. William S. Downer, superintendent of the Richmond Armory. The compiled military service records of Confederate general and staff officers including ordnance officers also contain copies of reports and returns that were

submitted to the Ordnance Bureau and invoices and receipts relating to ordnance stores. The letters-sent and letters-received files that are available for arsenals contain many letters to and from the Chief of the Bureau of Ordnance (see the descriptions below).

Correspondence files of arsenals and ordnance depots contain some letters to and from arsenals for which there are no separate records. Other correspondence and reports and returns relating to arsenals are also in the compiled military service records of Confederate general and staff officers. As some officers who became attached to the Niter and Mining Bureau had previously served as ordnance officers, their files in the compiled military service records of Confederate organizations contain documents on those duties. Some documents relating to ordnance officers are also likely to be found in the files of other subdivisions of the War Department, including the Office of the Secretary of War, the Adjutant and Inspector General's Office, and the Quartermaster General's Office. Confederate papers relating to citizens or business firms, described in chapter XI, include papers on arsenals, on industrial firms that had contracts with the Government, and on individuals employed by those firms. The payrolls of civilian employees described with the records of the Quartermaster General's Office include rolls for ordnance establishments. Inspection reports among the records of the Adjutant and Inspector General's Office include reports on arsenals.

Records in Other Custody. --The Josiah Gorgas papers in the University of Alabama Library include correspondence on his duties as Chief of the Bureau of Ordnance and diaries that cover the war period. Invoices of ordnance and ordnance stores, 1861-63 (1 vol.), are in the American Antiquarian Society collections. A list of women employed in the Ordnance Bureau, 1864, is in the Juliana Dorsey papers in the William and Mary College Library.

Frank E. Vandiver, ed., The Civil War Diary of General Josiah Gorgas (University, Ala., 1947). Letters of Maj. Smith Stansbury to Josiah Gorgas, the Secretary of War, Caleb Huse, Norman S. Walker, and others, June-Nov. 1863, are in Frank E. Vandiver, ed., Confederate Blockade Running Through Bermuda, 1861-1865; Letters and Cargo Manifests, p. 71-103 (Austin, Tex., 1947). The records of industrial firms, such as the Tredegar Iron Works in the Archives Division, Virginia State Library, and the Brierfield Iron Works and the Shelby Iron Company in the University of Alabama Library, document their dealings with the Confederate Government. James F. Doster, "The Shelby Iron Works Collection in the University of Alabama Library," Business History Society Bulletin, 26:214-217 (Dec. 1952). Papers of Joseph R. Anderson, the proprietor of the Tredegar Iron Works, are in the Henry E. Huntington Library. An account book (1861-63) of Edward R. Archer, the superintendent of the Tredegar gun foundry, is in the Virginia Historical Society collections.

Arsenals, Armories, and Ordnance Depots

The Bureau of Ordnance administered a system of ordnance establishments taken over from the States of the Confederacy or founded by the Confederate Government. Former U.S. arsenals at Augusta, Ga., Apalachicola, Fla., Baton Rouge, La., Charleston, S.C., Fayetteville, N.C., Harpers Ferry, Va., Little Rock, Ark., Mount Vernon, Ala., and San Antonio, Tex., became Confederate property in 1861. Since these old arsenals had been used chiefly for the storage of ordnance and ordnance stores and lacked machinery and skilled workmen, the Bureau had to provide manufacturing facilities not only for new arsenals but at the captured ones.

Officers on ordnance duty had charge of all arsenals, powder mills, ordnance depots, and magazines and furnished arms, ordnance, and ordnance stores to military commands on the receipt of proper requisitions. Arsenals usually contained armories for the manufacture or repair of arms and laboratories for the manufacture of cartridges, shells, and other munitions, in addition to leather, tin, carpenter, and machine shops. Authority given to the commanding officers of arsenals and ordnance depots in 1861 to contract for arms and ordnance stores was limited in 1863 to purchases or contracts amounting to less than $10,000 without prior clearance through the Bureau of Ordnance. Arsenal commanders sometimes assigned ordnance officers to arms factories for inspection duties.

Personnel of arsenals included soldiers attached to the corps of artillery, other detailed enlisted men, slaves hired from their owners, white mechanics exempted from the draft, and women and boys. An act of Mar. 6, 1861 (Prov. Cong. C.S.A. Stat. 50), authorized the enlistment of not more than 100 armorers, carriagemakers, blacksmiths, artificers, and laborers who were to be attached to the Corps of Artillery for ordnance service. In Nov. 1863 two-thirds of the 5,090 workers at arsenals, armories, and similar installations were nonconscripts, disabled soldiers, women, boys, and slaves. Attempts to import skilled mechanics were unsuccessful. Despite the shortage of workers, 742 employees of arsenals and contractors' factories of draft age had to be released to enrolling officers toward the end of 1864 (AIGO General Order 82, Oct. 20, 1864).

Lester J. Cappon, "A Note   Military Affairs, 4:94-102 (Summer
on Confederate Ordnance Records, "   1940).

Apalachicola Arsenal (Fla.)

The State of Florida seized this former U.S. arsenal on Jan. 6, 1861, and found a small quantity of arms, but the arsenal was not used for manufacturing during the war.

No records of this arsenal have been found.

Asheville Armory (N.C.)

Originally a private arms factory, this establishment was taken over by the Confederate Government early in the war. It manufactured rifles similar to the British Enfield. Near the end of 1863 the operatives and machinery were moved to the Columbia Arsenal (S.C.).

Successive commanders of this armory:

    Capt. Benjamin Sloan.
    Capt. C. C. McPhail, Sept. 1863.

Records in Other Custody. --The Archives Division of the Virginia State Library has a record book of the Asheville Armory, Dec. 24, 1861-May 31, 1864 (1 vol., 387 p.). It contains fair copies of letters sent to the Chief of Ordnance and other officers attached to the Bureau of Ordnance, the commanding officers of armories and arsenals at Richmond, Fayetteville, Macon, and Columbia, industrial and business firms, State military authorities, the commandant of conscripts of North Carolina, slaveowners, the Niter and Mining Bureau, and enrolling, ordnance, and quartermaster officers. Also in this book are reports on work done, orders to personnel of the armory, a record of furloughs, statements of money received and expended, lists of workmen, and statements of wages and personnel.

Atlanta Arsenal (Ga.)

This plant was established in 1862 in a number of buildings that were partly equipped with machinery from other ordnance works at Vicksburg, Holly Springs, Knoxville, and Nashville. No arms were made; but many were repaired, and ordnance stores were supplied to the Army of Tennessee. Before the capture of Atlanta by Sherman's army in Nov. 1864, the arsenal was moved to Columbus, Ga.

The commander of the arsenal was Maj. M. H. Wright.

Record Group 109. --Record books of the Atlanta Arsenal are in the War Department Collection of Confederate Records. Press copies of letters and telegrams sent, Mar. 6, 1862-July 21, 1863, and Feb. 5-July 9, 1864 (ch. IV, vol. 8, p. 109-230, and vols. 10-12 and 16), include communications from Captain Wright to the Chief of Ordnance in Richmond, commanders of arsenals, enrolling officers, ordnance and quartermaster and other Army officers, industrial and business firms, Ordnance Department agents, employees of the Atlanta Arsenal, and railroad agents. Other press copies of letters sent, Mar. 12-Aug. 23, 1862, Sept. 5, 1862-Feb. 5, 1864 (ch. IV, vol. 9, p. 208-498, and vols. 14 and 15), concern invoices and receipts for ordnance stores issued and received. A record of letters mailed, Apr. 1, 1862-July 8, 1864 (ch. IV, vol. 85), shows the date, the name of the person and place to which the letter was sent, and the cost of postage, and there is an order book, Mar. 26, 1862-Mar. 28, 1864 (ch. IV, vol. 77). The latter contains also an employees' furlough record. A memorandum book, Mar. 18-June 1, 1864 (ch. IV, vol. 79), contains copies of advertisements to be published in newspapers and instructions to personnel. A timebook of employees, Mar. 1862-Aug. 1864 (ch. IV, vols. 81, 84, 106, 112 1/2, and 130), shows employees' names, days worked, rate of pay, amounts paid, and occupations. There is also a record of contracts for ordnance, ordnance stores, and materials, Jan. 9, 1862-June 14, 1864 (ch. IV, vol. 78), showing quantities to be delivered, the price, and contractors' names. Record books of ordnance stores received and issued, Apr. 26, 1862-Mar. 20, 1863, Aug. 19-Nov. 30, 1863, and Dec. 1863-July 1864 (ch. IV, vols. 17-19, 79 1/2, 88), show the kinds of articles and the names of persons from whom received or to whom issued. With a similar record of a few pages for 1862 (ch. IV, vol. 86) there are, near the back of the same book, a record of conscripts assigned to contractors in 1864 and a record of employees in different departments of the arsenal in 1864. Some invoices for ordnance stores, office supplies, and lumber purchased, 1862 (ch. IV, vol. 80), are bound in a volume in chronological order. A record of ordnance stores passing through Atlanta, Mar. 1863-July 1864 (ch. IV, vol. 87), contains a daily record of the kinds of articles, the places from and to which shipped, and the names of railroads. Several other books relating in part to the Atlanta Arsenal are described under the Nashville Arsenal. Another book contains in one end a record of the repair and cleaning of machinery, Sept. 1864-Jan. 1865, and in the other end a record of the repair and cleaning of arms, Mar. -Nov. 1864 (ch. IV, vol. 82).

Augusta Arsenal and Powder Works (Ga.)

On Jan. 24, 1861, Georgia forces captured the U.S. Arsenal at Augusta, and in Sept. 1861 construction of Confederate powder works on the banks of the Augusta Canal began. The old arsenal was converted into an armory, and three private foundries and machine works were acquired and enlarged for manufacturing purposes. The powder works included saltpeter and sulphur refineries, charcoal furnaces, a laboratory, incorporating mills, granulating building, and a magazine. Large quantities of cartridges, fixed ammunition, signal rockets, fuses, primers, grenades, nitric acid, fulminate of mercury, and percussion caps were produced. The arsenal also manufactured bronze field artillery, gun carriages, caissons, battery wagons, limbers for field artillery, travelling forges, ammunition and powder

boxes, horseshoes, saddles, artillery harness, cartridge bags, knapsacks, and artillery projectiles.
Successive commanders of this arsenal:
  Capt. W. G. Gill, Aug. 3, 1861.
  Col. George W. Rains, Apr. 12, 1862.

George W. Rains, History of   (Augusta, Ga., 1882).
the Confederate Powder Works

Record Group 109. --Records of the Augusta Arsenal that were received from the Office of the Chief of Ordnance of the United States are now in the War Department Collection of Confederate Records. They include: daily reports of work performed in the powder factory, Nov. 30, 1862-Apr. 28, 1865 (2 vols.), a record of invoices of ordnance stores turned over to quartermasters for transportation by the military storekeeper, July 1, 1862-Nov. 25, 1863, a record of ordnance stores issued by the military storekeeper, Nov. 1863-Apr. 1865, a record of Government stores received and issued at the powder factory, Jan. 21, 1863-Feb. 9, 1865 (1 vol.), a record of ordnance and ordnance stores ready for shipment, Oct. 1, 1863-Feb. 8, 1865 (1 vol.), a record of ordnance and ordnance stores on hand and received and of deliveries made, Apr. 1-Oct. 17, 1864 (1 vol.), a record of expenditures, Sept. 12-Oct. 28, 1861, a record of stores received and issued by the powder factory, 1862-65, a record of receipts and issues of powder by the magazine, Apr. 1862-Apr. 1865, a record of damaged powder received and issued and of blasting powder made, issued, and on hand, Jan. 22, 1863-Apr. 3, 1865, weekly reports of operations, Jan. 1863-Apr. 1865, a record of invoices of ordnance stores and gunpowder turned over by the military storekeeper for transportation, Apr. 14, 1862-Nov. 19, 1865, and a record of receipts and issues of gunpowder by the military storekeeper, Nov. 1863-Jan. 1865.
Records in Other Custody. --The George W. Rains papers in the Southern Historical Collection in the University of North Carolina Library include a few letters from Josiah Gorgas, Gen. Benjamin Huger, J. H. Hammond, and Maj. Lachlan H. McIntosh, ordnance officer of the State of Georgia. Some photostats of Rains letters with the Texas Archives at the University of Texas Library include a few other letters from Gorgas and Hammond and a letter from Rains to Catesby ap R. Jones, commander of the Naval Ordnance Works at Selma, Ala. Correspondence and orders of Capt. Victor J. B. Girardy, adjutant of the arsenal, 1863-64 (1 vol.), are in Duke University Library.

Baton Rouge Arsenal (La.)

The U.S. arsenal at Baton Rouge was surrendered to Louisiana State forces on Jan. 10, 1861, and later transferred to Confederate control. By the fall of 1861 it was producing small-arms ammunition and preparing to make field artillery. Baton Rouge was held by Union troops from Dec. 17, 1862, until the end of the war.
The commander of this arsenal was Capt. John C. Booth.
No records of this arsenal have been found.

Bellona Arsenal (Va.)

An old U. S. arsenal at Bellona, in Chesterfield County, Va., 13 miles up the James River from Richmond, was being used as a private foundry by Dr. Junius L. Archer at the outbreak of the war. It was later taken over by the Confederate Government.

The commander of this arsenal during 1863-64 was Maj. R. Milton Cary.

No records of this arsenal have been found.

Charleston Arsenal (S. C.)

Seized by the State of South Carolina on Dec. 30, 1861, this arsenal was later turned over to the Confederate Government. It manufactured small-arms ammunition and projectiles for use by the defenses of Charleston harbor. The arsenal was evacuated in Feb. 1865.

Successive commanders of this arsenal:
Capt. Frederick L. Childs, July 1861.
Capt. J. T. Trezevant, ca. Jan. 1863.
Maj. Nathaniel R. Chambliss, Dec. 10, 1863.
Capt. C. C. Pinckney, 1864.
No records of this arsenal have been found.

Clarksville Ordnance Harness Shops (Va.)

In May 1862 this facility was moved from Richmond to Clarksville and continued in operation until the end of the war. It produced artillery and cavalry saddles and harness and cartridge and cap boxes.

Successive superintendents of the shops:
Henry Pride, 1862.
Capt. John Kane, 1864.
No records have been found for these shops, but the records of the Richmond Armory, to which the shops were subordinate, contain considerable correspondence with the superintendents.

Columbia Arsenal (S. C.)

This arsenal was established at the end of 1863, and the Asheville Armory (N. C.) was moved to Columbia to become part of it. The arsenal also included a laboratory. The armory produced few if any arms before its destruction along with the rest of the arsenal by General Sherman's army in Feb. 1865.

The commander of this arsenal was Maj. J. T. Trezevant.
No records of this arsenal have been found.

Columbus Arsenal (Ga.)

In 1862 Capt. F. C. Humphreys established this arsenal with machinery brought from Baton Rouge, La. Small-arms ammunition, artillery shells, harness, and knapsacks produced here were shipped to the Army of Tennessee and to troops on the coast south of Charleston, and toward the end of the war a pistol factory began operations under Maj. James Harding.

Successive commanders of this arsenal:
  Capt. F. C. Humphreys, 1862.
  Col. M. H. Wright, Sept. 5, 1864.
No records of this arsenal have been found.

Columbus (Briarfield) Arsenal (Miss.)

Early in 1862 after the Confederate defeat in Tennessee ordnance property was moved from there and a site selected for an arsenal in Columbus to manufacture and repair small arms and fabricate cartridges, fuses, and caps. The arsenal was moved early in 1863 to Selma, Ala.
Successive commanders of this arsenal:
  Maj. William R. Hunt, 1862.
  Capt. J. T. Trezevant, 1862.
  Lt. Col. James L. White, Dec. 1862.
Record Group 109.--There is an inventory of public property at the Columbus Arsenal, Sept. 30, 1862 (ch. IV, vol. 149).

Dalton Ordnance Depot (Ga.)

In Aug. 1862 Lt. Col. Hypolite Oladowski established a depot at Dalton to supply the Army of Tennessee.
Record Group 109.--Fair copies of letters and telegrams sent, Aug. 21, 1862-Apr. 6, 1863 (ch. IV, vol. 25, p. 37-202), are to commanders of arsenals at Atlanta, Charleston, and Augusta, to ordnance officers in Georgia, Tennessee, South Carolina, and Alabama, to Colonel Oladowski, to Col. Josiah Gorgas, and to quartermaster officers. A record book of the military storekeeper, Aug. 1862-Apr. 1863 (ch. IV, vols. 133 and 145), includes invoices of ordnance stores issued, Nov.-Dec. 1862. There are invoices of ordnance and ordnance stores transferred, Sept. 4, 1862-Apr. 3, 1863 (ch. IV, vol. 113), a record of supplies, Sept. 1862-Feb. 1863 (ch. IV, vol. 117), and invoices and receipts for ordnance and ordnance stores received, Aug. 1862-Mar. 1863 (ch. IV, vol. 79 1/2).

Danville Ordnance Depot (Va.)

The commander of this depot during 1862-65 was Capt. E. S. Hutter. No records of this establishment have been found.

Fayetteville Arsenal and Armory (N.C.)

Captured by North Carolina militia on Apr. 22, 1861, this arsenal was used by the State until transferred to the Confederate Government. The armory manufactured and repaired pistols and rifles, and the laboratory made ammunition. The arsenal was destroyed by Sherman's army in Mar. 1865.
Successive commanders of this arsenal:
  Capt. John C. Booth, July 1861.
  Lt. Col. Julius A. DeLagnel, 1862.
  Maj. Frederick L. Childs, Apr. 1863.
No records of this arsenal have been found.

Greensboro Ordnance Depot (N. C.)

AIGO General Order 13 of Jan. 31, 1863, announced that the depot at Greensboro was to be under the supervision of the War Department and was to receive orders directly from the Bureau of Ordnance.

Capt A. G. Brenizer had become the commander in 1862.

No records of this depot have been found.

Holly Springs Armory (Miss.)

In 1862 the Confederate Government bought the Holly Springs arms factory of Jones, McElwain & Co., which had been given a government contract in 1861 for the manufacture of arms. W. S. McElwain became the master armorer for the armory. Late in 1862 Union forces occupied Holly Springs.

The superintendent was William L. Broun.

No records of this armory have been found.

Jackson Arsenal (Miss.)

AIGO Special Order 241 of Oct. 15, 1862, announced that the ordnance depot at Jackson was to be an arsenal under the supervision of the Bureau of Ordnance.

The commander of this arsenal was Col. Philip Stockton.

No records of this arsenal have been found.

Lynchburg Ordnance Depot (Va.)

This ordnance depot included a laboratory that made cartridges and minié balls. General Gorgas stated in his "Notes" that the shops were moved to Danville.

The commander during 1862-63 was Capt. G. T. Getty.

No records of this depot have been found.

Macon Armory (Ga.)

In 1862 the Bureau of Ordnance began construction of a permanent armory at Macon. It manufactured gunstocks to send to the armories at Richmond and Fayetteville and repaired thousands of muskets, rifles, and carbines. Early in 1864 the Government bought the Spiller & Burr pistol factory at Atlanta and transferred the machinery to the Macon Armory for pistol manufacture. In Nov. 1864 the machinery was transported to Columbia, S. C.

Successive commanders of this armory:

Col. James H. Burton, 1862.

Col. Richard M. Cuyler, acting, May 1863.

Col. James H. Burton, 1863.

Record Group 109. --Correspondence, orders, and other records of the Macon Armory are in the War Department Collection of Confederate Records. Fair copies of letters and telegrams sent by the superintendent, June 4, 1862-Apr. 17, 1865 (ch. IV, vols. 20, 29, and 31), are to the Chief of the Bureau of Ordnance, commanders of arsenals and armories, the superintendent of the Central Laboratory at Macon, industrial and business firms, the War Department agent at Wilmington, officers attached to the armory, enrolling officers, superintendents of Niter and Mining Bureau districts, the Chief Commissary of the State of Georgia, the tax-in-kind agent, the provost marshal at Macon, the surgeon of the Macon hospital, owners of slaves hired, and others. These volumes contain also summary statements of work done on the construction of the armory. The superintendent's book, July 25, 1862-Apr. 4, 1865 (ch. IV, vol. 49), contains fair copies of orders regarding the administration and operation of the armory, the armory guard, the military company, musters, and personnel matters. Fair copies of letters sent by the master armorer (Jesse Fuss), Dec. 30, 1862-Apr. 11, 1865 (ch. IV, vol. 30), are to Colonel Burton, the foremen of shops, the paymaster and military storekeeper, and other employees.

The records include a roll of employees, 1863-65 (ch. IV, vol. 46), a list of employees on furlough, Mar. 17, 1864-Apr. 16, 1865 (ch. IV, vol. 72), a record of slaves employed by the master builder, 1864 (ch. IV, vol. 75), and a record of employees of the master armorer's office, n. d. (ch. IV, vol. 53).

Several account books show expenditures for materials and services. There are accounts with contractors, 1863-64 (ch. IV, vol. 76), machinery, building and other accounts, 1862-64 (ch. IV, vol. 40), a small account book, apparently of the master armorer, Dec. 1863-May 1864 (ch. IV, vol. 65), a record of machine department accounts approved for payment, Oct. 1862-Apr. 1864 (ch. IV, part of vol. 64), an account book for Oct. 2-15, 1862 (ch. IV, vol. 68), and a record book relating to lumber received, Dec. 1863-Feb. 1865 (ch. IV, vol. 69). Information regarding lumber purchased during Feb. 27-Mar. 27, 1863, is in an unnumbered booklet.

A record of gunstocks machined and pistols manufactured, Dec. 1862-Nov. 1864 (ch. IV, vols. 1 and 2), is available. Returns of employees and articles manufactured, June 1864-Feb. 1865 (ch. IV, vol. 42), consist of monthly records of the types and numbers of employees and the types and quantities of arms and appendages manufactured. A record of repairs and machine work performed, Oct. 1864-Mar. 1865 (ch. IV, vol. 35), shows for each employee the days worked during the month, the number of hours worked, and the kind of work. Returns of work done, Aug. 1862, July 1863-Aug. 1864, Jan. 1865 (4 in.), include returns of Negro laborers, carpenters, and bricklayers; white bricklayers and carpenters; and employees of the pistol and machine departments and stock shop. A foreman's monthly timebook, incompletely identified, June 1-Oct. 31, 1863 (ch. IV, vol. 119), may be a record of the Macon Armory.

Other records concern stores. A record of the delivery and receipt of ordnance stores and other supplies, Mar. 20, 1862-Oct. 7, 1863 (ch. IV, vols. 73 and 74), and a record of supplies, May 1862-July 1863 (ch. V, vol. 143), are available.

A few other brief records exist. Some requisitions for supplies and materials are in the form of brief letters sent by the superintendent, Sept. 23, 1862-Dec. 18, 1863 (ch. IV, vol. 66). Stubs of orders for articles, June 13, 1864-Mar. 24, 1865 (ch. IV, vol. 61 3/4), show the name of the person or firm from whom ordered, the kinds of articles, and the quantity. A master builder's department foreman's tool book, 1863-64 (1 vol.), shows the kinds, number, and value of tools received from the military storekeeper and the number and value of those on hand at different times. Single documents include an inventory of stores and machines in the workshops with a report of operations causing an increase or decrease since the last inventory,

June 30, 1864, and a return of materials and equipment on hand for the fourth quarter of 1864.

Records relating to the pistol department and its predecessor include an undated price book (ch. IV, vol. 55), showing the prices of components and of piece work performed, a record of work performed by or for different companies and persons, n. d. (ch. IV, vols. 56 and 57), a foreman's monthly timebook, Feb. 1864-Jan. 1865 (ch. IV, vol. 54), and a record of pistols fabricated, Oct. 1864-Feb. 1865. There are also timebooks of the pistol works, Sept. 1859- Mar. 1861 (ch. IV, vol. 47), and the Macon Pistol Manufacturing Co., 1863 (ch. IV, vol. 112).

Records in Other Custody. --Manuscripts of James H. Burton concerning his work in producing small arms for the Confederacy and his diary for the period are in Yale University Library (microfilm in the Texas Archives, University of Texas Library).

Macon Arsenal (Ga.)

In 1862 the ordnance laboratory at Savannah was moved to Macon for use with the arms factory of D. C. Hodgkins & Son and the Findlay Iron Works, which had been leased and converted as an arsenal. The arsenal fabricated and repaired field artillery, accoutrements, and edged weapons, and ammunition was made at the laboratory. The arsenal also stored powder for the Confederate Navy.

The commander of this arsenal was Capt. Richard M. Cuyler.

Record Group 109. --Correspondence and other records of the Macon Arsenal are in the War Department Collection of Confederate Records. There are press copies of letters sent, Apr. 4-17, 1865 (ch. IV, vol. 32), to Col. G. W. Rains, Col. J. H. Burton, Capt. J. W. Mallet, other Army officers, industrial firms, and Lt. Augustus McLaughlin, C. S. N., at Columbus, Ga. The telegrams in a press copy book of telegrams sent, May 9, 1862-Apr. 19, 1865 (ch. IV, vol. 101), are addressed mainly to Army officers, including the Chiefs of the Bureau of Ordnance and the Niter and Mining Bureau. A letters-received file, May-Oct. 1862 (ch. IV, vols. 3, 4, 6, and 36), contains letters from the same category of correspondents. A letters-sent book of the military storekeeper, Nov. 20, 1862-Jan. 12, 1864 (ch. IV, vol. 33), contains fair copies of communications from Richard Lambert to the Chief of Ordnance at Richmond, commanding officers of arsenals, other Army officers, industrial firms, the Assistant Treasurer at Charleston, and the depositary at Augusta. An order book, Sept. 19, 1862-May 12, 1863 (ch. IV, vol. 7), contains AIGO general and special orders and orders of the headquarters of the Department of South Carolina and Georgia concerning personnel, instructions and orders from the Ordnance Bureau, and circulars and memoranda of the Central Laboratory.

Other records relate to work performed, employees, equipment, and stores. Among these are a record of machine and other work performed, July-Dec. 1862 (ch. IV, vols. 21 and 22), a foreman's monthly timebook, Nov. 1863-Sept. 1864 (ch. IV, vol. 48), an inventory of tools and machines, 1863-64 (ch. IV, vol. 39), some daily reports of ordnance and ordnance stores on hand, Mar. 13, 1863-July 4, 1864 (ch. IV, vol. 58), receipts for ordnance stores, Jan. 23, 1864-Feb. 28, 1865 (ch. IV, vol. 83), stubs of orders for supplies obtained by the military storekeeper, Nov. 28, 1863-Apr. 1, 1865 (ch. IV, vol. 61 1/4), an inventory of ordnance and ordnance stores on hand, Jan. 1, 1864 (ch. IV, vol. 59 1/2), and a record of clothing and shoes issued to detailed soldiers and slaves, 1864-65 (ch. IV, vol. 60).

Macon Central Laboratory (Ga.)

After a visit to arsenals and laboratories in the southernmost part of the Confederacy in the summer of 1862, John W. Mallet, a chemist who had been employed by the Bureau of Ordnance, recommended establishing an ordnance laboratory at Macon. After receiving the necessary instructions from Lieutenant Colonel Gorgas, Mallet selected a site near Macon, and construction of the laboratory buildings was begun toward the end of the year. Like the armory buildings at Macon, these were intended to be large permanent structures, but they were only partially completed. Improving the quality of gunpowder and other pyrotechnics manufactured by Confederate ordnance laboratories was the objective of the Central Laboratory.
The commander of this laboratory was Col. John W. Mallet.

Walter A. Harris, "By Right of Conquest; the Confederate Laboratory at Macon," Georgia Bar Journal, 10:428-436 (May 1948); John W. Mallet, "Memoranda of My Life for My Children," manuscript in the University of Virginia Library; [John W. Mallet,] "Work of the Confederate Ordnance Bureau," Southern Historical Society Papers, 37:1-20 (1909); Vandiver, Gorgas, passim.

Record Group 94. --In Dec. 1899 the War Department received some Confederate military papers from John W. Mallet, who was then a member of the faculty of the University of Virginia. Some of these papers and a catalog of those received are in Record and Pension Office document file no. 568,231. They include correspondence between Mallet and Josiah Gorgas; letters and telegrams from ordnance officers; reports on experiments with powder, fuses, and artillery; a report of the board appointed to inquire into the causes of an explosion that occurred in the laboratory on Brown's Island, Richmond, in 1863; printed rules and examination questions for candidates for appointments in the artillery corps as ordnance officers; a report of operations of the laboratory department of the Augusta Arsenal, Apr. 1, 1864; and a list of the number and calibers of guns in the Department of the Gulf, Sept. 24, 1863. Plans or drawings of fuses, shell, a 30-pounder Parrot, and a 30-pounder rifled gun are in a separate container.
Record Group 109. --Correspondence and other records of the Central Laboratory are in the War Department Collection of Confederate Records. Letters-sent books, May 27, 1862-Apr. 12, 1864 (ch. IV, vols. 24 and 28), contain fair copies of outgoing communications. Letters of May-Oct. 1862 were written from Richmond and other points in the South where Major Mallet inspected arsenals and laboratories; letters from Macon begin on Oct. 7. The letters are addressed to Josiah Gorgas, Isaac M. St. John, commanders of arsenals and ordnance depots, industrial, mining, and business companies, superintendents of Niter and Mining Bureau districts, ordnance officers, quartermasters, commissaries, Col. W. M. Wadley, railroad presidents and agents, and slaveowners. These books also contain advertisements for proposals, consolidated returns of chemical laboratory stores on hand at arsenals, circulars sent to ordnance laboratories, and drawings as enclosures. There are also some fair copies of telegrams sent, Oct. 28, 1863-Apr. 17, 1865 (ch. IV, vol. 52), addressed to many of

those mentioned above. Letters and telegrams received, June 23, 1862-
Apr. 3, 1865 (ch. IV, vols. 5, 37, and 38), are from the above correspondents and from military officials of the State of Georgia, the headquarters
of the District of Georgia, and private individuals. Besides original letters
from the Chief of the Bureau of Ordnance there are letters written to him
by officers and others regarding inventions, powder, and cartridges. Letters and telegrams sent by the military storekeeper (W. H. McMain), Apr.
9, 1863-Apr. 14, 1865 (ch. IV, vol. 25, p. 202-260, and vols. 26, 27, and
34), are to Josiah Gorgas, commanding officers of ordnance works, businessmen, slaveowners, quartermasters, Niter and Mining Bureau officers,
and others.

Other records concern the administration of the laboratory, its personnel, and work performed. There are incomplete files of general orders,
Sept. 1, 1864-Mar. 8, 1865 (ch. IV, vol. 51), and special orders, Aug. 24,
1864-Apr. 8, 1865 (ch. IV, vol. 50). There is a return of hired men, Dec.
1862-Mar. 1865 (ch. IV, vol. 102); and in the same volume there are statements of appropriation receipts and expenditures, 1862-64, a rent roll of
quarters belonging to the Central Laboratory, Sept. 1864-Mar. 1865, a
statement of ordnance and ordnance stores sold to officers and contractors,
Sept.-Oct. 1864 and Jan.-Mar. 1865, and a statement of the tax in kind
received, 1864. A roll book of white employees, 1864-65 (ch. IV, vol. 43),
contains names, occupation, status (e.g., conscript, exempt, detailed,
medical disability, civilian), rate of pay, and information on leave, furlough, resignation, or desertion. A record of details, 1863-65 (ch. IV, vol.
71), shows name, rank or status, age, occupation, by whom detailed, dates
and expiration of detail, and sometimes additional information on renewal
of detail, relief for disability, and release to the Army. Daily reports of
operations, Mar. 2, 1863-Aug. 20, 1864 (ch. IV, vol. 59), show the number of employees present each day and the number and types of small arms
and field ammunition worked on, completed, issued or expended, and on
hand. An incompletely identified record of articles fabricated, Jan. 1863-
Apr. 1865 (ch. IV, vol. 121), may be a record of the Central Laboratory.
A record of tools and machines manufactured, Jan. 1863-Feb. 1865 (ch. IV,
vol. 64), shows for quarters the quantity, value, and kind of articles made.

Records of articles received, delivered, purchased, or issued usually show the kinds and quantities of articles, from whom received, or to
whom issued or delivered. These records include a record of receipts and
deliveries, Dec. 23, 1861-Feb. 11, 1862 (ch. IV, vol. 62), orders from the
superintendent to the military storekeeper to issue supplies, Sept. 28, 1864-
Apr. 14, 1865 (ch. IV, vols. 61 and 61 1/2), a record of articles received
from other ordnance officers, Nov. 17, 1862-Apr. 5, 1865 (ch. IV, vol. 45),
and a record of the issue of supplies to other ordnance officers, Dec. 8,
1862-Apr. 11, 1865 (ch. IV, vol. 44). The last volume contains also a list
of stores lost as a result of moving laboratory property on the approach of
Union forces in Nov. 1864.

Other records concern supplies, materials, tools, equipment, provisions, and other articles issued to employees of the laboratory and
building materials used for construction purposes. Included are a record
of receipts for articles purchased, Oct. 29, 1862-Dec. 31, 1863 (ch. IV,
vol. 67), a similar record for Dec. 10, 1862-Apr. 17, 1865 (ch. IV, vol.
111), an account book of articles purchased, July 1863-Feb. 1865 (ch. IV,
vol. 103), a ledger of accounts for materials and manufactured products,
Oct. 1863-Mar. 1865 (ch. IV, vol. 23), a record of "issues for expenditure

and use, " Oct. 29, 1862-Apr. 12, 1865 (ch. IV, vol. 41), and a record of "general issues, " Oct. 31, 1864-Apr. 17, 1865 (ch. IV, vol. 63).

A record of experiments with copper in the manufacture of percussion caps is in the form of a letter from Lt. James C. Calhoun to J. W. Mallet, Apr. 1, 1865 (ch. IV, vol. 70), and is accompanied by a brief report on the effects of the recoil on india-rubber blocks behind the trunnions of field guns.

Montgomery Arsenal (Ala.)

An arsenal was in operation at Montgomery by the end of 1861. Its shops repaired small arms and made leather equipment. The commander of this arsenal was Maj. C. G. Wagner. No records of this arsenal have been found.

Mount Vernon Arsenal (Ala.)

On Jan. 4, 1861, Alabama troops seized the U.S. Arsenal at Mount Vernon. After its transfer to the Confederacy in the spring of 1861, it was used to repair small arms and make ammunition. After the fall of New Orleans in 1862 the Mount Vernon Arsenal was moved to Selma, Ala. The commander of this arsenal was Capt. James L. White. No records of this arsenal have been found.

Nashville Arsenal (Tenn.)

This arsenal operated during 1861-62. In Dec. 1861 the ordnance depot was destroyed by fire, and in Feb. 1862 the arsenal was moved to Atlanta, Ga. The commander of this arsenal was Lt. M. H. Wright.

Record Group 109.--Press copies of letters and telegrams sent, Dec. 23, 1861-Feb. 16, 1862 (ch. IV, vol. 8), are to the Chief of Ordnance at Richmond, commanding officers of arsenals, ordnance officers and other Army officers, and industrial and business firms. There are press copies of letters sent regarding invoices for ordnance stores, Dec. 25, 1861-Feb. 14, 1862 (ch. IV, vol. 9). A contract book, Jan. 9-10, 1862 (ch. IV, vol. 78), contains copies of contracts for the manufacture of ordnance stores, and there are invoices, 1861 (ch. IV, vol. 80), for ordnance stores, lumber, and office supplies, with quantities and prices. A timebook of the percussion cap factory, June 29, 1861-Feb. 10, 1862 (ch. IV, vol. 124), contains a weekly record of employees. A list of ordnance and ordnance stores purchased, Sept. 25-Dec. 28, 1861 (ch. IV, vol. 19, p. 1-36), shows the voucher number, the firm from which purchased, date, the kind and quantity of articles purchased, and the total cost.

Other volumes, similar to the above, relate to both the Nashville and Atlanta arsenals. An account book of the percussion cap factory at the Nashville and Atlanta arsenals, 1861-62 (ch. IV, vol. 80 1/2), shows the number of percussion caps delivered, Sept. 23, 1861-Feb. 10, 1862, the number of pistol caps delivered, Nov. 20, 1861-Feb. 10, 1862, and materials received and delivered, Dec. 6, 1861-June 30, 1862. A cashbook of the Nashville and Atlanta arsenals, Jan. 2-May 7, 1862 (ch. IV, vol. 100), contains a record of salary payments to employees and payments to firms and persons for a variety of materials, equipment, and services. There are records of ordnance, ordnance stores, and other materials received and issued, Dec. 1861-Apr. 1862 (ch. IV, vols. 104 and 105), and some original invoices for ordnance stores and other supplies purchased, Apr. 1861-Aug. 1862 (ch. IV, vol. 80).

New Orleans Arsenal (La.)

The New Orleans Arsenal manufactured small-arms ammunition and served as a depot for ordnance stores during 1861-62.
The military storekeeper was Richard Lambert.
Record Group 109.--A letters-sent book, Dec. 21, 1861-Feb. 20, 1862 (ch. IV, vol. 144), contains fair copies of communications sent by Lambert to commanding officers of Louisiana forts, quartermasters, the Chief of the Bureau of Ordnance, and other Army officers.

Richmond Armory (Va.)

After the outbreak of war the State of Virginia began remodeling the old Virginia State Armory, a two-story brick structure at the southern end of Fifth Street between the James River and the canal. In June 1861 the armory was turned over to the Confederate Government, machinery from Harpers Ferry arsenal was installed, and in September the manufacture of rifle-muskets began. Early in 1863 the Confederate Government bought the S. C. Robinson Arms Manufactory and continued to make carbines with its machinery. The Richmond Armory manufactured rifle-muskets, muskets, and carbines, and repaired weapons retrieved from Virginia battlefields.
Successive commanders of this arsenal:
Lt. Col. James H. Burton, 1861.
Capt. Benjamin Sloan, Oct. 1862.
Maj. William S. Downer, 1862.
Maj. Frank F. Jones, Feb. 22, 1864.
Record Group 109.--Records of the Richmond Armory in the War Department Collection of Confederate Records include a record of the receipt of muskets altered from flint to percussion, Sept. 6-Nov. 30, 1861 (ch. IV, part of vol. 116), a timebook, July 1862-Apr. 1865 (ch. IV, part of vol. 116), a record of arms issued, July 1862-June 1863 (ch. IV, vol. 116 1/2), and stubs of orders for the shipment of ordnance and ordnance stores, Apr. 20-May 10, 1861 (ch. IV, vol. 109 1/2). An account book of supplies purchased, June-Oct. 1861 (ch. IV, vol. 95), also contains lists of arms and accoutrements on hand and arms received.

Richmond Arsenal (Va.)

The Richmond Arsenal was on Byrd Island at the foot of Seventh Street in several large buildings formerly used as tobacco warehouses. This large establishment made and/or distributed large quantities of ordnance and ordnance stores, chiefly to the Army of Northern Virginia. It received and issued guns and fieldpieces made by the Tredegar Iron Works, infantry and cavalry arms made or repaired by the Richmond Armory, ammunition, cartridges, infantry and cavalry accoutrements, edged weapons, and other equipment. The laboratory on Brown's Island at the foot of Seventh Street prepared ammunition for small arms and field artillery. The commanders of the ordnance depot included Maj. W. S. Downer, Capt.

A. W. Lawrence, Capt. O. W. Edwards, and Capt. James Dinwiddie.
The artillery store which issued field artillery and equipment was under
Capt. J. Wilcox Brown in 1863. Maj. Smith Stansbury had charge of the
artillery workshops in 1862.

    Successive commanders of this arsenal:
        Capt. Briscoe G. Baldwin, 1861.
        Lt. Col. Smith Stansbury, June 1862.
        Lt. Col. William L. Broun, June 1863.

    Record Group 109. --Letters and telegrams sent by the officers in
charge of the ordnance depot, Nov. 8, 1862-Jan. 30, 1864 (ch. IV, vol. 90,
fair copies), Apr. 20, 1864-Mar. 31, 1865 (ch. IV, vols. 91, 91 1/2, and
92, press copies), are to the Chief of Ordnance in Richmond, the Niter and
Mining Bureau, the Commissary General of Subsistence, the Quartermaster
General, railroad officials and agents, the superintendent of the Ordnance
Harness Shops at Clarksville, Va., the commander of the Richmond Arsenal, commanding officers of arsenals and ordnance depots, industrial
firms, ordnance officers and agents, quartermaster and other Army
officers, tanneries, navy ordnance officers (John M. Brooke and George
Minor), enrolling officers, the head of the Railroad Bureau, the Second
Auditor, and the Treasurer, C.S.A. An incomplete file of letters and
telegrams received, Mar. 1864-Jan. 1865 (ch. IV, vols. 93 and 94),
contains letters addressed to Capt. James Dinwiddie by most of those
listed above. A daybook of materials purchased by the ordnance depot, Nov. 11, 1861-Mar. 31, 1862 (ch. IV, vol. 96), shows the name of firm
or person, kind and quantity of materials, price, and notations as to payment. An abstract of contracts made by the ordnance depot, Sept. 1862-
June 1863 (ch. IV, vol. 96, p. 238-433), shows the contractor's name, the
kinds of stores, materials, and equipment contracted for, price, date of
delivery, and quantity delivered. Invoices of ordnance and ordnance stores,
Jan. 1-Mar. 5, 1862 (ch. IV, vol. 108 1/2), consist of printed forms showing the kind and quantity of stores turned over by Military Storekeeper O
W. Edwards to Capt. D. H. Wood for transportation to other named officers.
A timebook, Jan. 1863-Apr. 1865 (ch. IV, vol. 99), supplies an employment
record of women, showing names, days worked during the month, total
number of days, and pay. A miscellaneous record book of the ordnance
depot (ch. IV, vol. 97) contains the following: a record of requisitions for
articles to be furnished to the different departments of the arsenal, Nov.
1861-Sept. 1862; a record of orders on commercial firms for supplies and
materials, Jan. 13-June 1862; lists of soldiers detailed to contractors, Apr.-
June 1863; several agreements for the manufacture of leather, Mar.-Aug.
1862; an account with O. H. Chalkley for finishing leather, Mar.-June 1862,
and requisitions for materials for the Ordnance Harness Shops at Clarksville, Oct. 2, 1862-Jan. 12, 1863.

    Records in Other Custody. --Papers of W. L. Broun relating to his
Confederate Army service are in the Southern Historical Collection in the
University of North Carolina Library.

Salisbury Arsenal (N.C.)

    A foundry was in operation at Salisbury in 1863. AIGO General Order
70 of Aug. 29, 1864, designated the foundry, blacksmith shops, and laboratory as the Salisbury Arsenal. The arsenal made Parrott shells and horseshoes.

The commander of the foundry in 1863 was Capt. A. G. Brenizer. No records of this arsenal have been found.

Savannah Arsenal (Ga.)

AIGO General Order 42 of Apr. 14, 1864, designated the ordnance depot at Savannah, which had hitherto been regarded as a field depot under the command of the district commander, as an arsenal subject to the supervision of the Chief of Ordnance in Richmond. Its payroll indicates that it included a foundry, laboratory, magazine, warehouse, carpenter shop, blacksmith shop, gunsmith shop, and machine shop. The arsenal was operational until the evacuation of Savannah in Dec. 1864.
Successive commanders of this arsenal:
Capt. Richard M. Cuyler, 1861.
Lt. Col. John C. Moore, Apr. 1864.
Maj. W. V. Taylor, Sept. 1864.
Record Group 109.--A letters-sent press copy book, Oct. 8, 1861-May 5, 1862 (ch. IV, vol. 139), contains letters to the Chief of Ordnance in Richmond, commanding officers of arsenals, railroads, Gov. Joseph E. Brown, ordnance officers and ordnance agents, other Army officers, and industrial and business firms. A file of original letters received, Aug. 25, 1861-Apr. 1862 (ch. IV, vols. 134-138), includes letters from the same correspondents, from commanders of batteries, forts, and camps, from the headquarters of the 2nd Military District of the Department of Georgia, from the Savannah Naval Station, from the Second Auditor (W. H. S. Taylor) and the Treasurer, C. S. A. (E. C. Elmore). Letters received by Captain Cuyler at Savannah during Apr. 22-May 19, 1862, are in the Macon Arsenal letters-received file (ch. IV, vol. 36). A volume of orders and circulars, Aug. 29, 1861-Sept. 19, 1862 (ch. IV, vol. 140), includes orders from the Department of Georgia at Savannah, orders of the Bureau of Ordnance for the distribution of stores, AIGO general and special orders, and letters from the Chief of Ordnance in Richmond concerning work to be done or ordnance stores to be distributed.
Records in Other Custody.--In the Georgia Historical Society collections is a roll of conscripts and civilians employed at the Savannah Ordnance Depot, Feb. 1, 1864, showing employees' names, occupations, and places to which assigned.

Selma Arsenal (Ala.)

The Selma Arsenal probably began in 1862 as an ordnance depot. Buildings were constructed or remodeled and equipped with machinery for the manufacture of arms, ammunition, and equipment.
Successive commanders of this arsenal:
Capt. James L. White, 1862.
Comdr. James L. Henderson, C. S. N., Aug. 1862.
Maj. Nathaniel R. Chambliss, Oct. 1862.
Lt. Col. James L. White, Mar. 1863.
Lt. Col. John C. Moore, Sept. 1864.
No records of this arsenal have been found.

Tallassee Armory (Ala.)

   In the fall of 1864 the machinery for making carbines was moved from the Richmond Armory to buildings in Tallassee leased from the Tallassee Manufacturing Co., a textile mill owned by Barnett, Micon & Co. By the end of 1864, 150 workmen were employed in making carbines.
   Successive commanders of this armory:
      Capt. C. P. Bolles, 1864.
      Maj. W. V. Taylor, 1865.
   No records of this armory have been found.

ARMY INTELLIGENCE OFFICE

   On the suggestion of Chap. William A. Crocker of the 14th Virginia Volunteers, the War Department created by General Order 45 of June 26, 1862, the "General Intelligence Office," to collect information regarding the sick and wounded. AIGO Special Order 147 of June 26, 1862, designated Chaplain Crocker as superintendent of the "Army Intelligence Office," the designation by which the new office became known. Information obtained on sick and wounded men in hospitals and on deceased personnel was recorded in large books. A book was kept for each State and the information entered by regiments, battalions, or other independent commands of the Army and the Navy. The information was obtained from reports filed in the Surgeon General's Office and from the records of field commands visited by the superintendent and other persons. The Office supplied information to chaplains, relatives and friends of servicemen, and foreign governments, and exchanged lists of the dead with the U.S. Government. Lists of casualties were published in newspapers. In 1863 an auxiliary branch of the Army Intelligence Office was established in the Trans-Mississippi Department under R. S. Thomas.
   Successive superintendents:
      William A. Crocker, June 26, 1862.
      Robert Gatewood, Dec. 11, 1863.

   William A. Crocker, "The   erate Veteran, 8:118-119 (Mar. 1900).
Army Intelligence Office," Confed-

   The records of this office were destroyed on the evacuation of Richmond on Apr. 2-3, 1865.

   Correspondence of the super-   other documents are in the compiled
intendents is in the records of the   military service records of Confed-
Office of the Secretary of War and   erate general and staff officers.
the Adjutant and Inspector General's   These records are described in chap-
Office and correspondence and   ter XI of this Guide.

BUREAU OF EXCHANGE

   The parole and exchange of prisoners did not become general practice until 1862. Early in that year Brig. Gen. Howell Cobb, C.S.A., undertook negotiations for an exchange cartel. Arrangements were concluded on July 22 by Maj. Gen. Daniel H. Hill, C.S.A., and Maj. Gen. John A. Dix, U.S.A. The cartel provided for the exchange of all prisoners of war including those taken on privateers; the prisoners were to be exchanged "man for man and officer for officer; privateers to be placed upon the footing of officers and men of the Navy." Citizens were to be exchanged only for citizens, and captured sutlers, teamsters, and other civilians were to be exchanged for persons in similar positions. Prisoners were to be discharged on parole within 10 days after capture, and prisoners then held and those taken thereafter were "to be transported to the points mutually agreed upon at the expense of the capturing party." Surplus prisoners were not to be used for military duties until exchanged under the terms of the cartel. Both sides were to supply lists of prisoners discharged and relieved from parole. The exchange points were to be Aiken's Landing below Dutch Gap on the James River and Vicksburg on the Mississippi River, though the commanders of armies could arrange exchanges at other points. To effectuate the agreement each side was to appoint two agents for the exchange of prisoners of war "whose duty it shall be to communicate with each other by correspondence and otherwise, to prepare the lists of prisoners, to attend to the delivery of the prisoners at the places agreed on and to carry out promptly, effectually and in good faith all the details and provisions of the said articles of agreement."

Col. Robert Ould, appointed Confederate agent for the exchange of prisoners in July 1862, made arrangements with the U.S. agent for the exchange of prisoners. Prisoners from Richmond and elsewhere in the South were transported to Aiken's Landing whence they were taken on the U.S. flag-of-truce boat New York to Fort Monroe. Near the end of Sept. 1862, Secretary of War Randolph directed Ould to change the place of delivery to City Point (now a part of Hopewell) farther down the James River. Paroled men were kept in 1862 in a barracks at Petersburg, Va., where in 1863 there was a camp of paroled and exchanged prisoners commanded by Capt. Henry A. Cannon. Discharged prisoners were also assembled at Camp Lee near Richmond. At those places returned Confederate prisoners were paid and prepared for the field, and returned citizens liable for conscription were mustered into Confederate service.

Regular exchanges of prisoners under the cartel were suspended in 1863 when the number of Confederates captured exceeded the number of Union prisoners. But under special arrangements some exchanges took place. On Mar. 19, 1863, the War Department assigned Capt. William H. Hatch to assist Colonel Ould, and in 1864 sick and wounded prisoners were released by both sides. The Confederate Government's proposal for the resumption of exchanges was accepted early in 1865, and exchanges continued until the end of the war.

Exchanges of prisoners were also effected in the west by officers subordinate to Colonel Ould. On Aug. 14, 1862, the War Department designated Maj. N. G. Watts as exchange agent at Vicksburg (later at Mobile). A camp of paroled and exchanged prisoners at Jackson, Miss., was moved about June 1863 to Demopolis, Ala. On Aug. 14, 1863, the War Department assigned Capt. H. A. M. Henderson as assistant commissioner of exchange at Demopolis. He was evidently stationed at Cahaba, Ala., in May 1864. A parole camp for Confederates who had belonged to the Vicksburg and Port Hudson garrisons was established at Enterprise, Miss., in Nov. 1863. Lieutenant Colonel Watts moved his headquarters from Mobile to Jackson in Dec. 1863, but reestablished it at Mobile a few months later.

In Sept. 1863 Colonel Ould sent Maj. Ignatius Szymanski to the Trans-Mississippi Department as assistant agent for exchange with instructions to furnish Ould with corrected lists of paroles of Union prisoners and information about Union prisoners and captures of Confederates, to inform commanders of the proper method of preparing lists of paroles and the importance of forwarding lists of their captures, to hold prisoners when possible and, when not, to deliver them under a flag-of-truce at Vicksburg, and to assist in establishing parole camps. Major Szymanski established his headquarters at Alexandria, La., in Nov. 1863.

Successive agents for the exchange of prisoners:
Col. Robert Ould, July 1862.
Col. William Norris, Apr. 25, 1865.

Reports of Robert Ould as agent of exchange are in Official Records . . . Armies, ser. 2, as follows: Dec. 5, 1863, vol. 6, p. 654-657; May 2, 1864, vol. 7, p. 103-106; Nov. 1, 1864, vol. 7, p. 1078-1080; Nov. 18, 1864, vol. 7, p. 1139-1140. William B. Hesseltine, Civil War Prisons; a Study in War Psychology (Columbus, 1930); Official Records . . . Armies, ser. 2, vols. 4-8, passim; Robert Ould, "Captain Irving and the Steamer 'Convoy'--Supplies for Prisoners," Southern Historical Society Papers, 10:320-328 (July 1882); Morgan A. Powell, "Cotton for the Relief of Confederate Prisoners," Civil War History, 9:24-35 (Mar. 1963).

Record Group 109.--The endorsement book of the agent for the exchange of prisoners, July 15, 1863-Mar. 31, 1865 (ch. IX, vol. 228), gives names of writers of letters received, purport of the letters, date of the action, and endorsement. The writers were U.S. agents of exchange, Army officers, General Winder, former Confederate prisoners, relatives of prisoners, parolees, residents of the North, and others. Muster rolls of captured Confederates who had been paroled and exchanged, Mar. 1, 1863-Mar. 28, 1865 (folded papers, 2 1/2 ft.) give data as to payments made to the soldiers, their military organizations, enlistments, and the places where they were captured. The rolls are for men held at the following parole camps: Camp Lee, Va., Demopolis, Ala., Columbus, Ga., Jackson and Enterprise, Miss., Chattanooga (Camp Direction) and Jonesboro, Tenn., and Petersburg (Camp Lewis), Va. Also in this file is a list of Confederates exchanged at Cumberland Gap on Sept. 17, 1862. A copy of Ould's letters-sent book (described below), obtained by the War Records Office about 1878, is also in this record group. No letters received by the Bureau of Exchange have been found.

A compiled file of correspondence relating to the exchange of prisoners and the treatment of prisoners in Southern prisons, June 1861-Mar. 1865 (2 1/2 in.), consists of documents drawn from the letters received files of the Adjutant and Inspector General's Office, the Office of the Secretary of War, Congress, and the Department of Norfolk. The file contains correspondence between Brig. Gen. Benjamin Huger, commanding the Department of Norfolk, and Maj. Gen. John E. Wool, U.S.A., commanding the Department of Virginia, and the Secretary of War, correspondence between Brig. Gen. Howell Cobb and General Wool, and letters of Robert Ould, Brig. Gen. Gideon J. Pillow, and Jefferson Davis to the House of Representatives, Apr. 20 and Dec. 7, 1863. There are also notices, orders, and reports regarding the exchange of prisoners and reports and recommendations concerning prisons.

Other letters of Ould are in the correspondence file of the Office of the Secretary of War and the Adjutant and Inspector General's Office. Some of Ould's correspondence was published during the war; see C. S. A. Bureau of Exchange, Official Correspondence between the Agents of Exchange, Together with Mr. Ould's Report (Richmond, 1864). Correspondence of Ould is also in S. E. Doc. 17, 38 Cong., 1 sess., serial 1176 (Washington, 1864), and H. E. Doc. 32, 38 Cong., 2 sess., serial 1223 (Washington, 1865). Correspondence on the exchange of prisoners is also in "Report on the Treatment of Prisoners of War, by the Rebel Authorities, During the War of the Rebellion, " H. Rep. 45, 40 Cong., 3 sess., serial 1391 (Washington, 1869). Much of Ould's correspondence is in Official Records . . . Armies, ser. 2, vols. 4-8, passim. The records of the U. S. Commissioner of Exchange in Record Group 249 contain correspondence with the Confederate Agent for the Exchange of Prisoners.

Records in Other Custody. --The letters-sent book of the agent of exchange, Nov. 29, 1862-Mar. 31, 1865 (1 vol.), is in the Archives Division of the Virginia State Library. It contains fair copies of Robert Ould's letters to the Confederate agents of exchange, the Federal agents of exchange (Lt. Col. William H. Ludlow, Brig. Gen. Sullivan A. Meredith, Maj. John E. Mulford, and Maj. Gen. Ethan A. Hitchcock), Brig. Gen. John H. Winder, Brig. Gen. William M. Gardner, Maj. Gen. Lafayette McLaws, Lt. Gen. Edmund Kirby Smith, the Confederate Secretary of War, Lt. Gen. U. S. Grant, President Davis, Assistant Secretary of War John A. Campbell, Stephen R. Mallory, Maj. Gen. Leonidas Polk, Zebulon B. Vance, and others. A scrapbook of Col. William Norris in the University of Virginia Library contains a few letters of Apr. 1865 regarding the exchange of prisoners. Capt. James R. Curell's correspondence, 1864-65, while assistant exchange agent at Mobile, Ala., is in the Louisiana State Museum, New Orleans, La. Orders, Apr.-May 1865, of the paroled prisoners headquarters at Demopolis and Enterprise, Miss., are in the Chicago Historical Society collections.

The papers, Oct. 1864-Sept. 1865, of Brig. Gen. William N. R. Beall, C. S. A., relating to his activities as agent to supply Confederate prisoners of war in Northern prisons are in the Confederate Museum. They include correspondence, orders, and instructions concerning the shipment of cotton from Mobile and its sale in New York; letters from U. S. provost marshals general regarding the disposition to be made of supplies for prisoners of war; letters from committees of distribution at prisons with certificates on the distribution of supplies; statements of prisoners of war; a list of contracts for clothing; abstracts of purchases; memoranda of telegrams sent by Beall, Dec. 1864-Feb. 1865; correspondence with Maj. Gen. Halbert E. Paine; letters and bills on purchases in Baltimore; and records of the distribution of the supplies.

A calendar and description of the Beall papers is in Douglas S. Freeman, A Calendar of Confederate Papers, p. 73-125 (Richmond, 1908).

BUREAU OF CONSCRIPTION

The slowdown of volunteering in the winter of 1861-62 and losses of men in military action during the spring of 1862 necessitated the adoption of a national conscription act on Apr. 16, 1862 (1 Cong. C.S.A. Stat. 29). This act authorized the President to call up all resident white men between the ages of 18 and 35 for 3-year terms, bound men within those ages then in the Army to serve for 3 years, and allowed military organizations with enlistment terms of 12 months to reorganize and elect their own officers. With a direct call from the central Government, the part of the States in the recruitment of soldiers was downgraded. In 1862 the age limit was raised to 45, and in 1864 the lower limit was 17; an act of 1864 also authorized the enrollment of men between 45 and 50 in State Reserves for local defense and detail duty. In 1864 the enrollment of free Negroes and the employment of 20,000 slaves for auxiliary service was authorized. The number of men enrolled under the foregoing acts was greatly reduced, however, by legislative provision for substitutes and exemptions, and the number of those on active duty was decreased by details for industrial work.

The Adjutant and Inspector General's Office administered the conscription service initially, but the work increased so rapidly that on Dec. 30, 1862 (AIGO General Order 112), the Adjutant and Inspector General announced the establishment of a Bureau of Conscription and directed that all reports, returns, and communications from commandants of camps of instruction were to be addressed to that Bureau. In 1863 Lt. Col. A. C. Jones and Capt. Peyton N. Page were attached to the Bureau, and in the next year Lt. Col. Edward D. Blake was referred to as its registrar. Maj. Heros Von Borcke and Col. Thomas P. August also served in the Bureau. Near the end of 1864 Lt. Col. George W. Lay was designated as inspector-general of conscription to supervise the activities of inspectors of conscription who would be appointed for each State.

The Bureau of Conscription directed the activities of enrolling officers and commandants of conscripts. It prepared instructions in the form of AIGO general and special orders and Bureau circulars. It passed upon applications for exemptions and details forwarded by the county enrolling offices and received reports and kept records regarding enrollment, exemptions, and details. Its authority did not extend west of the Mississippi River where conscription was under the direction of the commanding general of the Trans-Mississippi Department. In Jan. 1863 Gen. Joseph E. Johnston was given jurisdiction over conscription in the Western Department embracing Tennessee, Alabama, and Mississippi.

By early 1865 the authority of the Bureau of Conscription was pretty generally disregarded, and the use of force was necessary to get enrollees to report at camps and to collect deserters and absentees from the army. An act of Mar. 7, 1865 (Ramsdell, Laws and Joint Resolutions, p. 86), abolished the Bureau of Conscription and placed the generals commanding the State Reserves in charge of the enforcement of conscription laws, exemptions, and details. The generals were to report to the Secretary of War through the Adjutant and Inspector General, in whose office was designated on Mar. 29, 1865, an "Officer of Conscription," who was to receive and arrange all returns and perform other duties connected with conscription.

Successive heads of the Bureau:
    Brig. Gen. Gabriel J. Rains, Dec. 30, 1862.
    Brig. Gen. Charles W. Field, May 25, 1863.

WAR DEPARTMENT

Lt. Col. George W. Lay (acting), June 23, 1863.
Col. John S. Preston, July 30, 1863.

Reports of the Bureau of Conscription are in the Official Records . . . Armies, ser. 4, as follows: Aug. 17, 1863, vol. 2, p. 723-726; Apr. 30, 1864, vol. 3, p. 354-364; Feb. 1865, vol. 3, p. 1099-1110. Memory F. Mitchell, Legal Aspects of Conscription and Exemption in North Carolina (Chapel Hill, 1965); Albert B. Moore, Conscription and Conflict in the Confederacy (New York, 1924); William L. Shaw, "The Confederate Conscription and Exemption Acts, " American Journal of Legal History, 6:368-405 (Oct. 1962).

On May 31, 1865, Maj. Robert N. Scott, U. S. A., sent to the War Department from Richmond a box of records relating to the Confederate conscription service. The records became part of the War Department Collection of Confederate Records, and some of them appear to be records of the central office of the Bureau of Conscription in Richmond although its records were reportedly burned at the end of the war.

Record Group 109. --Manuscript and printed circulars issued to commandants of conscripts and of camps of instruction, Feb. 27, 1863-Mar. 21, 1865, and Jan. 13-Dec. 14, 1864 (ch. I, vol. 258). A classification ledger of exemptions, Apr. 1864-Apr. 1865 (ch. I, vol. 254), shows the name of the man exempted, his age, occupation, duties, and date and term of exemption. The exemption classifications include agriculturists, Confederate and State officials, railroad employees, physicians, druggists, ministers, teachers, mail contractors, newspaper employees, and disabled persons. A classification ledger of details, Apr. 1864-Apr. 1865 (ch. I, vol. 255), shows name, age, duties, and date and term of detail. Types of details include agriculturists, tanners, millers, private necessity, blacksmiths, shoemakers, wheelwrights, Government bureaus, artisans and mechanics, contractors to furnish supplies, and telegraph companies. A ledger of details, Oct. 1864-Mar. 1865 (ch. I, vol. 259), shows name, to whom detailed, department in which detailed, official authorizing the detail, and date and term of detail. A record of payments for exemptions, Mar. 1862-Dec. 1864 (ch. I, vol. 262), shows the date, amount, by whom and to whom paid, cause of exemption, and residence of those paying for exemption. A register of applications for leaves of absence, transfers, and examinations by medical boards, Oct. 1, 1864-Jan. 12, 1865 (ch. I, vol. 246), shows name of applicant, his military organization or station, nature of the application, and date of action. A record of details delivered and papers filed, Nov. 1864 (ch. I, vol. 249), contains only a few entries.

A few lists of conscription and enrolling officers, 1863-65, show the organization of the commandant's office in Richmond on Dec. 15, 1863, and Dec. 19, 1864; in Albemarle County, Va., on Feb. 28, 1865; in Petersburg, Va., in Mar. 1865; in the State of Mississippi, n. d.; and in the Departments of Tennessee and Alabama, Mississippi, and East Louisiana in Jan. 1863. A few abstracts of payments made and accounts current of the quartermaster (Maj. George F. Maynard) at Camp Lee, Va., Sept.-Oct. 1864, and Jan.-Feb. 1865, show the names of officers and men stationed there to whom payments were made and the amounts paid. Another abstract of expenditures on the quartermaster's account shows the payments made by Capt. George B. Baker at Camp Holmes, N. C., during the quarter ending Dec. 31, 1863.

Correspondence of the heads of the Bureau of Conscription, of commandants of conscripts, of enrolling officers, and of other conscription officers is in the records of the Office of the Secretary of War and the Office of the Adjutant and Inspector General. Correspondence and other documents are in the compiled military service records of Confederate officers described in chapter XI of this Guide. Conscription officers corresponded with State authorities and with Confederate military and naval authorities, whose records should therefore be consulted. Among the records of the Adjutant and Inspector General's Office are inspection reports relating to the conscription service and camps of instruction. Correspondence, orders, circulars, and other documents relating to conscription are in Official Records . . .Armies, ser. 4, vols. 1-3. Letters Oct. 18-Dec. 18, 1864, of John S. Preston to James A. Seddon, President Davis, and John A. Campbell are in Rowland, ed., Jefferson Davis, 6:362-383, 422-423.

Records in Other Custody. --In the Emmett collection at the New York Public Library is a book containing abstracts of letters received and sent by the Bureau of Conscription, Oct. 27, 1863-Mar. 18, 1865. The letters are from enrolling officers and inhabitants of Tennessee and include petitions for exemption and applications from ironworks for details of mechanics; abstracts of letters sent are also entered in the book.

State Conscription Offices

The field organization for the enrollment and disposition of recruits was prescribed by AIGO General Order 30 of Apr. 28, 1862. Officers not below the rank of major were to be detailed for each State "to take charge of the enrollment, mustering in, subsistence, transportation, and disposition of the recruits . . ." The conscription act allowed the use of State officers for enrollment purposes, but on assuming charge of the Bureau of Conscription Colonel Preston found that they had been dilatory about forming the conscription organization and he began replacing them with Confederate officers. Commissioned officers were assigned to Congressional districts, and noncommissioned officers or privates to counties, cities, towns, districts, or parishes (AIGO General Order 82, Nov. 3, 1862). Officers and men disabled by wounds and acquainted with the localities where they were to serve were to be selected; individual assignments were made by AIGO special orders. The commissioned officer in each district superintended the enrollment and collection of conscripts. Enrolling officers prepared monthly rolls of conscripts, supervised boards of investigation that examined applications for exemption or detail, and arrested deserters and delivered them to the nearest camp of instruction. By the end of 1863 the conscription organization had been extended to all areas of the Confederacy.

An act of Oct. 11, 1862 (1 Cong. C.S.A. Stat. 75), authorized the establishment of rendezvous in cities, counties, parishes, or districts where enrollees were to be examined under regulations issued by the Secretary of War. Three surgeons who were to constitute examining boards were to be assigned to each Congressional district in the States. The rendezvous were established, but it was found inconvenient to hold them in all the prescribed places and enrollees were obliged to go longer distances for examination.

No more than two camps of instruction were to be established in each State, except by special permit (AIGO General Order 30, Apr. 28, 1862). Commandants were to apportion recruits among military organizations in existence on Apr. 16, 1862. An act of Oct. 8, 1862 (1 Cong. C. S. A. Stat. 69), provided legislative authority for the camps of instruction by empowering the President to establish them and to appoint officers in the Provisional Army to command them. AIGO General Order 82 of Nov. 3, 1862, announced that a commandant of conscripts who would be responsible for the enrollment and disposition of recruits would be appointed for each State. He was to recommend officers for appointment as his subordinates and the commandant of the other camp, if one was to be established. The commandants of conscripts east of the Mississippi River were to receive orders from the War Department only and not from department or army commanders. Commandants of conscripts west of the Mississippi were to report to and receive instructions from the commanding general of the Trans-Mississippi Department, who was to send consolidated monthly reports to the Adjutant and Inspector General. The commandants were to "distribute the conscripts of the state among its regiments, battalions, and companies thereof, in proportion to their respective deficiencies."

The appointment of commandants of conscripts and the establishment of camps of instruction began in the spring of 1862. By June 1862 commandants had been appointed in Virginia, North Carolina, South Carolina, Georgia, Alabama, Louisiana, and Texas, and camps of instruction had been established in most of those States. Officers and surgeons were assigned to the commandants for duty at the camps or for assignment as enrolling officers. By the beginning of 1863 commandants had been appointed in each State, and camps of instruction had been or were being established in each State. AIGO General Order 73 of Sept. 22, 1864, placed generals of State Reserves in control of the commandants of conscripts, the camps of instruction, and the enrolling officers in their respective States. It required all officers and men employed in the enrolling service who had not been retired or assigned to light duty by medical boards to be relieved by details from the Reserves and sent to the field. The same order provided that all applications for exemption and detail were to be sent to the Bureau of Conscription for decision. The office of Congressional district enrolling officer was abolished, and communications from local enrolling offices were to be sent through the commandants of conscripts to the generals of Reserves, who could assign officers to the Congressional districts as inspecting officers.

The conscription service that was organized throughout the Confederacy employed thousands of men. In Virginia there were enrolling officers in charge of each of the 13 Congressional districts and subordinate to them were the enrolling officers in 65 counties and Richmond and Charles City. In Dec. 1863 the organization in Virginia comprised 943 men including 676 in the conscript mounted guard.

The commandants of conscripts were as follows: Alabama: Maj. William G. Swanson and Lt. Col. H. C. Lockhart; Florida: Maj. S. St. George Rogers and Col. William Miller; Georgia: Maj. John Dunwody, Lt. Col. John B. Weems, and Col. William M. Browne; Kentucky: Maj. J. C. Johnston; Mississippi: Maj. D. O. Merwin, Maj. J. C. Denis, Maj. Thomas J. Hudson, and Capt. William Wren; Missouri: Maj. William C. Price; North Carolina: Col. Peter Mallett; South Carolina: Lt. Col. John S. Preston and Maj. C. D. Melton; Tennessee: Lt. Col. Edward D. Blake and Maj. J. C.

Johnston; and Virginia: Col. John C. Shields.

Camps of instruction were located in Alabama at Camp Watts (near Notasulga), Talladega, and Tuscumbia; in Florida at Gainesville and Madison; in Georgia at Calhoun, Camp Cooper (Macon), and Camp Randolph (Decatur); in Mississippi at Brookhaven, Enterprise, and Marion Station; in North Carolina at Camp Hill (near Statesville), Camp Holmes (near Raleigh), Camp Stokes, Camp Vance (near Morgantown), Garysburg, and Goldsboro; in South Carolina at Columbia; in Tennessee at Athens, Cleveland, McMinnville, and Strawberry Plains; and in Virginia at Camp Lee, Dublin Station, Petersburg, and Winchester.

Record Group 109.--The most extensive records on the conscription service in a State are those for Virginia. A register of officers and employees of the conscription service, May 1862-Mar. 1865 (ch. I, vol. 257), shows name of officer or employee, rank and organization, station, date of assignment, authority for assignment, and remarks. Statistical reports on conscripts in Virginia, Sept. 1862-Feb. 1865 (ch. I, vol. 250), were submitted by the commandant to the Adjutant and Inspector General's Office and the Reserve Forces of Virginia. There are a record of exemptions, Dec. 1862-Dec. 1863 and Feb.-Mar. 1864 (ch. I, vols. 251 and 244), and a commandant's exemption book, Mar. 1864-Jan. 1865 (ch. I, vols. 242 and 243). A record of officers employing exempted persons, 1863-64 (ch. I, vol. 245), shows the number of persons employed and their occupations. An agricultural exemption book, June 1864-Jan. 1865 (ch. I, vol. 235), shows the name of the person exempted, county, age, physical description, occupation, post office, number of farmhands, amount of supplies, penal sum, date of bond, names of sureties and witnesses, and date of exemption. A record of enlisted men detailed, Jan.-Nov. 1864 (ch. IV, vol. 107), shows the name, age, physical description, birthplace, occupation, by whom enrolled, where enrolled, and how detailed. Lists of details and exemptions, Feb. 17-Aug. 17, 1864 (ch. I, vol. 235 1/2), include a list of persons detailed for agricultural purposes with name of county and names of exempting officers; and a list of exempted persons, showing grounds of exemption. A register of officers' applications for details, July 18-Oct. 5, 1864 (ch. I, vol. 248), shows date, name of person to be detailed, and the nature of the detail. A list of conscripts recommended for discharge under general order 107, Aug.-Sept. 1863 (ch. I, vol. 238), shows the names of physically unfit conscripts, age, place and date of enrollment, and date of discharge or furlough. A record of the enrollment and disposition of conscripts at Camp Lee, Va., Jan.-Aug. 1864 (ch. I, vol. 250 1/2), shows name of conscript, when enrolled, and date and manner of disposition. Special orders for details issued at Camp Lee are dated Jan. 1, 1864-Feb. 22, 1865 (ch. I, vols. 223-229), with a gap for Aug. 25-Oct. 27, 1864. A record of details of free Negroes made at Camp Lee, 1864-65 (ch. I, vol. 240), shows date of detail, name of Negro, to whom detailed, and date of expiration of detail. A register of free Negroes enrolled and assigned, 1864-65 (ch. I, vol. 241), shows name, age, physical description, birthplace and occupation, circumstances of enlistment, and where assigned. There are circulars, received by the enrolling officer (Capt. J. A. Coke) of the Third Congressional District at Richmond (Jan. 21-Dec. 28, 1863), from the Conscript Office there and correspondence, Jan. 23, 1863-Feb. 19, 1864 (1/4 in.), from that office and other correspondents. An abstract of communications received and endorsements of the conscript inspector for Virginia (Capt. W. L. Riddick), Jan. 1864-Jan. 1865 (ch. I, vols. 230-234), shows the date received, name of writer, a brief of the communication, and the endorsement and its date. A miscellaneous record book (ch. I, vol. 239), contains a record of endorsements on reports returned to the enrolling officers, Dec. 3, 1864-Mar. 25, 1865, copies of letters sent to inspectors of conscription and enrolling officers, Nov. 14, 1864-Mar. 28, 1865; reports of exemptions and details; a statistical report on registration; a return of officers on duty, Nov. 23, 1864; and a report on the enrollment of free Negroes.

Volumes for Mississippi include copies of special orders issued by the commandant of conscripts (Majs. J. C. Denis and Thomas J. Hudson), June 1, 1864-May 6, 1864 (ch. I, vol. 222); a record of officers and employees of the commandant's office and of congressional district offices, 1864 (ch. I, vol. 263); a record of exemptions, Apr. 1864-Apr. 1865 (ch. I, vol. 253, and index, vol. 261); a record of details, Apr. 1864-May 1865 (ch. I, vol. 252); and a register of slaves impressed by enrolling officers, 1864-65 (ch. I, vol. 256). These supply information regarding the persons exempted, detailed, and impressed; the third book contains an index to counties.

There are a few telegrams received or sent, July 30-Sept. 10, 1863, by Maj. C. D. Melton, commandant of conscripts at Columbia, S. C.

Records in Other Custody.--The papers of Peter Mallett in the Southern Historical Collection in the University of North Carolina Library include records relating to North Carolina. A letters-sent book of the conscript office at Raleigh, May 19-July 2, 1864, is no. 7 of a series kept by Colonel Mallett, the commandant of conscripts. It contains fair copies of outgoing letters signed mostly by the adjutants in the office and addressed to the commandants at Camp Holmes and Camp Vance, enrolling officers, the Bureau of Conscription in Richmond, other offices of the War Department, and Army officers and State officials in North Carolina. There is a register of letters received by the same office, Feb.-Apr. 1863. A letters-sent press copy book of the commandant of Camp Holmes, June 23, 1862-Jan. 27, 1863, contains letters and telegrams sent by Colonel Mallett, Col. T. P. August, and Capt. L. J. Johnson (after Dec. 1862). The same repository also has some other papers, 1849-88, of Colonel Mallet concerning conscription and other military affairs. Some reports and other documents of enrollment officers of the 7th district, Feb.-June 1864, make up another volume.

Other records relate to South Carolina, Tennessee, and Virginia. In the South Caroliniana Library of the University of South Carolina is a roll book of the enrolling officer of the Orangeburg District of South Carolina, Apr. 1864-Jan. 1865, containing a descriptive list of persons reporting for enrollment, another list of persons enrolled for examination by the medical board, and rolls of persons exempt under the act of Feb. 17, 1864, of conscripts between 18 and 45 years of age, and of conscripts enrolled and detailed. A muster and descriptive roll of Kentucky and Tennessee conscripts, Jan. 1864-Mar. 1865, and a register of correspondence of the conscription office at Bristol, Tenn., are in the Emmett collection at the New York Public Library. The Manuscript Division of the Library of Congress has a few papers, Jan. 1863-May 1864, of Col. J. C. Shields, the commandant of conscripts in Virginia. In 1891 the Virginia Historical Society received as a gift two record books of J. W. G. Smith, the enrolling officer of Rockingham County, Va., 1862-64. These books contain descriptive rolls of conscripts, a descriptive roll of exempts giving the reason for exemption, a list of hands detailed, a roll of conscripts who obtained substitutes, a roll of conscripts sent forward, a list of reserves enrolled in Apr. 1864, a list of exemptions outstanding on Sept. 1, 1864, copies of letters from the Bureau of Conscription consisting largely of circulars and general and special orders embodying instructions and communicating the names of recruiting officers, copies of letters sent by the enrolling officer, and correspondence with the conscript office and the camp of instruction at Richmond, Va. (Camp Lee). The Society also has some records, 1864-65, of the enrolling officer of Scott County, Va., consisting of an enrolling book and papers kept by W. T. Fentress concerning conscripts, exemptions, and desertions; and correspondence, 1863-64, of Capt. John A. Coke, the enrolling officer of the 3d Congressional District, Richmond, Va. Other papers, 1862-65 (1,125 items), of Captain Coke in the New-York Historical Society collections include correspondence, orders, lists, and medical reports.

NITER AND MINING BUREAU

The Confederacy arranged promptly for the procurement of minerals necessary for the manufacture of powder. In 1861, for example, George W. Rains took action on behalf of the Bureau of Ordnance to obtain niter from private limestone works in eastern Tennessee, western Virginia, Alabama, North Carolina, and Georgia. Some of the works were lost as a result of military action, and throughout the war niter was imported from Europe and Mexico. Charcoal made from local woods and sulphur made from pyrites were combined with niter to make powder.

An act of Apr. 11, 1862 (1 Cong. C.S.A. Stat. 27), authorized the organization of a corps of officers for the purpose of procuring a supply of niter. Under the supervision of the Chief of Ordnance, the corps was to inaugurate and prosecute a system for working niter caves, procure niter within the Confederacy, inspect the niter caves and deposits and report the probable annual supply, and establish niter beds near the principal cities and towns.

An act of Apr. 22, 1863 (1 Cong. C.S.A. Stat. 114), placed this corps under an independent bureau of the War Department to be known as the Niter and Mining Bureau and to supervise the mining of other minerals needed for military purposes. The Bureau's superintendent could lease privately owned mines and obtain by contract or otherwise the necessary supplies of ore and coal. An act of June 9, 1864 (2 Cong. C.S.A. Stat. 263), raised the rank of the superintendent to colonel, increased the number of officers in the corps, and authorized the Secretary of War to appoint six chemists and six professional assistants.

Although the artificial niter beds (nitriaries) that were set up did not produce any niter before the end of the war, by the end of 1863 niter production had nearly doubled the output of the previous year. In 1864 important niter works in Virginia, Georgia, and Alabama were destroyed by the enemy, but at the end of Sept. 1864 there were 2,659 workmen at niter works and 633 at nitriaries.

To obtain iron, the Government subsidized the construction of new furnaces and the enlargement of old ones or operated others in Virginia, Alabama, Georgia, and Texas. Coal was mined in Virginia west of Richmond, in the Deep River region of central North Carolina, in Tennessee around Chattanooga, and in central Alabama. Copper mined in the Ducktown Basin of Polk County in southeastern Tennessee was rolled into sheet and bolt copper by the Tennessee Rolling Works at Cleveland, Tenn., and shipped by rail to Richmond and other points. Copper was also mined in Grayson and Carroll Counties, Va. Lead was mined in Wythe County, Va., near Jonesborough, Tenn., and in Davidson County, N.C. Copper and lead were imported from abroad through the blockade. Church bells, turpentine stills, and kettles for boiling sugar supplied copper for conversion into implements of war, and lead water pipes, window weights, and cistern linings were collected for the manufacture of bullets.

Supervision of the activities of the corps was decentralized in the spring of 1862 by dividing the Confederate States into niter districts. These later became niter and mining districts under the Niter and Mining Bureau. A return of officers and professional assistants attached to the bureau on Dec. 31, 1864, shows their assignments as follows:

Niter and Mining Districts

No.	State	Headquarters	Superintendent
1 & 2	Va.	Wytheville	David K. Tuttle
3	Va.	Fincastle	Capt. Robert C. Morton
4	Va.	Union	James B. Noyes
4 1/2	Va.	Staunton	Maj. James F. Jones
5	N.C.	Greensboro	Maj. Charles Barney
6	S.C.	Edgefield Courthouse	Francis S. Holmes
6 1/2	S.C.	Columbia	Joseph LeConte
7	Va.	Wytheville	Maj. T. J. Finnie
8 & 9	Ga. & N. Ala.	Montevallo, Ala.	Capt. William Gabbett
10	Ala.	Montgomery	Maj. William H. C. Price
12	Fla.	Tallahassee	Lt. C. H. Latrobe
14	Ga.	Macon	Henry P. Farrow
--	Trans- Miss.	San Antonio	Maj. Isaac Read

During 1862-63 there was a Niter and Mining District No. 11 with headquarters at Jackson, Miss., under Dr. D. R. Lemman. The return of Dec. 31, 1864, shows that Lt. James H. Mathews was then stationed in Mississippi, but attached to District No. 10.

By the end of 1864 a divisional organization seems to have been imposed on the districts. The 1st Division under Lieutenant Colonel Morton at Richmond controlled the niter and mining service in Virginia, North Carolina, and Tennessee. The 2d Division under Lt. Col. William R. Hunt at Selma, Ala., had charge of the iron and mining service in Alabama, Georgia, and South Carolina. Major Read's office at San Antonio constituted a 3d Division.

The Bureau established a number of special plants. In the spring of 1862, Dr. Aaron S. Piggot supervised the construction at Petersburg, Va., of a works for smelting lead, copper, and zinc. Military operations forced its abandonment in 1864 and John W. Goodwyn who was then the superintendent moved to a new one at Lexington, N.C. Charles H. Winston, another scientist in the employ of the Bureau, was superintendent of the sulphuric acid works at Charlotte, N.C.

Successive heads of the Bureau:

Col. Isaac M. St. John, Apr. 18, 1862.

Col. Richard Morton, Feb. 22, 1865.

Reports of the Niter and Mining Bureau of July 31 and Dec. 3, 1862, and Oct. 1, 1864, are in Official Records . . . Armies, ser. 4, vol. 2, p. 26-30, 222-223, vol. 3, p. 695-702. Robert E. Barclay, Ducktown Back in Raht's Time (Chapel Hill, 1946); Ralph W. Donnelly, "Confederate Copper," Civil War History, 1:355-370 (Dec. 1955), "The Confederate Lead Mines in Wythe County, Va.," ibid., 5:402-414 (Dec. 1959), "Scientists of the Confederate Nitre and Mining Bureau," ibid., 2:69-92 (Dec. 1956); Joseph LeConte, Instructions for the Manufacture of Saltpeter (Columbia, S. C., 1862); George W. Rains, Notes on Making Saltpetre from the Earth of the Caves (Augusta, Ga., 1861); Frank E. Vandiver, "The Shelby Iron Works in the Civil War; a Study of a Confederate Industry," Alabama Review, 1:12-26, 111-127, 203-217 (Jan., Apr., July 1948); Joseph H. Woodward, II, "Alabama Iron Manufacture, 1860-1865," ibid., 7:199-207 (July 1954).

Record Group 109. --Records, Apr. 14, 1862-Apr. 1, 1865 (1/2 in.), of the Niter and Mining Bureau include letters sent and received, a manuscript copy of the Bureau's report of July 31, 1862, a return of the commissioned officers and the scientific arm of the Bureau, Dec. 31, 1864, general and special orders, and a few other documents.

Other War Department records contain material concerning the Niter and Mining Bureau. Correspondence of the heads and other officers of the Bureau is in the letters-sent books and the letters-received files of the Office of the Secretary of War, the Adjutant and Inspector General's Office, and the Quartermaster General's Office. Other materials on the niter and mining districts are among the records of armories, arsenals, and local military commands. Inspection reports of the Adjutant and Inspector General's Office include reports on the mining and manufacturing operations of the Bureau.

Other materials are in the compiled files described in chapter XI of this Guide. The compiled military service records of Confederate general and staff officers contain envelope-jackets (2 ft.) for both commissioned officers and professional assistants attached to the Bureau. Among Confederate papers relating to citizens and business firms are records concerning mines, ironworks and leadworks, niter beds, niter contractors, and professional assistants; also the report made by Socrates Maupin to Col. Josiah Gorgas on the survey of central Alabama in 1862.

Records in Other Custody. --Duke University Library has a small collection of documents, 1861-65, relating to the Bureau. Papers of Thomas G. Clemson who was a superintendent at Shreveport, La., are in Clemson College Library. Joseph LeConte served as a chemist at Columbia, S. C., and as an inspector in the field; his papers are in the Southern Historical Collection in the University of North Carolina Library. His journal (1864-65) and other materials are in the South Caroliniana Library of the University of South Carolina. Letters of Charles W. Slagle, 1863-65, in the same repository concern his services at Franklin, N. C. George W. James, a Bureau employee, kept a notebook regarding the operation of a charcoal furnace; a photostatic copy is in the Archives Division of the Virginia State Library. Letters written by Robert A. Newell while traveling in Texas in the service of the Niter and Mining Bureau are in the Department of Archives of the Louisiana State University.

The dealings of the Niter and Mining Bureau with industrial firms are documented in records of the firms. Records of the Tredegar Iron Works are in the Archives Division of the Virginia State Library and in the University of Virginia Library. The Charles B. Mallett papers, 1862-67, in the Southern Historical Collection in the University of North Carolina relate to the firm of Mallett & Browne, operators of the Egypt coal mine in North Carolina. The Tennessee State Library and Archives has the papers of Julius E. Raht, superintendent of the Ducktown copper mines. Relations between Lt. Col. William R. Hunt, superintendent at Selma, Ala., and the Shelby Iron Company are documented in the company's records in the University of Alabama Library. Certain papers of William Weaver, proprietor of the Bath Iron Works at Buffalo Forge, Va., in Duke University Library concern the procurement of iron by the Confederate Government.

BUREAU OF FOREIGN SUPPLIES

In 1862 the Ordnance Bureau began operating its own blockade-runners between Bermuda and the Bahamas, to which supplies were brought from Europe, and Confederate ports. The War and Navy Departments also negotiated with companies operating blockade-runners for cargo space to carry out cotton and return war supplies. The War Department contracted with Alexander Collie and Company of Liverpool for the importation of Government freight on ships to be obtained by the company, and a blockade-running agreement was concluded with Crenshaw and Company of Richmond. In this way the War Department avoided paying the heavy freight charges levied by private blockade-runners and improved its financial position abroad.

The Ordnance Bureau placed Maj. Thomas L. Bayne in charge of its blockade-runners, and AIGO Special Order 174 of July 23, 1863, designated Major Bayne as the War Department representative in matters connected with the management of the steamers under the Collie contract. Later (AIGO Special Order 259, Oct. 31, 1863) he was also charged with matters connected with private steamers that carried out cotton and other produce and brought in supplies for the Government.

An act of Feb. 6, 1864 (1 Cong. C.S.A. Stat. 181), established Government control over the foreign commerce of the Confederacy. It prohibited the exportation of cotton, tobacco, military and naval stores, molasses, and rice except under regulations to be issued by the President. Another act of the same date prohibited the importation of luxuries. Regulations issued a month later required blockade-runners to allow the Government one-half their cargo space at fixed rates or two-thirds at a somewhat higher rate.

After the adoption of the above acts Lt. Col. Thomas L. Bayne was made the head of an office of the War Department that became known as the Bureau of Foreign Supplies. In addition to the duties assigned him by Special Orders 174 and 259 of 1863, he was to supervise the War Department's trade with Bermuda and the Bahamas and provide cotton to pay for foreign supplies bought by War Department bureaus (AIGO Special Order 64, Mar. 17, 1864). During 1864 large quantities of supplies were imported, but by early 1865 the chief ports on the Atlantic Coast with rail connections had been lost and the Bureau's work was made much more difficult.

Other than those noted below, no records of this Bureau have been found.

Record Group 109. --Copies of contracts made by Bayne, the Quartermaster General, and Thomas A. Harris for the importation of supplies; also related correspondence, Mar. 23, 1864-Mar. 8, 1865 (ch. VIII, vol. 371).

Correspondence of T. L. Bayne is in the records of the Office of the Secretary of War, the Adjutant and Inspector General's Office, and the Quartermaster General's Office. Files relating to Bayne and his associates are in the compiled military service records of Confederate general and staff officers described in chapter XI of this Guide. An autobiographical sketch written by Bayne in 1870 now in the custody of the Southern Historical Collection in the University of North Carolina Library contains information concerning the Bureau, life in New Orleans and Richmond, and relations between Bayne and the Assistant Secretary of War.

OFFICE OF THE COMMISSARY GENERAL OF PRISONERS

The Confederate Government never developed an efficient organization for the care of prisoners of war. An act of May 21, 1861 (Prov. Cong. C.S.A. Stat. 154), provided for the transfer of military and naval prisoners of war to the War Department and directed the Secretary of War to instruct the Quartermaster General to provide for their care. The War Department placed the 1,000 or more prisoners captured at Bull Run under the command of Brig. Gen. John H. Winder, who in June 1861 had been designated provost marshal of Richmond and inspector general of camps near that city. During the early part of the war Richmond became the principal center for the confinement of prisoners of war, and General Winder continued in control of them. He also exercised an undefined supervision over other prisons and received reports from them.

The system of military prisons that evolved was still without specialized direction in 1864. After the transfer of most of the prisoners from Richmond to Georgia, General Winder was assigned to the command of the military prisons in Georgia and Alabama, and Brig. Gen. William M. Gardner at Richmond was assigned to the command of the prisons in the other States east of the Mississippi; both were to receive orders from the Adjutant and Inspector General (AIGO Special Order 175, July 26, 1864). General Winder was later designated Commissary General of Prisoners, with responsibility for the custody, discipline, and administration of all prisoners east of the Mississippi River (AIGO General Order 84, Nov. 21, 1864).
Successive Commissaries General of Prisoners:
Brig. Gen. John H. Winder, Nov. 21, 1864.
Brig. Gen. Gideon J. Pillow, Feb. 14, 1865.
Brig. Gen. William M. Gardner, Mar. 20, 1865.
Brig. Gen. Daniel Ruggles, Mar. 24, 1865.

C.S.A. Congress, Joint Select Committee To Investigate the Condition and Treatment of Prisoners of War, Report . . . (Richmond, 1865); William B. Hesseltine, Civil War Prisons; a Study in War

Psychology (Columbus, 1930); John William Jones, comp., "The Treatment of Prisoners during the War Between the States," Southern Historical Society Papers, 1:113-327 (Mar. 1876); U.S. Congress, Report on the Treatment of Prisoners of War, by the Rebel Authorities, during the War of the Rebellion (H. Rep. 45, 40 Cong., 3 sess., Serial 1391, Washington, 1869); U.S. Judge Advocate General's Office (Army), United States Military Reservations, National Cemeteries, and Military Parks: Title, Jurisdiction, Etc. (Washington, 1916); U.S. Quartermaster's Department, Alphabetic Index to Places of Interment of Deceased Soldiers in the Various States and Territories as Specified in Rolls of Honor No. I-XIII Being Those Issued from the Quartermaster General's Office (Washington, 1868), Roll of Honor: Names of Soldiers Who Died in Defense of the American Union, Interred in National and Other Cemeteries . . . (27 vols.; Washington, 1865-71), Statement of the Disposition of Some of the Bodies of Deceased Union Soldiers and Prisoners of War Whose Remains Have Been Removed to National Cemeteries in the Southern and Western States (4 vols.; Washington, 1868-69); U.S. War Department, Official Records . . . Armies, ser. 2, vols. 1-8; U.S. Christian Commission, Record of the Federal Dead Buried from Libby, Belle Isle, Danville & Camp Lawton Prisons, and at City Point, and in the Field before Petersburg and Richmond (Philadelphia, 1866).

Confederate prison records that were captured by Union officers and forwarded to Washington in 1865 were placed in the custody of the Office of the Commissary General of Prisoners or the Archive Office of the Adjutant General's Office. They were used in supplying information to the Paymaster General, the Commissioner of Pensions, and the Second Auditor; in compiling death and burial records; and in verifying applications for commutation for rations for periods when soldiers were prisoners of war. An order of Aug. 19, 1867, abolished the Office of the Commissary General of Prisoners and transferred records in its custody to the Adjutant General's Office where a Division of Records of Prisoners of War was established. In order to answer inquiries regarding Federal prisoners held by the Confederates, the Record Division of the Office of the Secretary of War to which the Archive Office had been transferred in 1881 prepared in 1886 a list of the names of prisoners of war from the records. By an order of June 22, 1886, these records were transferred from that division to the Division of Records of Prisoners of War in the Adjutant General's Office. A list of the records thus transferred is in the Record and Pension Office, Document File 429,707. Most of the records were placed in consolidated files that are described below under Record Group 249.

In 1887 the Division of Records of Prisoners of War abstracted the data in the records on printed slips to which were added references to the sources. In 13 volumes, these slips serve as an index to the Confederate prison records under Record Group 249 described below. The records relating to both Confederate and Union prisons remained in the custody of the Adjutant General's Office until they were transferred on Nov. 14, 1938, to the National Archives where they are held as Records of the Commissary General of Prisoners (Record Group 249). Record Group 109 also includes records relating to Confederate prisons.

Record Group 109.--Records of several Commissaries General of Prisoners became part of the War Department Collection of Confederate

Records. In 1888 W. S. Winder of Baltimore lent to the War Department letters-sent books, telegram books, special-order books, an endorsement book, a registry book, and a general-order book of Brig. Gen. John H. Winder for 1864-65; special orders of Col. Henry Forno and Brig. Gens. W. M. Gardner and Daniel Ruggles, Feb.-Apr. 1865; and general orders of Forno and Gardner, Feb.-Mar. 1865. Copies made from these books were dispersed in different files, and the fate of the books themselves has not been ascertained. In 1883 and 1887 Daniel Ruggles lent correspondence, telegrams, and orders of Mar. and Apr. 1865 for copying.

Letters of General Winder, most of the other Commissaries General of Prisoners, and commissioners who examined political prisoners are in the correspondence of the Office of the Secretary of War, the Adjutant and Inspector General's Office, and other offices of the War Department described in this chapter. A reference file of cross-reference cards and copies of correspondence, 1861-65, in Record Group 109 is arranged alphabetically by name of prison or place. A U.S. War Department compilation, this file assists in locating the correspondence referred to above. It includes copies of correspondence of Robert Ould, some inspection reports of prisons, and lists of prisons and prison camps. Reports on prisons are among the inspection reports of the Adjutant and Inspector General's Office. Some compiled records relating to Federals in Confederate prisons are in the records of the U.S. Commissary General of Prisoners (Record Group 249). Correspondence and other documents relating to prisons are in Official Records . . .Armies, ser. 2, vols. 1-8.

Record Group 249. --Brief lists of prisoners, Mar. 1862 (misc. records, vol. 54), who escaped from or were received at Salisbury Military Prison, a roll of political prisoners there, and a list of prisoners captured at New Bern and paroled by General Burnside. Orders issued by the Inspector General of Camps and Prisons, June 29-Oct. 21, 1861 (misc. records, vol. 54, p. 1-13), include those of General Winder concerning the movement and transfer of soldiers, surveys of horses and property, courts-martial, details, and leaves of absence. A large file of miscellaneous rolls and records concerns Federal and Confederate prisoners of war, 1861-65 (10 ft.). It includes lists of prisoners captured, lists of prisoners in hospitals, lists of prisoners exchanged, rolls of prisoners who died in Confederate prisons, lists of prisoners paroled, individual parolees, lists of prisoners who took an oath to the Confederate States of America, lists of prisoners interred in Confederate cemeteries, lists of political prisoners, staffs of Confederate hospitals, and letters to the Confederate Agent for the Exchange of Prisoners. The rolls show prisoner's name and military organization (place of residence for civilian prisoners); place, date, and circumstances of capture; and charges. Information is sometimes given about occupations, behavior while in prison, and further disposition. A list of the rolls and lists in this file is available at the National Archives. Reports and correspondence of Sydney S. Baxter and Isaac H. Carrington relating to investigations of civilian prisoners held in Richmond, July 1863-Feb. 1864 (2 1/2 in.), concern both Unionists and Confederates. A register of reports by Baxter and Carrington is in ch. II, vol. 236, p. 146-149, Record Group 109. Monthly statistical reports of sick and wounded Federal prisoners of war in military prison hospitals at Richmond, Jan. -

Feb. 1865 (1/2 in.), show on printed forms the number of men sick and the diseases. Miscellaneous correspondence, reports, rolls, and lists of the Adjutant General's Office relating to prisoners of war, 1862-67 (3 in.), include lists of those who died in Confederate prisons in Richmond, Atlanta, Savannah, Florence, and Charleston; a list of Federal prisoners in the Salisbury military prison who enlisted in the Confederate Army; a list of prisoners who left Camp Lawton, ca. Nov. 1864; and an original register of deaths in the military prison hospital at Camp Lawton.

Records in Other Custody. --A small collection of John H. Winder papers in the Southern Historical Collection in the University of North Carolina Library contains a few documents of the war period. The papers of John D. Imboden, 1831-95, in the University of Virginia Library also contain wartime material.

Other files in Record Group 249 contain rolls, lists, and reports of Federal prisoners of war who were captured, paroled, or exchanged by the Confederates, enlisted in the Confederate Army, or who died in Confederate military prisons. The extensive file of rolls of Federal prisoners of war delivered on parole, 1862-65, contains rolls signed by Robert Ould and other Confederate officers for prisoners of war delivered at Aiken's Landing, Va., Charleston, S.C., City Point, Va., Wharf, Va., Graysville, Va., Harpers Ferry, Va., Jacksonville, Fla., Lafayette, Tenn., Lawrence County, Ky., Morris Island, S.C., Mumfordsville, Ky., North East Ferry, N.C., Red River Landing, La., Richmond, Ky., Richmond, Va., Savannah, Ga., Turkey Island Landing, Va., U.S. Ford, Va., and Woodbury, Tenn. See especially entries 28, 34, 37, and 58 in "Preliminary Inventory of the Records of the Office of the Commissary General of Prisoners" at the National Archives.

Information from prisoner-of-war records was abstracted on index record cards that are filed in the compiled military service records of Confederate military personnel described in chapter XI of this Guide.

Military Prisons

Andersonville, Ga.

Toward the end of 1863 when the need was greatest General Winder sent Capt. W. S. Winder to Georgia to select a site for a large prison. During the winter Capt. Richard B. Winder, an assistant quartermaster, superintended the construction of a stockade and prison buildings on a site chosen near Americus. The first prisoners were confined in Feb. 1864 and the total number of prisoners at Andersonville has been reliably set at 49,485. Of these, approximately 14,000 died.

On the approach of General Sherman's army in Sept. and Oct. 1864 all except 5,000 unable because of sickness to be moved were transferred to Savannah and Charleston. Early in 1865 some of the remaining ones were able to be marched to Wilmington, N.C., for exchange and others were transferred to Charlotte. In April 1865 the last of the prisoners were taken to Florida and then paroled. Successive commandants of this prison:

    Col. Alexander W. Persons, Feb. 1864.
    Brig. Gen. John H. Winder, June 17, 1864.

Col. George C. Gibbs, Oct. 1864.

Record Group 109.--A correspondence book, May 18, 1864-Mar. 19, 1865 (ch. IX, vol. 227), contains fair copies of a few letters sent and received by Capt. Henry Wirz, commander of the interior of the prison. A volume of reports on medical and sanitary conditions at Andersonville, 1864 (ch. IX, vol. 226), contains Surg. Joseph Jones' observations on diseases of Federal prisoners confined there and copies of letters and reports (Apr. 25-Sept. 16, 1864) of Isaiah H. White, chief surgeon at Andersonville military prison hospital, letters of R. R. Stevenson, surgeon in charge, and a report on gangrene by Asst. Surg. Amos Thornburgh.

Record Group 153.--A bound volume of press copies of letters sent by the post quartermaster at Camp Sumter (Capt. Richard B. Winder), Jan. 27-Sept. 28, 1864, accompanies the general-court-martial record of Capt. Henry Wirz in the records of the Office of the U.S. Judge Advocate General (file MM 2975). It contains letters to General Winder, the Quartermaster General, quartermasters, commissaries, and others; and appointments of and instructions to purchasing agents. In the same file is an order book of Captain Winder containing special orders to personnel, Oct. 4, 1864-Apr. 6, 1865, and a few orders received, Nov. 26, 1864-Mar. 28, 1865, from the Adjutant and Inspector General, the Quartermaster General, and Brig. Gen. William M. Gardner.

Record Group 249.--Records pertaining to Andersonville among the records of the Commissary General of Prisoners include a register of prisoners, Mar. 1864-Apr. 1865 (misc. records., vols. 2 and 3); consolidated morning reports of prisoners, Apr. 1, 1864-May 5, 1865 (misc. records, vol. 110); registers of patients in the military prison hospital, Feb. 24, 1864-Apr. 17, 1865 (misc. records, vol. 113), and Aug. 1864-Mar. 1865 (misc. records, vol. 4); an index to the registers (misc. records, vols. 111 and 112); a register of burials, Feb. 27, 1864-Apr. 28, 1865 (misc. records, vols. 114-118, [114-117 in one vol.]), which is probably the register prepared by Dorence Atwater (see below); and a register of burials, Mar. 1864-Mar. 1865 (5 in.), accompanied by a military prison hospital provision return, Aug. 1864-Mar. 1865 (1/8 in.).

The above records in Record Group 249, except those relating to deaths, have been indexed alphabetically by the U.S. War Department. The index is with the record group. See also the inventory of this record group at the National Archives. A record of U.S. money owed to Andersonville prisoners (misc. records, vol. 51 [2]) also appears to be a compilation of the U.S. War Department. Surgeon Jones' observations on diseases at Andersonville are published in Official Records . . . Armies, ser. 2, vol. 8, p. 588-625. The record of the proceedings of the trial of Captain Wirz is printed in "Trial of Henry Wirz," H. Ex. Doc. 23, 40 Cong., 2 sess., Serial 1331 (Washington, 1868), which also contains some wartime documents. Dorence Atwater, a Union prisoner at Andersonville, while paroled and detailed as a clerk in Surgeon White's office secretly made a copy of the prison hospital's death register. It was copied by the U.S. War Department in the summer of 1865. Atwater then published A List of Union Soldiers Buried at Andersonville, Copied from the Official Records in the Surgeon's Office at Andersonville (New York, 1866). See "Dorence Atwater," H. Ex. Doc. 149, 39 Cong., 1 sess., Serial 1267 (Washington, 1866).

Atlanta, Ga.

In 1863 a former slavepen south of Atlanta was used for the imprisonment of Union soldiers captured at Chickamauga. Confederate soldiers guilty of desertion and other infractions of military law were also confined there.

No records of this prison have been found.

Cahaba, Ala.

Late in 1863 an old cotton shed on the west bank of the Alabama River 10 miles south of Selma began to be used as a military prison. A wooden stockade was being erected around it at the end of Mar. 1864 when there were 660 prisoners on hand. Some prisoners were later taken to Andersonville, but by Oct. 1864 there were more than 2,000. Surgeon R. H. Whitfield was in charge of the small hospital at the prison. Most of the prisoners were removed early in 1865.

The commandant of this prison was Capt. H. A. M. Henderson.

William M. Armstrong, "Cahaba to Charleston: the Prison Odyssey of Lt. Edmund E. Ryan," Civil War History, 8:218-227 (June 1962); Peter A. Brannon, "The Cahaba Military Prison, 1863-1865," Alabama Review, 3:163-173 (July 1950).

Record Group 249.--A register of patients returned to prison or to duty, Oct. 1, 1864-Mar. 20, 1865 (misc. records, vol. 12, p. 374-396); a register of deaths, Jan. 1864-Apr. 1865 (misc. records, vol. 12, p. 398-403); and morning reports of patients, Nov. 2, 1864-May 2, 1865 (misc. records, vol. 12, p. 407-420).

Camp Lawton, Ga.

In Sept. 1864 a stockade was constructed near Millen, 80 miles north of Savannah, for prisoners of war from Andersonville and Savannah. In the enclosure of 44 acres the prisoners built huts from the timber felled in clearing the camp, and an inadequate hospital was also constructed. More than 10,000 prisoners were held at Camp Lawton in the fall of 1864, but as a result of General Sherman's operations they were removed in Nov. 1864 to Blackshear and Thomasville, Ga.

The commandant of this prison was Capt. D. W. Vowles.

No records of this prison have been found.

Charleston, S. C.

Prisoners of war were kept at several places in Charleston. In 1861 prisoners taken at the first battle of Bull Run were removed from Richmond to Castle Pinckney in Charleston Harbor. In 1862 prisoners were kept in the city jail. U. S. naval personnel from the gunboat Isaac Smith were held in Charleston in 1863, and in 1864 600 officers arrived from Macon. By Sept. 1864, 6,000 prisoners were held on the fairground on the outskirts of the city. The workhouse in Charleston was also used as a prison for officers.

Successive commandants of prisoners:
Col. John F. Iverson.
Capt. William J. Gayer.
Lt. Col. R. Stark Means, Sept. 27, 1864.
Records in Other Custody. --In Duke University Library is a guard report (1 vol.) of the military prison at Castle Pinckney, Aug. 29, 1864-Feb. 1, 1865. It gives names of soldiers on guard during different reliefs, their companies and regiments, places where posted, and names of sergeants and corporals of the guard. Included also is a list of names of prisoners with dates of imprisonment, charges, and sentences.

Columbia, S. C.

Prisoners of war were held at several places in and near Columbia. Late in 1861 they were kept in the city jail and at a fairground. On Jan. 28, 1862, the Secretary of War ordered Col. John S. Preston, commandant of the camp of instruction at Columbia, to assume command of the prisoners and the special guard. That summer prisoners sent from Charleston were turned over to his command. Capt. R. D. Senn, commander of the post guard at Columbia, was in charge of prisoners of war in the "Jailhouse Prison" there in 1864. In Oct. 1864 officer prisoners were transferred from Charleston to a field near Columbia where a makeshift prison was constructed. It became known as Camp Sorghum, from a principal item in the prison diet: sorghum molasses. So many escapes from Camp Sorghum occurred that a new prison for officers was established on the grounds of an asylum for the insane. In Feb. 1865 there were 1,200 prisoners at the new prison, known as Camp Asylum. At the same time a large prison was being constructed at Killian's Mills 11 miles from Columbia on the railroad line to Charlotte. In the middle of Feb. 1865 the prisoners were conducted from Camp Asylum to Charlotte, and soon afterward 1,003 officers were removed to Goldsboro and paroled.
Successive commandants of Camps Sorghum and Asylum:
Lt. Col. R. Stark Means, Oct. 1864.
Maj. Elias Griswold, Dec. 1864.
Record Group 109. --An account of a sutler at the Columbia military prison, Nov. 1, 1864-Feb. 19, 1865 (ch. IX, vol. 243), contains a chronological record of receipts for provisions, postage stamps, supplies, shoes, and tableware sold to prisoners.

Danville, Va.

On Nov. 11, 1863, 4,000 prisoners of war were transferred from Richmond to Danville where they were quartered in six tobacco factories. Other prisoners came from Richmond in 1864. During Feb. and Mar. 1865, most of the prisoners were removed for exchange, and when U.S. forces occupied Danville in April only 763 prisoners remained.
Successive commandants of this prison:
Capt. Henry McCoy, Nov. 1863.
Maj. Mason Morfit, Dec. 1863.
Lt. Col. Robert C. Smith, Oct. 25, 1864.

James I. Robertson, Jr., "Houses of Horror; Danville's   Civil War Prisons, " Virginia Magazine of History and Biography,

69:329-345 (July 1961).

Record Group 249.--A register of patients in the military prison hospital, Nov. 1863-Mar. 27, 1865 (misc. records, vol. 18); and a register of deaths in the hospital, Nov. 1863-Apr. 1865 (misc. records, vol. 12, p. 272-357).

Florence, S. C.

In Sept.-Oct. 1864 Maj. Gen. Samuel Jones, commander at Charleston, transferred prisoners of war from Charleston to Florence. A stockade was built around 23 acres, and by Oct. 12, 1864, there were 12,362 prisoners at Florence. Able-bodied prisoners were escorted away for exchange in Feb. 1865, and early in March the prison was abandoned. Successive commandants of this prison:
> Maj. F. F. Warley, Sept. 1864.
> Lt. Col. John F. Iverson, Dec. 6, 1864.

Record Group 249.--A register of prisoners, Sept.-Dec. 1864 (misc. records, vol. 12, p. 430-547), giving for names from S to W only the date of arrival, names, rank, company, regiment, place captured, branch of service, date and place of birth, and disposition.

Records in Other Custody.--The South Carolina Archives Department has a few records of the Florence prison, Nov. 1864-Jan. 1865, including correspondence, a court-martial proceeding, and a morning report.

Lynchburg, Va.

Prisoners captured by Gen. Thomas J. Jackson in the Shenandoah Valley were placed in stables at a fairground in Lynchburg. A tobacco warehouse and a hospital held 2,248 prisoners in July 1862. These were exchanged, but in 1864 others were held at Lynchburg. Successive commandants of this prison:
> Major Moffett.
> Col. George C. Gibbs.

No records of this prison have been found.

Macon, Ga.

Some officer prisoners were held at Macon by the post commandant, and when others arrived from Richmond in May 1864 they were placed in a 3-acre enclosure, which became known as Camp Oglethorpe, on a fairground just east of Macon. Late in July 1864 some of the prisoners were removed to Charleston and the others to Savannah. Successive commandants of this prison:
> Capt. W. K. Tabb.
> Capt. George C. Gibbs, May 25, 1864.

No records of this prison have been found.

Richmond, Va.

The War Department took over a number of tobacco factories, warehouses, and other buildings in Richmond for use as military prisons. In 1861 prisoners from Bull Run were placed in Liggon's and Harwood's factories, and later in 1861 General Winder commandeered a tobacco warehouse that had belonged to W. H. Gwathmey. These buildings were in the lower part of Richmond known as Rocketts. Officers were transferred from Liggon's factory to the neighboring Atkinson's tobacco factory. In 1862 the Confederate Government confined U. S. officers in a building at the corner of Cary and 20th Streets that had belonged to L. Libby & Son, ship chandlers and grocers. Nearby tobacco warehouses also became known after their owners as Scott's and Pemberton's Prisons. In Jan. 1863 the factory of R. H. Mayo was occupied, and early in the fall of 1863 Brigadier General Winder impressed James H. Grant's factory at Franklin and 19th Streets and Smith's factory on 21st Street. By late 1863 Yarborough's or Yarbrough's, W. H. Ross', Crew's, J. B. & A. L. Royster's, and Barrett's factories were also occupied. In June 1862 a prison camp was established on Belle Isle, a small island in the James River, where during the war more than 20,000 prisoners were received. During 1862-63 Capt. Norris Montgomery commanded the Belle Isle prison camp, and he was succeeded by Lt. Virginius Bossieux. In the summer of 1864, some Union prisoners were kept in the "Jailhouse Prison" (Richmond County Jail).

By late Nov. 1863 there were 10,590 prisoners in Richmond and by Jan. 1864 over 14,000, more than half on Belle Isle under very crowded conditions exposed to the weather. Some were transferred to Danville and many more to the newly established Andersonville military prison. Officers were removed from Richmond to Danville, Salisbury, and Macon; later, in Feb. 1865, many were brought back for exchange. The prisoners were escorted away on Richmond's evacuation in Apr. 1865 but escaped.

Before the designation of a Commissary General of Prisoners the commanders of the Department of Henrico had general charge of the military prisons in Richmond. AIGO Special Order 52 of Mar. 3, 1865, relieved Brigadier General Gardner from duty at Richmond and placed Lt. Gen. Richard S. Ewell, commander of the Department of Richmond, in charge of the prisons. Successive commandants of the military prisons:

> Capt. Archibald C. Godwin.
> Capt. Henry Wirz.
> Capt. George W. Alexander.
> Capt. Thomas P. Turner, Oct. 27, 1862.

Frank L. Byrne, "Libby Prison; a Study in Emotions," Journal of Southern History, 24:430-444 (Nov. 1958); C. S. A. Congress, House of Representatives, Committee To Enquire into the Treatment of Prisoners at Castle Thunder, Evidence Taken before the Committee of the House of Representatives, Appointed To Enquire into the Treatment of Prisoners at Castle Thunder ([n. p., 1863?]; printed also in Official Records . . . Armies, ser. 2, vol. 5, p. 871-924); William H. Jeffrey, Richmond Prisons, 1861-1862, Compiled from the Original Records Kept by the Confederate Government (St. Johnsbury, Vt., ca. 1893). A report of the Joint Select Committee on the Conduct of the War on "Returned Prisoners," May 9, 1864, H. Rep. 67, 38 Cong., 1 sess., Serial 1206 (Washington, 1864), contains testimony of Federal prisoners who had been confined in Confederate prisons in Richmond.

On May 2, 1865, Col. Richard D. Cutts, a U. S. officer who had been charged with collecting Confederate records in Richmond, forwarded to the

War Department three boxes of records of the headquarters of the Richmond military prisons and the next day he sent to Washington three large volumes. On July 17, 1865, Lt. Col. Albert Ordway, Provost Marshal General in Richmond, sent the letter book of Clarence Morfit to the Adjutant General in Washington. These records are described below.

Record Group 109.--A letter and order book of the Richmond military prisons office, Jan. 20, 1862-Dec. 15, 1863 (ch. IX, vol. 199 1/2), contains copies of letters and orders of General Winder and Captains Godwin, Wirz, Turner, and W. S. Winder, instructions to the commander of the prisons, letters received by the Winders, letters from S. S. Baxter and Robert Ould, and orders regarding the administration of the prisons. This book is a copy made by the War Records Office in 1886 from the original lent by Col. Edward H. Ripley of Rutland, Vt. A copy is also with the records of the Office of the U.S. Commissary General of Prisoners (Record Group 249, misc. records, vol. 106 1/2). A letters-sent press copy book, Mar. 7, 1863-Apr. 1, 1865 (ch. IX, vol. 232), of Capt. Clarence Morfit, quartermaster of the Richmond prisons, contains letters to General Winder, the Quartermaster General, the Richmond quartermaster, and others.

Record Group 249.--Registers of prisoners entitled "Nominal Lists of Prisoners of War Received at Richmond," July 23, 1861-Apr. 2, 1865 (misc. records, vols. 93, 94, 96, 97, 99, and 101-106), show the date of receipt, name, rank, company, regiment, State, date and place of capture, date and reason for discharge (transfer, parole, or exchange), by whose order discharged (General Winder or Colonel Ould), where sent, and additional information about prisoners paroled, exchanged, or deceased. They include Federal military and naval prisoners of war, political prisoners from the South and the North, and foreigners. A register of Federal officers kept in Libby Prison, Sept. 24, 1862-Mar. 25, 1865 (misc. records, vol. 100), contains similar information and is similarly arranged. A register of Negro prisoners, 1862-65 (misc. records, part of vol. 69), supplies abundant information on their status and disposition, and there is a register of civilian prisoners, 1862-63 (misc. records, vol. 98). Daybooks of arrivals at military prisons in Richmond, June 1861-Apr. 1865 (misc. records, vols. 32, 52-53, 58-61, and 63-67, 8 in.), give the prisoner's number and name, rank, company, regiment, place and date of capture, and sometimes information as to disposition. Daybooks of the arrival and disposition of prisoners, Nov. 15, 1862-Mar. 28, 1865 (misc. records, vols. 70-91, 10 in.), contain similar information. "Roll Call Books," Oct. 18, 1861-Jan. 24, 1865 (misc. records, vols. 119-127, 6 in.), contain morning and evening reports of the numbers of prisoners in the different prisons and hospitals.

Other records are more specialized. A list of noncommissioned officers and privates captured at Reams' Station, Va., Aug. 25, 1864, and received at Richmond, Aug. 27, 1864 (misc. records, vol. 68), shows the prisoner's name, rank, company, and place of birth. A daybook of prisoners received at Barrett's factory, prison no. 4, June 30-Sept. 2, 1862 (misc. records, vol. 55), shows the prisoner's number, name, rank, company, regiment, State, and place and date of capture. Morning reports of prisoners at Belle Isle Prison, Sept. 1-Oct. 8, 1864 (misc. records, vol. 34), give the prisoner's number, name, rank, company, regiment, date hospitalized, date discharged, and disease. A list of prisoners received at Libby Prison in May 1863 and paroled on May 13 (misc. records, vol. 62), and a list of vaccinated prisoners of war in Richmond prisons and hospitals, 1863-64 (misc. records, vol. 44), show the prisoner's name, rank, company, regiment, and age. Lists of prisoners of war released at City Point, Va., by Confederate authorities, July 19-Aug. 3, 1862 (misc. records, vol. 57), show prisoner's number, name, rank, company, regiment, and State. A register of visitors to prisoners in Richmond, July 8, 1861-Mar. 30, 1862 (misc. records, vol. 59, p. 1-15), shows names of visitors, names of prisoners visited, and kind of permit issued. Lists of prisoners of war received at military prisons in Richmond, June 1862 (2 in.), show the prisoner's name, rank, company, regiment, State, and where and when captured. A list of Federal prisoners paroled before the battles [1862] before Richmond, (1 1/2 in.), shows the same information. These lists were prepared for the Confederate Agent for the Exchange of Prisoners.

Incomplete records of the Military Prison Hospital (General Hospital No. 21) are also available. A register of patients, Mar. 1, 1863-June 9, 1864 (misc. records, vol. 66A), also lists names of hospital employees. There is a register of prisoners of war and U.S. Army deserters admitted to the hospital, Mar. 9, 1863-Apr. 2, 1865 (misc. records, vols. 20 and 21). For use with these records is an alphabetical name index ("Index to Miscellaneous Records of Prisoners of War--Except Deaths"). Other prison hospital records are described under the Surgeon General's Office, and other records relating to military prisoners in Richmond are described under the Department of Richmond.

Records in Other Custody.--The Ryder Collection of Confederate Archives in the Tufts College Library contains 455 morning reports of prisoners in the Richmond military prisons on printed forms, Mar. 22, 1862-Dec. 16, 1863. These reports show the number of prisoners of war, civilian prisoners, Confederates, Federal deserters, and Negroes on hand, received, or transferred each day. On other forms are 117 passes, Jan. 7, 1863-July 29, 1864, issued by order of Generals Winder and Gardner and Majors Turner and Carrington to visitors to Libby Prison. An alphabetical list of the names of persons to whom passes were issued is in Historical Records Survey, Massachusetts, A Calendar of the Ryder Collection of Confederate Archives at Tufts College, p. 157-159 (Boston, 1940).

Salisbury, N.C.

Early in Nov. 1861 the War Department bought an abandoned cotton factory at Salisbury for use as a military prison; the factory and five adjacent buildings were enclosed by a board fence and prepared for the reception of prisoners. In Dec. 1861 the first prisoners arrived, and on July 16, 1862, General Winder reported a total of 780 prisoners at Salisbury. Early in Oct. 1864 7,500 prisoners were transferred from Belle Isle (Richmond). The total number of prisoners held in Salisbury on Nov. 6, 1864, was 8,740. In Mar. 1865 more than 2,279 prisoners were sent to Richmond for exchange; the rest of the prisoners were later removed, and the prison was turned over to the Ordnance Department.

Successive commandants of this prison:

Maj. George C. Gibbs, Jan. 11, 1862.
Capt. Swift Galloway, Sept. 14, 1863.
Capt. George W. Alexander, May 1864.
Col. John A. Gilmer, Jr., June 8, 1864.
Maj. John H. Gee, Aug. 24, 1864.
Brig. Gen. Bradley T. Johnson, Dec. 20, 1864.

Adolphus W. Mangum, "Salisbury Prison," in Walter Clark, ed., Histories of the Several Regiments and Battalions from North Carolina in the Great War 1861-'65, vol. 4, p. 745-772 (5 vols.; Goldsboro, 1901); Ida B. Williams, "John Henry Gee, Physician and Soldier," Georgia Historical Quarterly, 45:238-244 (Sept. 1961).

Record Group 249. --An undated index of prisoners of war who enlisted in the Confederate service (misc. records, vol. 13) gives name, rank, regiment, company, arm, and State. Also in this record group are a register of patients in the military prison hospital, Oct. 1, 1864-Apr. 8, 1865 (misc. records, vol. 5), a register of hospital patients (prisoners and guards) returned to duty, May 2-Dec. 17, 1864 (misc. records, vol. 12, p. 80-122), and a register of patients dated May 1-Nov. 14, 1864 (misc. records, vol. 12, p. 1-75). A register of deaths, May 7, 1864-Feb. 19, 1865 (misc. records, vol. 12, p. 127-192 and 200-257), shows name, rank, company, regiment, disease, and date of death.

A list of the names of soldiers who had served court-martial sentences at Salisbury and who were to be restored to duty is in AIGO Special Order 285, Dec. 1, 1864. C.S.A. War Department, [Communication from the Secretary of War, Enclosing a List of the Civilian Prisoners in Custody at Salisbury, N.C., under Military Authority, Richmond, 1863] contains a list of 133 prisoners with residences, occupations, and causes of arrest. The proceedings of a military commission that tried Maj. John H. Gee at Raleigh, N.C., in 1866 (Record Group 153, Records of the Office of the U.S. Judge Advocate General, file MM 3972), contain wartime documents. Records of the prison hospital are described under the Surgeon General's Office.

Records in Other Custody. --The Bradley T. Johnson papers in Duke University Library contain correspondence, Feb. 1-Apr. 21, 1865, with the War Department and Gov. Zebulon B. Vance of North Carolina and telegrams, Jan.-Apr. 1865, concerning the administration of the Salisbury military prison. Included are a few communications from Capt. James M. Goodman and Maj. Mason Morfit, quartermasters.

Savannah, Ga.

In July 1864 Federal prisoners arrived at Savannah from Macon and Cahaba. The prison was located on grounds adjoining the old U.S. marine hospital. By the end of the first week in September there were 1,500 prisoners at Savannah. Since there were not enough soldiers to guard the prisoners, they were moved to Charleston, Millen, and Blackshear, Ga., within a short time. Savannah was occupied by U.S. forces on Dec. 21, 1864.
The commandant of this prison was Col. Richard A. Wayne.
No records of this prison have been found.

Tuscaloosa, Ala.

On instructions dated Oct. 28, 1861, Maj. J. L. Calhoun, assistant quartermaster at Montgomery, rented an abandoned papermill at Tuscaloosa for use as a military prison. Prisoners were brought from Richmond, Montgomery, and Pensacola. Early in Mar. 1862, 214 prisoners captured at Fort Donelson and held temporarily in Memphis were sent to Tuscaloosa. Although some prisoners at Tuscaloosa were exchanged later that year, in 1864 more than 4,000 prisoners were held there. Maj. Elias Griswold was designated as commandant on Nov. 21, 1861. No records of this prison have been found.

HEADQUARTERS OF THE ARMY

Under the Confederate Constitution the President was Commander in Chief of the Army and Navy, and because of his military background President Davis considered himself best qualified to establish military policy. Early in 1862 he vetoed an act providing for the appointment of a commanding general who was to be charged with the direction of military operations and the supply and discipline of the Army because it did not make the officer subordinate to the President. On Mar. 13, 1862, Gen. Robert E. Lee was assigned to duty at Richmond and charged with the direction of military operations under the President (AIGO General Order 14). The President continued to exercise his authority as Commander in Chief and Lee was referred to as military adviser. After Lee's departure from Richmond in June 1862, the position of military adviser was vacant until the assignment of Gen. Braxton Bragg on Feb. 24, 1864 (AIGO General Order 23). General Bragg left Richmond in Oct. 1864 to assume command of the Department of North Carolina. An act of Jan. 23, 1865 (Ramsdell, Laws and Joint Resolutions, p. 22), authorized the President to appoint a "General in Chief," who as ranking officer of the Army was to have command of the Confederate military forces. Appointed General in Chief on Feb. 9, 1865, General Lee continued to maintain his headquarters with the Army of Northern Virginia and to devote most of his attention to it.

Record Group 109.--Records of General Lee include copies of letters sent, Mar. 13-Aug. 13, 1862 (ch. II, vol. 83 1/2), to generals and other Army officers, War Department officials, Governors and other officials of States, post commanders, and others; general orders issued, Mar. 20 and Apr. 11, 1862, and a circular, Mar. 31, 1862 (ch. VIII, vol. 237, p. 21-22); special orders issued, Mar. 14-June 3, 1862 (ch. VIII, vol. 240, p. 171-180); a few circulars issued, Apr. 20-28, 1862; and an incomplete file of general orders issued, Feb. 11-28, 1865. There are copies of letters and telegrams sent by General Bragg, Apr. 8-July 27, 1864 (ch. II, part of vol. 359), to Army officers, Government officials, and the President.

Other Lee papers are described in the section of this chapter on the Army and Department of Northern Virginia. General Bragg's papers are described below under records of other commands and officers. The files of the Secretary of War and War Department bureaus contain correspondence of Generals Lee and Bragg.

TERRITORIAL COMMANDS AND ARMIES

The military forces of the Confederacy were organized into geographical units and armies commanded by general officers. Most of the geographical units were territorial departments which were subdivided into districts and subdistricts--a few territorial divisions included several departments. The fighting forces or mobile commands were organized into armies, corps, divisions, brigades, and regiments.

Extensive authority was delegated to the army commanders who operated largely without direction from Richmond. There was no general staff at the Capital to aid the President and the Secretary of War in planning and directing the operations of the Army. Distances were so great and communications so slow that effective control of operations from the Capital was not possible.

Generals in command of armies and territorial departments acquired staffs to assist them in developing plans for military operations, coordinating movements, and procuring supplies. The large armies had a Chief of Staff, an Assistant Adjutant General, an Inspector General, a Chief of Ordnance, a Chief Quartermaster, a Chief Engineer, a Chief of Subsistence, a Chief of Artillery, a Chief Signal Officer, and a Medical Director. These staff officers had subordinates of lower rank to assist them in handling the activities of their departments. The generals had aides-de-camp who took care of much of the paperwork connected with the preparation of dispatches and reports on operations. The staff officers served at the headquarters of the armies or the departments. Other quartermasters, commissaries, ordnance officers, and civilian employees served at other points attending to the procurement and transportation of supplies.

Provost marshals and provost guards were the military police of that day. Commanders of departments assigned provost marshals to cities, towns, and posts where there were hospitals or depots for more effective police protection. The provost marshals administered the passport system that was instituted to restrain stragglers and deserters, prevent communicating with the enemy, and detect spies. Provost marshals also conducted courts for the trial of Army personnel, guarded prisoners and deserters, posted guards on railroad trains, arrested drunk and disorderly soldiers and deserters, controlled the departure of vessels from ports, and impressed Negroes. Where martial law was proclaimed, such as in Richmond and Charleston, the provost marshals had charge of police departments and detectives and other civilians to assist in the operations.

Francis T. Miller and Robert S. Lanier, eds., "Confederate Armies and Generals, " in The Photographic History of the Civil War, vol. 10. p. 239-286 (New York and London, 1957); U.S. War Department, Atlas to Accompany the Official Records of the Union and Confederate Armies (2 vols.; Washington, 1891-95), Memorandum of Armies, Corps, and Geographical Commands in the Confederate States from 1861 to 1865 [Washington, n.d., reprinted in William F. Amann, ed., Personnel of the Civil War, 2 vols.; New York, 1961], "Special Index for the Principal Armies, Army Corps, Military Divisions and Departments, " in Official Records ...Armies, ser. 130, p. xliii-xlvii; Frank E. Vandiver, Rebel Brass; the Confederate Command System (Baton Rouge, 1956). See also the bibliography in the section of this chapter on the Adjutant and Inspector General's Office under "Appointment Records. " Instructions regarding records that were to be forwarded to the War Department bureaus in Richmond are in C.S.A. War Department, Regulations for the Army of the Confederate States, 1863 (Richmond, 1863). See also the citations to bureau regulations in other sections of this chapter.

Record Group 109. --Several files compiled apparently by the U.S. War Department relate to the Confederate Army as a whole or to many elements of the Army. A file (15 ft.) of post, department, and army returns, rosters, and lists, 1861-65, contains morning reports showing the number of men present and absent; periodic returns showing the locations of organizations and their strength; lists of deserters, paroled prisoners exchanged, men detailed, quartermasters, and medical officers; and rosters of officers. There is a file (3 ft.) of battle reports, 1862-64. A file (1 ft.) of general and special orders issued by minor commands, 1861-65, relates chiefly to Virginia.

In this record group are orders issued by the headquarters of the Western Department, the Central Army of Kentucky, the 1st and 4th Divisions of the Western Department, Gen. John S. Bowen's brigade, and the Army of the Mississippi, 1861-62 (ch. VIII, vol. 337); orders issued by the headquarters of the Army of the Mississippi, the Western Department, the Army of Tennessee, and by subordinate commands, 1862-63 (ch. VIII, vol. 342); and other orders issued by the Adjutant and Inspector General in Richmond, the Western Department, and the Army of Tennessee, 1862-63 (ch. VIII, vol. 347). There are circulars, letters, and orders (ch. II, vol. 223) from Gen. Charles Clark's command (forces near Corinth, Miss., and Union City, Tenn.), May-Aug. 1861; Gen. Felix K. Zollicoffer's brigade, Knoxville, Tenn., Aug.-Sept. 1861; and Gen. Simon B. Buckner's ("Tennessee") brigade, Central Division of Kentucky, and the Army of Kentucky, Sept. 1861-Feb. 1862.

Records of the 1st Kentucky Brigade were given to the War Department in 1887 by Fayette Hewitt, who had been assistant adjutant general of the brigade. The file of letters, reports, orders, and other papers, 1861-65 (1 ft.), includes letters received, general and special orders and circulars received and issued, surgeons' reports of sick and wounded men, reports on stoppages of ordnance stores, lists of ordnance and ordnance stores condemned, reports on wagons, statistical morning-strength reports, weekly reports of effective strength, and reports on the appraisement of horses. It also contains cross-reference cards for reports on casualties and rolls of commissioned officers that were withdrawn and placed in other files. The records of this brigade, then, include: letters and telegrams sent and received, Dec. 3, 1861-Nov. 19, 1863 (ch. II, vol. 311); general orders issued, Oct. 26, 1862-Aug. 18, 1863, and Oct. 4, 1863-Oct. 27, 1864 (ch. II, vol. 308, p. 100-134, and vol. 310, p. 375-380); special orders issued, Oct. 26, 1862-Sept. 5, 1863, and Sept. 25, 1863-Oct. 30, 1864 (ch. II, vol. 308, p. 2-89, 141-148, and vol. 310, p. 201-232); general orders and circulars received, Apr. 1862-May 1864 (ch. II, vol. 305, p. 1-79, vol. 306, p. 89-218, vol. 308, p. 273-337, vol. 309, and vol. 313, p. 1-12); general orders and circulars received and sent, Nov. 16, 1861-Apr. 12, 1864 (ch. II, vol. 307); special orders received, Apr. 14, 1862-Sept. 15, 1864 (ch. II, vol. 305, p. 89-131, vol. 306, p. 1-16, 20-81, vol. 308, p. 90-94, 174-272, 344, vol. 310, p. 301-366, and vol. 313, p. 62-92); special orders received from the headquarters of Maj. Gen. John C. Breckinridge, Nov. 16, 1861-Oct. 14, 1862 (ch. II, vol. 316); special orders received from the headquarters of the Reserve Corps of the Army of the Mississippi, Maj. Gen. J. C. Breckinridge commanding, Apr. 13-May 13, 1862 (ch. II, vol. 315, p. 1-24); general and special orders and circulars received, June 28, 1862-Aug. 24, 1863 (ch. II, vol. 312); and general and special orders and circulars received and issued, Mar. 15, 1863-Jan. 19, 1865 (ch. II, vol. 314). The orders were received from the Central Army of Kentucky, the Department of Mississippi and East Louisiana, the Army of the Mississippi, the Western Department, the Army of Tennessee, the Army of the West, the

Department of the West, the Adjutant and Inspector General's Office, and the Surgeon General's Office. There are copies and extracts of special orders received from the Adjutant and Inspector General's Office, Dec. 31, 1861-May 23, 1861 (ch. II, vol. 313, p. 51-61). Statistical morning-strength reports, Nov. 1861-Feb. 1862 (ch. II, vol. 317), May 1862-Jan. 1863 (ch. II, vol. 309, p. 10-55), and Nov. 1862-Nov. 1864 (ch. II, vol. 310, p. 2-161) give information regarding the regiments constituting the brigade. Semiweekly returns of the 1st Brigade, Reserve Corps, and of the Army of the Mississippi, May 7 and 11, 1862, are in vol. 309, p. 7 and 9. Also available are a record of details, discharges, resignations, furloughs, and transfers, July 12, 1862-June 29, 1863 (ch. II, vol. 315, p. 26-80), a list of men killed and wounded at Hartsville, Tenn., Dec. 7, 1862 (ch. II, vol. 308, p. 358), and a report on the appraisement of horses, Mar. 17, 1863 (ch. II, vol. 308, p. 356).

C.S.A. War Department, Official Reports of Battles Published by Order of Congress (Richmond, 1862). This compilation was reprinted with the title Southern History of the War; Official Reports of Battles as Published by Order of the Confederate Congress at Richmond (New York, 1863). C.S.A. War Department, Official Reports of Battles Published by Order of Congress (Richmond, 1864). Many of the records described below are published in Official Records ... Armies (available on microfilm as M 262). Supplementary documents are in U.S. Army Service Schools, Fort Leavenworth, Kans., Donelson Campaign Sources Supplementing Volume 7 of the Official Records ..., ed. by A. L. Conger ([Fort Leavenworth], 1912); U.S. General Service Schools, Fort Leavenworth, Kans., Fort Henry and Fort Donelson Campaigns, February 1862; Source Book, ed. by A. L. Conger and C. H. Lanza (Fort Leavenworth, 1923). Confederate military departments, districts, and armies issued general and special orders, circulars, and other documents in printed form. Collections of these have been assembled by many libraries and are listed in Crandall, Confederate Imprints, 1:119-142, and in Harwell, More Confederate Imprints, 1:29-45. Many documents relating to Army commands and military departments and districts are in the compiled military service records of Confederate officers described in chapter XI of this Guide.

Records in Other Custody. --Many of the repositories listed in this Guide hold miscellaneous collections of records relating to the Confederate Army. Repositories in both North and South have Confederate materials in miscellaneous files on the Civil War or in collections of personal papers. Such files should be checked for information regarding military organizations and officers.

Department of Alabama and West Florida

Established in Oct. 14, 1861, this department embraced Pensacola, Fla., and the State of Alabama, with headquarters at Mobile. It included the District of Alabama, commanded by Brig. Gen. Jones M. Withers and consisting of Alabama and that part of Mississippi east of the Pascagoula River. In Jan. 1862 this district was designated the Army of Mobile. The department and the army were discontinued on June 27, 1862.

Successive commanders of the department:

Maj. Gen. Braxton Bragg, Oct. 14, 1861.
Brig. Gen. Samuel Jones, Mar. 3, 1862.
Col. W. L. Powell (temp.), Mar. 24, 1862.
Brig. Gen. John H. Forney (temp.), Apr. 28, 1862.

Record Group 109.--General and special orders issued by the department and the Army of Mobile, 1861-62 (1 in.); letters-sent book of the Engineer Office at Mobile, Apr.-May 1862 (ch. III, vol. 15).

Department of Alabama, Mississippi, and East Louisiana

The Department of Mississippi and East Louisiana, embracing Mississippi and that part of Louisiana east of the Mississippi River, was established on Oct. 1, 1862, and divided into the 1st, 2d, and 3d Military Districts. In Jan. 1864 the department was merged into the Department of Alabama, Mississippi, and East Louisiana, which in Oct. 1864 became part of the Military Division of the West.

Successive commanders of the Department of Mississippi and East Louisiana:

Maj. Gen. John C. Pemberton, Oct. 1, 1862.
Lt. Gen. Leonidas Polk, Dec. 23, 1863.

Successive commanders of the Department of Alabama, Mississippi, and East Louisiana:

Lt. Gen. Leonidas Polk, Jan. 28, 1864.
Maj. Gen. Stephen D. Lee, May 9, 1864.
Lt. Gen. Richard Taylor, Sept. 23, 1864.
Maj. Gen. Dabney H. Maury (temp.), Nov. 22, 1864.
Lt. Gen. Richard Taylor, Dec. 12, 1864.

Record Group 36.--Records of Capt. L. R. Evans, ordnance officer, Sept. 1862-Nov. 1863 (2 in.), and requisitions for ordnance and ordnance stores, Jan. 1863 (1/2 in.), are with the records of the collector of customs at Mobile.

Record Group 109.--Records of the Department of Mississippi and East Louisiana include letters and telegrams sent, Oct. 17, 1862-Aug. 28, 1863 (ch. II, vols. 57 and 60); letters and telegrams sent, Oct. 25-Dec. 26, 1862 (4 in.; copies made by the War Records Office in 1879); letters sent relating to trade, Nov. 29, 1862-Mar. 23, 1863 (ch. II, vol. 56); letters, telegrams, and reports relating to operations around Vicksburg and its siege and surrender, Jan.-Dec. 1863 (4 in.); letters and telegrams received by General Pemberton, Jan. 1862-Aug. 1864 (1 ft.); endorsements on letters received, Oct. 19, 1862-Feb. 6, 1863 (ch. II, vol. 1 3/4); quartermaster records of Pemberton's command, Oct. 1862-May 1863 (1/8 in.), including returns, lists, requisitions, and reports; and letters sent by Maj. Theodore Johnston, chief of subsistence, Apr. 25-June 17, 1863 (ch. VIII, vol. 370). Other records include a record of general and special orders received, Jan. 7-Sept. 3, 1864 (ch. II, part of vol. 6); and a duty roster of the brigades of Gens. John Gregg, Samuel B. Maxey, and William N. R. Beall, 1863 (ch. I, vol. 106).

Records of the Department of Alabama, Mississippi, and East Louisiana include copies of letters sent by the commanding generals or their adjutants general, Jan. 13, 1864-May 11, 1865 (ch. II, vols. 8 1/2, 8 3/4, 14, and 1 index vol.); copies of telegrams sent, Jan. 2-Aug. 31, 1864, and Nov. 22, 1864-Apr. 22, 1865 (ch. II, parts of vols. 6 and 196, vols. 10, 11, and 236 1/4); letters and telegrams received, 1862-65 (1 ft. 6 in.); register of letters and telegrams received, 1862-65 (ch. II, vol. 7 1/2); endorsements on letters received, Nov. 1863-May 1865 (ch. II, vols. 3-5, and 2 index vols.); general and special orders and circulars issued by the departmental headquarters and subcommands, 1862-65 (4 in.); special orders issued, Jan. 1-May 9, 1865 (ch. II, vol. 199, with index in ch. II, vol. 13 1/2); commissary papers, 1862-65 (1 in.); and general orders issued chiefly by the provost marshal general, Jan. 27-July 8, 1864 (ch. II, part of vol. 196).

Records of subordinate officers and commands include an account book of Maj. A. B. Cooke, chief paymaster, May 1, 1862-May 8, 1865 (ch. V, vol. 235); letters and telegrams sent by the chief pay quartermaster, Sept. 24, 1863-Apr. 26, 1865 (ch. V, vols. 240 and 241); letters sent by Maj. John A. A. West, chief of artillery, Jan. 1, 1865-Mar. 25, 1865 (ch. II, vol. 9); press copies of letters sent by Col. Samuel H. Lockett, chief engineer, Oct. 11, 1864-May 8, 1865 (ch. III, vol. 11); press copies of letters sent by Capt. Walter J. Morris, acting chief engineer, Oct. 20, 1864-Feb. 7, 1865 (ch. III, vol. 6, p. 148-159); letters sent by the chief quartermaster (Majors R. M. Mason, John W. Young, and Thomas Peters), Mar. 8-Aug. 1, 1864 (ch. V, vol. 221); endorsements on letters received by cavalry headquarters in Mississippi commanded by Maj. Gen. Stephen D. Lee, Sept. 1863-Mar. 1864 (ch. II, vol. 2), with a memorandum of accounts paid, July 1864-May 1865; special orders issued by Maj. Gen. S. D. Lee, Sept. 4, 1863-Apr. 25, 1864 (1/4 in.); orders and letters sent and received by John Brownrigg, chief surgeon of Maj. Gen. S. D. Lee's cavalry corps, Oct. 16, 1863-May 6, 1864 (ch. VIII, vol. 343); records of subsistence and quartermaster stores received and issued at Camp Lewis, La., July-Dec. 1862 (ch. V, vol. 140); and provision returns and reports of stores on hand, 1863-65 (1 in.).

For the 3d Military District of the Department of Mississippi and East Louisiana commanded by Maj. Gen. Frank Gardner at Port Hudson, La., there are letters sent, Dec. 29, 1862-July 5, 1863 (ch. II, vol. 8); correspondence and reports, 1862-63 (2 in.); and general and special orders issued, Dec. 28, 1862-July 8, 1863 (ch. II, vol. 198).

Records in Other Custody.--Military telegrams of General Pemberton, Oct. 18, 1862-May 2, 1863, are in the U. S. Naval Academy Museum, and a few other papers of Pemberton are in the University of North Carolina Library. A letters-sent book of Lt. Gen. Richard Taylor, Sept. 25, 1864-May 9, 1865, and telegrams sent, Sept. 7, 1864-May 11, 1865 (4 notebooks), are in Tulane University Library. General orders issued, Department of Mississippi and East Louisiana, Feb. 10-May 24, 1864 (1 vol.), are in the Virginia Historical Society collections. Orders of Maj. Gen. Dabney H. Maury, Jan. 3-Apr. 17, 1863, and orders of Maj. Gen. John H. Forney, Apr. 17-Aug. 14, 1863, are in the Chicago Historical Society collections. Capt. John B. Vinet, an engineer officer, preserved some papers and maps of Alabama that are in the Department of Archives, Louisiana State University. That repository also has hospital inspection reports by Surg. Peter B. McKelvey, Oct. 1864-Apr. 1865 (1 notebook). A journal of events at Fort Morgan, Ala., by Hurieosco Austill, Aug. 1864, is in the Alabama Department of Archives and History.

Department No. 1

The Military District of Louisiana, embracing the city of New Orleans and its defenses, was established on Apr. 17, 1861. The district was merged on May 27, 1861, into Department No. 1 which included the State of Louisiana and the southern portions of Mississippi and Alabama, including Fort Morgan. In June 1862 Department No. 1 was merged into Department No. 2 (or Western Department). Early in 1861 the Louisiana State troops commanded by Maj. Gen. Braxton Bragg and by Col. Paul O. Hébert were designated the Army of Louisiana.

Successive commanders of the district and department:
  Maj. Gen. David E. Twiggs, Apr. 17, 1861.
  Maj. Gen. Mansfield Lovell, Oct. 7, 1861.

Record Group 109. --Press copies of letters sent by the Artillery and Engineer Department of the Army of Louisiana, Feb. 1861 (ch. III, vol. 19 1/2).

Records in Other Custody. --Letters sent by Col. Johnson K. Duncan, commander of Forts Jackson and St. Philip, Feb. 23, 1861-Jan. 11, 1862 (1 vol.), are in the Louisiana Historical Association collection on deposit in the Howard-Tilton Memorial Library of Tulane University.

The following wartime publications provide documentation: C.S.A. Congress, House of Representatives, Correspondence between the President, War Department and Governor T. O. Moore, Relating to the Defenses of New Orleans (Richmond, 1863); C.S.A. War Department, Correspondence between the War Department and General Lovell, Relating to the Defenses of New Orleans (Richmond, 1863), Proceedings of the Court of Inquiry, Relative to the Fall of New Orleans (Richmond, 1864).

Departments of East Tennessee and Western Virginia

The District of East Tennessee was established on July 26, 1861, and renamed the Department of East Tennessee in Mar. 1862. In that month it was extended to include Chattanooga and vicinity and in July to include part of northern Georgia. The Department of Southwestern Virginia was established on May 8, 1862, and in November of that year it was designated the Trans-Allegheny or Western Department of Virginia.

Successive commanders of the District of East Tennessee:
  Brig. Gen. Felix K. Zollicoffer, July 26, 1861.
  Maj. Gen. George B. Crittenden, Dec. 8, 1861.
  Maj. Gen. Edmund Kirby Smith, Mar. 8, 1862.

Successive commanders of the Department of East Tennessee:
  Maj. Gen. Edmund Kirby Smith, Mar. 1862.
  Maj. Gen. John P. McCown (temp.), Sept. 1, 1862.
  Maj. Gen. Samuel Jones, Sept. 23, 1862.
  Brig. Gen. Henry Heth, Dec. 19, 1862.
  Maj. Gen. Edmund Kirby Smith, Dec. 23, 1862.
  Brig. Gen. Daniel S. Donelson, Jan. 17, 1863.
  Brig. Gen. William G. M. Davis, spring 1863.
  Maj. Gen. Dabney H. Maury, Apr. 25, 1863.
  Maj. Gen. Simon B. Buckner, May 12, 1863.
  Brig. Gen. William Preston, July 4, 1863.

Lt. Gen. James Longstreet, Dec. 5, 1863.
Maj. Gen. Simon B. Buckner, Apr. 12, 1864.
Brig. Gen. William E. Jones, May 2, 1864.
Col. George B. Crittenden (temp.), May 31, 1864.
Brig. Gen. John H. Morgan (temp.), June 22, 1864.
Brig. Gen. John C. Breckinridge, Sept. 27, 1864.
Lt. Gen. Jubal A. Early, Mar. 25, 1865.

After the assignment of General Jones, the commanders of the Department of East Tennessee also commanded the Trans-Allegheny or Western Department of Virginia.

Successive commanders of the Department of Southwestern Virginia:
Maj. Gen. William W. Loring, May 8, 1862.
Brig. Gen. John Echols, Oct. 15, 1862.
Brig. Gen. John S. Williams, Nov. 19, 1862.

Record Group 109. --Records of the Department of East Tennessee include letters and telegrams sent, Mar.-Nov. 1862 (ch. II, vols. 51, 52, and 237); letters and telegrams sent and special orders, Aug.-Dec. 1862 (ch. II, vol. 52 1/2); endorsements on letters received, Nov. 22, 1862-Mar. 31, 1863, Oct. 11-Dec. 27, 1864 (ch. II, vol. 51 1/2; ch. VIII, vol. 357); general and special orders and circulars, 1861-64 (1 in.); orders and letters sent by General Zollicoffer's brigade, Aug. 1861-Jan. 1862 (ch. II, vol. 280); and copies of letters and telegrams received and sent by Col. William B. Wood, post commander at Knoxville, Oct. 14-Nov. 25, 1861 (ch. II, vol. 279). Records of the Department of East Tennessee, Provost Marshal's Office (Cols. William M. Churchwell and John E. Toole), include correspondence and other documents relating to Federal prisoners, Apr. 1862-June 1863 (2 1/2 in.); telegrams received, Jan. 1862-Aug. 1863 (1/2 in.); correspondence relating to passes, Apr. 1862-Aug. 1863 (3 in.); bonds for loyalty and good behavior, Apr. 1862-June 1863 (1 1/2 in.), index in ch. II, vol. 236; jailers' reports of prisoners in the Knoxville jail, Aug. 1862-Aug. 1863 (1/2 in.); and an undated record of passes issued (1 vol.) with a separately bound index.

Records of the Department of Western Virginia include letters and telegrams sent, Mar.-Oct. 1863 (ch. II, vols. 58, 61, and 65); letters sent, Oct. 1863-Jan. 1864 (ch. II, vol. 54); endorsements on letters received, Mar.-Dec. 1863 (ch. II, vol. 261); general orders and circulars, Dec. 10, 1862-Mar. 25, 1864 (ch. II, vol. 62); special orders, Dec. 10, 1862-Apr. 2, 1863, and Jan. 27-May 31, 1864 (ch. II, vols. 63 and 64); letters and telegrams sent by Maj. Gen. Samuel Jones' command, Aug. 1862-Feb. 1863 (ch. II, vol. 233); letters sent by Maj. T. M. Bowyer, chief of ordnance, Nov. 14, 1862-Jan. 23, 1864 (ch. IV, vol. 89); a personal data and clothing issue book of the post guard at Abingdon, 1861-65 (ch. VIII, vol. 89); and telegrams sent by Maj. J. Stoddard Johnston from Dublin, Dec. 17-20, 1864.

Records of the Departments of East Tennessee and Western Virginia include letters sent, orders, and circulars, Apr. 1863-Oct. 1864 (ch. II, vol. 234); telegrams sent, Apr. 1863-Sept. 1864 (ch. II, vol. 235); telegrams sent, Apr., May, and Dec. 1864 (1/4 in.); letters received, Jan. 1862-Mar. 1865 (6 in.); and telegrams received, Dec. 1862-Mar. 1864 (4 in.). Records of the Provost Marshal's Office include papers relating to political prisoners, miscellaneous papers, and correspondence, Oct. 1861-Feb. 1865 (8 in.).

Records in Other Custody. --Two letters sent by Gen. Edmund Kirby Smith, June 14 and Aug. 1862, are in Duke University Library. Orders issued and received by General Zollicoffer's brigade, Aug. 21, 1861-Jan. 17, 1862 (1 vol.), are in the Confederate Museum. Copies of letters sent, Apr. 14, 1862-Aug. 23, 1862, by Maj. William H. Thomas as chief commissary of the Department of East Tennessee and other papers of Major Thomas, Jan. 1862-Jan. 1863 (701 items), including copies of outgoing letters, vouchers for supplies issued at Knoxville, invoices, and returns of provisions, are in the Howard-Tilton Memorial Library of Tulane University. A letters-sent book of Maj. Gen. W. W. Loring in the Virginia State Library, Archives Division, contains copies of letters written from the headquarters of the Department of Southwestern Virginia, May 19-Sept. 1, 1862. Other papers of General Loring are in Duke University Library which also has letters received (with a few letters sent) of Capt. William E. Duncan, quartermaster at Giles Courthouse, Dec. 31, 1861-Aug. 18, 1862. A miscellaneous record book of the ordnance depot at Dublin, Va., containing letters, reports, and invoices, Nov. 1862-Jan. 1865, is in the New York Public Library. A correspondence and order book of Col. William B. Wood, 16th Alabama Infantry, Oct. 14, 1861-Jan. 11, 1862, in the Confederate Museum is chiefly for the period when he was post commander at Knoxville; he moved in Dec. 1861 to Camp Beach Grove, Ky.

District of the Gulf

Established in the Western Department on July 2, 1861, this district embraced the region east of the Pearl River to the Apalachicola and north to the 32d parallel. For a few months in the latter part of 1863 it was called the Department of the Gulf, and on Jan. 28, 1864, it was merged into the Department of Alabama, Mississippi, and East Louisiana.

Successive commanders of the district:

Brig. Gen. John H. Forney, July 2, 1862.
Brig. Gen. William W. Mackall (temp.), Dec. 8, 1862.
Brig. Gen. Simon B. Buckner, Dec. 14, 1862.
Maj. Gen. Frank Gardner (temp.), Apr. 27, 1863.
Maj. Gen. Dabney H. Maury, May 1863.

Record Group 36.--Press copies of letters sent by Capt. Samuel H. Lockett, engineer officer at Fort Morgan, Ala., Sept. 14-Oct. 27, 1861, with the records of the collector of customs at Mobile, are in a book that also contains letters sent by the Superintendent's Office, Mobile Harbor Improvement, Apr. 1854-Nov. 1857. A timebook for mechanics and slaves employed at Fort Morgan, May 1861-May 1862 (1 vol.), is in the same collection of records.

Record Group 109.--General and special orders issued from headquarters and from subcommands, 1862-65 (1/4 in.); endorsements on letters received, Jan.-Apr. 1865 (ch. II, vol. 98); press copy books of letters sent by the engineer office at Mobile, Jan. 10, 1863-May 3, 1865 (ch. III, vols. 10, 12, 13, and 16), containing outgoing letters, telegrams, and reports signed by Brig. Gen. Danville Leadbetter, Lt. Col. Victor von Sheilika, and Col. Samuel H. Lockett, chief engineer of the district; letters-sent book of the headquarters of the Eastern Division at Blakely, Ala., Mar. 14-Apr. 9, 1865, containing fair copies signed by Brig. Gen. St. John R. Liddell, commanding, and Capt. H. L. D. Lewis, acting assistant adjutant general; a dispatch and telegram book of the Eastern Division, Mar.-Apr. 1865 (ch. II, vol. 100); record of extra-duty men, civilian employees, and buildings and articles hired by Maj. E. G. Mohler, quartermaster at

Mobile, 1862-64 (ch. V, vol. 212); rolls of civilians, Negroes, and detailed men employed by Maj. J. E. Klumph, quartermaster at Mobile, 1864-65 (ch. VIII, vol. 96); and a record of slaves hired, 1864-65 (ch. V, vol. 135).

Department of Henrico

This department was established on Oct. 21, 1861, and embraced Henrico County, the seat of which was Richmond. In Mar. 1862 it was extended to include Petersburg and 10 miles of surrounding country, and on May 5, 1864, it was merged into the Department of Richmond. The departmental commander was also in charge of the President's Guard. On Mar. 4, 1862, the provost marshal of this department took over from the Office of the Secretary of War the function of issuing passports.

The commander of this department was Brig. Gen. John H. Winder.

Record Group 109. --Letters received by Brig. Gen. John H. Winder, 1862-65 (1 1/4 in.), are entered in a register (ch. II, vol. 236), for which there are alphabetical name indexes. A miscellaneous file, 1861-62 (1 in.), consists of lists of deserters delivered to Winder, memoranda, correspondence, payrolls of hospital guards, commutations of rations, reports, and accounts current. An account book of Capt. John H. Parkhill, Apr.-Dec. 1862 (ch. X, vol. 185), shows amounts received by draft, check, and cash, and the names of persons to whom disbursements were made, with the amounts. Another section on disbursements shows only check numbers and the amounts. Abstracts of disbursements on account of contingencies made by Col. John H. Parkhill, Oct. 28, 1862-Mar. 17, 1863 (ch. V. vol. 248 1/2), show amounts paid for quartermaster purposes. Other records that were begun by the Department of Henrico are described under the Department of Richmond.

Records in Other Custody. --In the Confederate Museum are general and special orders, May 14-Oct. 29, 1863 (1 vol.), including copies of many special orders to the provost marshal regarding the disposition of military and civilian prisoners held in Richmond prisons; letters sent, May 15-Oct. 27, 1863 (part of the same vol.), including copies of letters to the provost marshal and his assistant, prison commanders, and the agent for the exchange of prisoners; and appointments of clerks and detectives.

Army of the Kanawha

Troops that had been under the command of Brig. Gen. Henry A. Wise since June 1861 were organized on Aug. 12 of that year into the Army of the Kanawha. In Oct. 1861 the army was merged into the Department of Northern Virginia.

The commander of the army was Brig. Gen. John B. Floyd.

Record Group 109. --Letters-sent books, July-Sept. 1861 (ch. II, vols. 93 and 95); general and special orders, July-Dec. 1861 (ch. II, vols. 94 and 96); copies of correspondence between Generals Floyd and Wise, July-Sept. 1861 (ch. II, vol. 232); and letters, telegrams, and reports sent and received, 1861 (2 in.).

Records in Other Custody. --Other papers of General Floyd are in Duke University Library.

Central Army of Kentucky and the Army of Kentucky

Organized in Oct. 1861, the Central Army of Kentucky was united in Mar. 1862 with the Army of the Mississippi. The Army of Kentucky was organized on Aug. 25, 1862, and in November of that year these armies were merged into the Army of Tennessee.
Commanders of the Central Army of Kentucky:
Gen. Albert S. Johnston, Oct. 28, 1861.
Maj. Gen. William J. Hardee, Dec. 5, 1861.
The commander of the Army of Kentucky was Maj. Gen. Edmund Kirby Smith.
Record Group 109. --General and special orders of both armies, 1861-62 (1 in.); special orders, 2d Division, Central Army of Kentucky, Nov. 2, 1861-Feb. 6, 1862 (ch. II, vol. 225); and letters sent, Army of Kentucky, Sept.-Oct. 1862 (ch. II, vol. 82).
Records in Other Custody. --Papers of Surg. Charles J. Johnson, who treated men wounded in the battle of Shiloh, are in the Department of Archives of Louisiana State University.

Central Division of Kentucky

The Central Division of Kentucky was in existence from Sept. 1861 to Feb. 1862, with headquarters at Bowling Green.
The commander was Brig. Gen. Simon B. Buckner.
Record Group 109. --Letters, telegrams, and circulars sent, Sept. 1861-Feb. 1862 (ch. II, vol. 226), and general and special orders, 1861-62 (ch. II, vol. 224).

Army of the Mississippi (Western Department)

On Mar. 5, 1862, troops in the Western Department were organized as the Army of the Mississippi. It had two corps headed by Maj. Gens. Leonidas Polk and Braxton Bragg. When the Army of the Mississippi was united with the Central Army of Kentucky on Mar. 29, Gen. Albert S. Johnston took command. The larger Army of the Mississippi fought the battle of Shiloh on Apr. 6-7, 1862. In July the army was transferred to Chattanooga, and when General Bragg resumed command in Nov. 1862 it became the Army of Tennessee.
Successive commanders:
Maj. Gen. Braxton Bragg, Mar. 6, 1862.
Gen. Pierre G. T. Beauregard, Mar. 17, 1862.
Gen. Albert S. Johnston, Mar. 29, 1862.
Gen. Pierre G. T. Beauregard, Apr. 6, 1862.
Maj. Gen. Braxton Bragg, May 7, 1862.
Maj. Gen. William J. Hardee, July 5, 1862.
Maj. Gen. Leonidas Polk (temp.), Sept. 28, 1862.
Maj. Gen. Braxton Bragg, Nov. 7, 1862.
Record Group 109. --General and special orders and circulars issued, Mar. 4-Dec. 28, 1862 (2 1/2 in.); general and special orders issued by Brig. Gen. James P. Anderson's brigade, Mar. 24-June 29, 1862 (ch. VIII, vol. 338), with morning reports of the 1st Brigade, June 22-28, 1862; endorsements on letters received by Anderson's brigade, May 2, 1863-May 7, 1864 (ch. II, vol. 18 1/2); report of killed, wounded, and missing of the

2d Corps at the battle of Shiloh, 1862 (ch. II, vol. 220); letters and telegrams sent by the Corinth Ordnance Depot, Apr. 15-May 20, 1862 (ch. IV, vol. 25), including communications signed by William H. McMain, the military storekeeper and Capt. Hypolite Oladowski; and a record of ordnance and ordnance stores issued, Feb. 24-May 13, 1862 (ch. IV, vols. 122 and 123).

Records in Other Custody.--General orders and circulars, Mar. 5-Apr. 28, 1862 (1 vol.), are in the Louisiana Historical Association collection on deposit in the Howard-Tilton Memorial Library of Tulane University. An order book of Brig. Gen. John K. Jackson's brigade of Withers' division, Mar. 13, 1862-Jan. 10, 1863 (microfilm), is in the Southern Historical Collection in the University of North Carolina Library. Orders, circulars, reports, and returns of Brig. Gen. Charles Clark's division, Mar. 10-Aug. 4, 1862, are in the Mississippi Department of Archives and History. That repository also has returns of quartermaster and commissary stores, property accounts, and ordnance accounts, 1861-62, and copies of cash vouchers paid by Col. Madison McAfee, May-Dec. 1861. A record of requisitions for ordnance by Capt. John T. Champneys, ordnance officer at Columbus, Ky., Oct. 1861-Feb. 1862 (1 vol.), and his record of ammunition and ordnance stores on hand, received, and issued, Sept. 1861-Feb. 1862 (1 vol.), are in Emory University Library. Papers of Gen. A. S. Johnston are in the Chicago Historical Society collections, and a scrapbook is in the Texas Archives of the University of Texas Library.

Army of Mobile

The Army of Mobile was organized under the Department of Alabama and West Florida on Jan. 27, 1862. It comprised troops in, around, and south of Mobile and was discontinued on June 27, 1862.

Successive commanders:
Brig. Gen. Jones M. Withers, Jan. 27, 1862.
Col. John B. Villepigue (temp.), Feb. 28, 1862.
Brig. Gen. Samuel Jones, Mar. 15, 1862.

Record Group 109.--General and special orders issued, Mar.-May 1862 (1/8 in.).

Records in Other Custody.--Letters sent by Brig. Gen. Samuel Jones, Feb. 6-July 18, 1862, are in part of a volume with the Bragg papers in the Western Reserve Historical Society collections.

Department of North Carolina and the Department of North Carolina and Southern Virginia

The Department of North Carolina was established in the summer of 1861. On Sept. 29 the District of Cape Fear, including Wilmington and its defenses, was established and became a part of it. In Nov. 1861 the department was enlarged to include Roanoke Island and in June 1862 it was extended to the south bank of the James River and Drewry's Bluff. On Sept. 19, 1862, it was abolished, and the State of North Carolina became part of the Department of North Carolina and Southern Virginia, which included the defenses of Richmond. Reestablished on Apr. 1, 1863, the Department of North Carolina included the State of North Carolina, and it was extended on May 28, 1863, to include that part of the Department of Southern Virginia as far north as Petersburg and its environs and the Appomattox River.

On May 19, 1864, it became part of the Department of North Carolina and Southern Virginia.

Successive commanders of the District of Cape Fear:

Brig. Gen. Joseph R. Anderson, Oct. 5, 1861.
Brig. Gen. Samuel G. French, Mar. 15, 1862.
Brig. Gen. William H. C. Whiting, Dec. 1862.

Successive commanders of the Department of North Carolina:

Brig. Gen. Richard C. Gatlin, Aug. 20, 1861.
Brig. Gen. Joseph R. Anderson, Mar. 19, 1862.
Maj. Gen. Theophilus H. Holmes, Mar. 25, 1862.
Maj. Gen. Daniel H. Hill, July 17, 1862.
Maj. Gen. William H. C. Whiting, July 14, 1863.
Maj. Gen. George E. Pickett, Sept. 23, 1863.
Gen. Braxton Bragg, Nov. 27, 1864.

Successive commanders of the Department of North Carolina and Southern Virginia:

Maj. Gen. Gustavus W. Smith, Sept. 19, 1862.
Maj. Gen. Samuel G. French (temp.), Feb. 17, 1863.
Brig. Gen. James Longstreet, Feb. 26, 1863.
Gen. Pierre G. T. Beauregard, May 14, 1864.

Record Group 45. --Telegrams sent and received by Col. John J. Hedrick, commander of Fort Holmes, N.C., May 20-Dec. 3, 1864 (1 vol.).

Record Group 109. --Letters and telegrams sent, Aug. 25, 1861-Mar. 7, 1862 (ch. II, vol. 262 1/2); orders and circulars issued by the department headquarters and other commands, 1861-65 (2 in.); letters sent by Brig. Gen. Walter Gwynn, commanding the coast defenses, May-Aug. 1861 (ch. II, vol. 259 1/2); letters sent and orders issued by the Wilmington command, Apr.-May 1861 (ch. II, vol. 331); special orders, Department of North Carolina and Southern Virginia, Apr.-Oct. 1864 (ch. II, vol. 216); general and special orders of the 1st, 2d, and 3d Military Districts, 1864 (1/4 in.); rosters of officers in Gen. Thomas L. Clingman's brigade, 1861-62, and endorsements on letters received by the brigade, July 1863 (ch. II, vol. 345); and letters, orders, and circulars issued, Mar. 1863-June 1864 (ch. II, vol. 216 1/2).

Records of Maj. Gen. W. H. C. Whiting's command include letters sent, Nov. 1862-Jan. 1865 (ch. II, vols. 334-339); telegrams sent, Dec. 1862-Aug. 1863 (ch. II, vol. 326); telegrams received, Jan. 1865 (ch. II, vol. 328); a register of letters received and endorsements on letters received, Nov. 1862-May 1863 (ch. II, vol. 330); and endorsements on letters received, June 1863-Dec. 1864 (ch. II, vols. 344 and 346-348).

Other records relating to local commands include press copies of letters sent by Capt. James M. Goodman, post quartermaster at Salisbury, Mar. 14, 1864-Mar. 7, 1865 (ch. IX, vol. 233); a record of papers concerning personnel actions at Salisbury, 1864 (ch. VIII, vol. 99); a record of orders for quartermaster stores, June-Aug. 1861 (ch. VIII, vol. 88); and rosters of officers at Fort Johnson, Mar.-May 1863 (ch. I, vol. 110).

Records in Other Custody. --Wartime records of Maj. Gen. W. H. C. Whiting, including correspondence, military commissions, orders, and a letter book are in the North Carolina Department of Archives and History. Letters and telegrams sent, 1864-65 (1 vol.), are in the Palmer collection of the Western Reserve Historical Society. Records of A. D. Smith, a surgeon in the 62d Georgia Cavalry stationed near Greenville, N.C., in 1863, including correspondence, orders, reports, requisitions, and discharges, 1863-64 (photostats), are in the North Carolina Department of Archives and History. Three record books of Isaac S. Tanner, chief surgeon of Hoke's division, are in the Confederate Museum. One of these contains a report of the division's killed and wounded at the battle of Plymouth, N.C., Apr. 18-20, 1864 (p. 29-119), and a return of casualties near Kinston, N.C., Mar. 8-10, 1865 (p. 135-150). The second contains a report of the killed and wounded of the 24th North Carolina Regiment at the battle of Plymouth, Apr. 18-20, 1864; summaries of that regiment's sick and wounded, Apr. 1, 1862-Mar. 31, 1864; copies of invoices of medicines and hospital stores issued to Surgeon Tanner; a semiannual return of hospital stores and equipment, June 30, 1862-Dec. 31, 1864; and a monthly register of surgical cases, 21st North Carolina Regiment, May 1862-July 1863. The third volume is a correspondence and order book, Sept. 1862-Feb. 1865. Records of Capt. John F. Divine, assistant quartermaster at Fort Macon (Goldsboro, N.C.), in the Confederate Museum include press copies of letters sent, Nov. 22, 1861-Nov. 10, 1864 (1 vol.), and a cashbook containing a record of receipts and expenditures, Nov. 16, 1861-Mar. 31, 1865. Letters written by Joseph S. Fowler, Jr., a commissary officer at Kinston, N.C., are in Duke University Library. Records of Capt. James A. Bryan, an ordnance and quartermaster officer at New Bern and Kinston, in the Southern Historical Collection in the University of North Carolina Library include a letters-sent book, Oct. 27, 1861-May 1, 1862; a record of ordnance and ordnance stores received, bought, and shipped, Oct. 26, 1861-Jan. 30, 1862 (1 vol.); and a file of letters, reports, orders, bills, requisitions, vouchers, and invoices, 1861-64 (7 in.). Captain Bryan's record of ordnance and ordnance stores received and issued at New Bern, Aug. 30-Sept. 16, 1861 (1 vol.), is in the North Carolina Department of Archives and History. Records of Capt. Lewis C. Hanes, quartermaster at Salisbury, including a record of forage received and issued, Sept. 1864-Apr. 1865 (1 vol.), papers of Maj. William T. Sutherlin, quartermaster at Danville, Va., during 1862-65, and papers of Matthias M. Marshall, who became attached as a chaplain to General Hospital No. 1 at Kittrell's Springs, N.C., in 1864, are in the Southern Historical Collection in the University of North Carolina Library. Papers of Drury Lacy, who served as a chaplain at the hospital in Wilson in 1863 and at Camp Holmes and General Hospital No. 8 in Raleigh in 1864, are in the same repository.

Army and Department of Northern Virginia

The Department of Northern Virginia was established on Oct. 22, 1861. On that date the Army of the Potomac was merged into the department. At the end of 1861 the Army of the Kanawha also became a part of it. The department included the Aquia District, the Potomac District, and the Valley District. On Apr. 12, 1862, it was enlarged to include the Departments of Norfolk and the Peninsula; on June 1, 1862, the armies in eastern Virginia and North Carolina; and on Apr. 2, 1863, the post at Staunton, Va. Successive commanders of the Aquia District:
>Brig. Gen. Theophilus H. Holmes, Oct. 22, 1861.
>Col. R. Milton Cary (temp.), July 18, 1861.
>Brig. Gen. Gustavus W. Smith, Mar. 23, 1862.
Commander of the Potomac District:
>Brig. Gen. Pierre G. T. Beauregard.

Successive commanders of the Valley District:
Maj. Gen. Thomas J. Jackson, Nov. 1861.
Maj. Gen. Daniel H. Hill (temp.), Sept. 6, 1862.
Brig. Gen. William E. Jones (temp.), Dec. 29, 1862.
Maj. Gen. Jubal A. Early (temp.), June 15, 1863.
Brig. Gen. John D. Imboden, July 28, 1863.
Brig. Gen. Lunsford L. Lomax, Mar. 29, 1865.
Successive commanders of the Army of Northern Virginia:
Gen. Joseph E. Johnston, Oct. 22, 1861.
Maj. Gen. Gustavus W. Smith, May 31, 1862.
Gen. Robert E. Lee, June 1, 1862.

Record Group 109. --Records of the headquarters include letters and telegrams sent, Jan. 1862-Mar. 1864 (ch. II, vols. 82 1/2, 83, and 84); confidential letters sent, June, 1863-Oct. 1864 (ch. II, vol. 84 1/2); letters, telegrams, and other papers received by Gen. Robert E. Lee, 1862-65 (3 in.); a register of letters and telegrams received, 1862-65 (ch. VIII, part of vol. 232, p. 15-93, and part of an index vol.); registers of letters received, Department of Northern Virginia, 1862-64 (ch. II, vols. 85-87); a record of papers received and referred, 1862-63 (ch. VIII, vols. 355 and 356); battle reports, 1863 (ch. II, vol. 90); general and special orders and circulars issued, 1861-65 (7 in.); special orders issued, Dec. 1861-Sept. 1863 (ch. II, vols. 88 and 89); and accounts for telegrams sent, Apr. 1862-June 1863 (ch. II, vol. 264).

Records of subcommands and certain officers include battle reports, statistical reports and returns, and orders and circulars of Lt. Gen. Jubal A. Early's command, 1861-65 (6 in.); letters sent by the right wing commanded by Maj. Gen. John B. Magruder, June-Oct. 1862 (ch. II, vol. 232 1/2); the official diary of the 1st Corps commanded by Maj. Gen. Richard H. Anderson, May-Oct. 1864 (ch. II, vol. 281); general and special orders and circulars issued by Robert E. Rodes' and Cullen A. Battle's brigade, Nov. 1861-Mar. 1865 (ch. II, vol. 66); a miscellaneous record book of Brig. Gen. Thomas T. Munford, Apr. 1862-Sept. 1865 (ch. II, vol. 285 1/2); a letters-sent book of Maj. Gen. Richard H. Anderson, Feb. 1861-Aug. 1863 (ch. II, vol. 282); and letters and orders issued and received by Chief Surg. John T. Gilmore of Maj. Gen. Lafayette McLaws' division, Nov. 1862-Oct. 1864 (ch. VI, vol. 646). Records of Maj. Gen. William H. C. Whiting's command include letters sent, Mar.-Apr. 1862 (ch. II, vol. 333); letters sent and received, Mar.-July 1862 (ch. II, vol. 332); a register of letters received and endorsements on letters received, 1861-63 (ch. II, vol. 329); general and special orders issued, Sept. 1861-Feb. 1862 (ch. II, vol. 340); general orders and circulars, Feb.-July 1862 (ch. II, vol. 341); and special orders, Feb.-July 1862 (ch. II, vol. 342). Other records include copies of letters sent by Lt. Col. James L. Corley, the chief quartermaster, July 5-16, 1862 (ch. V, vol. 152, p. 1-5); a record of quartermaster stores issued and condemned, Sept. 1, 1862-Oct. 30, 1863 (ch. V, vols. 198 and 204); and an undated roster of officers of local defense troops and artillery battalions (ch. I, vol. 100). Records of topographers under the supervision of Capt. Albert H. Campbell include memoranda, a receipt book, circulars, instructions, and letters, 1862-64 (2 notebooks), of Lt. Benjamin L. Blackford; a sketchbook of F. Boylan, July 1863, and C. B. Denson, July-Aug. 1863, and sketchbooks and cashbooks, 1862-64, of William R. Martin.

Robert A. Brock, ed., Paroles of the Army of Northern Virginia (Southern Historical Society Papers, 15, 1887; reprinted, New York, 1962); C. S. A. Army, Department of Northern Virginia, Reports of the Operations of the Army of Northern Virginia, from June 1862, to and Including the Battle at Fredericksburg, Dec. 13, 1862 (2 vols.; Richmond, 1864); Clifford Dowdey and Louis H. Manarin, eds., The Wartime Papers of R. E. Lee (Boston, 1961); Douglas S. Freeman, ed., Lee's Dispatches; Unpublished Letters of General Robert E. Lee, C. S. A., to Jefferson Davis and the War Department of the Confederate States of America, 1862-65 (New York, 1915; reprinted with 10 additional dispatches, Grady McWhiney, ed., New York, 1957); John W. Jones, ed., Life and Letters of Robert Edward Lee, Soldier and Man (New York and Washington, 1906), "Roster of the Army of Northern Virginia," Army of Northern Virginia, Memorial Volume, p. 334-342 (Richmond, 1880); Robert E. Lee, Jr., Recollections and Letters of General Robert E. Lee (New York, 1904). Correspondence, reports, and orders of General Lee are in the Official Records . . . Armies.

Records in Other Custody. --Official correspondence, telegrams, orders, and reports, including some transcripts that were obtained by General Lee after the war, are in the Virginia Historical Society collections. In the Society's map collection are maps prepared under the direction of Capt. A. H. Campbell (see the section on the Engineer Bureau). In 1964 the Society received other official records of General Lee and letters written by him to members of his family. Some of this material relates to the Army of the Kanawha and the Army of the Northwest. The R. E. Lee papers, 1830-70, in the Washington and Lee University Library number 5,000 items. The Lee papers in the Virginia State Library, Archives Division, consist largely of photocopies obtained by the Virginia Civil War Centennial Commission for use in the compilation by Dowdey and Manarin cited above. For the war years more than 6,000 items of correspondence were found, and one-sixth of these were published. Telegrams from General Lee to the President and the War Department and military and family correspondence are in Duke University Library. Other Lee papers are in the Library of Congress, the Chicago Historical Society, the Confederate Museum, the Henry E. Huntington Library, the Maryland Historical Society, the Missouri Historical Society, the University of North Carolina Library, the North Carolina Department of Archives and History, the New York Public Library, the New-York Historical Society, the University of Texas Library, and the Palmer collection of the Western Reserve Historical Society. Other records of the Army of Northern Virginia are in the Louisiana Historical Association deposit in the Howard-Tilton Memorial Library, Tulane University.

George L. Christian, "General Lee's Headquarters Records and Papers--The Present Location of Some of These," Southern Historical Society Papers, 44:229-231 (June 1923).

Correspondence, telegrams, orders, reports on ordnance, journals, and diaries of Brig. Gen. E. Porter Alexander, chief of ordnance of the Army of Northern Virginia and chief of artillery of Longstreet's corps, are in the Southern Historical Collection in the University of North Carolina Library. A few other papers of his are in the Library of Congress.

Special and general orders issued by Brig. Gen. Joseph R. Anderson, Apr. 26-May 28, 1862, to the "Army of the Rappahannock" are in the Virginia Historical Society collections. Correspondence of Brig. Gen. Henry L. Benning, colonel of the 17th Georgia Infantry and later a brigade commander, are in the Southern Historical Collection in the University of North Carolina Library. A small quantity of wartime letters of Brig. Gen. Robert H. Chilton, chief of staff and inspector general, are in the Confederate Museum. Papers of Brig. Gen. James Conner, commander of the 22d North Carolina Infantry and of a brigade in Kershaw's division, are in the South Carolina Historical Society. Correspondence, telegrams, orders, and battle reports of Lt. Gen. Jubal A. Early, division commander, are in the Library of Congress. Other papers of General Early are in the Henry E. Huntington Library, the University of Virginia Library, the U. S. Military Academy Library, and the Virginia Historical Society collections. Official and personal correspondence of Lt. Gen. Richard S. Ewell, commander of the 2d Corps, is in the Library of Congress (microfilm with the Virginia Historical Society). Other Ewell papers are in the Southern Historical Collection in the University of North Carolina Library, the Tennessee State Library and Archives, and the William and Mary College Library. Papers of Brig. Gen. Richard B. Garnett, who served under Generals Jackson and Longstreet, are in the Archives Division, Virginia State Library. Papers of Brig. Gen. Martin W. Gary, commander of the Hampton legion and after 1864 of a brigade, are in the South Caroliniana Library of the University of South Carolina. Papers of Brig. Gen. James B. Gordon, commander of a brigade in Hampton's division, in the North Carolina Department of Archives and History include correspondence, commissions, and special orders, 1861-64. The same repository has papers of Maj. Gen. Bryan Grimes, commander of a brigade in Rodes' division, and other papers are in the Southern Historical Collection in the University of North Carolina Library. Papers of Lt. Gen. Wade Hampton, commander of the Hampton legion and later of a brigade in Stuart's cavalry corps and of the corps itself, are in the South Caroliniana Library of the University of South Carolina and in the Valentine Museum, Richmond, Va. In Apr. 1865 at Petersburg a Union captain found a letter book, June 6, 1862-June 1, 1863, of the light division commanded by Maj. Gen. Ambrose P. Hill; it is now in the New York Public Library. A register of Brig. Gen. John D. Imboden's command is in the University of Virginia Library (J. B. Christian papers). A variety of military records of Lt. Gen. Thomas J. Jackson, commander of the 2d Corps, are in Duke University Library, the University of North Carolina Library, the Virginia Historical Society collections, the Virginia Military Institute, and the Virginia State Library, Archives Division. In the Jedediah Hotchkiss papers in the Library of Congress are outgoing letters, 1861-63, and abstracts of Jackson's orders. Correspondence of Brig. Gen. Bradley T. Johnson, commander of Maryland infantry, is in Duke University Library. Papers of Brig. Gen. Joseph B. Kershaw, a brigade and division commander of the 1st Corps, are in the South Caroliniana Library of the University of South Carolina. Papers of Maj. Gen. William Mahone, a brigade and division commander, are in Duke University Library. Records of Brig. Gen. William N. Pendleton, chief of artillery, in the Confederate Museum include a letters-sent book, June 5, 1862-Apr. 1, 1865, and general and special orders and circulars issued by the artillery corps, June 17, 1862-Apr. 2, 1865 (1 vol.). Pendleton's papers in Duke University Library include correspondence, telegrams, commissions, orders, lists of ordnance, lists of quartermaster supplies, contracts for supplies, and officers' reports. His papers in the Southern Historical Collection in the University of North Carolina Library include military communications, orders, requisitions, statistical abstracts, and muster rolls of artillery. A few letters sent, 1862-63, are in the Virginia State Library, Archives Division. Correspondence and other documents of Maj. Gen. S. Dodson Ramseur, commander of the 49th North Carolina Infantry and later of a division, are in the North Carolina Department of Archives and History and the Southern Historical Collection in the University of North Carolina Library. Correspondence of Maj. Gen. Thomas L. Rosser, commander of the 5th Virginia Cavalry and later of a brigade, is in the University of Virginia Library. Papers of Brig. Gen. George H. Steuart, commander of a brigade in Johnson's division, in the Confederate Museum include letters, orders, reports, and invoices of commissary supplies, Jan.-Dec. 1863. Other papers of General Steuart are in Duke University Library. Lt. Gen. James E. B. Stuart's papers in the Henry E. Huntington Library include letters (more than 100 from R. E. Lee), orders, and addresses to his soldiers. In 1961 the Virginia Historical Society bought from the State Historical Society of Wisconsin some Stuart papers including a letters-sent book, Oct. 24, 1862-May 2, 1864, a fieldbook containing copies of battle reports, July 21, 1861-Apr. 25, 1863, and some letters and orders received. Other Stuart papers are in the Chicago Historical Society collections and in the Duke University Library. Papers of Maj. Gen. Isaac R. Trimble are in the Maryland Historical Society. Correspondence, orders, and battle reports, 1862-65, of Maj. Gen. Cadmus M. Wilcox are in the Library of Congress.

Records of some quartermaster officers are available. A cashbook of Maj. Alfred M. Barbour, a chief quartermaster, Sept. 19, 1861-Sept. 19, 1862, is in the Library of Congress. Extracts of letters, Feb. 2-May 27, 1862, written by Maj. John A. Harman to Col. A. W. Harman, post commander at Staunton, are with the Jedediah Hotchkiss papers in the Library of Congress. Major Harman was chief quartermaster of the 2d Corps commanded by General Jackson. Quartermaster records, Apr.-Sept. 1864, of 2d Corps Headquarters accumulated by Capt. Marshall Lake are in the Library of Congress. Capt. David Meade, quartermaster of the 11th Virginia Infantry, July-Dec. 1862, and of the supply train of Pickett's division, Dec. 1862-Dec. 1864, kept a record book, July 16, 1862-Dec. 31, 1864, now in the Confederate Museum. Records, Jan. 1862-Mar. 1863, of Capt. William Miller, quartermaster of the 7th Virginia Cavalry in the Valley District, are in Duke University Library (Thomas J. Jackson papers). Quartermaster records, 1862-65 (50 items), of Capt. George G. Thompson are in the Library of Congress. Bills of lading for articles transported over the Orange & Alexandria Railroad and received by Captain Thompson at Orange Courthouse, Mar. 1-18, 1863, and shipped from there, Dec. 9, 1863-Feb. 7, 1864, are in the Texas Archives, University of Texas Library. A letters-sent book of Capt. Charles E. Carr, assistant quartermaster at Norfolk, Va., June 30, 1861-May 7, 1862, is with the New-York Historical Society collections. Other quartermaster records, relating mainly to Virginia, 1861-65, are in the Confederate Museum.

Papers, Jan. 1862-Mar. 1864, of Maj. Wells J. Hawks, chief commissary in the Army of the Valley District, are in Duke University Library (Thomas J. Jackson papers). Records of Capt. John J. Halsey, assistant commissary of the 6th Virginia Cavalry, Dec. 1861-Mar. 1863, are in Duke

University Library.

Records of several engineer officers are available. Papers of Capt. James K. Boswell, chief engineer with the 2d Corps, including letters sent, 1862-63, and a diary, Jan. 1-Apr. 18, 1863, are in the Library of Congress (Jedediah Hotchkiss papers). Correspondence, orders, circulars, requisitions, supply lists, and other documents, of Capt. Hugh T. Douglas, 1st Engineer Troops (Pontoniers), Nov. 6, 1861-Aug. 11, 1864, are in the University of Virginia Library. An engineering journal (1861-65; microfilm) of Samuel S. Gause, who planned the fortifications at Aquia Creek on the Potomac River, is in the Tennessee State Library and Archives. Correspondence and diaries of Peter Guerrant are in the same repository. Correspondence and other documents of Lt. Col. Samuel R. Johnston are with the Virginia Historical Society collections. Correspondence, orders, accounts, agreements, muster rolls, payrolls, reports, drawings, and maps of Capt. Charles T. Mason concerning military works at Drewry's Bluff are in the same collections, as are also the papers of Col. T. M. R. Talcott, an aide and engineer under General Lee.

Several collections of papers of surgeons who served with the Army of Northern Virginia have been preserved. A record of military and civilian patients treated by Surg. James Bolton in Richmond, Oct. 1862-Nov. 1863, is in the Virginia State Library, Archives Division. A diary of Surg. James R. Boulware of the 6th South Carolina Volunteers, Apr. 17, 1862-May 10, 1863, in the same repository contains extensive casualty lists. Papers of Blair Burwell, who was attached to Gen. George E. Pickett's division, are in the William and Mary College Library. Papers of James W. Claiborne, surgeon with the 12th Virginia Infantry, are in the Virginia Historical Society collections. Correspondence, 1861-65, and a diary, Sept. 13, 1863-Feb. 5, 1865, of John F. Shaffner, surgeon with the 4th and later the 33d North Carolina Infantry, are in the North Carolina Department of Archives and History. Letters, 1861-62, of John Q. Winfield are in the Southern Historical Collection in the University of North Carolina Library.

Several collections of chaplains' papers are available. Papers of Robert L. Dabney, chaplain of the 18th Virginia Infantry, are in the Southern Historical Collection in the University of North Carolina Library, the Archives Division of the Virginia State Library, the Union Theological Seminary Library, and the University of Virginia Library. A diary of Francis M. Kennedy, chronicling his activities as a chaplain with the 28th North Carolina Infantry, 1863-64, is in the Southern Historical Collection in the University of North Carolina Library. A few letters, 1861-62, of Robert W. Watts are in the University of Virginia Library.

Joseph T. Durkin, ed., Confederate Chaplain; a War Journal of Rev. James B. Sheeran, C.S.S.R., 14th Louisiana, C.S.A. (Milwaukee, 1960).

In 1948 the Library of Congress acquired the papers and maps of Jedediah Hotchkiss, topographical engineer of the 2d Corps, Army of Northern Virginia. The papers include official and private correspondence, orders, and diaries relating to the military campaigns that he took part in. The nearly 200 military maps were prepared by Major Hotchkiss or other officers under his direction for the use of Generals Jackson and Lee. The maps relate to campaigns of the 2d Corps and the Army of Northern Virginia in Virginia and Maryland and to the West Virginia campaign of July

1861. In 1963 the Library of Congress acquired Hotchkiss' 1862 map of the Shenandoah Valley which had been retained by the Handley Library in Winchester, Va., where the Hotchkiss collection had previously been kept. The Handley Library now has three wartime Hotchkiss maps, and five others are in the University of Virginia Library which has another collection of Hotchkiss papers including some wartime material (microfilm in the Library of Congress).

Clara Egli LeGear, "The Hotchkiss Map Collection," Library of Congress Quarterly Journal, 6: 16-20 (Nov. 1948); Everard K. Meade, "Maps and Other Papers of Major Jedediah Hotchkiss, C. S. A.," in Clarke County Historical Association, Proceedings, 8:56-65 (1948); U.S. Library of Congress, Map Division, The Hotchkiss Map Collection; a List of Manuscript Maps, Many of the Civil War Period, Prepared by Major Jed. Hotchkiss, and Other Manuscript and Annotated Maps in His Possession, comp. by Clara Egli LeGear (Washington, 1951); Willard Webb, "The Hotchkiss Papers; an Additional Note," Library of Congress Quarterly Journal, 7: 23-24 (Nov. 1949). Mrs. LeGear's 1951 list indicates the Hotchkiss maps that are published in U.S. War Department, Atlas to Accompany the Official Records of the Union and Confederate Armies (3 vols.; Washington, 1891-95).

Papers of line officers who served with the Army of Northern Virginia are in various repositories. Papers of Col. Stapleton Crutchfield, 1862-65, in Princeton University Library, relate to the artillery of the 2d Corps. Correspondence, reports, and orders of Col. John S. Mosby, commander of the Partisan Rangers, June 1861-Apr. 1865 (photostats), are in the Library of Congress. Other wartime papers of Colonel Mosby are in Duke University Library, the Archives Division of the Virginia State Library, and the University of Virginia Library.

Papers of other officers who served in the Army of Northern Virginia in different capacities are available. Papers of Lt. Col. William Allan, chief ordnance officer in the 2d Corps, are in the Southern Historical Collection in the University of North Carolina Library. Correspondence of Capt. Robert A. Bright, who was attached to Pickett's division, is in the William and Mary College Library which also has letters of Maj. Campbell Brown, assistant adjutant general on General Ewell's staff. Correspondence of Capt. Holmes Conrad, an adjutant with the 11th Virginia Infantry, post commissary at Winchester and Woodstock, and a staff officer with Gen. John D. Imboden and Thomas L. Rosser, is in the Virginia Historical Society collections. Correspondence and diaries of Capt. John E. Cooke, who served under Generals Stuart and Pendleton, are in the University of Virginia Library, and other papers of Cooke are in Duke University Library. Papers of Capt. Francis W. Dawson, an ordnance officer, are in Duke University Library. Letters of Maj. Henry K. Douglas, a staff officer under Gens. T. J. Jackson, Elisha F. Paxton, Edward Johnson, and Jubal A. Early, are in the University of Virginia Library. Other papers of Douglas are in the Southern Historical Collection in the University of North Carolina Library. Papers of Capt. James M. Garnett, an ordnance officer, are in the Archives Division of the Virginia State Library and the University of Virginia Library. A miscellaneous record book of Maj. Walter Harrison, adjutant general and inspector general under Maj. Gen. George E. Pickett, Jan. 10, 1863-Feb. 1865, in the Southern Historical

Collection in the University of North Carolina Library contains in addition
to copies of inspection reports, a list of staff officers of the division, a
statistical report on field transportation available, a record of clothing
issued, and estimates of clothing and shoes needed for the division. A few
papers of Capt. Richard B. Kennon, who served as a staff officer with Generals Stuart and Rosser, are in the Archives Division of the Virginia State
Library. Some correspondence and reports of Maj. Henry B. McClellan,
assistant adjutant general to Generals Stuart and Hampton, are in the Virginia Historical Society collections. A diary of Capt. W. W. Old, June
13-Aug. 12, 1864, relating to General Early's campaigns in Virginia and
Maryland is with the Early papers in the Library of Congress. Correspondence of Col. John M. Patton, Jr., concerning his service with the 21st
Virginia Infantry is in the Virginia Historical Society collections. Letters
of Capt. Dudley D. Pendleton written while he was acting adjutant general
under his uncle, Brig. Gen. W. N. Pendleton, during 1862-64 are in Duke
University Library. Some papers of Lt. Col. William D. Simpson, inspec-
tor general under Brig. Gen. M. L. Bonham, are in the South Caroliniana
Library of the University of South Carolina. A "business diary" of Capt.
Edwin Taliaferro, Jan. 1-May 4, 1863, while he was an ordnance officer
with Maj. Gen. Lafayette McLaws, is in the Southern Historical Collection
in the University of North Carolina Library which also has papers of Lt.
Col. Charles S. Venable, assistant adjutant general to General Lee. Other
Venable papers are in the Texas Archives of the University of Texas Library. Papers of Maj. Andrew R. Venable, who served in the cavalry
corps, are among the Virginia Historical Society collections.

Edmund C. Burnett, ed.,
"Letters of a Confederate Surgeon:
Dr. Abner Embry McGarity, 1862-
1865, " Georgia Historical Quarterly,
29:76-114, 159-190, 222-253 (June,
Sept., Dec. 1945), 30:35-70 (Mar.
1946); C. G. Chamberlayne, ed.,
Ham Chamberlayne--Virginian;
Letters and Papers of an Artillery
Officer in the War for Southern In-
dependence, 1861-1865 (Richmond,
1932); Jay B. Hubbell, ed., "The
War Diary of John Esten Cooke, "
Journal of Southern History, 7:526-
540 (Nov. 1941); Frederick Maurice,
ed., An Aide-de-Camp of Lee; Being the Papers of Colonel Charles
Marshall (Boston, 1927); Mary C.

Moffett, ed., Letters of General
James Conner, C.S.A. (Columbia,
S.C., 1933); William S. Myers, ed.,
"The Civil War Diary of General
Isaac Ridgeway Trimble, " Maryland
Historical Magazine, 17:1-20 (Mar.
1922); Caroline L. Shaffner, ed.,
Diary of Dr. J. F. Shaffner, Sr.,
Commencing September 13, 1863,
Ending February 5, 1865 (Winston-
Salem, 1936); Harold B. Simpson, ed.,
Touched With Valor: Civil War Papers
and Casualty Reports of Hood's Texas
Brigade; Written and Collected by
General Jerome B. Robertson (Hills-
boro, Tex., 1964); Spencer G. Welch,
A Confederate Surgeon's Letters to
His Wife (New York & Washington, 1911).

Army and Department of the Peninsula

The Department of the Peninsula was established on May 21, 1861,
embracing at first the troops and military operations on the line to Hamp-
ton, Va. It was extended on June 14 to include the troops at Gloucester
Point, Va., on June 28 the military positions at West Point and Jamestown
Island, Va., and on Aug. 26 the counties of Gloucester, Mathews, and
Middlesex. In Apr. 1862 the department became the right wing of the Army

of Northern Virginia.
Successive commanders:
Col. John B. Magruder, May 21, 1861.
Col. Daniel H. Hill (acting), May 31, 1861.
Record Group 109. --Letters and telegrams sent, May 1861-May 1862 (ch. II, vols. 67, 69, 227, and 228); memoranda, orders, and letters sent by Capt. Andrew G. Dickinson, the assistant inspector general, Feb.-Apr. 1862 (ch. II, vol. 231); general orders, May 1861-Apr. 1862 (ch. II, vol. 229); special orders, Feb.-Apr. 1862 (ch. II, vol. 68); and letters sent by Col. Robert Johnston, commanding the cavalry, July 1861-Apr. 1862 (ch. II, vol. 275).

Records in Other Custody. --Other records in the Confederate Museum include a letters-sent book of Col. Robert Johnston, July 12, 1861-Sept. 7, 1862 (1 vol., p. 335-454); an index to letters received, June 21, 1861-Apr. 27, 1862 (p. 323-328 of the letters-sent book); an orders-received book of the 1st Division, Oct. 18-Dec. 22, 1861 (1 vol.); letters and orders received by Col. John B. Cary, May 16-Aug. 3, 1861 (1 vol.); and letters received by Asst. Quartermaster Colin D. Clarke, Aug. 1861-Mar. 1862.

Army of Pensacola

The Army of Pensacola was organized within the Department of Alabama and West Florida on Oct. 29, 1861. Composed of the troops at and around Pensacola, it was discontinued in Mar. 1862.
Successive commanders:
Gen. Braxton Bragg, Oct. 29, 1861.
Brig. Gen. Adley H. Gladden (temp.), Dec. 22, 1861.
Brig. Gen. Samuel Jones, Jan. 27, 1862.
Record Group 109. --General and special orders issued, Mar. 11, 1861-Jan. 27, 1862, and Mar. 3-9, 1862 (1 1/3 in.), including orders issued by the headquarters of the Confederate troops near Pensacola, Mar. 11-Oct. 22, 1861, and by the Army of Pensacola, Oct. 1861-Mar. 1862.

Records in Other Custody. --Letters sent by Gen. Braxton Bragg, Mar. 10, 1861-Jan. 21, 1862, and orders, letters, and other papers of the Medical Department relating to hospitals, Apr. 1861-Feb. 1862, are among the Bragg papers in the Western Reserve Historical Society collections.

Army of the Potomac

Organized on June 20, 1861, the Army of the Potomac became part of the Army and Department of Northern Virginia on Oct. 22, 1861.
Successive commanders:
Brig. Gen. Pierre G. T. Beauregard, June 20, 1861.
Brig. Gen. Joseph E. Johnston, July 20, 1861.
Record Group 109. --Orders and circulars issued, June 2, 1861-Mar. 2, 1862 (1 in.).
Records in Other Custody. --A soldiers' discharge book of the 1st Corps, Aug. 12-Oct. 14, 1861, is in the Manuscript Division of the Library of Congress. Papers of Brig. Gen. Philip St. G. Cocke, commander of the 5th Brigade in 1861, are in the University of Virginia Library. Papers of Brig. Gen. Milledge L. Bonham, commander of the 1st Brigade of the 1st Corps, are in the South Caroliniana Library of the University of South Carolina. Correspondence of Maj. William L. Cabell, chief quartermaster,

1861, is in the Confederate Museum. Other quartermaster records are in the W. P. Palmer collection of the Western Reserve Historical Society.

Department of Richmond

On Apr. 1, 1863, that part of the Department of North Carolina and Southern Virginia embracing the defenses of Richmond north of the James River was constituted the Department of Richmond. It was extended on Apr. 23, 1863, to include Drewry's Bluff on the James River below Richmond and Manchester south of the river. In May 1864 the Department of Henrico was merged with the Department of Richmond.

Several prisons were maintained by the department. Castle Thunder, also referred to in the records as Eastern District Military Prison, Eastern District Station, and the Provost Marshal's Prison, was a 3 1/2-story tobacco warehouse used for political prisoners (disloyal citizens of western Virginia), captured U.S. citizens, foreigners, deserters, Confederate soldiers undergoing punishment, court-martial prisoners, persons suspected of spying, and captured Negroes. Castle Lightning, another warehouse across the street, was used for the imprisonment of Confederate soldiers who had violated military and civil laws. Castle Godwin, in an alley behind Franklin Street, was used for the confinement of political prisoners and other civilian prisoners. During 1863-65 Army officers were appointed as commissioners to examine these prisoners and report on the circumstances of their detention. Officers who performed this duty included Maj. Isaac H. Carrington in 1863, Capt. D. W. Vowles and Maj. John D. Munford in 1864, and Capt. J. H. Sands in 1864-65.

Successive commanders of this Department:
> Maj. Gen. Arnold Elzey, Apr. 1, 1863.
> Maj. Gen. Robert Ransom, Jr., Apr. 25, 1864.
> Lt. Gen. Richard S. Ewell, June 13, 1864.

Record Group 109. --Letters received, 1862-65 (5 in.); telegrams received, 1862-64 (1 in.); general and special orders and circulars received, 1862-65 (mostly 1863; 3/4 in.); applications for forage, Mar. 1863-Mar. 1864 (1/2 in.); and inspection reports relating to military organizations and installations in and around Richmond and at Danville, 1863-64 (1/2 in.). The letters received and the telegrams are entered in a register (ch. II, vol. 236), for which there are alphabetical name indexes. A record of endorsements on letters received, Jan. 27-July 28, 1864 (ch. IX vols. 184 1/2 and 187), concerns applications for leaves of absence, furloughs, transfers, and requests to appear before examining boards. There is also a record of persons hired and buildings and land rented, Oct. 1, 1864-Mar. 1, 1865 (ch. V. vol. 248).

Records of the Provost Marshal's Office include special orders sent and received, Apr. 30-July 4 and July 16-Aug. 23, 1864 (ch. IX, vol. 250). A register of arrests of military personnel and civilians, Oct. 9, 1862-Mar. 25, 1863 (ch. IX, vol. 244), also includes names of foreigners arrested, Feb. 24, 1862-Dec. 16, 1863. For persons confined in Castle Thunder and Castle Lightning there is a register of arrests, Feb. 25, 1863-June 14, 1864 (ch. IX, vol. 100). Reports by Maj. Isaac H. Carrington on prisoners examined in Richmond, July-Dec. 1863 (1 in.), present the grounds for arrest and recommendations for disposition and are accompanied by related documents. A docket on prisoners examined by Captains Vowles and Sands, Mar. 16, 1864-Apr. 1, 1865 (ch. IX, vol. 229), has an alphabetical index.

The records of the Department of Richmond also include provost marshal passes, requests for passes, and citizens' passes, 1861-65 (3 ft.). Statistical reports relating to passports, Mar. 12, 1864-Mar. 25, 1865 (ch. IX, vol. 130, and unbound reports, 2 in.), show the number of passports received, issued, marked, and on hand. Registers of passports issued to military personnel and civilians, 1862-65 (ch. IX, vols. 101-109, 111-129, 131-137 1/2, 139-151 1/2, 152-173, 173 1/2, 174, 174 1/2-181 1/2, 182, 183, 183 1/2, and 258, 6 ft.), show date, name of person, destination, and purpose of travel. Separate registers were kept for passes issued for use in Richmond for certain groups of persons and for the different routes that were used in leaving Richmond, such as the Danville Railroad, Fredericksburg Railroad, Petersburg Railroad, Petersburg road, packet, turnpike, Virginia Central Railroad, and York River Railroad. There is a record of orders for the denial of passports and the arrest of applicants, June-Nov. 1864 (ch. IX, vol. 110). A record of arrivals of visitors at Richmond, Aug. 24, 1862-Mar. 3, 1863 (ch. IX, vol. 186), shows the name, place of residence, hotel, and date of arrival.

Record Group 249.--A record of employees in the office of the departmental commander, 1863-64 (misc. records, vol. 54, p. 27-65), and morning reports of prisoners in Castle Thunder Prison, Nov. 1, 1863-June 8, 1864 (nos. 819-874 in the miscellaneous rolls and related records of Federal and Confederate prisoners of war, 1861-65).

Other records concerning political prisoners are described above under Office of the Secretary of War and Office of the Commissary General of Prisoners.

Records in Other Custody.--In the New-York Historical Society collections is a letters-sent book of Maj. Seth B. French, Sept. 12, 1862-May 9, 1863, containing copies of his letters while chief commissary of the Department of Richmond. An order book, Jan. 2, 1864-Feb. 10, 1865, relating to the artillery defenses of Richmond, is in the Chicago Historical Society collections. The Louisiana State University Department of Archives has a list of officers and other employees of the Provost Marshal's Office, Apr. 5, 1864. Papers of Maj. Isaac H. Carrington in Duke University Library contain documents relating to his duties as provost marshal in Richmond.

Department of South Carolina, Georgia, and Florida

This department was established on Nov. 5, 1861, to consist of the coastal areas of South Carolina, Georgia, and Florida. It was extended in Apr. 1862 to include eastern and middle Florida as far west as the Choctawhatchee River, in October all of South Carolina and Georgia and that part of Florida east of the Apalachicola River, and in November the Districts of East and Middle Florida. In Nov. 1861 the department was divided into the First, Second, and Third Military Districts. In May 1862 the District of Georgia was established and in Oct. 1864 the District of South Carolina. The Districts of Middle and East Florida were consolidated in Feb. 1864 into the District of Florida. In Nov. 1864 the departmental limits were changed to include only that part of Georgia south of the Chattahoochee River; a further modification of the boundary in Georgia was made in Jan. 1865. The headquarters of the department was at Charleston.

Successive commanders of the Department of Middle and East Florida:

Brig. Gen. John B. Grayson, Aug. 21, 1861.
Brig. Gen. James H. Trapier, Oct. 22, 1861.
Col. William S. Dilworth (acting), Mar. 19, 1862.
Brig. Gen. Joseph Finegan, Apr. 8, 1862.
Successive commanders of the District of Florida:
Maj. Gen. James P. Anderson, Mar. 4, 1864.
Brig. Gen. John K. Jackson, Aug. 1864.
Brig. Gen. William Miller, Sept. 29, 1864.
Maj. Gen. Samuel Jones, Feb. 2, 1865.
Successive commanders of the Department of South Carolina, Georgia, and Florida:
Gen. Robert E. Lee, Nov. 5, 1861.
Maj. Gen. John C. Pemberton, Mar. 3, 1862.
Brig. Gen. P. G. T. Beauregard, Aug. 29, 1862.
Maj. Gen. Samuel Jones, Apr. 20, 1864.
Lt. Gen. William J. Hardee, Sept. 28, 1864.

Record Group 45.--A report of a board of Army officers that investigated the bursting of a Blakely rifled gun in Charleston in Sept. 1863 is in the Naval Records Collection of the Office of Naval Records and Library, subject file BG. A roll of slaves employed by the engineer office at Charleston, Aug. 1862-Sept. 1864 (1 vol.), is in the same record group.

Record Group 109.--Letters-sent books, Nov. 1861-Apr. 1864 (ch. II, vols. 22, 28, 31, 32, 183-185, and 3 index vols.); letters sent and received by Gen. J. C. Pemberton, Mar.-Sept. 1862 (ch. II, vol. 21); copies of letters sent, Jan. 1863-Nov. 1864 (1 ft. 2 in.); endorsements on letters received, Nov. 1861-May 1862 (ch. II, part of vol. 185); letters received, Oct. 1862-Nov. 1864 (3 1/2 ft.); registers of letters received, Oct. 1862-Nov. 1864 (ch. II, vols. 19, 20, 33, 34, and 2 index vols., 1 ft.); endorsements on letters received, Nov. 1862-Feb. 1864 (ch. II, vols. 23-27, 29, 30, 36, and 187; ch. VIII, vols. 351, 352, and 1 index vol., 2 ft.); telegrams sent, Sept. 1862-July 1864 (ch. II, vols. 45, 48, and 50); letters, telegrams, and orders issued and received, Mar. 1864 (ch. II, vol. 195); general and special orders issued, Nov. 1861-Sept. 1862 (ch. II, vol. 42 and 1 index vol.); general orders issued, July 1862-Jan. 1864 (ch. II, vols. 41 and 43); special orders and circulars issued, Sept. 1862-Dec. 1863 (ch. II, vol. 40 and 1 index vol.); orders and circulars issued, Sept. 1863-Mar. 1864 (ch. II, vol. 150 1/2); printed general court-martial orders, 1863 (ch. II, vol. 182); orders and circulars issued by departmental headquarters and subcommands, 1861-65 (1 1/2 ft.); general and special orders issued by subcommands, 1863-65 (ch. II, vol. 258 1/2); reports of operations, events, strength, ordnance stores, field transportation, enemy movements, and other matters, 1863-64 (6 in.); copies of letters, telegrams, and reports, 1861-62 (3 in., from originals in the custody of the Southern Historical Society); inspection reports on military units and stations, 1863-65 (8 in.); rolls of extra-duty men and lists and reports of persons and articles hired, Feb. 1863-Feb. 1864 (6 in.); a record of discharges, 1861-63 (ch. II, vol. 190); a record of resignations, 1862-64 (ch. II, vol. 191); company provision returns, 1861 (3 in.); undated receipts for general orders (2 1/2 in.); letters and telegrams sent and endorsements on letters received by the Engineer Office, 1863-64 (ch. III, vol. 9); press copies of letters sent by Maj. William H. Echols, chief engineer, July 1863-Feb. 1864 (ch. III, vols. 14, 17, and 19); letters sent by the Signal Office, Aug. 13, 1862-Feb. 7, 1863, and May 5, 1863-Feb. 8, 1865 (ch. VIII, vol. 30); a register of letters received by the Signal Office, 1862-65 (ch. VIII, vol. 28); special orders of the Signal Office, 1863-65 (ch. VIII, vol. 33); property accounts and oaths of enlisted men of the Signal Office, 1862-64 (ch. VIII, vol. 32 1/2); and an undated report of a board of artillery officers on the proper charges for heavy guns and the service of artillery (ch. IV, vol. 129).

Records of subdivisions of the department include telegrams received, 1st Military District, Apr. 7-July 29, 1863 (ch. II, vols. 47 and 189); telegrams sent and received, 1st Military District, Sept. 5, 1864-Feb. 15, 1865 (ch. II, vol. 45 1/2); orders and circulars, 1st Military District, 1862-63 (ch. II, vol. 37); special orders, 2d Military District, 1862 (ch. II, vol. 44); letters sent, District of Florida, Mar. 1864-May 1865 (ch. II, vols. 1 1/2 and 283); endorsements on communications received, 1864-65 (ch. II, vols. 1 1/4, 188, and 283 1/2); special orders, District of Florida, 1864 (ch. II, vol. 193); special orders, District of East Florida, 1862-64 (ch. II, vol. 1); letters sent, District of South Carolina, Nov. 23-Dec. 20, 1864 (ch. II, vol. 176); special orders, 2d and 3d subdistricts, District of South Carolina, 1865 (ch. II, vol. 49); and copies of general and special orders issued by Col. T. W. Brevard, commanding at Camp Finegan, Fla., Dec. 20, 1862-Sept. 30, 1863 (ch. II, vol. 38).

In Aug. 1863 Jeremy F. Gilmer who had been Chief Engineer in Richmond, was appointed to the temporary rank of major general and ordered to report to General Beauregard at Charleston for services connected with the defense of Charleston. During the succeeding months he also spent some time at Atlanta and Mobile, commanded the defenses of Savannah during Mar.-Apr. 1864, and during June-July 1864 was at Greensboro, N. C., before returning to Richmond to resume the post of Chief Engineer. He kept a record book in which are recorded copies of letters and telegrams sent, Aug. 1863-July 1864, and endorsements on communications received and forwarded, Sept. 1863-June 1864 (ch. III, vol. 9).

Other departmental records include reports and dispatches from Fort Sumter on enemy activity in Charleston Harbor, Feb. 1863-Sept. 1864 (3 in.); reports from signal stations on enemy activity July 1863-Nov. 1864 (1 ft.); daily reports of telegraph operators on duty at Charleston and at batteries and forts in the harbor, Jan. 24-Feb. 16, 1865 (ch. II, vol. 194); a journal of operations in Charleston Harbor, Sept. 1, 1863-Jan. 21, 1864 (ch. II, vol. 192); a report by Lt. John Johnson on the bombardment of Fort Sumter, July 20-Sept. 2, 1863 (1/2 in.); extracts from the journal kept at Fort Sumter, July 17 and Dec. 5, 1863 (1/2 in.); copies of daily reports from the commanding officers on James and Sullivan's Islands concerning the siege of Charleston, Dec. 30, 1864-Feb. 13, 1865 (ch. II, vol. 46 1/2); messages sent by the signal station at Charleston, Feb. 4-16, 1865 (ch. VIII, vol. 31); and abstracts of payments made by the assistant quartermaster at Charleston, May-Nov. 1863 (ch. V, vol. 237).

Records in Other Custody. --A letters-sent book, May 8, 1864-Jan. 5, 1865, of Maj. Gen. S. Jones is in the Confederate Museum. An order book, June 8-Aug. 20, 1862, is in Emory University Library, and another order book, June 1863-Mar. 1864, is in the Southern Historical Collection in the University of North Carolina. Special orders, Sept. 1862-Feb. 1863, are in the Palmer collection in the Western Reserve Historical Society. A collection of papers, 1862-65, is in Duke University Library. Records of Maj. H. Lee, quartermaster at Charleston, are in the South Carolina Historical Society collections.

Papers of Col. David B. Harris, General Beauregard's Chief Engineer, 1863-64, are in Duke University Library. Records of Maj. William H. Echols, an engineer officer in the department during 1863-65, in the South Caroliniana Library of the University of South Carolina include correspondence, reports, orders, payrolls, invoices, and receipts. Other records of the engineer office at Charleston, Feb. 1863-Jan. 1865 (31 items), including correspondence, lists, drawings, payrolls, and accounts, are in the Southern Historical Collection in the University of North Carolina Library which also has a record book, May 14-Aug. 20, 1862, of A. H. Brown, the provost marshal at Charleston.

Records of the 1st Military District, 1861-65 (1,021 items), in the South Carolina Historical Society collections include correspondence, telegrams, orders, court-martial proceedings, inspection reports, records of elections of officers, and ordnance, quartermaster, and signal corps reports. Official papers, Jan. 2-Apr. 30, 1861 (145 items), of Brig. Gen. R. G. M. Dunovant, who was in charge of the defense of Charleston Harbor, are in Duke University Library. Correspondence, a journal for July 20-Sept. 2, 1863, and other papers of Maj. John Johnson, engineer officer at Fort Sumter, are in the South Carolina Historical Society collections. With Johnson's papers are also an order book, 1863, and a letter book, 1864, of Col. Stephen Elliott, Jr., the commanding officer of Fort Sumter. Correspondence of Col. Lawrence M. Keitt in Duke University Library relates to Sullivan's Island during 1862-64. Daily reports of artillery operations at Legare's Point and Battery Simkins, Nov. 1863 (60 items, microfilm), are in the South Caroliniana Library of the University of South Carolina. In the same repository are: a letters-sent book of Capt. W. W. McCreery, Jr., ordnance officer at Pocataligo, S.C., Jan. 10-Apr. 30, 1862; a letters-sent book, Dec. 17, 1863-June 7, 1864, a record of subsistence stores issued, May 1, 1862-July 31, 1863 (2 vols.), and an account book, Aug. 1862-June 1864, of Capt. Isaac D. Witherspoon, assistant commissary at Columbia, S.C.; and correspondence and other papers of Capt. John S. Richardson, assistant quartermaster at Columbia, S.C., Jan. 2, 1864-Apr. 2, 1865 (1,711 items), concerning the construction and supply of military prisons. Capt. John T. Champneys, another engineer officer at Fort Sumter, kept a letter book, 1862-63, that is now in the University of Virginia Library. A few papers, 1863-64, of Capt. H. L. Simons, assistant commissary at Anderson Courthouse, S.C., are in the South Carolina Archives Department, and a miscellaneous record book of Captain Simons, 1864-65, is in the Schenectady County (N.Y.) Historical Society collections. Letters-sent books of A. S. Baldwin, chief surgeon for the District of East Florida, July 20, 1863-Feb. 8, 1864, and Jan. 31-May 12, 1865 (2 vols.), are in the Confederate Museum. Papers, 1859-65, of R. S. Butler, an assistant surgeon in South Carolina, are in the Palmer collection of the Western Reserve Historical Society. Papers of Capt. Henry W. Feilden, who was an assistant adjutant general on the staff of the commanding general of the department, are in the Library of Congress, the South Carolina Historical Society collections, and the University of Virginia Library.

Correspondence of Brig. Gens. Roswell S. Ripley, Thomas Jordan, and Col. Alfred Roman is in Correspondence Relating to Fortifications of Morris Island and Operations of Engineers (Charleston, 1863).

Department and District of Georgia

The Department of Georgia was established on Oct. 26, 1861, and was merged on Nov. 5, 1861, into the Department of South Carolina, Georgia, and Florida. Under this department the District of Georgia was established on May 28, 1862. In Dec. 1862 the district consisted of the State of Georgia except for the defenses of the Apalachicola River and its principal affluents.
Successive commanders of the district:

Brig. Gen. Alexander R. Lawton, Oct. 26, 1861.
Brig. Gen. Hugh W. Mercer, Dec. 28, 1862.
Lt. Gen. Daniel H. Hill, Jan. 21, 1865.

Record Group 109. --General and special orders and circulars issued by the headquarters and subcommands, 1861-65 (2 in.); letters sent by Col. M. H. Wright, commander of the troops at Atlanta, July 1863-May 1864 (ch. II, vol. 186); a register of communications received and forwarded by the headquarters of the defenses of Atlanta, 1863-64 (ch. VIII, vol. 349); press copies of letter sent by Lt. William D. Harden, Mar. 6, 1862-Jan. 2, 1863 (1 vol.), containing outgoing letters of the ordnance officer of the Skidaway District, Isle of Hope, and the Department of Georgia; abstracts of payments made by Capt. H. T. Massengale, quartermaster at Atlanta, July 1862-Mar. 1863 (ch. V, vols. 215, 215 1/2, and 242); a record of articles received and issued by Maj. F. W. Dillard, quartermaster at Columbus, Oct.-Dec. 1863 (ch. V, vol. 211); letters sent by Capt. Joseph Manigault, signal officer at Savannah, with endorsements on letters received, Nov. 11, 1862-Oct. 24, 1864 (ch. VIII, vol. 32); and the Savannah Signal Office's record of employees and property, 1862-64 (ch. VIII, vol. 29).

Records in Other Custody. --A letters-sent book, Jan. 22-Feb. 20, 1865, of Lt. Gen. D. H. Hill is in the North Carolina Department of Archives and History, which also has other records of Hill. Vouchers and other financial records of Maj. T. D. Hamilton, quartermaster at Rome, Nov. 1, 1861-Apr. 1, 1865 (165 items), are in the Mississippi Department of Archives and History. Press copies of letters sent by Capt. George Robertson, Jr., post commissary at Savannah, Apr. 1, 1864-Apr. 19, 1865 (1 vol.; after Feb. 15, 1865, he was at Macon) are in Duke University Library. Returns of provisions signed by Captain Robertson at Savannah, July 1861-Sept. 1862 and Feb. and Apr. 1863, are in the Georgia Historical Society collections. A register of passes issued by Capt. George H. Fulkerson, the provost marshal at Macon, May 7-Sept. 7 [1864], is in the Georgia Department of Archives and History. The diary of Col. Edward C. Anderson in the Southern Historical Collection in the University of North Carolina Library concerns his tours of duty at Savannah, Nov. 20, 1861-Mar. 13, 1862, and Nov. 2, 1863-Nov. 13, 1864.

Army and Department of Tennessee

On Nov. 20, 1862, the Army of Kentucky and the Army of Mississippi joined to form the Army of Tennessee. The commanders of this army were also commanders of the Department of Tennessee (formerly Department No. 2), organized on July 25, 1863, including also the Department of East Tennessee. The department included parts of Tennessee, western North Carolina, Alabama, and Georgia. It was renamed the Department of Tennessee and Georgia on Aug. 15, 1864.
Successive commanders of the army and the department:

Gen. Braxton Bragg, 1862.

Lt. Gen. Leonidas Polk (temp.), Aug., Dec. 1863.
Lt. Gen. William J. Hardee (temp.), Dec. 2-22, 1863.
Gen. Joseph E. Johnston, Dec. 27, 1863.
Gen. John B. Hood, July 18, 1864.
Gen. Joseph E. Johnston, Feb. 25, 1865.

Record Group 109. --Records of the Army of Tennessee include general orders issued, Nov. 24-Dec. 19, 1862, and telegrams sent, Jan. 19-Apr. 19, 1864 (ch. III, part of vol. 8); orders and circulars issued, Dec. 1863-Apr. 1865 (ch. II, vol. 350); special orders issued, Aug. 27-Dec. 22, 1863 (ch. II, vol. 19 1/2); special field orders and special orders issued, July 1864-Apr. 1865 (ch. II, vol. 349); special orders received from the Adjutant and Inspector General's Office, 1862-65 (6 in.); proceedings of examining boards relating to artillery officers, 1864-65 (3 in.); an undated register of officers (ch. VIII, vol. 358); miscellaneous records including correspondence, telegrams, orders, and lists of paroled prisoners, 1863-65 (3 in.); endorsements on letters received, copies of letters sent, and special orders, 1863-64 (ch. II, vol. 15 1/2); dispatches concerning actions and engagements, Mar.-May 1863 (ch. II, vol. 53 3/4); general and special orders and circulars issued by the Army of Tennessee and subordinate commands, Feb. 1863-Mar. 1864 (ch. II, vol. 53); orders and circulars of the Department and Army of Tennessee, 1862-65 (6 in.); and General Hood's field dispatches, July 27, 1864-Jan. 16, 1865 (1 vol.). Records of subordinate commands include copies of dispatches sent and orders and circulars issued by Lt. Gen. Leonidas Polk's corps, Sept. 1863 (ch. II, vol. 222 1/2); endorsements on letters received by General Polk's corps, Apr. 1863-Feb. 1864 (ch. II, vols. 222, 222A, and 222B); letters and telegrams sent and orders and circulars issued by General Polk, May 9-June 19, 1864 (ch. II, vol. 221 1/2); copies and extracts of general and special orders and circulars issued by General Hardee's corps, Feb. 1863-Mar. 1865 (ch. II, vol. 272); letters and circulars sent and orders issued by General Hood's corps (Maj. Gen. Stephen D. Lee's corps after July 1864), Mar. 1864-Feb. 1865 (ch. II, vol. 273); copies of letters and orders received by Maj. Gen. Patrick R. Cleburne's division, 1862-64 (ch. II, vol. 265); orders and circulars of Brig. Gen. William H. Jackson's cavalry division, June-Sept. 1864 (ch. II, vol. 271 1/2); orders and circulars of Lt. Gen. Nathan B. Forrest's cavalry, 1863-65 (1 in.); special orders of General Polk's corps, Dec. 1863 (ch. II, vol. 236 1/2); copies of general orders received by Polk's corps, Jan.-Aug. 1863 (ch. II, vol. 53 1/4); dispatches, orders, and circulars received by Polk's corps, Sept. 1863 (ch. II, vol. 273 1/2); a register of letters received by Maj. Gen. Thomas C. Hindman's division, Oct. 20, 1863-May 8, 1864 (ch. VIII, vol. 314); general and special orders received by Brig. Gen. John C. Brown's brigade, Jan. 7-Aug. 7, 1863 (ch. VIII, part of vol. 341); an undated roster of field, staff, and company officers of General Brown's brigade (ch. VIII, vol. 341, p. 126-135); letters, reports, and telegrams received and sent concerning Maj. Gen. Carter L. Stevenson's command, 1863-65 (3 in.); letters, orders, and circulars received relating to Brig. Gen. Edward C. Walthall's division, 1864-65 (3 in.); letters received and copies of letters sent by Maj. Gen. Joseph Wheeler, 1863-64 (1/3 in.); letters, telegrams, and orders relating to Brig. Gen. St. John R. Liddell's command, 1865; and strength returns of the brigades of Maj. Gen. J. C. Breckinridge's division, Jan. 1863-May 1863 (2 in.), that were received with records of the 1st Kentucky Brigade. Records of the Inspector General include letters sent and endorsements on letters received,

June 5, 1863-Apr. 29, 1864 (ch. II, vol. 158 1/4); and a letters-sent book, Nov. 12, 1864-Apr. 29, 1865 (ch. II, vol. 19 1/4).

Other records include: special orders of the headquarters of the Confederate forces at Chattanooga and of the District of Tennessee at Chattanooga, Nov. 22, 1862-July 3, 1863 (ch. II, vol. 249), signed by Brig. Gens. Benjamin H. Helm, William B. Bate, and John K. Jackson; a record book of Maj. A. L. Landis, a quartermaster officer, 1863-64 (ch. V, vol. 226); some notes of Lt. W. B. Richmond, aide-de-camp to General Polk, on the movement of the Army of Tennessee from Memphis to Chattanooga, June-Aug. 1863 (ch. II, vol. 272), with some copies of dispatches, orders, and circulars; and a brief diary of Lieutenant Richmond, Sept. 6-16, 1863 (ch. II, vol. 272 1/4). For the 1st Missouri Brigade that served with the Army of Tennessee the records include a cashbook of Capt. Albert Danner, assistant quartermaster, Nov. 1864-May 1865 (ch. V, vol. 139), and quartermaster accounts, Mar., Apr., and Aug.-Oct. 1864 (ch. VIII, vol. 90). Letters, orders, and circulars relating to hospitals in Alabama, Georgia, Mississippi, and Tennessee, Nov. 6, 1862-Apr. 27, 1865 (ch. VI, vol. 664), include those sent by Surgeons Carey B. Gamble and B. M. Wible. A return of medical officers of Anderson's division, Hardee's corps, is dated Shelbyville, Dec. 1, 1862 (ch. VI, vol. 664, p. 160-161).

Records in Other Custody. --Letters-sent books, Feb. 24, 1862-Mar. 29, 1864 (3 vols.); containing outgoing communications by Generals Bragg, Hardee, and Johnston, and telegrams, general and special orders, circulars, inspection reports, and a roster of officers, are in the W. P. Palmer collection in the Western Reserve Historical Society which also has a journal kept by Josiah S. Johnston, Oct. 1, 1862-Dec. 2, 1863, and letters of Gen. John B. Hood. Other letters of Hood are in the Henry E. Huntington Library. A letters-sent book of Lt. Gen. William J. Hardee, Dec. 20, 1862-Apr. 30, 1864, and letters to his wife during the period June 1-Aug. 30, 1864, are in the Alabama Department of Archives and History. Correspondence, orders, circulars, reports, returns, and other records, 1863-65 (545 items), of Brig. Gen. William W. Allen are in the same repository. A letters-sent book, Feb. 25-May 8, 1865, of Gen. Joseph E. Johnston and telegrams sent, Feb. 25-May 3, 1865 (4 vols.), are in the William and Mary College Library. General orders issued by Johnston, Jan. 3-Apr. 28, 1864, orders and circulars issued and received by the 2d Alabama Brigade commanded by Brig. Gen. Edmund W. Pettus, Sept. 30, 1863-Apr. 17, 1864 (1 vol.), and returns of men and materials, Jan. 1864-Apr. 1865, are in the Manuscript Division of the Library of Congress. The Tennessee State Library and Archives has papers of Capt. B. J. Semmes, chief depot commissary, and a register of a hospital at Memphis, 1861-62. Papers of Maj. Jerome P. Wilson, concerning in part Major General Hindman, and papers of Maj. William F. Ayer, a quartermaster officer, are in Emory University Library. Papers of Brig. Gen. Marcellus A. Stovall are in the Southern Historical Collection in the University of North Carolina Library. Another miscellaneous collection of documents is in the Louisiana Historical Association collection on deposit in the Howard-Tilton Memorial Library of Tulane University. Papers of Thomas J. McKean in the Mississippi Department of Archives and History relate mostly to the battle of Corinth, Miss., Oct. 1862. Papers of Capt. Irving A. Buck, assistant adjutant general of Maj. Gen Patrick R. Cleburne's division, in the Confederate Museum include battle reports, lists of casualties, orders and telegrams received from Hardee's headquarters, and field orders and circulars issued by Cleburne's division. A correspondence and order book of B. M. Wible, post surgeon at Tunnel Hill, Ga., Aug. 29-Dec. 14, 1862, is in the Stout collection in the Texas Archives of the University of Texas Library. Correspondence and a diary (Oct. 15, 1864-May 26, 1865) of Charles T. Quintard, chaplain of the 1st Tennessee Infantry, are in the University of the South Library (available on microfilm; microfilm copies in the Department of Archives of the Louisiana State University, the University of North Carolina Library, and the University of Chicago Library). Other correspondence of Quintard is in Duke University Library. Some property returns, requisitions, invoices, and reports, 1863, are in the Mississippi Department of Archives and History.

Trans-Mississippi Department

The State of Texas was set up as the Department of Texas on Apr. 21, 1861, and commanded successively by Col. Earl Van Dorn, Col. Henry E. McCulloch, and Brig. Gen. Paul O. Hébert. The District of Galveston was established within the department in Oct. 1861 and commanded by Col. John C. Moore and Col. E. B. Nichols. The District of Houston, established in Jan. 1862, was commanded by Col. John C. Moore. On Jan. 9 the Trans-Mississippi District, embracing parts of Louisiana, Indian Territory, Arkansas, and Missouri, was established and commanded by Maj. Gen. Earl Van Dorn. On May 26, 1862, it was joined with the Department of Texas to form the Trans-Mississippi Department. In 1863 Texas was divided into an eastern subdistrict under the successive commands of Col. Xavier B. Debray and Brig. Gens. William R. Scurry, Philip N. Luckett, and Henry E. McCulloch; a northern subdistrict commanded successively by Lt. Col. S. P. Bankhead and Brig. Gen. Henry E. McCulloch; and a western subdistrict commanded successively by Brig. Gens. Hamilton P. Bee and James E. Slaughter.

Generals Hébert and Holmes maintained their headquarters at Little Rock. General Smith established departmental headquarters at Alexandria, La., but moved it on Apr. 24, 1863, to Shreveport. By 1864 with the enemy occupying Arkansas and Louisiana, the department was greatly reduced in size.

The Trans-Mississippi Department, distant from the major sources of supply in the Confederacy, was left to its own resources in obtaining war supplies. Ordnance, quartermaster, and subsistence supplies were obtained from the northern states of Mexico and from abroad through Texas ports. Maj. Simeon Hart, a quartermaster officer at San Antonio, functioned as a purchasing agent for all services. In Nov. 1863 the department designated quartermaster depots in Texas at Bonham, Jefferson, San Antonio, and Houston, and in Louisiana at Shreveport. In Feb. 1865 depots for the manufacture of clothing and garrison equipage were located at Houston, Huntsville, Mount Prairie, and Gilmer, Tex., and at Shreveport. A chief inspector of field transportation had charge of the inspection, purchase, impressment, and issue of field transportation.

The U.S. arsenal at Little Rock was taken over and used during 1862-63 for the repair of arms, the manufacture of ammunition, and as an ordnance depot. Arsenals at Arkadelphia and Camden, Ark., repaired arms and manufactured ammunition. Ordnance shops were established at Alexandria and New Iberia, La.; in 1863 the ordnance stores at New Iberia were moved to Shreveport where an arsenal was established. In the same year the machinery and stores in Arkansas were moved to new arsenals at Marshall and Tyler, Tex. The arsenal at San Antonio, seized by Texas forces in Feb. 1861, was transferred later that year to the Confederate Government.

In 1863 after Union forces secured control of the Mississippi River, bureaus were established in the Trans-Mississippi Department to perform functions which were carried on for the cis-Mississippi region by the War Department bureaus in Richmond. Conscription, ordnance, subsistence, and quartermaster's bureaus were established under officers subordinate to General Smith. The chief of the Bureau of Conscription was referred to as the Commandant of Conscripts in the Trans-Mississippi Department; the conscription service had been subordinate to the commander of that department from its inception in 1862. The Cotton Bureau was concerned with the exportation of cotton owned by the Confederate Government and the importation of supplies. The Army Intelligence Office performed the same function as the office of the same name in Richmond. On Sept. 16, 1863, General Smith directed that all papers required by <u>Army Regulations</u> to be sent to the chiefs of the War Department bureaus at Richmond were to be sent to the chiefs of the bureaus at his headquarters. The administrative organization thus developed in the Trans-Mississippi Department was legalized by an act of Congress of Feb. 17, 1864 (1 Cong. C.S.A. Stat. 202), which stipulated that the bureaus established west of the Mississippi River were to be auxiliary to the similar bureaus of the War Department and were to perform duties as prescribed by the Secretary of War or the general commanding the Trans-Mississippi Department. The bureaus were at first located at General Smith's headquarters at Shreveport, La., but his order of May 30, 1864, directed that they were to be established at Marshall, Tex. Organizations added in 1864 included a Medical Bureau, an Agent of Exchange, a Tax in Kind Bureau, and an Engineer Bureau.

Successive commanders of the Trans-Mississippi Department:
    Brig. Gen. Paul O. Hébert (temp.), May 26, 1862.
    Maj. Gen. Theophilus H. Holmes, July 30, 1862.
    Lt. Gen. Edmund Kirby Smith, Mar. 7, 1863.
Chiefs of the Trans-Mississippi Bureaus:
    Bureau of Conscription: Brig. Gen. Elkanah Greer, June 3, 1863.
                            Brig. Gen. F. T. Nicholls, July 30, 1864.
    Bureau of Ordnance: Maj. Gen. Benjamin Huger, July 27, 1863.
    Niter and Mining Bureau: T. G. Clemson, July 11, 1863.
    Cotton Bureau: Lt. Col. W. A. Broadwell, Aug. 3, 1863.
    Subsistence Bureau: Maj. William B. Blair, Aug. 17, 1863.
    Quartermaster's Bureau: Lt. Col. L. W. O'Bannon, Sept. 4, 1863.
    Army Intelligence Office: R. S. Thomas, Nov. 12, 1863.
    Medical Bureau: Surg. John M. Haden, Mar. 25, 1864.
    Agent of Exchange: Maj. Ignatius Szymanski, July 4, 1864.
    Tax in Kind Bureau: Maj. Benjamin A. Botts, Sept. 1, 1864.
    Iron Works: Capt. R. H. Temple, Sept. 27, 1864.
    Supervisor of Mines: T. G. Clemson, Sept. 27, 1864.
    Engineer Bureau: Lt. Col. Henry T. Douglas, Mar. 6, 1865.

Florence E. Holladay, "The Powers of the Commander of the Confederate Trans-Mississippi Department, 1863-1865," Southwestern Historical Quarterly, 27:279-298, 333-359 (Jan., Apr. 1918); F. Lee Laurence and Robert W. Glover, Camp Ford, C.S.A.; the Story of Union Prisoners in Texas (Austin, 1964); Leon Mitchell, Jr., "Camp Ford, Confederate Military Prison," Southwestern Historical Quarterly, 66:1-16 (July 1962), "Camp Groce, Confederate Military Prison," ibid., 67:15-21 (July 1963); James L. Nichols, The Confederate Quartermaster in the Trans-Mississippi (Austin, 1964); Stephen B. Oates, "Supply for Confederate Cavalry in the Trans-Mississippi," Military Affairs, 25: 94-99 (Summer 1961).

Early in 1873 A. P. Tasker of the War Department's Archive Office examined records of the Trans-Mississippi Department that were then at Shreveport. In Mar. 1873 the War Department offered $2,500 for the records, and George Williamson acting for George L. Woodward of Caddo Parish accepted the offer and shipped the records to Washington. A schedule of these records is available (Archive Office, Letters Received, R 38 B). The War Department also acquired records from Gens. Thomas J. Churchill, Thomas C. Hindman, Theophilus H. Holmes, John S. Marmaduke, John B. Magruder, Sterling Price, Edmund Kirby Smith, and William Steele, and from Lt. Col. Gabriel H. Hill and Maj. Charles E. Carr.

Record Group 109.--Records of the Department of Texas include copies of letters sent, Sept. 16, 1861-Oct. 1862 (ch. II, vols. 129, 134, 135, and 135 1/2); general and special orders and circulars issued, 1861-64 (3 1/2 in.); endorsements on letters received, Nov. 1861-Oct. 1862 (ch. II, vol. 140); general orders issued, Oct. 2, 1861-Nov. 27, 1862 (ch. II, vol. 112); special orders issued, Sept. 13, 1861-Feb. 5, 1862 (ch. II, vol. 109); special orders issued by the Military District of Galveston, July 26, 1861-May 20, 1862 (ch. II, vol. 241); and general and special orders issued and received at Galveston, May 14, 1862-July 3, 1863 (ch. II, vol. 243).

Records of the Trans-Mississippi Department include copies of letters sent, Mar. 7, 1863-May 19, 1865 (ch. II, vols. 70-72 and 73 1/2); copies of confidential letters and telegrams sent, Jan. 6-Apr. 15, 1865 (ch. II, vol. 71 1/2; available on microfilm); letters and telegrams received, 1861-65 (4 in.); general orders issued, Oct. 1, 1862-May 16, 1865 (ch. II, vols. 74 and 81; mostly printed); general and special orders and circulars issued by headquarters and subcommands and the Bureau of Conscription, 1861-65 (6 in.; available on microfilm); general and special orders issued and received by various commands, 1862-63 (ch. II, vol. 80); and special orders issued, Nov. 22, 1862-May 10, 1865 (ch. II, vols. 77-79; available on microfilm).

Records of the eastern subdistrict of Texas include general orders issued, Feb. 13-Dec. 25, 1863 (ch. II, part of vol. 116); special orders issued, Feb. 13, 1863-Feb. 1, 1865 (ch. II, vol. 102); and an undated roster of commissioned officers (ch. I, vol. 102 1/2).

C.S.A. Army, Trans-Mississippi Department, General Orders, Headquarters, Trans-Mississippi Department, from March 6, 1863, to January 1, 1865 (Houston, 1865), Report of Major General Hindman, of His Operations in the Trans-Mississippi District (Richmond, 1864).

Other records include correspondence of Brig. Gen. John S. Marma-

duke, 1863-64 (3 in.; available on microfilm); copies of letters sent by
Brig. Gen. Thomas J. Churchill's division, Jan. 23-May 17, 1865 (ch. II,
vol. 263 1/2; available on microfilm); general and special orders issued by
various headquarters, Oct. 1861-Oct. 1862 (ch. II, vol. 242); copies of
special orders issued by Brig. Gen. Thomas Green's cavalry division, Nov.
12-Dec. 15, 1863, and rosters of the division (ch. VIII, vol. 393); a register of officers of Maj. Gen. Mosby M. Parsons' division of Missouri volunteers commissioned during 1862-63 (ch. VIII, vol. 394); general and special
orders issued by Maj. Waldemar Hyllested, provost marshal, and Lt. Col.
John J. Myers and Capt. Peter MacGreal, commanders of the post of
Houston, Jan. 27-Dec. 8, 1863 (ch. II, vol. 117); an observatory report
book of Lt. A. L. Lindsay, Signal Corps, Houston, July 9, 1863-Sept. 20,
1864 (ch. VIII, vol. 7); and special orders issued by the commanders of the
post of Houston, Dec. 3, 1863-Dec. 22, 1864 (ch. II, part of vol. 116), containing also copies of letters sent by Maj. N. B. Pearce, Dec. 18, 1863-
Jan. 14, 1864.

Records relating to ordnance works include a miscellaneous record
book of the Little Rock arsenal, Aug. 1862-Aug. 1863 (ch. IV, vol. 148);
letters sent by Lt. Col. Gabriel H. Hill, commander of the Tyler arsenal,
Mar. 4, 1864-May 26, 1865 (ch. IV, vol. 147; available on microfilm as
M 119); and a miscellaneous record book of the Tyler arsenal, Sept. 1863-
Apr. 1865 (ch. IV, part of vol. 148).

Most of the letters sent by   A. Albaugh, III, Tyler, Texas,
the Tyler arsenal are printed ver-   C.S.A. (Harrisburg, Pa., 1958).
batim or summarized in William

Record Group 365. --In 1873 the records of the Trans-Mississippi
Department's Cotton Bureau were purchased by the U.S. Commissioners
of Claims from J. P. Broadwell, a brother of Lt. Col. W. A. Broadwell
who had been the head of the bureau. An inventory of the records is in the
files of the War Department's Archive Office, Letters Received, R 38 C.
The commissioners later transferred them to the Treasury Department
from which they were received by the National Archives in 1939. The records are bound in volumes and all or nearly all the volumes contain name
indexes. They include: a press copy book of letters sent by W. A. Broadwell, Aug. 21, 1863-Apr. 18, 1864, to cotton agents, quartermasters, depositaries, other Government officials, business firms, private individuals, Gen. E. K. Smith and officers on his staff, and Lt. Col. W. J. Hut-
chins at Houston; correspondence and other records, Feb. 1864-May 1865
(3 1/2 ft.), consisting of letters received by Broadwell, copies and drafts
of outgoing letters and drafts of instructions, circulars and general and
special orders of the Trans-Mississippi Department, reports and permits,
and lists of exemptions and fiscal records; a register of letters received,
Feb. 1864-May 1865; a record of endorsements on letters received, Aug.
22, 1863-May 13, 1865; a record of cotton shipments, Oct. 1863-Apr. 1865;
statements of cotton purchased in Arkansas, Louisiana, and Texas by Government agents, 1864-65; a record of permits issued for exporting cotton
on private account, Oct. 6, 1864-Jan. 25, 1865; and a record of invoices of
ordnance supplies delivered and to be delivered by Bouldin, Riggs & Walker, Oct. 8, 1863.

Records that were accumulated by a branch of the Cotton Bureau at
Houston known as the Texas Cotton Office and now in this collection include:

press copies of letters sent, June 23, 1864-Oct. 5, 1865 (7 vols.); letters received, June 1864-Sept. 1865 (8 ft.); a register of letters received, June 1864-Aug. 1865 (2 vols.); a record of endorsements on letters received, Nov. 1863-May 1865 (1 vol.); and miscellaneous records, such as circulars, general and special orders from military headquarters, reports of purchasing agents, lists of agents and officials, payrolls, vouchers, quarterly returns of quartermaster stores, financial statements, registers of export duty on cotton, and papers concerning vessels.

Other book records of the Texas Cotton Office in the same collection include: weekly reports of cotton purchases by agents, July-Nov. 1864 (1 vol.); a record of shipments of cotton by transport agents, July 1864-Jan. 1865 (1 vol.); a record of deliveries of cotton by railroads, July 1864-Apr. 1865 (1 vol.); a record of cotton received and delivered, Jan. 1864-Apr. 1865 (1 vol.); a record of the receipt and delivery of bagging and rope, Feb. 1864-May 1865 (1 vol.); a cotton sales book, Aug. 1864-May 1865 (1 vol.); a record of purchases of cotton by agents, July-Dec. 1864 (1 vol.); a cotton cash account, July 15, 1864-May 20, 1865 (1 vol.); a record of certified cotton accounts, July 1864-Jan. 1865 (2 vols.); a ledger of certified accounts, Apr. 1864-May 1865 (1 vol.); and a record of the organization, Apr. 2, 1864, in Matamoras, Mex., of a joint-stock company in contract with the Texas Cotton Bureau to purchase arms and import them into Texas and, in turn, to ship cotton through the blockade. All the records listed here are described in detail in National Archives, Preliminary Inventory [No. 169] of the Treasury Department Collection of Confederate Records.

Records in Other Custody.--A letters-sent book of Gen. Edmund Kirby Smith, June 3, 1863-May 2, 1865, and a file of his correspondence and other papers, 1861-65, are in the Southern Historical Collection in the University of North Carolina Library (microfilm in the University of Texas Library). A register of letters received, Sept. 1864-May 25, 1865; and letters sent by Col. Ben Allston, the inspector general, July 11-Dec. 30, 1863 (1 vol.) are in the Louisiana Historical Association collection on deposit in the Howard-Tilton Memorial Library of Tulane University, which also has some printed general orders issued, Jan.-May 1865. The surrender agreement of May 26, 1865, endorsed by General Smith and Gen. Edward R. S. Canby in Galveston Harbor on June 2 is in the Virginia Historical Society collections. The Texas Archives of the University of Texas Library has a miscellaneous collection of documents relating to the Trans-Mississippi Department, such as the papers of Guy M. Bryan, an officer on the staff of General Smith. Some ordnance records, 1862-65, are in the Howard-Tilton Memorial Library of Tulane University.

The letters-sent books, June 30, 1861-May 15, 1865 (4 vols.), of Maj. Charles E. Carr, chief quartermaster from Oct. to Dec. 1862 and chief paymaster from Dec. 1862 to May 1865, are in the New-York Historical Society collections. Other records of his maintained while he was chief paymaster are in the Louisiana Historical Association deposit in the Howard-Tilton Memorial Library of Tulane University. Some papers of Maj. William L. Cabell, chief quartermaster from Dec. 1862 to Mar. 1863, are in the Dallas Historical Society collections. On Mar. 10, 1863, the appointment of Maj. William H. Thomas as chief of subsistence was announced and he continued in that office until the end of the war. His records in the Louisiana Historical Association deposit in the Howard-Tilton Memorial Library of Tulane University include press copies of letters sent, Apr.-Dec. 1863 and Feb. 1864-Feb. 1865 (4 vols.); miscellaneous papers, Mar.

20, 1865 (365 items), including letters received, drafts of letters sent, receipts, returns, orders, estimates of funds required, reports of persons employed, and accounts; a register of letters received, Feb. 20-Oct. 16, 1865 (1 vol.); a record of briefs of letters received and endorsements on letters forwarded, Aug. 8, 1863-May 26, 1865 (3 vols.); a return of provisions received and issued at Shreveport, Oct.-Dec. 1863; a cashbook, Aug. 19, 1864-Apr. 11, 1865; rosters of officers and agents of the Subsistence Department on duty in districts nos. 1 and 2, 1862-64; and an alphabetical roster of commissary officers, 1862-64. Some papers of Maj. John Reid, a commissary officer who served with Major Thomas during 1864-65, are in the Department of Archives of Louisiana State University. A letters-sent book of Maj. Benjamin A. Botts, inspector of the tax in kind, 1863-65, is with the Texas Archives of the University of Texas Library. Miscellaneous quartermaster records relating to the Trans-Mississippi Department are in the same repository and also in the Archives Division of the Texas State Library, where some commissary records are interfiled with them.

Records of other quartermaster officers have been located. Capt. N. A. Birge became post quartermaster at Monroe, La., late in 1862, then served as assistant quartermaster at Shreveport, and during 1864-65 he was agent for the impressment of cotton at Jefferson, Tex. An extensive collection of his records in the Texas Archives of the University of Texas Library includes correspondence, 1861-65 (3,173 items); reports on persons employed, Nov. 1861-Apr. 1864 (2 vols.); and a roll of noncommissioned officers and privates employed on extra duty as mechanics and laborers at Monroe, Shreveport, and Jefferson, 1862-65 (1 vol.). Other papers of Captain Birge in the Department of Archives of the Louisiana State University include letters received, a file of requisitions, vouchers, receipts, orders, and summary statements of funds, 1862-65; and a transportation record book, 1862-63. Capt. George C. Rives was a quartermaster officer on tax-in-kind service at Austin, Tex., during 1863-65. His correspondence and reports received by him from county agents are in the Archives Division of the Texas State Library. Thomas D. Miller, a quartermaster agent who headed a cotton agency at Alexandria, La., kept a letters-sent (fair copies) book, July 14, 1864-Jan. 30, 1865, which is now in the Department of Archives of the Louisiana State University. Fair copies of letters sent by Capt. Francis J. Lynch, Oct. 21, 1864-May 12, 1865 (1 vol.), relating to the cotton agency at Brownsville, Tex., are in the Archives Division of the Texas State Library.

Some incomplete collections of records relating to the conscription service in several of the States are available. General and special orders, telegrams, circulars, and other papers received by the enrolling officer of the 4th Division of Arkansas (Maj. James T. Elliott), Nov. 3, 1862-Feb. 15, 1865, are in the Manuscript Division of the Library of Congress. The Louisiana Adjutant General's Office at Jackson Barracks, New Orleans, has records of Col. E. G. Randolph, the commandant of conscripts at Shreveport, including orders, circulars, and letters sent to enrolling officers, and with these documents are a few papers, Dec. 1863-May 1865 (2 in.), of Lt. J. A. Prudhomme, enrolling officer at Natchitoches. In the same collection is a letters-sent book of Lieutenant Prudhomme, July 1864-May 1865, containing fair copies of letters to the commandant of conscripts, other enrolling officers, surgeons, post commanders, and others. Another record book of the Natchitoches Parish enrolling office, containing descriptive lists and reports of slaves and conscripts enrolled, June 1864-

Apr. 1865, is in the Louisiana Historical Association collection on deposit in the Howard-Tilton Memorial Library of Tulane University. A notebook in the John A. Spence papers in the Department of Archives of the Louisiana State University contains records of the Calcasieu Parish enrolling office, Aug. 1864-Apr. 1865, including descriptive lists of conscripts enrolled, special orders detailing men for duty, and a register of documents received.

District of Arkansas

The District of Arkansas, including the States of Arkansas and Missouri and the Indian country, was established on Aug. 20, 1862, as part of the Trans-Mississippi Department. By the end of 1863 the Confederates had been forced to retreat into southwestern Arkansas leaving most of Arkansas in Union control.

Successive commanders of the District:

Maj. Gen. Thomas C. Hindman, Aug. 20, 1862.
Lt. Gen. Theophilus H. Holmes, Mar. 18, 1863.
Maj. Gen. Sterling Price, Mar. 16, 1864.
Brig. Gen. Thomas J. Churchill, Aug. 1864.
Maj. Gen. John B. Magruder, Aug. 4, 1864.
Brig. Gen. Mosby M. Parsons, Jan. 29, 1865.
Maj. Gen. John B. Magruder, Feb. 1, 1865.
Brig. Gen. Mosby M. Parsons, Feb. 15, 1865.

Record Group 109.--Letters sent by Maj. Gen. John B. Magruder, Sept. 8, 1864-Jan. 18, 1865 (ch. II, vol. 201; available on microfilm); special orders, May 20-Oct. 17, 1864, and copies of letters sent by Brig. Gen. Joseph G. Shelby, May 19-Sept. 14, 1864 (ch. II, vol. 73; available on microfilm); and a statement of differences arising on the settlement of the accounts of Maj. George W. Clarke, quartermaster at Fort Smith, 1861-62 (ch. V, vol. 246).

Records in Other Custody.--Papers of Brig. Gen. Daniel M. Frost, who served under Generals Hindman and Price, are in the Missouri Historical Society collections.

District of Indian Territory

In 1861 the Indian country west of Arkansas and south of Kansas was made a separate military command, the Department of Indian Territory, its regiments composed of Creek, Cherokee, Choctaw, and Chickasaw Indians. In May 1862 the department was merged into the Trans-Mississippi Department, but a District of Indian Territory consisting of the same area was established within that department on July 21, 1864. The district commanders also served as Superintendents of Indian Affairs.

Successive commanders of the department and district:

Brig. Gen. Ben McCulloch, May 13, 1861.
Brig. Gen. Albert Pike, Nov. 22, 1861.
Brig. Gen. Douglas H. Cooper, Jan. 20, 1862.
Brig. Gen. William Steele, Jan. 1863.
Brig. Gen. Samuel B. Maxey, Dec. 11, 1863.
Brig. Gen. Douglas H. Cooper, July 21, 1864.

Record Group 109.--Letters-sent books, May 19, 1863-June 17, 1864, and May 10-27, 1865 (ch. II, vols. 258, 267, and 268); letters sent by Col. E. E. Portlock, Jr., inspector general, Apr. 23, 1864-May 15, 1865 (ch. II, vols. 259 and 260); letters received by Colonel Portlock from the inspector general of the Trans-Mississippi Department, June 14-Oct. 7, 1864; and miscellaneous papers, 1863-65 (1/2 in.), consisting of circulars, letters transmitting muster rolls, correspondence regarding prisoners and Federal raids, the proceedings of the grand council of the Confederate Indian tribes, Aug. 1864, memoranda on the military forces in the district, 1863, and the compact between the Confederate Indian tribes and the prairie tribes, 1865.

Records in Other Custody.--Papers of Generals Cooper, Maxey, and Stand Watie, commander of an Indian brigade, are in the University of Oklahoma Library. Some letters received by Stand Watie, Apr. 1862-Apr. 1865, are in the Texas Archives of the University of Texas Library. Papers of Capt. Bulow Marston, inspector general under Cooper, are in the Department of Archives, Louisiana State University. Papers of Charles B. Johnson in the Newberry Library, Chicago, include correspondence, reports, contracts, and vouchers relating to the subsistence of Indians of the Wichita and other agencies. A smaller quantity of similar papers of Johnson are in the University of Arkansas Library. John R. King's papers, 1861-62, in the Archives Division of the Texas State Library concern the procurement of provisions for McCulloch's regiment of mounted riflemen.

District of Texas, New Mexico, and Arizona

In the summer of 1861 Confederate forces under Lt. Col. John R. Baylor occupied the southern part of the Territory of New Mexico and organized it as part of the Territory of Arizona. The Army of New Mexico under Brig. Gen. Henry H. Sibley advanced northward and occupied Santa Fe briefly during Mar.-Apr. 1862 but was driven out of both territories in the summer. U.S. forces remained in control in those territories. The District of Texas, which was set up in Aug. 1862 under the Trans-Mississippi Department, became part of the District of Texas, New Mexico, and Arizona in Dec. 1862. In 1863 prisoner-of-war camps were established in Texas at Camp Ford near Tyler and at Camp Groce near Hempstead.
Successive commanders of the district:
> Brig. Gen. Paul O. Hébert, Aug. 20, 1862.
> Maj. Gen. John B. Magruder, Oct. 20, 1862.
> Maj. Gen. John G. Walker, Aug. 6, 1864.
> Maj. Gen. John B. Magruder, Mar. 31, 1865.

Record Group 109.--Letters-sent books. Dec. 1, 1862-May 22, 1865 (ch. II, vols. 121-128 and 130-133); telegrams sent, Mar. 22, 1864-May 22, 1865 (ch. II, vols. 136-138); letters received, reports, and other papers, 1861-65 (8 in.); letters received, Oct. 1, 1862-Dec. 27, 1863 (ch. II, vol. 251); letters received from the War Department, Nov. 14, 1862-Aug. 26, 1864 (ch. II, vol. 252); correspondence and telegrams of General Magruder, 1862-64 (3 in.); telegrams received, 1861-65 (6 in.); endorsements on letters received, July 1863-May 1865 (ch. II, vols. 139 and 141-149); general orders issued, Dec. 11, 1862-Nov. 8, 1863 (ch. II, vols. 246-248); general orders and circulars issued, Jan. 25-Dec. 31, 1863, and Jan. 1-May 26, 1865 (ch. II, vols. 113 and 114); special orders issued, Dec. 1, 1862-May 22, 1865 (ch. II, vols. 103-106, 106 1/2, 107, 108, 110, 111, and 118); extracts of special orders received, July 9, 1862-Dec. 22, 1864 (ch. II, vol. 256 1/2); a record of men detailed, 1864-65 (ch. II, vol. 254); a statement of enlisted men detailed in staff departments, 1862-63 (ch. II, vol. 253); a record of orders and blank forms furnished, 1863-65 (ch. II, vol. 255); and an index to special orders issued, apparently by a Texas command (ch. II, vol. 244).

Martin H. Hall, "The Muster in Sibley's New Mexico Campaign, Rolls of the Army of New Mexico," p. 227-329 (Austin, 1960).

Record Group 365. --Letters received by the headquarters of the Department of Texas and the District of Texas, New Mexico, and Arizona from Maj. Sackfield Maclin and other correspondence, Oct. 8, 1861-Mar. 24, 1865 (1 in.), relating to him are with the records of the Texas Cotton Office (Letters Received, file 4013). Major Maclin served as the chief quartermaster in the Department of Texas in 1861, as principal commissary of subsistence and chief ordnance officer in 1862-63, and as chief purchasing commissary for the State of Texas in 1863-65.

Correspondence, Mar. 1862-Oct. 1864, of military authorities with foreign consuls and attorneys relates to the conscription of aliens and their discharge from military service. Correspondence, Mar. 1863, of Brig. Gen. Hamilton P. Bee concerns relations with Mexicans along the Rio Grande. Some miscellaneous correspondence and papers include material on the mustering of Capt. Ashbel Smith's company, material concerning John S. Greer, ordnance officer at Fort Brown, and a letter, Nov. 30, 1863, of Colin J. McRae with a copy of a contract between Maj. William H. Haynes, Chief of the Clothing Bureau of the Trans-Mississippi Department, and John Chiles of St. Louis, Mo.

Records in Other Custody. --General and special orders issued by Maj. Gen. John B. Magruder, Dec. 1862-Mar. 1863, are in the Texas Archives of the University of Texas Library. In the Library of Congress is a correspondence book of Brig. Gen. Hamilton P. Bee, Feb. 3-May 17, 1863, containing copies of his correspondence with Gov. Albino Lopez of Tamaulipas, Mex., concerning an extradition treaty, the passage of armed parties across the border, and other matters. In the same repository are papers of Col. James A. Bourland, commander of a cavalry regiment, concerning activities on the Red River. Records of Col. John S. Ford, 2d Texas cavalry, in the Archives Division of the Texas State Library include letters-sent books, Feb. 18-Apr. 25, Sept. 22-Nov. 29, 1864, and Aug. 24-Dec. 30, 1864 (3 vols.), and general and special orders issued by Colonel Ford, Apr. 1863-May 1865. Ford's memoirs in the Texas Archives of the University of Texas Library contain some documents of the war period. Papers of Col. John R. Baylor are in the Department of Archives, Louisiana State University. Records of Capt. James M. Holmsley, who served in Texas, in the University of Texas Library include orders, returns, lists, invoices, and letters, 1861-64. A folder of papers of Capt. John R. King, Jan. 11, 1861-Nov. 11, 1862, in the Archives Division of the Texas State Library concern his activities as commissary of Col. H. E. McCulloch's regiment of mounted riflemen. A. R. Roessler's narrative descriptions of military routes of the Confederate Army in Texas are in the same repository. Papers of Maj. William T. Mechling in the University of Texas Library (Jeremiah Y. Dashiell papers) concern his service in Texas. Correspondence and papers of Capt. Milton G. Howe, Jan. 3, 1863-May 9, 1865 (4 in.), in the Texas Archives of the University of Texas Library concern engineering duties performed by Howe with Co. E, 1st Battalion, engineer troops at Galveston and Houston. A correspondence and order book, Sept. 1862-

May 1865, of the military headquarters at Tyler, Tex., is in the custody of F. Lee Lawrence of Tyler. Correspondence and other papers of Surg. George Cuppler, 1861-63 (100 items), are in the Archives Division of the Texas State Library. Letters of Edward A. Pye, who served as a surgeon in hospitals at Niblett's Bluff, Beaumont, and Houston have been published (Frank E. Vandiver, ed., "Letters from the Confederate Medical Service in Texas, 1863-1865," Southwestern Historical Quarterly, 55:378-393, 459-474 (Jan., Apr. 1952).

A record of a military commission that met at San Antonio to try persons suspected of being Unionists is in the University of Texas Library and has been published (Alwyn Barr, ed., "Records of the Confederate Military Commission in San Antonio, July 2-October 10, 1862," Southwestern Historical Quarterly, 70:93-109, 289-313, 623-644 (July, Oct. 1966, Apr. 1967). A letters-sent book, Dec. 1862-May 1864, of the chief engineer of the Eastern Subdistrict of Texas is in the State Historical Society of Wisconsin.

District of West Louisiana

On Aug. 20, 1862, that part of the State of Louisiana west of the Mississippi was established as the District of West Louisiana. It was consolidated with the District of Arkansas on Apr. 19, 1865.

Successive commanders of the district:
Maj. Gen. Richard Taylor, Aug. 20, 1862.
Maj. Gen. John G. Walker, June 10, 1864.
Maj. Gen. Simon B. Buckner, Aug. 4, 1864.

Record Group 109.--Letters sent, Jan. 13-Feb. 22, 1864 (ch. II, vols. 75 and 76), a transcript of a press copy book made in 1874.

Records in Other Custody.--A letters-sent and order book of Major General Taylor, Apr. 11-May 19, 1864, is in the Louisiana Historical Association collection on deposit in the Howard-Tilton Memorial Library of Tulane University. In the same library are the records of Col. Joseph L. Brent as chief of ordnance and artillery, including letters-sent books, Oct. 22, 1862-Oct. 11, 1864 (2 vols.); letters received, Jan. 27, 1862-May 14, 1865, with drafts of some letters sent; and miscellaneous papers, Jan. 5, 1862-May 16, 1865, consisting of orders, invoices of ordnance and ordnance stores, receipts, reports, returns, abstracts of disbursements, estimates of harness and horses required, reports of the workshop at Jackson's bridge, summary statements of work done at the New Iberia arsenal, and reports of artillery operations. Letters sent by Brig. Gen. Joseph L. Brent as commander, Forces Front Lines, Apr. 18-June 3, 1865 (2 notebooks), and special orders of Brent's Louisiana cavalry brigade, Nov. 14, 1864-May 27, 1865 (1 vol.), are also in that library. Correspondence and orders of Joseph L. Brent, July 1862-May 1865 (3 in.), are in the Louisiana Adjutant General's Office, Jackson Barracks, New Orleans, where there are also other records of Brent's brigade, Jan.-May 1865 (4 in.). Correspondence and other documents, 1861-1905, of Brent are in the Henry E. Huntington Library. A letter book of Capt. J. W. Sims, post quartermaster at Natchitoches, and papers of Capt. David F. Boyd, chief engineer of the District, are in the Department of Archives of the Louisiana State University.

Army of the West

Organized on Mar. 4, 1862, the Army of the West consisted largely of the Missouri State Guard. After fighting in Arkansas the Army of the West crossed to the eastern side of the Mississippi and was united with the Army of Tennessee at the battle of Corinth in Oct. 1862.

Successive commanders of the Army of the West:

Maj. Gen. Earl Van Dorn, Mar. 4, 1862.
Maj. Gen. John P. McCown, June 20, 1862.
Brig. Gen. Dabney H. Maury, June 27, 1862.
Maj. Gen. Sterling Price, July 3, 1862.

Record Group 109. --Endorsements on letters received, May 12-Dec. 31, 1862 (ch. II, vol. 180); general and special orders and circulars issued, Mar.-Dec. 1862 (1 in.); rosters of officers, 1861-62 (ch. I, vols. 107 1/4 and 108 1/2); letters sent and general and special orders issued by the artillery brigade, Apr.-July 1862 (ch. II, vol. 266), containing copies of letters signed by Col. M. L. Clark, Lt. Col. James P. Major, and Col. George W. McCown; and general and special orders received by Col. M. L. Clark, chief of artillery, Feb.-Aug. 1862 (ch. II, vol. 212); returns of ordnance and ordnance stores, Brig. Gen. Martin Green's brigade, Bowen's division, 1862 (ch. IV, vol. 131); and a record of quartermaster stores transferred to Capt. J. E. Klumph, Sept. 1, 1862-May 30, 1863, and accounts of quartermaster stores supplied to various officers, Sept. 1862-May 1863 (ch. V, vol. 213).

Records in Other Custody. --In the Minnesota Historical Society collections is an order book, 1862-64 (2 vols.), containing copies of general and special orders issued by Brig. Gen. D. H. Maury and others. A letters-sent book, Aug. 6, 1862-Dec. 1, 1863, containing copies of letters by Brig. Gens. John S. Bowen, Francis M. Cockrell, and Martin E. Green is in the Virginia Historical Society collections. Papers of Maj. John Reid, who served as chief of subsistence to General Price during 1862-63, are in the Department of Archives of the Louisiana State University.

Department of the West

Established on Nov. 24, 1862, this department embraced in the next year the region west of the line between Georgia and Alabama to the Mississippi River, north to the Tennessee River and the Kentucky border, and south to the Gulf.

The commander of this department was Gen. Joseph E. Johnston.

Record Group 109. --A letters-sent book, Feb. 16-Dec. 16, 1863 (ch. II, vol. 18 1/4); copies of telegrams sent, June-Dec. 1863 (ch. II, vol. 236 3/4); letters and telegrams received, 1862-63 (1 in.); general and specila orders and circulars issued, Dec. 1862-Dec. 1863 (1 in.); and special orders issued, May-Aug. 25, 1863 (ch. II, vol. 181).

Military Division of the West

On Oct. 17, 1864, Gen. Pierre G. T. Beauregard assumed command of the Military Division of the West which comprised the Department of Tennessee and Georgia commanded by Gen. John B. Hood and the Department of Alabama, Mississippi, and East Louisiana commanded by Lt. Gen. Richard Taylor.

Record Group 109. --General and special orders and special field orders and circulars issued, 1864-65 (1/4 in.).

Records in Other Custody. --Letters-sent books, Oct. 23, 1864-Mar. 7, 1865 (3 vols.); telegrams sent, Oct. 18, 1864-Mar. 17, 1865 (1 vol.); and general orders issued, Oct. 17, 1864-Feb. 4, 1865 (1 vol.), are in the Louisiana Historical Association collection on deposit in the Howard-Tilton Memorial Library of Tulane University. Letters-sent books, Oct. 11, 1864-Mar. 16, 1865 (2 vols.); letters sent and orders issued, Feb. 11-Apr. 10, 1865 (1 vol.); special orders issued, Oct. 18-Dec. 30, 1864 (1 vol.); field orders, Oct. 23, 1864-Mar. 6, 1865 (1 vol.); and letters sent by Maj. Henry Bryan, assistant inspector general, Nov. 30, 1864-Mar. 9, 1865 (1 vol.), are in the Manuscript Division of the Library of Congress.

Western Department

The Western Department, also called Department No. 2, was established on June 25, 1861. Its boundaries were frequently changed and it included at times all or parts of the States of Alabama, Florida, Tennessee, Mississippi, Louisiana, Arkansas, and Missouri. In Jan. 1862 the Trans-Mississippi District, embracing parts of Louisiana, Indian Territory, Arkansas, and Missouri, was established within the Western Department. That district was transferred in May 1862 to the Trans-Mississippi Department. In Mar. 1862 the Army of the Mississippi under Gen. Braxton Bragg was organized in the Western Department, and in Nov. 1862 it was renamed the Army of Tennessee. In July 1863 the Western Department was designated the Department of Tennessee. Brig. Gen. Gideon J. Pillow was assigned to a Volunteer and Conscript Bureau in this department on Jan. 14, 1863. It acted independently of the Bureau of Conscription in Richmond until it was abolished in Dec. 1863.

Arrangements were also made for examining political prisoners. General Johnston appointed Judge John J. Burnham of Kentucky and Maj. J. J. Williams, a provost marshal, to hear and determine the cases of persons held by military authorities. A departmental order of June 8, 1862, directed the formation of a military commission at Columbus, Miss., to investigate charges against political prisoners.

Successive commanders of the department:
Maj. Gen. Leonidas Polk, July 13, 1861.
Gen. Albert S. Johnston, Sept. 15, 1861.
Gen. Pierre G. T. Beauregard, Apr. 6, 1862.
Gen. Braxton Bragg, June 17, 1862.

Record Group 109. --Letters and telegrams sent, Sept. 14, 1861-Apr. 3, 1862 (ch. II, part of vol. 217 and vol. 218); copies of letters and telegrams received, May 6, 1861-Apr. 4, 1862 (ch. II, vol. 217, p. 417-441); registers of letters received, 1861-62 (ch. II, vol. 158 1/2); endorsements on letters received, Aug.-Sept. 1862 (ch. II, vol. 19 3/4); telegrams received and sent, 1861-62 (8 in.); general and special orders and circulars issued, 1861-63 (5 in.); orders and special orders issued, Oct. 24, 1862-Mar. 22, 1862 (ch. II, vol. 220); special orders, Sept. 15-Oct. 23, 1861 (ch. II, vol. 217, p. 261-280); letters sent by Maj. J. F. Gilmer, chief engineer, Nov. 11, 1861-Jan. 28, 1862 (ch. III, vol. 8, p. 1-42); a record of discharges on surgeon's certificate of disability, July-Sept. 1861 (ch. II, vol. 217, p. 2-7); letters and telegrams sent, Trans-Mississippi District, Feb.-Apr. 1862 (ch. II, vol. 271); and letters sent, Western Department

and Army of the Mississippi, Sept. 1861-Aug. 1862 (2 in.).
Records of the Volunteer and Conscript Bureau include letters and
orders, Jan.-May 1863 (ch. I, vol. 260, p. 130-512); letters sent by Brig.
Gen. Gideon J. Pillow, Jan. 17, 1863-May 30, 1864 (1/3 in.); letters and
dispatches received, Feb. 6-Sept. 2, 1863 (1/4 in.); telegrams received,
Jan. 1863-May 1864 (3 in.); orders and circulars issued, Feb. 3-Aug. 10,
1863 (1/4 in.); orders and circulars received, Jan.-Dec. 1863 (1 in.); and
a register of supernumerary officers ordered for conscript duty, a list of
officers commanding rendezvous, reports of officers commanding rendezvous, and an undated list of rendezvous (ch. VIII, vol. 358, p. 51-59, 60,
62-63, and 86)

Records in Other Custody. --Records of the Western Department in
the Louisiana Historical Association collection on deposit in the Howard-
Tilton Memorial Library of Tulane University include letters-sent books,
Sept. 14, 1861-Apr. 4, 1862, and Oct. 24, 1861-Mar. 19, 1862 (2 vols.);
special orders issued, Oct. 24, 1861-Mar. 28, 1862 (1 vol.); and general
orders issued, Apr. 30-Aug. 24, 1862 (1 vol.). The same repository has
papers of Gen. A. S. Johnston, Sept. 1861-Apr. 1862, including correspondence, telegrams, and orders; and copies of correspondence, telegrams,
and memoranda exchanged between Generals Johnston and Beauregard, Mar.
2-17, 1862 (1 vol.). A few other papers of General Johnston are in the Library of Congress. A letter and order book of the Okolona (Miss.) Ordnance Depot, July 8-Oct. 19, 1862, in Emory University Library contains
copies of letters sent by Capt. John T. Champneys and Lt. M. Levy, letters
received, and orders. Correspondence of Maj. Gen. Gideon J. Pillow,
June-Oct. 1863, is in the Texas Archives of the University of Texas Library.

REGIMENTS, BATTALIONS, AND COMPANIES

An act of Feb. 28, 1861 (Prov. Cong. C.S.A. Stat. 43), authorized the
President to receive into the service of the Confederate Government as part
of the Provisional Army of the Confederate States such forces in the service
of the States as might be tendered or that might volunteer for not less than
12 months. They could be received as companies, battalions, or regiments.
Additional legislation for the purpose of recruiting and reenlisting volunteers was enacted on Mar. 6, May 8, Aug. 8, and Dec. 11, 1861, and Jan.
27, 1862 (Prov. Cong. C.S.A. Stats. 45, 104, 176, 223, and 254). The Confederate Army was largely composed of volunteers raised under this legislation, and almost all the regiments enrolled in 1861 continued in service
throughout the war.

The sources available in the States for service in the Confederate
Government included the militia, old volunteer organizations, and new volunteer
organizations. State militia systems were based on the Federal militia act
of 1792 which with some exemptions required all men between 18 and 45
years of age to undergo military training. Men enrolled in the company and
regiment of the districts in which they lived. The militia in the States became greatly depleted because of volunteering, drafts, and the conscription
acts. Old volunteer organizations included the Washington Artillery of New
Orleans, the Richmond Howitzers, the Chatham Artillery of Savannah, the
Richmond Light Infantry Blues, the Alexandria Riflemen, and the Norfolk
Light Artillery. Most such organizations were promptly mustered into Confederate service and some were soon on the way to northern Virginia. Under
legislation adopted in 1861 the States organized new volunteer bodies to

meet the Confederate Government's calls for volunteers. Thus, for example, by July 18, 1861, North Carolina had transferred 14 volunteer regiments organized under its act of May 1, 1861.

An act of Mar. 6, 1861 (Prov. Cong. C. S. A. Stat. 47), provided for the establishment and organization of a Regular Army in the Confederacy to be composed of one corps of engineers, one corps of artillery, six regiments of infantry, one regiment of cavalry, and the staff departments already established. All Regular Army officers were to be appointed by the President and the rank and file were to be enlisted for not less than 3 nor more than 5 years. A total of 750 officers and cadets were appointed in the Regular Army, but efforts to enlist privates were largely unsuccessful. The officers were assigned to duty with the Provisional Army.

Further legislation added other types of military organizations to the Confederate Army. Regiments and battalions of cavalry, infantry, and mounted rifles were raised among the Cherokee, Chickasaw, Choctaw, Creek, Seminole, and Osage Indians who inhabited the country west of Arkansas and became confederated in 1861 with the Confederacy. In May 1861 Congress authorized mustering companies of light artillery into Confederate service. A Corps of Engineers originally authorized for the Provisional Army in Dec. 1861 was enlarged by an act of Apr. 21, 1862 (1 Cong. C. S. A. Stat. 49). An act of Mar. 20, 1863 (1 Cong. C. S. A. Stat. 98), authorized the organization of companies of engineer troops into regiments of ten companies each. Two companies in each regiment were to be pontonier companies each of which was to be furnished with bridge trains. A Signal Corps that originated in Apr. 1862 was enlarged in September of that year. Bands of partisan rangers that were organized under the authority of an act of Apr. 21, 1862 (1 Cong. C. S. A. Stat. 48), were usually mounted on detached duty; they became so troublesome to loyal Confederates that they were abolished in Feb. 1864, except for those operating in enemy territory. An act of Apr. 21, 1862 (1 Cong. C. S. A. Stat. 51), authorized the organization of battalions of sharpshooters who were to be armed with long-range muskets or rifles. Though legislative provision had been made on Aug. 21, 1861 (Prov. Cong. C. S. A. Stat. 186), for the employment by the Confederacy of volunteers for local defense in the States, such troops were not mustered into Confederate service until 1863 (AIGO General Order 86, June 22, 1863). The organization of the local defense corps was to conform to that prescribed for companies, battalions, and regiments of the Provisional Army; only infantry and cavalry were to be organized and the latter had to furnish their own horses. They were not to go beyond the limits of their States and were to serve only for periods of emergency. The work of the corps of officers authorized on Apr. 11, 1862, for the procurement of niter is described above under the section on the Niter and Mining Bureau.

An act of Feb. 17, 1864 (1 Cong. C. S. A. Stat. 211), provided for the conscription of 17-year-old youths and men between the ages of 45 and 50 and their enrollment in State reserve forces for local defense and detail duty under Confederate control. The Bureau of Conscription enrolled, organized, and mustered the reserves which thereafter came under the control of generals of reserves appointed by the President. Reserve forces were used as prison guards and as reinforcements for active forces under the command of district, department, or army commanders. AIGO General Order 63 of Aug. 6, 1864, required detailed men including those between the ages of 18 and 45 to report to generals of reserves to be organized into companies and regiments, and the order allowed men who were exempted also to enroll in these companies. Early in 1865 the generals of reserves were directed to employ men in apprehending deserters and absentees. When the Bureau of Conscription was abolished in Mar. 1865, the generals of reserves were given charge of conscription.

Generals of reserves:

Alabama: Maj. Gen. Jones M. Withers, Apr. 30, 1864.

Florida: Maj. Gen. James P. Anderson, Apr. 30, 1864.

Brig. Gen. William Miller, Sept. 8, 1864.

Georgia: Maj. Gen. Howell Cobb, Mar. 30, 1864.

Mississippi: Brig. Gen. William L. Brandon, July 23, 1864.

North Carolina: Lt. Gen. Theophilus H. Holmes, Apr. 18, 1864.

South Carolina: Brig. Gen. James Chesnut, Jr., Apr. 30, 1864.

Texas: Brig. Gen. Jerome B. Robertson, June 24, 1864.

Virginia: Brig. Gen. James L. Kemper, Apr. 30, 1864.

Regiments and companies kept the same kinds of records. Regiments recorded general and special orders issued and received. Outgoing letters were copied into letters-sent books, and letters received were filed in order and registered. Rosters were used to record officers' names, rank, dates of commission, and personnel actions. Other records that were kept by regimental officers are described below. Descriptive books of companies contain lists of officers and noncommissioned officers showing name, rank, date of appointment, promotion, and death. These books also contain registers of transfers, discharges, deaths, and desertions, and company rolls that give physical descriptions of men, enlistment information, and remarks as to discharge, death, promotion, capture, transfer, and wounds. Clothing account books show the name and rank of men, date and place of enlistment, articles of clothing issued and their value, and signatures of men and of witnesses. Order books contain special and general orders and circulars. Morning reports give information regarding the number of officers, noncommissioned officers, and men present or absent, and the number sick, under arrest, detached on leave, absent without leave, deceased, discharged, transferred, resigned, or returned to service. These records are often in the same volume. The company records sometimes supply information as to the name of company officers and superior officers, the geographical locations of the companies, affiliations with higher commands, and nicknames.

C. E. Dornbusch, Military Bibliography of the Civil War, Volume 2, Regimental Publications and Personal Narratives: Southern, Border, and Western States and Territories; Federal Troops, Union and Confederate Biographies (New York, 1967). Adam R. Johnson, The Partisan Rangers of the Confederate States Army, William J. Davis, ed. (Louisville, 1904), contains a roster of the rangers on p. 308-342. James L. Nichols, Confederate Engineers (Tuscaloosa, 1957); U.S. War Department, Local Designations of Confederate Troops [Washington, n.d.]; Richard P. Weinert, "The Confederate Regular Army," Military Affairs, 26:97-107 (Fall 1962).

Records in Other Custody. --Records relating to Confederate military organizations are in many repositories. These are usually diverse in content, but they are often arranged systematically, making it possible for the repositories to furnish specific information. A collection of regimental papers of U.S. and Confederate organizations in the W. P. Palmer

collection in the Western Reserve Historical Society contains correspondence, official orders, muster rolls, ordnance and quartermaster reports,
lists of casualties, memoirs, diaries, and descriptions of engagements.
A collection of records concerning Mississippi organizations is in the Mississippi Department of Archives and History.

Records of Alabama Troops

Record Group 109.--A register of patients of the 17th Infantry, Dec.
1863-Nov. 1864 (ch. VIII, vol. 5); a clothing account book of Company A,
19th Infantry, 1862-64 (ch. VIII, vol. 37); a clothing account book of Company B, 24th Infantry, 1861-64 (ch. VIII, vol. 42); an account book of expenditures of Company I, 24th Infantry, 1861-63 (ch. VIII, vol. 39); morning reports of Company F, 25th Infantry, Nov. 1863-Mar. 1864 (ch. VIII,
vol. 38 3/4); statistical morning-strength reports of Company G, 25th Infantry, Dec. 1861-Dec. 1863 (ch. VIII, vol. 38 1/2); a clothing account book
of Company G, 25th Alabama Infantry, 1862-64 (ch. VIII, vol. 38), with a
muster roll of Oct. 14, 1861; a clothing account book of Company E, 28th
Infantry, 1862-64 (ch. VIII, vol. 40); a descriptive roll of men and a clothing account of the 34th Infantry, 1862-64 (ch. VIII, vol. 43); a roster of officers and men of the 34th Infantry, 1862 (ch. I, vol. 109); with copies of
special orders issued; a clothing account book of Company C, 39th Infantry,
1862-64 (ch. VIII, vol. 41); a record book of Company H, 39th Infantry, 1862-
64 (ch. VIII, vol. 44), containing descriptive lists of men, reports of ordnance stores, lists of men absent and furloughed, and certificates relating
to enlistments; a roster of officers of the 39th Infantry, 1862-63 (ch. I, vol.
108); a record book of Company C, 45th Infantry, and Company G, 1st Infantry, 1862-65 (ch. VIII, vol. 4), containing for Company C a descriptive
roll of men, a record of clothing and equipment issued, and lists of men,
and for Company G a muster roll.

James G. Terry, comp.,
"Record of the Alabama State Artillery from Its Organization in May
1836 to the Surrender in April 1865
and from Its Re-organization Jany
1872 to Jany 1875, " Alabama Historical Quarterly, 20:141-443 (Summer
1958).

Records of Arkansas Troops

Record Group 109.--Clothing account book of Company D, 1st Mounted
Riflemen, 1861-62 (ch. VIII, vol. 45).

Muster rolls appear in the
following publications: Calvin L.
Collier, "They'll Do To Tie To!";
the Story of the Third Regiment Arkansas Infantry, C.S.A., p. 15-32
(Little Rock? 1959); V. Y. Cook,
"List of General and Field Officers,
Arkansas Troops, C.S.A., and State
Troops, " Arkansas Historical Association Publications, 1:411-422 (1906);
John C. Hammock, With Honor Un-
tarnished; the Story of the First Arkansas Infantry Regiment, Confederate States Army, p. 143-158 (Little
Rock, 1961).

Records of Florida Troops

Records in Other Custody. --A list of deserters of the 11th Infantry,

May 4, 1864-Feb. 15, 1865, is in the Buffalo and Erie County Historical Society collections.

Records of Georgia Troops

Record Group 109. --An undated roster of commissioned and noncommissioned officers of the 10th Infantry (ch. I, vol. 111).

Records in Other Custody. --The records noted here are in the Georgia Historical Society collections. Records of the Chatham Artillery (Capt. Joseph S. Claghorn's company of artillery detached from the 1st Georgia Volunteers) include a register, 1861-65 (1 vol.), containing lists of commissioned and noncommissioned officers, men transferred, discharged, deceased, and deserted, and a descriptive roll of men; a roll book, 1861-65, containing a record of enrollments, discharges, deaths, promotions, transfers, desertions, and departures from Savannah; a clothing account book, Jan. 1863-Apr. 1865; and some clothing receipts, muster rolls, and proceedings of general courts-martial convened at James Island, S. C. Other records include general and special orders issued by the headquarters of the 24th Battalion Georgia Cavalry (Randolph Rangers, Capt. Edward C. Anderson, Jr.), Aug. 6, 1863-Mar. 30, 1864 (1 vol.); a record book of Company A, 1st Georgia Volunteers (Irish Jasper Greens), containing minutes of meetings at Savannah, Jan. 31, 1856-Jan. 30, 1862, lists of men who served at Fort Pulaski, 1861, and rolls of men mustered into Confederate service, 1861-62; a regimental order book of the 47th Infantry, Cols. G. W. M. Williams and A. C. Edwards commanding, July 9-Nov. 29, 1864, containing general and special orders issued at the regimental and post headquarters at Secessionville, S. C., and other orders and circulars received from the headquarters of the 7th Military District, West Lines, East Lines, and the Department of South Carolina, Georgia, and Florida; correspondence, orders, and other documents of the same regiment, 1862-64; a regimental report book, Oct. 1861-Jan. 1862, of Col. C. B. Harkie, apparently with the 55th Infantry; and a map of the environs of Vicksburg, June 1, 1863.

Materials documenting Howell Cobb's services as general of the reserve forces of Georgia and, after Sept. 28, 1864, as commander of the Military District of Georgia and also his activities during 1863-64 in organizing the Georgia militia are among his papers in the University of Georgia Library. They include letters-sent books, Sept. 12, 1863-Apr. 18, 1865 (4 vols.), containing copies of letters and telegrams; endorsements on letters forwarded, Apr. 1864-Apr. 1865 (2 vols.); special orders issued, Apr. 14, 1864-Apr. 17, 1865 (1 vol.); and letters received and other papers, 1861-65.

Records of Kentucky Troops

Record Group 109. --Undated quartermaster accounts relating to articles issued to the 2d, 4th, 5th, 6th, and 9th Infantry (ch. VIII, vols. 67 and 68); quartermaster accounts of stores issued to the same regiments, Dec. 1863-1865 (ch. VIII, vol. 72), with a report on horses and mules in the 9th; quartermaster accounts, 4th Infantry, 1862-64 (ch. VIII, vol. 70); a transportation account, a record of requisitions, an account of clothing sold to officers, and a record of the disbursement of pay to officers of the 4th and other Kentucky regiments; quartermaster accounts of W. S.

Phillips, 4th Infantry, 1862 (ch. VIII, vol. 71), containing a record of stores issued to the companies, cash accounts, clothing accounts, a list of articles received, and a list of Negroes hired as regimental cooks; and a clothing account book of Company C, 4th Infantry, 1862-64 (ch. VIII, vol. 69).

Records of Louisiana Troops

Record Group 109. --A medical record book of the 7th Infantry, Aug.-Dec. 1861 (ch. VI, part of vol. 37), containing statistical reports of sick and wounded men, lists of men discharged on surgeon's certificates, lists of deaths, and reports of Surg. S. A. Smith to the medical director of the Army of the Potomac; a clothing account book of the 7th Infantry, Oct.-Dec. 1862 (ch. V, vol. 205); and quartermaster's cash accounts, 1863-64 (ch. V, vol. 486). Miscellaneous record books of the Louisiana brigade commanded by Brig. Gens. Daniel W. Adams and Randall L. Gibson, 1862-65 (ch. II, vols. 302-304), contain orders, letters, lists, battle reports, circulars, memoranda, and strength returns. These books relate to the brigade's service in the Army of Tennessee, the Army of the Mississippi, and the District of the Gulf.

Records in Other Custody. --Records of the Washington Artillery Battalion of New Orleans in the Louisiana Historical Association collection on deposit in the Howard-Tilton Memorial Library of Tulane University include correspondence, orders, circulars, instructions, and court-martial proceedings, 1861-65 (2 in.); a minute book, Nov. 8, 1860-Mar. 7, 1862; statistical morning-strength reports, 1861-63 (2 vols.); 5th Company records, Mar. 11, 1862-May 8, 1865 (2 vols.); and extracts from Brig. Gen. Randall L. Gibson's dispatches from Spanish Fort, Mar.-Apr. 1865. A miscellaneous record book of Company A, 2d Cavalry, 1863-65, in the Department of Archives of Louisiana State University contains muster and payroll notes; records of clothing issues, furloughs, and details; and copies of special orders. A record book of Company D, 1st Infantry, 1862-64, in the Howard-Tilton Memorial Library of Tulane University contains lists of officers and noncommissioned officers, registers of transfers, deaths, desertions, and a descriptive roll of enlisted men. General and special orders of the 2d Infantry, 1861, are in the Department of Archives of the Louisiana State University. Orders issued and received and circulars received of the 7th Infantry, Oct. 2, 1862-Jan. 22, 1864 (1 vol.), are in the New York Public Library. Muster rolls of Company D, 16th Infantry, Mar. 1862-Dec. 1863, and other muster rolls of Company H of that regiment, July 1862-Apr. 1863 and July-Dec. 1863, are in the Department of Archives of the Louisiana State University. A letter and order book of the Crescent Regiment, Louisiana Infantry, Sept. 12, 1862-Sept. 13, 1863, is in the Louisiana Historical Association collection on deposit in the Howard-Tilton Memorial Library of Tulane University.

John S. Kendall, ed., "Muster Rolls of the Fourth Louisiana Regiment of Volunteers, Confederate States Army," Louisiana Historical Quarterly, 30:381-522 (Apr. 1947).

Records of Mississippi Troops

Record Group 109. --Statistical morning-strength reports of the 3d Infantry, Nov. 14, 1861-June 3, 1862 (ch. I, vol. 140); a descriptive book

of Company D, 7th Infantry, 1861-63 (ch. VIII, vol. 102); a descriptive book
of Company G, 7th Infantry, 1861-62 (ch. VIII, vol. 50); a record book of
Company H, 7th Infantry, 1862-63 (ch. VIII, vol. 311), containing ordnance
and clothing accounts and muster rolls and payrolls; statistical morning-
strength reports of Company H, 7th Infantry, Oct. 1861-May 1864 (ch. I, vol.
141); statistical morning-strength reports and inventories of ordnance stores,
Company I, 7th Infantry, 1862-64 (ch. IV, vol. 110); a record book of the 7th
and 9th Infantry, 1863 (ch. VIII, vol. 101), containing morning reports, rosters and lists of officers and men, and quartermaster and ordnance accounts;
daily reports of camp guards and rosters of officers, 7th and 9th Infantry,
Feb. 1862-June 1863 (ch. VIII, vol. 360); a medical record book of the 21st
Infantry, 1863-64 (ch. VI, vol. 295), containing statistical reports of sick
and wounded men, a register of patients, invoices of medical and hospital
supplies, and lists of casualties at Gettysburg, Pa., and Berryville, Va.;
statistical morning-strength reports of Companies A and F, 24th Infantry,
1863-64 (ch. VIII, vol. 359); statistical morning-strength reports of Company E, 24th Infantry, 1863-64 (ch. VIII, vol. 359); general and special
orders issued and received, 24th and 29th Infantry, Apr. 24, 1862-May 1,
1863 (ch. VIII, vol. 98); statistical morning-strength reports, 27th Infantry,
1862-63 (ch. VIII, vol. 103); statistical morning-strength reports, Company
F, 27th Infantry, 1862-64 (ch. VIII, vol. 104); statistical morning-strength
reports, Companies H and L, 27th Infantry, 1863-64 (ch. VIII, vol. 359 1/4);
a clothing account book of Company H, 29th Infantry, 1863-64 (ch. VIII, vol.
47); a clothing account book of Company H, 29th Infantry, 1863-64 (ch. VIII,
vol. 48); general and special orders received, 30th Infantry, Apr. 16, 1862-
Apr. 18, 1863 (ch. VIII, vol. 347); statistical morning-strength reports,
30th Infantry, 1862 (ch. VIII, vol. 359 1/2); statistical morning-strength
reports of Company H, 30th Infantry, 1863-64 (ch. VIII, vol. 105); statistical morning-strength reports of Company B, 34th Infantry, and Company
B, 37th Infantry, 1862-63 (ch. VIII, vol. 106); a descriptive book of Company H, 34th Infantry, 1862-64 (ch. VIII, vol. 100), with quartermaster and
ordnance accounts and a list of men who received bounty payments at Holly
Springs, Miss.; a company book of Company A, 40th Infantry, 1862-64 (ch.
VIII, vol. 51), with descriptive records of men and clothing and ordnance
accounts; and a company book of Company I, 41st Infantry, 1861-64 (ch. VIII,
vol. 95), with descriptive records of men, clothing and ordnance accounts,
and copies of a few general orders received in June 1862. Records of the
reserve forces of Mississippi include general and special orders issued,
July 23, 1864-May 5, 1865 (ch. VIII, vols. 279 and 280).

Records in Other Custody. --Records of Company M, Wirt Adams
Cavalry (Harvey's Scouts), are in the Wiley N. Nash papers in the Mississippi State University Library. A few records of the 3d Battalion Missis-
sippi Cavalry, 1864-65, are in the Mississippi Department of Archives and
History. Records of the 10th Infantry in the same repository include general
orders, 1861, reports of the guard mounted at Pensacola, May 28, 1861-
Mar. 6, 1862, and statistical morning-strength reports, May 28, 1861-Mar.
6, 1862. A descriptive book of Company E, 21st Infantry, 1862-65, is in the
Manuscript Division of the Library of Congress. A record book of Company
C, 22d Infantry (microfilm), is in the New-York Historical Society collec-
tions.

Records of Missouri Troops

Record Group 109. --Clothing account books of Companies C and G, 1st Infantry, 1863-64 (ch. VIII, vol. 92); clothing account books of Companies A-I, and K, 2d and 6th Infantry, 1863-65 (ch. VIII, vol. 91 in 10 parts); clothing account books of Companies A-H, 3d and 5th Infantry, 1863-65 (ch. VIII, vol. 91 1/2 in 9 parts); and a record book of the 1st Military District, Missouri State Guard, Brig. Gen. M. Jeff Thompson commanding, July 1861-June 1862 (ch. II, vol. 207 1/2), containing copies of letters sent, a record of resignations and discharges, reports of operations, and rosters of officers.

Records of North Carolina Troops

Record Group 98. --Consolidated morning reports of the 1st Infantry Battalion, Oct. 9, 1861-Feb. 19, 1862, are in vol. 66, N.C. and Va. 9th Army Corps, in Record Group 98 (Records of United States Army Commands).

Record Group 109. --A descriptive list of the 5th North Carolina State Troops, 1861-62 (ch. VIII, vol. 94); a clothing and descriptive book of Company D, 5th State Troops, 1862-63 (ch. VIII, vol. 46); a clothing account book of Company F, 5th State Troops, 1863-64 (ch. VIII, vol. 46 1/2); account books, 1861-62 (ch. VIII, vols. 53 and 244), and a clothing account book (ch. VIII, vol. 52) of Company E, 12th State Troops (2d N.C. Volunteers); a clothing and descriptive book (ch. VIII, vol. 54) of Company H, 12th State Troops (2d N.C. Volunteers), 1863-64; a company book (ch. VIII, vol. 55) of Company K, 12th State Troops (2d N.C. Volunteers), containing a muster roll, a list of men discharged and killed, clothing accounts, and a list of articles drawn by men later killed, discharged, or not accounted for; a company book (ch. VIII, vol. 57) of Company B, 20th State Troops (10th N.C. Volunteers), 1861-65, containing notes on the organization of the company, a list of members, clothing and equipment accounts, and returns of ordnance stores; a company book (ch. VIII, vol. 58 1/2) of Company E, 20th State Troops (10th N.C. Volunteers), 1863-65, containing clothing and ordnance accounts, lists of deaths, discharges, transfers, and desertions, and a descriptive roll of officers; a clothing account book (ch. VIII, vol. 58) of Company I, 20th State Troops (10th N.C. Volunteers), 1861-64; general and special orders issued and received (ch. VIII, vol. 262) by the 23d State Troops (13th N.C. Volunteers), Oct. 22, 1862-Feb. 1, 1865; a record of ordnance and ordnance stores issued to companies of the 23d State Troops (13th N.C. Volunteers), 1863-64 (ch. VIII, vol. 64); a company book of Company B, 23d State Troops (13th N.C. Volunteers), 1861-63 (ch. VIII, vol. 66), containing lists of deaths and discharges and men who received bounty payments, reports of ordnance stores issued, clothing and ordnance accounts, and copies of letters, orders, and circulars; a clothing account book (ch. VIII, vol. 59) of Company D, 23d State Troops (13th N.C. Volunteers), 1861-65; a clothing account book (ch. VIII, vols. 62 and 63) of Company E, 23d State Troops (13th N.C. Volunteers), 1862-65; a clothing and ordnance account book (ch. VIII, vol. 65) of Company F, 23d State Troops (13th N.C. Volunteers), 1861-63; a clothing account book (ch. VIII, vol. 60) of Company H, 23d State Troops (13th N.C. Volunteers), 1861-64; a clothing and equipment account book (ch. VIII, vol. 61) of Company K, 23d State Troops (13th N.C. Volunteers), 1861-64; and statistical morning-strength reports (ch. VIII, vol. 107) of the 60th State Troops, 1862-64. Records of the reserve forces of North Carolina include copies of telegrams sent, May 14, 1864-Apr. 10, 1865 (ch. II, vol. 354); a record of communications sent, Oct. 1864-Feb. 1865 (ch. II, vol. 355); a register of letters received, May-Sept. 1864 (ch. II, vol. 351); endorsements on letters received, June 8, 1864-Jan. 30, 1865 (ch. II, vol. 352); and special orders issued, May 16, 1864-Apr. 10, 1865 (ch. II, vol. 357).

Records in Other Custody. --A journal of Company B, 10th Artillery, 1861-65, and a journal of the 38th State Troops, 1862-64, are with the Hoke papers in the Southern Historical Collection in the University of North Carolina Library. A medical record book of the 21st State Troops (11th N.C. Volunteers), 1862-64, in the Confederate Museum contains a register of patients, a list of men killed, monthly reports on surgical cases, a medical examining board record, orders, invoices of medicines and medical supplies, and summaries of sick and wounded men. Various records relating to the 12th Infantry are in the North Carolina Department of Archives and History. Muster rolls of Company C, 13th State Troops (3d N.C. Volunteers), Feb. 28-June 30, 1862, are in the Buffalo Historical Society collections. General order books (2 vols.) of the 37th State Troops, 1862-64, containing also some correspondence, and a quartermaster record of the 49th State Troops, 1863-64, are in the North Carolina Department of Archives and History which has an extensive collection of miscellaneous regimental records. A descriptive roll of Company G, 27th Infantry (Orange Guards of Hillsboro, N.C.), giving service records of officers and privates of the company, is in the Southern Historical Collection in the University of North Carolina Library. It has been published together with letters written from camps in North Carolina and Virginia by James A. Graham, a captain of the company, in H. M. Wagstaff, ed., The James A. Graham Papers, 1861-1884 (Chapel Hill, 1928).

Records of South Carolina Troops

Record Group 109. --A clothing account book, 19th Infantry, 1862 (ch. VIII, vol. 73), containing also descriptive lists; lists of deaths, discharges, furloughs, resignations, promotions, and absentees; and notes on military action and elections of officers.

Records in Other Custody. --Unless otherwise indicated the following records are in the South Caroliniana Library of the University of South Carolina. A record book of Company E, 1st Artillery, 1862, contains a descriptive roll of men, a roll of men sent to the hospital, a list of clothing issued, and a list of discharges. A file of records (140 items) of the 2d Artillery, June 1862-Nov. 1864, in Emory University Library includes correspondence, special orders, a list of details, and reports of events, battles, operations, and inspections. Record books (2 vols.) of the Washington Artillery of Charleston, 1862, contain lists of officers, guns, ammunition, and drivers. A roll of men in the Palmetto Guards (Company I, 2d Infantry) is one compiled in 1926 by the last surviving member of the company. An order book of Company I, 3d Cavalry, Aug. 3, 1862-Nov. 22, 1864, contains general and special orders and circulars received, including some from the 2d and 3d Military Districts of South Carolina, and orders issued by the company. A record book of Company K, 4th Infantry, June 1861-Apr. 1862, contains lists of guard and work details and clothing accounts. Muster rolls of Company E, 6th Infantry, 1862-63, and a roll of honor and roll of officers of Company D, 14th Infantry, 1861-65. Notes on surgical cases,

14th Infantry, are in the Confederate Museum. A clothing account book of Company D, 15th Infantry, 1860-65, and a muster roll of Company A, 17th Infantry, May 1-July 1, 1862. A daily record of leaves of absence (1 vol.) of the 25th Infantry, July 1862-June 1863, is in the Southern Historical Collection in the University of North Carolina Library. Copies of letters sent and received by Col. J. F. Marshall, commander of the 1st Regiment of South Carolina Rifles, Feb. 16-July 22, 1862, and a register of officers, rosters of companies, and record of guard details of the same regiment (microfilmed from the original in Clemson College Library). A printed roll (photostat) of Company C, Holcombe legion, 1861-65. A letters-sent book of Brig. Gen. James Chesnut, Jr., May 26, 1864-Apr. 25, 1865, containing copies of letters issued from the headquarters of the reserve forces at Columbia, S. C., is in Emory University Library. Other papers of Chesnut in Duke University Library include some wartime material.

Cornelius I. Walker, Rolls and Historical Sketch of the Tenth Regiment, South Carolina Volunteers, in the Army of the Confederate States (Charleston, 1881), contains rolls compiled from information supplied by survivors.

Records of Tennessee Troops

Record Group 109. --A record book of Company F (McClellan Troop) 5th Cavalry Battalion, 1861-62 (ch. VIII, vol. 97), contains clothing and provision accounts, a roll of the troop, and copies of orders and circulars received from superior commands. A record book (ch. VIII, vol. 109) of the 1st Infantry, Col. Peter Turney commanding, contains a morning-strength report of May 4, 1864, General Order 5 of Feb. 21, 1865, issued by the Army of Northern Virginia, and cash accounts, May 1864. Letters and orders received by the 7th Infantry, July 19, 1861-Mar. 12, 1862 (ch. VIII, vol. 348 1/2); orders issued by the same regiment, July 14, 1861-Apr. 14, 1862 (ch. VIII, vol. 108), were those of Col. Robert Hatton, mostly in Virginia. Strength reports of the 18th Infantry, 1863-64 (ch. VIII, vol. 108), with a few reports of the 26th Infantry; clothing and ordnance accounts of Company A, 26th Infantry, 1862-64 (ch. VIII, vol. 75), with a roll of men; general and special orders received and issued, Sept. 24, 1862-May 1, 1864 (ch. VIII, vol. 339); a clothing account book of Company C, 32d Infantry, 1862-64 (ch. VIII, vol. 78), with a roll of the company; a clothing account book of Company G, 32d Infantry, 1863-64 (ch. VIII, vol. 79); a clothing and descriptive book of Companies H and K, 32d Infantry, 1863-64 (ch. VIII, vol. 80); a clothing and descriptive book of Company K, 32d Infantry, 1861-62 (ch. VIII, vol. 80 1/2); a record book of Company B, 45th Infantry, 1862-64 (ch. VIII, vol. 76), containing morning reports, clothing and ordnance accounts, and orders; a clothing and ordnance account book of Company F, 45th Infantry, 1862-63 (ch. VIII, vol. 77); letters and telegrams sent and received by the 23d Infantry Battalion, Col. Tazewell W. Newman commanding, Oct. 20, 1862-May 1, 1863 (ch. II, vol. 238); general and special orders received and issued by Colonel Newman's battalion, Nov. 28, 1862-Aug. 11, 1864 (ch. VIII, vol. 340); statistical morning-strength reports of Colonel Newman's battalion, 1863 (ch. VIII, vol. 110); and a clothing account book of Company D, 23d Battalion, Tennessee Volunteers, 1863-64 (ch. VIII, vol. 74).

Records of Texas Troops

Record Group 109.--Special orders issued by the 1st Artillery, May 12, 1863-Nov. 5, 1864 (ch. II, vol. 240); statistical morning-strength reports of the 1st Artillery, 1863-65 (ch. VIII, vols. 111-113); clothing accounts of Company H, 1st Artillery, 1863 (ch. II, vol. 250); a record book of the 1st Cavalry, 1863-65 (ch. VIII, vol. 395), containing a list of commissioned officers, a register of men discharged, and a descriptive roll of men; and general and special orders and circulars received by the 13th Volunteers, Lt. Col. Joseph Bates commanding, Mar. 26, 1862-Feb. 19, 1864 (ch. II, vol. 239).

Records in Other Custody.--The Texas Archives of the University of Texas Library has statistical morning-strength reports of Company F, Stevens' dismounted cavalry, 1863-65 (1 vol., photostat), and orders issued by the headquarters at Velasco of the 2d Battalion, 4th Volunteers, Nov. 13, 1861-Mar. 4, 1862 (1 vol., photostat), with a roster of officers, a muster roll of Bates' rangers, and a register of countersigns.

Records of Virginia Troops

Record Group 109.--Ordnance return and appraisement of horses, Company D, 6th Cavalry, 1864-65 (ch. VIII, vol. 242); abstracts showing articles received and payments made by Capt. Thomas Tabb, quartermaster, 3d Infantry, 1863-64 (ch. V, vol. 216), with a record of the tax in kind collected; general and special orders received by the 15th Infantry, Dec. 27, 1861-Apr. 28, 1862 (ch. II, vol. 285); general orders issued and received by the 45th Infantry, June 6-Aug. 25, 1861 (ch. VIII, vol. 243); letters and general and special orders and circulars received, Oct. 24, 1861-Apr. 30, 1864 (ch. VIII, vol. 346); a clothing and descriptive book of Company K, 54th Infantry, 1861-64 (ch. VIII, vol. 84); a record book of Company A, 54th Infantry, 1862-63 (ch. VIII, vol. 83), containing clothing, ordnance, and equipment accounts and a descriptive roll of men; a clothing account book of Company F, 54th Infantry, 1862-64 (ch. VIII, vol. 81); a record book of Company H, 54th Infantry, 1862-63 (ch. VIII, vol. 82), containing a descriptive roll of men, a company roll, clothing accounts, a list of deserters, and a list of alterations; a clothing and descriptive book of Company I, 63d Infantry, 1862-64 (ch. VIII, vol. 86); a clothing account book of Company C, 63d Infantry, 1862-63 (ch. VIII, vol. 85); and a clothing account book of Company D, Local Defense Troops, 1863 (ch. V, vol. 203). Records of the reserve forces of Virginia include letters sent by Col. Robert Johnston, commander of the Petersburg district, May 20-Oct. 5, 1864 (ch. II, vol. 286), and general and special orders and circulars, May 30, 1864-Mar. 21, 1865 (1/4 in.).

Records in Other Custody.--Artillery records in the Virginia Historical Society collections include a record book of the Powhatan Artillery (1st Virginia Artillery); an order book, May 11, 1861-Feb. 24, 1862, muster rolls, and ordnance, clothing, and equipment reports, 1863-64, of the Richmond Howitzers; and records of the 20th Artillery Battalion. Documents relating to the 1st Cavalry are in the West Virginia University Library. Statistical morning-strength reports of the 4th Cavalry, 1863-64, are in the Confederate Museum. Company rolls of the 5th Cavalry (1 vol.), with a record of equipment issued to men, Feb. 1862, are in the William and Mary College Library. An account book of Company A, 14th Cavalry, kept by Lt.

Samuel W. N. Feamster, Apr. 1862-May 1864, is in the Manuscript Division of the Library of Congress. Documents relating to the 36th Cavalry Battalion are in the West Virginia University Library. A roster of the 1st Infantry and Edwin B. Loving's diary of its activities, 1861-65, are in the Archives Division of the Virginia State Library which also has an order book of that regiment, 1861-62. Records of Company J, 1st Infantry, Capt. B. F. Howard commanding, 1861-65, in the Confederate Museum include a statement of the organization of the company, a descriptive roll of men, and a journal of operations. Documents relating to the 2d Infantry are in the West Virginia University Library. A record book (microfilm) of Company K, 5th Infantry, 1861-65, is in the Southern Historical Collection in the University of North Carolina Library. Muster rolls of the 9th Infantry, 1862-63, officer-of-the-guard reports of the 10th Infantry, Aug. 1861-Jan. 1863, and muster rolls of the hospital department and detached soldiers of the 12th Infantry, Apr. 30, 1862-Oct. 21, 1864, are in the Archives Division of the Virginia State Library. Commissary records of Company A, 12th Infantry, kept by Capt. John P. May are in the University of Virginia Library. Documents relating to the 13th Infantry are in the West Virginia University Library. Records of Company F, 21st Infantry, are in the Henry E. Huntington Library. Records of Company H, 25th Infantry, and returns of Company I, 26th Infantry, June 30, 1862-Aug. 31, 1862, are in the Archives Division of the Virginia State Library. Clothing accounts of Company B, 31st Infantry, 1861-62, are in the Confederate Museum, and other records of that regiment are in the West Virginia University Library. A record book of Company F, 32d Infantry, containing a descriptive roll of men, an account, and a muster roll, is in the Archives Division of the Virginia State Library. Records of Company K, 40th Infantry, 1862 and 1864, in the New York Public Library include a muster roll, a letter, and reports of casualties. Some records of Company E (Dixie Grays), 42d Infantry, 1861-65, are in the University of Virginia Library. Quartermaster records (244 items) of the 44th Infantry, 1861-65, including vouchers, correspondence, memoranda, receipts, lists of rations, payrolls, and soldiers' furlough certificates, are in the Manuscript Division of the Library of Congress. A record book of the 51st Infantry in the Virginia Historical Society collections contains a diary of its operations and a list of casualties. Hospital rolls of the 54th Infantry are in the Virginia State Library. Letters-sent books (2 vols.) of the 59th Infantry, Col. William B. Tabb commanding, Jan. 4-Mar. 6, 1863, are in the Virginia Historical Society. A clerk's book of the 42d Virginia Militia is in the University of Virginia Library. An extensive collection of the papers of Maj. Gen. James L. Kemper, commander of the reserve forces, in the University of Virginia Library includes material on his wartime service.

W. A. Christian, "Official Rosters of the Richmond Companies Mustered into the Service of the Confederacy, 1861-1865," Richmond; Her Past and Present, p. 547-576 (Richmond, 1912); "Extracts from an Old 'Order Book' of the First Company, Richmond Howitzers," Contributions to a History of the Richmond Howitzers; Pamphlet No. 4, p. 33-64 (Richmond, 1878).

STATE COMMANDS

On Apr. 23, 1861, Robert E. Lee assumed command of the military and naval forces of Virginia. On May 10 the Confederate Secretary of War directed him to take command of the Confederate forces in Virginia and on May 14 his appointment as a brigadier general in the Confederate Army was confirmed. From his office at Richmond with the aid of a small staff General Lee directed the organization and training of the Virginia forces and the development and construction of defense works. Under the provisions of the convention of Apr. 25, 1861, between Virginia and the Confederate Government, the Virginia forces were transferred to the Confederacy in June. Until late in 1861, however, General Lee continued to serve in Virginia, acting as military adviser to the President, directing the defense of the eastern part of the State, and coordinating operations in western Virginia. A division headquarters that was set up in Richmond on Apr. 26, 1861, to command all of the State forces in and around that city was commanded successively by Maj. Gen. Joseph E. Johnston, Col. John B. Magruder, Brig. Gen. Thomas T. Fauntleroy, and Col. Charles Dimmock, before its discontinuance on Nov. 5, 1861.

Douglas S. Freeman, R. E. Lee; a Biography, 1:488, 501, 528,   529, 541 (4 vols.; New York, 1934-36).

Record Group 109. --Records of General Lee's headquarters include letters sent, Apr. 24-Nov. 4, 1861 (ch. VIII, vol. 234); a file of letters, telegrams, and other papers, Apr.-Nov. 1861 (1 ft. 4 in.), including orders, lists of men, statements of arms and ammunition on hand, court-martial proceedings, statistical morning-strength reports, letters referred by the President, and cross-references to documents filed elsewhere; a register of letters received, Apr. 13-Nov. 30, 1861 (ch. VIII, vol. 232, p. 1-13, 95-428, vol. 233); endorsements on letters received, May 8-Dec. 3, 1861 (ch. VIII, vol. 236); general and special orders issued, Apr. 23-Nov. 5, 1861 (ch. VIII, vols. 237 and 240); a list of officers appointed in the volunteer forces of Virginia, Apr.-Nov. 1861 (ch. I, vol. 126); a list of officers appointed in the Provisional Army of Virginia, Apr.-July 1861 (ch. I, vol. 125); and a list of discharged men, July-Sept. 1861 (ch. VIII, vol. 236, p. 458-469).

Records of the division headquarters commanding the forces in and around Richmond include letters sent, May 1-Oct. 9, 1861 (ch. VIII, vol. 235); letters and orders received, Apr. 27-Nov. 5, 1861 (ch. VIII, vol. 238); general and special orders issued, Apr. 27-Oct. 18, 1861 (ch. VIII, vol. 239); and consolidated morning-strength reports, May-Nov. 1861 (ch. VIII, vol. 241).

Other State records include: a register of officers' commissions, Mississippi State troops, 1861-65 (ch. VIII, vol. 6; a copy made by the U.S. War Department in 1905); a register of officers of the Provisional Army of Tennessee, 1861-65 (ch. I, part of vol. 97, with an index vol.); general and special orders issued by the East Tennessee Brigade, Provisional Army of Tennessee, May 11-Oct. 6, 1861 (ch. VIII, vol. 396); special orders issued by the Adjutant General of Texas, Jan. 4, 1862-May 10, 1865 (ch. VIII, vol. 277); and a roster of officers, Texas State Troops, Dec. 5 and Dec. 21, 1863 (ch. I, vol. 104 1/2). Eighty volumes of records of the State of Louisiana relating to its troops, which are described in National Archives, Preliminary Inventory [No. 101] of the War Department Collection of Confederate Records, p. 197 and 211-213, were returned to Louisiana in Oct. 1961.

COMMANDERS, STAFF OFFICERS, AND OTHER PERSONNEL
FOR WHOM ADDITIONAL PAPERS ARE AVAILABLE

J. D. Alison
    A diary of Surgeon Alison, May 9, 1861-July 4, 1863, is in the Alabama Department of Archives and History.

Richard H. Anderson (Maj. Gen.)
    A letters-sent book, May 29, 1861-Aug. 23, 1863, in the Confederate Museum relates to his services in South Carolina, Florida, and Virginia

Charles H. Andrews
    Andrews' papers in the Southern Historical Collection in the University of North Carolina Library concern in part his wartime service.

John H. Ash (Lt.)
    Papers relating to his service with the 5th Georgia Cavalry in Georgia, Florida, and South Carolina are in Emory University Library.

John Bannon
    Bannon's diary, 1861-63, concerning his activities as a chaplain, is in the South Caroliniana Library of the University of South Carolina.

James B. Barry (Lt. Col.)
    Barry's papers in the Texas Archives of the University of Texas Library include muster rolls and battalion reports of troops at Fort Belknap and Camp Cooper, Tex.

Robert Battey
    Battey's papers in Emory University Library include some documents relating to his service as a surgeon in Georgia and Mississippi.

Pierre G. T. Beauregard (Gen.)
    General Beauregard's commands included in 1861 the Confederate forces at Charleston, S. C., the Department of Alexandria, and the Army of the Potomac; in 1862 Department No. 2; in 1862-65 the Department of South Carolina, Georgia, and Florida; and in 1865 he was second to General Johnston in command of the Army of Tennessee. The following are in Record Group 109: press copies of letters and telegrams sent, Mar. 3-May 27, 1861 (ch. II, vol. 263); letters and telegrams received, Mar. 1-May 27, 1861 (ch. II, vol. 256); copies of letters and telegrams sent, May 19, 1862-Apr. 19, 1864 (ch. II, vol. 35); and correspondence, telegrams, reports, and other papers, 1862-64 (3 in.).
    General Beauregard's correspondence, military orders, and other documents, 1861-65 (500 items), are in Columbia University Library. Additional correspondence, orders, and other documents, 1861-65 (45 items), are in the Confederate Museum. Copies of letters sent and telegrams, letters received, general orders, special orders, and battle reports, 1861-65, are in the Library of Congress; some of these are in the Alfred Roman collection. Other papers of General Beauregard are in the Charleston Library Society collections, Duke University Library, Emory University Library, the Department of Archives of Louisiana State University, the Missouri Historical Society, the North Carolina Department of

Archives and History, the South Caroliniana Library of the University of South Carolina, the Texas Archives of the University of Texas Library, the Louisiana Historical Association collection on deposit in the Howard-Tilton Memorial Library of Tulane University, the Archives Division of the Virginia State Library, the Western Reserve Historical Society collections, and Yale University Library.

Taylor Beatty (Col.)
    Beatty's diary, Jan. 18, 1861-June 9, 1865, in the Southern Historical Collection in the University of North Carolina Library relates to his service in Florida and Tennessee.

John W. Beckwith
    The papers of Beckwith, who was appointed a chaplain in Feb. 1865 to serve at Demopolis, Ala., are in the Southern Historical Collection in the University of North Carolina Library.

Hamilton P. Bee (Brig. Gen.)
    Bee's papers in the Texas Archives of the University of Texas Library include wartime documents relating to Texas, Louisiana, and Indian Territory.

Samuel M. Bemiss
    Bemiss was a surgeon in Virginia and Georgia. His papers are on deposit in the Virginia Historical Society building.

William N. Berkeley (Maj.)
    Berkeley was an officer of the 8th Virginia Infantry. His papers are in the University of Virginia Library.

Alexander D. Betts
    Some papers of Betts, a chaplain of the 30th North Carolina Infantry, are in the Southern Historical Collection in the University of North Carolina Library.

John S. Bowen (Maj. Gen.)
    In Record Group 109 are copies of letters sent, Aug. 1862-Nov. 1863 (ch. II, vol. 274), relating to the Army of the West and the Army of the Mississippi.

Alexander H. Boykin (Capt.)
    The military papers and orders of Boykin's rangers (Company A, 2d South Carolina Cavalry), 1861-62, are in the Southern Historical Collection in the Univeristy of North Carolina Library.

Braxton Bragg (Gen.)
    General Bragg's commands included in 1861 the troops and defenses at Pensacola, in 1861-62 the Department of Alabama and West Florida, in 1862 the Army of the Mississippi and the Western Department, in 1863 the Army and Department of Tennessee, in 1864-65 the Department of North Carolina, and in 1865 the defense of Wilmington. In 1864 he served as military adviser to the President at Richmond. In Record Group 109 are copies of special orders issued, Mar. 7, 1862-May 7, 1864 (ch. II, vol. 221), and

copies of letters and telegrams sent, June 13-Dec. 14, 1863 (ch. II, vol. 359, p. 1-85).
    General Bragg's papers, Feb. 1861-Mar. 1865 (2 ft.), in the W. P. Palmer collection in the Western Reserve Historical Society include letters-sent books, 1861-64 (4 vols.), and a file of correspondence, telegrams, reports on battles and operations, orders, and memoranda, Feb. 25, 1861-Feb. 28, 1865. Smaller collections of his papers are in the Alabama Department of Archives and History, Duke University Library, Emory University Library, the Henry E. Huntington Library, the Louisiana State Museum, Miami University Library, the Missouri Historical Society, the Rosenberg Library at Galveston, Tex., the University of Georgia Library, and the University of Texas Library.

Junius N. Bragg
    Surgeon Bragg served in Arkansas, Louisiana, and Texas. His wartime letters have been published; see Mrs. T. J. Gaughan, ed., Letters of a Confederate Surgeon, 1861-65 (Camden, Ark., 1960).

Lawrence O'B. Branch (Brig. Gen.)
    Branch's papers in the North Carolina Department of Archives and History include materials relating to the activities of his brigade in North Carolina and Virginia in 1862.

John C. Breckinridge (Gen.)
    In Record Group 109 are copies of Breckinridge's letters, telegrams, and orders received and sent, Dec. 1861-Nov. 1863 (ch. II, vol. 311), relating to the Central Army of Kentucky, the Army of the Mississippi, and the Army of Tennessee. See also the section in this chapter on the Office of the Secretary of War.

William C. P. Breckinridge (Col.)
    Breckinridge was the commander of the 9th Kentucky Cavalry. His papers are in the Manuscript Division of the Library of Congress.

George W. Brent (Col.)
    Brent was a staff officer under Generals Beauregard, Bragg, and Smith. His papers are in Duke University Library and in the Louisiana Historical Association collection on deposit in the Howard-Tilton Memorial Library of Tulane University.

Louis A. Bringier (Col.)
    Papers of Colonel Bringier, an officer of the 4th and 7th Louisiana Cavalry, 1862-65, are in the Archives Department of Louisiana State University.

John M. Bronough
    Papers of Surgeon Bronough, who served with the 5th Texas Mounted Volunteers, 1861-65, are in Baylor University Library.

John T. Brown (Col.)
    Papers of Brown, an artillery officer in the Army of the Peninsula and the Army of Northern Virginia, in the Confederate Museum include correspondence, general and special orders, returns, receipts, requisitions,

and invoices, June 1861-Apr. 1864.

Simon B. Buckner (Lt. Gen.)
       General Buckner's commands included in 1861-62 the Central Army of
Kentucky, a division in the Army of the Mississippi, and the District of the
Gulf, in 1863-64 the Department of East Tennessee, in 1864 the District of
West Louisiana, and in 1865 the District of Arkansas and West Louisiana.
His wartime papers are in the Henry E. Huntington Library.

Robert F. Bunting
       A transcript of letters written by Bunting, chaplain of Terry's Texas
Rangers, to newspapers, 1861-65, is in the University of Texas Library,
Texas Archives.

William H. S. Burgwynn (Capt.)
       Letters of Burgwynn, an officer of the 35th North Carolina Infantry,
are in the North Carolina Department of Archives and History.

Ellison Capers (Brig. Gen.)
       Records of Capers, commander of the 24th South Carolina Infantry
and a brigadier general in the Army of Tennessee in 1865, in Duke University Library include correspondence on military operations and maps.
Other papers of his are in the South Caroliniana Library of the University
of South Carolina.

Leonidas D. Carrington (Capt.)
       Correspondence and quartermaster returns, 1862-64, prepared while
Carrington was attached to the 16th Texas Infantry are in the University of
Texas Library, Texas Archives.

David M. Carter (Lt. Col.)
       Carter was an officer in the 4th North Carolina Infantry; his papers
are in the Southern Historical Collection in the University of North Carolina Library.

William R. Carter (Lt. Col.)
       A diary of Carter, who died in July 1864, is in the Hampden-Sydney
College Library. He served with the 3d Virginia Cavalry.

James R. Chalmers (Brig. Gen.)
       Chalmers had commands in 1862 in the Army of the Mississippi, in
1863 in the Department of Mississippi and East Louisiana, and later in the
1st Division of Maj. Gen. N. B. Forrest's cavalry corps. In Record Group
109 are copies of letters and telegrams sent, Feb. 1862-Apr. 1865 (ch. II,
vols. 288-290); letters, telegrams, orders, and circulars received, Nov.
1861-Mar. 1865 (ch. II, vols. 292-297); telegrams received, Mar. 1863-
Mar. 1865 (ch. II, vol. 291); general and special orders and circulars, Feb.
1862-Aug. 1864 (ch. II, vols. 298-300); special orders, Jan.-Apr. 1865
(ch. II, part of vol. 301); and correspondence and other documents, 1861-
65 (2 in.).

Benjamin F. Cheatham (Maj. Gen.)
      Correspondence, reports, orders, and other documents (microfilm),
are in the Southern Historical Collection in the University of North Carolina Library.

Alexander R. Chisholm (Lt.)
      Chisholm was an aide-de-camp to General Beauregard; his papers are
in the New-York Historical Society.

Charles Clark (Brig. Gen.)
      In Record Group 109 are general orders issued, June-July 1861 (ch.
II, vol. 284). Clark served in Mississippi and Tennessee.

Edward Clark (Col.)
      Correspondence of Clark, colonel of the 14th Texas Infantry, is in the
Texas Archives of the University of Texas Library.

Lewis M. Clark (Col.)
      Abstracts of receipts and disbursements by Clark, 1862-64, are in
the Mississippi Department of Archives and History. Clark served in the
Army of the West and the District of Tennessee.

William J. Clarke (Col.)
      Correspondence and other papers of Clarke, colonel of the 24th North
Carolina Infantry, are in the Southern Historical Collection in the University of North Carolina Library.

Henry D. Clayton (Maj. Gen.)
      Clayton commanded the 1st and later the 39th Alabama Infantry and
served in Kentucky under General Bragg and with the Army of Tennessee. Correspondence, quartermaster and ordnance records, and muster
rolls are with his papers in the University of Alabama Library.

Thomas L. Clingman (Brig. Gen.)
      Correspondence and other papers relating to his services in North
and South Carolina and Virginia are in Duke University Library and in the
Southern Historical Collection in the University of North Carolina Library.

W. G. Crenshaw (Capt.)
      Correspondence of Crenshaw while serving at Camp Lee, Va., Feb.-
June 1862, is in the Archives Division of the Virginia State Library.

Raleigh E. Colston (Brig Gen.)
      Colston commanded the 16th Virginia Infantry, a brigade in the
peninsular campaign, and a brigade in Gen. T. J. Jackson's corps before
being transferred to Petersburg to serve under General Beauregard and
later at Lynchburg. Correspondence, reports, orders, and other documents are in the Southern Historical Collection in the University of North
Carolina Library.

Alexander M. Davis (Lt. Col.)
      Letters of Davis, an officer of the 45th Virginia Infantry, are in the
William and Mary College Library.

COMMANDERS, STAFF OFFICERS, AND OTHER PERSONNEL 319

Nicholas A. Davis
    A microfilm of the papers of Davis, who served as chaplain to the
4th Texas Volunteers of Hood's Texas Brigade, is in Trinity University
Library, San Antonio, Tex. See Donald E. Everett, ed., Chaplain Davis
and Hood's Texas Brigade (San Antonio, 1962).

Nathaniel H. R. Dawson (Capt.)
    Papers relating to Dawson's services with the 4th Alabama Infantry
during 1861-62 in Virginia, South Carolina, and North Carolina are in the
Southern Historical Collection in the University of North Carolina Library.

Henry W. Feilden (Col.)
    Papers of Feilden, who served as assistant adjutant general to Gen-
eral Beauregard, 1862-65, are in the Library of Congress, the South Carolina Historical Society collections, and the University of Virginia Library.

Samuel W. Ferguson (Brig. Gen.)
    After serving on General Beauregard's staff in 1861-62, Ferguson was
on cavalry duty in the Vicksburg campaign and commanded a brigade in Gen.
William H. Jackson's division in Mississippi, Georgia, and the Carolinas
in 1863-65. His papers are in the Department of Archives of the Louisiana
State University.

George A. Ferris
    Papers of Ferris, a surgeon from Texas, are in the Archives Divi-
sion of the Texas State Library.

Nathan N. Fleming (Capt.)
    Miscellaneous quartermaster records relating to the 46th North Caro-
lina Infantry, 1862-64 (1 vol.), are in the North Carolina Department of Archives and History.

Andrew J. Foard
    Letters received by Surgeon Foard relating to his service in Florida
and Mississippi are in the Stout collection in Emory University Library.

Edward Fontaine (Capt.)
    Papers of Fontaine, an officer of the 18th Mississippi Infantry, are
in the Mississippi State University Library.

Nathan B. Forrest (Lt. Gen.)
    Correspondence, orders, and other papers, 1862-66 (393 items), con-
sisting chiefly of communications to army surgeons, are in Duke University
Library. Forrest was a cavalry officer in the Army of the Mississippi and
the Army of Tennessee, and commander in 1865 of the District of Mississippi and East Louisiana.

Samuel G. French (Maj. Gen.)
    In Record Group 109 are letters, telegrams, orders, and circulars
received and copies of letters sent, 1861-65 (2 in.). After serving in the
Army of the Potomac, French commanded in 1862 the Department of North
Carolina and in 1863 the Department of Southern Virginia. He later served
in the Department of Mississippi and East Louisiana, the Army of Tennessee,

and at Mobile. Papers relating chiefly to his service under Gen. Joseph
E. Johnston in 1864 are in the Mississippi Department of Archives and
History.

Wade H. Gibbes (Maj.)
     Papers of Gibbes, an officer of the 13th Battalion Virginia Artillery,
are in the South Caroliniana Library of the University of South Carolina.

Jeremy F. Gilmer (Maj. Gen.)
     Correspondence and other documents of the war period among his pa-
pers in the Southern Historical Collection in the University of North Carolina Library relate to his service as an engineer officer in Tennessee,
South Carolina, Alabama, and Georgia, and as Chief of the Engineer Bureau at Richmond.

Harry W. Gilmor (Lt. Col.)
     Papers of Gilmor, an officer of the 2d Battalion Maryland Cavalry,
1862-65, are in the Maryland Historical Society.

Henry Ginder (Lt.)
     Ginder's papers, 1862-65, in the Howard-Tilton Memorial Library of
Tulane University concern in part his duties as an engineer officer.

Thomas J. Goree (Capt.)
     Goree was an aide to General Longstreet; his wartime letters are in
the Department of Archives of the Louisiana State University.

James A. Graham (Lt.)
     Letters Lieutenant Graham wrote from camps in North Carolina and
Virginia, 1861-65, are in the Southern Historical Collection in the University of North Carolina Library.

George St. Leger Grenfel (Col.)
     Copies of letters written by Grenfel, inspector general under Gener-
al Bragg, are in the Filson Club, Louisville, Ky.

Bryan Grimes (Lt. Col.)
     Papers of Grimes, an officer of the 4th North Carolina Infantry, are
in the North Carolina Department of Archives and History.

Thomas D. Hamilton (Maj.)
     Hamilton served as a quartermaster at Saltillo, Miss., Tunnel Hill
and Rome, Ga., and in Florida. Vouchers prepared by him during the period Nov. 1, 1861-Apr. 1, 1865, are in the Mississippi Department of Archives and History.

Lewis C. Hanes (Capt.)
     Records of Hanes as quartermaster of the 48th North Carolina Infan-
try are in the Southern Historical Collection in the University of North
Carolina Library.

William J. Hardee (Lt. Gen.)
     Letters written by General Hardee during 1861-62 concerning his

operations in Arkansas, Tennessee, and Kentucky are in the Library of Congress.

David B. Harris (Maj.)
    Reconnaissance sketch maps of the operations of the Army of Tennessee and maps of the coast defenses of South Carolina are in Duke University Library.

Alexander C. Haskell (Col.)
    Letters Haskell wrote while he was assistant adjutant general of Gen. Maxcy Gregg's brigade in South Carolina and Virginia are in the Southern Historical Collection in the University of North Carolina Library.

Benjamin H. Helm (Brig. Gen.)
    Papers of Helm, who served in the Army of the Mississippi, the District of the Gulf, the Department of Mississippi and East Louisiana, and the Army of Tennessee are in the University of Kentucky Library.

Patrick Henry (Maj.)
    Henry's papers in the Mississippi Department of Archives and History include some for the war period.

Henry Heth (Maj. Gen.)
    Heth was a division commander in the Army of East Tennessee and the Army of Northern Virginia. His papers are in the University of Virginia Library.

William Hicks
    Hicks' order book is in the University of Texas Library, Texas Archives.

Daniel H. Hill (Lt. Gen.)
    Papers of Hill, who served in Virginia, North Carolina, Tennessee, and Georgia, are in Duke University Library, the New-York Historical Society, the North Carolina Department of Archives and History, and the Archives Division of the Virginia State Library.

Thomas C. Hindman (Maj. Gen.)
    In Record Group 109 are correspondence and other papers, 1861-64 (1 in.). Hindman served in 1862 in the Army of the Mississippi and in the Trans-Mississippi Department, and in 1863-64 in the Army of Tennessee.

James M. Holloway
    Correspondence relating to his service as a surgeon in the Army of the Potomac, the Army of Northern Virginia, and the Department of South Carolina, Georgia, and Florida is in the Virginia Historical Society collections.

Theophilus H. Holmes (Lt. Gen.)
    In Record Group 109 are copies of letters sent by Holmes, May 5, 1861-Mar. 8, 1864 (ch. II, vol. 358), relating to his commands in North Carolina, the District of Arkansas, and the Trans-Mississippi Department. Papers of Holmes as commander of the reserve forces of North Carolina,

1864-65, are in Duke University Library.

William J. Holt
    Papers of Holt, a surgeon with the 19th Alabama Infantry, are in the South Caroliniana Library of the University of South Carolina.

John B. Hood (Gen.)
    In Record Group 109 are correspondence and other papers, 1862-65 (2 in.), including outgoing and incoming letters, reports on operations, and casualty returns. After commanding a division in the Army of Northern Virginia, Hood became commander of the Army of Tennessee in July 1864.

John D. Imboden (Brig. Gen.)
    Papers of Imboden in the University of Kentucky Library include wartime letters concerning his service in western Virginia and the Valley District.

J. L. Irion
    Papers of Assistant Surgeon Irion, who served with the 20th Texas Infantry, are in the Archives Division of the Texas State Library.

Henry R. Jackson (Brig. Gen.)
    A few communications received by Jackson in 1861, when he commanded the Army of the Northwest, are in the Telamon Cuyler collection in the University of Georgia Library.

John K. Jackson (Brig. Gen.)
    In Record Group 109 are morning reports of Jackson's brigade, 1862-64 (ch. II, vol. 245). The brigade was part of the Army of the Mississippi in 1862 and later of the Army of Tennessee.

Thomas J. Jackson (Lt. Gen.)
    An order book, Apr. 28-July 22, 1861, in the Confederate Museum contains copies of general and special orders issued when Jackson was in command at Harpers Ferry and in the Shenandoah Valley. For other collections see above under Army and Department of Northern Virginia. Letters and other papers (originals and copies) of Jackson, 1838-63, are in the Roy Bird Cook collection in the West Virginia University Library.

William H. Jackson (Brig. Gen.)
    In Record Group 109 are papers that were kept by Capt. George Moorman, Jackson's adjutant, including orders, telegrams, letters, and circulars, 1861-65 (2 in.). The collection includes copies of general and special orders issued by Jackson's cavalry corps, 1863-65. Jackson served in the Western Department and the Department of Mississippi and East Louisiana.

Bushrod R. Johnson (Maj. Gen.)
    In Record Group 109 are letters sent, June 30, 1864-Mar. 9, 1864 (ch. II, vol. 287), and communications received, 1862-65 (1/4 in.), relating to Johnson's commands in the Army of Tennessee, the Department of North Carolina and Southern Virginia, and the Army of Northern Virginia.

Joseph E. Johnston (Gen.)
Records of General Johnston, commander of the Army of the Potomac, the Department of Northern Virginia, the Department of the West, and the Army of Tennessee, are in several repositories. Records in the William and Mary College Library include: copies of outgoing dispatches, May 30, 1861-Apr. 27, 1865 (5 vols.); copies of letters sent, Jan. 28, 1862-Oct. 20, 1864, and Feb. 25-May 8, 1865 (3 vols.); a book containing copies of letters sent and received, Dec. 28, 1863-June 27, 1864, Col. Benjamin S. Ewell's diary regarding an official visit to Richmond, Apr. 13-Aug. 5, 1864, and special orders issued, Dec. 14-21, 1862; copies of telegrams sent, May 9, 1863-May 6, 1864, and Feb. 25-May 3, 1865 (6 vols.); general orders issued, Dec. 4, 1862-Dec. 22, 1863 (1 vol.), also containing a scrapbook; a casualty report on the battle of Ball's Bluff, Oct. 21, 1862; a copy of a report on the battle of Seven Pines; a few monthly reports; and a letter regarding the condition of the 33d Virginia Volunteers after First Manassas. The Henry E. Huntington Library has other Johnston papers, 1861-65 (523 items), including correspondence, telegrams, battle reports, division and brigade reports, and maps. Other correspondence, 1861-64, is in the Samuel Richey collection in Miami University Library. Other Johnston papers are in the Confederate Museum, Duke University Library, and the San Francisco College for Women.

Robert M. Hughes, ed., "Some War Letters of General Joseph E. Johnston," Journal of the Military Service Institution of the United States, 50:319-328 (May-June 1912); Joseph E. Johnston, Narrative of Military Operations, Directed, during the Late War between the States (New York, 1874); Fred B. Joyner, "Calendar of General Joseph E. Johnston Papers, Miami University," Civil War History, 8:86-90 (Mar. 1962); Earl G. Swem, "Joseph E. Johnston Papers [and] John Marshall Papers in the Library of William and Mary College," William and Mary College Bulletin, 33 (Nov. 1939).

Samuel Jones (Maj. Gen.)
In Record Group 109 are correspondence and telegrams, 1861-64 (1 1/2 in.). Jones served in 1862 in Virginia and Florida and commanded the Department of Alabama and West Florida and a division of the Army of the Mississippi; in 1863-64, the Western Department of Virginia; in 1864, the Department of South Carolina; and in 1864-65, the District of Florida.

Thomas Jordan (Brig. Gen.)
Correspondence and other documents of Jordan, a staff officer under Gen. A. S. Johnston and Generals Beauregard and Bragg, and commander in 1865 of the 3d Military District of South Carolina, are in Duke University Library.

John F. King (Lt.)
Ordnance records of King, an officer with the 1st Georgia Regulars, 1861, are in the Southern Historical Collection in the University of North Carolina Library.

Jesse R. Kirkland (Capt.)
Kirkland was an assistant commissary with the 14th and 16th Mississippi Volunteers. His papers, 1861-63, are in the Mississippi Department

of Archives and History.

Richard F. Langdon (Capt.)
Quartermaster records, 1863, when Langdon was with the 3d North Carolina Infantry (3d State Troops), are in the Southern Historical Collection in the University of North Carolina Library.

Evander M. Law (Maj. Gen.)
Law's correspondence, orders, and reports (microfilm) are in the Southern Historical Collection in the University of North Carolina Library.

Henry Lay
Lay's papers in the Southern Historical Collection in the University of North Carolina Library cover his wartime service as a chaplain.

John W. Lea (Col.)
In Record Group 109 are Lea's diary and account book, 1863 (ch. VIII, vol. 363). Lea was commander of the 5th North Carolina State Troops.

Richard Leach
Some papers of Leach, a surgeon with the 2d Battalion North Carolina Infantry, are in Duke University Library.

Stephen D. Lee (Lt. Gen.)
Lee's correspondence, reports, orders, and commissions are in the Southern Historical Collection in the University of North Carolina Library. After serving as an artillery officer in Virginia and at Vicksburg, Lee commanded cavalry in the Department of Alabama, Mississippi, and East Louisiana, commanded that department, and then became a corps commander in the Army of Tennessee.

St. John R. Liddell (Brig. Gen.)
Papers of Liddell, who served in the Army of the Mississippi, Department No. 2, the Army of Tennessee, and the Department of Alabama, Mississippi, and East Louisiana, are in the Department of Archives of the Louisiana State University.

Charles E. Lippitt
Lippitt's papers in the Southern Historical Collection in the University of North Carolina Library relate to his service as a surgeon with the 57th Virginia Volunteers in Virginia, Pennsylvania, and North Carolina.

Samuel H. Lockett (Col.)
Lockett was an engineer officer who served in Florida and as chief engineer of the District of the Gulf and the Department of Mississippi, Alabama, and East Louisiana. His papers in the Southern Historical Collection in the University of North Carolina Library include material on an inspection tour of forts in Alabama and Florida in 1861 and reports from engineer officers during the siege of Vicksburg.

George W. Logan (Lt. Col.)
Military records, 1861-65, of Colonel Logan, who commanded a battalion of Louisiana Heavy Artillery at Fort Beauregard, La., and other places,

are in the Southern Historical Collection in the University of North Carolina Library.

James Longstreet (Lt. Gen.)
     In Record Group 109 are copies of letters and telegrams sent, Oct. 26, 1863-Mar. 16, 1864, and Feb. 25-Mar. 20, 1865 (ch. II, vol. 277); an undated roster of officers and organizations (ch. II, vol. 277 1/2); copies of letters sent, Jan. 1, 1864-Feb. 16, 1865 (ch. II, vol. 276); and copies of confidential letters and telegrams sent, Feb. 26, 1863-Feb. 23, 1865 (ch. II, vol. 269). Copies of letters, telegrams, and circulars sent, Dec. 31, 1862-Feb. 1, 1865 (1 vol.), are in the Texas Archives of the University of Texas Library. Other Longstreet papers are in Duke University Library and in the custody of the Georgia Department of Archives and History.

William W. Loring (Maj. Gen.)
     Loring's letters-sent book in the Archives Division of the Virginia State Library includes copies of letters written from the 1st Division of the Department of Norfolk at Suffolk, Va., Apr. 2-May 11, 1862, and from the headquarters of the Department of Southwestern Virginia, May 19-Sept. 1, 1862.

Mansfield Lovell (Maj. Gen.)
     Lovell commanded Department No. 1 at New Orleans and then a division in the Army of the Mississippi. A collection of letters received, 1860-69, in the Library of Congress contains only a few items of the war period.

James S. McCoy (Capt.)
     McCoy was an officer of the 26th Alabama Infantry. His papers, 1859-65 (715 items), are in the University of Oklahoma Library.

Marshall McDonald (Capt.)
     An extensive collection of McDonald's papers in Duke University Library includes 500 wartime items. He served as an ordnance officer at Vicksburg, later at Selma, Ala., and then as an engineer in Virginia and North Carolina.

Lafayette McLaws (Maj. Gen.)
     McLaws served in 1861 in Georgia and in the Army of the Peninsula, in 1862-63 in the Army of Northern Virginia, and in 1864 in the Department of South Carolina, Georgia, and Florida. In Record Group 109 are correspondence and other documents, 1861-65 (1 1/2 in.) of General McLaws. His papers in Duke University Library are mainly concerned with General Pemberton's charges against him in connection with the attack on Knoxville, Tenn., in 1863. Papers in the Southern Historical Collection in the University of North Carolina Library include wartime correspondence, military records, and maps. Other papers of McLaws are in the Western Reserve Historical Society collections.

John K. McLean
     Letters written by Surgeon McLean from South Carolina, Georgia, and Virginia are in the South Caroliniana Library of the University of South Carolina.

Fitz William McMaster (Lt. Col.)
      Letters of McMaster, an officer of the 17th South Carolina Infantry,
are in the South Caroliniana Library of the University of South Carolina.

Duncan K. MacRae (Col.)
      MacRae was a colonel of the 15th North Carolina Infantry. His papers
are in the Southern Historical Collection in the University of North Carolina
Library.

John B. Magruder (Maj. Gen.)
      Magruder commanded in 1861 the Department of the Peninsula, in
1862 the Trans-Mississippi District, in 1862-63 the District of Texas, New
Mexico, and Arizona, and in 1864-65 the District of Arkansas. In Record
Group 109 are correspondence and telegrams, 1862-65 (1/2 in.). A few of
his papers are in the Confederate Museum.

C. K. Mallory (Capt.)
      A memorandum book of Mallory as assistant quartermaster at Liber-
ty, Va., 1862-63, is in the Manuscript Division of the Library of Congress.

George E. Maney (Brig. Gen.)
      Papers of Maney, who had commands in three different armies, are
in the University of North Carolina Library.

Gabriel E. Manigault (Lt.)
      Papers of Manigault, adjutant of the 4th South Carolina Cavalry, are
in the South Carolina Historical Society.

Thomas R. Markham
      Papers of Markham, a chaplain of the 1st Mississippi Light Artillery,
are in the Department of Archives of Louisiana State University.

Samuel B. Maxey (Brig. Gen.)
      In Record Group 109 are copies of letters and telegrams received by
Maxey as commanding officer at Chattanooga, Tenn., Mar. 19-Oct. 31,
1862 (ch. II, vol. 257), with lists of men in various military units.

Samuel W. Melton (Maj.)
      Letters written by Melton from Columbia and Charleston, S. C.,
Richmond (Adjutant and Inspector General's Department), and camps in
Virginia and North Carolina are in the South Caroliniana Library of the
University of South Carolina.

Thomas B. Memminger
      Some official papers, 1864, of Surgeon Memminger are in the South-
ern Historical Collection in the University of North Carolina Library.

Frank Moore (Capt.)
      The papers of Captain Moore in the Henry E. Huntington Library
are concerned mainly with the defense of Mobile.

John W. Moore (Maj.)
      Major Moore was an officer of the 3d Battalion North Carolina Light

Artillery. His correspondence and other papers are in the Southern Historical Collection in the University of North Carolina Library.

James T. Morehead, Jr. (Col.)
  Morehead commanded the 53d North Carolina Infantry. His papers are in the Southern Historical Collection in the University of North Carolina Library.

John H. Morgan (Brig. Gen.)
  Morgan was a cavalry commander in the Army of Tennessee and commander of the Department of East Tennessee and Western Virginia. His military correspondence, telegrams, orders, reports, lists, and maps are in the Southern Historical Collection in the University of North Carolina Library.

John T. Morgan (Brig. Gen.)
  After serving with the 5th Alabama Infantry and as colonel of the 51st Alabama Partisan Rangers, Morgan commanded a brigade in the Army of Northern Virginia and the Army of Tennessee. His papers are in the Alabama Department of Archives and History.

Beverly P. Morriss
  Papers of Morriss, a Confederate surgeon from Virginia, are in Duke University Library.

Peter M. Mull (Capt.)
  A few papers of Mull, who was an officer of the 55th North Carolina Infantry, are in the North Carolina Department of Archives and History.

Thomas T. Munford (Col.)
  Munford was the colonel of the 2d (also called 30th) Virginia Cavalry. His papers are in Duke University Library.

Robert P. Myers
  Myers was a surgeon at Oglethorpe Barracks, Savannah, Ga., and Camp Drayton during 1861-62. A correspondence book, Oct. 2, 1861-May 2, 1862, and a diary, June 15, 1863-May 1, 1865, when he was with the 16th Georgia Infantry, are in the Confederate Museum.

Henry D. Ogden (Col.)
  Ogden was on the staffs of Maj. Gen. Mansfield Lovell, Gov. Thomas O. Moore, and Lt. Gen. Richard Taylor. Correspondence and other documents, Apr. 1862-Sept. 1863, are in the Howard-Tilton Memorial Library of Tulane University.

Charles H. Olmstead (Col.)
  Colonel Olmstead was the commander of the 1st Georgia Infantry which served in Georgia and South Carolina. Correspondence and other documents, 1860-65, are in the Southern Historical Collection in the University of North Carolina Library.

Edwin A. Osborne (Col.)
  Osborne commanded the 4th North Carolina Infantry. His papers are

in the Southern Historical Collection in the University of North Carolina Library.

John M. Otey (Lt. Col.)
Some papers of Otey, who served as a staff officer under General Beauregard in 1861-65 and also under General Bragg in 1862, are in Duke University Library.

F. J. Paine (Maj.)
Letters of Paine, an officer of the 16th Battalion Tennessee Cavalry, are in the Tennessee State Library and Archives.

John O. Paris
As a chaplain with the 54th North Carolina Infantry, Paris kept a diary concerning military activities, Jan. 7, 1863-Oct. 22, 1864, and Feb. 4-Apr. 14, 1865, which is in the Southern Historical Collection in the University of North Carolina Library.

William D. Pender (Maj. Gen.)
Letters sent by General Pender from Virginia and North Carolina, Mar. 1861-June 1863, are in the Southern Historical Collection in the University of North Carolina Library. See William W. Hassler, ed., The General to His Lady; the Civil War Letters of William Dorsey Pender to Fanny Pender (Chapel Hill, 1965).

J. Johnston Pettigrew (Brig. Gen.)
After initial service at Charleston, Pettigrew was elected colonel of the 22d North Carolina Infantry, served in the peninsular campaign, commanded the defenses of Petersburg, and participated in an expedition into North Carolina. He was killed during the retreat of the Army of Northern Virginia from Gettysburg. Papers of Pettigrew are in the North Carolina Department of Archives and History and in the Southern Historical Collection in the University of North Carolina Library.

George E. Pickett (Maj. Gen.)
After commanding the defenses of the lower Rappahannock River, Pickett led a brigade in the Army of the Peninsula and a division in the Army of Northern Virginia before he became commander of the Department of North Carolina in 1863. In Jan. 1865 he again became a division commander in the Army of Northern Virginia. A small collection of papers is in Duke University Library; others are in the Henry E. Huntington Library and in the Western Reserve Historical Society collections.

Harnet Pinson
Papers of Pinson, a surgeon from Arkansas who served in Alabama and Louisiana, are in the Department of Archives of the Louisiana State University.

Gideon J. Pillow (Maj. Gen.)
Pillow served in 1861 in Missouri, in 1862 in the Western Department, in 1863 as head of the Volunteer and Conscript Bureau of that department, and in 1864 in northern Alabama. In Record Group 109 are copies of special orders, letters sent, battle reports, and correspondence with the

Secretary of War on the surrender of Fort Donelson, Nov. 13, 1861-May 9, 1863 (ch. II, vol. 18); and letters, telegrams, and orders received and sent, 1861-64 (1 1/3 in.).

Leonidas Polk (Lt. Gen.)
    Polk commanded the Western Department in 1861, organized the Army of the Mississippi in 1862, commanded a corps in the Army of Tennessee in 1863, and in 1864 the headquarters of paroled and exchanged prisoners at Enterprise, Miss., and the Department of Alabama, Mississippi, and East Louisiana. In Record Group 109 are copies of letters sent, May 21, 1862-May 23, 1864 (ch. II, vol. 13 and index vol. 13 1/2); copies of telegrams sent, Mar. 18, 1863-Jan. 12, 1864 (ch. II, vol. 222 3/4); letters, reports, telegrams received and sent, and orders and circulars received, 1861-64 (1 ft.); a register of letters received, July 1861-Dec. 1862 (ch. II, vols. 12 and 52 1/4 and an index vol.); endorsements on letters received, July 12, 1861-Apr. 9, 1863 (ch. II, vol. 52 1/8 and an index vol.); extracts of special orders received, June 1862-Aug. 1863 (ch. II, vol. 53 1/2); and special orders issued by the commands of Gens. Polk, Stephen D. Lee, Dabney H. Maury, and Richard Taylor, Mar. 26, 1862-Dec. 9, 1864 (ch. II, vol. 15 and an index vol.).
    Correspondence, diaries, and other papers of General Polk are in the University of the South Library at Sewanee, Tenn. A volume in the Library of Congress contains copies of general and special orders and incoming and outgoing communications, July 20, 1861-Apr. 12, 1864. A few items of correspondence are in Duke University Library. The Southern Historical Collection in the University of North Carolina Library has correspondence relating to operations in Kentucky, Tennessee, and Georgia, 1861-64, consisting partly of microfilm of the material in the University of the South Library. Other Polk papers are in the Palmer collection of the Western Reserve Historical Society.

Sterling Price (Maj. Gen.)
    Price commanded in 1861 the Missouri State Guard and in 1862 the Army of the West; in 1862-63 he served in the Department of Mississippi and East Louisiana and in 1864 commanded the District of Arkansas and later the cavalry and the Missouri division in that district. In Record Group 109 are copies of letters sent, Apr. 24, 1862-Mar. 9, 1865 (ch. II, vols. 177, 178, and 178 1/2); endorsements on letters received and forwarded, Jan. 2, 1863-Mar. 10, 1865 (ch. II, vols. 203 and 204); general orders issued by the Army of the West and General Price's division, Apr. 29, 1862-Dec. 8, 1863 (ch. II, vol. 211); orders and circulars issued, Jan. 1, 1864-Mar. 8, 1865 (ch. II, vol. 209); special orders issued, Army of the West, District of the Tennessee, and General Price's division, May 16, 1862-Dec. 31, 1863 (ch. II, vol. 208); a record of applications for furlough, Apr.-June 1863 (ch. II, vol. 205); a record book containing rosters of officers and data concerning promotions, elections, resignations, assignments, and deaths, Feb. 1863-Mar. 1864 (ch. I, vol. 109 1/2); a roster of officers of Price's division, 1862-63 (ch. I, vol. 110 1/2 and an index vol.); a record book of Price's command, 1862-63 (ch. II, vol. 202); and a record book of the 8th Division of the Missouri State Guard, including troops under General Price, 1861-64 (ch. I, vol. 107 1/4). Fair copies of letters sent by General Price, July 19, 1861-Mar. 2, 1862, are with the Albert S. Johnston papers in the Howard-Tilton Memorial Library of Tulane University.

J. R. Purvis (Col.)
    Purvis was assistant adjutant general in the Missouri State Guard
and later (1862) a purchasing agent at Little Rock. A small collection of
papers in the Southern Historical Collection in the University of North Carolina Library includes wartime correspondence and orders.

William Quayle (Lt. Col.)
    Quayle was an officer of the 9th Texas Cavalry. His correspondence,
1862-64, is in the University of Alabama Library.

John Reid (Maj.)
    Reid served as a commissary officer under Maj. Gen. Sterling Price
in the Army of the West, the District of Tennessee, the Army of the Mississippi, the District of Arkansas, and in Texas. Correspondence and
other documents of Major Reid, 1862-65, are in the Department of Archives
of Louisiana State University.

Alexander W. Reynolds (Brig. Gen.)
    Reynolds commanded the 50th Virginia Infantry in western Virginia
and in Mississippi and was a brigadier general in the Army of Tennessee.
His papers are in the West Virginia University Library.

Oran M. Roberts (Col.)
    Papers of Roberts, the commander of the 11th Texas Infantry, are in
the Texas Archives, University of Texas Library.

Sion H. Rogers (Col.)
    Correspondence of Rogers, commander of the 47th North Carolina In-
fantry, is in Duke University Library.

Alfred Roman (Lt. Col.)
    Correspondence, telegrams, reports, and memoranda of Colonel
Roman in the Library of Congress relate mainly to the career of General
Beauregard under whom Roman served as an assistant adjutant general and
inspector general during most of the war.

Lawrence Ross (Col.)
    Ross was commander of the 6th Texas Cavalry. His papers are in
Baylor University Library.

Daniel Ruggles (Brig. Gen.)
    Ruggles' command was at New Orleans, Camp Benjamin, La., and
at Corinth, Miss. In Record Group 109 are general and special orders
issued, Nov. 1, 1861-Feb. 22, 1862 (ch. II, vol. 278). Correspondence,
telegrams, reports, and other documents of General Ruggles are in Duke
University Library. Telegrams and other records on the Shiloh campaign
and a book containing copies of orders and letters concerning operations in
the western theater, 1862-65, are in the Fredericksburg and Spotsylvania
National Military Park Library. Other correspondence and telegrams,
1862-65 (315 items), are in the Mississippi Department of Archives and
History. A few other letters and telegrams, 1861-63, are in Emory University Library.

Joseph H. Saunders (Col.)
Papers of Saunders, commander of the 33d North Carolina Infantry, are in the Southern Historical Collection in the University of North Carolina Library.

Andrew G. Scott (Maj.)
In Record Group 109 are quartermaster accounts, 1863-64 (ch. VIII, vol. 49), with copies of general and special orders received, relating to Scott's service as a quartermaster with the 14th Mississippi Volunteers, as a brigade quartermaster with Brig. Gen. William E. Baldwin's brigade in the Department of Mississippi and East Louisiana, and with Brig. Gen. Claudius W. Sears' brigade in the Army of Tennessee.

William L. Scott (Lt. Col.)
Papers of Scott, an officer attached to the 21st North Carolina Infantry, are in Duke University Library.

Henry C. Semple (Maj.)
Semple served in the Army of Tennessee and was transferred in 1864 to Mobile, Ala. Some of his correspondence in the Alabama Department of Archives and History concerns his military service.

J. F. Sessions (Maj.)
Major Sessions was an officer of the 7th Mississippi Infantry and Power's Louisiana and Mississippi cavalry. His correspondence, orders, reports, and other papers, 1862-65 (160 items), are in the Mississippi Department of Archives and History.

Joseph F. Sessions (Capt.)
Captain Sessions was an officer of the 8th Mississippi Infantry. A few of his papers, 1861-65, are in the Mississippi Department of Archives and History.

Thomas L. Settle
Part of the papers of Settle, a surgeon from Virginia, relate to the war period. They are in Duke University Library.

Samuel R. Simpson (Capt.)
Papers of Simpson, an assistant quartermaster with the 30th Tennessee Infantry, are in the Tennessee State Library and Archives.

William D. Simpson (Lt. Col.)
Some of Simpson's papers in the South Caroliniana Library of the University of South Carolina and in Duke University Library concern his war service with the 14th South Carolina Infantry.

Gustavus W. Smith (Maj. Gen.)
See Gustavus W. Smith, Confederate War Papers; Fairfax Court House, New Orleans, Seven Pines, Richmond and North Carolina (New York, 1884).

Ashbel Smith (Col.)
Correspondence, orders, and reports of Smith, commander of the

2d Texas Infantry, are in the Texas Archives of the University of Texas Library.

Dabney H. Smith (Col.)
    Smith's papers in the Kentucky Historical Society collections contain military rosters, casualty lists of Morgan's cavalry, and correspondence regarding Smith's service with the 5th Kentucky Cavalry.

Robert A. Smith (Col.)
    Papers of Smith, commander of the 10th Mississippi Infantry, 1861-64 (88 items), are in the Mississippi Department of Archives and History.

William D. Somers
    Papers of Somers, a surgeon who served in hospitals at LaGrange, Tenn., Jackson and Shubuta, Miss., and Cahaba and Selma, Ala., are in Duke University Library.

Charles M. Stedman (Maj.)
    Stedman was attached to the 44th North Carolina Infantry; his papers are in the Southern Historical Collection in the University of North Carolina Library.

William Steele (Brig. Gen.)
    Steele commanded the 7th Texas Cavalry, served in the Army of New Mexico in 1862, and commanded the Indian Territory in 1863. In Record Group 109 are copies of letters sent, Mar. 7, 1862-May 18, 1863 (ch. II, vol. 270).

William B. Taliaferro (Brig. Gen.)
    In Record Group 109 are general and special orders and circulars issued, Apr. 14, 1862-Apr. 7, 1863 (ch. II, vol. 16), with a casualty list of May 8, 1862; a list of absentees without leave from the 3d Brigade, June-July 1862; a roster of regimental officers of the Army of Northern Virginia, 1862; and lists of officers and men taken prisoner, July, 1861-June 1862. General and special orders and circulars and letters received, Apr. 4, 1862-Apr. 4, 1863 (ch. II, vol. 7), also contain casualty lists and battle reports.
    Taliaferro commanded the 23d Virginia Infantry, served in the Army of the Northwest in western Virginia in 1861, and Jackson's Army of the Valley in 1862-63. He later served in South Carolina, Georgia, and Florida. A sizable collection of Taliaferro's papers, Nov. 1861-May 1865, in the Confederate Museum includes correspondence, telegrams, orders, battle reports, field returns of brigades of Jackson's division, rolls of men on extra duty, lists of employees, lists, registers, and statements of troops, morning reports of military organizations in the Army of the Valley, and reports of inspection, ordnance, and means of transportation. Other Taliaferro papers, 1861-65 (254 items), in the William and Mary College Library include correspondence, reports, and reminiscences concerning Gen. T. J. Jackson.

John B. Tapscott (Lt.)
    Tapscott served as an engineer officer in Richmond in 1862, on the defenses of Petersburg and on a topographical survey of New Kent County,

Va., in 1863, on the defenses of eastern North Carolina in 1864, and with the Army of Northern Virginia in 1864-65. His scrapbook is in the Henry E. Huntington Library.

Samuel McD. Tate (Lt. Col.)
Papers of Tate, an officer who served with the 6th North Carolina Infantry, are in the Southern Historical Collection in the University of North Carolina Library.

Richard Taylor (Lt. Gen.)
Taylor commanded the 9th Louisiana Infantry, served under General Jackson in the Army of the Valley, commanded the District of West Louisiana during 1863-64, and became commander of the Department of Alabama, Mississippi, and East Louisiana in Sept. 1864. Papers of General Taylor in the Louisiana State Museum at New Orleans include correspondence, telegrams, soldiers' paroles, and rolls of prisoners of war surrendered. Other papers of Taylor, Apr. 1863-May 1865, in the Louisiana Adjutant General's Archives, Jackson Barracks, New Orleans, include correspondence and reports. Taylor's letter books, 1864-65, are in the Howard-Tilton Memorial Library of Tulane University.

George S. Thompson (Maj.)
Major Thompson served as a quartermaster with the 28th North Carolina Infantry and with Brig. Gen. James H. Lane in Virginia during 1861-63. He became depot quartermaster at Tallahassee, Fla., in Nov. 1864 but soon transferred to Quincy, Fla., where he continued as post quartermaster until the end of the war. His quartermaster records, 1861-65 (ca. 1,000 items), in the Southern Historical Collection in the University of North Carolina Library include requisitions for supplies, muster rolls, pay records, vouchers, receipts, and military orders.

Meriwether Jeff Thompson (Brig. Gen.)
An officer of the Missouri State Guard, Thompson served in Missouri and Arkansas. Papers in the Southern Historical Collection in the University of North Carolina Library include correspondence, rosters, and muster rolls chiefly of the Army of the Northern Sub-District of Arkansas, paroles, a Confederate cipher invented by Thompson, an autobiography, and reminiscences. Other papers of Thompson are in the Howard-Tilton Memorial Library of Tulane University.

Edward A. Thorne (Lt.)
Papers relating to Thorne's service as an ordnance officer with the 24th North Carolina Infantry in Virginia and North Carolina are in Duke University Library.

Earl Van Dorn (Maj. Gen.)
In 1861 Van Dorn commanded the Department of Texas and served in the Army of the Potomac; in 1862 he commanded the Trans-Mississippi District, the Army of the West, and the Department of Southern Mississippi and East Louisiana in the defense of Vicksburg. After the battle of Corinth he commanded the cavalry under General Pemberton. In Record Group 109 are copies of letters and telegrams sent, Jan. 23-May 24, 1862 (ch. II, vol. 179); endorsements on letters received, Feb.-May 1862 (ch. II, vol. 206);

special orders issued, Jan. 29-May 15, 1862 (ch. II, vol. 210; available on microfilm); and general and special orders and circulars issued, June 1862-Feb. 1863 (1 1/2 in.). His papers in the Alabama Department of Archives and History include correspondence, telegrams, orders, reports, and maps. Copies of letters, orders, and telegrams sent, Jan. 23-June 22, 1862 (1 vol.), are in the Confederate Museum. Other letters and telegrams originating mainly in Tennessee and Mississippi are in the Manuscript Division of the Library of Congress. Other papers of Van Dorn are in the Missouri State Historical Society.

Alfred M. Waddell (Lt. Col.)
    Papers of Waddell, an officer of the 3d North Carolina Cavalry, are in the Southern Historical Collection in the University of North Carolina Library.

John G. Walker (Maj. Gen.)
    After serving as a brigade and division commander in the Army of Northern Virginia in 1862, Walker transferred to the Trans-Mississippi Department where he participated in the Red River campaign and commanded the District of West Louisiana in 1864 and the District of Texas, New Mexico, and Arizona in 1864-65. His papers, 1862-64, in the Southern Historical Collection in the University of North Carolina Library include correspondence, orders, messages, and reports.

William H. T. Walker (Brig. Gen.)
    Walker served at Pensacola and in northern Virginia in 1861, with the Army of the Mississippi in 1862, and with the Army of Tennessee in 1863-64. Some correspondence of Walker is in Duke University Library.

Harvey W. Walter (Lt. Col.)
    Walter served as judge advocate on General Bragg's staff, and letters received by him from the general, Dec. 1861-Oct. 1863, are in the Southern Historical Collection in the University of North Carolina Library.

James B. Walton (Col.)
    Walton commanded the Washington Artillery Battalion in northern Virginia during 1861-63, and after June 1862 served also as chief of artillery under General Longstreet. At the end of May 1863 he was relieved of the command of the Washington Artillery Battalion and at the end of 1863 he was ordered to the vicinity of Petersburg to assume command of the light artillery under Longstreet. After inspection duty during part of 1864, he resigned on July 8, 1864. Walton's records in the Louisiana Historical Association collection on deposit in the Howard-Tilton Memorial Library of Tulane University include a file of correspondence, telegrams, general and special orders, court-martial proceedings, and reports of boards of survey on ordnance and ordnance stores and on horses, Apr. 27, 1861-Dec. 26, 1862 (198 items); letters sent and orders issued, Apr. 14, 1863-Jan. 8, 1864 (1 vol.); orders received and issued, Feb. 15, 1863-Jan. 23, 1864 (1 vol.); and a register of papers forwarded, Aug. 1863-Jan. 1864 (1 vol.). Another file of correspondence, orders, receipts, statistical reports on batteries, recommendations for personnel actions, reports of boards of survey on property, and surgeons' morning reports, Aug. 1861-Nov. 1863 (1 in.) is in the Lousiana Adjutant General's Office, Jackson Barracks, New Orleans.

Henry C. Watkins (Maj.)
     An extensive collection of correspondence and other papers, Mar. 1863-Mar. 1864, in the Confederate Museum relates to Watkins' service as a quartermaster under Brig. Gen. Henry A. Wise in Virginia and in the Department of South Carolina, Georgia, and Florida (Sixth Military District).

Joseph Wheeler (Maj. Gen.)
     Correspondence, orders, and other military records of Wheeler as a cavalry leader in the Army of Mississippi and the Army of Tennessee are in the Alabama Department of Archives and History.

George D. White
     Copies of letters of White, a surgeon who served with the 29th Virginia Infantry, in charge of the Farmville (Va.) General Hospital, and medical director of Colquitt's brigade in the Department of North Carolina and Southern Virginia, are in the Columbia University Libraries.

Octavius A. White
     Papers of White, a surgeon who served in North and South Carolina, are in the Southern Historical Collection in the University of North Carolina Library.

William H. C. Whiting (Maj. Gen.)
     General Whiting commanded a division in the Army of Northern Virginia until his transfer late in 1862 to the command of the Cape Fear River and the defenses of Wilmington. In Record Group 109 are correspondence, orders, battle reports, inspection notes, and maps, 1861-65 (2 in.). A few copies of letters sent, orders, and commissions of Whiting are in the North Carolina Department of Archives and History.

Edward Willis (Col.)
     Colonel Willis served on the staff of Maj. Gen. Edward Johnson, commander of the Army of the Northwest, during 1861-62, as an artillery and ordnance officer on Maj. Gen. T. J. Jackson's staff in 1862, and as colonel of the 12th Georgia Infantry in 1863-64. Correspondence, orders, and other papers of Willis, 1861-64 (506 items), are in the Henry E. Huntington Library.

Edward Willis (Maj.)
     Willis served as a quartermaster under Brig. Gen. Thomas F. Drayton in the Department of South Carolina during 1861-62, as post quartermaster at Charleston from about Dec. 1862 to Apr. 1864, as Chief Quartermaster on the staff of General Beauregard in the Department of North Carolina and Southern Virginia, May-Oct. 1864, and as Chief Quartermaster under Beauregard in the Military Division of the West. Records of Willis in the Library of Congress include press copies of letters sent, Oct. 20, 1861-May 23, 1864 (5 vols.); correspondence, telegrams, orders, and memoranda, Apr. 22, 1864-Jan. 28, 1865 (4 vols.); requisitions for supplies, Oct. 1861-Oct. 1864 (2 vols.); a record of expenditures, Oct. 1861-July 1862 (1 vol.); a receipt book, Oct. 30, 1861-Nov. 13, 1864; a list of quartermasters who served under Willis, 1862-64; and records relating to blockade runners.

Claudius C. Wilson (Col.)

    Papers of Wilson, commander of the 25th Georgia Infantry, 1861-63, are in the Georgia Historical Society.

David R. E. Winn (Lt. Col.)

    Winn was an officer of the 4th Georgia Infantry. His letters, 1861-63 (54 items), are in Emory University Library.

Henry A. Wise (Brig. Gen.)

    In 1861 Wise commanded the Wise legion in the Kanawha Valley and served at Richmond, in 1862 in North Carolina and in the Army of Northern Virginia, in 1863 in South Carolina, in 1864 in the Department of North Carolina and Southern Virginia, and in 1865 in the Army of Northern Virginia. In Record Group 109 are copies of letters sent, June 29, 1861-May 4, 1864 (ch. II, vols. 318-322); special orders issued, Aug. 7, 1861-May 13, 1864 (ch. II, vols. 323 and 324); and a miscellaneous record book, 1861-63 (ch. II, vol. 325), containing rosters of officers, a record of leave granted, and a record of papers passing through the brigade adjutant's office.

Sterling A. M. Wood (Brig. Gen.)

    After commanding the 7th Alabama Infantry in Florida in 1861, Wood served in the Army of the Mississippi and the Army of Tennessee. Copies of Wood's papers, Nov. 21, 1860-Oct. 9, 1863, in the Alabama Department of Archives and History include correspondence, orders, battle reports, and court-martial proceedings.

George Wortham (Col.)

    Some papers of Wortham, commander of the 50th North Carolina Infantry, in the North Carolina Department of Archives and History relate to the settlement of claims for damaged property and runaway slaves.

John C. Wrenshall (Capt.)

    Captain Wrenshall was an engineer officer in Tennessee and Georgia. After July 1864 he was stationed at Macon, Ga. Papers that had been preserved by Wrenshall were presented by his daughter in 1931 to the Office of the Chief of Engineers. Now in Record Group 77 (Records of the Office of the Chief of Engineers), these papers, 1862-65, include reports on reconnaissances of roads, rivers, trails, bridges, fords, ferries, and fortifications in Tennessee, Alabama, and Georgia; reports on the condition of the Macon & Western Railroad and the Western & Atlantic Railroad; maps and plans of topographical features, fortifications, battlefields, and railroad lines; correspondence; and other documents. Some of the material concerns a depot of engineer supplies and a photographic department that were maintained at Macon.

Augustus R. Wright (Col.)

    Papers of Wright, commander of the 38th Georgia Infantry, are in the University of Georgia Library.

Howard C. Wright (Lt.)

    Letters of Wright relating to the siege of Port Hudson, La., and his imprisonment at Johnson's Island are in the New-York Historical Society.

VIII

NAVY DEPARTMENT

The Confederate Navy Department was established by an act of Feb. 21, 1861 (Prov. Cong. C.S.A. Stat. 33), which also provided for a Secretary of the Navy and several clerks. An act passed 2 weeks later authorized a chief clerk, who was also to serve as disbursing and corresponding clerk, three other clerks, and a messenger (Prov. Cong. C.S.A. Stat. 53). Edward M. Tidball of Virginia was appointed chief clerk on Mar. 13 and continued in that capacity throughout the war.

An act of Mar. 16, 1861, providing for the organization of the Navy (Prov. Cong. C.S.A. Stat. 74), authorized a Marine Corps and the assignment to the Navy Department of officers who became the heads of the Office of Ordnance and Hydrography, the Office of Orders and Detail, the Office of Provisions and Clothing, and the Office of Medicine and Surgery. Other legislation that is referred to below resulted in the formation of additional offices that became known as the Office of Special Service, Engineer-in-Chief, Chief Constructor, and the Torpedo Bureau. Since the former U.S. naval officers who could fill the assignments authorized by the act of Mar. 16, 1861, were then serving in State navies, the appointment of officers to the Navy Department was delayed until June 1861.

The maximum strength initially authorized for the Confederate Navy was 3,000, but the authorized strength for officers was increased by an act of Apr. 21, 1862 (1 Cong. C.S.A. Stat. 50). Commissions were given primarily to former officers of the U.S. Navy. In May 1863 a Provisional Navy was authorized (1 Cong. C.S.A. Stat. 161), in an attempt to increase the naval personnel. Officers appointed in it were to hold commissions only during the war, and the necessary personnel and vessels were to be transferred from the Regular to the Provisional Navy. Both were to be governed by the same laws and regulations. In his report of Apr. 30, 1864, Secretary Mallory stated that the Provisional Navy had been organized; its composition was given in the 1864 Navy Register.

Seamen for the Confederate Navy were obtained largely by recruiting, but this method did not obtain enough men. An act of Oct. 2, 1862 (1 Cong. C.S.A. Stat. 67), permitted men subject to conscription for military service to enlist in the Navy, but naval officers sent to conscript camps had little success in recruiting. Bounties were authorized to encourage enlistments and reenlistments in the Navy and Marine Corps. Authorization for men to transfer from the Army to the Navy was ineffective; by a War Department order of early 1864, 960 men were transferred from the Army to the Navy. In April 1864 the Confederate Navy included 4,460 enlisted men and 753 officers.

The number of vessels in the Confederate Navy at its peak strength was about 200, and Confederate efforts to acquire auxiliary navies were largely unsuccessful. Privateers were authorized by Presidential proclamation on Apr. 17, 1861, and rules controlling them were enacted on May 6, 1861 (Prov. Cong. C.S.A. Stat. 100). Many prizes were captured during the first year of war, but the Union blockade and the refusal of foreign nations to permit the entry of prizes into their ports soon resulted in the disappearance of Confederate privateers from the seas. In Apr. 1863 the Government agreed to accept privately armed vessels into its service and to organize them as a Volunteer Navy (1 Cong. C.S.A. Stat. 111). Capital for the construction and arming of such vessels was lacking, however, and this auxiliary navy did not materialize.

Stephen R. Mallory was sworn in as Secretary of the Navy on Mar. 8, 1861, and served throughout the war.

Reports of the Confederate Navy Department were published in pamphlet form during the war, but they are now more accessible in U.S. Navy Department, Official Records of the Union and Confederate Navies in the War of the Rebellion (31 vols.; Washington, 1894-1927), hereafter cited as Official Records ...Navies. The reports are in ser. 2, vol. 2, as follows: Apr. 26, 1861, p. 51-57; July 18, 1861, p. 76-79; Feb. 27, 1861, p. 149-159; Mar. 29, 1862, p. 174-176; Aug. 16, 1862, p. 241-253; Nov. 30, 1863, p. 528-561; Apr. 30, 1864, p. 630-648; Nov. 5, 1864, p. 743-763. The last four reports are useful in showing bureau activities. Reports of Nov. 18, 1861, and Jan. 10, 1863, are missing. Information on individual naval vessels is in "Confederate States Vessels," in Official Records ...Navies, ser. 2, vol. 1, p. 247-272, and a list of privateers is in ser. 1, p. 818-819. A more complete alphabetical list of naval vessels is in U.S. Navy Department, Office of the Chief of Naval Operations, Naval History Division, "Confederate Forces Afloat," in Dictionary of American Naval Fighting Ships, 2:487-589 (Washington, 1963). Joseph T. Durkin, Stephen R. Mallory, Confederate Navy Chief (Chapel Hill, 1954); William M. Robinson, Jr., The Confederate Privateers (New Haven, 1928); William N. Still, Jr., "Confederate Naval Strategy; the Ironclad," Journal of Southern History, 27:330-343 (Aug. 1961).

Most of the records of the Navy Department were "destroyed upon, & soon after, the evacuation of Richmond" in 1865 (Stephen R. Mallory to James H. Rochelle, May 21, 1867, Rochelle Papers, Duke University Library). At the end of the war the Navy Department was housed in the War Department building, and records were probably burned or pillaged when that structure was destroyed by fire. Some records were taken south by train on the evacuation of Richmond, but these records, deposited at the Charlotte Navy Yard, apparently were deliberately destroyed.

Some Navy Department records, however, were among captured Confederate War Department records taken north to Washington. Only part of the records of Confederate naval vessels and stations remain, and these records are dispersed, usually among the papers of commanding officers, in numerous repositories in both the North and the South. Naval battles and the abandonment of naval stations and ships resulted in the destruction of records, while some records were carried off by officers retreating from captured stations or from vessels set afire.

NAVAL RECORDS COLLECTION OF THE OFFICE OF
NAVAL RECORDS AND LIBRARY

Record Group 45. --The largest body of documents on the Confederate Navy is in Record Group 45 (Naval Records Collection of the Office of Naval Records and Library). The U.S. Navy Department began acquiring documents relating to the Confederate States Navy while the war was in progress. Papers obtained by Union officers and forwarded to the Department can still be found in its files with letters attesting to their origin. A systematic program for obtaining records was initiated after the Naval War Records Office was authorized in 1884 to undertake the publication of documents on the Union and Confederate Navies in the War of the Rebellion. The Office employed for many years an agent whose task was to locate, examine, and obtain as gifts or loans papers in private or institutional hands for use in the publication. In order to insure the success of the program, a former Confederate naval officer, Hardin B. Littlepage, was employed in 1889. The position was continued until about 1920. A total of 2,232 documents, or copies of documents, were procured from many different sources, including former Confederate naval officers and other officials or members of their families, the Confederate Museum, the John Thomas Scharf Collection now in the collections of the Maryland Historical Society, the Confederate State Department papers in the Library of Congress, the Louisiana Historical Association, the Southern Historical Society, and the Virginia Historical Society.

The Office of Naval Records and Library obtained other records relating to the Confederate Navy from departments of the Federal Government. In 1930 the Office received from the War Department more than 600 papers relating to personnel of the Navy and Marine Corps, 2 muster rolls, 26 clothing rolls, a Marine Corps payroll, and registers of the hospital ship Gaines. A receipt signed by Capt. Dudley W. Knox is accompanied by lists of the names of the personnel to whom the papers relate (Adjutant General's Office, General Correspondence File, 314. 81 ORD). In June 1934 some 30 documents relating to naval inventions were received from the War Department. In 1909 the Office received from the Treasury Department records relating to officers and enlisted personnel of the Confederate States Navy (Office of the Secretary of the Navy, General Correspondence File, 27149).

Officers and others whose records were deposited in or lent to the Office of Naval Records and Library are as follows:

Averett, Samuel W.	Chalaron, J. A.	Hoge, Francis L.
Baker, James McC.	Cooke, James W.	Hollins, George N.
Baker, Thomas Harrison	Duvall, R. C.	Hunter, William W.
Barney, Joseph N.	Eggleston, Everard T.	Ingraham, Duncan N.
Barron, Samuel	Eggleston, John R.	Jackson, Thomas A.
Benjamin, Judah P.	Faries, T. A.	Jones, Catesby ap R.
Brent, Thomas W.	Farrand, Ebenezer	Jones, C. Lucian
Bragg, Braxton	Forrest, French	Kennedy, Charles H.
Brooke, John M.	Galt, George W.	Littlepage, Hardin B.
Buchanan, Franklin	Goodwyn, Matthew P.	Loyal, Benjamin P.
Bulloch, James D.	Gregg, A.	McCarrick, James W.
Carter, Jonathan H.	Gunther, C. F.	McCarrick, Patrick H.
Carter, William F.	Guthrie, John J.	Maffitt, John N.
Cary, Clarence	Hodges, W. R.	Mallory, Stephen R.

Mason, James M.	Putnam, W. L.	Stone, S. G., Jr.
Maxwell, John	Ramsay, Henry A.	Swain, Edward A.
Minor, Robert D.	Randolph, Victor M.	Tattnall, Josiah
Mitchell, John K.	Ruggles, Edward S.	Tomb, James H.
Mitchell, K.	Russell, Lord John	Tucker, John R.
Morgan, James M.	Sage, B. J.	Waddell, James I.
Murdaugh, William H.	Sanders, George N.	Ware, Thomas R.
North, James H.	Semmes, Raphael	Webb, William A.
Page, Thomas J.	Simms, Charles C.	Warley, Alexander F.
Pointdexter, Carter B.	Sinclair, Arthur	Wilson, John A.
Porter, John L.	Sinclair, George T.	Wood, John Taylor
Porter, J. W. H.	Slidell, James	Wright, Marcus J.

Instead of maintaining the records of offices and the officers' papers intact in the series or collections in which it received them, the Office of Naval Records and Library arranged them in two large conglomerate files: the area file and the subject file. The origin of these files is described in Guide to Federal Archives Relating to the Civil War, p. 450-451. Since that guide was published the documents in these files relating to the Confederate Navy have been segregated but left in their old arrangement by area and subject.

The area file (1 1/4 ft.; available on microfilm as M 625) includes documents relating to parts of the Confederacy and the waters in which the Confederate Navy operated. The pertinent areas are described below; areas 1-3 are not pertinent. It contains original correspondence and copies of correspondence of the Navy Department, naval and privateer and military officers, the First Auditor, the Secretary of the Treasury, the War Department, the Post Office Department, telegrams, paymasters' vouchers for services and provisions, receipts for funds and supplies, printed materials, edited copy prepared for the Official Records. . .Navies, naval officers' recollections, invoices, certificates of the commissioning of vessels, contracts for work on naval vessels, reports of commanding officers of vessels, bills for pilotage, and travel orders and vouchers. The file for area 4 (eastern part of the Atlantic Ocean and all of the South Atlantic Ocean, including the waters off the coast of South America) contains correspondence and other documents relating to operations of Confederate cruisers and the Confederate naval headquarters in Paris. The file for area 5 (Mississippi River and its tributaries) contains documents relating to the Mississippi River Squadron and the New Orleans, Little Rock, Shreveport, and Yazoo City Naval Stations. The file for area 6 (Gulf of Mexico) contains documents relating to the Mobile Squadron; the defense of Ship Island and Apalachicola; the Mobile, Columbus, Pensacola, Selma, Galveston, and Shreveport Naval Stations; the Selma Naval Gun Foundry; the Augusta and Atlanta Naval Ordnance Works; and the Oven Bluff Shipyard. The file for area 7 (North Atlantic Ocean) contains documents relating to the Norfolk Navy Yard, the Virginia Navy, the naval defenses of North Carolina and Virginia, naval gun batteries and obstructions on Virginia rivers, the James River Squadron, the North Carolina Squadron, the submarine torpedo service, the Wilmington Naval Station, and the Selma Naval Gun Foundry. The file for area 8 (South Atlantic Ocean) contains documents relating to the Charleston and Savannah Squadrons, the Charlotte, Charleston, Marion Courthouse, Savannah, and Wilmington Naval Stations, and the operations of privateers. A card index to the area file, prepared by the Office of

Naval Records and Library, is mainly to names of persons and ships. The subject file, 1861-65 (ca. 24 ft.), contains a much larger quantity and greater variety of documents. The main divisions of the alphabetic classification adopted for this are as follows:

A. Naval Ships: Design, Construction, etc.
B. Ordnance
D. Communication
E. Engineering
H. Battles and Casualties to Ships
I. Instructions
K. Nautical Technology and Science
M. Medical
N. Personnel
O. Operations of Naval Ships and Fleet Units
P. Bases, Naval
R. Prisoners and Prisons
S. Merchant Ships and Commerce
V. Governmental Relationships--Domestic and Foreign
X. Supplies (including Finance)
Y. Pensions and Pensioners
Z. History

Much of the correspondence in the above records is in the Official Records . . . Navies, ser. 1 and 2. Considerable correspondence derived from captured Confederate records in the custody of the War, Navy, and Treasury Departments, relating to the activities of Confederate cruisers, had previously been published in the U.S. Department of State, Correspondence Concerning Claims Against Great Britain. . . (7 vols.; Washington, 1869-71), published also as S. Ex. Doc. 11, 41 Cong., 1 sess., Serials 1394-1398).

Official publications of the Confederate Navy Department include annual reports, circulars, communications to Congress, findings and opinions of courts-martial and courts of inquiry, general orders, instructions, registers, regulations, and special reports. Lists of these publications, which are in the category of rare books, are in Crandall, Confederate Imprints, 1:148-153, and Harwell, More Confederate Imprints, 1:48-49.

Records in Other Custody. --Custody of subject file Z (History) has been retained by the Naval History Division of the U.S. Navy Department quartered in the National Archives Building. Subdivisions of file Z on naval officers, ships, or stations consist mostly of data compiled by the division and correspondence relating to inquiries on naval history, but the files contain some original documents or copies concerning particular officers, ships, or stations.

OFFICE OF THE SECRETARY OF THE NAVY

Record Group 45. --The materials assembled by the Office of Naval Records and Library, embracing area and subject files that are described above, included many of Secretary Mallory's letters. The area file includes letters sent by Mallory to naval officers, the chiefs of Navy

Department offices, President Davis, the Secretary of War, the Secretary of the Treasury, the First Auditor (Bolling Baker), the chairmen of the Committees on Naval Affairs of the Congress, and letters received from many of the same. Correspondence with many persons on the business of the Navy Department is in the subject file. Some correspondence with B. J. Sage, a master in the Confederate Navy, concerns the establishment of a volunteer navy.

Record Group 59.--In the general records of the Department of State are copies of letters sent by the Secretary of the Navy, Feb. 24-May 10, 1862 (1 in.). These are addressed to Capts. Franklin Buchanan, French Forrest, Josiah Tattnall, and Sidney S. Lee and concern the naval defense of Virginia and the construction of the ironclads Virginia and Richmond, the obstruction of Elizabeth River, and the removal of the Confederate Navy from Norfolk.

Records in Other Custody.--Most of Secretary Mallory's papers were destroyed on his instructions, but his papers, 1846-72 (93 items; on microfilm), in the Southern Historical Collection in the University of North Carolina Library include some wartime correspondence containing information on naval matters. His diary, May 30, 1861-Jan. 24, 1866 (2 vols.), in the same repository (typescript in the Library of Congress) gives information on naval affairs, cabinet meetings, political conditions, relations between the President and Congress, the flight of the Cabinet after the evacuation of Richmond, and his imprisonment.

Correspondence of Secretary Mallory is in Official Records... Navies, ser. 1 and 2; Official Records... Armies, ser. 4, vols. 1-3; Correspondence Concerning Claims Against Great Britain, cited above, and in C.S.A. Congress, Joint Special Committee, Report of Evidence Taken before a Joint Special Committee of Both Houses of the Confederate Congress To Investigate the Affairs of the Navy Department (Richmond, 1863?), largely reprinted in Official Records... Navies, ser. 2, vol. 1, p. 431-809. This compilation contains documentary material on naval activities at New Orleans and the operations of the Mississippi River Squadron during 1861-62. Other Mallory letters are among the records of naval squadrons and stations described below and with the papers of President Davis and the records of Congress and the executive departments described in other chapters of this Guide.

OFFICE OF ORDERS AND DETAIL

An act of Mar. 16, 1861 (Prov. Cong. C.S.A. Stat. 74), provided that the officer in charge of this bureau was to "prepare and issue all orders and details for service, and...have charge of all matters and things connected with courts martial and courts of enquiry, and with the custody of all records and papers thereunto appertaining." The Navy Regulations issued in Apr. 1862 directed this office to keep a register of the service of officers and service records of officers containing applications, declinations, explanations for leaving assignment before completion, and charges and complaints and their disposition. An act of Apr. 4, 1863 (1 Cong. C.S.A. Stat. 105), provided for the position of registrar. James S. Jones transferred to this position from that of chief clerk in which he was followed by George L. Brent. A circular of July 18, 1863, directed the sending of communications to this office on the "equipment of vessels, except ordnance; recruiting service; transfers from the army to the navy; receiving ships; supplies of coal; all matters connected with courts martial and courts of inquiry and the details of stations generally; all acknowledgments of orders; all applications for service and change of service, and for leave of absence." Recruiting stations were maintained by officers at Richmond, Raleigh, Macon, Savannah, Mobile, and New Orleans. Receiving ships for the temporary accommodation of recruits and seamen detached from vessels were maintained at most of the navy yards and stations. Supervision of a ropewalk that opened at Petersburg, Va., in Jan. 1863 was placed under this office on Apr. 1.

The circular quoted above evidently transferred the business of procuring coal from the Office of Provisions and Clothing to the Office of Orders and Detail. An "Office of Superintendent of Coal Contracts" was established in the Navy Department late in 1862 under Comdr. John K. Mitchell. He became head of the Office of Orders and Detail in Mar. 1863 and cognizance over coal supply was placed under that office.

Courts-martial and courts of inquiry were conducted by the Navy Department to determine the responsibility of officers in cases in which they were involved. For example, in July 1862 in Richmond a court-martial tried Capt. Josiah Tattnall for ordering the destruction of the Virginia and decided that his action had been justified. In Jan. 1863 Comdr. John K. Mitchell's conduct as commander of the Confederate fleet in the battle of New Orleans was investigated and he was exonerated.

C.S. Navy Department, Proceedings of a Naval General Court Martial, in the Case of Captain Josiah Tattnall (Richmond, 1862), Finding and Opinion of a Naval

Court of Inquiry Convened in the City of Richmond, Va., January 5th, 1863 [To Investigate the Conduct of Comdr. John K. Mitchell] (Richmond, 1863).

After the Secretary of the Navy was authorized by an act of Apr. 4, 1863 (1 Cong. C.S.A. Stat. 105), to employ pilots for Government-owned blockade-runners, naval officers were sent to Wilmington, N.C., and other ports to assign pilots and signalmen to the vessels. The port officer at Wilmington established lights, signals, and sailing directions, and exercised general supervision over trading vessels.

Successive Chiefs of the Office:
      Capt. Samuel Barron, June 1861.
      Capt. Lawrence Rousseau, July 1861.
      Capt. William F. Lynch, Aug. 1861.
      Capt. Franklin Buchanan, Sept. 1861.
      Capt. French Forrest, May 1862.
      Capt. John K. Mitchell, Mar. 1863.
      Capt. Sidney S. Lee, May 1864.

Record Group 45. --In subject file N (Personnel) are documents that would also have been in the files of the Office of Orders and Detail. The subdivisions containing material on the Confederate Navy are as follows:

NA. Complements, Rolls, Lists of Persons Serving in or with Vessels of Stations
NC. Ceremonies, Salutes, Courtesies, Honors, etc.
NE. Drills, Training, and Education
NF. Distribution and Transfers

NH. Heroic Acts, Commendations, Honors, Memorials, and Medals
NI. Promotion and Privileges; Rank, Retirement and Reinstatement
NJ. Discipline (Minor) and Minor Delinquencies
NK. Technical and Professional Examinations of Individuals
NL. Living Conditions, Customs, etc.
NN. Commissions, Appointments, Applications, Acceptances, Oaths, Resignations, Discharges, and Similar Documents
NO. Courts-martial, etc.
NP. Pilots
NR. Recruiting and Enlistments, Shipping Articles, etc.
NU. Uniforms, Characteristics
NV. Miscellaneous Material Relative to Personnel
NZ. Desertions and Straggling

In the Naval Records Collection are rolls relating to personnel of the Confederate Navy. Muster rolls and payrolls of naval vessels, May 1861-Apr. 1865 (1 ft.), are arranged alphabetically by name of vessel and thereunder chronologically. They show the names and rank of men, the pay period, the amount of pay per month, the total amount paid, the amount allowed for undrawn rations, the amount due from other vessels, the amount paid in clothing, and the date of enlistment. Some rolls include officers and enlisted men, others are for officers, and still others are for men transferred from one vessel to another. Included are requisitions for small stores, lists of clothing issued to crews, and registers of allotments made by crew members. Muster rolls and payrolls for naval stations and squadrons, June 1861-Sept. 1864 (7 vols., 1 ft. 9 in.), give the same information for the stations at Charleston, Jackson, Mobile, New Orleans, Richmond, Savannah, and Wilmington and the squadrons on the James River and off the coasts of North and South Carolina.

Other muster rolls, payrolls, and lists of naval and marine personnel, 1861-65 (1 ft.), are in subject file NA in the Naval Records Collection. These are for vessels, stations, squadrons, privateers, blockade-runners, and naval shore batteries. Payrolls, receipts, and accounts of revenue cutter officers, 1861-65 (1/2 in.), in subject file OV are for officers who served with the Navy in the Mississippi River Squadron and the Mobile Squadron.

Shipping articles, May 1861-Feb. 1865 (1 vol.), consist of printed forms with the statement in the heading that those signing agreed to enlist in the Confederate Navy, to go on board such vessels as they might be ordered to, and to obey the naval laws and regulations. Grouped together by recruiting station or vessel, the forms give the date of enlistment, the signature or mark of the recruit, the name of the recruit, rating, monthly wages advanced, bounty paid, signature of surety for advance wages and bounty, and witnesses' names. Other shipping articles are in the payrolls of civilian employees described below. An alphabetical name index to the shipping articles, which was prepared by the Office of Naval Records and Library, contains more than 5,000 names.

A list of muster rolls of Confederate vessels and lists of the names of officers and men on the rolls are in Official Records . . . Navies, ser. 2, vol. 1, p. 273-323, which is indexed. The Confederate Navy Department published a Register of the Officers of the Confederate Navy in three volumes during 1862-64. The Office of Naval Records

and Library published a consolidated register in 1898, and a revised
edition appeared in 1931. Other pay
and muster rolls of naval vessels
and stations are described in chapter VI of this Guide under the section on the First Auditor.

Many orders from the Chief
of the Office of Orders and Detail
are in the Office of Naval Records
and Library area file described
above. Some general orders and
circulars signed by the same official and a few general orders signed
by Secretary Mallory for the period
Sept. 20, 1862-June 15, 1864, are in
the Register of the Commissioned
and Warrant Officers of the Navy of
the Confederate States to January 1,
1864, p. 82-93 (Richmond, 1864).
See the records of Congress for nominations of men for commissions in
the Navy, the Marine Corps, and the
Provisional Navy. Carded service
records of naval and marine personnel compiled by the U.S. War Department are described in chapter
XI of this Guide.

Record Group 56.--In the records of the U.S. Department of the
Treasury, Captured and Abandoned Property Records (file 5997) are a
few payrolls and muster rolls of the James River Squadron. These include
a payroll of the squadron itself, fourth quarter 1863, and transfer, pay,
receipt, and muster rolls of crews of the Beaufort and Roanoke transferred
to Wilmington, Sept. 30, 1864, of the naval battery at Drewry's Bluff transferred to Charleston, Sept. 30, 1863, and a roll of the Roanoke, Nov. 15,
1863.

Records in Other Custody.--During May-July 1861, Comdr. William
W. Hunter conducted a recruiting station at New Orleans. His correspondence for that period, including communications from the Office of Orders
and Detail, is in the Louisiana Historical Association collection on deposit
in the Howard-Tilton Memorial Library of Tulane University.

The papers of William Phi-
neas Browne, a coal-mine operator
who furnished coal to naval establishments, are in a collection at
the Alabama Department of Archives
and History. A long letter from
Browne to Comdr. John K. Mitchell,
Feb. 26, 1863, concerns difficulties
encountered in mining coal and transporting it. Letters from Julius A.
Pratt, then attached to the Selma
Naval Station, from the foundry
there, and from J. L. M. Curry,
Representative from Alabama, are
also in the collection.

OFFICE OF ORDNANCE AND HYDROGRAPHY

Under the provisions of an act of Mar. 16, 1861 (Prov. Cong. C.S.A.
Stat. 74), this Office purchased or manufactured ordnance, ordnance stores
and equipment, and attended to duties connected with hydrography. Heavy
guns, shells, and powder captured at the Norfolk Navy Yard provided an
immediate supply of ordnance that was distributed to naval vessels, batteries, and stations. An act of Jan. 14, 1862 (Prov Cong. C.S.A. Stat. 240),
authorized the appointment of a draftsman for the Office, and Frederick
Volck was assigned to the post. Other draftsmen employed by the Office in
1862 included A. von Fischer and John Barker. Other employees in 1863
included Lt. John M. Brooke, assistant to the chief, Chief Clerk J. O.
McCorkle, and Elliott Lacey, a mathematician. The Office directed naval
ordnance works at Richmond, Charlotte, Selma, Columbia, Atlanta, New
Orleans, Augusta, Columbus, and the Naval Academy on the James River.

Assistant inspectors of ordnance attached to navy yards corresponded with the Office through the commandants of the yards on subjects under its cognizance.

The Office procured ordnance, iron products, and other metals. Through contracts with Tredegar Iron Works in Richmond, the Etowah Iron Works in Cass County, Ga., the Shelby Iron Works in Shelby County, Ala., F. B. Deane, Jr., & Son in Lynchburg, and the Bellona Foundry in Chesterfield County, Va., it obtained heavy guns, projectiles, armor plate, and boiler iron. Naval inspectors of ordnance were usually assigned to private ordnance plants. In 1862 the Office contracted with many companies in Virginia, North Carolina, Alabama, Tennessee, Georgia, and Louisiana to manufacture iron (see the list of agreements in Official Records . . . Navies, ser. 2, vol. 2, p. 248-249). Agents employed to purchase, collect, and distribute iron, including scrap iron, were James G. Miner in Georgia, W. W. Shackelford in Georgia and North Carolina, David Pender in North Carolina, and Charles F. M. Garnett in Virginia. Scarce metals, such as steel, copper, tin, and zinc, and tools and other articles were imported from abroad, chiefly through Wilmington, N. C.

As a user of metals the Office was concerned with the discovery and development of mineral resources. In 1863 Comdr. Archibald B. Fairfax, Prof. Oscar J. Heinrich, and Capt. Mitchell Tate, Army quartermaster, conducted experimental research. P. Melinaud made ordnance experiments. In 1864 Commander Fairfax was on special duty in charge of mining coal and iron ore in Botetourt County, Va., an undertaking in which Professor Heinrich assisted on a contract basis.

The hydrographic duties of the Office involved the procurement and distribution of nautical instruments, books and charts, and the drafting of charts. Late in 1861 Charles J. Ost was added to the staff as a hydrographic draftsman.

Successive Chiefs of the Office:

    Capt. Duncan N. Ingraham, June 1861.
    Capt. George B. Minor, Dec. 1861.
    Comdr. John M. Brooke, Mar. 1863.

C. S. A. Navy Department, Ordnance Instructions for the Confederate States Navy (London, 1864); Charles B. Dew, Ironmaker to the Confederacy; Joseph R. Anderson and the Tredegar Iron Works (New Haven and London, 1966); Official Records . . . Navies, passim; Frank E. Vandiver, "The Shelby Iron Company in the Civil War; a Study of a Confederate Industry," Alabama Review, 1:12-26, 111-127, 203-207 (Jan. - July 1948).

Record Group 37.--In the records of the U.S. Hydrographic Office is a chart by Charles J. Ost of the entrance to Mobile Bay showing soundings and the locations of lighthouses and beacons.

Record Group 45.--Records on naval ordnance assembled by the Office of Naval Records and Library were placed in the area and subject files described above. Original papers of John M. Brooke and Robert D. Minor are in those files. In the area file (areas 5-8) are many orders from the heads of the Office of Ordnance and Hydrography assigning duties or giving directions to officers or to civilian agents for the transportation of guns and ordnance stores to naval stations. Subject file B (Ordnance) contains correspondence, drawings, reports, and other documents on the design, production, and testing of guns, ammunition, hand weapons, submarine batteries, torpedoes, and armor.

Record Group 74. --A file of plans, drawings, and sketches in the records of the Bureau of Ordnance, U.S. Navy Department, includes some plans of Confederate guns. A file of ordnance drawings kept by a naval ordnance plant of that Bureau at Louisville, Ky., includes a drawing of a shell for the 8-inch gun designed by John M. Brooke.

Record Group 109. --In the War Department Collection of Confederate Records is a letters-sent book of the Office of Ordnance and Hydrography for the period Nov. 5, 1864-Mar. 25, 1865. This is presumably the only surviving volume of fair copies of outgoing letters. The volume was apparently obtained by the Adjutant General's Office in 1872 from L. S. Thompson of St. Paul, Minn. In it are letters of John M. Brooke to Secretary Mallory reporting on the activities of the Office and of naval ordnance works, instructions to the superintendent of the Naval Powder Works at Columbia, S.C., letters to Navy agents on the handling of small arms and ordnance materials, to industrial firms on the manufacture of ordnance, and to Josiah Gorgas, Gabriel J. Rains, Isaac M. St. John, and other Army officers or agents requesting ordnance, supplies, publications, passes, and transportation.

Records in Other Custody. --A few wartime letters of John M. Brooke are in the Southern Historical Collection in the University of North Carolina Library. Other Brooke papers are owned by George M. Brooke, Jr., Virginia Military Institute.

Some correspondence of the heads of the Office and of Lt. Robert D. Minor is in Official Records... Navies, ser. 1 and 2. Letter books, contract books, and other records of the Tredegar Iron Works in the Archives Division of the Virginia State Library document its work for the Office of Ordnance and Hydrography. Some records of Talbott & Bros., operators of the Schockoe Foundry at Richmond, in the Virginia Historical Society collections include materials relating to the use of the foundry by the Confederate Navy Department. The Shelby Iron Works records in the University of Alabama Library contain correspondence with Capts. William F. Lynch and George Minor and Secretary Mallory. See also the section on the Bureau of Ordnance in chapter VIII of this Guide.

OFFICE OF PROVISIONS AND CLOTHING

A paymaster was attached to the Navy Department by the act of Mar. 16, 1861 (Prov. Cong. C.S.A. Stat. 74), to procure food, clothing, and coal. William F. Howell, Navy agent at Augusta, Ga., sent out agents to obtain wheat in order to supply the naval stations and squadrons at Savannah, Mobile, and Charleston. Paymaster William W. J. Kelly, of the Savannah station opened a meat-packing plant at Albany, Ga., in 1863, and in the following year a flour mill and bakery were established there under the supervision of Asst. Paymaster Nelson Tift.

Provisions obtained in southwest Virginia in 1864 were stored at the Richmond (Rocketts) Navy Yard. Other storehouses were located at Montgomery, Ala., Augusta, Ga., and the naval stations at Mobile, Savannah, Charleston, and Wilmington. In 1863 canvas shoes were made at Mobile and in 1864 the manufacture of shoes was begun at Augusta. The Navy was obliged to purchase high-priced cloth brought in by blockade-runners or to arrange for its procurement abroad. A procurement agent, C. Girard, was in England and France in 1863. Clothing was manufactured at Richmond, Augusta, Savannah, and Mobile. Materials brought through the blockade at Wilmington, N.C., were distributed by William H. Peters, the Navy agent there. Contracts were made with Robert Jemison, Jr., of Tuscaloosa, Ala., for the delivery of coal at Mobile, with William P. Browne of Montevallo, Ala., for supplying coal to Mobile and to naval works in Georgia, and with James Brown of Charleston, S.C., for the delivery of coal at Charleston, Savannah, and Wilmington. J. G. Miner, Navy agent at Atlanta, Ga., in 1862, attended to the transportation of coal to naval stations and works. In 1863 the Office of Orders and Detail became responsible for procuring coal.

Paymasters attached to naval stations, vessels, squadrons, and naval batteries functioned as disbursing officers for the Navy, expending funds for the pay, travel, allotments, and allowances of naval personnel, and for the purchase of provisions, cloth, coal, ordnance, ordnance stores, and equipment. Some paymasters also disbursed funds to contractors employed by the Navy Department.

Successive paymasters in charge of the Office:

         John de Bree, June 1861.

         James A. Semple, Aug. 1864.

Record Group 45. --Some correspondence of Paymaster de Bree is in the area and subject files described above. Many vouchers for expenditures made by paymasters at naval stations and on board vessels are also in the subject file. These were derived from the records of paymasters and assistant paymasters obtained by the Office of Naval Records and Library and also from the records of the Confederate First Auditor of the Treasury that were transferred by the U.S. Treasury Department to the Office of Naval Records and Library. A record of requisitions for funds drawn on naval appropriations ("Requisition Book"), Apr. 13, 1864-Mar. 29, 1865 (1 vol.), is not marked as to office origin, but it may be a record of the Office of Provisions and Clothing. It shows the requisition number, date, name of paymaster for whom drawn, appropriation charged to, and the amount. In front of the volume is an index, and on p. 1-4 is a list of accounts reported to the comptroller, Mar. 17-Dec. 16, 1862.

The records of a number of paymasters have survived and are described below under records of squadrons and stations. See also the description of the records of the First Auditor of the Treasury in chapter VI of this Guide.

OFFICE OF MEDICINE AND SURGERY

The act of Mar. 16, 1861 (Prov. Cong. C.S.A. Stat. 74), providing for the organization of the Navy authorized a surgeon who under the direction of the Secretary of the Navy was to purchase medicines and medical supplies for the Navy. In practice, the chief medical officer supervised the treatment of the sick and wounded. A purveyor's department established to obtain medicines, surgical instruments, and appliances succeeded in obtaining them from abroad through the blockade until the end of 1864. But the tightening of the blockade forced the Office to authorize naval stations to purchase medicines on their own. Apothecaries hired by the Office manufactured, received, packed, and issued medicines. They took turns conveying medical supplies to the stations south of Richmond. Naval hospitals were maintained at Richmond, Wilmington, Charleston, Savannah, Mobile, Charlotte, and during 1861-62 at Norfolk and Pensacola. The receiving ship St. Philip was used as a hospital ship at New Orleans where naval patients were also treated at the Charity Hospital, a State institution. Naval surgeons served at hospitals, naval stations, shore batteries, recruiting stations, and on vessels. In 1864 the Navy Department issued instructions to medical officers prescribing their duties, forms to be used, and records to be kept.

Surg. William A. W. Spotswood was head of the Office from June 10, 1861, until 1864 or 1865.

C.S.A. Navy Department, Instructions for the Guidance of the   Medical Officers of the Navy of the Confederate States (Richmond, 1864).

Record Group 45.--In subject file M (Medical, 8 in.) of the Naval Records Collection are some records that contain information on the administration of the medical affairs of the Navy. Most of the material consists of vouchers for disbursements by paymasters for medical supplies and equipment for hospitals, vessels, and naval stations, travel of doctors, pay of civilian doctors, transportation of patients, undertakers' bills, and records of deaths and interments. Included is a small quantity of correspondence of W. A. W. Spotswood and other surgeons.

OFFICE OF SPECIAL SERVICE

Acts of Dec. 24, 1861 (Ramsdell, Laws and Joint Resolutions, p. 161 and 162), authorized the construction of 100 wooden gunboats for coast defense according to plans that had been submitted by Comdr. Matthew F. Maury. The Office of Special Service, which developed as a result of that statute, operated shipyards in Virginia at Keswick, Fluvanna, Indian Town, Romancoke, Fredericksburg, Deep Creek, Richmond, and West Point, maintained lumber camps, and sent agents to other areas to obtain timber, materials, and supplies.

Successive heads of the Office:
Comdr. Matthew F. Maury, 1862.
Comdr. Thomas T. Rootes, ca. Sept. 1862.
Lt. John H. Parker, ca. Dec. 1862.

No separate records of this Office have been found, but there are documents concerning its activities in the area file (area 7) and the subject file (PL and XS) described above under Naval Records Collection of the Office of Naval Records and Library.

ENGINEER-IN-CHIEF

No corollary to the U.S. Navy's Bureau of Steam Engineering was provided by the act of Feb. 21, 1861, establishing the Confederate Navy Department, but an Engineer-in-Chief was eventually appointed. William P. Williamson worked with John L. Porter and Lt. John M. Brooke on the conversion of the Merrimack to the ironclad Virginia at the Norfolk Navy Yard. On Oct. 17, 1861, Williamson was ordered to superintend for the Department the planning, construction, and fitting up of engines, boilers, and steam machinery of naval vessels. An act of Apr. 21, 1862 (1 Cong. C.S.A. Stat. 50), provided for an Engineer-in-Chief and 12 engineers.

Later in 1862 Williamson was appointed Engineer-in-Chief. A Navy Department general order of July 18, 1863, directed that all communications relating to the construction and repair of steam machinery were to be addressed to the Engineer-in-Chief. In 1864 there were nine chief engineers and many assistant engineers attached to naval steam vessels, stations, ordnance works, and squadrons.

The Engineer-in-Chief was William P. Williamson.

Record Group 45.--Subject file E (Engineering, 2 in.) of the Naval Records Collection contains some records relating to engines, boilers, auxiliary machinery, and propellers. Most of the material consists of vouchers for purchases of and work on engines, but there are also some letters and orders of Secretary Mallory appointing engineers at naval installations.

CHIEF CONSTRUCTOR

Congress did not provide for an Office of Construction and Repair such as the U.S. Navy Department's. After the evacuation of the Norfolk Navy Yard where he had worked on the conversion of the Merrimack, Naval Constructor John L. Porter was attached to Rocketts Navy Yard in Richmond, functioning as Chief Constructor for the Secretary of the Navy. He prepared hull and inboard plans and models for vessels, examined plans and propositions submitted by others to the Department, adapted vessels to machinery found in the South, and inspected shipbuilding activities at many points. On Sept. 20, 1862, Secretary Mallory recommended to the Senate Committee on Naval Affairs that Porter be designated as Chief Constructor, thereby raising him to the same status as the Engineer-in-Chief. An act of Apr. 30, 1863 (1 Cong. C.S.A. Stat. 131), authorized a Chief Constructor and Porter was appointed. A Navy Department general order of July 18, 1863, directed that all communications relating to the construction and repair of vessels be addressed to the Chief Constructor of the Confederate States Navy. John W. Borum served as chief clerk. Naval constructors served at Richmond, Selma, and McIntosh Bluff and Oven Bluff, Ala.

The Chief Constructor was John L. Porter.

Record Group 19.--The ship plans file of the Bureau of Ships of the U.S. Navy Department contains drawings and sketches of some Confederate naval vessels and blockade-runners.

Record Group 45.--Records assembled by the Office of Naval Records and Library concerning the purchase, conversion, design, construction, fitting, and equipment of all types of naval vessels and some blockade-runners are in subject file A (Naval Ships, 3 ft.). More than half of the material is in file AC (Construction). The records include paymasters' vouchers, statements of paymasters' accounts, recapitulations of payrolls, requests for transportation, railroad waybills, accounts, requisitions, bills, certificates, and correspondence. Ship plans are available for a number of vessels; those for the Virginia include photostats of John L. Porter's plans and others presented by the Mariners' Museum, Newport News, Va. The records concern the construction and repair of Confederate vessesls in Europe also.

Record Group 109.--In the War Department Collection of Confederate Records are plans of the C.S.S. Alabama, including a profile of inboard works, masts and spars, and the lower deck, all dated at the Birkenhead ironworks of John Laird Sons & Co. in Oct. 1861. Photographs of these plans are in Record Group 19 and in the University of Alabama Library.

Plans, sketches, and photographs of some Confederate naval vessels are in Official Records. . . Navies. A file in Record Group 109 that contains some documents relating to naval vessels is described in chapter XI of this Guide.

Records in Other Custody. --The original plans of the Virginia (Merrimack) are in the Confederate Museum. Other plans of that vessel by John L. Porter are in the Virginia Historical Society collections and in the Mariners' Museum at Newport News. The Mariners' Museum also has Porter's plans for an iron warship whose construction was begun in England but not completed.

At the Smithsonian Institution in the Division of Transportation is a large collection of photocopies of plans, specifications, contracts, and other documents relating to Confederate naval vessels. In order to prepare exhibits and a history of Confederate naval vessel construction, the Division reconstructed plans of the vessels from existing models that were located.

TORPEDO BUREAU

Although not provided for by law except by the appropriation of funds, the Navy Department maintained an office that was concerned with the development of submarine mines and torpedoes. Comdr. Matthew F. Maury began experiments with batteries in 1861. He laid mines in the James River and connected them by insulated wire with shore stations. Lt. Hunter Davidson grounded the Teaser in the James River in July 1862 and it was captured by the Federals, along with Maury's descriptions, instructions, and diagrams. But the mines played an important part in preventing the ascent of Union vessels up the river to Richmond.
Successive Chiefs of the Bureau:
Comdr. Matthew F. Maury, 1861.
Brig. Gen. Gabriel J. Rains, June 1862.
Lt. Hunter Davidson, Sept. 1862.
No records of this Bureau have been found, but it is possible that documents are in the area and subject files of the Naval Records Collection.

R. O. Crowley, "The Confederate Torpedo Service, " Century Magazine, 56:290-300 (June 1898); Hunter Davidson, "Mines and Torpedoes During the Rebellion, " Magazine of History, 8:255-261 (Nov. 1908); Milton F. Perry, Infernal Machines; the Story of Confederate Submarine and Mine Warfare (Baton Rouge, 1965); Frances L. Williams, Matthew Fontaine Maury; Scientist of the Sea (New Brunswick, N. J., 1963).

MARINE CORPS

The act of Mar. 16, 1861, providing for the organization of the Navy (Prov. Cong. C. S. A. Stat. 74), authorized a corps of marines to consist of one major, one quartermaster, one paymaster, one adjutant, one sergeant major, one quartermaster sergeant, and six companies of 100 men

each. An amendatory act of May 20, 1861 (Prov. Cong. C.S.A. Stat. 121),
enlarged its numbers and raised the rank of its principal officers. The
commandant recommended on Dec. 17, 1861, that authorization be obtained
for the pay of a clerk to keep books, records, and returns of the corps.
On Sept. 30, 1864, the corps consisted of 539 officers and men and 32 recruits.

Marines were distributed in small detachments at shore stations and
on board vessels. Recruits were trained at Camp Beall at Drewry's Bluff
on the James River where they also manned gun batteries. Guard detachments were kept at the naval stations at Richmond, Wilmington, Charleston,
Savannah, Mobile, and Charlotte. Marines were assigned to most of the
larger vessels of the Navy, including the Alabama, Tallahassee, Chickamauga, and Sumter. Marines participated in the defense of seacoast fortifications and in the naval battles of Hampton Roads, New Orleans, Wassaw
Sound, and Mobile Bay.

Staff officers of the Marine Corps:

    Col. Lloyd J. Beall, Commandant, May 23, 1861.
    Capt. Israel Greene, Adjutant, June 19, 1861.
    Maj. Richard T. Allison, Paymaster, May 10, 1861.
    Maj. Algernon S. Taylor, Quartermaster, Dec. 4, 1861.

The headquarters records of the Marine Corps were destroyed largely
at the time of the evacuation of Richmond on Apr. 2, 1865, or soon afterward. Some of the records of the corps that were kept in Colonel Beall's
house were destroyed by fire near the end of the war. At the end of the war
books and papers relating to the corps were burned by order of the Secretary of the Navy (Beall to Capt. Henry C. Cochrane, Sept. 21, 1880, "Personal Journal of Henry C. Cochrane, 1863-1905," U.S. Marine Corps Museum, Quantico, Va.). Lt. Nathaniel E. Venable, assistant to Major
Taylor, took the quartermaster records to Danville where they were destroyed. Historians have been unable to locate records of any of the departments of the corps.

Ralph W. Donnelly, "Battle Honors and Services of Confederate Marines," Military Affairs, 23:37- 40 (Spring 1959); Navy Register, Jan. 1, 1864, p. 34-37.

Record Group 45.--Some of the records collected by the Office of
Naval Records and Library relate to the Confederate Marine Corps. The
muster rolls described under the Office of Orders and Detail contain data
relating to marines attached to naval vessels and stations. The marines
are sometimes listed on rolls giving the entire complements of vessels and
stations and sometimes on separate rolls. Other rolls and lists pertaining
to marines are in subject file NA, also described above. In subject file OV
are bills; vouchers; correspondence; certificates of deposit; invoices; abstracts of expenditures; accounts; receipts; special orders relating to provisions, clothing, and equipment for marine detachments; returns of ordnance and ordnance stores; returns of clothing and equipment; and
transportation requests.

Lists of names of marines on muster rolls are in Official Records ...Navies, ser. 2, vol. 1, p. 280-320. Some carded service records relating to Marine Corps personnel are described in chapter XI of this Guide.

Records in Other Custody. --Alfred C. Van Benthuysen of Louisiana served as a captain in the Marine Corps at New Orleans and Pensacola in 1861, at Drewry's Bluff in 1862-64, and at Mobile and Wilmington in 1864, before his capture at Fort Fisher in Jan. 1865. Van Benthuysen's papers, Mar. 30, 1861-Jan. 10, 1865 (130 pieces), in Tulane University Library contain a few letters from Secretary Mallory, general orders from Marine Corps headquarters, orders and circulars from General Bragg's headquarters near Pensacola, instructions from the headquarters of the 2d Brigade, Department of Alabama and West Florida, abstracts of disbursements and of clothing and equipment received, and personal letters. Other items are Van Benthuysen's report on the handling of the battery at the Pensacola Navy Yard during the bombardment of Nov. 1861; Capt. John D. Simms' report on the defense of Drewry's Bluff in May 1862; court-martial records of Van Benthuysen and Lt. Henry B. Tyler, Jr.; seven muster rolls of Company B, June 1861-Apr. 1862; two payrolls, Apr.-June 1861, and Sept.-Oct. 1861; three company returns, Aug., Sept., and Dec. 1861, and July 1862; and a return of Van Benthuysen's detachment, Oct.-Nov. 1864. Another statistical return of Company B, Nov. 1864, is in the William and Mary College Library.

Less extensive are the papers of other Marine Corps officers. A letter book, Oct. 8, 1862-June 7, 1864, of Capt. Julius E. Meiere, commander of the marine guard at Mobile, is in the records of the probate court of Mobile County, Ala. Edward Crenshaw served first in the 58th Alabama Infantry, and after recovering from a wound suffered at Chickamauga joined the Marine Corps. He kept a diary, July 4, 1861-Sept. 19, 1863, and July 1, 1864-June 19, 1865, the second part of which concerns the role played by the marines in planning the abortive expedition of Comdr. John Taylor Wood designed to free Confederate prisoners at Point Lookout, Md., the cruise on the Tallahassee against Union shipping, service at Drewry's Bluff, and the retreat to the south in 1865. The letters written by Lt. Henry L. Graves to members of his family, Oct. 1862-Mar. 1865, in the Southern Historical Collection in the University of North Carolina Library give some information about his service at Drewry's Bluff, Nov. 1862-Jan. 1863, with the Savannah naval station and squadron, Feb. 1863-Nov. 1864, and at Charleston naval station, Dec. 1864-Jan. 1865. Like Crenshaw and Graves, Lt. Ruffin Thomson had prior service in the Army and did not join the Marine Corps until Feb. 1864. A few letters he wrote from Camp Beall near Drewry's Bluff in 1864 and 1865 in the Southern Historical Collection in the University of North Carolina Library concern conditions there and his activities as a marine officer. Correspondence of John L. Rapier, a marine lieutenant who served at Drewry's Bluff, 1863-64, and at Mobile, 1864-65, was recently in the custody of a granddaughter, Mrs. E. M. Trigg of Savannah, Ga.

"Diary of Captain Edward Crenshaw, " Alabama Historical Quarterly, 1:261-270, 438-452 (1939), 2:52-71, 221-238, 365-385, 465-382 (1940); Richard B. Harwell, ed., A Confederate Marine; a Sketch of Henry Lea Graves with Excerpts from the Graves Family Correspondence (Tuscaloosa, Ala., 1963).

NAVAL SQUADRONS

The Confederate Navy maintained a few small squadrons for the defense of its coasts, seaports, and rivers. They placed obstructions in rivers and harbors, laid mines, reconnoitered U.S. positions, manned naval batteries, cooperated with the Confederate Army, raided blockading vessels, and fought enemy fleets. The superior strength of the U.S. Navy limited their activities, but they were persistently maintained despite reverses.

The published reports of the Secretary of the Navy cited above give some information regarding the naval squadrons. Information on individual vessels of the Confederate Navy is in Official Records . . .Navies, ser. 2, vol. 1, p. 247-272, and in U.S. Navy Department, Dictionary of American Naval Fighting Ships, 2:487-589. See the records of district courts in chapter III of this Guide for material on the operations of naval vessels connected with the seizure of prize vessels on Confederate coasts.

Record Group 45.--Several subdivisions of the subject file in the Naval Records Collection contain documents on Confederate naval vessels, particularly file H (Battles and Casualties to Ships) and file O (Operations of Naval Ships and Fleet Units). File Z (History), containing alphabetical files on ships and operations, is in the National Archives Building but in the custody of the Naval History Division of the Navy Department.

Information regarding Confederate naval vessels is also in the compiled vessel papers that are described in chapter XI of this Guide.

James River Squadron

In July 1861 a squadron consisting of the Patrick Henry, the Jamestown, the St. Nicholas, the George Page, the Raleigh, the Edwards, and the Ellis was organized for the naval defense of Virginia and North Carolina. Early in Mar. 1862 the squadron was composed of the Virginia (Merrimack), the Patrick Henry, the Jamestown, the Teaser, the Raleigh, and the Beaufort. After the Monitor-Merrimack battle in Hampton Roads and the fall of Norfolk, the squadron retreated in May 1862 up the James River, except for the Virginia which drew too much water and was burned. Late in 1862 the squadron was composed of the Richmond, the Patrick Henry, the Hampton, the Nansemond, the Torpedo, the Drewry, and the Beaufort; additions in 1864 included the Virginia II, the Fredericksburg, and the Roanoke.
Successive commanders of this squadron:
        Capt. Samuel Barron, July 29, 1861.
        Capt. William F. Lynch, 1861.
        Capt. Franklin Buchanan, Mar. 4, 1862.
        Capt. Josiah Tattnall, Mar. 29, 1862.
        Capt. Samuel Barron, Nov. 1862.
        Capt. French Forrest, Mar. 1863.
        Capt. John K. Mitchell, May 7, 1864.
        Rear Adm. Raphael Semmes, Feb. 18, 1865.
Record Group 45.--Flag and other officers attached to the James River Squadron, including Joseph N. Barney, Barron, Buchanan, Forrest, Robert D. Minor, Mitchell, and Tattnall, loaned their papers to the Office of Naval Records and Library. Copies of their correspondence are filed in

the area file (area 7) described above. A letters-sent book of Lt. Joseph N. Barney, Dec. 3, 1861-Apr. 20, 1863, is still intact and contains fair copies of letters he wrote while commanding the Jamestown to Captains Lynch, Tattnall, and Sidney S. Lee; Secretary Mallory; the Office of Orders and Detail; the Office of Ordnance and Hydrography; and enlisted personnel. A report of Mar. 27, 1862, by Captain Buchanan and a narrative by H. Ashton Ramsay, chief engineer, C.S.N., of the Monitor-Merrimack battle on Mar. 8-9, 1862, is in subject file HA.

A register of money, clothing, and small stores paid out or issued during Nov. 1861-Feb. 1862 (2 vols.), is also in the Naval Records Collection. It was apparently kept by Asst. Paymaster James O. Moore who was probably attached at the time to the naval forces of Virginia and North Carolina.

Documents from the records	ser. 1, vol. 6, p. 710-781, vol. 7, p.
described above and other sources	748-801, vol. 10, p. 625-805, and
are in Official Records...Navies,	vols. 8-10, passim.

Records in Other Custody. --Samuel Barron's papers in the William and Mary College Library contain correspondence relating to his two tours of duty in Virginia. Letters-sent books, July 20-Aug. 27, 1861, and Oct. 2, 1862-Mar. 4, 1865 (2 vols.), contain letters to Secretary Mallory and Capt. French Forrest, the commandant of the Norfolk Navy Yard, regarding the formation and equipment of the squadron, instructions to officers commanding vessels in the squadron, and copies of orders from the Navy Department.

A letters-sent book of Capt. Franklin Buchanan, Mar. 3, 1862-Nov. 20, 1863, in the Southern Historical Collection in the University of North Carolina Library contains fair copies of letters and reports to Secretary Mallory relating to his activities as flag officer of the naval forces in Virginia, his hospitalization at the Norfolk Naval Hospital, and his recuperation at Greensboro, N.C. Also included are letters to the officers of the squadron and to the Office of Orders and Detail.

Letters-sent press copy books of Capt. French Forrest, Dec. 1, 1863-May 6, 1864 (2 vols.), are in the Archives Division of the Virginia State Library. Letters to officers commanding vessels concern operations, provisions, equipment, personnel, inspection of marines, pilots, and leaves of absence. Other letters are to the Secretary of the Navy, Navy Department offices, and Comdr. Robert G. Robb of the Rocketts Navy Yard. An order book, Dec. 1, 1861-Jan. 31, 1864, and orders, Feb. 1-May 6, 1864 (microfilm), are in the Southern Historical Collection in the University of North Carolina Library.

A diary of Raphael Semmes, Sept. 28, 1864-May 27, 1865, in Duke University Library, chronicles events from the time of his landing in England after the sinking of the Alabama until his arrival in Alabama after the war.

Smaller lots of officers' papers provide further documentation. The papers of Lt. James H. Rochelle in Duke University Library contain correspondence relating to his service on the Patrick Henry and on the Nansemond. Included are letters from the flag officers of the squadron, the commanding officer of the Patrick Henry, the Office of Orders and Detail, the Office of Ordnance and Hydrography, Paymaster de Bree, and Secretary Mallory. The Minor family papers in the Virginia Historical Society collections contain some reports, May-June 1864, received by Lt. Robert D. Minor, ordnance

officer of the squadron regarding ordnance and ordnance stores on board
vessels. Official records of Marsden Bellamy, assistant paymaster on the
Richmond in 1864, in the Southern Historical Collection in the University
of North Carolina Library include appointment letters from Secretary Mallory, orders, rolls of officers and men, transfer accounts, muster rolls,
and returns of provisions, clothing, and small stores. The letters of Comdr.
John M. Kell, commanding the Richmond in 1865, in Duke University Library contain some information on his naval duties. Two letters of appreciation from Secretary Mallory to Lt. Catesby ap R. Jones for services on
the Merrimack during the battle with the Monitor are in the Manuscript
Division of the Library of Congress.

North Carolina Squadron

This squadron was formed in 1861 with a nucleus of vessels of the
North Carolina State Navy, including the Winslow, the Ellis, the Raleigh,
and the Beaufort. In the same year the Winslow was wrecked while on a
rescue mission, and the Forrest and the Sea Bird were acquired. The
squadron operated first as a part of the naval defenses of Virginia and North
Carolina under Capt. Samuel Barron and then Capt. William F. Lynch, but
after Buchanan assumed command in Virginia in Mar. 1862 Captain Lynch
commanded only in North Carolina. In an engagement with a superior U. S.
fleet off Roanoke Island on Feb. 7, 1862, the Curlew was sunk, and in the
battle of Elizabeth City on Feb. 10 Lynch's flagship, the Sea Bird, was sunk,
the Ellis captured, and the Forrest burned. Additions to the squadron in
1863 included the North Carolina and the Arctic, and in 1864 the Raleigh,
the Yadkin, the Equator, and the Squib. The Albemarle completed in the
same year on the Roanoke River and the Neuse on the Neuse River served
on those rivers. The North Carolina sank in the Cape Fear River from a
leak in Sept. 1864, and in the next month the Albemarle was torpedoed. The
Equator, the Arctic, and the Yadkin were burned when Wilmington was
captured in Jan. 1865, and the Neuse met the same fate on the approach of
Sherman's army.
Successive commanders of this squadron:
Capt. William F. Lynch, Mar. 1862.
Capt. Robert F. Pinkney, 1864.
Record Group 45.--Some documents on the activities of naval vessels
off the coast of North Carolina are in the area file (area 7) in the Naval
Records Collection. The logbook of the Ellis, Aug. 2, 1861-Feb. 6, 1862
(captured at Elizabeth City on Feb. 10, 1862), gives information about its
cruise with the squadron off the coast of North Carolina, the transportation
of Confederate troops, the return to Norfolk in Nov. 1861 for repairs, and
further cruising with the squadron. For the Raleigh there is an 1861 record
of clothing and small stores and provisions issued and contingent expenditures and invoices of materials received at the Norfolk Navy Yard.
Records in Other Custody.--A letter from Secretary Mallory to the
flag officer at Wilmington, Nov. 5, 1864, is in the North Carolina Department of Archives and History.
In Mar. 1952 the Georgia Historical Society bought the official records
of C. Lucian Jones, assistant paymaster on the North Carolina from Dec.
1863 to Mar. 1865. Incoming letters are from Secretary Mallory, Paymaster de Bree, Captain Lynch, Capt. Robert F. Pinkney (the commandant at
Wilmington), the Office of Orders and Detail, W. H. Peters (naval store-

keeper at Charlotte), enclosing invoices of stores shipped and requests
from ship commanders for rations, and from Comdr. John Taylor Wood
regarding the purchase of supplies for the proposed expedition against Point
Lookout, Md. Records that document the procurement and distribution of
supplies, travel, pay of naval personnel, the handling of funds, and accounting include abstracts of expenditures, accounts current, certificates of
deposit, vouchers, receipts, invoices, requisitions, muster rolls and payrolls, lists of men transferred, lists of deserters, and acknowledgments
of the receipt and approval of bounty pay. An accompanying list shows the
materials for each vessel. For Battery Buchanan at Wilmington there are
returns of men received, a roster of the marine guard, lists of deserters
and of men hospitalized, and abstracts of clothing issued.

Some papers of Samuel Barron, Jr., in the William and Mary College
Library, include his orders of 1862 to report to the Beaufort and later to the
Raleigh. The papers of James R. Randall, secretary to Flag Officer Lynch
at Wilmington in 1864, are in the Southern Historical Collection in the University of North Carolina Library.

Documents on naval activities   1, vols. 6-12, passim. An abstract
off the coast of North Carolina are   of the logbook of the Ellis is in vol.
in Official Records...Navies, ser.   6, p. 781-789.

Charleston Squadron

The command of the naval defenses of South Carolina was united with
that of Georgia under Capt. Josiah Tattnall until the beginning of 1862 when
Comdr. Duncan N. Ingraham arrived in Charleston to assume charge there
of a separate squadron. During 1863 the Charleston Squadron consisted of
the ironclads Chicora, Charleston, and Palmetto State and the tender Juno.
On the evacuation of Charleston in Feb. 1865 the squadron was destroyed to
prevent its capture by U.S. forces.

Successive commanders of this squadron:
    Comdr. Duncan N. Ingraham, 1862.
    Comdr. John R. Tucker, Mar. 1863.

Record Group 45.--The Naval Records Collection includes records
obtained from Flag Officers Tattnall and Tucker and small lots from Comdr.
William A. Webb and Chief Engr. James H. Tomb who served with the
Charleston Squadron. Letters of flag officers of this squadron, the Secretary of the Navy, Navy Department offices, and commanding officers of
naval squadrons, vessels, and stations are in the area file (area 8), and
correspondence and other documents are in the subject file.

Some original manuscripts of Comdr. William A. Webb in subject
file OM consist of letters he received in Apr. 1863, while he was attached
to the squadron, from Flag Officer Tucker and Army officers regarding
preparations for the defense of the harbor. Some original manuscripts of
James H. Tomb in subject file HA consist of letters from Tucker and Army
officers, Nov.-Dec. 1864, concerning preparations to test torpedo boats.

Documents relating to opera-   lina waters are in Official Records
tions of naval forces in South Caro-   ...Navies, ser. 1, vols. 12-16, passim.

Records in Other Custody.--Papers of Chief Engr. James H. Tomb
given to the Southern Historical Collection in the University of North

Carolina Library by the Tomb family include original correspondence and a memoir of his experiences in the Confederate Navy. A report by Tomb of Aug. 8, 1863, concerns the capture of a launch and a report of Oct. 6, 1863, concerns the attack by the David on the U.S.S. New Ironsides. A copy of Tomb's memoir and some of his correspondence is in the South Caroliniana Library of the University of South Carolina and another copy of the memoir is in the Naval History Division's subject file ZB in the National Archives Building. An extensive group of papers of Lt. James H. Rochelle, 1850-69, in Duke University Library includes letters of the war period relating to his services with the Charleston Squadron and the Charleston station. A letter from Rochelle to Secretary Mallory, June 8, 1863, gives an account of the grounding of the C.S.S. Stono. Two letters Rochelle wrote while on the C.S.S. Palmetto State at Charleston, July 17, 1864, in the New-York Historical Society collections concern officers' promotions and assignments, the expedition against Point Lookout, Md., movements of vessels, and attacks on Fort Johnson and James Island, S.C.

Savannah River Squadron

In 1861 the former passenger boat Savannah and the tugs Sampson, Resolute, and Lady Davis were assembled as a squadron at Savannah and by Feb. 1862 the Huntress and five gunboats had been added. When the command at Savannah was divided in Mar. 1863, Captain Tattnall was given command of the naval station, and Comdr. Richard L. Page, the squadron. Late in that year the squadron comprised the Savannah, Georgia, Isondiga, Sampson, Resolute, and Firefly; the captured Water Witch and the Macon were added in 1864. When Savannah was bombarded in Dec. 1864, some vessels of the squadron were burned, blown up, or sunk, and the Resolute was captured during the retreat up the Savannah River. Captain Hunter remained at Augusta with the Sampson and the Macon until he surrendered on May 4, 1865.
   Successive commanders of this squadron:
   Capt. Josiah Tattnall, 1861.
   Lt. John N. Maffitt (acting), Mar. 1862.
   Capt. Josiah Tattnall, 1862.
   Comdr. Richard L. Page, Mar. 1863.
   Comdr. William A. Webb, May 1863.
   Capt. William W. Hunter, June 1863.

   Charles C. Jones, Jr., The   Josiah Tattnall (Savannah, 1878).
Life and Services of Commodore

   Record Group 45. --The Naval Records Collection includes records received from Tattnall, Webb, and Hunter. The original records obtained from Comdr. William A. Webb are in subject file OM. His letters-sent book, May 22-June 15, 1863, contains fair copies of letters to Secretary Mallory, Navy Department offices, Captain Tattnall, and to Army officers at Savannah and the camps of instruction near Macon and Atlanta. Lists and inventories of stores and some letters from Lucius S. Seymour to Commanders Page and Webb are included.
   Several volumes of paymaster's records relate to the Savannah River Squadron. A record of provisions and small stores received and expended and a record of clothing received on board the Georgia and the Isondiga,

Oct. 1863-Sept. 1864, was kept by DeWitt C. Seymour. Some steward's weekly returns of provisions expended, May 1861-Dec. 1864 (3 vols.), show on printed forms the number of men subsisted each day and the quantities and kinds of provisions expended, with notations in the remarks column on discharges, transfers, detachments, desertions, and the arrival of men, sometimes with their names. These volumes contain returns of varying dates for the Savannah, Oconee, Resolute, Firefly, Gunboat No. 1, Georgia, and Isondiga. A "general pay and receipt book" of the Georgia, Oct. 1862-Sept. 1863, kept by DeWitt C. Seymour contains individual accounts showing name, rank, and amounts of payments to officers and crew for pay, clothing, small stores, grog, undrawn rations, and hospital expenses. In this volume are copies of detachment orders of officers and notations as to transfers of men among vessels of the squadron, dates of reporting, discharges, ratings, medical surveys, and disratings.

Published documents in Official Records...Navies, ser. 1, vol. 14, p. 689 ff., vol. 15, p. 691-773 (Apr. 13, 1863-May 1, 1865), include correspondence, orders, reports, and appointments.

Records in Other Custody. --Savannah River Squadron records, including letters of Page, Webb, and Hunter and other documents, Dec. 27, 1862-Apr. 19, 1865 (600 pieces), are in the Keith Read Confederate Collection in Emory University Library. Incoming communications include letters, instructions, and general and special orders from Secretary Mallory, offices of the Navy Department, and military headquarters at Savannah, Augusta, and Charleston. Other communications from the commandant of the Savannah Naval Station, the Columbus Naval Iron Works, the paymaster at Savannah, surgeons attached to the squadron, and the flag officer commanding the Charleston Squadron concern the training of marines, personnel, ship repairs, fuel, and the health of crews. Copies of returns of guns on board vessels that were made to the Office of Ordnance and Hydrography are also in this collection.

In the Louisiana Historical Association collection on deposit in the Howard-Tilton Memorial Library of Tulane University are other records of the Savannah River Squadron, Apr. 10, 1863-May 1, 1865 (651 pieces). A letter and order book, Apr. 10-June 12, 1863, contains copies of letters and orders by Page, Webb, and Hunter to commanding officers of vessels in the squadron. Letters-sent books, June 28, 1863-Apr. 27, 1865 (3 vols.), contain a chronological record of fair copies of letters and telegrams to Secretary Mallory and offices of the Navy Department regarding the operations, supply, and personnel of the squadron. Other communications are to Capt. Josiah Tattnall (commandant of the Savannah Naval Station), Capt. J. R. Tucker (flag officer at Charleston), Col. Lloyd J. Beall, Lt. Gen. W. J. Hardee, and the Navy agent at Augusta. Also included are letters of appointment as acting mates. Letters and orders, June 30, 1863-May 1, 1865 (3 vols.), are to commanding officers of vessels in the squadron regarding their operations, personnel, marines, prisoners, and orders to surgeons, assistant engineers, assistant paymasters, gunners, and pilots. Other records for Aug. 1863-Apr. 1865 include letters received from Secretary Mallory, offices of the Navy Department, Josiah Tattnall, D. C. Seymour, the Navy agent at Augusta, Brig. Gen. H. W. Mercer, commanding the Military District of Georgia, and Capt. J. R. Tucker; drafts of letters sent; returns of punishment; lists of officers on vessels, signals, countersigns, stores, and clothing required; reports on men incapacitated; report on ammunition aboard; telegrams; and a journal of the Sampson, Dec. 10-25, 1864.

Additional letters received by Captain Hunter, Apr.-Oct. 1864, are in the Texas Archives in the University of Texas Library. Letters from officers and mates commanding vessels of the squadron concern repairs, personnel, deserters, pilots, and testing of engines. Other communications are from Capt. Josiah Tattnall, the fleet surgeon and other surgeons, Paymaster William W. Kelly at Savannah, the naval storekeeper at Savannah, Capt. J. R. Tucker, the Office of Orders and Detail, the marine barracks and the naval hospital at Savannah, Army headquarters in Savannah, and, from others, applications for and acceptances of appointments.

Other correspondence of Captain Hunter, 1864-65 (103 pieces), in Duke University Library is with Secretary Mallory, Capt. Sidney S. Lee and Comdr. John M. Brooke of the Navy Department, naval officers, and others concerning squadron vessels, supplies, personnel, the Water Witch, and torpedo-laying in Savannah harbor.

In other repositories are materials relating to the services of other officers in the Savannah River Squadron. Personal letters of Lt. George W. Gift, who was attached to the Savannah in 1864, are in the Southern Historical Collection in the University of North Carolina Library. An engineering notebook kept by Asst. Engr. George W. Tennent, 1861-64, in the Virginia Historical Society collections contains a list of Confederate officers captured at Fort Pulaski, Ga., on Apr. 11, 1862, and a drawing of the C.S.S. Atlanta. A diary kept by Passed Mid. Dabney M. Scales on board the Atlanta, Dec. 10, 1862-Apr. 17, 1863, is in Duke University Library.

Mobile Squadron

The squadron formed at Mobile early in 1862 consisted of the gunboats Morgan and Gaines and the schooner Alert. In 1863 it consisted of the Morgan, Gaines, floating batteries Tuscaloosa and Huntsville, ram Baltic, and the gunboat Selma. Additions to the squadron in 1864 included the Nashville and the Tennessee which Admiral Buchanan made his flagship. In the battle of Mobile Bay on Aug. 5, 1864, the Tennessee and the Selma were captured and the Gaines was beached, but the Morgan escaped to Mobile. On the approach of U.S. forces in Mar. 1865, Capt. Ebenezer Farrand sank the Tuscaloosa and the Huntsville and fled up the Tombigbee River where he was blockaded. He surrendered on May 10.

Successive commanders of this squadron:
    Capt. Victor M. Randolph, 1862.
    Adm. Franklin Buchanan, Aug. 1862.
    Capt. Ebenezer Farrand, Aug. 1864.

Record Group 45.--Correspondence of the flag officers of the Mobile Squadron (Randolph, Buchanan, and Farrand) and of other officers concerning the squadron is in the area file (area 6) and in the subject file. Some original records of Captain Randolph, Feb. 15, 1862-Feb. 23, 1863 (1/4 in.), in subject file PB consist of copies of letters sent to the Office of Orders and Detail, to Secretary Mallory recommending the construction of ironclads, to Gov. John G. Shorter on defense measures, to Sen. William L. Yancey requesting the submission of the matter of his promotion to Congress, and to Comdr. Charles H. Kennedy, the commanding officer of the Morgan. Incoming letters are from Commander Kennedy, the Office of Orders and

Detail, and the Secretary of War.
Also in the Naval Records Collection are the following: a logbook of the Tennessee, Feb. 16-July 31, 1864, Lt. James D. Johnston commanding; and two medical record books of the Gaines, May 1, 1862-Aug. 31, 1863, kept by Asst. Surg. Osborn S. Iglehart (subject file MM).

Documents relating to the   Records . . . Navies, ser. 1, vols.
Mobile Squadron are in Official   20-22, passim.

Records in Other Custody. --Admiral Buchanan's letter book, Mar. 3, 1863, in the Southern Historical Collection in the University of North Carolina Library contains letters, orders, and reports written from the "Naval Commandant's Office" at Mobile, Sept. 12, 1862-Nov. 20, 1863. Letters addressed to Secretary Mallory, the Office of Orders and Detail, the Office of Medicine and Surgery, Col. Lloyd J. Beall, President Davis, and officers of the squadron and nearby naval stations concern the operations of the squadron, work on the cruiser Florida at the naval station, the construction of vessels at Mobile, Oven Bluff, and Selma, the defense of Mobile Bay, personnel matters, the marine guard, the procurement of iron, coal and ordnance, the disposition of men from the Mississippi River Squadron, and discipline and court-martial cases.

In the same repository are a journal of the Florida (renamed the Selma), Feb. 12-July 4, 1862, by Acting Mid. Thomas L. Moore; a microfilm of letters and orders of Lt. Thomas L. Harrison, commander of the Morgan, 1862-64, and of the Nashville, 1865; personal letters, 1862-63, of Charles I. Graves; and letters of Lt. George W. Gift from the Baltic and Gaines in 1863. For the Tennessee a few documents of 1864 are in the Library of Congress, a descriptive list of the crew, Feb. 1864, is in the Confederate Museum, and quarter and fire bills, 1864, are in the Ohio Historical Society collections.

An extensive collection of official records of John M. Pearl, 1863-65 (600 items), accumulated while he was assistant paymaster on the Morgan, Mobile Squadron, is in the Connecticut State Library. The correspondence includes letters from Admiral Buchanan, Captain Farrand, Secretary Mallory, and Comdr. George W. Harrison. There are also military orders, copies of transfer and discharge orders, payrolls, a payroll account book, checks, orders to the storekeeper, bills of exchange on Richmond, letters of introduction, surgeons' reports, and printed Confederate Navy circulars.

Mississippi River Squadron

During 1861 the Navy built up a squadron for the defense of the Mississippi River and the coast of Louisiana. Navy officers sent to New Orleans acquired and had converted into warships the side-wheel steamers Bienville, Carondelet, Ivy, Jackson, Livingston, Maurepas, Pamlico, and Pontchartrain. They purchased and armed the steamers Florida, General Polk, McRae, and Mobile, fitted out the floating batteries New Orleans and Memphis, and took over the revenue cutters Morgan and Pickens. Other vessels built locally under contract included the ironclads Louisiana, Manassas, and Mississippi. Late in 1861 part of the squadron ascended the Mississippi to cooperate with the Army in stopping the descent of U. S. vessels; some of the squadron's vessels were destroyed and others took flight. In Apr. 1862 another part of the squadron was largely destroyed in a battle below New

Orleans. The Arkansas assisted Gen. Earl Van Dorn in thwarting the attempt of the U.S. fleet to take Vicksburg, but it developed engine trouble and had to be blown up. In 1863 the Pontchartrain was burned in the Arkansas River and the Ivy and the Mobile in the Yazoo River to prevent their capture by Union forces which thereafter controlled the Mississippi River.
Successive commanders of this squadron:
    Capt. Lawrence Rousseau, Mar. 1861.
    Capt. George N. Hollins, Aug. 1861.
    Comdr. John K. Mitchell, Apr. 20, 1862.
    Capt. William F. Lynch, June 1862.
    Record Group 45. --Flag Officers Hollins and Mitchell gave a few manuscripts to the Office of Naval Records and Library. The area file (area 5) and the subject file in the Naval Records Collection contain correspondence by the flag officers and others. Commander Mitchell's report of Aug. 19, 1862, on the naval battle of Apr. 24 with 14 enclosures is in subject file HA. In the same place are letters received by Lt. John J. Guthrie, Feb.-Mar. 1862, while commanding a floating battery on the Mississippi River under Captain Hollins. A notebook diary of Mid. John A. Wilson relating to his service on the Arkansas in the summer of 1862 is in the Naval Records Collection.

Mitchell's report and enclosures referred to above, records of the court of inquiry concerning the naval defeat on the Mississippi, and other documents are in Official Records . . . Navies, ser. 1, vol. 1, p. 289-334, and passim.

Red River Squadron

In Sept. 1863 the ironclad steam gunboat Missouri was delivered to the naval defenses of western Louisiana, whose headquarters was at Alexandria on the Red River. Although guns were mounted on the Missouri, its activities were limited to transporting and mining between Alexandria and Shreveport. The Cotton accompanied it as a tender, and the wooden ram William H. Webb also became part of the squadron. In Apr. 1865 the William H. Webb was burned by its crew, and in June the Missouri surrendered at Alexandria and the Cotton was seized.
Successive commanders of this squadron:
    Comdr. Thomas W. Brent, 1863.
    Lt. Jonathan H. Carter, Nov. 1863.
    Record Group 45. --On taking command of the Red River Squadron, Lieutenant Carter continued to record outgoing letters in the volume he had used as commandant of the station at Shreveport. These letters, Nov. 4, 1863-May 5, 1865 (p. 52-150), to Secretary Mallory, the Office of Orders and Detail, and Asst. Paymaster Edward McKean at Shreveport concern the condition of command and personnel matters; others to Army officers at Shreveport and Houston concern the crew of the Missouri and supplies for the vessels of the squadron. The volume is in the Naval Records Collection.
    Records in Other Custody. --A few records of the Red River Squadron, Mar.-Oct. 1863, when Commander Brent was in command, are in the Manuscript Division of the Library of Congress. They include a muster roll, lists of officers, orders to officers, engineers' requisitions for tools, orders to officers from the Office of Orders and Detail, and shipping articles

of enlisted men.

Galveston Squadron

In the summer of 1861 Comdr. William W. Hunter, after reporting to the War Department on orders of the Secretary of the Navy, went to Texas where he was placed in charge of the naval defenses of Galveston. In this position he was subordinate to Brig. Gen. Paul O. Hébert, commander of the Military Department of Texas. For more than a year Hunter worked with the Army in building up the fortifications of Galveston. He armed and manned the schooner Royal Yacht for use in communicating with the mainland, placed a crew on the former revenue schooner Henry Dodge, and chartered the former mailboat Bayou City. When the Union expedition appeared, however, the Confederates decided that Galveston was not strong enough to resist attack and withdrew on Oct. 8, 1862. Afterward Hunter disputed with the Army the disposition to be made of the Henry Dodge and its ordnance, but despite his protests the crew and arms of that vessel were transferred to the Bayou City which the Army planned to use with other vessels in an attack on Galveston. Galveston was recaptured on Jan. 1, 1863, and with it the U.S.S. Harriet Lane, which soon afterward was transferred to the Confederate Navy. On Apr. 15, 1863, Hunter transferred the men under his command to Lt. Joseph N. Barney for service on the Harriet Lane. Barney's command was brief, for the Secretary of the Navy ordered the return of that vessel to the Army.

Successive commanders of this squadron:
Comdr. William W. Hunter, 1861.
Lt. Joseph N. Barney, Apr. 15, 1863.

Record Group 45. --The area file (area 6) in the Naval Records Collection contains some correspondence relating to the Galveston Squadron. Part of the letters-sent book of Comdr. Joseph N. Barney covers the period of his command of the Harriet Lane, Feb. 13-Apr. 20, 1863 (p. 68-98). The book contains fair copies of letters to Secretary Mallory and the Office of Orders and Detail concerning the condition, equipment, and personnel of the Harriet Lane and to Army officers regarding its movements, coal, and armament.

Correspondence of Commander Hunter is in the file of naval service records which is described in chapter XI of this Guide.

Records in Other Custody. --Official records of the Galveston Squadron are in the W. W. Hunter papers, Aug. 1861-Apr. 1863, in the Louisiana Historical Association collection on deposit in the Howard-Tilton Memorial Library of Tulane University. Correspondence, including drafts of letters sent and received, is with Secretary Mallory, offices of the Navy Department, commanding officers of vessels, Paymaster John W. Nixon at New Orleans, Brig. Gen. P. O. Hébert and other Army officers, and business firms and individuals from whom vessels were chartered. Other materials include lists of steam vessels in Galveston Bay, charter parties of vessels hired for the use of the Navy, a transcript of the journal of the Dodge, Oct. 1861, lists of seamen, and orders of the Military Department of Texas. A logbook of the Bayou City, Sept. 26, 1861-Oct. 28, 1862 (with a journal for Dec. 16, 1862-Apr. 24, 1863), supplies information about its activities and those of the squadron.

Other correspondence of Commander Hunter, July 1861-May 1863 (ca. 80 items), is in the Texas Archives of the University of Texas Library. It includes reports to Secretary Mallory, instructions to officers, correspondence with Paymaster John W. Nixon at New Orleans and Jackson, Miss., communications with General Hébert and other Army officers regarding the operations of the squadron and the placement of guns, and acceptances of appointments.

Correspondence, reports, and orders relating to the Galveston Squadron are in Official Records . . . Navies, ser. 1, vol. 16, p. 835-859, vol. 17, p. 149-169, vol. 18, p. 823-855, vol. 19, p. 785-842, and vol. 20, p. 804-822. For an abstract of the logbook of the Bayou City, Master Philip F. Appel commanding, see vol. 16, p. 859-869, vol. 17, p. 170-175, and vol. 18, p. 825-829. For an abstract of Hunter's journal, Dec. 16, 1862-Apr. 24, 1863, see vol. 19, p. 813-817.

NAVAL BATTERIES

In 1861 the Confederate Navy Department assigned naval officers to command batteries on rivers and at seaports. Batteries that had been erected by the Virginia Navy were transferred to Confederate service in June 1861 along with the personnel manning them. The batteries on the Elizabeth River and in its vicinity were located at Fort Norfolk, Fort Nelson Naval Hospital, Craney Island, Bush's Bluff, Pinner's Point, Sewell's Point, Lambert's Point, Barrett's Point, Town Point, and Pig Point. On the York River batteries under naval command were at West Point, Gloucester Point, and Yorktown. Lowry's Point on the Rappahannock River was the site of another battery. To protect routes leading from the Potomac River to Richmond, including the terminus of the Richmond, Fredericksburg, and Potomac Railroad on Aquia Creek, batteries were constructed at the mouth of Aquia Creek, at nearby Simms' Point, at Potomac Creek, and at Potomac Creek Bridge. Batteries established at Evansport on the Potomac River in Sept. 1861 under the command of Comdr. Ebenezer Farrand were abandoned in Mar. 1862. The first batteries on the James River were at Fort Powhatan and Jamestown Island. In May 1862 after the Union invasion of southern Virginia began, strong fortifications were built at Drewry's Bluff on the west bank of the James River 7 miles below Richmond and at Chaffin's Bluff 1 1/2 miles below Drewry's Bluff on the opposite side of the river. Farrand's command of the naval, marine, and army personnel manning the batteries and entrenchments at Drewry's Bluff was brief. Capt. Sidney S. Lee assumed that command in May 1862 and exercised it until 1864 when he was succeeded by Lt. Col. George H. Terrett, C.S.M.C. In Oct. 1864, Capt. John K. Mitchell, as flag officer of the James River Squadron, assigned some of his officers and enlisted personnel to Batteries Brooke, Semmes, and Wood on the James River. On Nov. 15, 1864, Mitchell transferred command of these batteries to Lt. William Bradford. Farther south there were naval batteries at Indian Wells, N.C., and Battery Buchanan at Wilmington. Naval officers also participated in the construction of batteries at other points on the coast including Charleston, Apalachicola, Mobile, Ship Island, and Galveston, and naval gunners were sometimes assigned to them.

A list of the naval defenses of
Virginia, June 1861, in Official
Records . . . Navies, ser. 1, vol.
5, p. 804-806, includes the names
of officers commanding batteries.

William M. Robinson, Jr., "Drewry's
Bluff: Naval Defense of Richmond,
1862, " Civil War History, 7:167-175
(June 1961).

Record Group 45. --A logbook of Battery Brooke on the James River,
Oct. 28, 1864-Apr. 2, 1865, when it was commanded by Lt. John H. Ingraham and then Lt. Charles Borum, is in the Naval Records Collection. It
gives information on personnel, supplies, the activities of the battery, and
the mounting and firing of guns, with some references to other batteries.
A diary of Mid. John A. Wilson describes activities at Drewry's Bluff from
Oct. 1862 to Apr. 1863.

Records in Other Custody. --The papers of Lt. John Taylor Wood in
the Southern Historical Collection in the University of North Carolina Library include many letters written from Drewry's Bluff to his wife in 1862.
Letters of Lt. William L. Maury, who was stationed at Sewell's Point on
the Elizabeth River in 1861, are in the University of Virginia Library.

NAVAL PROCUREMENT IN EUROPE

Throughout the war the Confederate Navy Department maintained an
agent in England whose duty was to purchase or contract for the building of
vessels and to obtain naval supplies. The agent selected for this secret
mission was Comdr. James D. Bulloch who reached Liverpool on June 4,
1861. He succeeded in acquiring for the Confederate Navy the cruisers
Florida, Alabama, Alexandra, Georgiana, and Shenandoah which did much
damage to U. S. shipping during the war. These vessels went to sea as
merchant ships, but they were met at prearranged rendezvous by tenders
from which were transferred the armament that was used to fit them out as
warships. Bulloch contracted with the Messrs. Laird of Birkenhead for
two ironclad rams, but a threat of war by the United States resulted in their
purchase by the British Navy. In 1863 Bulloch contracted with a shipbuilder
at Bordeaux, France, for the construction of four wooden screw corvettes
and two ironclads, but under pressure from the U. S. minister the French
Government prevented the delivery of these vessels. By devious means,
however, one of the corvettes was acquired by the Confederacy and became
the Stonewall. Bulloch was designated in 1864 for the purchase and construction of Government blockade-runners employed for exporting cotton and importing war supplies. Other officers who served with Bulloch included Lt.
John Low and Lt. Robert R. Carter.

Lt. James H. North contracted with a Clyde River shipbuilder for an
ironclad vessel that he was to command, but the British Government inter-
fered and the vessel was sold to Denmark. Comdr. Matthew F. Maury,
who reached London in Dec. 1862, was authorized to purchase a cruiser.
In Mar. 1863 he bought a new steamer that he then had converted into the
Georgia. Late in 1863 he negotiated the purchase of another steamer that
became the Rappahannock when Confederate naval officers assumed command of her in the English Channel. He gathered information on torpedoes
and guns, conducted laboratory experiments on torpedoes, and sent data
and equipment to the Navy Department in Richmond. On a mission similar
to North's, Lt. George T. Sinclair contracted with a shipyard at Glasgow
for a steamer, but it was seized by the British government before it was

completed. Lt. William H. Murdaugh inspected and arranged for the transportation of ordnance stores.

James D. Bulloch, The Secret Service of the Confederate States in Europe; or, How the Confederate Cruisers Were Equipped (2 vols.; New York, 1884); Williams, Matthew Fontaine Maury.

Record Group 45.--Records accumulated by Comdr. James D. Bulloch in England during the war included correspondence with the Secretary of the Navy, Confederate commissioners in Europe, shipbuilders, agents, and others. In 1894 the Office of Naval Records and Library borrowed two lots of Bulloch's papers through his nephew, the Hon. Theodore Roosevelt, had them copied, and returned them. Efforts of historians to locate the original Bulloch papers in recent years have been unsuccessful.

Comdr. James H. North also loaned his papers to the Office of Naval Records and Library for copying (190 documents were returned to him). Included was correspondence with Secretary Mallory, Bulloch, Barron, Maury, other naval officers, British shipyards and firms, James M. Mason (the Confederate commissioner in England), and Colin J. McRae (the Confederate financial agent in Europe).

Bulloch used his own papers and other documentary sources in preparing his Secret Service of the Confederate States in Europe, in which he published some of his correspondence of 1861-63 with Secretary Mallory, letters to naval officers, and the report of Lt. Thomas K. Porter, Feb. 20, 1865, on the capture of the Florida by the U.S.S. Wachusett. Other correspondence on the construction of Confederate cruisers in England including letters of Bulloch is in U.S. Department of State, Correspondence Concerning Claims Against Great Britain . . . (7 vols.; Washington, 1869-71). A much larger quantity of correspondence on the same subject, particularly with Secretary Mallory, Lt. James H. North, and others, is in Official Records . . . Navies, ser. 2, vol. 2. Documents from North's papers also appear in this volume.

Records in Other Custody.--Matthew F. Maury's papers in the Manuscript Division of the Library of Congress contain some wartime correspondence relating to his activities in Europe including instructions of Feb. 21, 1863, from Secretary Mallory and a record book concerning his experiments with electric torpedoes, Dec. 1864-May 1865. Other Maury papers are in Duke University Library, the Henry E. Huntington Library, and the Virginia Historical Society collections.

CONFEDERATE STATES NAVAL FORCES IN EUROPE

Capt. Samuel Barron and his staff went to England in the summer of 1863 to obtain crews for the ironclad rams under construction at Birkenhead. When those vessels were purchased by the British Navy, Barron moved to Paris where he established his headquarters as Flag Officer Commanding Confederate States Naval Forces in Europe. His staff included in May 1864 Commanders North, Sinclair, and Joseph N. Barney; and Lts. Henry B. Claiborne and John H. Ingraham. They were concerned with the construction of ironclads in France, the repair and fitting out of the Georgia and the Stonewall, the manning of cruisers, and the procurement

of naval supplies for shipment on blockade-runners. Felix Senac served
as paymaster under Barron, 1863-65.
    Records in Other Custody. --Samuel Barron's papers were given to
the William and Mary College Library in 1942. Part of them relate to his
activities as Flag Officer Commanding Confederate States Naval Forces in
Europe. A letters-sent book, Jan. 5, 1864-Mar. 4, 1865, contains copies
of letters to Secretary Mallory; to officers commanding the Florida (J. N.
Barney and Charles M. Morris), the Georgia (William L. Maury and William E. Evans), and the Rappahannock (Lt. W. P. A. Campbell); to M. F.
Maury, G. T. Sinclair, J. D. Bulloch, J. H. North, and other officers in
Europe; to the Office of Ordnance and Hydrography; and to James M. Ma-
son, the Confederate commissioner in England. Letters were received
from most of these officers, from Lt. Charles M. Fauntleroy aboard the
Rappahannock at Calais, from Secretary Mallory, and from Capt. Raphael
Semmes while he was aboard the Alabama at Cherbourg and in England.
The correspondence and reports concern the operations of the cruisers and
their supply, repair, personnel, and disposition. Other documents include
lists of officers and crews, vessels captured by the Florida, the crew of
the Alabama saved by the British ship Deerhound, and the crew and prisoners of the Alabama. A diary of James H. North in the Southern Historical
Collection in the University of North Carolina Library contains entries for
1861 on duties performed for the Navy in the Confederacy and at Liverpool,
London, and Paris.
    A diary of Lt. Francis T. Chew, May 16, 1863-Sept. 16, 1864, is in
the same repository. It concerns his trip to Europe with a party of naval
officers including John Grimball, Edmund G. Read, William F. Carter,
Alexander M. Mason, Thomas J. Charlton, Bennett W. Green, and Samuel S. Gregory.
    The William C. Whittle collection in the Norfolk Museum of Arts and
Sciences contains other correspondence relating to the activities of the Confederate Navy in Europe. Included are letters from Bulloch to Barron, Mar.
14, 1864-Feb. 16, 1865 (40 items), manuscripts relating to the Rappahannock,
July 8, 1864-Aug. 12, 1864 (34 items), letters from Secretary Mallory to
Barron, Oct. 1863-Apr. 6, 1864 (3 items), and letters from various officers to Barron, Feb. 9, 1864-Feb. 14, 1865 (27 items).

                                CRUISERS

    Though most Confederate naval vessels remained in home waters, a
few preyed upon U.S. merchant ships on the high seas. The Sumter ran
the blockade of the Mississippi River on June 30, 1861, then cruised in the
Caribbean and the Atlantic under Comdr. Raphael Semmes before it was
abandoned at Gibraltar in Jan. 1862. Lt. Robert B. Pegram commanded
the Nashville on a cruise from Charleston to England in the fall of 1861. A
British-built steamer left Liverpool in July 1862, and as the Alabama under
Capt. Raphael Semmes raided U.S. shipping in the Atlantic, the West
Indies, and the Pacific before it was sunk by the U.S.S. Kearsarge off the
coast of France in June 1864. The Tuscaloosa, an American bark captured
by the Alabama in June 1863, made a cruise toward the Cape of Good Hope
under Lt. John Low. The Florida, another steamer that sailed from England in 1862, cruised under Capt. John N. Maffitt, Comdr. Joseph N. Barney, and Lt. Charles M. Morris in the North Atlantic, the West Indies, the
Gulf of Mexico, and the South Atlantic; it was rammed and seized in a

Brazilian port in Oct. 1864 by the U.S.S. Wachusett. Transferring from the Florida to a captured brig, the Clarence, in May 1863, Lt. Charles W. Read cruised off the Atlantic coast in that vessel and two other captures, the Tacony and the Archer, until his capture off the coast of New England in June. Acquired on the Clyde River in Scotland in Mar. 1863, the Georgia operated in the Atlantic under Comdr. William L. Maury and later Lt. William E. Evans; it was sold at Liverpool in June 1864. The Georgiana, a steamer built at Glasgow, was disabled by gunfire and later burned by Union blockaders after attempting to run into Charleston in Mar. 1865. After departing from the Thames River in Nov. 1863, the Rappahannock drifted to Calais where it was detained by the French Government; the commanding officers there were Lt. William F. Carter and Lt. Charles M. Fauntleroy. A converted blockade-runner, the Tallahassee, made a destructive cruise under Comdr. John T. Wood from Cape Hatteras to Halifax in the summer of 1864. This vessel left Wilmington as the Olustee at the end of Oct. 1864 under Lt. W. H. Ward and captured some ships off the Capes of Delaware. The Confederate Government then bought the Chickamauga at Wilmington and sent it on a raid up the Atlantic coast under Lt. John Wilkinson. The ironclad ram Stonewall, built in France and purchased in Denmark, was blockaded by U.S. vessels at Ferrol, Spain, and escaped across the Atlantic too late in 1865 to engage in any attacks on Union vessels. From Glasgow the Shenandoah, a former East Indiaman, sailed around the Cape of Good Hope and sank most of the Union whaling fleet in the northern Pacific in 1865. All together, Confederate cruisers sank or captured 260 merchant ships with cargoes valued at more than $20 million.

Edna and Frank Bradlow, Here Comes the Alabama; the Career of a Confederate Raider (Cape Town, 1958); Benjamin F. Gilbert, "Confederate Warships off Brazil," American Neptune, 15:287-302 (Oct. 1955); Jim Dan Hill, Sea Dogs of the Sixties; Farragut and Seven Contemporaries (Minneapolis, 1935); William S. Hoole, Four Years in the Confederate Navy; the Career of Captain John Low on the C.S.S.

Fingal, Florida, Alabama, Tuscaloosa, and Ajax (Athens, 1964); Stanley F. Horn, Gallant Rebel, the Fabulous Cruise of the C.S.S. Shenandoah (New Brunswick, 1947); Murray C. Morgan, Dixie Raider; the Saga of the C.S.S. Shenandoah (New York, 1948); Frank L. Owsley, Jr., The C.S.S. Florida; Her Building and Operations (Philadelphia, 1965); Walter A. Roberts, Semmes of the Alabama (Indianapolis, 1938).

Record Group 45. --Some Confederate naval officers who commanded cruisers lent their papers to the Office of Naval Records and Library for copying. Among them were Joseph N. Barney, commander of the Florida, 1863-64, William F. Carter, commander of the Rappahannock, 1863-64, John N. Maffitt, commander of the Florida, 1862-63, Thomas J. Page, commander of the Stonewall, 1864-65, Raphael Semmes, commander of the Sumter and later of the Alabama, George T. Sinclair, commander of the Georgiana, 1863, James I. Waddell, commander of the Shenandoah, 1864-65, and John T. Wood, commander of the Tallahassee, 1864. Copies of these papers were placed in the area file (area 4) and the subject file of the Naval Records Collection. Among the book records is a smooth copy of the logbook of the Florida, Jan. 9-Sept. 8, 1864, made on a printed form similar to two of the logbooks of this vessel in Record Group 76. An abstract of the logbook of the Florida, Aug. 17, 1862-May 31, 1863, prepared by

Mid. George D. Bryan is in a separate volume; like the other logbook for this vessel it helps to fill the gap in the series described under Record Group 76. In the same book is the log of the Lapwing (Mar. 30-Apr. 15, 1863), which was captured by the Florida and cruised briefly in the South Atlantic. Also included in Record Group 45 is a copy of the journal of Mid. Clarence Cary which is described below under Record Group 76.

In the Official Records . . . Navies, ser. 1, vols. 1-3, are more than 600 pages of documents relating to the operations of the Confederate cruisers. Included are records of Semmes relating to the cruise of the Sumter, 1861-62 (vol. 1, p. 613-686), extracts of his journal on the Sumter, May 24, 1861-Apr. 11, 1862 (vol. 1, p. 691-744); and extracts of his journal on the Alabama, Aug. 20, 1862-June 1864 (vol. 1, p. 783-817, vol. 2, p. 720-807, and vol. 3, p. 669-677). Documents are printed also in Raphael Semmes, The Log of the "Alabama" and the "Sumter" from the Private Journals and Other Papers of Commander R. Semmes, C.S.N., and Other Officers (London and New York, 1864); Laird Brothers, Birkenhead, Birkenhead Iron-Clads; Correspondence between Her Majesty's Government and Messrs. Laird Brothers; and an Appendix . . . Respecting the Iron-Clad Vessels Building at Birkenhead, 1863-4 (London, 1864). For copies of Semmes' correspondence relating to the Sumter, see the chapter on the State Department in this Guide. Reproductions of British Foreign Office records, Feb. 1863-June 1864, relating to the ironclads built at Birkenhead are in the Manuscript

Division of the Library of Congress. Papers relating to cruisers and their tenders are in the Foreign Office records in the British Public Record Office, London, England. The records include books containing crew lists and meager log entries on ship movements, copies of certificates of registration, permits for sale, and documents about the sale and repurchase of vessels. The vessels include the Agrippina, Ajax, Alar, Bahama, Bermuda, Chickamauga (Edith), Georgia, Georgiana, Hawk, Hercules, Louisa, Ann Fanny, Shenandoah, Southerner, Tallahassee, and Virginia. See Great Britain, Public Record Office, List of Foreign Office Records to 1878 Preserved in the Public Record Office, p. 20 (London, 1929). Registry documents concerning the Agrippina, the Alar, the Bahama, and the Florida, and probably others are in the General Register and Record Office of Shipping and Seamen (Ministry of Transport and Civil Aviation, Cardiff, Wales). Other manuscripts relating to the Alabama and other Confederate cruisers are described in Bernard R. Crick and Miriam Alman, eds., A Guide to Manuscripts Relating to America in Great Britain and Ireland (London and New York, 1961).

Record Group 59.--Some intercepted papers of Confederates in the general records of the Department of State relate to the C.S.S. Florida. These include letters received by Commanders Barney and Charles M. Morris, 1863-64, concerning the Florida's cruise, machinery, and repairs; and appointments by Barney of men in the ship's company, 1863-64. Records of Richard Taylor, assistant paymaster of the Florida, include letters received, vouchers, a payroll of officers, and a quarterly return of disbursements, 1863-64.

Record Group 76.--Among the records of the Geneva Tribunal of Arbitration are logbooks and other records of the C.S.S. Florida (available on microfilm as T 716). The logbooks (4 vols.) are for the periods Aug. 17, 1862-Jan. 22, 1863, and Sept. 17, 1863-Oct. 3, 1864. The other records include receipts for payments by Asst. Paymaster Richard Taylor, Sept. 1863-Oct. 1864; a medical journal kept by Asst. Surgeons Thomas J. Charlton and Thomas Emory, Feb. 1-Sept. 29, 1864; a list of the officers and crew of the Florida on Mar. 29, 1864, the date of the capture of the Avon; and the proceedings of a court held in Sept. 1864 to try eight crewmen on charges of mutinous conduct and sodomy.

Also in this record group is the journal of Mid. Clarence Cary, Sept. 24, 1864-Dec. 28, 1864 (microfilm in the University of Virginia Library), with quarter and station bills of the C.S.S. Palmetto State, notes on seamanship, remarks on events between Jan. 15 and Mar. 18, 1865, and ink or pencil sketches of the Chickamauga, the Drewry, the Frolic, the Roanoke, the Moultrie, the United States, and the Tallahassee. Lt. James Parker, U.S.N., sent this diary to the Navy Department at Washington after the war (Mrs. Burton N. Harrison, Recollections Grave and Gay, New York, 1911, p. 193).

A letter book of Lt. Charles M. Morris, Jan. 31-Sept. 29, 1864, contains copies of letters sent while he commanded the Florida and some letters received. They concern the cruise of the Florida, repairs to its engines, the procurement of supplies and fuel, and personnel matters. Included also is an engineering logbook of the Florida, Jan. 2-Oct. 4, 1864.

Cary's diary is reproduced in Brooks Thompson and Frank L. Owsley, Jr., eds., "The War Journal of Midshipman Cary," Civil War History, 9:187-202 (June 1963).

Record Group 84. --Copies of letters received by Lt. C. M. Morris from Commander Bulloch, Jan. 14, 1864, and from Commander Barney, Feb. 5, 1864 (enclosures in a letter from Secretary of State Seward to C. F. Adams, Dec. 21, 1864), are in the records of the U.S. Embassy in Great Britain in Record Group 84 (Records of the Foreign Service Posts of the Department of State). Bulloch's letter concerns the recruitment of men for service on the Florida; Barney's letter contains remarks on the use of the Florida's engines, on the payment of allotments made by crew members, and other matters.

Records in Other Custody. --The logbook of the Alabama, July 29, 1862-June 14, 1864, is in the Mobile Public Library, having been bought for the library in Dec. 1963 at Sotheby's in London for $3,640. A photographic copy of Lt. John Low's journal of the Alabama, July 28, 1862-June 20, 1863, is in the University of Alabama Library. William S. Hoole, whose work on Low is cited above, located this journal and that of the Tuscaloosa (see below) in 1957 in the hands of Low's descendants in England. An engineering logbook of the Florida, Jan. -Sept. 1863, is in the New-York Historical Society collections. Kept by Engineers John Spidel and Charles W. Quinn, it concerns a cruise from Mobile under Comdr. John N. Maffitt. The logbook of the Georgia, Apr. 9, 1863-Jan. 18, 1864, Lt. William L. Maury commanding, is in the Virginia Historical Society collections and another copy is in the Confederate Museum. The logbook of the Shenandoah, Oct. 20, 1864-Nov. 5, 1865 (2 vols.), Lt. James I. Waddell commanding, was acquired by the North Carolina Department of Archives and History in 1949 (microfilm in the Library of Congress and the University of North Carolina Library). The logbook of the Tuscaloosa kept by Lt. John Low, June 21-

Dec. 31, 1863, is in the University of Alabama Library. The engineering
logbook of the Stonewall, Jan. 25-May 17, 1865, Capt. Thomas J. Page
commanding, is in the Confederate Museum.
A journal of Lt. Francis T. Chew, Nov. 2, 1864-Nov. 4, 1865, concerning the cruise of the Shenandoah is in the Southern Historical Collection
in the University of North Carolina Library. While serving as an assistant
paymaster at Calais, France, during 1863-65, Douglas F. Forrest kept a
diary (Nov. 26, 1863-Dec. 13, 1864, and Mar. 5-June 25, 1865) now in the
Archives Division of the Virginia State Library. It describes activities on
the Rappahannock which was tied up at Calais and contacts with southerners
who visited France, including Mrs. Rose O'Neal Greenhow, naval officers,
and blockade-runners. Autobiographical notes, 1861-65, and a diary, Jan.
24-May 20, 1865, of Bennett W. Green, a naval surgeon, are in the University of Virginia Library. The diary concerns the voyage of the Stonewall
from Quiberon Bay to Coruna and Ferrol, Spain, and thence to Cuba. Asst.
Surg. Charles E. Lining kept diaries, 1855-76, that were purchased by the
Texas Archives of the University of Texas Library. A journal kept by Dr.
Lining on board the Shenandoah, Oct. 18, 1864-Nov. 8, 1865, is in the Confederate Museum (reproduced in Freeman, Calendar of Confederate Papers,
p. 126-163). Charles W. Quinn, assistant engineer of the Florida, kept a
journal of the cruise of that vessel, Jan. 1, 1863-Apr. 4, 1864; often it is
more detailed than the official logbook. It is in the Confederate Museum,
as is also Mid. John T. Mason's journal of the Shenandoah, Oct. 19, 1864-
Nov. 5, 1865.
        Records kept by Richard Taylor, assistant paymaster on the Florida,
1863-64, and at Liverpool, 1864-65, are in the possession of Harvey Smith
(1 Lexington Ave., New York, N.Y., 10010). They are for 1864-65 and include correspondence, orders, bills, vouchers, payrolls, check stubs,
canceled checks, receipts, allotments, officers' transfer accounts, notebooks, and accounts of crew members and officers of the Florida, Alabama,
Stonewall, and Shenandoah. Various papers of Lt. Samuel Barron, Jr.,
1863-64, when he served abroad, are with Taylor's papers.
        Wartime papers of Comdr. John N. Maffitt, Aug. 18, 1861-Feb. 24.
1865 (1 in.), relating to his command of the Florida during 1862-63 and later of the blockade-runners Florrie, Lilian, and Owl, were presented to
the Southern Historical Collection in the University of North Carolina Library in 1950 by a granddaughter. In the same repository are Raphael
Semmes' commissions as captain, June 2, 1864, and as rear admiral, Feb.
10, 1865. The papers of Lt. James I. Waddell in the North Carolina Department of Archives and History include a letter to Lord John Russell, Nov.
5, 1865, giving an account of the cruise of the Shenandoah during 1864-65
and its surrender to the British Government. The letters of Comdr. William L. Maury in the University of Virginia Library supply information regarding his command of the Georgia, Jan. 1863-Jan. 1864, earlier assignments at Sewell's Point, Va., and Charlotte, N.C., and his duties during
1864-65 at Wilmington and Richmond. In Duke University Library are letters by Comdr. John M. Kell concerning his command of the Savannah, his
cruises as executive officer on the Sumter and the Alabama, and his command of the Richmond in the James River Squadron. In the same repository is a long letter by Lt. John Grimball, Dec. 23, 1864, concerning the
cruise of the Shenandoah. The morning order book of William C. Whittle,
Jr., executive officer of the Shenandoah, is in the Norfolk Museum of Arts
and Sciences.

Some paymaster's vouchers pertaining to the C.S.S. Sumter, May 10-Sept. 14, 1861 (15 items), are in the Library of Congress. A pay, receipt, and muster roll of the Sumter, Apr. 1-Sept. 30, 1861, is in the Georgia Historical Society collections.

Correspondence between Commander Maffitt and Secretary Mallory, extracts from his journal, and letters to his family are in Emma M. Maffitt, The Life and Services of John Newland Maffitt (New York and Washington, 1906). See also Arthur Sinclair, Two Years on the Alabama (Boston and London, 1896); John McIntosh Kell, Recollections of a Naval Life, Including the Cruises of the Confederate States Steamers "Sumter" and "Alabama" (Washington, 1900); James I. Waddell, Shenandoah; the Memoirs of Lieutenant James I. Waddell, ed. by James D. Horan (New York, 1960). The contract made in 1861 by James D. Bulloch with John Laird Sons & Co., Shipbuilders, Birkenhead, England, for the construction of the Alabama, the specifications and principal dimensions, and a scale model are in the custody of Cammell Laird & Co., Birkenhead, England. Photographic copies of the documents are in the University of Alabama Library and in the Southern Historical Collection in the University of North Carolina Library.

Fawcett Preston & Co., Ltd., Wirral, Cheshire, England, has an order (or engine) book containing information regarding the engines built for the Florida and the Alexandra.

BLOCKADE-RUNNERS

Naval officers commanded blockade-runners that were acquired by the Confederate Government to transport arms, ammunition, and other supplies needed by the Confederacy. In the summer of 1861 Comdr. James D. Bulloch purchased the Bermuda in Liverpool and sent it to Savannah with a cargo of war supplies. In the fall of that year he bought the Fingal for the Navy and War Departments, loaded it with a valuable cargo of war supplies, and took it into Savannah. During 1862-63, Lt. John Wilkinson took the R. E. Lee through the blockade into Wilmington, and in 1864 he commanded the Chameleon on a voyage from that port to Bermuda. Comdr. John N. Maffitt ran the Gordon into the same port in 1862, and later commanded the Lilian and the Florrie. Unable to make port at either Wilmington or Charleston early in 1865, he took the Owl to Galveston, and then on the orders of the Secretary of the Navy delivered it to Fraser, Trenholm & Co. in Liverpool. On being appointed a lieutenant in 1863, Richard H. Gayle was assigned to the command of the Cornubia at Bermuda. Lt. Joseph Fry commanded the Eugenie and later the Agnes E. Fry on runs between Bermuda and Wilmington. The blockade-runners transported cotton from Wilmington to the sea islands and brought back war supplies. The Coquette purchased by Bulloch and commanded by Lt. Robert R. Carter took a load of engines and hardware from Liverpool to Bermuda and after taking on additional cargo went into Wilmington. Bulloch also bought by 1864 four steamers constructed for blockade-running: the Owl, the Bat, the Stag, and the Deer. In 1864 Lt. Gayle assumed command of the Stag, which was captured in Jan. 1865 when attempting to enter the port of Wilmington. The City of Richmond, a blockade-runner chartered by the Confederacy and commanded by Comdr. Hunter Davidson, carried officers, men, and stores to the Stonewall off Quiberon late in 1864.

Francis B. C. Bradlee, Blockade Running during the Civil War (Salem, Mass., 1925); Marcus W. Price, "Ships That Tested the Blockade of the Carolina Ports, 1861-65, " American Neptune, 8:196-241 (July 1948); Jeanie M. Walker, Life of Capt. Joseph Fry (Hartford, Conn., 1874).

Record Group 45. --A journal of the Cornubia, Sept. -Nov. 1863, kept by J. T. Gordon on runs between Wilmington and St. George, Bermuda, is in the Naval Records Collection. Besides shipboard incidents, the journal notes activities at Wilmington, the arrival and departure of vessels from St. George, and the names of passengers. This journal was seized along with the vessel's papers when the Cornubia was captured by a Union blockader on Nov. 8, 1863.

Record Group 56. --Among the captured and abandoned property records of the U.S. Treasury Department is the logbook of the Coquette, Nov. 4, 1863-Aug. 7, 1864 (file no. 6100), covering the voyage from Liverpool to St. George, Bermuda, and several trips between Bermuda and Wilmington.

Ships' papers relating to the blockade-runners Atalanta (Chameleon, Olustee), Atlanta (Fingal), City of Richmond, Laurel, and Phantom are with the Foreign Office records in the British Public Record Office (cited above under the section on cruisers). Registry documents concerning blockade-runners purchased in Great Britain are in the General Register and Record Office of Shipping and Seamen (Ministry of Transport and Civil Aviation, Cardiff, Wales).

Records in Other Custody. --Letters of Lt. R. H. Gayle to Josiah Gorgas and Mrs. Gorgas and others describing his wartime experiences are in the Gorgas papers in the University of Alabama Library. An 1863 diary of Lt. William C. Whittle, Jr., relating to blockade-running aboard the Cornubia is in the Norfolk Museum of Arts and Sciences.

NAVY YARDS AND NAVAL STATIONS AND WORKS

A resolution adopted by the Confederate Congress on Mar. 15, 1861 (Prov. Cong. C.S.A. Stat. 94), recommended in part that the States cede the navy yards within their limits to the Confederacy. Accordingly, the navy yards at Norfolk and Pensacola were transferred to the Confederate Navy Department, which established other yards and works at seaports, on rivers, and in the interior to construct and repair vessels and to manufacture, store, and issue machines, equipment, and stores.

C.S. Navy Department, Navy Register, 1863, 1864, Regulations for the Navy of the Confederate States (Richmond, 1862); Albert L. Kelln, "Confederate Submarines, " Virginia Magazine of History and Biography, 61:293-303 (July 1953); Fletcher Pratt, "The Rebel Rams, " U.S. Naval Institute Proceedings, 64:1021-1028 (July 1938); William N. Still, Jr., "Facilities for the Construction of War Vessels in the Confederacy, " Journal of Southern History, 31:285-304 (Aug. 1965).

Record Group 45. --In the Naval Records Collection is a file of payrolls of civilian personnel of naval shore establishments, May 1861-Dec. 1864 (2 ft.). The payrolls give the names of employees, occupations, rate of pay per day, number of days worked, total pay due, signatures of employees and a witness, and approval signatures of foremen and commandants.

Several subdivisions of the subject file in the Naval Records Collection contain materials relating to naval stations and works. File OL (Mobilization and Demobilization) contains records about the fitting out of vessels. These records are largely paymasters' vouchers for the procurement of ordnance and ordnance stores, materials, provisions, services, freight, drayage, office rent, and pay of naval personnel. The file also includes statements of receipts and expenditures, telegrams, paymasters' letters, and instructions of Secretary Mallory. Subject file P (Naval Bases) contains records on naval stations (4 ft.). File PB (Administration of Stations) contains paymasters' vouchers for administrative expenses. File PI (Industrial Activity) contains paymasters' vouchers, abstracts of disbursements, accounts, receipts, and correspondence. File PL (Labor and Civilian Personnel) contains vouchers, payrolls, and receipts. This file also contains some correspondence between Secretary Mallory and paymasters and other correspondence of commandants and flag officers. File PN (Plant) contains vouchers for material, supplies, and services paid for by naval paymasters and instructions of Navy Department offices and station commandants. Subject file XS (Naval Supplies Ashore, 9 in.) contains vouchers, invoices, receipts, statements of disbursements, statements of accounts, and Secretary Mallory's appointments and instructions relating to the procurement of iron, copper, coal, timber, hemp, and other supplies.

The files described above and just below contain documents on most and probably all the Confederate naval shore establishments. For most of these there are no other records.

Record Group 109. --The War Department Collection of Confederate Records contains some payrolls for civilian employees of naval shore establishments (see under Quartermaster General's Office in chapter VII of this Guide). There is an index to the names of employees on the rolls but no list of stations for which rolls are available.

Atlanta Naval Ordnance Works

In the spring of 1862, Lt. David P. McCorkle and Acting Master W. A. Robbins moved ordnance and laboratory stores that had been evacuated from New Orleans to Atlanta where new works were erected on leased land. Projectiles, gun carriages, and stores manufactured there were shipped to vessels at Charleston, Savannah, and Mobile. In June 1864 the Atlanta ordnance plant was moved to Augusta, Ga.

The commandant was Lt. David P. McCorkle.

No records of this establishment have been found.

Augusta Naval Ordnance Works

Temporary structures were built at Augusta and the manufacture of projectiles, gun carriages, and ordnance equipment continued presumably until the capture of Augusta in the spring of 1865.

The commandant was Lt. David P. McCorkle.

No records of this establishment have been found.

YARDS AND STATIONS 375

Charleston Naval Station

Late in 1861 Capt. Duncan N. Ingraham was ordered to Charleston, S. C., to direct naval activities. He assisted in the preparation and armament of batteries and supervised the construction of gunboats by Kirkwood & Knox and J. G. & D. C. March and ironclads by James M. Eason and F. M. Jones. The station thus established served as a base for the squadron made up of these vessels, and for a while Ingraham commanded both the squadron and the station. After Mar. 1863 he commanded only the station. An old wooden vessel, Indian Chief, served as receiving ship. Lt. Nicholas H. Van Zandt supervised the manufacture of gun carriages, projectiles, and ordnance stores at Charleston in 1863.

The commandant was Capt. Duncan N. Ingraham.

No records of this station have been found.

Charlotte Naval Works

In May 1862 machines, tools, stores, and workmen were moved from the Norfolk Navy Yard, then in danger of capture, to Charlotte, N. C. Shops erected on land purchased by the Navy Department produced gun carriages, wrought-iron rifle bolts and shot, torpedoes, and other ordnance equipment principally for the naval stations at Charleston and Savannah. The shops also made heavy forgings, such as propeller shafting, crank shafts and other equipment for gunboats, and crank axles for locomotives. Locomotives and the machinery of neighboring cotton and woolen mills were repaired there.

Successive commandants of this naval works:
Comdr. Richard L. Page, 1862.
Chief Engr. Henry A. Ramsay, 1863.

Ralph W. Donnelly, "The Yard, C.S.N.," Civil War History, Charlotte, North Carolina, Navy 5:72-79 (Mar. 1959).

Records in Other Custody.--Four payrolls of civilian employees of the Charlotte Naval Station, Jan.-Apr. 1865, are in the North Carolina Department of Archives and History.

Columbia Naval Powder Works

In the summer of 1862 the powder works at Petersburg, Va., were moved to Columbia, S. C., where a new plant was built under the direction of Chief Engr. Thomas A. Jackson. The Columbia mills produced different kinds of powder for the several types of guns used by the Navy. The works were destroyed in Feb. 1865.

The superintendent was P. B. Garesché.

No records of this establishment have been found.

Columbus Naval Ironworks

On Oct. 3, 1861, Secretary Mallory instructed Lt. Augustus McLaughlin to undertake the construction of an ironclad steamer. McLaughlin located a plant at Columbus, Ga., on the Chattahoochee River and was joined there later by Chief Engr. James H. Warner, who leased the Columbus Ironworks in the spring of 1862 and converted it into a naval ironworks. The establishment became a foundry, ironworks, and shipyard. The foundry cast brass, bronze, and wrought-iron cannon. The works built engines and boilers for steamers under construction at Wilmington, Charleston, Savannah, on the Tombigbee River, and at Columbus. During 1862-64 Lieutenant McLaughlin superintended the construction of the ironclad Muscogee. During 1863-64 the Wm. Penny & Co. works at Prattville, Ala., were operated as a branch of the ironworks at Columbus.

The commandant of this establishment was Lt. Augustus McLaughlin.

Records in Other Custody.--Some of the records of James H. Warner are in the Columbus Museum of Arts and Crafts, Inc. Engineering drawings are available for engines, boilers, and other naval machinery manufactured at the Columbus Naval Ironworks. The employees of the works were organized into three military companies for which there is an 1864 roster. Three letters written late in 1861 list materials needed at the works. A press copy book of letters sent of J. H. Warner, 1862-65, is in the Buffalo Historical Society collections.

Halifax Naval Station

In an improvised shipyard in a cornfield on the Roanoke River in Halifax County, N.C., Gilbert Elliott built the ironclad steamer Albemarle for the Confederate Navy. William A. Graves was assigned to the station as acting naval constructor. The Albemarle was completed in 1864, but the station continued in operation; an unfinished gunboat was seized there on May 12, 1865.

Successive commandants of this naval station:
Lt. James L. Johnston, 1863.
Comdr. James W. Cooke, 1864.

Records in Other Custody.--The Southern Historical Collection in the University of North Carolina Library contains papers of Peter E. Smith regarding his inventions and patents and his work with Elliott on the Albemarle. The same repository has papers of William F. and James G. Martin that include correspondence between Elliott and Secretary Mallory concerning the construction of naval vessels.

Jackson Naval Station

After the fall of New Orleans in 1862, the headquarters for the naval forces on the Mississippi River and its tributaries were located at Jackson, Miss.

The commandant of this station was Capt. William F. Lynch.

No records of this station have been found.

Kinston Naval Station

Late in 1862 construction of the ironclad gunboat Neuse began at Whitehall on the Neuse River in North Carolina. The hull was turned over to the Navy in the spring of 1863 and towed to Kinston for completion. After its first voyage down the river during which it grounded on a sandbar, the Neuse returned to Kinston and was scuttled there in Mar. 1865 on the approach of U.S. forces.

Successive commanders of the station and vessel:
Lt. William Sharp, 1863?
Lt. Benjamin P. Loyall, ca. Feb. 1864.
Comdr. Joseph Price, Aug. 25, 1864.

Richard S. Grant, "Captain William Sharp, of Norfolk, Virginia, U.S.N.-C.S.N.," Virginia Magazine of History and Biography, 57: 44-54 (Jan. 1949); William M. Still, Jr., "The Career of the Confederate Ironclad Neuse," North Carolina Historical Review, 43:1-13 (Jan. 1966).

No records of this station have been found.

Little Rock Naval Station

During 1862-63 repairs were made on the steamer Pontchartrain at this station. This vessel was burned on the White River in Oct. 1863 to prevent its capture.
The commandant was Lt. John W. Dunnington.
No records of this station have been found.

Mobile Naval Station

A naval station was established at Mobile, Ala., in 1862 when a squadron was formed for the defense of the harbor. Under the direction of the flag officers of the Mobile Squadron, the force at the station repaired vessels and fitted out two ironclad gunboats constructed at Oven Bluff on the Tombigbee River. During 1862-63 the Florida was repaired and equipped at Mobile, and in 1863-64 the ironclad ram Tennessee was completed. The floating batteries Huntsville and Tuscaloosa built at Selma and the ironclad steamer Nashville built at Montgomery were brought to Mobile in 1863 and completed there. Another floating battery, the Phoenix, was built at Mobile, and the submarine torpedo boat Hunley was built there in 1863. In 1864 Henry D. Bassett was attached to the yard as assistant naval constructor, and at McIntosh Bluff, where ironclad steamers were being built in 1864, William M. Hope served as acting constructor. The Navy Department assumed control of the construction of the gunboats at Oven Bluff in 1863 and assigned Sidney D. Porter there as naval constructor.
Record Group 45.--In 1929 some records of Thomas R. Ware, naval paymaster at Mobile, were presented by his family to the Office of Naval Records and Library. In 1939 other Ware papers in the custody of the National Bank of Fredericksburg were placed in the Fredericksburg and Spotsylvania National Military Park. In 1965 they were transferred to the National Archives. Press copies of letters sent, June 14, 1862-Oct. 29, 1864 (2 vols.), contain letters from Ware to Paymaster John de Bree, Secretary Mallory, Bolling Baker (First Auditor), Paymaster John W. Nixon at Jackson, Miss., Paymaster William W. J. Kelly at Augusta, Depositary T. W. Sanford at Montgomery, Flag Officer Victor M. Randolph at Mobile, Maj. A. S. Taylor, C.S.M.C., the Office of Orders and Detail, William P. Browne, coal contractor at Montevallo, Ala., Army quartermasters, and others. Letters and telegrams received, June 1861-Feb. 1865 (4 in.), are mostly from the same correspondents and also from assistant paymasters at shore stations and aboard ships, shipbuilders, Navy officers and engineers, Army officers, E. C. Elmore (Treasurer), Comdr. George

NAVY DEPARTMENT

Minor regarding saltpeter, and Capt. Ebenezer Farrand at Selma concerning coal delivered by W. P. Browne. Also in Record Group 45 are vouchers, 1862-65 (8 in.), and a record of expenditures, July 1862-Feb. 1865 (1 vol.), with abstracts. Small quantities of other types of records include: some contracts, May 1862-June 1864 (1/4 in.); records relating to the marine detachment, 1862-64 (1/2 in.), chiefly concerning personnel actions; some cash statements, July 1862-Oct. 1864 (1/4 in.); receipts for payments to officers and employees, 1863-64 (1/2 in.); and miscellaneous records, 1861-65 (3 in.).

Records in Other Custody. --Three collections of material relating to the Hunley have been assembled. In 1960 the Southern Historical Collection in the University of North Carolina Library bought from Eustace L. Williams of Van Nuys, Calif., copies of documents on the construction and services of that vessel, an engraving of it, and photographs of James R. McClintock, one of its designers, and of Horace L. Hunley, its financial backer. Other sets of the documents collected by Williams are in the Smithsonian Institution's Museum of History and Technology Library, the University of Texas Library, and the University of Washington Library. Transcripts of letters and other records, photographs of the Hunley, and some material on other torpedo boats collected by Louis J. Genella are in the Tulane University Library. The Department of Archives of Louisiana State University has copies of letters, other documents, and photographs, 1863-64 (35 items), relating to the Hunley and a submarine built in New Orleans by Hunley and McClintock.

In the University of Virginia Library (Lewis W. Minor papers) with the register of naval patients in the Charity Hospital at New Orleans is a list of men discharged from service by the naval hospital at Mobile on the recommendation of medical surveys during Jan.-Nov. 1863.

The press copy books of letters sent by Colin J. McRae, Sept. 28, 1861-Dec. 15, 1862, and Sept. 4-Dec. 18, 1862 (2 vols.), in the Alabama Department of Archives and History contain letters and telegrams to Secretary Mallory relating to the conversion of the side-wheeler steamers Morgan and Gaines into gunboats for the Confederate Navy.

An inventory of medicine on board the Baltic prepared by Surg. William F. Carrington, who served on that vessel in 1862-63, is in Duke University Library.

Naval Academy (Drewy's Bluff, Va.)

At first midshipmen were trained on naval vessels and at shore batteries. Considering this unsatisfactory, Secretary Mallory recommended in his report of Feb. 27, 1862, that a school be provided. An act of Apr. 21, 1862 (1 Cong. C.S.A. Stat. 50), authorized the appointment of 20 passed midshipmen and 106 acting midshipmen. The Patrick Henry of the James River Squadron was designated as a schoolship for midshipmen and was remodeled for that purpose. Lt. William H. Parker, who had graduated from and taught at the U.S. Naval Academy, was appointed commandant and under Comdr. John M. Brooke of the Office of Ordnance and Hydrography he organized and prepared regulations for the academy. It opened in Oct. 1863 aboard the Patrick Henry off Drewry's Bluff on the James River with an enrollment of about 50 midshipmen.

G. Melvin Herndon, "The Confederate States Naval Academy, " Virginia Magazine of History and Biography, 69:300-323 (July 1961), contains a roster of midshipmen appointed to the academy; lists of midshipmen are also in the Navy Register. See also C.S. Navy Department, Regulations for the Confederate States School-Ship Patrick Henry [Richmond, 1863]; William H. Parker, Recollections of a Naval Officer, 1841-1865 (New York, 1883). During the war Parker published textbooks for the use of the midshipmen.

Record Group 109. --In the War Department Collection of Confederate Records is a record of the board for examining midshipmen, 1861-62 (ch. VIII, vol. 294). It includes a list of the subjects in which the classes were examined, copies of examinations, the names of examiners and of members of the board, a journal of proceedings of the board, and information as to midshipmen examined.

Records in Other Custody. --The Archives Division of the Virginia State Library has a roster of midshipmen enrolled in the Naval Academy, 1863, and a photostat copy of an autobiography of Henry St. George T. Brooke, a midshipman who later served in the James River Squadron. Some material relating to the Patrick Henry is in the Fredericksburg and Spotsylvania National Military Park collections. Papers of James M. Morgan, who after earlier naval service became attached to the Patrick Henry as a midshipman in 1864, are in the South Caroliniana Library of the University of South Carolina.

New Orleans Naval Station

Established in the spring of 1861, this station converted steamers purchased in New Orleans into naval vessels; among them were the Sumter, the McRae, and the Florida. The commandant also arranged with private shipyards for the conversion or reconstruction of other vessels into gunboats, requisitioned an ironclad ram that became the Manassas, acquired six stern-wheelers, and made contracts for the ironclad steamers Louisiana and Mississippi. The U.S.S. Star of the West, captured at Indianola, Tex., was brought to New Orleans for use as a receiving ship and renamed the St. Philip. The manufacture of ordnance, ordnance stores, and powder was begun. Lt. Beverly Kennon arrived in the summer of 1861 to supervise this work; he was succeeded late in 1861 by Lt. John R. Eggleston. W. A. Robbins was superintendent of the pyrotechnic laboratory. A coal depot at Algiers on the west bank of the Mississippi River was superintended by Henry Willett, and John Roy operated a gun carriage shop in the new customhouse.

Successive commandants of this station:

Capt. Lawrence Rousseau, Mar. 1861.
Capt. George N. Hollins, Aug. 1861.
Comdr. John K. Mitchell, Jan. 1862.
Capt. William C. Whittle, Mar. 29, 1862.

C.S.A. Congress, Report of Evidence Taken before a Joint Special Committee of Both Houses of the Confederate Congress To Investigate the Affairs of the Navy Department (Richmond, 1863?); Charles L. Dufour, The Night the War Was Lost (New York, 1960); James M. Merrill, "Confederate Shipbuilding at New Orleans, " Journal of Southern

History, 28:87-93 (Feb. 1962).

Records in Other Custody. --A register of patients is among the papers of Surg. Lewis W. Minor in the University of Virginia Library. It contains a list of eight patients from vessels of the Mississippi River Squadron that were cared for in the Charity Hospital in New Orleans in Nov. 1861 (2 p.) and a list of patients on the hospital ship St. Philip, Oct. 1861-Apr. 1862 (12 p.).

A diary of John Roy, Apr. 23, 1861-Sept. 4, 1862 (microfilm), in the Department of Archives of Louisiana State University (also in Tulane University Library) gives some information about naval ship construction at New Orleans. Instructions of Captain Hollins to Lt. Joseph Fry, Jan. 4, 1862, and to Thomas Garrett, Sept. 17, 1861, are in the New York Public Library. An instruction of Lieutenant Fry, commandant pro tempore of the New Orleans Naval Station, to Lt. Francis E. Shepperd, July 30, 1861, ordering him to report to the Florida is in the North Carolina Department of Archives and History. Papers of Lt. Beverly Kennon are in the James W. Eldridge collection in the Henry E. Huntington Library. A diary, Nov. 6, 1861-Feb. 8, 1862, of Lt. Robert D. Minor, who was ordered to New Orleans for duty as an ordnance officer in Nov. 1861, is in the Virginia Historical Society collections.

Norfolk Navy Yard

On the night of Apr. 20, 1861, the U.S. Navy withdrew from this extensive navy yard fronting on the Elizabeth River. Vessels then at the yard were scuttled, buildings were set afire, and ordnance and other property were destroyed. Confederate military forces immediately occupied the yard and extinguished the fires. Steps were quickly taken by the Virginia Navy to salvage material and ready the yard for work. About 1,000 guns, shot and shells, and 2,000 barrels of powder that were captured supplied the immediate needs of the Confederacy. The yard and the Virginia Navy officers serving in it were transferred to the Confederate Navy on June 10, 1861. A laboratory was organized to manufacture fuses, caps, bullets, shot, shells, and shrapnel. The sunken Union vessels, Merrimack, Plymouth, and Germantown were raised and the conversion of the Merrimack into the ironclad Virginia was undertaken. The Germantown was fitted out as a floating battery and the United States was pumped out and used as a receiving ship at the yard. The yard repaired vessels attached to the naval defenses of Virginia and North Carolina. Construction of the ironclad gunboat Richmond began. The acquisition of a steam hammer from the Tredegar Iron Works made it possible to manufacture steam engines. But early in May 1862 after Union forces had landed north of Norfolk, machines and ordnance stores were removed from the yard, the Richmond was towed to the James River, and on the night of May 9 the Confederate Navy set fire to and evacuated the Norfolk Navy Yard.

Successive commandants of this navy yard:
    Capt. French Forrest, Apr. 22, 1861.
    Capt. Sidney S. Lee, Mar. 27, 1862.

Record Group 59. --Among the general records of the Department of State for the Civil War period are some records of John Johnson, paymaster at the Norfolk Navy Yard. Summary statements of receipts and expenditures, July-Dec. 1861, show expenditures for various purposes, including the conversion of the Merrimack and work on gunboats. A number of payrolls of civilian employees of various departments of the yard are dated May 1862.

Records in Other Custody. --A press copy book of letters sent by Capt. French Forrest, Oct. 9, 1861-Mar. 27, 1862, in the Archives Division of the Virginia State Library includes letters to officers attached to the yard, Flag Officer W. F. Lynch, and Gen. Benjamin Huger and other Army officers in the area. The volume contains an alphabetical index. An order book, Apr. 22-Oct. 15, 1861, also indexed, contains orders relating to the appointment of men to posts in the yard, the employment of men, the procurement of tools, the mounting of guns, assignments to duty, the opening of a recruiting rendezvous, the detail of workmen for guncrews, and the delivery of guns.

Besides microfilms of the two volumes described above, the Southern Historical Collection in the University of North Carolina Library has microfilms of an order book, Dec. 1, 1861-Jan. 31, 1864, and of a few other documents, including Forrest's commissions.

An autobiography of Henry St. George T. Brooke, who served as an acting midshipman on the receiving ship United States at Norfolk, 1861-62, and on the Nansemond, James River Squadron, 1862-63, is in the Virginia Historical Society collections.

Records relating to the Norfolk Navy Yard are published in	Official Records . . . Navies, ser. 1, vols. 4-7.

Pee Dee (Mars Bluff) Navy Yard

This navy yard was established late in 1862 at Mars Bluff on the Marion County (S. C.) side of the Pee Dee River. The wooden steamer Peedee was completed there in 1864 and a steamer and a torpedo boat were under construction in 1864-65. In Mar. 1865, after the fall of Charleston and Wilmington, both the yard and the Peedee were destroyed.

Successive commandants of this navy yard:
Lt. Van Renssalaer Morgan, 1862.
Lt. Edward J. Means, 1864.

Maxwell C. Orvin, In South Carolina Waters, 1861-1865 [Charleston?, 1961]; Leah Townsend, "The	Confederate Gunboat 'Pedee', " South Carolina Historical Magazine, 60:66-73 (Apr. 1959).

Records in Other Custody. --The letters-sent press copy book of Lt. Edward J. Means, Sept. 17, 1864-Mar. 1, 1865 (1 vol.), is in the Department of Archives of Louisiana State University. Letters to Secretary Mallory, E. C. Murray, John L. Porter, the Office of Orders and Detail, and Maj. C. D. Melton, commandant of conscripts at Columbia, S. C., concern work on vessels, the recapture of Federal prisoners who had escaped from a nearby prison, naval personnel for the yard, and the assignment of conscripts to work there. Other documents include requisitions for men, food, clothing, and medical supplies; discharges and transfers of men; and a list of men employed at the yard.

Pensacola Navy Yard

On Jan. 12, 1861, the commissioners of the State of Florida, backed by a strong military force, demanded and received the surrender of this yard. The labor force was retained and repair work was done on vessels. The yard was of limited use to the Confederates because it was within cannon range of Union-held Fort Pickens across the bay on Santa Rosa Island. Naval officers removed the drydock, sank it in the channel as an obstruction, and assisted in the construction of batteries for the defense of the port. Before the yard was evacuated on May 10, 1862, the Confederates removed guns, munitions, machines, commissary stores, and other property, and then set fire to the yard, forts, and public buildings in the town. Union forces immediately occupied the yard and continued in control thereafter.

Successive commandants of this navy yard:
  Capt. Victor M. Randolph, Jan. 12, 1861.
  Capt. Duncan N. Ingraham, 1861.
  Comdr. Thomas W. Brent, 1861.

Record Group 45. --Original records of Captain Randolph, Jan. 12- Nov. 5, 1861, are in the Naval Records Collection, subject file PB (1/2 in.). They include correspondence with officers attached to the yard and with Army officers in the area, a few letters addressed to Captain Brent, Randolph's general and special orders regarding activities at the yard, his appointments in the Confederate Navy, vouchers for the cost of lighting the yard, the terms of the surrender of the yard (Jan. 12, 1861), an estimate for wharf repair, a hospital sicklist, and orders of the Pensacola Military District.

Original letters and other records of Captain Brent, Mar. 28, 1861- Feb. 13, 1862, in subject file PB (1 1/2 in.), include letters from officers and employees attached to the yard, from the commandant of the New Orleans Naval Station, from Army officers in the area, and from others relating to materials for and work on the Fulton at the yard. Other documents include requisitions for funds, vouchers, contracts, and specifications for buildings to be constructed in Pensacola, returns of labor, returns of naval stores, reports of boards of survey on provisions, and orders of the Pensacola Military District.

Petersburg Naval Powder Works

This works operated during 1861-62 at Petersburg, Va., but in 1862 it was moved to Columbia, S.C.

Successive superintendents were Chief Engrs. Thomas A. Jackson and P. B. Garesché.

No records of this establishment have been found.

Petersburg Naval Ropewalk

This plant opened in Jan. 1863 and was still operating in Dec. 1864. It supplied cotton cordage to the Navy, Army, coal mines, and railroad and canal companies. A cotton yarn factory with a separate work force under Foreman William P. Gill was also under the same command.

Successive superintendents of this ropewalk:
  Chief Engr. Thomas A. Jackson.

Lt. S. Wellford Corbin.
Lt. Maxwell T. Clarke.
No records of this establishment have been found.

Richmond Naval Ordnance Works

By early fall of 1861 operations had begun at the naval laboratory which with other shops developed into the Richmond Naval Ordnance Works. James D. McCloskey supervised the work at the laboratory, first as acting gunner and then as superintendent from the end of 1862 until 1865. Operations apparently began about June 1862 at the gun-carriage shop under George T. Guy. In Sept. 1862 John B. Rooke was foreman of the finishing shop, and Charles Sneed was foreman of the blacksmith shop. During 1862-63 James A. Mahone kept an ordnance store at the laboratory. In 1863 a powder magazine, a shell house, a storehouse, and a laboratory were built on a leased site. The Richmond Naval Ordnance Works supplied ordnance and gun carriages to vessels on the James River and at Wilmington and to shore batteries.
Successive superintendents of this naval ordnance works:
Lt. Robert D. Minor, 1861.
Lt. Alexander M. DeBree, 1863.
Asst. Engr. Richard B. Wright, 1864.
Records in Other Custody.--Official papers of Lieutenant Minor in the Virginia Historical Society collections include correspondence with Navy Department officials. A record book of ammunition issued by the naval laboratory of the Richmond Naval Ordnance Works, 1861-65, is in Washington's Headquarters Museum, Newburgh, N.Y.

Richmond Navy Yards

After the Confederate evacuation of Norfolk in 1862, the Navy Department established a navy yard in the lower part of Richmond on the James River. It came to be known as Rocketts Navy Yard after its locality, named for Robert Rockett who in the 18th century had operated a ferry in that part of the river. On the opposite side of the James was another navy yard that was sometimes referred to as Grave's Navy Yard. The ironclad steamers Richmond, Virginia II, Fredericksburg, and Texas were constructed at Rocketts Navy Yard; all but the Texas were added to the James River Squadron before the end of the war. Other vessels attached to that squadron were repaired at Richmond. The torpedo launchers Squib, Hornet, Scorpion, and Wasp were also built at Richmond, and two of four wooden gunboats were completed. After 1863 Lt. John H. Parker was in charge of gunboat construction at Grave's Navy Yard.
Successive commandants of the Richmond Navy Yard:
Comdr. Ebenezer Farrand, 1862.
Comdr. Robert G. Robb, 1862.
No records of these yards have been found.

Saffold Navy Yard

The Chattahoochee, a wooden gunboat, was built at Saffold, Ga., during 1862-63 by D. S. Johnson.
The superintendent at this navy yard was Lt. Catesby ap R. Jones.

Harriet Gift Castlen, Hope Bids Me Onward; Biography of George Gift Arranged by His Daughter from Letters George Gift Wrote to Her Mother before They Married (Savannah, 1945). Lt. Gift was attached to the Chattahoochee during 1862-63 and 1864; texts of his letters written from that vessel are in this book.

No records of this yard have been found.

St. Marks Naval Station

This station in Florida served as a base for the Spray. Successive commanders of the station and the vessel:
  Lt. Charles P. McGary, 1862.
  Lt. Charles W. Hays, 1863.
  Lt. Henry H. Lewis, 1864.
No records of this station have been found.

Savannah Naval Station

The formation of the Savannah River Squadron in 1861 for the defense of Georgia and South Carolina necessitated a naval station at Savannah. Besides fitting out and supplying the squadron, the station worked with the shipyards of Willink & Miller, and Krenson & Hawkes with whom contracts were made by the Navy Department in 1861 for the construction of ironclad gunboats and with the brothers Asa and Nelson Tift who converted the blockade-runner Fingal into the ironclad Atlanta. On the approach of Sherman's army in Dec. 1864, the naval station, a large quantity of ship timber, and the incomplete vessels at the shipyards were burned.
Successive commandants of this station:
  Capt. Josiah Tattnall, 1861.
  Comdr. Thomas W. Brent, 1862.
  Capt. Josiah Tattnall, 1862.
Record Group 45. --A record of payments made by Asst. Paymaster Dewitt C. Seymour, Nov. 1862-June 1863 (1 vol.), is in the Naval Records Collection. The volume includes an alphabetical index.
Records in Other Custody. --A few papers of Henry F. Willink, Jr., Nov. 2, 1861-Aug. 11, 1862, are in Emory University Library. Willink was a member of the Savannah shipbuilding firm of Willink & Miller with whom the Navy Department contracted for the construction of two gunboats. His papers include correspondence with Secretary Mallory and Commander Brent, the contract and specifications for the gunboats, and plans for the Milledgeville, an ironclad steamer that Willink was completing when Savannah was captured.

Selma Naval Gun Foundry and Ordnance Works

In 1863 the Confederate Government bought Colin J. McRae's iron foundry at Selma, Ala. It was operated jointly by the War and Navy Departments until June 1, 1863, when control of the entire works was assumed by the Navy Department. Additional shops were erected and the plant made Brooke and other heavy guns and ammunition that were sent to the naval squadrons at Mobile, Charleston, and Wilmington and to shore defenses there and elsewhere. In 1863 the commandant was assigned the additional

responsibility of obtaining and transporting coal for Selma and Montgomery. When Selma was captured by U.S. forces on Apr. 2, 1865, Commander Jones escaped with the foundry records.
Successive commandants of the foundry and ordnance works:
Comdr. Archibald B. Fairfax, 1863.
Comdr. Catesby ap R. Jones, 1863.

W. S. Mabry, Brief Sketch of the Career of Captain Catesby Ap R. Jones (Selma, Ala., 1912); Walter W. Stephens, "The Brooke Guns from Selma, " Alabama Historical Quarterly, 20:462-475 (Fall 1958); William N. Still, Jr., "Selma and the Confederate States Navy, " Alabama Review, 15:19-37 (Jan. 1962).

Record Group 45. --Records of the Naval Gun Foundry and Ordnance Works that were in the care of Commander Jones at the end of the war are now in the Naval Records Collection. Press copy books of letters sent, May 23, 1863-Mar. 21, 1865 (4 vols.), contain many letters to the Office of Ordnance and Hydrography, Secretary Mallory, Admiral Buchanan, Captain Farrand, the Office of Orders and Detail, the commandants of naval stations in Georgia, South Carolina, and North Carolina, officers and mechanics employed at the foundry, Army officers, industrial and business firms, and individuals. Part of the first press copy book (p. 1-93) contains letters sent by Colin J. McRae, the original owner of the foundry, during the period Dec. 20, 1862-Feb. 26, 1863, and in another volume are some handwritten copies of letters sent by McRae, June 17-Aug. 8, 1862. The first volume contains letters to Commander Farrand and Joseph Pierce at the Selma Naval Station; and the second, letters to Secretary Mallory, July 13 and Aug. 1, 1862, recommending the construction of ironclads at Selma by Otis and Templeton, and to the Office of Ordnance and Hydrography. Other letters sent by Commander Jones, Jan. 25-Mar. 31, 1865, are on unbound press copy sheets in subject file PI.
Original letters received are in several subdivisions of the subject file in the Naval Records Collection. Those in file BA for June 19, 1863-Jan. 19, 1865 (1/4 in.), are chiefly from John M. Brooke and concern the manufacture and distribution of guns and ammunition, experiments with powder, and the submission of monthly returns. Other letters for June 3, 1863-Jan. 28, 1865 (1/2 in.), in subject file BG include some from Brooke, the naval ordnance works at Atlanta and Charlotte, and the Army arsenal and laboratory at Macon. Some tracings of gun parts and pattern drawings are included. Letters of May 27, 1863-Apr. 27, 1865 (1 in.), in subject file PI are from Brooke, Secretary Mallory, Lt. Col. George W. Rains of the Augusta Arsenal, the Office of Orders and Detail, and others. Other letters received by Commander Jones are in the area file (area 6).
Records concerning the guns and ammunition made at Selma are also in the Naval Records Collection. A record of guns manufactured, July 1863-Jan. 1865 (2 vols.), contains individual records on each gun cast (125 in the 2 vols.) with data on each step in the process and the name of the Navy or Army officer to whose command the gun was shipped. Available also are records of guns cast, a report of the results of experiments with sabots for rifle projectiles, drawings of guns and gun carriages, calculations and measurements of guns, drawings of foundry structures, reports of extreme proof of a 7-inch gun, and specifications of a welding machine invented by John Blackadder, master machinist at Selma (subject file BG, 1 1/2 in.).

In the book containing McRae's 1862 letters are other foundry records of all types for July 1863-Dec. 1864 (p. 65-144).

Records in Other Custody. --Other correspondence of Colin J. McRae is in the Alabama Department of Archives and History. Press copy books of letters sent, Sept. 28, 1861-Dec. 15, 1862, and Sept. 4-Dec. 18, 1862 (2 vols.), contain letters and telegrams to Secretary Mallory about assistance rendered Commander Farrand in converting the Morgan and Gaines into gunboats for the Confederate Navy and the defense of Mobile, and letters to George Minor of the Office of Ordnance and Hydrography concerning McRae's contract with the War and Navy Departments for the production of guns and ammunition. Among the letters received by McRae are a few from Minor concerning the manufacture of guns and ship plates and from William P. Browne and J. W. Lapsley concerning coal.

Correspondence of Comdr. Archibald B. Fairfax in the Texas Archives of the University of Texas Library relates to the Navy's early interest in and acquisition of the Selma foundry. There are letters sent, Oct. 24, 1862-Feb. 25, 1863, and received, Sept. 25, 1862-April 22, 1863.

Selma Naval Station

In the spring of 1862, Henry D. Bassett, who had contracted with the Navy Department to build two floating batteries, selected a site for a shipyard above Selma on the Alabama River 200 miles from the Gulf of Mexico. The following September Comdr. Ebenezer Farrand arrived to superintend naval ship construction. Naval constructors assigned to Selma included Joseph Pierce and, later, E. C. Murray. When the Tuscaloosa and the Huntsville were launched by Bassett early in 1863, they were moved down to Mobile to be completed; they later joined the Mobile Squadron. Farrand superintended the building of the ironclad ram Tennessee; it also was completed at Mobile and became Admiral Buchanan's flagship. Two other contractors, John T. Shirley and D. D. DeHaven, built an ironclad steamer at Selma during 1863-64, but it was damaged when launched and was sold by the Navy.

The commandant of this naval station was Comdr. Ebenezer Farrand.

William N. Still, Jr., "Selma   Alabama Review, 15:30-36 (Jan. and the Confederate States Navy,"   1962).

No records of this station have been found.

Shreveport Naval Station

Preparations began at Shreveport, La., in the fall of 1862 to construct gunboats to protect the Red River. The gunboat Missouri was launched in Apr. 1863, and the work of fitting it out proceeded. John Roy supervised the making of gun carriages and other ordnance supplies. In 1864 mechanics at this station worked on the Missouri, the Webb, and the Cotton of the Red River Squadron.

The commandant of this naval station was Lt. Jonathan H. Carter.

Record Group 45. --Lieutenant Carter's letters-sent book, Feb. 1, 1863-May 5, 1865, was presented to the Office of Naval Records and Library in Mar. 1935. Part of this volume (p. 1-51) contains fair copies of letters he sent as commandant of the Shreveport Naval Station to Secretary Mallory, naval officers, and Army officers in the Trans-Mississippi Department concerning the construction, armament, and crew of the Missouri.

Records in Other Custody. --A few vouchers for the Shreveport Naval Station, 1863-64, in Duke University Library are for travel expenses, equipment and repair of steamers, and supplies. Some papers relating to this station and to the Red River Squadron are in the Scharf collection with the Maryland Historical Society.

Wilmington Naval Station

Ships for service in North Carolina waters were built at Wilmington. During 1862 Comdr. William T. Muse superintended gunboat construction at Wilmington. Berry & Bros. built the ironclad steamer North Carolina in 1863, and J. L. Cassidy & Sons built the steam sloop Raleigh in 1863-64. A tender for those vessels was also constructed. Hugh Lindsay was superintendent of gunboat construction in 1863; in the next year the gunboat Yadkin was completed. All these vessels served in North Carolina waters.

The flag officers commanding the North Carolina naval defenses had general direction of the shipbuilding for the Confederacy at Wilmington.

No records of this station have been found.

Yazoo City Naval Station

In 1862 the Arkansas was moved from Memphis to the Yazoo River. While still a mere hull it was floated downstream from Greenwood to Yazoo City where a large force of mechanics from the Army armored the vessel with railroad iron and installed engines. After the Arkansas' brief career on the Mississippi River in 1862, the commander returned to the station at Yazoo City. The Mobile was repaired in the fall of 1862 and by the end of that year gunboats were being constructed there. When an enemy flotilla attacked Yazoo City on July 14, 1863, the heavy battery under Lieutenant Brown's command repulsed them, but when the Confederate infantry retreated he was also obliged to withdraw after destroying the river transports.

The commandant of this naval station was Lt. Isaac N. Brown.

Isaac N. Brown, "The Confederate Gun-Boat 'Arkansas, ' " in R. U. Johnson and C. C. Buel, eds., Battles and Leaders of the Civil War, 3:572-580 (4 vols.; New York, 1887-88).

No records of this station have been found.

IX

POST OFFICE DEPARTMENT

The Post Office Department was established by an act of Feb. 21, 1861 (Prov. Cong. C.S.A. Stat. 33), providing for a Postmaster General to administer post offices and post routes. An act of Mar. 9, 1861 (Prov. Cong. C.S.A. Stat. 57), provided for an organization similar to that of the U.S. Post Office Department, including a Contract Bureau, an Appointment Bureau, a Finance Bureau, a chief clerk, a draftsman, 20 clerks, and such additional clerks as might be required.

C.S.A. Post Office Department, Report of the Postmaster General (Richmond, 1861-64), issued irregularly with the following dates: Apr. 29 and Nov. 27, 1861; Feb. 28 and Sept. 29, 1862; Jan. 12, Feb. 12, and Dec. 7, 1863; May 2 and Nov. 7, 1864. Ben H. Procter, Not Without Honor; the Life of John H. Reagan (Austin, 1962); John H. Reagan, Memoirs, with Special Reference to Secession and Civil War, ed. by Walter F. McCaleb (New York and Washington, 1906); Cedric O. Reynolds, "The Postal System of the Southern Confederacy," West Virginia History, 12:200-279 (Apr. 1951).

Soon after the war the U.S. War Department acquired part of the records of the Confederate Post Office Department. Some had been shipped to Charlotte, N.C., before the evacuation of Richmond. On Apr. 2, 1865, Henry St. G. Offutt left Richmond with other records which he placed in storage in Chester, S.C.; at the end of May a U.S. Army officer recovered part of them. They were sent to the Archive Office of the War Department in Washington and are described in the report of Francis Lieber, head of the Archive Office, to the Secretary of War, Jan. 18, 1866.

On Mar. 14, 1866, Postmaster General Dennison wrote to the Secretary of War requesting all records relating to post offices in the Confederate States for use in the examination of claims of Southern postmasters for services before and at the beginning of the war. The Archive Office transferred these records to the Post Office Department on Mar. 27, 1866; an inventory of the records is in the Archive Office, Letters Received, file P 8.

On June 10, 1896, Judson Harmon, the Attorney General, offered to the Secretary of War 51 volumes of Confederate Post Office Department records which according to Harmon the Department of Justice had purchased some years before for use in connection with suits then pending in the Court of Claims. The War Department accessioned these records on June 23, 1896; an inexact list of the records in a letter from the Attorney General to the Secretary of War of that date indicates that most of these records were part of those that the War Department had transferred to the Post Office

Department on Mar. 27, 1866. Since the War Department stamped each volume as an accession from the Department of Justice on June 23, 1896, it is possible to identify the volumes received. They are described below under Record Group 109.

On Nov. 1, 1906, the Librarian of Congress requested the Postmaster General to transfer the letter books of the Postmaster General of the Confederacy to the Library of Congress. This was done and in his letter of acknowledgment of Nov. 27, 1906, the Librarian included a list of the volumes that had been received. (This letter is reproduced in the Post Office Department's press copy book of letters sent.) They are the records described below now in the custody of the Library of Congress.

Some other Confederate Post Office Department records that were bought by the U. S. Government in 1893 were placed in the custody of the Auditor for the Post Office Department. The records have since disappeared, but descriptions of them are available in Official Opinions of the Attorneys General of the United States, 20:261-269 (Oct. 20, 1891); in a memorandum from McGrew & Small to Assistant Attorney General John B. Cotton, Sept. 25, 1892 (Department of Justice, Letters Received, file 9454, in Record Group 60, General Records of the Department of Justice); and in Claude H. Van Tyne and Waldo G. Leland, Guide to the Archives of the Government of the United States in Washington, p. 94-96 (Washington, 1907).

OFFICE OF THE POSTMASTER GENERAL

In Mar. 1861 at Montgomery the Postmaster General began to organize the Department in a room in the Exchange Hotel, but he soon moved to a new building on Bibb Street. He sent an agent to Washington with letters to Post Office officials offering them positions in the Confederate Post Office Department. Several accepted, and the Department thus began with some experienced personnel. Washington D. Miller of Texas was appointed chief clerk; and Joseph F. Lewis, disbursing clerk. After its removal to Richmond the Department was located in Goddin's Hall at the corner of Bank and 11th Streets.

An act of May 9, 1861 (Prov. Cong. C. S. A. Stat. 105), authorized the Postmaster General to issue a proclamation announcing the date on which he would take control of the postal service of the Confederate States. In his proclamation of May 13 the Postmaster General notified all postmasters, contractors, special agents, and route agents within the limits of the Confederate States that he would assume charge on June 1, directed them to continue in the performance of duties, and requested them to forward their names to the Appointment Bureau at Montgomery in order that they could be issued new commissions. Contractors, mail messengers, and special contractors were authorized to continue their services subject to such changes as might be found necessary and were required to send information regarding their routes to the Contract Bureau.

John H. Reagan was appointed Postmaster General on Mar. 6, 1861, and served throughout the war.

Record Group 109. --A small collection of miscellaneous papers, 1861-65 (1 1/3 in.), includes copies of outgoing letters of bureau heads, payrolls of the Post Office Department agency in the Trans-Mississippi West, a list of mail routes in Louisiana, printed circulars, letters received from special agents, and an 1861 bill of the Southwestern Telegraph Co. Proposals for contracts, Mar. -May 1861 (1/3 in.), consist of letters from business firms stating the terms on which they would supply postage stamps, stamped envelopes, stationery, and other supplies and equipment. With the proposals are printed advertisements of the Post Office Department inviting the proposals. Materials appended to the reports of the Postmaster General, 1861-64 (2 in.), consist of tabular statements, statistical reports, estimates, lists, letters, and a report on the curtailment of mail routes.

Records in Other Custody. --Part of the Confederate records received by the Library of Congress in 1906 originated in the Office of the Postmaster General. The letters-sent book, Mar. 7, 1861-Oct. 12, 1863, contains fair copies of letters and telegrams. Many letters to the President concern the operations of the Department, recommendations for appointments as postmasters, and the exemption of Department employees. Communications to the Secretary of the Treasury concern estimates for appropriations, the conveyance of funds in mail cars by Treasury couriers, and requisitions for funds to be supplied to depositories. Letters to the Secretary of State inform him of the receipt of postmasters' bonds and request the issue of their commissions. Letters to postmasters, special and route agents, mail contractors, and railroad presidents concern the operation of the mail service and conscription. Instructions to chiefs and principal clerks of bureaus and acceptances of Department employees' resignations supply information on the operations of the Department. Other letters are to the Secretary of War, the Attorney General, telegraph operators, Army officers, printers, State Governors, and the First Auditor. Letters to Congressmen concern appointments, postmasters' claims, postmasters' and mail contractors' accounts, the exemption of mail carriers, and legislation for the Department. Parts of the book are devoted to the Postmaster General's reports, which are also available in printed form. In the front of the volume is an index. A few incoming communications copied in the book include a statement of the First Auditor of amounts claimed by contractors and others, several opinions of the Attorney General, a letter from J. O. Stegar, the postmaster at Richmond, and one from the Secretary of the Treasury.

A miscellaneous record book of the Postmaster General labeled "Record Journal and Orders, " Mar. 6, 1861-Mar. 26, 1862, in the Library of Congress is concerned with both personnel and postal service matters.

Small quantities of papers relating to the Post Office Department are in other repositories. Collections of the papers of John H. Reagan in the University of Texas Library and the Texas State Archives contain a few copies of documents but no original wartime manuscripts. Ben H. Procter, biographer of Reagan, plans to publish a compilation of his papers. The Texas State Archives has a collection of papers of W. D. Miller for the war period.

C. S. A. Post Office Department, Correspondence between the President of the Virginia Central Railroad Company and the Postmaster General in Relation to Postal Service (Richmond, 1864). Advertisements inviting proposals for delivering the mail, communications to Congress, and reports are listed in Crandall, Confederate Imprints, 1:155-158, and in Harwell, More Confederate Imprints, 1:49-50.

APPOINTMENT BUREAU

This Bureau was concerned with the establishment and discontinuance of post offices, changes of their sites and names, the appointment and removal of postmasters and route and special agents, the procurement and distribution of supplies, and the preparation and distribution of circulars, instructions, blank forms, form letters, appointment books, and the like.

On Mar. 20, 1861, the Confederate Postmaster General instructed postmasters to retain in their possession for the benefit of the Confederate States all property belonging to the U.S. postal service and to return full inventories to the Chief of the Appointment Bureau. G. A. Schwarzman, the former head of the Dead Letter Office of the U.S. Post Office Department, was appointed chief clerk of this Bureau on July 25, 1861. Bartholomew Fuller of North Carolina succeeded him on Sept. 2, 1861, followed by John Heart on Jan. 12, 1862.

An act of Mar. 15, 1861 (C.S.A. Stat. 66), authorized the Postmaster General to continue in office the postmasters and other employees then engaged in postal service until other appointments could be made. When the Confederate Post Office Department assumed control of the postal service in the Southern States on June 1, 1861, there were 8,411 post offices. By the end of Nov. 1861, 6,261 postmasters had been appointed and 950 had resigned. See the published Journal of the Congress for lists of postmaster appointments. Replacements resulted in the appointment of 7,009 postmasters by the end of Feb. 1862 and an additional 1,480 by the end of 1863. At that time there were 8,287 post offices. In appointing postmasters and route agents the Department selected persons exempt from military service because of age or disability. Women were appointed to smaller post offices.

Route and special agents were the traveling representatives of the Department. Route agents accompanied mail cars on railroad lines and mail steamers on water routes to handle the mail. From June to Aug. 1861, seven special agents were appointed, and in 1863 there were ten. Besides observing the operation of the postal system to see that regulations were followed, special agents installed postmasters, established mail service for Confederate armies, examined and revised the "mailing books" of newspaper offices, investigated mail depredations and losses and delays in mail deliveries, and assisted railroads in scheduling.

Benjamin N. Clements became Chief of this Bureau on Mar. 22, 1861, and served throughout the war.

C.S.A. Post Office Department, Instructions to Post Masters (Richmond, 1861), Instructions to the Special Agents of the Post Office Department... (Richmond, 1861), and A List of Establishments, Discontinuances, and Changes in Name of the Post Offices in the Confederate States, since 1861 [Richmond, 186?]. Useful tables on the postal service in the Southern States at the time the United States terminated that service on May 31, 1861, are in U.S. Post Office Department, Report of the Postmaster General...1861, p. 54, 74, and 75.

Record Group 109. -- The War Department Collection of Confederate Records contains two books that were evidently kept by the Appointment Bureau. One is simply an undated list of post offices in Kentucky, by counties. The other consists of two lists of post offices, for Texas and Arkansas, with the names of counties and route numbers.

Records in Other Custody. --In the Manuscript Division of the Library

of Congress are the Appointment Bureau letters-sent books, Apr. 6, 1861-
Jan. 17, 1865 (4 vols.), containing fair copies of outgoing letters. Most of
them are to postmasters, assistant postmasters, and acting postmasters
concerning appointments, bonds, oaths, the employment of deputies and
substitutes, the discontinuance and changes of sites of post offices, commissions paid on money received, and requests for comments or information. Letters to route agents concern appointments and oaths, the appointment of associate agents, the employment of substitutes, and instructions
on duties. Communications were also sent to special agents, local agents,
railroad mail agents, individuals, State Governors, Members of Congress,
printers, the Superintendent of Public Printing, applicants for appointments
as postmasters, and to petitioners for appointments. A list of post offices
in Arkansas, Louisiana, Texas, and Indian Territory, 1861-65 (1 vol.),
gives names of postmasters and dates of their appointment and the dates of
establishment, discontinuance, suspension, and reestablishment of post
offices. A list of postmasters, Apr. 16, 1863-May 8, 1865 (1 vol.), gives
appointment dates, names of persons replaced and the reason, names and
locations of the post offices, date of bond, date of commission, sureties'
names, and occasional remarks concerning new appointments, changes of
name, establishment, reestablishment, or discontinuance.

A list of postmasters in Texas compiled from the record in the Library of Congress is in Grover C. Ramsey, Confederate Postmasters in Texas, 1861-1865 (Waco, 1963). Upon receiving lists of postmasters confirmed by the Senate, the Department of State issued commissions; see chapter V of this Guide under appointment records.

CONTRACT BUREAU

The Contract Bureau negotiated mail contracts and made other arrangements for carrying the mail, prepared contract books and circular
letters, and procured stamps and equipment. An act of Mar. 16, 1861 (Prov.
Cong. C.S.A. Stat. 66), authorized the Postmaster General to renew the
contracts under which the mail was then being carried and to enter into new
contracts on post routes other than railroads and steamboats. Express and
other charter companies were to be allowed to carry mail. An act of May
9, 1861 (Prov. Cong. C.S.A. Stat. 105), authorized the Postmaster General
to annul mail contracts or to discontinue or reduce service. A series of
acts of Congress passed during 1861-65 described the post routes to be established and sometimes authorized the Postmaster General to make contracts without advertising for bids.

In order to make the postal service self-supporting as required by
the Constitution, some post routes taken over from the U.S. were discontinued and others shortened. On June 1, 1861, there were 2,207 post routes
under contract in the Southern States. Contracts were sent in duplicate to
postmasters for execution by contractors on 1,372 routes, and by the end of
Feb. 1862, 1,306 contracts had been returned and 319 were still outstanding.
Eleven steamship routes were stopped in 1861 by the Union blockade of the
coast, but steam packets carried mail on the lower Mississippi River until
the capture of New Orleans in Apr. 1862. The Federal occupation of Kentucky and Missouri prevented the establishment of the Confederate postal
service in those States, and for the same reason it was not extended to
western Virginia. By mid-1862, other areas on the periphery of the

Confederacy in Tennessee, Arkansas, Louisiana, Mississippi, Florida, and eastern North Carolina had been lost to U.S. forces; the number of mail contracts then active in the Confederacy was 1,519. At the end of June 1863, there were 1,253 mail contractors in the 11 States in which the postal service operated.

The bureau also made contracts with railroads for mail transportation. Postmaster General Reagan met with representatives of 35 railroads in Montgomery on Apr. 26, 1861, and arranged for the classification of railroads according to the quantities of mail they carried and the rates to be paid them in order to lower the cost of the service. The classification and rates agreed upon were embodied in the act of May 9, 1861. Of 109 railroads and branches known to the Department, 55 had made contracts by the end of Feb. 1862, and these included most of the important railroads in the South. At the end of 1863, however, some railroads still refused to make contracts even though they had been offered the maximum rate for first-class railroads. Some were allowed to carry mail although it was against the law to permit them to do so without signing contracts.

Mail carriers and contractors were exempt from military service. An act of Apr. 21, 1862 (1 Cong. C.S.A. Stat. 51), exempted all mail carriers and ferrymen on post routes. After this act was repealed in Oct. 1862, the Department experienced difficulty in finding contractors; therefore an act of Apr. 14, 1863 (1 Cong. C.S.A. Stat. 107), exempted mail contractors and drivers of coaches and hacks carrying mail as long as so employed. But the provisions of the law were not clear, and the Department found it difficult to prevent the conscription of carriers.

Arrangements for carrying foreign mail were no more than makeshift. On a mission abroad in 1861 T. Butler King failed to negotiate contracts for carrying mail between Europe and the Confederacy. The Union naval blockade discouraged steamship lines from undertaking such service, but blockade-runners carried mail between Confederate ports and Cuba, Bermuda, Nassau, Canada, and Mexico where it was usually transferred to English and French vessels. Diplomatic agents, naval officers, and others considered trustworthy carried official mail to Europe or to Nassau or Bermuda whence Confederate agents forwarded it to the Confederate representatives. Even the State Department did not regularly employ couriers.

Henry St. George Offutt was appointed Chief of the Contract Bureau on Mar. 27, 1861, and served throughout the war.

August Dietz, The Postal Service of the Confederate States of America (Richmond, 1929); Van Dyk MacBride, Lawrence L. Shenfield, and others, eds., Dietz Confederate States Catalog and Handbook of the Postage Stamps and Envelopes of the Confederate States of America (Richmond, 1959); Lawrence L. Shenfield, Confederate States of America; the Special Postal Routes (New York, 1961); George H. Shirk, "Confederate Postal System in the Indian Territory," Chronicles of Oklahoma, 41:160-218 (Summer 1963).

Record Group 109. --Letters-sent books, Apr. 12, 1861-May 26, 1864 (ch. XI, vols. 31-34, 9 in.), contain fair copies of letters written by Henry St. G. Offutt to postmasters, mail contractors, special agents and route agents, and to railroad presidents, Congressmen, and the First Auditor. Indexes to names of persons and places are available for vols. 31, 32, and 34.

Mail contracts, 1861-64 (ch. XI, vols. 6-9, 12-15, 22, and 23, 3 ft.), are available for Alabama, Arkansas, Florida, Georgia, Louisiana, North Carolina, South Carolina, and Virginia. They are bound numerically by route numbers for each State. Route books, 1861-65 (ch. XI, vols. 17-19, 21, 22 1/2, 23 1/2, 24-30, 47, 55, and 56, 2 ft.), are available for all Confederate States except Missouri. Included in these books are descriptions of the routes, the number of trips made each week, identification of the contractor, and orders on changes in service. A record of proposals to carry the mail, 1862-63 (ch. XI, vols. 35-43, 2 ft.), includes printed clippings of advertisements. Given in longhand are names of bidders and their addresses, the amounts of the bids, descriptions of the service proposed, and notations as to the bid accepted and the date of notification to the bidder.

Records in Other Custody.--Records of the Contract Bureau were accessioned by the Library of Congress in 1906. A mail contract book for Mississippi, Nov. 1861-Nov. 1862, is similar in content to the series of contract books in Record Group 109 and is evidently a part of that series. Post route papers, 1861-64 (2 ft.), include miscellaneous materials for Mississippi and Virginia. Letters in this file to the chief of the Contract Bureau and the Postmaster General concern the execution of contracts, the employment of temporary carriers, changes in routes and service, discontinuation of service, and failures of contractors. Other documents include schedules of mail arrivals and departures, postmasters' registers of arrivals and departures, affidavits of mail contractors, petitions to the Postmaster General on the establishment and changing of mail routes and the appointment of mail carriers, printed instructions of the Inspection Office, and crude, hand-drawn maps of mail routes.

FINANCE BUREAU

The Finance Bureau received from postmasters quarterly returns of moneys received, recorded the revenues deposited by them in the Treasury and its branches, and passed on the returns to the Auditor. It distributed postage stamps and stamped envelopes through the mails to postmasters and kept related accounts. It issued warrants and drafts in payment of amounts due to mail contractors and other persons. Undeliverable mail ("dead letters") was disposed of in various ways. Some such letters containing money were returned to the senders. Letters containing bills of exchange, drafts, and notes belonging to citizens of the United States were delivered to officers of Confederate district courts for disposal under the sequestration act. In 1863 lists were made of dead letters containing money so that returns could be made in the future, and the money was deposited in the Treasury.

The Department attempted to make the postal service self-sustaining by curtailing services and increasing postage rates. At the same time appropriations had to be made in 1861-62 to meet deficiencies in the postal revenues. The Postmaster General reported to the President on Sept. 29, 1862, that further reductions in expenditures could be made only by depriving sections of the country of necessary mail facilities. In the next year, however, revenues increased, and the Department had a surplus. Throughout the war the employees of the Department in Richmond were on the civil list; funds for their salaries and other Departmental expenses were included in general appropriation acts.

An act of Aug. 30, 1861 (Prov. Cong. C.S.A. Stat. 199), directed the Postmaster General to collect from postmasters moneys not turned over when the Confederates States took charge of the postal service on June 1, 1861, and to keep the funds in a separate account for the payment of claims for services rendered before that date. A proclamation issued by the Postmaster General on Sept. 18, 1861, required persons having claims to present them to the Auditor of the Treasury for the Post Office Department on or before Mar. 13, 1862, and instructed postmasters to render accounts on moneys collected on behalf of the United States. Reports submitted by postmasters were imperfect and tardy, and the Auditor was unable at the end of Feb. 1862 to inform the Postmaster General of the balances in the hands of postmasters or the amounts due mail contractors. An act of Sept. 27, 1862 (1 Cong. C.S.A. Stat. 62), authorized the Postmaster General to pay for postal services rendered under contracts or appointments made by the U.S. Government, and an act of Oct. 13, 1862 (1 Cong. C.S.A. Stat. 82), appropriated $800,000 for this purpose.

Successive Chiefs of the Finance Bureau:

John L. Harrell, Apr. 5, 1861.

Alexander Dimitry, Oct. 24, 1864.

Record Group 109.--Accounts of depositaries in Texas, Louisiana, and Arkansas, July 1864-May 1865 (ch. XI, vol. 53), show their names and locations, the names of postmasters or post offices, amounts of deposits and drafts, and dates. An index is in the front of this volume. Some depositaries' accounts are in two parts: one on account of the Post Office Department and another on account of the Agent of the Post Office Department for the Trans-Mississippi West. An account of John Dickinson, the principal depositary, Trans-Mississippi Department, relating to the mail service and an account of the Confederate Treasurer showing amounts transferred from depositaries' accounts are also in this volume. A volume of returns of postmasters in Texas, Louisiana, and Arkansas, 1864-65 (ch. XI, vol. 54), shows the amounts of monetary returns reported by them in the third and fourth quarters of 1864 and the first quarter of 1865. A dead-letter register, 1864-65 (ch. XI, vol. 52), shows the post office and State to which letters were addressed, the name of persons addressed, name of writer, nature of contents, office sent to, date sent, and remarks. Some statements of accounts of mail contractors for carrying U.S. mail, 1861-62 (1/3 in.), claiming compensation for services rendered during Jan. 1-May 31, 1861, show contractors' names, route numbers, annual rate of compensation, date of and amount of payment on account, fines and deductions, and the balance due. Eight accounts of William R. Vance, postmaster at Columbus, Ky., Sept.-Nov. 1861, show the offices to which letters were sent, the number sent, and money due or received.

For many years after the Civil War the U.S. Auditor for the Post Office Department and the U.S. Court of Claims were concerned with the settlement of claims of Southern mail contractors for carrying the mail before May 31, 1861. The names of claimants are in statements published in S. Doc. 92, 57 Cong., 2 sess., Serial 4422 (Washington, 1903) and H. Rep. 477, 64 Cong., 1 sess., Serial 6908 (Washington, 1916).

Depositaries' journals of Post Office Department accounts are described in chapter VI of this Guide under records of field offices.

Records in Other Custody. --The Manuscript Division of the Library of Congress has a register of accounts current of post offices in Tennessee, Texas, Arkansas, and Florida, June 1, 1861-Mar. 31, 1862 (1 vol.). A packet of quarterly accounts current on Sept. 30, 1864, with J. R. Sneed, depositary at Savannah, Ga., is in the Ryder Collection of Confederate Archives in the Tufts College Library.

INSPECTION OFFICE

Toward the end of June 1861, Benjamin N. Clements, the Chief of the Appointment Bureau, began acting as the head of the Inspection Office. Bartholomew Fuller conducted the business of the Office after his appointment as its principal clerk, which probably occurred in Oct. 1861 since he signed the letters sent from the 18th of that month. Fuller continued in charge of the Office although he was later designated chief clerk of the Department.

The Inspection Office had the duty of overseeing the performance of mail contractors and route agents and to some extent that of postmasters. It received and examined registers of arrivals and departures of mails, imposed fines on contractors for negligence in fulfilling their contracts, and made deductions in their compensation for failures and irregularities. It also examined certificates of the service of route agents and required from them explanations of irregularities. It supplied blanks for mail registers and reports of mail failures; and mailbags, locks, and keys. It supervised the work of special agents in investigating mail depredations and losses. The special agents were required to record in a journal any observations regarding the neglect of duty or violation of regulations by postmasters, mail contractors, and route agents and to forward with their monthly accounts any part of the journal not included in a report.

Record Group 109. --The letters-sent books of the Inspection Office, June 26, 1861-Feb. 3, 1864 (ch. XI, vols. 44-46, 9 in.), contain fair copies of outgoing letters; the record for 1864-65 has presumably been lost. The letters are to postmasters, route agents, and mail contractors concerning mail supplies and service and to special agents regarding investigations of mail depredations and other matters. Other letters are to railroad presidents, the First Auditor, the Chief of the Contract Bureau, and to Congressmen.

Records in Other Custody. --In the Southern Historical Collection in the University of North Carolina Library are the papers of G. G. Lynch, a special postal agent and railroad agent at Weldon, N.C., 1860-65 (109 items). They include letters from the Postmaster General and the chiefs of the bureaus of the Post Office Department.

OFFICE OF MILITARY TELEGRAPHS

An act of May 11, 1861 (Prov. Cong. C.S.A. Stat. 106), authorized the President to take control of telegraph lines and offices and to employ operators as agents of the Government. He was also authorized to contract for the extension of existing telegraph lines at Government expense. Since telegraph lines were a means of communication, the authority given to the President was vested by him in the Postmaster General, who under an act of May 21, 1861 (Prov. Cong. C.S.A. Stat. 125), was authorized to employ officers of the telegraph companies as agents to perform the services specified in the act of May 11.

The Confederate Government used existing telegraph lines and constructed others. In May 1861 the Southern Telegraph Co. took over that part of the American Telegraph Co.'s line running from Alexandria, Va., to New Orleans. William S. Morris of Lynchburg, Va., who had been a director of the latter company, and James R. Dowell who had been its general superintendent, became president and general superintendent, respectively, of the Southern Telegraph Co., incorporated in Virginia with headquarters in Richmond. Farther west the Southwestern Telegraph Co. operated lines southward from Louisville through Kentucky, Tennessee, Alabama, Mississippi, and Louisiana to New Orleans. The lines of this company in Kentucky and Tennessee were cut by military operations, and the lines farther south came under military control. New telegraph lines constructed in 1861 with Government funds included one from Houston to New Orleans by the Texas Telegraph Co. and one from Little Rock to Fort Smith by the Arkansas State Telegraph Co. Other telegraph lines were constructed and operated by the Army independently. After being designated manager of the Office of Military Telegraphs, William S. Morris continued to serve as president of the Southern Telegraph Co. J. T. Coldwell became superintendent of the military telegraph lines. In 1862 telegraph operators were exempted from military duty, but so scarce were they that operators who had already enlisted had to be detailed to the Military Telegraphs Office, the Southern Telegraph Co., and the Southwestern Telegraph Co. Richmond, Augusta, Wilmington, Montgomery, Atlanta, and Lynchburg each had facilities to handle the heavy traffic.

The manager of this Office was William S. Morris.

J. Cutler Andrews, "The Southern Telegraph Company, 1861-1865; a Chapter in the History of Wartime Communication," Journal of Southern History, 30:319-344 (Aug. 1964); C.S.A. Post Office Department, Report of the Postmaster General in Answer to the Resolution of the House of Representatives of October 13, 1862 [Richmond? 1863]; Robert L. Thompson, Wiring a Continent; the History of the Telegraph Industry in the United States, 1832-1866 (Princeton, 1947).

Record Group 109. --Some military telegraph accounts, 1863-64 (5 in.), supply information about the lines. There are abstracts of accounts and accompanying vouchers of William S. Morris and monthly accounts of telegraph stations.

The file of Confederate papers relating to citizens or business firms, described in chapter XI of this Guide, contains vouchers, abstracts of accounts, telegrams, and correspondence under the names of J. T. Coldwell, Charles C. Clute (Texas Telegraph Co.), J. R. Dowell, W. S. Morris, telegraph companies, John Van Horne (Southwestern Telegraph Co.), and B. Welford Wrenn (Southern Telegraph Co.). The file for telegraph companies includes some lengthy documents from the records of Congress.

The records of the Southern Telegraph Company in the Carnegie Library of Pittsburgh contain reports to stockholders and correspondence between William S. Morris and Postmaster General Reagan and other Confederate officials.

POST OFFICE DEPARTMENT AGENT FOR THE TRANS-MISSISSIPPI WEST

The maintenance of mail service in the Trans-Mississippi West depended upon the ability of the Post Office Department to communicate with that region. During 1862-63 special arrangements were made for the conveyance of mail between the eastern part of the Confederacy and the Trans-Mississippi West, but by the end of 1863 communication had become so uncertain, owing to stronger U.S. control on the Mississippi, that the Postmaster General recommended the appointment of an officer to administer the postal business in that region. Accordingly, on Feb. 10, 1864 (1 Cong. C.S.A. Stat. 184), the President was authorized to appoint an agent of the Post Office Department to be stationed west of the Mississippi River. On Mar. 12 the Postmaster General informed the newly appointed agent that clerks had been assigned to him from the Department and directed him to employ additional clerical assistance, to draw on the Assistant Treasurer for funds, and to rent an office building in Marshall, Tex.

James H. Starr was appointed Agent of the Post Office Department for the Trans-Mississippi West on Mar. 12, 1864.

John N. Cravens, James Harper Starr; Financier of the Republic of Texas, p. 136-145 (Austin, 1950); Lawrence L. Shenfield, "Confederate States Trans-Mississippi Express Mail," American Philatelist, 65:423-430 (Mar. 1952).

Record Group 109. --Only a minor part of the records of the agent of the Post Office Department for the Trans-Mississippi West that have survived are in the War Department Collection of Confederate Records. There is a small letters-received file, June 1864-May 1865 (4 in.). Letters from postmasters concern stamps, funds on hand and deposits of money, reports, dead letters, and accounts. Letters from depositaries at several places enclose reports of deposits by postmasters and statements of funds. Communications from the Finance Bureau of the Post Office Department relate to stamps, funds, and the disposition of Treasury notes found in dead letters. Other correspondents were officials of the Treasury Department at Marshall, Tex., the Postmaster General, special agents, and the Army headquarters at Shreveport. The file also includes receipts for dead letters delivered to the Army and monthly registers of mail arrivals and departures. Post route papers for Arkansas, Louisiana, and Texas, 1864-65 (8 in.), include contracts with mail carriers, invitations for proposals, proposals setting forth the terms on which bidders would agree to carry the mail, notices of acceptance of bids, and petitions from citizens regarding mail route changes. There are some financial returns of postmasters and related correspondence, 1864-65 (1 1/2 in.). Depositaries' reports, Jan.-Apr. 1865 (1/2 in.), show deposits by postmasters and the amounts of warrants drawn on the Treasurer of the Confederate States by James H. Starr on account of Post Office funds. A few receipts of Capt. H. P. Pratt for dead letters from the postmaster at Shreveport are dated Dec. 1864.

Records in Other Custody. --The correspondence of James H. Starr presented to the University of Texas Library in 1932 contains pertinent material. In the letters-sent press copy books, 1864-65, are letters to Postmaster General Reagan, special agents, Gen. E. K. Smith, Gen. H. W. Allen, and Congressman Franklin B. Sexton. In Starr's letters-received file are letters from Reagan, Sexton, Special Agents Morris R.

Reagan and R. M. Gains, postmasters, and military officers.

POST OFFICES

Record Group 75. --Among the records of the Bureau of Indian Affairs are some records of the post office at Fort Smith, Ark., 1858-62 (1 in.), including letters received, copies of letters sent, vouchers, receipts, affidavits, statements of accounts current, schedules and registers of arrivals and departures of mail, and other records kept by Abraham G. Mayers, who was first the U.S. and later the Confederate postmaster there.

Record Group 109. --An account book of the Richmond, Va., post office, Jan. 1855-Jan. 1865 (ch. XI, vol. 51, 1861-65, p. 10-18), is in the War Department Collection of Confederate Records. It contains a chronological record of payments to the Confederate Treasurer, the clerk, and other payments for rent, a mail messenger, firewood, and office supplies. It also shows amounts collected from postmasters, amounts due the Post Office Department, and amounts received in stamps.

Records in Other Custody. --Papers of William D. Coleman, postmaster at Danville, Va., in the University of Virginia Library contain post office appointments for 1861-65. In the same repository are an account of the mails received at the post office at Peytonsburg, Pittsylvania County, Va., Apr. 4, 1851-Mar. 27, 1864, and accounts of the Halifax County, Va., post office. The papers of Erasmus H. Coston in Duke University Library include manuscripts relating to his work as postmaster in Palo Alto, Onslow County, N. C. The papers of John L. Riddell, postmaster at New Orleans, are in the Howard-Tilton Memorial Library of Tulane University.

X

DEPARTMENT OF JUSTICE

An act of Feb. 21, 1861 (Prov. Cong. C. S. A. Stat. 33), established a Department of Justice to be headed by an Attorney General. He was empowered to prosecute all suits in the Supreme Court in which the Confederate States were concerned, to give his advice and opinions on questions of law when required by the President or when requested by any of the heads of departments, to supervise the accounts of court officials, and to handle all claims against the Confederate States. An act of Mar. 7, 1861 (Prov. Cong. C. S. A. Stat. 53), authorized an Assistant Attorney General for the Department, and Wade Keyes of Montgomery, Ala., was so appointed on Mar. 8. Other employees of the Office of the Attorney General included Jules St. Martin, chief clerk, James M. Matthews, law clerk, and Patrick Doran, messenger.

While interpreting the law became the main duty of the Attorney General (a Supreme Court was never established), his other duties included supervising district attorneys and suits in district courts and representing the Confederate Government in all cases considered by the Board of Claims Commissioners. Since no Department of the Interior was established the Department of Justice also supervised the Bureau of Public Printing, the Patent Office, and territorial affairs.

Successive Attorneys General:

    Judah P. Benjamin, Feb. 25, 1861.
    Wade Keyes (acting), Sept. 17, 1861.
    Thomas Bragg, Nov. 21, 1861.
    Thomas H. Watts, Apr. 9, 1862.
    Wades Keyes (acting), Oct. 1, 1863.
    George Davis, Jan. 4, 1864.

C. S. A. Department of Justice, Report of the Attorney General, Feb. 26, 1862, Jan. 1, 1863, Nov. 18, 1863, Apr. 25, 1864, Nov. 1, 1864 [Richmond, 1862-64]; Rembert W. Patrick, Jefferson Davis and His Cabinet (Baton Rouge, 1944); William M. Robinson, Jr., Justice in Grey; a History of the Judicial System of the Confederate States of America, p. 27-38, 510-538 (Cambridge, Mass., 1941).

Records of the Department of Justice were moved south when Richmond was evacuated on Apr. 2, 1865. Among the materials found soon after at Chester, S. C., by Felix G. De Fontaine was the opinion book of the Attorney General. Much later, in Nov. 1897, the New York Public Library bought the opinion book, together with a typewritten copy, from W. Hampton De Fontaine for $500.

OFFICE OF THE ATTORNEY GENERAL

Record Group 109. --Fourteen opinions of the Attorney General now in the War Department Collection of Confederate Records include 11 manuscript ones and three printed. All are printed in the compilation edited by Patrick cited below except one of Sept. 17, 1861, by Judah P. Benjamin relating to the status of prisoners who had been captured by privateers and were being maintained by a deputy marshal of Florida. Other papers include: a list dated June 24, 1863, of district judges, attorneys, and commissioners; an estimate of salaries and other expenses, Dec. 14, 1861; an undated list of Department employees; and letters to President Davis, Apr. 29, 1861, regarding appointments during the recess of Congress, and Nov. 28, 1864, submitting a list of Department employees. Reports of the Attorney General are in both manuscript and printed form. There are also manuscript and printed reports of the Commissioner of Patents and the Superintendent of Public Printing.

The few extant records of the Department of Justice can be considerably supplemented by letters to and from the Attorney General and his bureau heads in the correspondence of the other executive departments, Congress, and the other agencies of the Confederate Government. Several communications of the Attorney General are in print (Crandall, Confederate Imprints, 1:144). Another Communication from the Attorney General... March 13, 1863 [Richmond, 1863] contains his reports on specific claims for damages to land on which Confederate fortifications had been erected, for the loss of slaves who escaped or were killed while working on fortifications, for damage to property by the Confederate Army, and for land taken for the Richmond defenses.

Records in Other Custody. --The opinion book of the Attorney General, Apr. 1, 1861-Mar. 24, 1865 (1 vol.), in the New York Public Library contains fair copies of 217 opinions, including some prepared by Asst. Attorney General Wade Keyes. It is indexed by the names of the officials to whom the opinions were given. A photostat of this book is in the University of Texas Library, and a microfilm copy is in the Southern Historical Collection of the University of North Carolina Library.

C.S.A. Department of Justice, The Opinions of the Confederate Attorneys General, 1861-1865, ed. by Rembert W. Patrick (Buffalo, 1950). Included is the opinion of Apr. 22, 1865, given at Charlotte, N.C., on the advisability of the surrender of the Confederacy on the basis of the convention of Apr. 18 between Generals Johnston and Sherman. The original opinions sent to the Departments are in their files with copies of letters requesting opinions.

The Thomas H. Watts papers, 1818-92, in the Alabama Department of Archives and History include requests from President Davis for opinions, 1862-63, Watts' resignation of Sept. 1863 and its acceptance, and a printed circular of the Attorney General, Oct. 22, 1862, on enforcement of the sequestration act.

The diary of Thomas Bragg, Jan. 1861-Nov. 1862 (1 vol.), in the Southern Historical Collection of the University of North Carolina Library contains references to President Davis, Vice President Stephens, Judah P.

Benjamin, Gens. Thomas J. Jackson, Gideon J. Pillow, Leonidas Polk,
P. G. T. Beauregard, and Richard Gatling; a record of the comments of
Davis on public matters; and information on political activities in Richmond
and on matters discussed at Cabinet meetings during the period Dec. 6,
1861-Apr. 4, 1862.

> University of North Carolina   Edition of the Thomas Bragg Diary, ed.
> Library, Guide to the Microfilm   by Clyde E. Pitts (Chapel Hill, 1966).

PATENT OFFICE

The Patent Office had an informal beginning in a resolution of Mar.
4, 1861 (Prov. Cong. C.S.A. Stat. 93), authorizing persons who wished to
procure patents or file caveats for inventions and useful discoveries and
improvements to file specifications and descriptive drawings in the office of
the Attorney General. An act of May 21, 1861 (Prov. Cong. C.S.A. Stat.
136), established the Patent Office under a Commissioner of Patents who
was to be appointed by the President and placed under the direction of the
Attorney General. Under an act of Aug. 30, 1861 (Prov. Cong. C.S.A. Stat.
199), the Commissioner of Patents was authorized to appoint assistant
patent examiners as required and a messenger.

The Commissioner of Patents assembled a staff of examiners and
clerks and a technical library for which appropriations of $500 were made
by the act of May 21, 1861, and an act of Apr. 16, 1863 (1 Cong. C.S.A. Stat.
110). In Feb. 1862 the Patent Office staff included William W. Lester, chief
clerk; Americus Featherman and Thomas R. Duval, assistant examiners;
Howard H. Young, recording clerk; C. H. Ely, temporary recording clerk;
and E. A. Baughman, messenger.

The Commissioner of Patents was Rufus R. Rhodes, May 22, 1861.

> Robinson, Justice in Grey, p. 539-554. C.S.A. Patent Office, Report of the Commissioner of Patents, 1862-65 [Richmond, 1862-65]. The reports contain lists of patents by classes, which by 1865 included the following: agriculture, metallurgy, manufacture of fibrous tissues, chemicals, steam engines, navigation, mathematical instruments, civil engineering, land conveyance, hydraulics, lumber, leather, household furniture, fine arts, firearms, and surgical instruments. Other lists give name of patentee, his residence, the number and nature of the invention, and the date of the patent. C.S.A. Patent Office, Rules and Directions for Proceedings in the Confederate States Patent Office (Richmond, 1861), is based on the act of May 21, 1861, and contains samples of applications and other documents for use in applying for patents.

Record Group 109. --Patent No. 162 for an improved instrument for
measuring distances issued to John J. Daly of New Orleans on Apr. 18,
1863, is in the War Department Collection of Confederate Records.

Records in Other Custody. --A letters-sent book of the Commissioner
of Patents, June 26, 1863-Mar. 21, 1865 (1 vol.), in the Confederate Museum
at Richmond contains fair copies of letters mainly to individuals concerning
the form in which petitions and specifications were to be submitted, the
amendment of specifications, the reexamination of applications, information
regarding patents, acknowledgment of fees, explanation of the rejection of

applications, and requests for models. A record of assignments, June 26, 1861-Feb. 3, 1865 (1 vol.), in the Confederate Museum contains assignments of rights in improvements in inventions for which applications for patents had been made, with the names of parties and signatures of applicants and witnesses. Copies of patents Nos. 267-274 issued during the period Jan. 16-Mar. 21, 1865, with specifications are in the same record of assignments. These are additions to the list in the Commissioner's printed report of Jan. 1865. Patent No. 202 issued to Z. McDaniel of Glasgow, Ky., on Sept. 21, 1863, for an improvement in torpedoes, with specifications, is also in the Confederate Museum.

Papers in the University of Virginia Library relating to a projectile for a rifled siege gun invented by John B. Read include drawings, specifications, and correspondence.

Correspondence of the Commissioners of Patents with the heads of other Government departments and bureaus can be found in their records, described in this Guide. Other correspondence of the Patent Office, patents, drawings, and specifications are in collections of personal papers. Patent No. 9 issued to Thomas W. Cofer for a revolver, Aug. 12, 1861, and a drawing are published in William A. Albaugh, III, Hugh Benet, Jr., and Edward N. Simmons, Confederate Handguns: Concerning the Guns, the Men Who Made Them, and the Time of Their Use, p. 141-143 (Philadelphia, 1962). Patent No. 100 issued to Lt. John M. Brooke for his design of the ironclad Virginia, with specifications and drawings, is included in his "The Virginia, or Merrimac; Her Real Projector," Southern Historical Society Papers, 19:27-30 (Jan. 1891).

BUREAU OF PUBLIC PRINTING

An act of Feb. 27, 1861 (Prov. Cong. C.S.A. Stat. 41), established in the Department of Justice a Bureau of Public Printing under a Superintendent of Public Printing to be appointed by the President. The duty of the superintendent was to "supervise, direct and control all the printing done by order of Congress, or under contract with any executive department, as to the quality of paper to be used, the character of type, the style of binding, and the general execution of the work; and also as to the time and order in which the same shall be completed." Legislation enacted May 14, 1861, Aug. 5, 1861 (Prov. Cong. C.S.A. Stats. 111 and 172), and June 3, 1864 (2 Cong. C.S.A. Stat. 257), outlined the Superintendent's duties in more detail. The appropriation acts of 1862 and 1863 provided for a clerk and a messenger, and the act of 1864 for "clerks"; Edward G. Dill was the clerk in 1863.

The appointment of George E. W. Nelson as Superintendent was confirmed on May 6, 1861, and he held the position throughout the war.

Robinson, Justice in Grey, p. 555-564. Reports of the Superintendent of Public Printing of Jan. 5 and Nov. 18, 1863, and Apr. 26 and Oct. 26, 1864, are in The Virginia State Library, Bulletin, 4:47-65 (Jan. 1911). Letters of the Superintendent are in the letters-sent books and the letters-received files of other departments and bureaus of the Confederate Government that are described in this Guide.

XI

RECORDS COMPILED
BY THE
U.S. WAR DEPARTMENT

In the years after the Civil War the Archive Office of the U.S. War Department was frequently called on to furnish information from Confederate records to the Southern Claims Commission and the U.S. Court of Claims for use in substantiating the many claims of Southerners for property loss or damage. The Archive Office used these records also to assist the Pension Office in acting on applications from Union veterans who had been in Southern prisons and hospitals. At the same time the War Department received many requests from State officials, historical societies, and patriotic or memorial associations for transcripts of Confederate military records. Obviously there was need to preserve the original records and yet make them available for ready reference. To this end several compilations of Confederate records were undertaken by the U.S. War Department.

COMPILED MILITARY SERVICE RECORDS

In 1902 the Secretary of War recommended to the Senate Committee on Printing the compilation and publication of a roster of officers and men of the Union and Confederate armies as a supplement to the Official Records...Armies. It was pointed out that such a compilation would relieve Congress from the demands that were made upon it each year for legislation to provide information on the military records of State troops and that it would give public recognition to the enlisted men. Accordingly, an act of Feb. 25, 1903 (32 Stat., pt. 1, 884), authorized the chief of the Record and Pension Office of the U.S. War Department to compile a complete roster of the officers and enlisted men of the Union and Confederate Armies from official records in the possession of the United States and other authentic records that might be borrowed from States and other sources. The compilation was undertaken according to a system that had been inaugurated in 1887 by Capt. Fred C. Ainsworth, the head of the Record and Pension Office, for the officers and enlisted men of the Union Army. The information regarding individual servicemen in military and medical records was abstracted on cards that were printed for each record series; on them clerks filled in by hand the soldier's name, rank, and military organization, the volume and page number of the records, and the copyist's name. These index-record cards, as they were named, were supplemented by original one-name documents drawn from the files of the Confederate War Department. The compiled military service records that were thus built up replaced the dilapidated muster rolls and book records and were much easier to use.

The preparation of the compiled military service records was a major undertaking that required the services of many clerks over a period of years. The carding was actually started shortly before the passage of the act of Feb. 25, 1903, and for more than 10 years priority was given to the records of men belonging to State organizations. For several years after 1908, approximately 700,000 cards were made each year, and after the State organizations were completed in 1914 there were on June 30 of that year 7,767,898 military record cards and 113,011 medical records cards. The carding of medical records, the records of Confederate organizations, and of general and staff officers continued until 1917. On June 30 of that year there were 8,518,421 military record cards and 741,009 medical record cards. Resumed in 1920, the carding was completed by the end of the decade.

The Confederate War Department records that were used in compiling the military service records were chiefly those of the Adjutant and Inspector General's Office and included muster rolls and payrolls, registers of appointments, rosters, casualty lists, and inspection reports. The medical record cards were compiled chiefly from hospital registers and muster rolls. Records of the Second Auditor of the Confederate Treasury Department relating to deceased soldiers were also used. Supplementing the Confederate records that were in some cases incomplete were U.S. War Department records relating to Confederate prisoners of war (available on microfilm as M 598), hospital registers, and rolls of men paroled during and at the end of the war. Some of the Southern States responded to the Secretary of War's request of 1903 by furnishing muster rolls and other records for copying, and many individuals in the South also forwarded their official records.

The index-record cards are preserved in jacket-envelopes. In order to have a more complete record of the service of Confederate military personnel, the Adjutant General's Office collected single-name documents from the files of the various bureaus and offices of the Confederate Government in its custody and filed them with the appropriate index-record cards. Most such original documents are filed chiefly with the service records of officers, and they include requisitions for supplies, pay vouchers, receipts for ordnance and ordnance stores, receipts for commutation of quarters and fuel, paroles and amnesty oaths, abstracts and certifications of accounts, provost marshal passes, invoices of property transferred, vouchers for and abstracts of disbursements, abstracts of articles received, applications and recommendations for appointments, property returns, extracts of special orders, Second Auditor's accounts, mileage vouchers, and the like. Cross-references to documents in other compiled files are provided.

Many pieces of correspondence were removed from the letters-received files of the Office of the Secretary of War, the Adjutant and Inspector General's Office, the Quartermaster General's Department, the Ordnance Department, the Subsistence Department, and from the records of Congress and the Second Auditor and filed in the jacket-envelopes. The officers' papers that were received by the War Department after the war were also placed there. The files drawn upon were thus considerably diminished by this operation, which explains their present small volume and the great size of the compiled military service records.

Record Group 109. --The compiled military service records are in three parts. Part 1 (parts 2 and 3 are described below) consists of jacket-envelopes for men who served in organizations connected with one of the

Confederate States, 1861-65 (12,443 ft.), arranged alphabetically by State, thereunder by branch of service (cavalry, artillery, and infantry), thereunder by designation of organization, and thereunder alphabetically by name of person; after the jackets for men in each of the branches are jackets for men in reserve, militia, local defense, conscript, prison guard, instruction, and other organizations. A general index to all the compiled military service records is available on cards (1,027 ft.). The cards give the soldier's or officer's name, rank, and organization, and frequently information about the organization's origin. Indexes for the different States are available as separate microfilm publications.

The compiled military service records of State regiments and other military organizations are all available on microfilm. Pamphlets describing the rolls of microfilm and listing the military organizations included are available on request from the National Archives. The number of the microcopy for the records of each State, the microcopy number of the index (M 253 is the consolidated index described below), and repositories where they may be available for use are as follows:

State	Microcopy No.	Repositories
Alabama	M 311 (508 rolls) Index: M 374 (49 rolls)	---
Arizona 　Territory	M 318 (1 roll) Index: M 375 (1 roll)	Arizona Historical Foundation Phoenix, Ariz. (lacks M 253)
Arkansas	M 317 (256 rolls) Index: M 376 (26 rolls)	Arkansas History Commission Little Rock, Ark. (lacks M 376)
Florida	M 251 (104 rolls) Index: M 225 (9 rolls)	State Comptroller Tallahassee, Fla. (lacks M 225) United Daughters of the Confederacy, Florida Division (M 225 only)
Georgia	M 266 (607 rolls) Index: M 226 (67 rolls)	Georgia Department of Archives 　and History Atlanta, Ga. (lacks M 253)
Kentucky	M 319 (136 rolls) Index: M 377 (14 rolls)	---
Louisiana	M 320 (414 rolls) Index: M 378 (31 rolls)	Louisiana Department, Louisiana 　State Library Baton Rouge, La. (M 320 only)
Mississippi	M 269 (427 rolls) Index: M 232 (45 rolls)	University of Southern Mississippi Hattiesburg, Miss. (lacks M 253)
Missouri	M 322 (193 rolls) Index: M380 (16 rolls)	---

North Carolina	M 270 (580 rolls) Index: M 230 (43 rolls)	North Carolina Department of Archives and History Raleigh, N. C. (M 230 only)
South Carolina	M 267 (392 rolls) Index: M 381 (35 rolls)	South Carolina Archives Dept. Columbia, S. C. (M 267 only)
Tennessee	M 268 (359 rolls) Index: M 231 (48 rolls)	Cossitt-Goodwyn Libraries 33 S. Front Street Memphis, Tenn. (lacks M 253) Tennessee Polytechnic Institute Cookeville, Tenn. (M 231 only) Tennessee State Library and Archives Nashville, Tenn. (lacks M 253)
Texas	M 323 (445 rolls) Index: M 227 (41 rolls)	Fort Worth Public Library Fort Worth, Tex. (M 227 only) Stephen F. Austin State College Nacogdoches, Tex. (M 227 only) Texas State Historical Survey Commission Texas Historical Foundation Austin, Tex. (M 227 only)
Virginia	M 324 (1,075 rolls) Index: M 382 (62 rolls)	West Virginia Department of Archives and History Charleston, W. Va. (M 324 only) Virginia State Library, Archives Division Richmond, Va. (lacks M 253)

Since some records of the Confederate Army were lost during the war and at its close, the compiled military service records are not complete. Moreover, some soldiers served in State militia units that were not mustered into Confederate service. Records of military service that have been collected and compiled by most of the Southern States should therefore be consulted. An act of Feb. 16, 1864 (1 Cong. C. S. A. Stat. 190), authorized the Secretary of War to grant passports and transportation to State officers duly commissioned to communicate with and to perfect records of their troops. During 1864-65 some of the Southern States designated recorders or superintendents to collect information regarding their troops, and special orders issued by the Adjutant and Inspector General's Office directed that aid be extended to them in accordance with the act of Feb. 16. After the war the adjutants general or commissioners of military records of the former States of the Confederacy continued to collect muster rolls, commissions, appointments, orders, and other military records, to prepare compilations of military service records, and to index them. The published rosters that are cited below are not always comprehensive because, except for North Carolina, the compilers did not make adequate use of the compiled military service records in the War Department collection of Confederate records in the National Archives. Repositories of the Confederate military service records, and related bibliography, are as follows:

Alabama. Alabama Department of Archives and History, Montgomery, Ala.

Arkansas. Arkansas History Commission, Little Rock, Ark. Marcus J. Wright, Arkansas in the War, 1861-1865 (Batesville, Ark., 1963).

Florida. Office of the Adjutant General, State Arsenal, St. Augustine, Fla. Florida, Board of State Institutions, Soldiers of Florida in the Seminole, Indian, Civil, and Spanish-American Wars (Live Oak, Fla., 1909?).

Georgia. Georgia Department of Archives and History, Atlanta, Ga. Georgia, State Division of Confederate Pensions and Records, Roster of the Confederate Soldiers of Georgia, 1861-1865, comp. by Lillian Henderson (6 vols.; Hapeville, Ga., 1959-64). Charles E. Jones, Georgia in the War, 1861-1865 (Atlanta, 1909), containing information regarding military organizations, officers, and campaigns, and local designations of Georgia troops.

Kentucky. Kentucky Historical Society, Frankfort, Ky. Kentucky, Adjutant General's Office, Report... Confederate Kentucky Volunteers, 1861-65, comp. by Abner Harris (2 vols.; Frankfort, 1915, 1919).

Louisiana. Adjutant General's Office, Jackson Barracks, New Orleans, La. Napier Bartlett, Military Record of Louisiana, Including Biographical and Historical Papers

Relating to the Military Organizations of the State (Baton Rouge, 1964); Andrew B. Booth, "Louisiana Confederate Military Records," Louisiana Historical Quarterly, 4:369-418 (July 1921); Louisiana, Adjutant General, Annual Report, 1891 (New Orleans, 1892), containing lists of officers and military organizations; Louisiana, Commissioner of Military Records, Records of Louisiana Confederate Soldiers and Louisiana Confederate Commands, comp. by Andrew B. Booth (3 vols.; New Orleans, 1920).

Maryland. William W. Goldsborough, The Maryland Line in the Confederate Army, 1861-1865 (Baltimore, 1900). Maryland, Hall of Records Commission, Index to the Maryland Line in the Confederate Army, 1861-1865, comp. by Mrs. Louise Q. Lewis ([Annapolis, 1944]).

Mississippi. Mississippi Department of Archives and History, Jackson, Miss.

Missouri. U.S. Record and Pension Office, Organization and Status of Missouri Troops, Union and Confederate, in Service during the Civil War (Washington, 1902, published also as S. Doc. 412, 57 Cong., 1 sess.; Serial 4247).

North Carolina. North Carolina Department of Archives and History, Raleigh, N.C. North Carolina, Adjutant General's Office, Roster of North Carolina Troops in the War between the States, comp. by John W. Moore (4 vols.; Raleigh, 1882). A card index to this roster is in the North Carolina Department of Archives and History. North Carolina Confederate Centennial Commission, A Guide to Military Organizations and Installations, North Carolina, 1861-1865, comp. by Louis H. Manarin (Raleigh, 1961); North Carolina Department of Archives and History, Guide to Civil War Records in the North Carolina State Archives (Raleigh, 1966), North Carolina Troops, 1861-1865; a Roster, Vol. 1. Artillery, comp. by Louis H. Manarin and others (Raleigh, 1966). South Carolina. South Carolina Archives Department, Columbia, S. C. South Carolina Historical Commission, South Carolina Troops in Confederate Service, comp. by Alexander S. Salley (3 vols.; Columbia, S. C., 1913, 1914, 1930). Tennessee. Tennessee State Library and Archives, Nashville, Tenn. Tennessee, Civil War Centennial Commission, Tennesseans in the Civil War; a Military History of Confederate and Union Units with Available Rosters of Personnel (Nashville, 1964); Marcus J. Wright, Tennessee in the War, 1861-1865; Lists of Military Organizations and Officers from Tennessee in Both the Confederate and Union Armies (Williamsbridge, N. Y., 1908). Texas. Texas State Library, Archives Division, Austin, Tex. James M. Day, "Sources for Military History in the Texas State Archives, " Texas Military History, 2:113-125 (May 1962); Lester N. Fitzhugh, Texas Batteries, Battalions, Regiments, Commanders and Field Officers, Confederate States Army, 1861-1865 (Midlothian, Tex., 1959); Harry M. Henderson, "Regiments, Battalions and Batteries from Texas in the Confederacy, " in Texas in the Confederacy, p. 119-149 (San Antonio, 1955). Information concerning Texas military organizations is in Marcus J. Wright, comp., and Harold B. Simpson, ed., Texas in the War, 1861-1865 (Hillsboro, Tex., 1965). Virginia. Virginia State Library, Archives Division, Richmond, Va. Meriwether Stuart, "The Record of Virginia Forces; a Study in the Compilation of Civil War Records, " Virginia Magazine of History and Biography, 68:3-57 (Jan. 1960); Lee A. Wallace, Jr., A Guide to Virginia Military Organizations, 1861-1865 (Richmond, 1964).

Part 2 of the compiled military service records consists of jacket-envelopes (290 ft.; available on microfilm as M 258) for men who served in organizations raised directly by the Confederate Government and not identified with any one State (Confederate and Indian organizations designated by name, such as Morgan's Cavalry, Cherokee Mounted Rifles, Signal Corps, Engineers, Sappers and Miners, Invalid Corps, Brush Battalion, Exchanged Battalion, and President's Guard).

Part 3 consists of a group of jackets (272 ft.; available on microfilm as M 331) known as the General and Staff Officers' Papers, containing the carded records of general officers, officers and enlisted men of the staff departments (Adjutant and Inspector General's Department, Quartermaster General's Department, Commissary General's Department, Medical Department, and Ordnance Department), officers attached to army corps, division, and brigade staffs, chiefs of military courts, regimental officers of State units, aides-de-camp, agents, chaplains, couriers, drillmasters, enrolling officers, hospital stewards, surgeons, provost marshals, and civilian employees of the War Department. Files for Navy officers who were assigned to the Army are also in these records.

The three sections of compiled military service records described above are all indexed in the consolidated card index to compiled military service records of Confederate soldiers (999 ft.; available on microfilm as M 253). This master card index contains the names of all military personnel (soldiers, noncommissioned officers, and officers) in the compiled military service records. The cards give the name of the soldier, his rating or rank, the designation of the unit with which he served, and often information concerning the origin of the unit.

Other compiled aids to research are available. An alphabetical name index to Confederate and staff compiled military service records (43 ft.), relates to parts 2 and 3 of the compiled service records. Also in Record Group 109 are two other small files of compiled military service records. One concerns officers and noncommissioned officers attached to corps, division, and brigade staffs and bands. The other concerns miscellaneous assignments.

OTHER COMPILED RECORDS

A file compiled by the U.S. War Department on individual Confederate citizens or business firms, 1861-65 (1,240 ft.; available on microfilm as M 346), contains original documents, with cross-references to other compiled files and to book records. Vouchers, receipts, affidavits, and correspondence relate to payments for materials purchased by or services performed for the Army, with some for the Navy. Other documents include abstracts of expenditures, contracts for armament, contractors' bonds, certificates of deposit, passes, powers of attorney, lists of prepayment certificates received at offices of State commissioners of taxes, requests for warrants, Treasurer's receipts and warrants, reports of the Second Auditor on claims, recommendations for appointments, applications for clerkships in the Treasury Department, and receipts for salary payments. These documents concern banks, claims of survivors of deceased military personnel, claims for lost property and Negro slaves, coal and iron mining companies, commissary agents, commissioners to examine political prisoners, Confederate officials, Congressmen, county jails, drydock associations, Government contractors, home guards, hotels, industrial plants, insurance companies, ironworks, jailers, leadworks, militiamen, naval personnel, newspapers, niter beds, ordnance agents, penitentiaries, political prisoners, post offices, quartermaster agents, railroads, scientists of the Niter and Mining Bureau, stagelines, steamship companies, tanneries, telegraph companies and operators, utility companies, and widows of servicemen. The quantity of material is sometimes significant, as in the case of a number of the railroads, the Tredegar Iron Works, and Christopher G. Memminger, Secretary of the Treasury. Many Government activities are documented in these records, but to find the pertinent records the names of individuals connected with them will be needed, for there is no subject or place-name index.

During the 1880's the War Department compiled from Confederate records a file of vessel papers (23 ft.), containing materials relating to Government and non-Government vessels, British naval vessels, State vessels, and U.S. vessels. This file covers Confederate naval vessels, steamers, sailing vessels, flatboats, canalboats, blockade-runners, revenue cutters, privately owned vessels chartered by the Army or the Navy to carry freight or personnel, and vessels sunk to obstruct the passage of rivers and harbors. It contains correspondence, charters, bills, vouchers, payrolls, shipping articles, lists of officers and crews, soldiers' transportation tickets, quartermasters' transportation orders, insurance policies, provision returns, polls of soldiers' votes, ships' documents, requisitions, statements regarding the destruction of vessels, reports of the war claims commission, reports of boards of survey, bills for the relief of shipowners, cargo manifests, pictures, and cross-references to other records. An alphabetical index to ships' names gives the types of vessels and file numbers.

The Union provost marshals' file of one-name papers relating to civilians, 1861-67 (410 ft.; available on microfilm as M 345), consists chiefly of records of provost marshals who served in occupied areas of the South, the border States, Washington, D. C., and the Territory of New Mexico. The correspondence and other papers relate to the arrest and trial of persons suspected of aiding or spying for the enemy, using disloyal language, violating military orders, fighting as bushwhackers, claiming compensation for property used or seized by Union military authorities or for supplies or services furnished to the Army, to civilian and military prisoners, to persons charged with criminal offenses, and to persons requesting passes to cross the lines into the Confederacy or permits to visit persons in prisons. The correspondence also includes offers to testify against men charged with disloyalty, requests for permission to bear arms and for commissions as detectives, and statements regarding persons arrested. Other documents include affidavits, protests of persons arrested, orders for the confinement or release of prisoners, reports of military commissions, travel passes, loyalty and amnesty oaths, bonds and paroles of prisoners, bonds to keep the peace, and telegrams regarding the administration of telegraphers' oaths.

The Union provost marshals' file of two-or-more-name papers, 1861-67 (74 ft.; available on microfilm as M 416), contains records of provost marshals in the same areas relating to two or more persons. Correspondence in this file concerns the arrest of persons suspected of disloyalty, the transmittal of oaths of allegiance, the capture of contraband of war and slaves, the disposition of slaves, introductions and recommendations of persons, complaints against arbitrary arrests, the departure of men to join the Confederacy, requests to be placed on parole, applications for passes and the release of prisoners, contracts, and information against disloyal persons and spies. Lists and rolls of names cover bonded persons, committees of public safety, Confederate deserters, Confederate sympathizers, contrabands, detectives, employees at Government installations, guerrillas, hostages, Negro laborers, oaths and bonds, paroled prisoners, passes issued, patrol duty, planters, political prisoners, police, civilian prisoners, railroad employees, refugees, registered enemies, secessionists, slaveowners, stockholders in utility companies, and teamsters. The names of persons appearing on these lists and rolls are indexed alphabetically in the Union provost marshals' file of one-name papers relating to civilians, described above.

A file relating to military and civilian personnel, 1861-65 (480 ft.; available on microfilm as M 347), contains correspondence, other documents, card abstracts, and cross-reference slips relating to officers, soldiers, civilian employees, citizens, Confederates in Union prisons, and Federals in Confederate prisons, and British subjects in Confederate service, arranged alphabetically by surnames. The materials are similar to those in the compiled military service records, the citizens' file, and the Union provost marshals' files. The papers were placed in this file because they could not be identified positively for filing with the military service records, because no military service records had been established, and because they could not be correctly placed in any other file. The card abstracts were from the same sources that were used for the compiled military service records. The cross-references are to many different types of documents including receipt rolls for clothing and pay, detail and extra-duty rolls, registers and rolls of prisoners and deserters, hospital prescription books, oaths of allegiance, reports of operations and casualties, reports of prison guards, post returns, reports of sick and wounded, hospital returns, inspection reports, and muster rolls. The original documents include certificates for undertakers, certificates of discharge, certificates of enlistment and examination, correspondence, final statement regarding deceased soldiers for the Second Auditor, oaths and paroles of prisoners of war, pay vouchers, requisitions for forage, requisitions for stationery, and statements of prisoners. This file relates to the following civilian employees and citizens: blacksmiths, boatmen, carpenters and wheelwrights, clerks, Confederate sympathizers, conscripts, deserters, engineers, gunsmiths, harnessmakers, herdsmen, Invalid Corpsmen, laborers, laundresses, masons, mechanics, patternmakers, seamstresses, slaves, spies, tailoresses, tanners, teamsters, trimmers, and turners.

A miscellaneous collection of manuscripts, 1861-65 (28 ft.), consists of Confederate and some Union materials including correspondence concerning prisoners, deserters, and bushwhackers; lists and rolls of prisoners, deserters, burials, promotions, recruits, extra-duty men, and casualties; election returns of Confederate organizations, lists of employees in Confederate Government departments and installations; payrolls; vouchers; orders; quarterly reports of expenditures, receipts, prisoners' paroles, and reports on employees and extra-duty men in the niter and mining service and at ironworks and arsenals; and records of boards of inquiry, boards of survey, and courts-martial.

Record Group 109. --A file of carded naval service records, 1861-65 (6 1/2 ft.; available on microfilm as M 260), is in the War Department Collection of Confederate Records. Compiled by the Adjutant General's Office of the U.S. War Department from the Confederate records in its possession and other sources, the file consists mainly of cards giving the name and rank of naval personnel and references to a compiled file of vessel papers, payrolls, muster rolls, and volumes in which information relating to them can be found. The file covers officers and privateersmen as well as enlisted personnel. Original papers, including correspondence and paymasters' requisitions, are sometimes filed with the cards.

A file of carded hospital and prison records of naval and marine personnel, 1862-65 (7 ft.; available on microfilm as M 260), consists of printed cards showing the name of the person, his ship or station, the date and place of capture, release, or parole, place of confinement, and hospital treatment and discharge. This file also contains cards for personnel of privateers and other ships, and it sometimes gives information as to place of residence, age, and physical description. The cards were compiled from Union and Confederate hospital registers and prescription books; Union registers, rolls, and lists of prisoners; registers of oaths of allegiance; receipt rolls for clothing; rolls of rebel deserters and refugees; records of transportation issued; and other records. Cross-references to other compiled files are also in this file.

A small file of carded Marine Corps service records, 1861-65 (9 in.; available on microfilm as M 260), consists mainly of cards bearing references to other files in this record group, including payrolls, vessel papers, naval service records, and conscript rolls that supply data relating to marines. Some of the jackets in this file also contain original records.

APPENDIXES

I. WAR DEPARTMENT COLLECTION OF CONFEDERATE RECORDS

Before the Confederate Government evacuated Richmond some of its archives were moved southward. A joint resolution of May 27, 1864 (Ramsdell, Laws, p. 172), authorized the President, whenever the public exigencies required, to remove the archives and the executive departments to such places as he might designate. An act of Mar. 14, 1865, made a similar authorization. During 1864 some Government bureaus moved to more southern cities and in Mar. 1865 the Government agencies in Richmond shipped records from the Capital over the Richmond and Danville Railroad.

On Apr. 2, 1865, the Union Army penetrated the defenses of Petersburg, forcing a Confederate retreat from the southern approach to Richmond. On that day President Davis directed all department heads to complete arrangements for leaving the Capital. Some records were then boxed for rail transportation; clerks piled up other records in the streets and set them afire and other records were simply abandoned in the Government offices. Some records were saved by Union Army officers who entered the city and some were carried off by soldiers and individuals. Government offices were set aflame and most of the buildings that had been occupied by Confederate Government departments and agencies were destroyed along with quantities of records.

On occupying Richmond and other points in the South, the U.S. Army seized considerable quantities of Confederate records and sent them to the War Department at Washington. When Maj. Gen. Henry W. Halleck assumed command at Richmond on Apr. 22, 1865, he found that his predecessors there, Maj. Gen. Godfrey Weitzel and Maj. Gen. Edward O. C. Ord, had not taken adequate steps to preserve the official and private papers of Confederate leaders. He immediately designated Col. Richard D. Cutts to take charge of Confederate archives, and Colonel Cutts sent to Washington in May many boxes and barrels of records.

AGO General Order 127, July 21, 1865, established a bureau in the Adjutant General's Office for the "collection, safe-keeping, and publication of the Rebel Archives" that had been acquired. The order also announced the appointment of Francis Lieber as chief of the new bureau, and in August his son, Lt. Col. G. Norman Lieber, was designated his assistant. With the help of a dozen clerks, Norman Lieber examined, arranged, and classified the Confederate records, consisting of 428 boxes, 71 barrels, and 120 bags of undelivered mail. More than half of the records were found to consist of quartermasters' accounts (126 boxes and bbls.), Second

Auditor's accounts (118 boxes and bbls.), and muster rolls and payrolls (24 boxes). The accounts were in such disorder that it was considered impossible to arrange them and they were stored in the Winder Building. In Jan. 1866 Francis Lieber submitted to the Secretary of War a report with lists of the records of the Confederate executive departments. The lists are useful in showing what records were assembled. The records were largely those of Congress and the War, Treasury, and Post Office Departments. Not all of these records remained in the custody of the Archive Office, as the Bureau of Rebel Archives was officially designated by the Adjutant General's regulation of Aug. 23, 1865. In 1866 Confederate court records of North Carolina were transferred to the Attorney General, and the Post Office Department records were transferred to the U.S. Postmaster General.

An order of the Secretary of War of Aug. 19, 1867, merging the Archive Office into the Adjutant General's Office resulted in the retirement of Francis Lieber, and since Norman Lieber had already left for another assignment, the principal clerk, Bazaleel Wells, took charge of the office. On Aug. 1, 1871, A. P. Tasker became the head of the office, where he had been a clerk since its organization. Tasker and four clerks were kept busy examining the Confederate records to determine the loyalty of persons whose claims for wartime damages and losses were being investigated by the Treasury Department, the Department of Justice, the Quartermaster General's Office, and the Southern Claims Commission. Beginning in 1872 annual appropriations were made to enable the War Department to have the Confederate archives examined and transcribed for these agencies. The Archive Office also cooperated in the task of assembling documents for publication.

In later years the Office of the Secretary of War and the Adjutant General's Office had custody of the Confederate archives. In 1881 the Archive Office was merged into the Record Division of the Office of the Secretary of War of which Samuel Hodgkins was the chief. In that division it became the Archive Branch under Frank Jones. However, the work done by that branch was similar to work performed on Federal records in the Adjutant General's Office, and in 1888 Secretary of War William Endicott transferred the Archive Branch to that office where it was designated the Confederate Archives Division. As head clerk, Frank Jones had under him in 1889 ten clerks to arrange, index, and search the files. Most of the searching concerned, as before, investigations of the loyalty of claimants before U.S. agencies and applications for pensions by U.S. soldiers who had been in Confederate prisons and hospitals.

The offices having custody of the Confederate archives undertook to make them more usable for searches regarding claimants and pension applicants and to facilitate the publishing work of the War Records Office. The Archives Division classified the bound volumes roughly according to provenance into groups designated "chapters," the volumes numbered serially in each chapter. The volumes are still arranged on the shelves in the National Archives according to this classification and the chapters are as follows:

    I. Adjutant and Inspector General's Department
    II. Military Commands
    III. Engineer Department
    IV. Ordnance Department
    V. Quartermaster General's Department

VI. Medical Department
VII. Legislative Records
VIII. Miscellaneous Records
IX. Office of the Secretary of War
X. Treasury Department
XI. Post Office Department
XII. Judiciary

A subject index to the collection is available in a printed "General Index of the Books, Documents and Papers in the Archives Office, War Department."

After the War Department established a program for the publication of wartime records, it became desirable to acquire additional Confederate records, particularly the records of Army commands. In the 1870's the Department bought a collection of battle reports and the papers of Gen. Albert S. Johnston and Col. Thomas L. Snead. But acquiring records by purchase promised to be very expensive, and the practice was discontinued in 1879 when Congress refused to appropriate funds to buy the papers of Generals Pendleton, Polk, and Bragg.

In the meantime, on July 1, 1878, the War Department appointed Marcus J. Wright, a former Confederate brigadier general, its agent for the collection of Confederate records in what proved to be a successful effort to obtain by persuasion what was too costly to buy. Wright was instructed to visit persons and places in the South to procure original records as donations or loans for copying. He immediately opened correspondence with surviving Army officers and officials of the Confederacy or their widows or representatives and advertised in newspapers his appointment and the interest of the War Department in obtaining original Confederate records for publication. He arranged with the Southern Historical Society, which had been founded in New Orleans in 1869 by former officers of the Confederacy for the purpose of collecting, preserving, and publishing records, for the use of its collections. Wright functioned as the agent of the War Department for about 25 years and through his efforts the Department obtained the papers of many Confederate officers. In the case of papers that were borrowed the general practice was for the War Records Office to copy only those documents of which it did not already have copies. Some papers that were borrowed for copying were later acquired as donations, but more usually the papers after being returned by Wright found their way to other repositories. The list of Confederate papers below includes papers that were donated to other bureaus of the War Department and transferred to the Adjutant General's Office.

Name	Donation	Copies	Loan
Alexander, E. Porter, Gen.			X'
Andrews, Garnett, Col.			X
Archer, F. H., Col.	X		X
Archer, James J., Brig. Gen.	X		X
Avery, I. W., Col.			
Barksdale, William, Brig. Gen.	X		
Bate, William B., Brig. Gen.		X	
Beall, William N. R., Brig. Gen.		X	
Beauregard, Pierre G. T., Gen.*	X	X	
Bee, Hamilton P., Brig. Gen.		X	X
Benning, Henry L., Brig. Gen.			X

Name	Donation	Copies	Loan
Bragg, Braxton, Gen.	X	X	X
Branch, Lawrence O'B., Brig. Gen.			X
Brander, Thomas A., Col.			X
Breckinridge, John C., Gen.		X	
Brent, Joseph L., Maj.			X
Brown, Campbell, Maj.			X
Brown, John C., Gov. (Tenn.)			
Brown, Joseph E., Gov. (Ga.)		X	
Brownlow, John B., Col.		X	
Cabell, James L., Surg.	X		
Cantwell, John L., Col.	X		X
Capers, Ellison, Brig. Gen.	X	X	X
Carr, Charles E., Maj.			X
Carroll, William H., Col.	X		
Chaillé, Stanford E., Surg.	X		
Chalmers, James R., Brig. Gen.*	X		X
Churchill, Thomas J., Maj. Gen.			X
Claiborne, Thomas, Col.			X
Colston, Raleigh E., Brig. Gen.		X	X
Cooper, Douglas H., Brig. Gen.			
Crittenden, George B., Brig. Gen.		X	
Dashiell, R. R., Surg.			
Davis, Jefferson		X	
Douglas, Hugh T., Capt.		X	X
Duvall, Eli, Capt.		X	
Early, Jubal A., Gen.*	X	X	X
Echols, William H., Maj.			
Faries, Thomas A., Col.		X	
Finegan, Joseph, Brig. Gen.	X		
Flewellen, Edward A., Surg.	X		
Floyd, John B., Brig. Gen.*	X		
Forrest, Nathan B., Maj. Gen.	X		
French, Samuel G., Maj. Gen.*	X		X
Gatlin, Richard C., Brig. Gen.	X		
Gibson, Randall L., Brig. Gen.		X	
Goggin, James M., Maj.	X		X
Goodman, W. A., Maj.	X		
Grimes, Bryan, Brig. Gen.			X
Guerrant, Edward O., Capt.			X
Guild, Lafayette, Surg.	X		
Hagood, Johnson, Brig. Gen.		X	
Hampton, Henry, Maj.			X
Hampton, Wade, Maj. Gen.		X	X
Hardee, William J., Lt. Gen.			X
Harvie, Edwin J., Col.		X	
Hatton, Robert, Brig. Gen.	X		
Heiston, Thornton B., Capt.	X		
Helm, Benjamin H., Brig. Gen.			X
Hewitt, Fayette, Capt.	X		
Hill, Benjamin H., Brig. Gen.	X		X
Hill, Daniel H., Lt. Gen.	X		X

Name	Donation	Copies	Loan
Hill, Gabriel H., Col.	X		
Hindman, Thomas C., Maj. Gen.	X		
Hines, Peter E., Surg.	X		
Hodge, George B., Brig. Gen.			X
Holmes, Theophilus H., Lt. Gen.	X		
Hood, John B., Gen. *	X		
Hyatt, A. W., Col.			X
Jackson, Henry R., Brig. Gen.	X		
Jackson, John K., Brig. Gen.			X
Jackson, Thomas J., Lt. Gen.	X		
Jackson, William H., Brig. Gen.	X		X
Johnson, Bushrod R., Maj. Gen. *	X		
Johnson, Bradley T., Brig. Gen.		X	X
Johnston, Albert S., Gen. (purchase)			
Johnston, Joseph E., Gen.	X		X
Jones, J. A., Col.		X	
Jones, Samuel, Maj. Gen. *	X		X
Kershaw, Joseph B., Maj. Gen.	X		
Lane, James H., Brig. Gen.		X	
Law, Evander M., Brig. Gen.	X	X	
Lee, Robert E., Gen. *	X		X
Lee, Stephen D., Lt. Gen.	X	X	X
Liddell, St. John R., Brig. Gen.	X		
Lockett, Samuel H., Col.			X
Lomax, Lunsford L., Maj. Gen.			
Longstreet, James, Lt. Gen.			X
Loring, William W., Maj. Gen.	X		
Magruder, John B., Maj. Gen. *	X		
Mallet, John W., Col.	X		
Mangum, S. H., Col.		X	
Manning, Richard I., Maj.			X
Marshall, Charles, Col.		X	
Mathes, J. Harvey, Capt.	X		
McCann, J. R., Capt.		X	
McCarthy, Carlton, Capt.			X
McClellan, Henry B., Maj.		X	
McGowan, Robert, Capt.	X		
McLaws, Lafayette, Maj. Gen. *	X		
Miller, Andrew J., Capt.	X		
Moore, Samuel J. S., Capt.			X
Moore, W. S., Lt. Col.	X		
Moorman, George, Capt. *	X		
Morfit, Mason, Maj.	X		
Mosby, John S., Col.		X	
Munford, Thomas T., Brig. Gen.			X
Oliver, John N., Col.		X	
Ould, Robert, Col.		X	X
Owen, W. Miller, Col.		X	
Pemberton, John C., Lt. Gen. *	X	X	X
Peterkin, George W., Lt.			X
Pickett, George E., Maj. Gen.	X		

Name	Donation	Copies	Loan
Pike, Albert, Brig. Gen.	X		
Pillow, Gideon J., Brig. Gen.*	X		
Polk, Leonidas, Lt. Gen.*	X		X
Preston, William, Brig. Gen.			
Price, Sterling, Maj. Gen.	X		
Ransom, Robert, Jr., Maj. Gen.	X		
Ransom, Thomas D., Capt.			X
Ripley, Roswell S., Brig. Gen.			
Ritter, William S., Capt.			X
Ross, Lawrence S., Brig. Gen.			X
Roy, T. B., Col.	X		
Ruggles, Daniel, Brig. Gen.			X
Scott, C. C., Capt.	X		
Semmes, Paul J., Brig. Gen.	X		
Smith, Edmund Kirby, Gen.	X		
Snead, Thomas L., Col.	X		
Spence, P. B., Col.	X		
Steele, William, Brig. Gen.	X		
Stevenson, Carter L., Brig. Gen.*	X		
Stevenson, Randolph R., Surg.	X		
Stewart, Alexander P., Lt. Gen.			
Stuart, James E. B., Maj. Gen.			X
Taliaferro, William B., Maj. Gen.	X		
Tappan, James C., Brig. Gen.			X
Thomas, Bryan M., Brig. Gen.	X		
Trabue, Robert P., Col.			X
Vaughan, John C., Brig. Gen.			X
Walthall, Edward C., Brig. Gen.*	X		X
Wharton, John A., Maj. Gen.			
Wheeler, Joseph, Maj. Gen.*	X	X	X
Whiting, William H. C., Brig. Gen.	X		
Winder, John H., Brig. Gen.		X	
Wise, Henry A., Brig. Gen.	X		
Wright, Marcus J., Brig. Gen.	X		

The documents obtained from the officers listed above or their survivors and those acquired from historical societies and other repositories were placed in several files. All or part of the papers of the officers whose names are starred in the list were left intact as personal papers. Other papers are in the "Publication File," consisting of documents printed in the Official Records . . . Armies; these documents usually bear notations as to the source from which they were obtained. Other documents from officers' papers are in the compiled military service records described in chapter XI. Some records that were obtained from officers are described in this Guide as the records of territorial commands and armies. A small collection (1 ft.) of longhand and typewritten copies of documents that were evidently made by the War Records Office contains some original manuscript letters of Confederate officers and official wartime copies.

An appropriation of $14,600 was made under an act of May 13, 1892 (27 Stat. 36), for the preparation of a general card index to the books, muster rolls, orders, and other official papers in the Confederate archives,

and a like amount was appropriated the following year (27 Stat. 600). By
Sept. 1892 an index to the Secretary of War's letters received had been
completed, and a year later card indexes had been completed for the Adjutant and Inspector General's and the Quartermaster General's letters received and letter books. During 1892-94, 1,391 boxes of Confederate muster rolls were indexed on 1,563,000 cards. As soon as they were available
these indexes were in constant service by the Confederate Archives Division and the War Records Office. The indexes to the correspondence files
are still available for research and are referred to in chapter VII of this
Guide. The index cards to the muster rolls were presumably incorporated
into the compiled military service records described in chapter XI.

The War Department offices having custody of the Confederate archives also compiled several smaller indexes. These included a card index to appointments of Army officers, 1861-65; a card index to subscribers
to Confederate loans, 1861-65; an index to local Confederate military organizations (1 vol.); an index to field returns, morning reports, organizations,
etc., 1861-65 (1 vol.), showing the types of documents on file for commands;
and a general information index.

Some reference files were also compiled by the War Department offices. One consists of jackets containing newspaper clippings, citations to
published sources and to Confederate and U.S. War Department records,
and data compiled while searching records. A file of compilations of historical and strength data relating to Confederate Army commands is arranged by designation of command. It contains references to the Official
Records . . . Armies. A chronology of battles, with losses of both Union
and Confederate Armies, 1862-63, also refers to the Official Records. . .
Armies. Card memoranda relating to staff officers, 1861-65, contain data
relating to their services. A record of staff officers serving with general
officers is arranged alphabetically by name of general officer. A reference
file for State military organizations contains information on their formation,
officers, and local designations of companies. A reference file for officers
commanding Army corps, brigades, legions, and districts gives the composition of their successive commands. A reference file for medical officers contains citations to records. A reference file for Confederate and
U.S. Army posts, camps, stations, and batteries gives locations and citations to maps in the Atlas to Accompany the Official Records . . . Armies.
Other files relate to signatures of commissioned officers in records, Union
prisoners who joined the Confederate Army, State officials, and staff officers. A printed compilation entitled "Troops Tendered to the Confederate
War Department" gives information on those who offered troops or requested
authority to raise troops in 1861. In Record Group 94 is an historical and
statistical record of the principal military commands in the Union and Confederate Armies, 1861-62.

Although the compilation of the wartime records for publication was
authorized in 1864, it did not get well under way until more than 10 years
later. Funds were appropriated by an act of June 23, 1874 (18 Stat. 222),
and the Secretary of War was directed "to have copied for the Public Printer
all reports, letters, telegrams, and general orders not heretofore copied
or printed and properly arranged in chronological order." This resulted
in the preparation during the 1870's and 1880's of 30 sets of "preliminary
prints" of the Confederate records for the Official Records . . . Armies,
in the following series:

War Dept. letters received, Mar. 2-Dec. 30, 1861.	1 vol.
War Dept. letters sent, Feb. 23-Dec. 28, 1861.	1 vol.
War Dept. telegrams received, Feb. 22-Dec. 31, 1861.	7 vols.
War Dept. telegrams sent, Feb. 25-Dec. 30, 1861.	1 vol.
Adjutant and Inspector General's correspondence and orders and correspondence of Quartermaster General's Department, Ordnance Department, and Engineer Bureau, Feb. 19-Dec. 30, 1861.	1 vol.
AIGO special orders, Mar. 7, 1861-Apr. 14, 1865.	5 vols.
Correspondence and orders of military departments and commands, May 25-Dec. 31, 1861.	1 vol.
Reports of military operations, 1861-65.	21 vols.

Incomplete sets of these volumes are in the Library of Congress, the National Archives, and the National War College Library. The "preliminary prints" were used as printer's copy for the published compilation.

In Dec. 1877, Capt. Robert N. Scott was placed in charge of the Publication Office, War Records (later known as the War Records Office). An appropriation for printing and binding was made in 1880 and in the next year publication began. Col. Henry M. Lazelle became the head of the Office in 1887, and from 1889 to 1898 a Board of Publication headed by an Army officer supervised the project. After the dissolution of the board the work was placed under Col. Fred C. Ainsworth, head of the Record and Pension Office, and on July 1, 1899, the War Records Office became the Publication Branch of the Record and Pension Office. Joseph W. Kirkley, who had been with the project since its inception and who had been a member of the Board of Publication, became chief of the Publication Branch. The last volume of the Official Records . . . Armies was published in 1901.

The published Official Records . . . Armies (available on microfilm as M 262) are organized in series as follows: "I. Formal reports, both Union and Confederate, of the first seizures of United States property in the Southern States, and of all military operations in the field, with the correspondence, orders, and returns relating specially thereto, and, as proposed, is to be accompanied by an Atlas. II. Correspondence, orders, reports, and returns, Union and Confederate, relating to prisoners of war, and (so far as the military authorities were concerned) to state or political prisoners. III. Correspondence, orders, reports, and returns of the Union authorities (embracing their correspondence with the Confederate officials) not relating specially to the subjects of the first and second series. It will set forth the annual and special reports of the Secretary of War, of the General-in-Chief, and of the chiefs of the several staff corps and departments; the calls for troops, and the correspondence between the National and the several State authorities. IV. Correspondence, orders, reports, and returns of the Confederate authorities, similar to that indicated for the Union officials, as of the third series, but excluding the correspondence between the Union and Confederate authorities given in that series."

The original documents that were selected from the Confederate archives in the custody of the War Department for publication in the Official Records were placed in a "Publication File, " arranged in the order in which the documents were published. For documents from bound volumes in that file there are printed cross-reference cards on which are cited the chapter, volume number, and page number of the documents. Transcripts of documents obtained from collections in historical societies or other repositories or from private papers are also in jackets on which are usually indicated the sources from which the documents were copied. The War Records Office drew not only upon the Confederate War Department records in its custody but also upon the records of other Confederate departments and of the Congress, particularly for series IV of the Official Records, and these documents are also in the "Publication File." Therefore, in cases where questions arise in connection with published documents, it is possible to check the original document. After the last volume of the Official Records appeared the War Department continued to receive original Confederate records, and it was planned to publish more documents in volumes to be added to series I but no additional volumes have ever appeared.

In 1938 the Confederate records (2,153 cu. ft.) were transferred from the Old Records Division of the Adjutant General's Office to the National Archives. Of these, 425 cu. ft. have since been destroyed by the National Archives. Many of the remaining volumes have been rebound; some series have been microfilmed, and the microfilming of others is in progress.

Mabel E. Deutrich, Struggle for Supremacy; the Career of General Fred C. Ainsworth (Washington, 1962); Dallas D. Irvine, "The Archive Office of the War Department; Repository of Captured Confederate Archives, 1865-1881," Military Affairs, 10:93-111 (Spring 1946), "The Fate of Confederate Archives," American Historical Review, 44:823-841 (July 1939), "The Genesis of the Official Records," Mississippi Valley Historical Review, 24:221-229 (Sept. 1937); Carl L. Lokke, "The Captured Confederate Records under Francis Lieber," American Archivist, 9:277-319 (Oct. 1946); "The Southern Historical Society; Its Origin and History," Southern Historical Society Papers, 18:349-365 (1890); National Archives, Preliminary Inventory of the War Department Collection of Confederate Records (Record Group 109), comp. by Elizabeth Bethel (Washington, 1957); U. S. War Department, Report . . . 1865-1921 (Washington, 1865-1921), including reports of the Adjutant General, the War Records Office, and the Records and Pension Office, The War of the Rebellion; a Compilation of the Official Records of the Union and Confederate Armies (Washington, 1881-1901. 130 "serials" comprising 70 vols., general index, and atlas; available also on microfilm as M 262); U. S. War Records Publication Office, Records of the Confederate Armies in the Southern Historical Society at Richmond, Va. (Washington, 1880). Pertinent files in the following record series were also used: Office of the Adjutant General, Document File, 1890-1917; Record and Pension Office, Document File, 1889-1904.

II. LIST OF RECORD GROUPS CONTAINING CONFEDERATE RECORDS

The records in the National Archives and in the Federal Records Centers are organized by record group. A record group usually consists of the records of a single agency (and its predecessors) at the bureau level in the framework of government. There are approximately 400 of these record groups. Most of the Confederate records are in Record Group 109 (War Department Collection of Confederate Records), Record Group 365 (Treasury Department Collection of Confederate Records), and Record Group 45 (Naval Records Collection of the Office of Naval Records and Library). But óther Confederate records are in the regular series of record groups consisting mainly of records of U.S. agencies which had preceded the Confederate bureaus and which were reestablished during or after the war. Some other Confederate records are among the records of other U.S. agencies which acquired them in various ways.

There follows a list, in order of record group number, of all the record groups specified in this Guide as containing Confederate records. After each record group title appear the names of the agencies concerned and the page number or numbers of this Guide on which the descriptions of their records begin.

19. Records of the Bureau of Ships.
     Navy Department: Chief Constructor (p. 350).
21. Records of District Courts of the United States.
     Judiciary: Confederate District Courts (p. 43-57, passim).
     Treasury Department: Records of Field Offices-Alabama (p. 123).
26. Records of the United States Coast Guard.
     Treasury Department: Records of Field Offices-South Carolina
        (p. 130).
28. Records of the Post Office Department.
     Treasury Department: Office of the First Auditor (p. 109).
36. Records of the Bureau of Customs.
     Treasury Department: Records of Field Offices (p. 123-133, passim).
     War Department: Territorial Commands and Armies--Department
        of Alabama, Mississippi, and East Louisiana (p. 263); District of
        the Gulf (p. 267).
37. Records of the Hydrographic Office.
     Navy Department: Office of Ordnance and Hydrography (p. 346).
39. Records of the Bureau of Accounts (Treasury).
     Treasury Department: Treasury Note Bureau (p. 119).
41. Records of the Bureau of Marine Inspection and Navigation.
     Treasury Department: Records of Field Offices (p. 214-133, passim).
45. Naval Records Collection of the Office of Naval Records and Library.
     Department of State: Records of Commissioners and Agents (p. 86).
     Treasury Department: Office of the First Auditor (p. 109);
        Lighthouse Bureau (p. 114); Records of Field Offices-Tennessee
        (p. 132).
     War Department: Territorial Commands and Armies--Department
        of North Carolina and Southern Virginia (p. 271); Department of
        South Carolina, Georgia, and Florida (p. 283).
     Navy Department: Office of Orders and Detail (p. 343); Office of
        Ordnance and Hydrography (p. 346); Office of Provisions and
        Clothing (p. 348); Office of Medicine and Surgery (p. 349);

Engineer-in-Chief (p. 350); Chief Constructor (p. 350);
Marine Corps (p. 352); Naval Squadrons (p. 354-363, passim);
Naval Batteries (p. 365); Naval Procurement in Europe (p. 366);
Navy Yards and Naval Stations and Works (p. 373-386, passim);
Blockade-Runners (p. 373); Cruisers (p. 368).

56. General Records of the Department of the Treasury.
War Department: Engineer Bureau (p. 206).
Navy Department: Office of Orders and Detail (p. 345); Blockade-
Runners (p. 373).

59. General Records of the Department of State.
Department of State (p. 76).
War Department: Office of the Chief of Ordnance (p. 216).
Navy Department: Office of the Secretary of the Navy (p. 342);
Cruisers (p. 369); Navy Yards and Naval Stations and Works--
Norfolk Navy Yard (p. 380).

74. Records of the Bureau of Ordnance.
Navy Department: Office of Ordnance and Hydrography (p. 347).

75. Records of the Bureau of Indian Affairs.
War Department: Bureau of Indian Affairs (p. 213).
Post Office Department: Post Offices (p. 399).

76. Records of Boundary and Claims Commissions and Arbitrations.
Navy Department: Cruisers (p. 369).

77. Records of the Office of the Chief of Engineers.
War Department: Engineer Bureau--Cartographic Records (p. 207);
Commanders, Staff Officers, and Other Personnel--Capt. John
C. Wrenshall (p. 336).

84. Records of the Foreign Service Posts of the Department of State.
Navy Department: Cruisers (p. 370).

92. Records of the Office of the Quartermaster General.
War Department: Engineer Bureau--Cartographic Records (p. 208).

94. Records of the Adjutant General's Office.
War Department: Engineer Bureau--Cartographic Records (p. 208);
Office of the Chief of Ordnance--Arsenals, Armories, and Ord-
nance Depots, Macon Central Laboratory (p. 227).

98. Records of United States Army Commands, 1784-1821.
War Department: Regiments, Battalions, and Companies--North
Carolina Troops (p. 308).

104. Records of the Bureau of the Mint.
Treasury Department: Records of Field Offices, North Carolina
(p. 130).

109. War Department Collection of Confederate Records.
General Records of the Confederate States Government: Constitu-
tional Convention (p. 3); Laws and Resolutions (p. 6); Electoral
Papers (p. 7); Indian Treaties (p. 7).
Congress: Provisional Congress (p. 13); Congress (p. 17); Senate
(p. 23); House of Representatives (p. 31).
Presidency (p. 65).
Judiciary: District Court of North Carolina (p. 51); District Court
of South Carolina (p. 52).
Department of State: Records of Commissioners and Agents (p. 86).
Treasury Department: Office of the Secretary of the Treasury
(p. 94); Office of the Treasurer (p. 100); Office of the Comptroller
(p. 102); Office of the Register (p. 106); Office of the First Auditor

(p. 109); Office of the Second Auditor (p. 111); Office of the Commissioner of Taxes (p. 117); Treasury Note Bureau (p. 119); Treasury Agent for the Trans-Mississippi West (p. 121); Records of Field Offices (p. 125-133, passim).

War Department: Office of the Secretary of War (p. 136); Adjutant and Inspector General's Office (p. 141); Quartermaster General's Office (p. 155), Pay Bureau (p. 161), Office of the Inspector General of Field Transportation (p. 163), Railroad Bureau (p. 165), Tax in Kind Bureau (p. 167); Commissary General's Office and Subsistence Department (p. 169); Surgeon General's Office and the Medical Department--Surgeon General's Office (p. 171), Medical Directors (p. 173-177, passim), Medical Purveyors (p. 178), Hospitals (p. 181-204, passim); Engineer Bureau (p. 206), Cartographic Records (p. 208); Bureau of Indian Affairs (p. 214); Office of the Chief of Ordnance (p. 216), Arsenals, Armories and Ordnance Depots (p. 220-232, passim); Bureau of Exchange (p. 235); Bureau of Conscription (p. 238), State Conscription Offices (p. 241); Niter and Mining Bureau (p. 245); Bureau of Foreign Supplies (p. 247); Office of the Commissary General of Prisoners (p. 248), Military Prisons (p. 251-256, passim); Headquarters of the Army (p. 259); Territorial Commands and Armies (p. 260-300, passim); Regiments, Battalions, and Companies (p. 304-311, passim); State Commands (p. 313); Commanders, Staff Officers, and Other Personnel (p. 314-336, passim).

Navy Department: Office of Ordnance and Hydrography (p. 347); Chief Constructor (p. 350); Navy Yards and Naval Stations and Works (p. 374, 379).

Post Office Department: Office of the Postmaster General (p. 389); Appointment Bureau (p. 391); Contract Bureau (p. 393); Finance Bureau (p. 395); Inspection Office (p. 396); Office of Military Telegraphs (p. 397); Agent for the Trans-Mississippi West (p. 398), Post Offices (p. 399).

Justice Department: Office of the Attorney General (p. 401); Patent Office (p. 402).

153. Records of the Office of the Judge Advocate General (Army).
War Department: Office of the Commissary General of Prisoners-- Military Prisons, Andersonville (p. 251).

249. Records of the Commissary General of Prisoners.
War Department: Office of the Commissary General of Prisoners (p. 249), Military Prisons (p. 251-258, passim); Territorial Commands and Armies--Department of Richmond (p. 282).

365. Treasury Department Collection of Confederate Records.
Judiciary: District Court, Southern Division of Georgia (p. 47); District Court, Eastern District of Texas (p. 54).
Treasury Department: Office of the Secretary (p. 96); Office of the Treasurer (p. 101); Office of the Comptroller (p. 102); Office of the First Auditor (p. 109); Office of the Second Auditor (p. 113); Office of the Third Auditor (p. 113); Lighthouse Bureau (p. 114); Produce Loan Office (p. 116); Office of the Commissioner of Taxes (p. 118); Treasury Note Bureau (p. 120); Records of Field Offices (p. 124-133, passim).
War Department: Territorial Commands and Armies--Trans-Mississippi Department (p. 292), District of Texas, New Mexico,

and Arizona (p. 297).
366. Records of Civil War Special Agencies of the Treasury Department. Treasury Department: Records of Field Offices, South Carolina (p. 132).

INDEX

Abbeville, S. C. , 64
Aberdeen, Miss. , depositary, 129;
estimates of tax in kind, 167
Abingdon, Va. , 57; post guard, 266
Abolitionists, 85
Accounts, 106, 150; administrators',
40; AIGO, 141; Ala. Inf. , 24th,
304; Alexander, 82; Ariz. Terr.
officials, 59; Army, 93, 139;
Army officers, 112, 405; Army
pay, 161; Army paymasters, 161,
264; Asst. Treasurer at Mobile,
124; Asso. for the Relief of
Maimed Soldiers, 174; auditors',
102, 405; bakery, 196; Barksdale,
162; Camp Holmes, 238; Camp
Lee, 238; certification, 102, 104,
108, 109, 110; Charlotte mint,
130; clothing, 192, 201, 303, 304,
305, 306, 307, 308, 309, 310,
311, 312; commercial agents, 82;
commissaries, 93; Confederate
agents, 99; Confederate officials
at Sherman, Tex. , 214-215; cotton shipped, 100; court officials,
52, 400; cruisers, 371; customs
collectors, 102, 104, 123, 133;
deceased soldiers, 102; De Leon,
89; Dept. of Henrico, 268; depositaries, 125, 127, 130, 133; disbursing officers, 113, 128; drayage, 179; engineer office at
Charleston, 285; engineers, 206,
207; equipment, 308,
311; examination, 102, 108; foreign service, 80, 82; Fraser,
Trenholm & Co. , 100; fuel, 201;
Hines, 90; hospital: 194, 195,
196, 198, 199, Army of Tennessee hospitals, 176, First Louisiana at Charleston, 189, general at
Farmville, 192, general at Savannah, 185, general at Wilmington,
189, Howard's Grove, 202, Lake
City General, 182, Ocmulgee, 184,
Robertson, 203, Wayside at
Columbia, 189; hospital property,
199; hospital supplies, 179, 184,
191, 199, 200, 201; Hotze, 89; Indian agents, 212; Indian commrs. ,
215; Josselyn, 98; Justice Dept. ,
98, 108; laundry, 200, 204; Lea,
324; Lee's cavalry corps, 264;
letters re, 110; lighthouses, 114;
loan commr. , 126; McRae, 88;
Macon Armory, 225; mail contractors, 113, 390, 395; mail messengers, 113; Marine Corps, 109,
352; marshals, 47, 55, 98; materials, 228; medical officers, 93;
medical purveyors, 171, 179; medical supplies, 179, 184; mess, 179;
Military Telegraph Lines, 99,
397; naval officers, 109, 371; naval personnel, 371; naval stations,
374; Navy Dept. , 108; navy paymasters, 109, 350, 357, 374; ordnance,
270, 307, 308, 310, 311; Ordnance
Bur. , 215; ordnance officers, 93;
pay, 206; Pickett, 90; port surveyor, New Orleans, 128; Post
Office Dept. , 92, 108, 109, 113,
120, 128; postage stamps, 394;
postal agents, 113; postal moneys
collected for the U.S. , 395; postmasters, 113, 390, 395, 396, 399;
Produce Loan agents, 116, 124,
125; property, 270, 284; provisions, 188, 200, 201, 310; public
debt, 104; public money, 104;

personnel, 360, 364, 369, 374; Navy, 344; nominations, 11; Post Office Dept., 390; postmasters, 391, 392; post route agents, 392; Presidential, 14, 19, 21, 23, 31, 63, 65, 66, 68, 69, 80, 81, 116, 117, 401; prize commrs., 40; Produce Loan subagents, 95; Provisional Congress, 13; purchasing agents, 251; quartermasters, 153, 157; recommendations re, 97, 110, 410; records, 82; Secretary of the Navy, 110; Senators, 14, 23; State Dept., 80; surgeons, 170; tax collectors, 117; Treasury Dept., 94, 95, 97, 101. See also District attorneys, Clerks of court, Judges, Marshals, Sequestration receivers

Appomattox River, 270

Appraisers, appointment, 41

Appropriations, documents re, 97; estimates: customs collectors, 102, 104, depositaries, 130, executive depts., 14, 17, field transportation, 163, Lighthouse Bur., 114, Quartermaster General, 156, State Dept., 80, 82, tax collectors, 118, Treasury Dept., 94, 95, 98, 390, War Dept., 136; Post Office Dept., 394; War Dept., 140

Aquia Creek, 277, 364

Aquia District, Dept. of Northern Va., 272

Arapahoe Indians, agency records, 214

Archer, Edward R., 218

Archer, F. H., 415

Archer, James J., 415

Archer, Junius L., 222

Archer, C.S.S., 368

Archer & Daly, 118

Arctic, C.S.S., 356

Arizona, part of Ariz. Terr., 58

Arizona County, Ariz. Terr., 58, 59

Arizona Historical Foundation, 406

Arizona Territory, accounts, 98; appointment of officials, 63; corresp., 81; delegate, 9, 24; district courts, 58, 59; military

service records, 406; occupied by U.S. forces, 59; organized by Baylor, 296; secretary, 62

Arkadelphia, Ark., pharmaceutical laboratory, 178

Arkadelphia Arsenal, Ark., 289

Arkansas, 302; admitted to Confederacy, 9; Army of the West in, 299; capital removed to Washington, 44; chief tax collector, 116, 117; contested election, 32; cotton purchases in, 292; district courts, 44; enrolling officer, 294; Indians west of, 210; judicial district, 60; mail contracts, 394; maps, 209; military service records, 406; naturalization records, 42; number of Representatives, 15; occupied by U.S., 289, 295, 393; officers serve in: Hardee, 321, Thompson, 333; part of: the Dist. of Ark., 295, Trans-Miss. Dept., 289, Trans-Miss. Dist., 300, Western Dept., 300; persons who sold cotton, 116; post offices, 391, 392, 395, 396; post routes, 398; Produce Loan agent, 115; purveyors of medical supplies, 178; quartermaster purchasing officer, 154; records of troops, 304; regimental officers, 147, 148; secession ordinance, 5; surgeons serve in, 316; Treasury Agent and, 121; Treasury Dept. field offices, 125

Arkansas, C.S.S., 362, 387

Arkansas and Red River Superintendency, 60, 212-214

Arkansas History Commission, 406, 408

Arkansas River, 44; Pontchartrain burned in, 362

Arkansas State Telegraph Co., 397

Arkansas University Library, Johnson papers, 296; Stephens papers, 71

Armament, Army, 139; contracts, 410; manufacture, 216; supplied to cruisers, 365

Arman, Paul, 99

Armies, 146, 240, 259-262; chief commissaries, 168; chief quartermasters, 162; composition, 150; east. Va., 272; engineering work,

Attorney General, corresp., 401;
distributes laws, 6; duties, 400;
letters to, 390; opinions, 102,
390, 400, 401; publishes laws,
5; recommend court officials,
38; recommends re court fees,
38; records, 401; reports, 18,
400, 401; returns submitted to,
38; to represent the Govt. before the Board of Claims
Commrs., 61
Attorneys, 297; admitted to district
courts, 40; Ala., 43; fees, 40;
Fla., 45; names recorded, 40;
report re confiscable property, 39; soldiers', 113; to be
appointed for sequestration
cases, 39; Va., 57. See also
District attorneys
Atwater, Dorence, 251
Auburn (Maine) Public Library, 99
Auditor, Trans-Mississippi West,
120
Auditors of the Treasury, settlement of accounts, 102; First:
390, corresp., 340, duties, 108,
letters to, 96, 206, 342, 390,
393, 396, records, 93, 109-110,
348, reports, 98, 99, 104, reports on operations, 110; Second:
accounts, 405, 414, duties, 111,
letters sent, 100, 156, letters to,
156, 206, 231, organization of
office, 111, records, 92, 93, 111-
113, 405, reports, 18, 206, 410,
statement re deceased soldiers,
412; Third: 394, claims presented to, 395, records, 92, 113
August, Thomas P., 237, 242
Augusta, Ga., 12; board of loan
commrs. at, 105; depositary,
126, 127, 226; district court seat,
46; Engineer Bur. workshop,
205; field transportation hdqrs.,
162; Hunter surrenders at, 358;
military hdqrs., 359; naval
clothing factory, 348; naval ordnance works, 345; naval storehouse, 347; navy agent, 347,
359; navy paymaster, 377; Produce Loan agent, 115; quartermaster depot, 153, 154; quartermaster purchasing officer, 153;

railroad accounts paid at, 165;
records seized at, 47; shoe fac-
tory, 347; telegraph office, 397
Augusta Arsenal and Powder Works,
Ga., 218, 220-221, 223, 227, 385
Augusta Naval Ordnance Works, 340,
345, 374
Austill, Hurieosco, 264
Austin, William T., 53, 56
Austin, Tex., district court seat,
53, 54, 55; tax-in-kind quarter-
master, 294
Autobiographies, Bayne, 247;
Brooke, 379; Pike, 215; Thomp-
son, 333
Autopsies, 182
Avegno, Bernard, 73, 78, 79
Averett, Samuel W., 339
Avery, I. W., 415
Avery Island, La., salt mines, 167
Avon, 370
Ayer, Lewis M., 26, 30
Ayer, William F., 288
Aylett, Patrick H., 56

Badge of distinction, 140
Baggage, 183, 188, 193, 194, 201
Bagging, 293
Bahama, C.S.S., 369
Bahamas, blockade-runners from,
246
Bailey, W. H., 50
Bailey, William, 105
Bailiffs, 38
Baker, Bolling, 109, 377
Baker, George B., 238
Baker, James M., 20, 22, 33
Baker, James McC., 339
Baker, Thomas H., 339
Bakeries, 347; accounts, 196
Baldwin, A. S., 285
Baldwin, Briscoe G., 231
Baldwin, John B., 27, 28, 29, 30
Baldwin, William E., 331
Ballinger, William P., 53, 54, 55,
56
Balloons, 205
Ball's Bluff, Va., battle, 323
Baltic, C.S.S., 360, 361, 378
Baltimore, Md., supplies procured
in, 236
Baltzell, G. F., 45
Bank of Montgomery, Ala., 82

Post Office Dept., 391; Chief Constructor's Office, 350; Commr. of Taxes, 117; First Auditor's Office, 108; Justice Dept., 400; Lighthouse Bur., 114; Navy Dept., 337, 342; Ordnance and Hydrography Office, 345; Patent Office, 402; Post Office Dept., 388, 389, 396; Produce Loan Office, 115; Second Auditor's Office, 111; State Dept., 72; Third Auditor's Office, 113; Treasurer's Office, 100; Treasury Dept., 94, 95, 99, 106

Chief Constructor, Navy Department, 337, 350-351

Chief Engineer, 205

Chief Medical Purveyor, 178; contracts, 103

Chief of Ordnance, letters sent, 228, 232; letters to, 219, 220, 224, 226, 229, 230, 231, 232

Chihuahua, Mexico, Quintero's despatches from, 79

Childs, Frederick L., 222, 223

Chiles, John, 297

Chilton, Robert H., 140, 275

Chilton, William P., 1, 11, 24, 25, 27, 29

Chimborazo General Hospital, Richmond, Va., 31, 196-197

Chisholm, Alexander R., 318

Chisman, Samuel R., 162

Chisolm, William G., 33

Choctaw Indians, 295; agent to, 212; delegate in Congress, 24, 81; judicial district, 60; location, 210; military organizations, 302; records, 214

Choctaw Nation, Cherokee flee to, 211

Choctawhatchee River, 282

Chrisman, James S., 26

Churches, bells, 244; donations to the Govt., 98; subscribe to Govt. loans, 107

Churchill, Benjamin P., 73

Churchill, Thomas J., 291, 292, 295, 416

Churchwell, William M., 266

Cincinnati, Ohio, 67

Ciphers, 333

Cities, conscription in, 239;

general hospitals in, 172; maps, 208; provost marshals at, 260

Citizens, donations to Govt., 98; exchange, 234; judicial cases involving, 37; letters sent, 100; obtain subscriptions to produce loan, 115; records re, 410, 411, 412; to report re confiscable property, 39. See also Individuals

Citizenship, British, 85; declaration of, 37; S.C., 52

City of Richmond, blockade-runner, 372, 373

City Point, Va., burials at, 248; negotiations at, 70; prisoner exchange point, 234, 250, 257

Civil cases, Ariz. Terr., 59; La., 48; N.C., 51; Va., 57

Civil engineering, patents, 402

Civil engineers, employed by the Engineer Bureau, 205

Civil jurisdiction, in occupied areas, 143

Civilian employees, 260; appointments, 13, 63; Ariz. Terr., 59; Army, 142, 159; Asheville Armory, 219; Atlanta Arsenal, 220, 229; Commr. of Taxes Office, 118; commissions, 8, 81, 82; Comptroller's Office, 102, 103; conscription service in Miss., 242; Corps of Engineers, 207; customs service, 104; Dept. of Richmond, 282; departmental, 108; Engineer Bur., 206; First Auditor's Office, 110; foreign service, 82; form Richmond defense brigade, 63; Govt., 412; general hospitals: Farmville, 193, Richmond, 196, 197, 200, 201, 202; hospitals, 203, 257; Justice Dept., 401; Lighthouse Bur., 114; Macon Armory, 225; Macon Central Laboratory, 228; military hospitals, 176, 188, 191; Military Telegraph Lines, 99, 397; Nashville Arsenal, 229; naval stations: 373, 374, Charlotte, 375, Mobile, 378; navy yards, 98, 110, 381; ordnance establishments, 218; payments to, 110; payrolls, 412; Post Office Dept., 390, 392, 394; quartermasters, 267, 268, 294; records re,

411, 412; Register's Office, 107; removal, 63; Richmond Arsenal, 231; Savannah Ordnance Depot, 232; Savannah signal office, 286; Subsistence Bur., Trans-Miss. Dept., 294; Third Auditor's Office, 113; Treasurer's Office, 100; Treasury Dept., 94, 95, 96, 97, 410; Treasury Note Bur., 120; War Dept., 409. See also Chief Clerks, Clerks, Clerks of court, Disbursing officers, Payrolls, Personnel records

Claghorn, Joseph S., 305

Claiborne, Henry B., 366

Claiborne, Herbert A., 170

Claiborne, James W., 277

Claiborne, John H., 194

Claiborne, Thomas, 416

Claimants, letters to, 156; loyalty investigation, 414; names, 160

Claims, 103, 113, 161; against Treasury Dept., 95, 96; against U.S. Govt., 121; animals, 111, 153; Army supplies, 121; Attorney Gen. and, 400, 401; Auditor's reports, 410; British merchants, 83; deceased soldiers, 93, 102, 103, 111, 112, 113; destruction of ships, 85; equipment, 112, 113; filed in the State Dept., 74; Ga., 46; horses, 111, 112, 113; letters re, 80, 94, 137, 156; mail contractors, 395; military personnel, 112; pay, 113; postal services, 108; postmasters, 388, 390; property, 84, 153, 410, 411; quartermaster supplies, 160; slave hire, 113; slaves, 120, 155, 410; Southerners, 75, 404; States, 112; supplies, 111, 112, 411; Trans-Mississippi West, 120; wagons, 111; Yazoo River defense materials, 129

Claims, House Special Committee on the Payment of, 29

Claims, House Standing Committee on, 24

Claims, Senate Standing Committee on, 20

Claims, Standing Committee on, 11

Claims Against the Confederate Government, House Select Committee on State, 30

Claims commissioners, 63

Claims Commissioners, Board of, established, 61, 400. See also War claims commission

Claims Division, Second Auditor's Office, 111, 113

Claims of Deceased Soldiers Division, Second Auditor's Office, 111

Clapp, J. W., 26, 27, 28, 115, 129

Clarence, C.S.S., 368

Clark, Charles, 261, 270, 318

Clark, Edward, 81, 318

Clark, John B., 20, 31

Clark, Lewis M., 318

Clark, Micajah H., 62, 64, 100, 101

Clark, M. L., 299

Clark, Robert A., 49

Clark, William W., 26, 27, 28

Clarke, Colin D., 280

Clarke, George W., 295

Clarke, Maxwell T., 383

Clarke, William J., 318

Clarksburg, W. Va., 57

Clarksville Ordnance Harness Shops, Va., 222, 231

Clay, Clement C., 20, 21, 33, 73, 75, 79, 86, 87, 90

Clay, Hugh L., 140

Clayton, Alexander M., 2, 11

Clayton, Henry D., 318

Clayton, Philip, 94

Clayton, Philip A., 46, 49

Cleary, William W., 113

Cleburne, Patrick R., 287, 288, 289

Clements, Benjamin N., 391, 396

Clements, Jesse B., 52

Clemson, Thomas G., 245, 290

Clemson College Library, Clemson papers, 245

Clerk of the House of Representatives, corresp., 32

Clerks, military organizations, 110; Navy Dept., 337; Produce Loan Office, 116; Quartermaster General's Office, 157; records re, 412; Second Auditor's Office, 113; Third Auditor's Office, 113; Treasury Dept., 97; War Dept., 136

Clerks of court, 38; accounts, 52; Ala., 42; Ariz. Terr., 58; bills, 40; duties, 38, 39; Fla., 44, 45; Ga., 46; Indian judicial district, 60;

voyage to, 371; Sumter in ports of, 83
Culpeper Courthouse, Va., general hospital, 191
Cumberland Gap, Confederates exchanged at, 235
Cunningham, John W., 50
Cuppler, George, 298
Curell, James R., 236
Curlew, C.S.S., 356
Currency, acquired by U.S. Treasury Dept., 93; counterfeit, 95; credited to disbursing officers, 101; printing, 97; tax on, 117; transportation, 133. See also Treasury notes
Currency, House Special Committee on the, 27
Currency, Senate Select Committee on Bill To Tax, Fund, and Limit the Currency, 22
Curry, Jabez L. M., 24, 27, 28, 33, 345
Customhouses, condition, 96; funds for, 104; inventories of property, 104; records remain in, 122; seized, 121
Customs, collection, 94; duties, 15; 96, 97; officers, 102, 103, 104; receipts, 101, 122; surveyors, 96. See also Import duties
Customs collectors, accounts, 102, 104; appointment, 63; bonds, 103; corresp., 104; deposits, 104; estimates, 102; funds, 98, 102; letters sent, 81, 83, 95, 97, 100, 103, 104, 107, 110; letters to, 80, 94, 95, 101, 102, 106; lists, 122; personal corresp., 104; ports: Charleston, 132, Galveston, 133, Laredo, 133, Mobile, 123, New Orleans, 127, 129, Plymouth, 130, Point Isabel, 133, Sabine, 133, St. Marks, 126, Savannah, 127; returns, 96, 105; serve as depositaries, 122; telegrams to, 96
Customs Division, First Auditor's Office, 108
Customs of war, 142
Customs service, administration, 97; employees, 104; operations, 102; records re, 104;

requisitions for funds, 96
Cuthbert, John A., 42
Cuthbert, Ga., Hood Hospital, 183
Cutlar, DuBrutz, 50
Cutts, Richard D., 92, 155, 170, 205, 255, 413
Cuyler, George A., 165
Cuyler, Richard M., 224, 226, 232
Cuyler, Telamon, 322

Dabney, Robert L., 277
Dahlonega, Ga., mint seized, 122
Dallas Historical Society, 67, 293
Dalton, Ga., military hospital, 183, 184
Dalton Ordnance Depot, Ga., 223
Daly, John J., 402
Damage suits, Ariz. Terr., 59
Dameron, W. H., 168
Dana, Charles A., 135
Dandridge, Philip P., 72
Daniell, William C., 46, 47, 48
Danner, Albert, 288
Danville, Va., 281; commissary depot, 168; Confederate Govt. at, 64; Davis flees to, 135; general hospital, 192; hospitals, 175, 193; Marine Corps records destroyed at, 352; military prison, 248, 253-254; ordnance shops moved to, 224; postmaster, 399; prisoners transferred to, 255
Danville Female Academy, 75
Danville Ordnance Depot, Va., 223
Danville Railroad, 282
Darien, Ga., shipping, 83
Darlington, S.C., depositary, 132
Dashiell, R. R., 416
David, C.S.S., 358
Davidson, Hunter, 351, 372
Davidson, J. E. A., 180
Davidson, Robert H. M., 44
Davidson County, N.C., 244
Davis, Alexander N., 318
Davis, George, 20, 400
Davis, Jefferson, addresses, 68; appoints: Ariz. Terr. officials, 59, peace commrs., 70; attitude towards peace, 70; Benjamin furnishes papers to, 77; capture, 64; comments on public affairs, 402; corresp., 66, 71, 77, 139, 239; departs from Richmond, 64,

135; elected President, 9, 62; flight to south, 69; inaugurated, 62; information re, 401; letters sent, 72, 78, 235, 401; letters to, 78, 86, 150, 236, 342, 361, 401; messages, 68; orders removal from Richmond, 413; papers, 64-69, 342, 416; reports to, 169; sends commrs. to Washington, 86; shrine at Beauvoir, 68; signatures, 6; speeches, 66; submits conventions to Congress, 9; transmits corresp. to the House, 32; trial, 64, 67, 68
Davis, Joseph R., 62, 63
Davis, Nicholas A., 319
Davis, Zebulon P., 43
Davis, Varina H., 65, 66, 67
Davis, William G. M., 265
Davis' Bridge, Tenn., 209
Dawson, George, 74, 79
Dawson, Henry K., 278
Dawson, Nathaniel H. R., 319
Dead letters, 109, 394, 395, 398
Deane, F. B., Jr., & Son, Lynchburg, Va., 346
Deas, George, 134, 141
Deaths, Army of Tenn., 176; Army officers, 146, 148, 149; Camp Jackson, Va., 191; Chatham Artillery, 305; General Hospitals: Culpeper Courthouse, 191, Danville, 192, Farmville, 192, Raleigh, 187, Richmond, 196, 197, 200, 201, Wilmington, 188; military hospitals: 171, 180, High Point Wayside, 187, Lynchburg, 194, Petersburg, 195, Richmond, 195, 198, 199; La. Inf., 306; military prisons: 248, 249, 250, Andersonville, 250, 251, Cahaba, 252, Camp Lawton, 250, Danville, 254, Richmond, 256, Salisbury, 258; naval personnel, 349; N. C. Inf., 308; Price's command, 329; quartermasters, 147; registers, 233, 303; S. C. Inf., 309; soldiers, 177
De Bellot, Ernest, 83
De Bow, James D. B., 95, 115, 116, 129

Debray, Xavier B., 289
De Bree, Alexander M., 383
De Bree, John, 348, 355, 356, 377
Debt cases, Ariz. Terr., 59; Tex., 55; Va., 57
Debtors, southern, 52
Debts, due Confederate States, 102; sequestration, 40, 47, 48
Decatur, Ga., camp of instruction, 241
De Clouet, Alexander, 2, 34
Deep Creek, Va., 349
Deep River, N.C., 243
Deer, blockade-runner, 372
Deerhound, British ship, 367
Defaulters, 102
Defenses, Bridgeport, Ala., 208; coastal, 98; maps, 208; plans, 207; reports on, 207; river, 98. See also place names
De Fontaine, Felix G., 3, 4, 400
De Fontaine, W. Hampton, 400
De Give, Laurent M. J., 85
DeHaven, D. D., 386
De Jarnette, Daniel C., 27, 30
DeLagnel, Julius A., 215, 223
Delano, Columbus, 76, 90
Delaware Indians, 211, 213
De Leon, David C., 170, 177
De Leon, Edwin, 73, 74, 77, 78, 79, 88, 89
Delevan Hospital, Charlottesville, Va., 191
Demopolis, Ala., asst. commr. of exchange, 234, 236; chaplain, 315; Engineer Bur. workshop, 205; medical depot, 180; medical purveyor, 178; parole camp, 234, 235
Denegre, James D., 105
Denham, Andrew, 105
Denis, J. C., 240, 242
Denmark, 77, 365, 368
Dennison, William, 388
Denson, C. B., 273
Department No. 1, 265, 325
Department No. 2, 176, 265, 314, 324
Department of Alabama and West Florida, 262-263, 270, 280, 353; Bragg comdr., 315; Jones comdr., 323
Department of Alabama, Mississippi,

distributed to, 6; letters sent,
13, 14, 17, 23, 32, 66, 67, 70, 87,
97, 137; letters to, 66, 80, 102,
108; office space, 11; officials'
bonds, 103; opinions rendered to,
400, 401; recommendations for
appointments, 23; records, 414,
421; reports, 18; salaries, 98;
seats in Congress not provided,
10. See also Cabinet
Executive Departments, Committee
To Organize, 10, 69
Executive Departments, House
Standing Committee on, 25
Executive mansion, Montgomery,
68; Richmond, 62
Executive Office, 69; accounts, 96;
letters sent, 81. See also Davis,
Jefferson; President
Exemption of State Officers, House
Special Committee on the, 30
Exemptions, 84, 237, 241; applications, 239, 240; certificates,
113; classifications, 238;
foreigners, 84; letters re, 137;
list of, 292; mail carriers, 390,
393; mail contractors, 58, 393;
militia, 301; payments for, 238;
Post Office Dept. employees,
390; printers, 28; State officers,
30; telegraph operators, 397;
Va., 241, 242, 243
Exempts, House Select Committee
on Lessening the Number of, 30
Expenditures, Army, 410; Marine
Corps, 352; naval, 380-381; re-
ports on, 412. See also Accounts,
Disbursements, Financial records
Explosion, Brown's Island, 227
Export duties, 94; cotton, 104
Exports, Charleston, 131; cotton,
292; Mobile, 123, 124
Express, merchant ship, 83
Express agents, accounts, 113
Express companies, carry mail,
392; payments to by Govt., 98

Factories, 216; arms, 219, 224;
cotton yarn, 382; shoe, 174;
soldiers detailed to, 160
Fairfax, Archibald B., 346, 385,
386

Fairfax Court House, Va., 331
Fairground Hospital, Raleigh,
N.C., 187
Fairground (Old) Hospital, Rich-
mond, Va., 203
Fairgrounds, Charleston, 252;
Columbia, 253; Lynchburg, 194,
254; Macon, 254
Falls County, Tex., 53
Fanny, schooner, 46
Faries, Thomas A., 339, 416
Farley, James A., 115, 125
Farmers, required to pay tax in
kind, 166
Farmville, Va., hospital trans-
ferred to, 194; Wayside Hospital,
193
Farmville General Hospital, Va.,
192, 335
Farrand, Ebenezer, 114, 339, 360,
361, 364, 378, 383, 385, 386
Farrow, James, 30
Farrow, Henry P., 244
Fauntleroy, Charles M., 367, 368
Fauntleroy, Thomas T., 57, 313
Fawcett Preston & Co., Ltd.,
Wirral, Cheshire, England, 372
Fayette County, Tex., 53
Fayetteville, N.C., commissary
depot, 168
Fayetteville Arsenal, N.C., 218
Fayetteville Arsenal and Armory,
N.C., 219, 223, 224
Feamster, Samuel W. N., 312
Fearn, John W., 78
Featherman, Americus, 402
Federal citizens, taken prisoner,
138
Federal forces, occupy Ark., 44
Federal garrisons, driven out of
Ariz. Terr., 58
Federal gunboats, raid southern
coast, 167
Federal Records Center, East Point,
Ga., district court records: Ala.,
43, Ga., 45, 46, 47, Miss., 49,
N.C., 51, Tenn., 53
Federal Records Center, Fort Worth,
Tex., district court records,
Tex., 55
Federal Records Centers, district
court records in, 42
Federal troops, destroy property, 81

of reserves, 303; in the Dist. of
Ga., 286; iron agent, 346; iron
furnaces, 243; iron manufacture,
346; Jackson's division in, 319;
limestone works, 243; loan
commrs., 127; local defense
forces, 148; mail contracts, 394;
maps, 209, 336; medical purveyor in, 179; military hospitals,
175, 176, 182-183, 288; military
officials' corresp., 228; military operations in, 207; military
prisons, 247; military service
records, 406, 408; muster rolls,
145; naval defenses, 357, 384;
niter and mining service, 243,
244; number of Representatives,
14; officers serve in: Ash, 314,
Gilmer, 320, Hill, 321, McLaws,
325, Olmstead, 327, Polk, 329,
Taliaferro, 332; officials'
corresp., 71; ordnance officers
in, 221, 223; ordnance works,
216; part of: Dept. of E. Tenn.,
265, Dept. of S.C., Ga., and
Fla., 282, Dept. of Tenn., 286;
persons who sold cotton, 116;
Produce Loan agent, 115; quartermaster purchasing officer,
153; quartermasters in, 164;
railroads, 165; records of troops,
305; regimental officers, 147,
148; sales of property, 98; seizes
arsenal, 220; Stephens: commr.
to, 69, delegate from, 62, 69,
returns to, 70; surgeons serve
in: Battey, 314, Bemiss, 315,
McLean, 325; tax-in-kind estimates, 118; tax returns, 118;
Treasury Dept. field offices,
126-127
Georgia, C.S.S., 110, 358, 359,
365, 366, 367, 369, 370, 371
Georgia Department of Archives
and History, May Hospital records, 185; military service records, 406, 408; papers of Army
officers: Fulkerson, 286,
Longstreet, 325
Georgia Historical Society, cargo
manifests, 127; papers of Army
officers: Robertson, 286, Stout,
176, Wilson, 336, Wright, 336;

records held by: Chatham Artil-
lery, 305, Cavalry, 305, hospital
account book, 198, Savannah
Ordnance Depot roll, 232, Sumter
muster roll, 372
Georgia Relief and Hospital Associ-
ation in Richmond, 81
Georgia University Library, papers
of Army officers: Bragg, 316,
Cobb, 305, Jackson, 322; papers
of officials: Cobb, 33, Davis, 67,
Stephens, 71, Wright, 35; Perma-
nent Constitution, 3-4
Georgiana, C.S.S., 99, 365, 368,
369
Georgians, letters of, 70
German correspondents, 89
Germantown, C.S.S., 380
Getty, G. T., 224
Gettysburg, Pa., 70; casualties at,
307; retreat of Army of N. Va.
from, 328
Gholson, Thomas S., 29
Gibbes, Allen S., 115
Gibbes, James G., 108
Gibbes, Wade H., 320
Gibboney, William, 57
Gibbons, William H., 163
Gibbs, George C., 251, 255, 257
Gibraltar, Sumter at, 83
Gibson, Randall L., 306, 416
Giddings, J. D., 54, 55
Gift, George W., 360, 361, 384
Giles, Thomas T., 57
Giles Courthouse, Va., 267
Gill, W. G., 221
Gill, William P., 382
Gillaspie, W. M., 154
Gilmer, Jeremy F., 205, 206, 207,
208, 209, 284, 300, 320
Gilmer, John A., 24, 31, 257
Gilmer, Tex., manufacturing at,
289
Gilmor, Harry W., 320
Gilmore, John T., 273
Ginder, Henry, 320
Girard, C., 347
Girard, Charles F., 73, 74
Girardy, Victor J. B., 221
Gladden, Adley H., 280
Gladney, James B., 115
Glasgow, Scotland, 365, 368
Glass, W. S., 54

General Hospital at Charlottesville, 191

Louisiana State University, Department of Archives, diaries: Roy, 380; Miller papers, 294; papers of Army officers: Baylor, 297, Beauregard, 314, Birge, 294, Boyd, 298, Bringier, 316, Cabell, 191, Ferguson, 319, Goree, 320, Johnson, 269, Jones, 182, Liddell, 324, Marston, 296, Reid, 294, 299, 330, Vinet, 264; papers of Chaplains Markham, 326, Quintard, 289; papers of naval officers: Means, 381; papers of officials: Kenner, 88, Mann, 88, Vignaud, 88; papers of surgeons: Pinson, 328; personal papers: Newell, 246, Roman, 86; records held by: enrolling officer, 295, La. Cavalry, 306, La. Inf., 306, Provost Marshal's Office, Richmond, 282; records re the Hunley, 378

Louisville, Ky., 347; telegraph line to New Orleans, 397

Louisville (Ky.) Public Library, 18

Love, Samuel L., 50

Lovell, Mansfield, 265, 325, 327

Loving, Edwin B., 312

Lovingston Hospital, Winchester, Va., 204

Low, John, 365, 367, 368, 370

Lowry's Point, Va., 364

Loyalists, claims, 75

Loyall, Benjamin P., 339, 377

Lubbock, Francis R., 63, 64, 69

Luckett, Phillip N., 79, 289

Ludlow, William H., 81, 236

Lumber, 220, 225, 229, 349, 402

Lunatic Hospital, Richmond, Va., 199

Lusher, Robert A., 117

Luxuries, 246

Lynch, Francis J., 294

Lynch, G. G., 396

Lynch, Patrick N., 72, 78, 80, 88

Lynch, William F., 343, 347, 354, 355, 356, 357, 362, 376, 381

Lynchburg, Va., Colston serves at, 318; commissary depot, 168; depositary, 133; military

hospitals, 175, 193, 194; military prison, 254; records captured at, 155; telegraph instruments in, 397; wheat ground in, 167

Lynchburg Ordnance Depot, Va., 224

Lyon, Francis S., 25, 26, 27, 30

Lyon, George G., 42

Lyons, James, 25, 27, 28, 34, 105

Lyons, Richard B. P., 85

McAdoo, William G., 52

McCall, J. L. L., 54

McCampbell, John S., 54

McCance, Thomas W., 105

McCann, J. R., 417

McCarrick, James W., 339

McCarrick, Patrick, 339

McCarthy, Carlton, 417

McCaw, James B., 196

McClellan, Henry B., 279, 417

McClellan, James F., 44, 45

McClintock, James R., 378

McCloskey, James D., 383

McCorkle, David P., 374

McCorkle, J. O., 345

McCown, John P., 265

McCoy, A. A., 50

McCoy, Henry, 253

McCoy, James S., 325

McCreary, John, 53, 54, 55

McCreery, W. W., Jr., 285

McCulloch, Ben, 215, 295, 296

McCulloch, Henry E., 289, 297

McDaniel, Z., 403

McDonald, Marshall, 325

McDonough, Benjamin F., 133

McDowell, Thomas D., 34

McElroy, Robert M., 67

McElwain, W. S., 224

McFarland, James E., 82, 87

Macfarland, William H., 11, 105

McFee, Madison, 270

McGarity, Abner E., 279

McGary, Charles P., 384

McGhee, Charles M., 53

McGowan, Robert, 417

McGown, George W., 299

McGown, John P., 299

MacGreal, Peter, 292

McGrew & Small, 389

McGuire, Hunter H., 178

McHenry, George, 73, 83, 89

Military Telegraphs Office, Post Office Department, 396
Military units, muster rolls, 144; offers to organize, 137
Military works, constructing, 204
Militia, 10, 20, 407; commanded by the President, 63; decisions re conscription of, 41; Ga., 305; officers authorized for, 145; records re, 406; rolls, 145; State systems, 301; Va., 28, 312
Militiamen, records re, 410
Milledgeville, Ga., depositary, 127
Millegeville, C.S.S., 384
Millen, Ga., 252, 258
Miller, Andrew J., 417
Miller, Fleming B., 57
Miller, Henry C., 48
Miller, Robert C., 211
Miller, Samuel A., 28, 29, 30
Miller, Thomas D., 294
Miller, Washington D., 389, 390
Miller, William, 240, 276, 283, 303
Miller Hospital, Mobile, Ala., patients, 177
Millers, 238
Milligan, Joseph, 105
Mims, Livingston, 153, 154
Miner, James G., 346, 348
Minerals, development, 346; procurement, 243
Mines and Mineral Works Supervison, Trans-Mississippi Department, 290
Minié balls, 224
Mining, 215, 245; companies, 227, 228; supervised by Niter and Mining Bur., 243
Ministers, 238
Minnesota Historical Society, records held by: Army of the West, 299, hospital order book, 186
Minor, George, 231, 346, 347, 378, 386
Minor, Lewis W., 380
Minor, Robert D., 340, 346, 354, 355, 380, 383
Minot, revenue cutter, 123
Minter, J. F., 121
Mints, Charlotte, 130; coin and bullion at, 101; funds received by, 98; New Orleans, 128; letters

sent, 97; letters to, 95, 102; operation, 102; seizure, 122; suspension, 94, 122
Miscellaneous Division, First Auditor's Office, 108
Missionary, 212
Mississippi, adopts secession, 1; Cavalry hdqrs., 264; chief commissary, 168; chief tax collector, 116, 117; commandant of conscripts, 240; conscription service, 238, 242; cotton purchased in, 124; Davis arrives from, 62; delegate signs Constitution, 2; depositaries, 129; district court, 49; estimates of tax in kind, 167; field transportation, 162; general of reserves, 303; Jackson's division in, 319; Josselyn from, 62; mail contracts, 394; mail routes, 394; medical purveyor in, 179; military hospitals, 176, 185-186, 288; military organizations, 304; military service records, 406, 408; naturalization records, 42; niter and mining officer, 244; number of Representatives, 14; occupied by Union forces, 393; officers serve in: Clark, 318, Reynolds, 330, Van Dorn, 334; part of: Dept. of Miss. and E. La., 263, Dept. No. 1, 265, District of Ala., 262, Western Dept., 237; persons who sold cotton, 116; Produce Loan agent, 95, 115, 116; quartermaster purchasing officer, 153; quartermasters in, 164; records, 93; records of troops, 306-307; regimental officers, 147, 148; reserve forces, 307; sales of property, 98; secession ordinance, 5; State troops, 313; surgeons in, 314, 319; telegraph line through, 397; volunteers, 323
Mississippi, C.S.S., 361, 379
Mississippi Department of Archives and History, military service records, 408; papers of Army officers: Clark, 318, Hamilton, 286, 320, Henry, 321, Johnston, 320, McKean, 288, Ruggles, 330, Sessions, 331, Smith, 332, Walthall, 69; papers of officials:

Municipalities, currency, 93
Munitions, imported, 73, 216;
manufacture, 215, 216, 218;
seized at Pensacola, 382; trans-
shipment of, 74. See also
Ammunition, Ordnance, Powder
Munnerlyn, Charles J., 27
Murdaugh, William H., 90, 340,
366
Murder cases, Ariz. Terr., 58
Murray, E. C., 381, 386
Murray, John P., 29
Murrow, J. S., 212
Muscogee, C.S.S., 376
Muse, William T., 387
Muskegon (Mich.), Hackley Public
Library, Pickett papers, 90
Muskets, 224, 230
Muskogee, Okla., 214
Muster rolls, 405, 412, 414; Ala.
Inf., 318; Ala. troops, 304; Ark.
troops, 304; Army, 140, 144-145,
151, 276, 304; Army of N. Mex.,
297; Bates' rangers, 311;
Chatham Artillery, 305; collec-
ted by States, 407; exchanged
prisoners, 235; hospitals, 171;
index, 419; La. Inf., 306; La.
Vols., 306; Marine Corps
personnel, 352, 353; Miss. Inf.,
307; naval, 110, 339, 343, 344,
345, 356, 357, 362, 372, 412;
N.C. Inf., 308, 309; reserve
company, 113; Richmond
Howitzers, 311; S.C. Inf., 310;
Va. Inf., 312
Myers, Abraham, Quartermaster
General, 155
Myers, E. T. D., 210
Myers, John J., 292
Myers, Robert P., 327

Nacogdoches, Tex., 56
Nansemond, C.S.S., 354, 355, 381
Napoleon, Emperor, 73, 77
Napoleon, Ark., marine hospital,
123
Narratives, personal, 303
Nash, Wiley N., 307
Nashville, Tenn., board of loan
commrs. at, 105; commissary
depot, 168; depositary, 133;
district court seat, 52; Gordon

Hospital, 177; ordnance works,
219; surrender, 26; withdrawal of
Confederates, 53
Nashville Arsenal, Tenn., 229-230
Nashville, C.S.S., 81, 360, 361,
367, 377
Nassau, New Providence, commer-
cial agent at, 74, 79, 92;
Florida at, 110; mail service to,
393; shipping, 83; steamship
service, 216; supplies transferred
at, 134; U.S. attempt to recover
property in, 99
Natchitoches, La., quartermaster,
298
Natchitoches Parish, La., 294
National Bank Note Co., 118
National Bank of Fredericksburg,
377
National War College Library, 420
Naturalization, 10, 40; district
courts and, 37; district court
records: Ala., 43, Ark., 42,
Miss., 42; foreigners in military
service, 56
Nautical instruments, procurement,
346
Naval Academy (Drewry's Bluff,
Va.), 345, 378-379
Naval Affairs, House Standing Com-
mittee on, 25, 32
Naval Affairs, Senate Standing Com-
mittee on, 20
Naval Affairs, Standing Committee
on, 11
Naval battles, marines in, 352;
Mobile Bay, 360; New Orleans,
343, 352, 361-362
Naval constructors, 350; Halifax,
376; McIntosh Bluff, 377; Mobile,
377; Oven Bluff, 377; Selma
Naval Station, 386
Naval engineering, records, 341
Naval engineers, 349, 350, 362;
Charleston Squadron, 357;
Florida, 371; letters sent, 377;
Petersburg, 382; Savannah River
Squadron, 360
Naval officers, accounts, 109, 371;
activities in France, 371; allot-
ments, 109; appointment, 337;
assignments, 346; at naval bat-
teries, 364; bonds, 103; carry

Ramsey, James G. M., 132, 133
Ramsey, Joseph, 130
Ramsour, Darius F., 50
Randall, James R., 357
Randolph, E. G., 294
Randolph, George W., 134, 139, 234
Randolph, Victor M., 340, 360, 377, 382
Randolph, William M., 44
Randolph Rangers, 305
Randolph's Hospital, Richmond, Va., 201
Rangers. See Partisan rangers
Ransom, Robert, Jr., 281, 418
Ransom, Thomas D., 418
Rapier, John L., 353
Rappahannock, C. S. S., 88, 365, 367, 368, 371
Rappahannock River, defenses, 328; naval battery on, 364
Rations, 207, 268; commutation of, 159, 167; navy, 359
Rawlins, John A., 75
Read, Charles W., 368
Read, Edmund G., 367
Read, Henry E., 29
Read, Isaac, 244
Read, John B., 403
Read, Keith M., 85, 359
Reagan, John H., accompanies the President, 64; attends railroad convention, 393; Congressman, 10, 34; letters sent, 83, 398; memoirs, 69, 388; papers, 390; Postmaster General, 389; Secretary of the Treasury, 94
Reagan, Morris R., 398-399
Reagan, William R., 54
Real estate, war tax on, 116
Reams' Station, Va., 256
Receivers. See Sequestration receivers
Receiving ships, 343; Charleston, 375; New Orleans, 379; Norfolk Navy Yard, 380
Reception Office, Adjutant and Inspector General's Office, 140
Recollections, naval officers, 340
Reconnaissances, 204, 205, 336; maps, 208
Recruiting, Army: 139, 159, in Europe, 79, letters re, 136,

officers, 93, 145, 243; in Ireland, 73; Navy: 337, 370, 381, records, 344, stations, 343, 345, 349; volunteers, 301
Recruiting Service, Adjutant and Inspector General's Office, 141, 142
Recruits, 412; naval, 344
Rector, Elias, 212, 213
Red River, 297; campaign, 334; Indians north of, 210; naval protection, 386; Reserve Indians near, 212; valley, 211
Red River Landing, La., 250
Red River Squadron, 362-363, 386, 387
Refugees, 411, 412; vote for Representatives, 15
Regiments, 146; comdrs., 150; Indian tribes, 302; legislation for, 301; officers, 147, 409; publications, 146, 303; quartermasters, 157; records, 303; returns, 145, 150; rosters of officers, 147-148; surgeons assigned to, 172. See also Artillery regiments, Cavalry regiments, Infantry regiments
Register Division, Third Auditor's Office, 113
Register of the Treasury, 102; duties, 104; letters sent, 126; lists of employees, 107; records, 92, 106-108; supervises Produce Loan Office, 115
Registers of vessels, blockade-runners, 373; British, 369; cruisers, 369; Galveston, 133; Mobile, 124; New Orleans, 128; Savannah, 126
Regulations, Army, 142; Commr. of Taxes, 117; Comptroller's Office, 102; hospital, 193, 194; Indian affairs, 213; Medical Dept., 170, 180; Ordnance Dept., 216; Quartermaster General's Dept., 155, 157; Subsistence Dept., 168; Treasury Note Bur., 120
Reid, Charles H., & Co., 216
Reid, John, 294, 299, 330
Reid & Shorter, 80
Reily, James, 74
Relics, 62
Reminiscences, Thompson, 333

Talbott & Bros., Richmond, Va., 347

Talcott, T. M. R., 277

Taliaferro, Edwin, 279

Taliaferro, William B., 332, 418

Talladega, Ala., camp of instruction, 241

Tallahassee, Fla., board of loan commrs. at, 105; controlling quartermaster at, 167; depositary, 126; district court seat, 44, 45; medical purveyor, 178; niter and mining dist. hdqrs., 244; Produce Loan agent, 115; quartermaster depot, 333

Tallahassee, C.S.S., 352, 353, 368, 369, 370

Tallassee Armory, Ala., 99, 233

Tallassee Manufacturing Co., 233

Talley, Robert, 215

Tamaulipas, Mexico, 73, 297

Tangipahoa, La., depositary, 129

Tanner, Isaac S., 272

Tanneries, 410; letters to, 231

Tanners, 238, 412

Tappan, James C., 418

Tapscott, John B., 332

Tariff act, enforcement, 95

Tarrant County, Tex., 53

Tasker, A. P., 291, 414

Tate, Mitchell, 346

Tate, Samuel M., 333

Tattnall, Josiah, 340, 342, 343, 354, 355, 357, 358, 359, 360, 384

Tax assessors, 116, 117, 118; accounts, 118; Ala., 123; appointments, 117; list, 167; N.C., 130

Tax collectors, accounts, 117, 118; Ala., 123, 124, 125; appointments, 117; bonds, 103; commissions, 117; deposits by, 101; letters sent, 97, 118; letters to, 117; lists, 118; reports, 121; statements of money received, 118; Tenth Va. Dist., 92

Tax in kind, accounts, 160; agents, 157; collected in Va., 311; collection, 117; cotton acquired under, 115; Fort Bend County, Tex., 133; levied on agricultural produce, 166; payments on, 129; quartermasters collect, 157;

records re, 167; returns, 158; statement, 228

Tax-in-kind agent, 225

Tax in Kind Bureau, Quartermaster General's Office, 166

Tax in Kind Bureau, Trans-Mississippi Dept., 290, 294

Taxes, Ariz. Terr., 59; collection in Trans-Miss. West, 121; Congress and, 10; increase in, 117; returns, 37, 118; revenue from, 122; to be levied by Congress, 15. See also War tax

Taxes, House Select Committee on Additional, 31

Taxpayers, appraise the value of crops, 166; names, 118

Taxpayers, House Special Committee on the Relief of, 30

Taylor, Algernon S., 353, 377

Taylor, Charles E., 153

Taylor, J. H., 29

Taylor, Richard, 67, 263, 264, 298, 299, 327, 329, 333, 369, 370, 371

Taylor, W. V., 232, 233

Taylor, Walter H. S., 111, 169, 232

Tazewell Courthouse, Va., 170

Teachers, 238

Teamsters, 234; taken prisoner by Confederates, 138; records re, 411

Teasdale, H. R., 153

Teaser, C.S.S., 351, 354

Technology, nautical, records, 341

Telegraph companies, 238; payments to by Govt., 98; records re, 410

Telegraph lines, 99; construction of, 397; control of assumed by the Govt., 396; erected by signalman, 152; records re, 397. See also Military Telegraph Lines

Telegraph operators, 138, 396; Charleston, 284; exemption, 397; letters to, 390; records re, 410

Telegraph stations, accounts, 397

Telegraphers, 411

Teller, 100

Temple, R. H., 290

Tennant, S. B., 153

Tennent, George W., 360

Tennessee, admitted to Confederacy, 9; chief commissary, 168; chief tax collector, 116, 117; coal

Records and Library, 339, 348
U.S. War Department, 95, 112,
260, 313; Archive Office: 13, 17,
47, 93, 291, 388, 404, transfers
Surgeon General's Office records, 171; buys State Dept.
records, 76; compiled records,
171, 404, 410; copies Confederate
letters, 136; Davis' papers sent
to, 65; examines Confederate
archives, 414; gives up Davis'
corresp., 65; indexes prepared
by, 251, 419; records, 405;
records held by Navy Dept., 341;
records lent to, 249; records
received by: Army officers'
papers, 405, 415-418, battle reports, 415, Confederate maps,
207, Congress, 13, 17, conscription service, 238, Ga.
district court, 47, Post Office
Dept., 388, Trans-Mississippi
Dept., 291, Treasury Dept., 93;
records shipped to, 206, 413;
reference files compiled by,
419; Secretary of War's letter
book, 135; transfers records to
the Office of Naval Records and
Library, 339; uses rosters, 148
U.S. War Records Office, 144,
256, 263; compiles Official
Records . . . Armies, 414, 419-
420; copies Confederate papers,
415, 418
Undertakers, 349, 412
Uniforms, Army, 157; Navy, 344
Union, Va., 244
Union blockader, captures Cornubia, 373
Union City, Tenn., 261
Union forces, approach: Kinston,
376, Macon, 228, Mobile, 360;
capture cotton, 115; control
Miss. River, 167, 290, 362;
destroy records, 92; land north
of Norfolk, 380; places occupied
by, 208; occupy: areas in the
South, 393, Ark., 289, Baton
Rouge, 221, Chester, S.C., 3,
coast, 114, Fort Smith, 213,
Holly Springs, 224, Huntsville,
43, La., 289, N. Mex., 296,
Pensacola Navy Yard, 382,

Savannah, 258, Selma, 385
Union officers, forward records,
339
Union provost marshals, 47, 236,
411
Union shipping, Tallahassee's
cruise against, 353
Union soldiers, applications for
pensions, 414; deaths, 192;
patients at Danville General
Hospital, 192; relief, 70
Union Springs, Ala., hospital, 184
Union Theological Seminary Library,
Dabney papers, 277
Union whaling fleet, attacked by the
Shenandoah, 368
Unionists, Tex., 298
United Daughters of the Confederacy,
Florida Division, 406
United States, arsenals, 218; census
of 1860, 15; citizens imprisoned
in Richmond, 281; Confederate
agents in, 152; confiscation of
Confederate property, 39, 61;
consuls, 73; controls: Indian
country, 211, Mississippi River,
398, Mo. and Ky., 15; criminal law,
37; currency in Confederacy, 37;
customs collectors, 122, 127;
customs service, 104; forts, 208;
laws, 11; lighthouse system, 114;
medicines imported from, 178;
merchant ships, 80, 367, 368;
military hospitals, 404; military
prisons, 73, 87; militiamen, 9;
minister in France, 365; postage,
108; postal service property, 391;
postmasters, 109; property
seized, 5, 97, 420; raids on from
Canada, 73, 150; shipping damage,
365; threat of war against England, 365; vessels: captured by
Confederates, 40, on the Miss.
River, 361, records re, 410;
withdraws troops from Indian
country, 210. See also Enemy,
Federal forces, North, Union
forces
United States, C.S.S., 370, 380,
381
University Hospital, Oxford, Miss.,
186
University of the South Library,